Politics and Society in
Mid Thirteenth-Century England

Politics and Society in Mid Thirteenth-Century England

The Troubled Realm

PETER COSS

OXFORD
UNIVERSITY PRESS

Great Clarendon Street, Oxford, OX2 6DP,
United Kingdom

Oxford University Press is a department of the University of Oxford.
It furthers the University's objective of excellence in research, scholarship,
and education by publishing worldwide. Oxford is a registered trade mark of
Oxford University Press in the UK and in certain other countries

© Peter Coss 2024

The moral rights of the author have been asserted

All rights reserved. No part of this publication may be reproduced, stored in
a retrieval system, or transmitted, in any form or by any means, without the
prior permission in writing of Oxford University Press, or as expressly permitted
by law, by licence or under terms agreed with the appropriate reprographics
rights organization. Enquiries concerning reproduction outside the scope of the
above should be sent to the Rights Department, Oxford University Press, at the
address above

You must not circulate this work in any other form
and you must impose this same condition on any acquirer

Published in the United States of America by Oxford University Press
198 Madison Avenue, New York, NY 10016, United States of America

British Library Cataloguing in Publication Data
Data available

Library of Congress Control Number: 2024933874

ISBN 9780198924289

DOI: 10.1093/9780198924319.001.0001

Printed and bound in the UK by
Clays Ltd, Elcograf S.p.A.

Links to third party websites are provided by Oxford in good faith and
for information only. Oxford disclaims any responsibility for the materials
contained in any third party website referenced in this work.

In memory of Angela Coss, my wife, best friend, and soulmate

Preface

In 1984, Simon Lloyd of Newcastle University suggested that he and I should organize a conference on thirteenth-century England. It was a propitious time for doing so. After a comparative lull, there was a general renewal of interest in thirteenth-century studies. To the first Newcastle conference, held in September 1985, came established scholars and many others who were at the beginning of their careers. The conference was held biennially thereafter and migrated first to Durham, then to Lampeter and Aberystwyth, and subsequently to Cambridge. A total of nineteen conferences have been held to date. As a result of the work presented, both at and outside of the conferences, knowledge and understanding of the thirteenth century has expanded exponentially over the past forty years. In bringing together much of this work in a new study of the politics and society of mid-thirteenth-century England, this book is in part a celebration of this achievement. At the same time, however, it offers a reinterpretation of what I prefer to call the 'crisis' rather than the 'revolution' of mid-thirteenth-century England. Paradoxically, given the multidirectional nature of modern research, the interpretation of the political history of this period remains locked into a traditional framework bequeathed by the mid twentieth-century historian R. F. Treharne, and embellished by the emphases and accentuations of his present-day successors. With its high-flown interpretation of concepts like community, its constitutionalism, its ready identification of a national enterprise, and its predilection for idealism and progressive thinking, this interpretation remains uncomfortably close to the Whig interpretation of English history. It is reinforced by a continuation of a rather ahistorical reverence for the baronial leader, Simon de Montfort. In this book I offer an alternative, less idealistic, and more down-to-earth approach which is anchored in the social mores and cultural values of thirteenth-century England. More emphasis is placed upon the interests, ambitions, and needs of contemporaries, upon social networks of various kinds, and upon how interests both clashed and cohered as people strove to improve or preserve their positions. It was a crisis born of political instability, but in the context of institutional, administrative, and legal growth, that is to say at a particular point in the evolution of the state. This book deals, then, with the generation of the crisis, the factors which influenced its course, and its (partial) resolution. In short, it explores the anatomy and physiology of a troubled realm.

Preface

Acknowledgements

I would like to offer my sincere thanks to the staff of OUP for the work they have put into the production of this book, and most especially to Thomas Stonor, Acquisition Editor, Jo Spillane, Project Editor, and Jothi Aloysia Stephenson, Project Manager. I would also like to thank Rachel Cooper, copy editor and Bob Mariott, for producing the index. I am most grateful to the two anonymous readers commissioned by the press for engaging so fully with my text and for pushing me in the right direction. Needless to say, whatever its demerits might be, it is a much better book for their intervention. I discussed the contents on various occasions with two friends – Chris Wickham and George Demidowicz – and I am grateful for their input. Many other scholarly debts are present and evident in the book.

Contents

List of Figures	xiii
List of Abbreviations	xv
1. The Whig Interpretation of Thirteenth-Century England	1
2. The Angevin Legacy and the Kingship of Henry III	15
3. The Impact of Royal Policy on the Nobility: Patronage, Appeasement, and Privatization	38
4. Power and Profit in the Provinces	66
5. Reform and the Knights of 1258	86
6. Faction, Party, and Affinity	127
7. Civil War	157
8. Simon de Montfort and His Support	196
9. Public Authority and the Provisions of Westminster	229
10. Resolution and Equilibrium, 1267–90	244
11. Conclusion	272
Bibliography	277
Index	291

List of Figures

1. Seizure of Property by the Earl of Gloucester from his Adherents   149
2. Restorations by the Earl of Gloucester to Pre-Evesham Incumbents   150
3. Members of the Sub-Retinue of Brian de Gouiz   152

List of Abbreviations

Ann. Mon.	*Annales Monastici*, ed. H. R. Luard, 5 vols., Rolls Series (London, 1864–9).
Book of Fees	*Liber feodorum. The Book of Fees commonly called Testa de Nevill*, 3 vols. (London, 1920–32).
CAD	*Calendar of Ancient Deeds.*
C & S	*Councils & Synods with other documents relating to the English Church*, vol. 2: 1205–1313, eds. F. M. Powicke and C. R. Cheney (Oxford, 1964).
CChR	*Calendar of Charter Rolls.*
CFR	*Calendar of Fine Rolls.*
CIM	*Calendar of Inquisitions Miscellaneous*, vol. 1.
CIPM	*Calendar of Inquisitions Post Mortem.*
CLR	*Calendar of Liberate Rolls.*
CPR	*Calendar of Patent Rolls.*
CR	*Close Rolls.*
De Antiquis Legibus	*De Antiquis Legibus Liber: Cronica Maiorum et Vicecomitum Londiniarum*, ed. T. Stapleton, Camden Society (London, 1846).
DBM	Documents of the Period of Reform and Rebellion, 1258–67, ed. R. F. Treharne and I. J. Sanders, Oxford Medieval Texts (Oxford, 1973).
DNB	Dictionary of National Biography.
EHR	English Historical Review.
Eyton, Shropshire	Eyton, R. W., Antiquities of Shropshire, 12 vols. (London, 1854–60).
Feudal Aids	Inquisitions and Assessments relating to Feudal Aids, 6 vols. (1899–1920).
Fine Rolls, H III	Calendar of the Fine Rolls of the Reign of Henry III. Publications of Fine Roll Project headed by D. Carpenter, available at https://finerollshenry3.org.uk/home.html, and as Calendar of the Fine Rolls of the Reign of Henry III, 1216–42, 3 vols., ed. P. Dryburgh and B. Hartland (Woodbridge, 2007–9).
Flores Historiarum	Flores Historiarum, ed. H. R. Luard, 3 vols., Rolls Series (London, 1890).
Foedera	Foedera, Conventiones, Litterae et Acta Publica, ed. T. Rymer, new edn., ed. A. Clark and F. Holbrooke, Record Commission (London, 1816), vol. 1.
GEC	Complete Peerage, ed. G. E. Cokayne, revised by V. Gibbs and others (London, 1910–57).

xvi   LIST OF ABBREVIATIONS

Hundred Rolls	Rotuli Hundredorum, ed. W. Illingworth, 2 vols., Record Commission (London, 1812–18).
JMH	Journal of Medieval History.
ODNB	Oxford Dictionary of National Biography.
Paris, CM	Matthaei Parisiensis, Monachi Sancti Albani, Chronica Majora, ed. H. R. Luard, 7 vols., Rolls Series (London, 1872–83).
Paris, GA	Gesta Abbatum Monasterii Sancti Albani, ed. H. T. Riley, 3 vols., Rolls Series (London, 28, 1867–9).
P&P	*Past and Present.*
PROME	*Parliamentary Rolls of Medieval England.*
RBE	Red Book of the Exchequer.
Rishanger	The Chronicle of William de Rishanger of the Barons' Wars, ed. J. O. Halliwell, Camden Society (London, 1840).
Royal	Letters Royal and Other Historical Letters Illustrative of the Reign of Henry III, ed. W. W., Shirley, Rolls Series (London, 1866).
RHS	Royal Historical Society.
TCE	Thirteenth Century England.
TNA	The National Archives.
TRHS	Transactions of the Royal Historical Society.
VCH	Victoria County History.
Wendover	The Flowers of History by Roger of Wendover, ed. H. G. Hewlett, 3 vols., Rolls Series (London, 1886–9).
Wykes	Chronicon vulgo dictum Chronicon Thomae Wykes, 1066–1288, *Ann. Mon.*, iv.

1
The Whig Interpretation of Thirteenth-Century England

The standard interpretation of the mid-thirteenth-century crisis and its significance in the history of England stems in large measure from the seminal work of R. F. Treharne, entitled *The Baronial Plan of Reform*. First published in 1932, it has remained deeply influential among historians and their readers to this day. So much so that it is necessary to begin any reinterpretation with a reminder of his persuasive evocation of the era, employing a modicum of italicization to emphasize the essential essence of his argument and beliefs. Treharne wrote that:

> The movement for reform begun by the English barons in April, 1258, was, in depth and intensity, unique among the many efforts of organised political opposition in medieval England. The *noblest idealism* and the loftiest hopes accompanied its inception, for *the entire baronage* combined to redress *all the wrongs of the nation*; and so profoundly did their challenge effect *the imagination of men of all classes*, that within a few weeks the reformers had won the sympathy and aroused the eager expectations of the whole country ... No other movement in medieval English politics attempted so much, and few came so near to success. But as promises were made and plans announced only to be broken or thwarted before they could reach fulfilment, the hopeful goodwill of the early days turned to sullen disappointment, awakening the most bitter passions and widespread hates. The failure of the reformers resulted in a peculiarly disastrous civil war, for *public feeling* had spread so far beyond the limits of the political classes that the *humblest peasants and townsmen were ranged with barons and knights in a bitter, passionate conflict,* for a cause which they deemed their very own.

He adds:

> The true outcome lies deeper than law or royal policy, in the swift development of *social consciousness among classes previously inarticulate and obscure.* The movement of 1258 was, in truth, one of the decisive crises of English history.[1]

---

[1] R. F. Treharne, *The Baronial Plan of Reform, 1258–63* (Manchester, 1932), 1–6.

2 POLITICS AND SOCIETY IN MID THIRTEENTH-CENTURY ENGLAND

Treharne then dismisses a counter view:

> This great movement has been traditionally regarded as a protest against Henry [III]'s ineffective foreign policy, his extravagance, and his galling reliance upon his alien kinsmen and his low-born officials in all matters of national importance. Many historians fastening upon the baronial demand for a monopoly of counsel, and upon the undeniably aristocratic nature of the constitution devised at the Parliament of Oxford, have overstressed the baronial character of the movement, ignoring its wider *national appeal* even while they proclaimed its importance in *the origins of parliamentary institutions.*

Rather, he says:

> ... when at last this King's incompetent direction of his powerful machine threatened disaster to the whole nation, the baronage, as the only class capable of decisive and independent action in 1258, assumed control of the government in self-defence and *in the interests of the entire nation,* and not merely from selfish class-motives and desire for power.

To his belief in and enthusiasm for 'the baronial plan', Treharne adds one other important ingredient: Simon de Montfort:

> It is not easy to explain [he admits] why the baronage rose in 1258 to *heights of idealism* never attained by their class at any later time.

The opposition to King John and the forcing of Magna Carta from him and the long minority of Henry III must have played a part in this, he concedes, but:

> Probably it was *the idealism of Simon de Montfort* which moulded and inspired this promising material, for, though our meagre evidence of the transactions of the Hoketide Parliament and the Oxford Parliament of 1258 afford no conclusive proof of Simon's leadership, we know that from the end of 1263 he was himself the embodiment of the plan of reform, and that the movement died with him at Evesham. Already by February, 1259, he was the chief protagonist of reform and the merciless exposer of all faltering in the great task, and what we learn of him in 1258 accords well with the belief that it was he who inspired the whole movement, breathing upon the dead bones of dull, negative obstruction the quickening breath of a call to justice and service for the common good. The contemporary chroniclers do not give him in 1258 the outstanding pre-eminence which they accorded to him a few years later, but contrasting the movement of 1258 with the barren futility of the opposition during the previous years, when Simon had not been available as leader, it seems almost certain that it was he

WHIG INTERPRETATION 3

who lifted the baronial opposition to a far loftier plain than at any other time, save perhaps in 1214. And, despite the bitter failure of 1260, during the eighteen months after the Parliament of Oxford the baronage showed itself to be capable, as a class, of united effort and unselfish labour for the good of the whole land.

Treharne argued his case not merely with enthusiasm, but eloquently and with passion. The depth and quality of his research, moreover, was unequalled in his day, except perhaps by his contemporary E. F. Jacob.[2] Treharne's framework became the predominant one within which the crisis of mid-thirteenth-century England has been understood. Subsequent scholars have built upon Treharne's interpretation. First, there is the emphasis upon the term and the concept of the community of the realm (*communitas regni Anglie*). It was popularized by F. M. Powicke, who used it as the subtitle to his *King Henry III and the Lord Edward*, published in 1947.[3] It had clear contemporary resonance, appearing in the argument put forwards by the baronial opposition to Henry III before Louis IX of France in January 1264.[4] However, there are earlier usages which, even if they lack the same resounding force, carry more or less the same import.[5] The realm as community seems to appear for the first time in Henry II's Assize of Arms of 1181, which had defined the arms to be held by 'the whole commune of free men (*tota communa liberorum hominum*)'. The language was used again by King John on his plans to repel invasion in 1205. The whole realm, he said, should become a commune (*per totum regnum fieret communa*) for its defence and draw upon the lesser communes of shire, hundred, and vill. In John Maddicott's view, 'As this suggests, the concept of realm as commune ultimately came up from below, from the smaller communities of the localities which had a real existence prior to and more concrete than that of the more nebulous "community of the realm"'.[6] The idea soon grew up that the magnates could represent the whole community, a stance that was fully operative in Magna Carta in 1215. Not only was this a grant by King John to 'all the free men of our realm', but the 'commune of the whole land (*communa tocius terre*)' could be called upon to compel the king to abide by it. 'No longer an abstraction', says Maddicott, "the community of the realm" represented by its barons had acquired a novel solidity'.[7]

---

[2] E. F. Jacob, *Studies in the Period of Baronial Reform and Rebellion, 1258–67*, Oxford Studies in Social and Legal History, vol. 8 (Oxford, 1925).

[3] F. M. Powicke, *King Henry III and the Lord Edward*, 2 vols. (Oxford, 1947). This was followed by his *The Thirteenth Century, 1216–1307* (Oxford, 1953).

[4] *DBM*, no. 37B, clause 3 (258–9).

[5] For what follows see J. R. Maddicott, *The Origins of the English Parliament 924–1327* (Oxford, 2010), and the references given there. For a discussion of communitarianism, see Susan Reynolds, *Kingdoms and Communities in Western Europe 900–1300* (Oxford, 1984 and 1997), most especially the introduction to the second edition.

[6] Maddicott, *Origins of the English Parliament*, 142.   [7] Ibid., 143.

4 POLITICS AND SOCIETY IN MID THIRTEENTH-CENTURY ENGLAND

In 1984 John Maddicott proffered his own influential extension to the Treharne paradigm. In a powerful essay he laid novel stress on the role played by the shires and their knights in the process of reform:

> The Reform Movement of 1258–65 was distinguished from all similar movements in the past by the attentiveness of its leaders to the local opinion of the shires. It was a movement for the reform not only of central government but also of local government ... In that process the knights and substantial freeholders who were at the centre of local society, courted and placated by both king and barons, added to their political weight and were drawn still further into political affairs. ... For the first time we can see the emergence of the gentry of the shires as a political force.[8]

The last point is clearly reminiscent of an essay by Treharne on the knights and the rise of a new class.[9] However, behind the new capacity of 'the gentry', says Maddicott, 'lay a lengthy evolution'. The county community is now introduced:

> The county community, where the gentry found a voice, predated the Conquest and had long given the corporate expression to public opinion, whether in answering the questions put by the king's eyre justices, in electing knights to attend the king's court, or ... in bargaining with the crown for local privilege.

He emphasizes the 'political aspirations which underlay the assertiveness of the local community in the period of reform and rebellion'. This owed much to Magna Carta and to the Charter of the Forest 'which gave the men of the shires a touchstone of good government'.[10] However, Magna Carta, he says, never quite met their needs. He takes us in detail through local demands for reform in local government and the grievances felt by knights and freeholders in the counties, laying emphasis upon the solidarity of communities. The reader will have noted that he links these communities with their forebears in the remote past. In the final section he connects them, too, to their successors of the fourteenth century:

> 'Much of what was sought by individual counties under John and Henry became the policy of the Commons in parliament a century later', and the 'continuity between the local inspiration of John's reign and parliamentary politics of Edwardian England was partly ensured by the reform movement of 1258–9,

---

[8] J. R. Maddicott, 'Magna Carta and the Local Community 1215–1259', *P&P*, no. 102 (February 1984), 25–65. The quotation is drawn from the opening paragraph of the essay.

[9] R. F. Treharne, 'The Knights in the Period of Reform and Rebellion, 1258–67: A Critical Phase in the Rise of a New Social Class', *BIHR*, 21 (1946–8), 1–12.

[10] Maddicott, 'Magna Carta and the Local Community', 26.

when for the first time the requests of individual counties were translated into collective demands.[11]

In subsequent essays Maddicott dealt in particular with the rise of constituencies and the two-way interactions between them and parliament,[12] and in 2010 he published his magisterial book on the origins of the English Parliament based on his Ford Lectures of 2004 where he sets out his interpretation in broader terms. This, too, requires our attention. In his preface he presents his central platform:

> Taxation by consent, legislation by statute, county and borough representation, relations between lords and commons, the identity of assembly and nation, and new forms of two-way contact between royal government and provincial England, all move to the centre of the stage, giving the English parliament a general character which it would retain for many hundreds of years.[13]

He is, as one would expect, much concerned with representation. Via the ecclesiastical world came the Roman maxim that 'what touches all should be approved by all' and the idea of proctors, where one man represented others. For the parliament of April 1254, 'these clerical practices were adopted as a model for the representation of the laity'.[14] Two knights were to come from each county, chosen by the counties, 'in place of each and all in their counties (*vice omnium et singulorum eorundem comitatuum*)', with the clear intent that they should agree to taxation. This was a unique occurrence as far as the parliaments of Henry III's middle years were concerned, but an important precedent for the future. On this one occasion, elected knights representing the counties replaced the minor tenants-in-chief, many of whom were themselves knights.[15] Finally, when it comes to the 'dynamics of parliamentary politics', Maddicott argues that Magna Carta's insistence on the presence of the lesser tenants-in-chief at tax parliaments indicates that they were expected to participate. On this basis he suggests that the knights were already becoming an independent presence in parliament, with their own interests and grievances which did not necessarily match those of the magnates.[16] While admitting that we can 'see only through a glass darkly', he contends that 'we can be reasonably sure that the knights spoke up, and fairly sure that

---

[11] Ibid., 61.
[12] J. R. Maddicott, 'The County Community and the Making of Public Opinion in Fourteenth Century England', *TRHS*, 5th ser., 28 (1978), 27–43; 'Parliament and the Constituencies, 1272–1377', in R. G. Davies and J. H. Denton (eds.), *The English Parliament in the Middle Ages* (Manchester, 1981), 61–87.
[13] Maddicott, *Origins of the English Parliament*, viii.   [14] Ibid., 210.
[15] For the context and significance of this parliament, see Maddicott, *Origins of the English Parliament*, 210–18.
[16] Ibid., 221–2.

6 POLITICS AND SOCIETY IN MID THIRTEENTH-CENTURY ENGLAND

sometimes the burgesses did too', making them 'an essential component of the community of the realm'.[17]

Maddicott's interpretation is cloaked in scarcely disguised constitutionalism. David Carpenter, the leading authority on the politics of Henry III's reign and the king's biographer, also puts a great deal of emphasis upon the constitution. In a recent book we hear of the constitutional legacy of the king's minority and of the 'constitutionality' of the thirteenth-century legal thesis known under the title 'Bracton'.[18] When Ralph de Neville claimed that having received the great seal 'by the common counsel of the kingdom' he could not resign it without 'common consent',[19] this was putting 'the authority of the great council on a par with that of the king ... a statement of constitutional significance', while the crisis over Montfort's marriage to the king's sister 'quickly evaporated without Henry making constitutional concessions'.[20] Carpenter speaks, too, of the 'constitutional limits on royal power', and, following Maddicott, of the 'constitutional significance' of knights representing their counties in 1254.[21] Finally, he writes of 'the cardinal political and constitutional development of Henry's personal rule: the sudden emergence of parliamentary power'.[22] Meanwhile, in his study of the minority of Henry III, he had, rather startlingly, glossed a statement by the earl of Salisbury to the effect that an order requires the assent and counsel of the king's chief men with the comment that the 'earl considered himself something of a constitutional expert'.[23]

And then there is the use of the term 'revolution' to describe either what happened specifically in 1258 or to categorize the years 1258–67. Since Jacob and Treharne historians have generally written of this crisis as 'the period of reform and rebellion', this becoming the title of the edition of key documents published by Treharne and I. J. Sanders.[24] The term revolution surfaces from time to time in the historiography, and Carpenter uses it frequently in his biography. Thus, he speaks of 'ingredients of the revolution of 1258' and to phenomena that took place 'after the revolution of 1258'.[25] We also find 'the revolutionary government of 1258–9', revolution being used seemingly for the first phase in 'the period of reform and rebellion', which phrase of course he continues to use.[26] However, he does not confine the term 'revolution' to 1258. The phrase 'revolution in government'

---

[17] Ibid., 225–6.

[18] David Carpenter, *Henry III: The Rise to Power and Personal Rule 1207–1258* (New Haven and London, 2020), 49, 161.

[19] Paris, *CM* iii, 363–4.   [20] Carpenter, *Henry III: 1207–1258*, 188, 202.

[21] Ibid., 542, 580.   [22] Ibid., 709.

[23] D. A. Carpenter, *The Minority of Henry III* (London, 1990), 209. For a more positive view than mine of constitutionalism in a thirteenth-century context, see Andrew M. Spencer, 'Dealing with Inadequate Kingship: Uncertain Responses from Magna Carta to Deposition, 1199–1327', *TCE*, xvi (Woodbridge, 2017), 71–87.

[24] Jacob, *Studies in the Period of Baronial Reform and Rebellion*; R. F. Treharne and I. J. Sanders, *Documents of the Baronial Movement of Reform and Rebellion* (Oxford, 1973).

[25] Carpenter, *Henry III: 1207–1258*, 415, 544, 557, 708.   [26] Ibid., 580, 625.

is used to describe the monopolization of power by Peter de Rivallis after the fall of the justiciar Hubert de Burgh in 1232, while the parliamentary demands for the right to appoint and dismiss the great officers of state 'according to custom and for the common utility of the kingdom' is referred to as 'the revolutionary demands of 1244'.[27] There is perhaps a difference in scale involved here. On one occasion he refers to the 'great revolution' which 'brought Henry's government crashing to the ground'.[28]

The concept of revolution in English history has, of course, wider connotations and no historian of English politics can be unaware of this. It is difficult not to have one eye on the seventeenth century, more specifically on the Glorious Revolution of 1688 which is perceived as establishing constitutional monarchy. This is the 'Whig interpretation' of Thomas Babington Macauley, G. M. Trevelyan, and Bishop Stubbs, with its accent on the historical importance of parliament and the superiority and moral integrity of British institutions.[29] Implicit in the dominant framework within which thirteenth-century history has been couched, this has now become manifest. Adrian Jobson entitles his book on the period 1258–67 *The First English Revolution*.[30] The initial legacy of the revolution of 1258–67 was a seeking of consensus. However, 'reform began stalling in the early 1290s', and there followed 'the baronage's perennial struggle to curb the crown's perceived misuse of its power'. However: 'Only in the traumatic upheavals of Charles I's reign did an opposition movement emerge that was even more revolutionary than that led by Montfort'. Constitutional lawyers, Jobson points out, 'frequently drew upon thirteenth-century precedents to argue that the royal prerogative was subject to clearly defined legal limits', while 'Charles's most vociferous critics were the shire's elected parliamentary representatives'. Widespread grievances were articulated 'that were often reminiscent of those in 1258'. In the event, 'The public execution of Charles I may have been an unprecedented act in English history, but it can be seen as a natural development in a cumulative process that had originated in the 1260s'. Moving forwards, he writes: 'In the nineteenth century, the emergence of academic historians led to renewed interest in the events of 1258–67. Simon de Montfort was accorded a place in Britain's pantheon of national heroes as the pioneer of democratic government. William Stubbs noted, for example, that the "idea of representative government ripened under his hand"'. Finally, after a discussion of recent debates, Jobson adds that 'More than 700 years may have passed since the baronial confederates confronted Henry III in Westminster Hall, but the principles they championed still remain entirely relevant to us here in the early twenty-first century'.[31]

---

[27] Ibid., 118, 616.   [28] Ibid., 611.

[29] Herbert Butterfield, *The Whig Interpretation of History* (Penguin edition, Harmonsworth, 1973; first published 1931).

[30] Adrian Jobson, *The First English Revolution: Simon de Montfort, Henry III and the Barons' War* (London, 2012).

[31] Ibid., 169–74.

8 POLITICS AND SOCIETY IN MID THIRTEENTH-CENTURY ENGLAND

There is a further dimension which is of particular relevance in the present context. This is the emphasis placed upon the entire nation in the reform movement. A number of scholars have stressed the growth of national feeling in the thirteenth century.[32] Carpenter has recently suggested that it provides a framework for the understanding of the reign of Henry III.[33] He supports Huw Ridgeway's observation that anti-alien feeling grew exponentially during the period of reform,[34] and absorbs the paradox that Simon de Montfort was 'the shield and defender of the English, the enemy and expeller of aliens, although he himself was one of them by nation', as articulated by the Melrose chronicler.[35] Equally, and in keeping with Treharne, he emphasizes the involvement of the humblest peasants in the reform movement,[36] both in the sense that they were involved in armies and in the plundering bands of the civil war and in the sense of their general support for the enterprise. Indeed, they participated with 'passion'.[37] 'When', he says, 'Simon de Montfort described the movement of reform as "the common enterprise", he meant that everyone "in common" was involved in it'.[38] Moreover, if 'the movement of reform redressed peasant grievances, it did so out of a mixture of self-interest and idealism, not from a fear of peasant revolt'.[39] This leads us to one final comment in relation to the Treharne framework: historians' work on the reform movement thereafter has been peppered with the ascription of idealism to participants, both high and low.

It goes without saying that the 'standard' interpretation we have foregrounded is predicated upon outstanding scholarship. It remains undeniable, too, that this framework has an internal coherence to it, and that its components played their parts in the political conflicts of thirteenth-century England. Moreover, the thirteenth century was the century of Magna Carta, the most famous document in Western constitutional history, and it is hardly surprising that this should have determined the manner in which thirteenth-century political conflict is approached.[40] Essentially a by-product of the struggle between King John and his aristocratic opposition, it became embedded in the political structure during the minority of his successor. If it had broader implications, this was because the

---

[32] See, for example, M. T. Clanchy, *England and its Rulers, 1066–1272* (Glasgow, 1983), 241–4, and M. Prestwich, *English Politics in the Thirteenth Century* (London, 1990), Ch. 5. See also, more recently, H. M. Thomas, *The English and the Normans: Ethnic Hostility, Assimilation and Identity 1066–c.1220* (Oxford, 2003).

[33] Carpenter, *Henry III: 1207–1258*, 50.

[34] H. W. Ridgeway, 'King Henry III and the "Aliens" 1236–72', *TCE*, ii (Woodbridge, 1988), 81–92, at 90–1.

[35] D. A. Carpenter, 'King Henry III's "Statute" against the Aliens: July 1263', in *EHR*, 95 (1980), 925–44; repr. in *The Reign of Henry III* (London, 1996), 261–80, at 274, citing A. O and M. O. Anderson (eds.), *The Chronicle of Melrose* (London, 1961), 127.

[36] D. A. Carpenter, 'English Peasants in Politics, 1258–1267', *P&P*, 136 (1992), 3–22; repr. in *The Reign of Henry III*, 309–48.

[37] Ibid., 320, 339.   [38] Ibid., 328.   [39] Ibid., 348.

[40] What follows is adapted from Coss, 'Presentism and the "Myth" of Magna Carta', *P&P*, 234 (February 2017), 227–36.

king's opponents endeavoured to carry the widest possible constituency with them. The commemoration of Magna Carta in 2015 added additional impetus to the ongoing exploration by professional historians of the charter's generation, contextualization, and significance for the understanding of thirteenth-century society and politics, most notably through the Magna Carta Project, led by David Carpenter and Nicholas Vincent. The project has furthered understanding in many directions.[41] The broad narrative, however, remains unchanged. Indeed, it is arguably one of the few grand narratives that remains substantially in place today. The outline is as follows:

A period of governmental advance, and in particular the crystallisation of the common law and its courts [otherwise known as the Angevin Reforms] was followed by a tyranny [in the form of King John] and this in turn by a reaction [encapsulated in Magna Carta]. Magna Carta contained two particularly resounding clauses, nos 39 and 40:

'No free man is to be arrested, or imprisoned, or dispossessed or outlawed, or exiled, or in any way destroyed, nor will we go against him, nor will we send against him, save by the lawful judgement of his peers or by the law of the land'.

And

'To no one will we sell, to no one will we deny or delay, right or justice'.

A third clause (no. 14) requires the 'common counsel of the realm' before the king can indulge in important forms of irregular taxation. The placing of these restrictions upon the king is universally considered to be a major constitutional advance and, indeed, a later version of Magna Carta came to be regarded as a statute of the realm. In the meantime, it was not the 1215 version but the amended reissues by the advisers of the boy-king Henry III and then by the king himself which sealed its reputation. Henceforth it could be reaffirmed by a king to pull the carpet from under his enemies and it could be evoked by baronial opposition to the king, most famously in 1258, to advance the cause of reform. Furthermore, it was prized and debated by lawyers thereafter and was called upon from time to time by litigants in the law courts of the later Middle Ages. Magna Carta became ingrained in English consciousness. Nor does the significance of Magna Carta end there. The restrictions it placed upon the king and especially the argument for what was in effect 'no national taxation without consent' led directly to the institution of parliament; that is to say, to national assemblies with wide representation, knights from the counties, and later burgesses from the towns, creating the germ of the institution we know today. Earl Simon de Montfort, a great promoter of

---

[41] For the project see http://magnacartaresearch.org. Many of the project's findings to date are discussed in David Carpenter, *Magna Carta* (London, 2015).

10 POLITICS AND SOCIETY IN MID THIRTEENTH-CENTURY ENGLAND

parliament, was killed—effectively martyred—in a clash with the royal forces at Evesham on 4 August 1265. Though the war was resolved in the king's favour, parliament lived on. Moreover, the two episodes—the reaction against King John and its aftermath and the struggle to establish 'parliamentary restraint' upon Henry III—have tended to be elided as a heroic period in English constitutional history when the king and his government were brought within the law, liberties were proclaimed, and representation established.

This, then, is the essential narrative. The commemoration of Magna Carta has inevitably led to new studies of King John. Two scholarly biographies appeared in 2015, entitled, respectively, 'King John: England, Magna Carta, and the Making of a Tyrant' and 'King John: Treachery, Tyranny and the Road to Magna Carta'.[42] It is not only in the titles that the grand narrative is evoked. In the first of these Stephen Church writes:

> 'He [John] managed his kingdom to a point where many of those over whom he ruled decided to gather themselves together behind a set of principles (outlined in the document called Magna Carta) firstly to force John to rule according to the terms of a written constitution and then, when they failed, to unseat him from his throne and offer it to another [Louis, eldest son of the king of France]'.[43]

And again: 'for the emerging community of the realm, which was being infected by the twin ideas that the kingdom should be run for the public good and that the king had a duty to take counsel, a king accountable only to God was increasingly unacceptable'.[44] Finally, Magna Carta is described as 'the corner-stone of English liberty, law and democracy', with a 'legacy that has had and continues to have enduring worldwide influence', quoting UNESCO's inscription of Magna Carta in its Memory of the World Register.[45] The second biography, by Marc Morris, is more of a racy narrative but his conclusions are essentially in line. Future kings, he tells us, would have to rule 'within the law. This was the lasting legacy of King John ... His oppressions led to the creation of a document that ensured they would not be repeated, and which still symbolises the right of the subject against the power of the tyrant'.[46]

Nonetheless, when all of this has been said, the recourse made to Magna Carta during the reign of Henry III and beyond has encouraged scholars, arguably, to lay too much stress upon constitutional issues and allied matters when seeking to explain events and to reinforce Treharne's framework as the predominant one within which mid-thirteenth-century politics is understood. Although there are other foci within thirteenth-century studies—the growth of government and

---

[42] Stephen Church, *King John: England, Magna Carta and the Making of a Tyrant* (London, 2015); Marc Morris, *King John: Treachery, Tyranny and the Road to Magna Carta* (London, 2015).
[43] Church, *King John*, xx.   [44] Ibid., xxxi.   [45] Ibid., xxix.
[46] Morris, *King John*, 298.

the common law, power and the aristocracy within the British Isles, and so on—
Treharne's remains the pre-eminent one, at least as far as the mid-thirteenth century is concerned. How might we characterize it? The very year before Treharne
published *The Baronial Plan of Reform*, Herbert Butterfield launched his attack
on what he called the Whig interpretation of history, with its 'deep-seated tendency' to interpret the period of the Reformation as a watershed, its study of the
past with reference to the present, its championing of progress, and its quest for
the origins of liberty, religious tolerance, and constitutional government. Some of
Butterfield's statements are well known and pertinent here: 'It is astonishing to
what an extent the historian has been Protestant, progressive, and Whig, and the
very model of the nineteenth-century gentleman'; the Whig historian divides the
world into 'the friends and enemies of progress'; he 'diverts our attention from
what is the real historical process'; 'he is apt to imagine the British constitution as
coming down to us by virtue of the work of long generations of Whigs and in
spite of the obstruction of a long line of tyrants and Tories'; he 'is interested in
discovering agency in history ... It is characteristic of his method that he should
be interested in agency rather than process'; his '"fervour" ... very often comes
from what is really the transference into the past of an enthusiasm for something
in the present, an enthusiasm for democracy or freedom of thought or the liberal
tradition'; the 'sin in historical composition is the organization of the story in
such a way that bias cannot be recognized'; and, most famous of all, 'The study of
the past with one eye, so to speak, upon the present is the source of all sins and
sophistries in history, starting with the simplest of them: anachronism.'[47]

Butterfield's little book was about modern history, and his target was the rather
crude formulations which he believed stemmed from abridged histories as
opposed to historical research. Nonetheless, when we have toned down some of
Butterfield's rhetoric, much of the content of his Whig interpretation is present in
Treharne's work and remains prevalent in the study of the politics of thirteenth-
century England. I would pick out eight tendencies. These are: an emphasis upon
the constitution and constitutionalism, highlighting in particular the linkage
between Magna Carta on the one hand and the evolution of parliament on the
other; the identification of a quest for freedom from oppressive government as a
key motivation for political action; a celebration of progress in the political
sphere; an emphasis upon historical agency, in the sense of those who supported
or retarded progress, the key figure being Simon de Montfort, but with an allied
tendency to invoke 'county knights' and 'the county community' as a forwards-
looking force; an attention to the growth of national feeling in the thirteenth
century and an insistence upon involvement in the 'revolution' across a wide
spectrum of society; a national church applauded both for its opposition to the
crown and for its high standards (although, of course, there is no Protestantism);

---

[47] Butterfield, *Whig Interpretation of History*, 13, 32, 35–6, 42, 71–2, 77.

12 POLITICS AND SOCIETY IN MID THIRTEENTH-CENTURY ENGLAND

a predilection for seeking idealism among thirteenth-century actors; and a rather romanticized view of English politics.

The emphasis that is still placed on the constitution reminds one that long ago K. B. McFarlane is supposed to have sent Stubbsian constitutional history packing.[48] As far as the thirteenth century is concerned, however, it does not seem to have gone very far. Some time ago I warned that the ghost of constitutional history still walks among us, a warning that has not been heeded.[49] This is not to say that contemporary historians are unaware of the dangers. John Maddicott, for example, has acknowledged that 'In setting out the various episodes in this story there is an obvious danger of falling into an antiquated and Whiggish teleology of necessary progress.'[50] 'The argument', he adds, 'seeks to avoid this trap by emphasizing the countervailing elements of the contingent and the unexpected which went to parliament's making'. Maddicott thereby repudiates the Whig interpretation *stricto sensu*. It could be argued, however, and indeed is argued here, that the Whig interpretation is to be found not only in teleology, but also in the choice of where to concentrate one's research, in the themes chosen, in the tone, and in underlying assumptions. Maddicott, moreover, reinforces the direction of his work by championing English exceptionalism. As has been said, not all of the work on thirteenth-century England is directly or explicitly concerned with these issues. Nonetheless, the Whig interpretation tends to run like a leitmotiv throughout the study of its politics.[51]

What I want to explore in this book is an alternative approach, one that is more than embryonic in major contributions by John Maddicott and David Carpenter themselves. This centres upon power, upon material and social interests, and upon 'political' culture. Maddicott's biography of Simon de Montfort[52] is a multi-faceted portrait which takes account of both Simon's contemporary aura, emphasized by 'Whig' history, and his predilection for up-fronting his own interests, a characteristic feature already emphasized in the discordant voices of Clive Knowles and Margaret Wade Labarge.[53] Carpenter, in a famous essay, broke with Treharne and Powicke over the genesis of the crisis of April–May 1258.[54] In place of the view that the king accepted baronial reform to avoid the papal sanctions of excommunication and interdict over his failure to raise significant funds for his second son, Edmund, to take the throne of Sicily, Carpenter shows that the king

---

[48] K. B. McFarlane, *The Nobility of Later Medieval England* (Oxford, 1973), 1–3, 279–82.

[49] P. R. Coss, 'Knighthood and the Early Thirteenth Century County Court', *TCE*, ii (Woodbridge, 1988), 45–57.

[50] Maddicott, *Origins of the English Parliament*, ix.

[51] I owe this observation to one of the anonymous readers for the press.

[52] J. R. Maddicott, *Simon de Montfort* (Cambridge, 1994).

[53] Margaret Wade Labarge, *Simon de Montfort* (London, 1962) and C. H. Knowles, *Simon de Montfort*, Historical Association Pamphlet (London, 1965). There is a balanced summary of Montfort's characteristics in Carpenter, *Henry III: 1258–1272*, 453–7.

[54] Carpenter, 'What Happened in 1258?', in J. Gillingham and J. C. Holt (eds.), *War and Government in the Middle Ages: Essays in Honour of J. O. Prestwich* (Woodbridge, 1984), 106–19; repr. in Carpenter, *The Reign of Henry III*, 183–98.

capitulated before an armed demonstration by a group of magnates. The primary cause was 'a revolution [sic] within the court of Henry'. A group of courtiers, native barons plus Simon de Montfort and Peter of Savoy, 'turned on' the Lusignans, Henry's half-brothers, and 'imposed reform on the king'.[55] The Lusignans were violent, arrogant, and quarrelsome, and they appeared to be above the law. Moreover, they had gone a long way towards monopolizing royal patronage. It was primarily against these that the famous confederation of seven barons was formed on 12 April 1258, with the expectation that force would be required. The barons arrived armed at the Oxford parliament in June, took measures to increase security against royal reaction, and proposed an act for the resumption of royal lands and castles, causing the Lusignans to depart the realm. A series of reforms ensued. Carpenter followed this with another important essay which reassessed Henry III's period of personal rule in relation to the magnates. He found that Henry treated them with considerable leniency in relation to debt, to the judicial system, and to their exercise of local power. His aim was to achieve peace and stability within the realm, and while he granted great favours to his relatives, he aimed to integrate these and his native barons into a single entity. Unfortunately, he lacked the political skill to accomplish this. Moreover, his subjects in general experienced his government as increasingly grasping and oppressive.

It is my view that this approach offers the best starting point for a reassessment of the crisis of 1258–67 and its significance, and of the validity of the traditional framework within which this period has been understood. In what follows I will take a broad approach, drawing on much modern scholarship in addition to my own research. Chapter 2 deals with the Angevin legacy as mediated through the minority of Henry III and with the evolving system of governance, before examining the nature of Henry's kingship as addressed by modern historians. It is not necessary to offer an overall verdict on his rule to appreciate that his style, judgement, and preferences left him open to the possibility of a major insurrection. The character of his kingship certainly conditioned what happened in 1258, but it does not entirely explain it. To fully understand the crisis, we must turn to the impact of his rule upon the higher nobility. Chapter 3 concentrates on this through the issues of patronage, appeasement, and privatization. The fourth chapter takes us further into the provinces and to an exploration of magnate power in its principal dimensions: material resources, social pre-eminence and the affinity, and the institutional framework of control. Power at the centre and power in the provinces are shown to be intimately interconnected, and this interconnection has potentially serious consequences.

Chapter 5 turns to the crucial issue of the role of knights and of the county community in the reform and rebellion, examining the knights chosen to bring complaints before the justiciar in 1258, the sheriffs appointed by the baronial

---

[55] Ibid., 190–1. It is noticeable that this is not far away from the counter interpretation which Treharne had dismissed.

regime, reactions to the royalist revanche of 1261, and the involvement of knights in the subsequent warfare against the king. Its findings suggest that the relationship between the reforming barons and county knights championed by Treharne and by subsequent scholars is not in fact sustainable. To comprehend more fully how knights behaved during the political debacle of 1258–67, it is necessary to return to how aristocratic society functioned when it came to vantage-seeking and to conflict. Chapter 6 will look in detail therefore at the behaviour of factions across the reign of Henry III, and then at the operation of a political party during and immediately after the Montfortian period. It will conclude with some observations on the contours of the thirteenth-century affinity. Chapter 7 deals with the civil war, concentrating less on the battles and high politics and more on the struggle on the ground. In doing so it engages with a broader cross section of the population. What it will reveal primarily is a desperate struggle for control, one that highlights pragmatism and opportunities for advancement rather than the exercise of principle and the prevalence of idealism. With this in mind, Chapter 8 is a reappraisal of Simon de Montfort, emphasizing his charismatic qualities but also his populist leadership, exacerbating and manipulating the xenophobia of his day. He was less prescient in his views than some have thought, and his underlying values were largely contemporary aristocratic ones. A master of propaganda, 'Simon took his support from wherever he could find it'.[56] The chapter concludes with the battle of Evesham.

Much of the discussion up to this point has aimed to demonstrate that the baronial drive to control the executive was the primary dimension to reform. Although reform of the legal and administrative system was, by contrast, secondary, it was by no means without significance. What was at stake here was the exercise of public authority. Chapter 9 deals with the purpose, process, and significance of the ensuing legislation: the Provisions of Westminster of 1259 and the Statute of Marlborough of 1267. The final substantive chapter deals with the aftermath of the crisis and the first two decades of the reign of Edward I. The aim here is to examine the nature of the polity that ensued. It follows traditional lines in first examining these years in terms of resolution. Three principal dimensions are discerned: reconciliation, the restoration of harmony, and reform. The chapter ends, however, by suggesting another way of approaching these years, the creation of a new equilibrium in both politics and society. The conclusion offers an alternative framework for understanding the period as a whole.

Politics and Society in Mid Thirteenth-Century England: The Troubled Realm. Peter Coss, Oxford University Press.
© Peter Coss 2024. DOI: 10.1093/9780198924319.003.0001

---

[56] Knowles, *Simon de Montfort*, 27.

2

The Angevin Legacy and
the Kingship of Henry III

Historians examining the events of 1258–67 have naturally turned to the quality of Henry III's kingship as at least part explanation of what happened. In this chapter I will follow suit with a synthesis of the research undertaken in recent decades. Inevitably this will draw upon the published work of many scholars, and I will restrict myself to rehearsing the broad outlines, while emphasizing those features which I believe have a direct bearing on the outbreak and unfolding of the crisis.

The legacy which King John bequeathed to his son was complex, and even to some extent contradictory. On the one hand was the mystique of kingship itself and the status of the king as head of one of Christendom's leading dynasties. On the other was a problematic relationship with the nobility. There was also a central paradox in that the king, or the crown, was the custodian of the public interest and of public authority, and yet successive kings treated the realm as essentially a resource on which to draw for sustenance and to maintain their personal power. This legacy was passed on to the 9-year-old king through the ministers and supporters of King John. They kept the system afloat through initially dire circumstances. They supported the king when it came to the reissue of Magna Carta and maintaining support for his rule, when it came to taxation, and when it came to his overseas interests, as in the campaign to Poitou. Henry III's minority was a prism through which he learned to appreciate his future power and his role.

The Minority

What, then, happened during the minority? It extended, strictly speaking, from Henry III's coronation, aged 9, on 28 October 1216 until the king assumed the fulness of power in January 1227, although he was not yet 21. Modern understanding of the minority owes much to the thorough work of David Carpenter.[1] There was,

---

[1] David Carpenter, *The Minority of Henry III* (London, 1990). There is a very useful précis of events in the same author's *The Struggle for Mastery: Britain 1066–1284* (Oxford, 2003), Ch.10, of which I have made great use here. For a broader treatment of child monarchy, see Emily Joan Ward, *Royal Childhood and Child Kingship* (Cambridge, 2002).

however, as he points out, no formal end to the minority, and the king's personal rule is generally seen by historians as dating from 1234. There is certainly a case for regarding the period 1216–34 as a single unit, even though it comprised four more-or-less distinct regimes: the regency of William the Marshal; the triumvirate of the papal legate, the justiciar Hubert de Burgh, and the king's tutor Peter des Roches; the rule of Hubert de Burgh; and 'the Poitevin interlude' when the country was run formally by Peter de Rivallis and informally by his uncle—or father—Peter des Roches. With the fall of the latter, the young king may be said to have finally been in actual control.

Under the regency of the prestigious figure of William the Marshal and with the support of the papal legate, the motley collection of loyalist barons, officers, and mercenaries whom David Carpenter calls 'the Henricians' fought a successful war against the majority of the baronage and the army of Prince Louis of France. In September 2017 Louis resigned his claim to the English throne and his supporters were restored to their lands. In November 1216 'the Henricians', in a bid for wider support, had issued a new version of Magna Carta without the clauses that were most injurious to royal power. This was reissued in November 1217 together with a new charter, the Charter of the Forests. The war, in addition to wrecking royal finances, had seen, as Carpenter has emphasized, 'a huge transfer of power from the centre to the localities'.[2] John's castellans, whether native barons or foreign soldiers, had learned to handle the revenue from their sheriffdoms themselves and had taken over royal lands. Peace itself was not likely to reverse this, not least because they claimed to have taken an oath to King John not to surrender their offices until his son came of age.[3] With the departure of Peter des Roches and the papal legate in 1221, Hubert de Burgh gained sole power, which he retained until his fall in 1232. He set about restoring the authority of the crown which, of course, meant in the short term his own. This involved recovering crown lands and dismissing the powerful sheriffs and castellans, a move that was in line with papal policy since 1219. The most difficult to prise out was the Norman Falkes de Bréauté, who controlled no less than six Midland counties. The move against him ended with the siege of Bedford castle, his power base, the execution of its castellan, who was his brother, and finally his exile in 1224. Hubert was able to accomplish his task by making allies, principally William Marshall II, earl of Pembroke, and the archbishop of Canterbury, Stephen Langton. The purge of 1223–4 was quite extensive and involved not only shrievalties and castles but also membership of the royal household.

While the siege of Bedford was going on, King Louis VIII of France, who as prince had invaded England, now conquered Poitou, and Hugh de Lusignan, husband of King John's erstwhile queen, Isabella, overran much of Gascony.

---

[2] Carpenter, *Struggle for Mastery*, 303.   [3] Ibid.

Hubert once again proved himself up to the task of defending royal interests, and in 1225 an army was duly sent. It seems that the French king was satisfied with Poitou so that, with Bordeaux and Bayonne being loyal, Gascony was saved. In order to mount this operation, however, considerable funds had been required. A great council agreed to a tax of one fifth on movables. The price was another—though very similar—version of Magna Carta and the Charter of the Forests. It was sealed by the king himself and issued as before in the pursuit of the widest possible support.[4] Paradoxically, although the need for general consent to taxation had been dropped from the text, the linkage between the issue of Magna Carta and the tax seems to have played a major part in fixing the principle of consent. The reissue, which became the definitive version, probably also reinforced the idea that the king was not above the law.

The campaign to save Gascony appears to have had a big effect upon the king, dominating his thinking for some time to come.[5] In 1230 he campaigned in Brittany. Henry, however, failed to engage with the enemy and showed no military aptitude whatsoever. Nonetheless, his continental ambitions, predicated upon his family's past, continued to drive him. Meanwhile, a by-product of Henry's assumption of full power in January 1227 was that he could now make grants by charter and Hubert de Burgh could finally expect the rewards of service. However, he was becoming increasingly isolated, and the stage was set for the return to power of Peter des Roches, who reappeared in England in August 1231. In June and July 1232, the king placed much of central and local government in the hands of Peter de Rivallis, and Hubert fell.

As Carpenter says, at the heart of this new regime was a faction comprising the sheriffs, castellans, and minsters whom Hubert de Burgh had pushed out, men like Peter de Maulay, Engelard de Cigogné, and Brian de Lisle.[6] They aimed not only to have revenge on Hubert, but also to regain their power and influence. This could only lead to conflict. In February 1233 the manor of Upavon in Wiltshire was taken from Gilbert Basset and given back to Peter de Maulay. However, there would be consequences. Gilbert was connected with Richard Marshal. Moreover, other disseisins 'by the will of the king' followed. In effect, Peter des Roches and his nephew had encouraged the king to return to the bad days of his father, disseising men without due process of law, negating the effects of Magna Carta. It was, however, a failed experiment and, according to some historians, Henry III's first lesson in kingship.[7] The new regime fell in turn in 1234, and Gilbert Basset was restored to Upavon. According to Carpenter, 'Bishop Peter's regime had tested the most fundamental principle of Magna Carta and proved its strength. The king was indeed now subject to the law, and could not

---

[4] Ibid., 307.   [5] Ibid., 310.   [6] Ibid., 305.
[7] This stems from F. M. Powicke, *King Henry III and the Lord Edward*, 2 vols. (Oxford, 1947), i, Ch. 4, 'Henry III's Lesson in Kingship'.

18   POLITICS AND SOCIETY IN MID THIRTEENTH-CENTURY ENGLAND

arbitrarily deprive his subjects of their rights and property'. Furthermore, and ominously, he adds, 'The events of 1232–4 were a terrible indictment of Henry's weakness and poor judgement'.[8]

Looking back from 1234 it is clear that the various regimes ruling in the name of Henry III had been dominated by faction. Moreover, their behaviour reinforced the Angevin norm that there should be a fairly lavish system of reward, in terms of grants to ministers and councillors and, indeed, extending further down the line. The prevailing culture in this respect can be illustrated by looking briefly at William the Marshal and his sons. The former was deeply concerned to preserve the rights of the crown. Yet, as David Carpenter tells us, the regent was 'under intense pressure' to secure rewards for his supporters, as well as wanting them 'for himself'.[9] His regime did a great deal in implementing the terms of the peace treaty, in restoring royal administration, and in dispensing justice. At the same time, however, it 'sanctioned the continuing passage of power into the hands of the great men of the regime'.[10] The regent also looked after his own men.[11] More widely, the regent yielded to the importunate demands for patronage and was responsible for a flow of grants and confirmations from the royal demesne. Magnates and *curiales* did well, as did the regent himself, securing land in hereditary right.[12] When the regent did take action against others, there was often strong resistance to royal agents. This, then, was a land of 'great regional governors', as Carpenter calls them.[13]

It was not only the king's patronage that was politically and socially significant. It was also the knock-on patronage of his supporters. They needed to be able to step in to reward and aid their followers. To take one example, in July 1219 William Marshal II, earl of Pembroke, and son of the regent, wrote to Hubert de Burgh begging 'as my dearest friend for love of me' to give full justice to his sergeant William de Bricheville, 'and, if you please, cause his land to be repledged to him, acting in such a way that he may feel that he has benefited from my prayers proffered to you and so that I owe you on his behalf deeds of thanks'.[14] Similarly, he wrote to Hubert again later in the year: 'I ask you as my dearest friend not to permit my knight and man [William de Ros] to be treated and molested unjustly [by Falkes de Bréauté], although I myself, my concerns and my affairs, through the will of certain people, which I deplore, are so treated'.[15] On 28 December 1221 Pembroke received a large amount of game from the king, while his knight, Thomas Basset, was confirmed in possession of the royal manor of Slaughter. In March 1224 Basset acquired William de Bréauté's manor of Kirtlington from the

---

[8] Carpenter, *Struggle for Mastery*, 316.   [9] Carpenter, *The Minority*, 55.
[10] Ibid., 55.   [11] Ibid., 68.
[12] Ibid., 91–2. At the same time, as Carpenter points out, the prohibition on permanent alienation of royal lands and rights 'limited the freedom of the government and frustrated the widespread desire for permanent rewards': ibid., 95.
[13] Ibid., 120.   [14] Ibid., 158.   [15] Ibid., 165 and 175.

king.[16] In 1227 it was the turn of Gilbert Basset, another Marshal familiar, to receive a reward. On 27 April the king had given the earl of Pembroke a grand house in London, once the property of a Jew. This was only days after he had taken the manor of Upavon in Wiltshire from Peter Maulay and given it to Gilbert. The following year Gilbert was given this in hereditary right and made a knight of the royal household. At court he would naturally represent the Marshal interest. Both Gilbert and Thomas Basset had already received escheats in hereditary right. Gilbert was to play a major part in the civil war between Richard Marshal earl of Pembroke, brother of William II, and the Poitevins, which led directly to the fall of the regime.[17]

Historians looking at the period before Henry III's personal rule have tended to stress two particular features. One is the triumph of Magna Carta as the foundation on which future government should be based, both in fact and in imagination. The other is the restoration of royal rights and, to a degree, royal finances. David Carpenter has recently re-emphasized and reinforced the importance of a third: the ubiquity or near-ubiquity of the great council as the place where policy was determined. As he stresses, councils could be one of two types; the routine council, as it were, of the king and his ministers, and the great council attended by the king, his ministers, and magnates.[18] They are not always clearly distinguished in the sources, and indeed the term 'great council' seems to be an invention by historians. Nevertheless, the role of the latter type in this period is startling, and it was to carry expectations into the future. Terms that were used include: 'by the counsel of our court'; 'by the common counsel of our kingdom'; and 'by the counsel of the archbishops, bishops and magnates of the land'. In 1220 both Robert de Vieuxpont and the earl of Salisbury made it clear that in their view important decisions needed to go before the wider council of magnates.[19] Carpenter sees such developments during the minority and the early majority of Henry III in constitutional terms. Thus: 'The minority of Henry III ... had a dual *constitutional* significance [my italics here and below]. It planted the Charter into English political life and it also engendered the belief that great councils, or as they were soon to be called parliaments, should have a large say in deciding the personnel and policies of the king's government'.[20] In part, the conflicts of Henry's reign were foreshadowed in the minority. Yet they were also the result of his dispensing with great officers of state like the justiciar, which lapsed in 1234, and refusing to allow appointments and policies to be determined by great councils. While Henry continued to summon great councils, he was determined to decide questions of

---

[16] Ibid., 271, 347.

[17] For lists of the Marshal followers, see Carpenter, *Henry III: 1207–1258*, 140, 157.

[18] Carpenter, *The Minority*, 54. For the significance of the council at particular points, see, for example, 229, 362, 376, and for the importance of the council to the regent and to Hubert, 84, 183, 263.

[19] Ibid., 209.   [20] Ibid., 402.

appointments, patronage, and policy himself, as his ancestors had done. In Carpenter's words, the 'minority made Magna Carta a fundamental feature of English political life. It also saw the genesis of the *constitutional* programme over which king and country were still fighting in the seventeenth century'.[21] This is, of course, an interpretation from a particular perspective, one which is consistent with the Whig interpretation discussed earlier. More neutrally, however, one can understand the events of these years simply in terms of the exercise of power. The plain fact is that the disaster that was John's reign had weakened the crown in terms of its control over the aristocracy, and this weakness continued into the reign of Henry III. Carpenter certainly recognizes this. 'In the localities', he points out, 'magnates and local communities were determined to profit from the weakness of royal authority and exploit the concessions in Magna Carta and the Charter of the Forest'.[22] The young king also knew that he had to conciliate the great magnates much as Hubert de Burgh had done, although he applied himself with less skill. In the style of his personal rule, at least, Henry remained a product of the minority.

Yet another feature of the minority which had a lasting effect was an emphasis upon ceremony and the grandeur of kingship. In addition to great ceremonies such as the second coronation and the translation of Becket into his new shrine in 1220, there were the Christmas courts. That of 1220 at Oxford greatly impressed the St Albans chronicler Roger of Wendover, while of the Northampton court in 1223 the Dunstable annalist wrote that with 'so many bishops, earls, barons and armed knights, neither in the days of the king's father, nor afterwards, is such a feast known to have been celebrated in England'.[23]

Finally, we must ask what the study of these years indicates about the personality and capacity of the king. Here we can turn to the first part of David Carpenter's fine biography.[24] We observe a traditional though very extravagant piety and a penchant for religious iconography. There is a love of ceremony, of dressing up and displaying the magnificence of kingship. There is his tendency to short-lived outbursts of intense anger. There is a passionate desire to restore his family's position in France, despite an obvious lack of military prowess. All the indications are, however, that he was a man of limited political intelligence who was easily manipulated. Henry was charged from time to time with 'simplicity'. At Christmas 1221 Roger of Wendover described the king as 'still perplexed by great simplicity'.[25] The same chronicler called him '*rex simplex*' in allowing himself to be counselled in the way that he was by Peter des Roches.[26] He had shown

---

[21] Ibid., 412. [22] Ibid., 397. [23] Ibid., 227, 325. The quotation is from *Ann. Mon.* iii, 84.

[24] Carpenter, *Henry III: 1207–1258.*

[25] Wendover, iii, 164–5; Carpenter, *Henry III: 1207–1258*, 78.

[26] Carpenter, *Henry III: 1207–1258*, 134, and Wendover, iii, 241.

himself, in his early years, to be weak in political intelligence. Perhaps Henry was not very intelligent per se?

The minority schooled Henry III in kingship and revealed traits that would characterize his rule. At the same time it raised aristocratic expectations in what could be expected from a compliant king.

The System of Government

Before turning to the character of Henry III's personal rule it is necessary to outline the system of government through which he operated. How was the country ruled? To all intents and purposes this was still Angevin England, although the system was an evolving one, and it continued to evolve throughout Henry's personal rule. As Robert Stacey has written, 'in its essence' the Angevin administrative system was 'unimpaired' by the 1217 charters.[27] Magna Carta had sought 'to regularize' but also to extend royal justice.[28] The common law continued to provide new remedies while the royal courts attracted increasing numbers of litigants. The king's travelling justices went on eyre again, and the judicial world continued to draw upon knights and free men as appropriate in providing juries of various kinds. Government departments flourished and their business grew.[29] Organized around its central departments, the government became 'progressively more complex and bureaucratic, encouraging the emergence of an administrative caste of highly educated and professional administrators'.[30] Of these departments, the exchequer had long gone out of court and was established at Westminster, that is to say it had separated from the royal household. Its operation was badly hit by the civil war between John and his barons, but it recovered steadily and was soon to return to normal. Royal revenues remained problematic, however, with the erosion of the county farms under Richard I and the limitations imposed on the king's finances as a result of Magna Carta.[31] The chancery, by contrast, did not go out of court until the fourteenth century, and the thirteenth century has been described as its 'greatest age'.[32] At the very beginning of the century, it began to enrol copies of the charters and letters sent out. To the rolls of charters, letters

[27] R. C. Stacey, *Politics, Policy and Finance under Henry III, 1216–45* (Oxford, 1987), 8.
[28] Ibid., 6.
[29] The historiography and the development of the royal archive have recently been reviewed by Adrian Jobson in his introduction to *English Government in the Thirteenth Century* (Woodbridge, 2004), 1–15.
[30] Ibid., 1.
[31] See Nick Barratt, 'Finance on a Shoestring: The Exchequer in the Thirteenth Century', in Jobson (ed.), *English Government in the Thirteenth Century*, 71–86, at 73. The royal revenue increased from just over £4,000 per annum in 1218 to 'a far healthier' £18,000. See also his 'The English Revenue of Richard I', *EHR*, 116 (2001), 635–56, and 'The Revenues of King John', *EHR*, cxi (1996), 835–55.
[32] See David Carpenter, 'The English Chancery in the Thirteenth Century', in Jobson (ed.), *English Government in the Thirteenth Century*, 49–69, at 49–50.

22 POLITICS AND SOCIETY IN MID THIRTEENTH-CENTURY ENGLAND

patent, and letters close were later added fine rolls,[33] *originalia* rolls,[34] and in 1226 *liberate* rolls.[35] The chancery played a crucial role in maintaining central control and in conveying the king's wishes, but the huge increase in its business during the thirteenth century was due in large measure to the steadily increasing popularity of litigation in the royal courts.[36] Michael Clanchy pointed out that whereas in the late 1220s a little over 3 lbs of wax was used for sealing writs each week, by the late 1260s this had become 30 lbs per week.[37]

The expansion of the central law courts in the thirteenth century is well known. Paul Brand sees a doubling of business dealt with by the court between 1200 and 1242–3, another doubling between then and 1260, and a further doubling between 1260 and 1280.[38]

Although Magna Carta had imposed restraints, it is important to remember that the royal courts were still the king's courts and the judges royal officials, answerable to the king.[39] A by-product of the development of the law courts was the increasing professionalism of its justices, observable from early in the reign and mirrored elsewhere in the king's administration.[40] In addition to the bench and the justices travelling on eyre, there was also the court *coram rege* (king's bench), which had a continuous life from 1234.[41] Much was owed to William de Raleigh, not least the compilation of the treatise on royal justice, which has come down to us as 'Bracton'. Nonetheless, it would be a mistake to lay all the developments of these years solely at the door of the king, his ministers, and his magnates. At the same time, we need to appreciate that royal justice was popular and increasingly so. It can hardly be overstressed that the expansion was due not only

---

[33] These were, in Carpenter's words, rolls 'which recorded the fines or financial proffers made by individuals and institutions to the crown in return for a whole variety of concessions and favours'.

[34] These were copies of the fine rolls informing the exchequer of monies that needed to be collected.

[35] These were rolls of writs authorizing expenditure.

[36] The fine rolls include the writs involving the payment of ½ mark or more for special favour and not the standard writs 'of course' (*de cursu*), which began litigation but were not enrolled. As Carpenter says, the steady issue of these standard writs meant that the work of the chancery was 'absolutely colossal': ibid., 55.

[37] M. Clanchy, *From Memory to Written Record: England 1066–1307* (London, 1979), 43–4.

[38] Paul Brand, *The Origins of the English Legal Profession* (London, 1992), 23. There was then a 78 per cent increase between 1280 and 1290, and roughly a further doubling between 1290 and 1306. Moreover, as David Carpenter has pointed out in his introduction to the calendar of the fine rolls, the huge expansion in payments for writs to begin and continue legal actions is 'key evidence for the widening of the common law': David Carpenter, in *Calendar of the Fine Rolls of the Reign of Henry III*, vol. i, 1216–24, ed. P. Dryburgh and B. Hartland (Woodbridge and National Archives, 2007), xxiii. Looking at the size of the plea rolls themselves as an indication of the number of cases, there appears to be a jump around 1250. Furthermore, the bench remained in session during the eyre of 1252–8, whereas before it had been suspended during the eyre. Presumably, this change is to be explained by the extent of business.

[39] Stacey, *Politics, Policy and Finance*, 7.

[40] See Ralph V. Turner, *The English Justiciary in the Age of Glanvill and Bracton, c.1176–1239* (Cambridge, 1985), and for a broader chronological perspective, Brand, *Origins of the English Legal Profession*.

[41] Carpenter, *Henry III: 1207–1258*, 153.

ANGEVIN LEGACY AND THE KINGSHIP OF HENRY III   23

to the capacity of the legal system to expand, but also to the increasing desire of the free population to invoke the royal courts.[42]

Another by-product of the expansion of the central courts was the serious impact upon the county courts. These seem to have lost much of their previous jurisdiction rather rapidly around the middle of the thirteenth century. Early legal works such as Glanvill and the registers of writs indicate that most actions concerning real property actions had traditionally begun in the county courts. The same is indicated by the appointments of attorneys recorded on the close rolls between 1225 and 1238, as well as by the relatively light load coming before the *curia regis*. When we examine the meetings of the county court in the round, however, a rather different picture emerges.[43] Except when the royal justices were present, they seem to have been rather lack-lustre affairs, dominated by routine administration and judicial business. The magnates no longer attended, sending their stewards to look after their business. Suit of court, that is to say attendance based on land tenure, was in decline, and there is evidence showing low attendance. As John Maddicott has said, men found the meetings of local courts 'vexacious, expensive and open to exploitation'.[44] By and large, county courts were not large gatherings of knights and freeholders eager to take part in 'self-government at the king's command'.[45] Most knights probably avoided the detailed business except where their interests, personal or shared, were concerned. Sheriffs must often have found it difficult to deal with the volume of business, especially when faced with uncooperative suitors. Notwithstanding these features, the loss of judicial business mid-century was significant. At the same time, however, it is necessary to remember that the court did have business other than judicial. It had a particular significance from the government's point of view in offering an important channel of communication between the court and the country.

And so, we come to the sheriff. The sheriff was the key figure in local government and the link between the localities and the centre.[46] Traditionally, he had

---

[42] Further evidence of the expansion of the royal courts has been offered by David Carpenter and Tony Moore. Moore has looked at the number of fines for legal writs recorded on the fine rolls, which survive in almost complete sequence for the whole of Henry's reign. It seems that the rule at the beginning of Henry's reign was that the writs *de cursu* brought cases to the eyre, whereas those *de gratia* took them to the bench or *coram rege*. After about 1250, most of the fines were for writs *de gratia*. By the end of the reign, the fine rolls had been almost entirely taken over by judicial business. This was one of the main drivers of the general expansion of the business before the bench. There are indications of a change in 1242–3. However, the main change came about around 1250.

[43] For what follows, see Coss, *Origins*, 121, and 'Knighthood and the Early Thirteenth-Century County Court', 45–57.

[44] Maddicott, 'Magna Carta and the Local Community 1215–1259', 36.

[45] The phrase comes from the famous work by A. B. White, *Self-Government at the King's Command* (Minneapolis, 1933; reprinted Westport, CT, 1974).

[46] The starting point for the modern study of the sheriff in this period is David Carpenter, 'The Decline of the Curial Sheriff in England', 1194–1258, *EHR*, 101 (1976), 1–32; repr. in Carpenter, *The Reign of Henry III*, 151–82.

24   POLITICS AND SOCIETY IN MID THIRTEENTH-CENTURY ENGLAND

been 'a general purpose regional governor'.[47] From the late twelfth century onwards, however, the sheriff's independent powers were decreasing and his routine duties and responsibilities increasing. On the one hand are the effects of the justices on eyre and the coroners (introduced in 1194), and on the other those deriving from Henry II's assizes and their continual development in the thirteenth century. The sheriff accounted financially at the exchequer. He was traditionally responsible for what was known as the farm of his county, a fixed amount drawn from various dues (like sheriff's aid), the proceeds of the shire and hundred courts, and the income from the royal demesne manors. While the sheriff was a farmer, any remaining income above this went into his own pocket. In order to secure a greater share of the total income coming from the counties, the exchequer developed two methods. One was to introduce fixed annual increments above the farm. The other was to turn the sheriff into a custodian so that he rendered all the income and was made an allowance. There was intermittent usage of these methods, and moments of experiment.[48] Two opposing principles were at work: the need to maximize revenue on the one hand; security and patronage on the other. For various reasons *curiales* or *familiares regis* continued to play a particularly significant role as sheriff until 1236. In that year the curial hold on the sheriffdoms was finally broken, allowing for the exaction of greater profits.

A few further observations need to be made. The king was advised by his counsellors, that is to say his ministers and his barons, but the government departments recruited their own personnel. By 1225, as the men who had staffed the council died away, the king's household stewards rose to prominence: Ralph fitz Nicholas, Geoffrey de Crowcombe, and William de Cantilupe. These men served the king in a variety of additional capacities and were naturally recipients of his patronage.[49] They were products of Hubert de Burgh's rule. The king also drew on a variety of servants, some of them relatively low-born who functioned as forest justices and in other capacities, including sometimes as sheriffs. And then, of course, the system drew on knights and on free men in the counties, the latter for juries in particular, and knights for the grand assize and for other specific judicial duties which required their status. Knights functioned on a variety of commissions, including assizes (until 1241), gaol delivery, tallage collection, and so on. In this sense these men were all part of the Angevin system.

Aspects of Henry III's Kingship

This, then, was the world which Henry III inherited. What did he make of his legacy? Two features stand out immediately. One is the emphasis upon the

---

[47]   Ibid., 155.

[48]   Ibid., 160–3, and for the details Mabel Mills, 'Experiments in Exchequer Procedures (1200–1232)', *TRHS*, 4th ser. vii (1925), 151–70.

[49]   Stacey, *Politics, Policy and Finance*, 34.

ANGEVIN LEGACY AND THE KINGSHIP OF HENRY III   25

mystique of kingship. The other is the accent placed on the family and dynastic ambition. In some respects they are interrelated. Nonetheless, for ease of analysis, let us take each in turn. The key to understanding Henry seems to lie in his extreme, one might even say extravagant, piety. He was *rex piissimus*.[50] Henry also enjoyed the magnificence of kingship. He was keen to impress with his court, with his entourage, and indeed with his person. His table was lavish, as were his liveries and gifts to individuals. Much attention was paid to the architecture of his homes, and to the adorning of chambers and chapels. This is where his devotion and his love of finery especially intertwined. In some ways he was not a strong character, and he had a tendency to lean on others. This must have stemmed in part from his long tutelage by Hubert de Burgh, but Hubert was followed not only by Peter des Roches but also by William de Savoy, bishop-elect of Valence, and by Cardinal Otto. He was later to lean somewhat upon his family, including his brothers and his queen. He was a man of ambition but rather lazy. He was touchy and prone to violent rages, although he usually calmed down and for the most part at least did not bear grudges for long. These features are no doubt connected to his self-image and its intermittent puncturing. He was, says Carpenter, 'a king very conscious of his name and fame'.[51]

Henry III was not alone among kings in being heavily into symbolism, ceremony, and ritual, and we must pursue this dimension to his kingship a little more.[52] Royal hospitality and splendour are in evidence, for example, in the festivities for Queen Eleanor's coronation in 1236,[53] and in the *convivium* which Henry arranged for the marriage between his brother, Richard of Cornwall, and Sanchia of Provence in 1243.[54] Assemblies such as parliaments were also occasions for royal hospitality and splendour. Celebrations were put on in London to mark the departure of the king's daughter Eleanor to wed the German emperor in 1235 and the reception of Eleanor of Castile, his future daughter-in-law, in 1255. Symbolic acts were performed on religious feast days and when gifts were made to the church. And then there were Christmas festivities. The chronicler Matthew Paris remarked (favourably) on that of 1235 which preceded Queen Eleanor's coronation. Celebrations could mark reconciliations and could also involve symbolic

---

[50] For what follows see especially Carpenter, *Henry III: 1207–1258*, especially Chs. 6 and 7.

[51] Carpenter, *Henry III: 1207–1258*, 467.

[52] See Björn Weiler, 'Symbolism and Politics in the Reign of Henry III', *TCE*, ix (2013), 15-41, from which the following comments and instances are drawn. This is a subject of international discussion stemming largely from the work of Gerd Althoff, *Spielregeln der Politik in Mittelalter. Kommunikation in Frieden unde Fehde* (Darmstadt, 1997), and 'Zur Bedeutung symbolischer Kommunikation für das Verständnis des Mittelalters', in *Frühmittelalters Studien*, 31 (1997), 370–89. Symbolic communication refers to 'ideas, concepts and claims conveyed largely through gestures, ceremonies and rituals' (Weiler, 'Symbolism and Politics', 17). In an important adjunct to this line of inquiry Tim Reuter stresses how the spoken word remains active within the process of symbolic communication: T. Reuter, 'Velle Sibi Fier in forma hac. Symbolisches Handeln im Beckestreit', in *Formen und Funktionen öffentlicher Kommunikation im Mittelalter*, ed. G. Althoff, *Vortäge und Forschungen*, 51 (Stuttgart, 2001), 201–25.

[53] Paris, *CM* iii, 336–8. For the full details of the coronation, see also Margaret Howell, *Eleanor of Provence: Queenship in Thirteenth Century England* (Oxford, 1998), 16–20.

[54] *Ann Mon.* ii (Waverley), 330. See also Weiler, 'Symbolism and Politics', 20, n. 30.

26 POLITICS AND SOCIETY IN MID THIRTEENTH-CENTURY ENGLAND

knightings. In 1234 the reconciliation between the king and Gilbert Marshal involved Henry knighting him and granting him his inheritance, while in 1240 the inauguration of a period of peace in Anglo–Welsh relations was marked by the knighting of Dafydd, the son of Llewelyn the Great. The festivities around the translation of the Holy Blood at Westminster in 1247 also involved the knighting of young noblemen, including the king's half-brother, William de Valence. As Björn Weiler points out, feasts were about honour as well as patronage.[55] The full panoply of symbolism and ceremony is shown in 1253 when, on the eve of the king's departure for Gascony, Magna Carta was confirmed. The archbishop of Canterbury, assisted by thirteen bishops, dressed in pontifical garb and burning candles, then excommunicated all who would infringe it.[56]

The prestige of kingship and of the royal dynasty seem to have been high on the list of the king's priorities, and recent historians have paid much attention to ceremony and to symbolism in respect of it. His position was symbiotic with that of other dynasties, most particularly the Capetian. The rebuilding of Westminster, however much an act of piety, can also be seen in this light.[57] Henry's continental ambitions were very much connected. As we have seen, he dreamed of the reconquest of the Plantagenet lands. Although his Breton campaign was a failure, campaigning against the French monarchy was always there in the background. Hence the money and the energy he spent on diplomacy. It partly explains his marrying his sister, Isabella, to the emperor, Frederick II, on 20 July 1235. Then, of course, there was the prestige of being connected to the imperial dynasty. It was an expensive arrangement, involving a dowry of 30,000 marks.[58] In 1242 Henry finally had the opportunity to mount a reconquest of Poitou and sought taxation from parliament. This was denied and the campaign was an abject failure, although his presence in Gascony secured his power there the following year. Only with the Treaty of Paris in 1259 did Henry final renounce his other claims/ pretensions in France. Meanwhile he had made his eldest son, Edward, lord of Gascony as part of his appanage and was very taken with his brother, Richard of Cornwall, being elected king of Germany. Henry's ambitions and greed for dynastic prestige explain his acceptance of the papal offer for his younger son, Edmund, to become king of Sicily. Not that these ambitions were Henry's alone. His Lusignan half-brothers helped to keep his focus on Gascony, while his wife's family, the Savoyards, supported his ambition to establish his dynasty as a Mediterranean power. Sicily was in a sense 'an enterprise of the Savoyards'.[59]

[55] Weiler, 'Symbolism and Politics', 24.

[56] *De Antiquis Legibus*, 18–19; Weiler, 'Symbolism and Politics', 25.

[57] N. Vincent, *The Holy Blood: King Henry III and the Westminster Blood Relic* (Cambridge, 2001), 7–9. See also Paul Binski, *Westminster Abbey and the Plantagenets: Kingship and the Representation of Power 1200–1400* (New Haven and London, 1995), 142–3.

[58] The latest account is in Carpenter, *Henry III: 1207–1258*, 172–5. See B. Weiler, *Henry III of England and the Staufen Empire, 1216–1272* (Woodbridge, 2006), Ch. 2.

[59] See Carpenter, *Henry III: 1207–1258*, 585–6.

At one with all of this was the lavish patronage which he bestowed on the Savoyard relatives of the queen, Eleanor of Provence, and from 1247 on his own Lusignan half-brothers, sons of his mother, Isabella of Angoulême, by her second marriage to Hugh de Lusignan. To these and other recipients of royal patronage Henry gave land, cash, wardships, and marriages, the consequences of which we will return to in the course of this study.[60]

The Royal Finances

Given his ambitions and his style of rule it is hardly surprising that Henry was constantly in need of money. His outgoings were very considerable. The attempt at the reconquest of Poitou in 1242 cost a total of at least £80,000,[61] while the expense incurred by the expedition to Gascony in 1253–4 has been calculated as £42,458.[62] Worse was to follow. Seeking the crown of Sicily for Edmund meant underwriting of the papal debts amounting to some £90,000. Meanwhile, the rebuilding of Westminster Abbey on a grand scale cost some £55,000 over the course of the reign, £28,000 of it before 1259.[63] There was also the cost of Lord Edward's appanage, some £10,000 per annum in total. If Henry's finances were nonetheless relatively buoyant during the 1240s, the following decade saw increasing difficulties.[64] In raising money, the king was restricted by Magna Carta, not only in terms of feudal resources, fines, and amercements, but also through the stipulation in the original charter that no general aid should be levied 'without common consent'. Henry gained direct taxation in 1225 and 1232, and with more difficulty in 1237. 'For Henry', says Maddicott, 'direct taxation was the great honeypot. But between the king and his subjects' wealth there now stood parliament, the firm controller of the honeypot's lid'.[65] The king's subsequent attempts to raise money via parliament came to nought. In Maddicott's words, 'The exchanges between king and magnates occasioned by such requests provided the stuff of parliamentary politics during these years'.[66] In 1242 they told him that he had planned to campaign in Poitou without consulting them, while in 1248 they attacked him for his patronage of aliens, for his illegal seizing of supplies for his household, for keeping bishoprics and abbacies vacant so that he could take the revenues, for failing to appoint a justiciar and chancellor, and for appointing a treasurer 'without common counsel'. These great officers of state

---

[60] See below 38–60.

[61] These figures are from Maddicott, *The Origins of the English Parliament, 924–1327*, 170. See also Stacey, *Politics, Policy and Finance*, 199, and Maddicott, *Simon de Montfort*, 125.

[62] Carpenter, *Henry III: 1207–1258*, 598.

[63] H. M. Colvin, R. A. Brown, and A. J. Taylor, *The History of the King's Works*, vol. i (London, 1963), 155–7.

[64] For Henry's financial situation during the 1240s, see Carpenter, *Henry III: 1207–1258*, 449–52.

[65] Maddicott, *Origins of Parliament*, 172.   [66] Ibid., 174.

28 POLITICS AND SOCIETY IN MID THIRTEENTH-CENTURY ENGLAND

were a major issue with the magnates, and they repeatedly attempted to secure their appointment. Famously, in the parliament of 1244, the 'Paper Constitution' proposed the election of these together with four councillors to be attendant upon the king.[67] The attempts, however, were without effect.

For money, then, Henry had to look elsewhere. In fact, he and his advisors were 'fertile in schemes for increasing royal revenues and resources'.[68] By far the most lucrative was tallaging the Jews.[69] Another major resource was the king's income from the counties. This brings us back to the sheriff. In 1236 changes were introduced following the arrival of William de Savoy as Henry's chief councillor.[70] They were intended to increase the king's revenue.[71] Thirteen sheriffs were removed, involving seventeen counties. Curial sheriffs were replaced by lesser men, many of whom had property in the counties to which they were appointed and had already been employed there as escheators, assessors and collectors of taxes, justices, under-sheriffs, and the like. Royal manors were now withdrawn from the sheriffs and put into the hands of separate keepers, who would manage them more efficiently. Increments were abandoned. The new sheriffs were all custodians and operated with much less generous allowances. They also swore an oath not to take bribes. Between 1236–41 the majority of the sheriffs were custodians, operating in this way. In 1241, however, increments were reintroduced, making the sheriffs worse off than those of 1236–41. After 1242 the pressure was turned up. In Carpenter's words, 'What happened between 1241–58 was that the increments had become so large that they often left, even after raising the farms of the hundreds, insufficient revenue for the sheriff's sustenance, and thus he resorted increasingly to the imposition of fees and the exploitation of his traditional rights of hospitality'.[72] We now see men fining to be exempted from the office. Those who did take on the role dispensed with under-sheriffs and ran the show themselves. The period 1236–58 also saw the separation of castles and counties, with the former being handed to curial castellans and the latter being placed under non-curial sheriffs. These policies, however, helped to aggravate the endemic corruption of local government, especially when the exchequer turned to employing

---

[67] Ibid., 180 and references given there. For a recent, thorough discussion, see Carpenter, *Henry III: 1207–1258*, 452–63.

[68] Ibid., 451.

[69] See R. C. Stacey, '"1240–60"': A Watershed in Anglo-Jewish relations?' *Historical Research*, 61 (1988), 135–50.

[70] For what follows see David Carpenter, 'Decline of the Curial Sheriff in England, 1194–1258', *EHR*, 101 (1976), 166–78.

[71] Carpenter also claims that the changes were a 'subtly conceived reform of administration in the counties, which was designed to be popular with local society' (ibid., 166), that they were 'cleverly packaged to meet the aspirations and grievances of county society', and that William of Savoy was 'able to outmanoeuvre the opposition to his dominance at court by appealing to local society' (ibid., 167). No evidence is given for these assertions, although he does later cite Paris, *CM* iii, 363.

[72] Ibid., 173.

men from outside the counties to which they were appointed and, indeed, men of obscure background.

Richard Cassidy has looked in more detail at the functioning of the sheriffs between 1242 and 1258 from the point of view of royal finances.[73] Throughout the 1240s and 1250s the counties were expected to pay increasing amounts from their regular revenue. This level of extraction by the government was mirrored in other areas. The forests were exploited, as were the general eyres.[74] Cassidy sums up the situation as follows: 'The eyres were treated as a money-raising expedient, with the collective penalties *ante judicium* much resented. The same was true of the sums collected at county and hundred courts as *beaupleader* fines, imposed on communities rather than individuals'. These last were payments in advance, described by Paul Brand as 'a kind of institutional bribe to the king through the justices'.[75] Further money was raised from fines paid for charters and privileges. It is little wonder that Matthew Paris described the king as an indefatigable searcher after money.

It would be a mistake, however, to think that the government saw all of this money. Cassidy has calculated that in the case of the 1257 farm and profit, the sheriffs handed over some 80 per cent within a year or so. But this was not true in all cases. The sheriff of Northumberland delivered only 30 per cent of the amercements from the eyre. William Heron, the sheriff, had in fact collected the debts but kept them himself. Heron is a well-known example of shrieval dishonesty.[76] But what were sheriffs to do when their targets were raised? The articles of the eyre and the Hundred Rolls enquiry of 1255 asked for information on corrupt officials, and plenty came through. The sheriffs were up there on the front line. Two published eyres— those for Surrey in 1255 and Shropshire in 1256—reveal complaints of extortion. These included unjust imprisonment and payment to gain release, as well as bribes to avoid arrest, amercements taken more than once, and sheriffs using their office to advance their own private quarrels. There were clearly two factors at work. On the one hand, there was corruption for the sake of personal gain. On the other hand, there was pressure from the centre for increasing amounts of cash.

Henry III and the Public Interest

What, then, of Henry's attitude towards the public interest? He must certainly have been aware of his obligations. After all his coronation oath 'bound him to

[73] R. Cassidy, 'Bad Sheriffs, Custodial Sheriffs and Control of the Counties', *TCE*, xv (Woodbridge, 2015), 35–49.

[74] See Cassidy, 'Bad Sheriffs', 37, n. 10 and the references given there.

[75] Paul Brand, *Kings, Barons, and Justices: The Making and Enforcement of Legislation in Thirteenth-Century England* (Cambridge, 2003), 89.

[76] See Richard Cassidy, 'William Heron, "Hammer of the Poor, Persecutor of the Religious", Sheriff of Northumberland, 1246–58', *Northern History*, 50 (2013), 9–19.

30 POLITICS AND SOCIETY IN MID THIRTEENTH-CENTURY ENGLAND

rule for the welfare of his people',[77] not to mention the strictures of Magna Carta. Some time ago Michael Clanchy reacted against the general dismissal of Henry III's kingship by major historians as, among other things, lacking in direction, arguing to the contrary that the king did indeed have a coherent policy.[78] His essay is built around a lecture which the king delivered at the exchequer on 7 October 1250 to all sheriffs, recorded on a memoranda roll.[79] Clanchy argued that Henry's recorded statements have generally been under-studied by historians because they stem largely from the *Chronica Majora* of Matthew Paris whose general tendency to hyperbole, to say the least, renders him untrustworthy in this respect. Clanchy showed, however, that the king's propensity to make pronouncements from time to time is substantiated by the memoranda rolls, that the times and places Paris describes for these addresses can often be corroborated, and that the views Paris attributes to him are paralleled in other sources. Looking carefully at the memorandum of 1250 and separating out the high-flown components of royal status, what we actually see is the king expressing his role as the protector of public authority. His emphasis on how the magnates treat their men is a direct reference to Magna Carta's extension of the king's responsibilities to their own tenants. Stressed by Henry from time to time, this became a leitmotiv during the 1250s as Henry counterattacked against his critics.[80] As Matthew Paris has him say in 1255, 'Why do not these bishops and magnates ... observe towards their subjects this Charter for which they make such clamour?'[81] The problem was that this was largely rhetoric and did not extend to the king's friends and those he favoured. Carpenter has asked why Henry did not undertake a reform of the system, especially after he had taken the cross in 1250 when it was imperative that he cleanse his conscience? Why did he not copy Louis IX with his *enquêtes*, which offered reparations for the wrongs committed by the king and his officials?[82] As Carpenter writes, 'Louis's sense of his responsibilities spread the benefits of reparation over all the kingdom, with commensurate benefits to the whole standing of his kingship'.[83] He offers two explanations. The first is that Henry, with his extreme piety and almsgiving, did not see his situation in this way. And so, he 'missed the opportunity to reform the realm'.[84] The second is more practical, and more fundamental: 'Henry simply lacked the single-minded drive and sense of

[77] Carpenter, *The Reign of Henry III*, 457.
[78] M. T. Clanchy, 'Did Henry III Have a Policy', *History*, 53/178 (1968), 203–16.
[79] TNA E/368/25 m. 2. Clanchy gives the Latin text on 215–16.
[80] Maddicott, 'Magna Carta and the Local Community', 52–3.
[81] *Chronica Majora*, v, p. 501; Maddicott, 'Magna Carta and the Local Community', 53; Clanchy, 'Did Henry III Have a Policy?', 208.
[82] See the discussion in Carpenter, *Henry III: 1207–1258*, 527–33.
[83] Ibid., 714, citing M. Dejoux, *Les Enquêtes de Saint Louis: Gouverner et Sauvor son Âme* (Paris 2014), Ch. 8.
[84] Carpenter, *Henry III: 1207–1258*, 567.

ANGEVIN LEGACY AND THE KINGSHIP OF HENRY III   31

duty to carry through a great reform of the realm in face of the vested interests of himself and his ministers'.[85]

Clanchy pointed to a second important dimension to the 1250 memorandum. Implicit in Henry's statements is that the magnates are his subjects, hence his oversight of their behaviour and transgressions. At parliament in July 1248 he had already emphasized 'his unique position as sovereign lord'. Paris has him say:

> No more should vassals judge their prince or confine him to their conditions, than servants would their lord. For, whosoever are deemed inferiors have rather to be directed at the will (*arbitrium*) of the lord and the pleasure (*voluntas*) of the ordinary.[86]

Henry's expressed view is echoed in the treatise on the laws and customs of England known as 'Bracton': 'the king is under no man, he has no peer, no one should presume to dispute his acts, an aggrieved supplicant against him must wait the vengeance of God'. Furthermore, 'the interpretation of royal charters and acts depends ultimately upon the king's pleasure (*voluntas*); ordinary jurisdiction must always remain with the king'.[87] In the summer of 1255, Henry initiated a nationwide inquest into the infringements of royal rights which included a question 'concerning those who claim to have liberties without a royal charter, and which ones'.[88] But Henry's imperious concept of kingship was not transformed into practice.[89] He did not, for the most part at least, act in a high-handed way towards his magnates. As Carpenter says, they were not threatened by 'absolutist theories'.[90] But this does not prove that Henry did not subscribe to a high-flown conception of his powers. He was simply unable to act on them or had no stomach for attempting to do so.

Another insight into Henry III's conception of kingship is provided by the proem to the *Dictum of Kenilworth* in 1266.[91] In the opinion of Benjamin Wild, '*The Dictum of Kenilworth* was inspired by imperial, papal and Capetian rhetoric and ideology, but in its presentation of ideas touching royal authority it reflects the attitude of Henry himself'.[92] Wild makes a series of points. Henry is introduced as 'the most Christian prince', a title normally reserved to the Capetian kings of

---

[85] Ibid., 537.

[86] Paris, *CM* v, p. 20. Clanchy explains that an ordinary, in the sense drawn from Roman law by the canonists, was 'one who exercised jurisdiction *suo jure* [in his own right] and not by delegation'.

[87] *De Legibus et Consuetudinibus Angliae*, ed. G. E. Woodbine/*Bracton on the Laws and Customs of England*, trans. S. E. Thorne, 4 vols. (Cambridge, Mass, 1968), ii, 33, 109, 167.

[88] *Annales Monastici* i, 338 (Annals of Burton); Clanchy, 'Did Henry III Have a Policy?', 210. Clanchy argues that Paris was probably right in his assertion that Henry derived his ideas from papal practice. 'Bracton' was expert in this, as were John of Lexington and William of Kilkenny, successive keepers of the seal during the years 1245–55. Henry's views were also echoed in the *Liber Augustalis* of the emperor Frederick II: ibid.

[89] Carpenter, *The Reign of Henry III*, 75–106.   [90] Ibid., 85.

[91] For the context, see below 245–7.   [92] Ibid., 256.

32   POLITICS AND SOCIETY IN MID THIRTEENTH-CENTURY ENGLAND

France. There are references to consultation and consent, but the 'councillors' have God alone before their eyes and prefer the head to the members, echoing papal and imperial rhetoric. Henry is called 'illustrious', following the standard papal address to rulers. In Wild's view the proem is distinctive in elevating the king to a position of sole authority, eschewing the idea that lawmaking was a joint enterprise involving king and barons.

Henry III's occasionally revealed views on kingship do not seem to explain very much in terms of his actual governance, apart from helping to understand the shifts between stubbornness and vacillation that characterized his rule, and perhaps the way he moved from vindictiveness to a reasoned position between the battle of Evesham and the publication of the *Dictum of Kenilworth*. Henry's grievances against the council in March 1261[93] and the royalist position at Amiens in 1264 are more concerned with the practicalities of governing and the actual restrictions imposed upon him. It should be noted, though, that they contain references to his power and royal dignity, the rights of the crown, homage and fealty, and the coronation oath. Scholars have wondered why, having regained power in 1261, Henry restored the status quo rather than embracing reform, and have essentially condemned him for it. He was not a man of high political intelligence, but even if he had been it is doubtful that he could have achieved it. Not only did his ministers have other ideas and their own esprit de corps which militated against it, but there was a whole raft of people who were associated with his regime and profited from it. They would have baulked at reform. In any case there is nothing to indicate that Henry would have favoured it.

Finally, Clanchy raised yet a third dimension to the memorandum of 1250, asking whether Henry had a sacramental view of kingship. A contradiction has been seen between Henry's piety on the one hand and his reported expressions of anticlericalism on the other. But this is perfectly explicable, writes Clanchy, in that, 'Henry opposed clerics not as a secularist, but on religious grounds. In his view he was obliged by the sanctity of his office to supervise ecclesiastical affairs'. This is shown in preambles to chancery mandates. In 1246, for example, he wrote: 'By reason of our government of churches and their liberties, we have been given by divine clemency the duty to defend them from injurious violence committed by any sort of persons on any sort of occasion'.[94] The recipient here was the bishop of Coventry, who was being ordered to reverse an excommunication. 'If', says Clanchy, 'it is accepted that Henry had a sacramental view of the king's office, his combination of piety with opposition to the clergy makes sense'.[95]

---

[93] For the relationship between the three extant versions, see now Huw Ridgeway, 'King Henry III's Grievances against the Council in 1261: A New Version and a Letter Describing Political Events', *Historical Research*, 6/145 (1988), 227–42.

[94] *Close Rolls* 1237–42, 435.

[95] Clanchy, 'Did Henry III Have a Policy?', 213. Matthew Paris reports Henry acting in a sacramental manner in the disputed Winchester election of 1250. He has him process into the cathedral 'as though he were a bishop or a prior' and deliver his sermon from the president's seat in the chapter house': Paris, *CM* v, 180.

ANGEVIN LEGACY AND THE KINGSHIP OF HENRY III   33

'Bracton', Clanchy points out, acknowledges the king as Christ's viceregent and uses the ancient title of vicar of God. We are reminded that Henry's instructions to the sheriff in 1250 included actions against blasphemers. Clanchy also points to Henry's extraordinarily frequent use of the *Laudes Regiae* (the ancient hymns of praise for the ruler) as well as his devotion to Edward the Confessor and his reconstruction of Westminster abbey.[96]

However, as Clanchy himself was aware, care is needed in interpreting Henry's beliefs and actions here. Nicholas Vincent and David Carpenter have both drawn attention to the religious symbolism involved in Henry's expression of royal dignity.[97] On the one hand, as Carpenter stresses, Henry claimed no priestly powers. When Henry asked Bishop Grosseteste what unction added to the royal dignity, the bishop replied in terms of the responsibilities imposed and told him roundly that it did not place the king on the same level as a priest. Henry appears to have acknowledged this, for according to Matthew Paris he refused to hold a candle during an excommunication in 1253 because 'he was not a priest'.[98] On the other hand, however, 'No other English layman wore a crown and, if Henry claimed no priestly power, his dalmatic with its jewels and orphreys was still very much an ecclesiastical garment worn by bishops and deacons on festal occasions, most notably when celebrating mass'.[99]

Contemporary Perceptions of Henry III

But how was Henry perceived by his contemporaries? Carpenter says that Henry looked every inch a king.[100] But did he? He was, of course, clothed in and surrounded by glitter. There were surely some who could see through the sumptuous attire. And there were others who interpreted Henry's sense of theatre less sympathetically. Here we come face to face with the St Albans chronicler,

---

[96] Moreover, Henry was also interested in the other canonized English kings, whose names he was able to recall to Matthew Paris: Clanchy, 'Did Henry III Have a Policy?', 214.

[97] N. Vincent, *The Holy Blood: King Henry III and the Westminster Blood Relic* (Cambridge, 2001), 190–6, and 'The Pilgrimages of the Angevin Kings of England, 1154–27', in C. Morris and P. Roberts (eds.), *Pilgrimage: The English Experience from Becket to Bunyan* (Cambridge, 2002), 31–45; Carpenter, 'The Burial of King Henry III, the Regalia and Royal Ideology', in *The Reign of Henry III*, 28–54. See also P. Binski, *Westminster Abbey and the Plantagenets: Kingship and the Representations of Power, 1200–1400* (New Haven, 1995), 121–48, and S. Dixon-Smith, 'The Image and Reality of Alms-giving in the Great Halls of Henry III', *Journal of the British Archaeological Association*, 152 (1999), 79–96. Vincent has countered the argument of G. Koziol that the post-conquest English kings, unlike their Capetian rivals, faced difficulties when trying to use ritualized actions to buttress their dignity and authority: Vincent, *Holy Blood*, 189–96, and 'Pilgrimages', 39–40; G. Koziol, 'England, France and the Problem of Sacrality in Twelfth-Century Ritual', in T. N. Bisson (ed.), *Cultures of Power, Lordship, Status and Process in Twelfth-Century Europe* (Philadelphia, 1995), 124–48. See also B. Weiler, 'Knighting, Homage, and the Meaning of Ritual: The Kings of England and their Neighbours in the Thirteenth Century', *Viator*, 37 (2006), 275–99.

[98] Carpenter, 'The Burial of King Henry III', 437.   [99] Ibid., 438.

[100] Carpenter, *Henry III: 1207–1258*, 711.

34 POLITICS AND SOCIETY IN MID THIRTEENTH-CENTURY ENGLAND

Matthew Paris.[101] Lars Kjær draws on his work to give a fascinating account of the Christmas festivities provided by Henry III.[102] He begins by restating Paris' overall message: 'Henry was overly affectionate towards foreigners and alienated the native aristocracy. He wasted his money prodigally upon his favourites but was miserly and greedy towards his own subjects. Finally, he was a weak and naïve king who listened to bad counsel.'[103] According to Paris, Christmas 1240 was the first where Henry's love of foreigners became apparent. At the request of the papal legate, 'whom he very much desired to please', the king knighted Otto's nephew, Advocatus, and granted him an income of £30. At the banquet he installed Otto in the royal seat and sat him at his right hand so that all the bishops and nobles had to move one seat down the table 'according to the king's plan and will', undermining the traditional order and provoking 'angry looks'. In writing this Paris was of course aware of the theological and hence politically charged connotations of ruling by will (*voluntas*). Henry's honorands, moreover, were not worthy of the favours bestowed upon them. Advocatus immediately sold the gift he had been given by the king.[104]

Henry spent Christmas 1250 at the vacant see of Winchester, and while he was there he had the trees from its woods cut down and sold them. Divine displeasure was shown by a thunderstorm on Christmas night. Paris also reports that Henry gave no clothes to his knights and his household that year and reduced the expenses of his table. At this time, too, he began demanding hospitality and gifts from religious houses as of right. In addition to his general parsimony, he ceased to show any gratitude for the gifts that were given him, as was evident at Christmas 1252.[105] Meanwhile, in December 1251, came the marriage between Henry's daughter, Margaret, and the young King Alexander III of Scotland. According to Paris the wedding and the festivities were marred by the two kings vying with one another in the costly livery worn by their numerous knights and in holding sumptuous feasts. The whole tone was marred by their 'theatrical, worldly vanity'.[106]

Matthew Paris makes it clear that it was not just the lack of decorum which people objected to but the profaning of Christmas itself. Whereas Henry should have been concerned with divine matters and with promoting the happiness of his subjects and the harmony of his kingdom, he was concerned with worldly matters: with his favourites, his treasury, and his political aims, associating him with bad rulers of the past and comparing him, Kjær tells us, with Louis IX. 'In placing the affairs of the royal Christmas at the opening of each year, following on

---

[101] For the question of his reliability, see R. Vaughan, *Matthew Paris* (Cambridge, 1958) and B. Weiler, 'Matthew Paris and the Writing of History', *JMH*, 35 (2009), 254–78.

[102] Lars Kjær, 'Matthew Paris and the Royal Christmas: Ritualised Communication in Text and Practice', *TCE*, xiv (2003), 141–54. The quotation is at 143.

[103] Ibid., 153.   [104] Paris, *CM* iv, 83–4.   [105] Ibid., v, 199.

[106] ... *mundi vanitas theatralis*: Paris, *CM* v, 266–70. For the wedding see K. Staniland, 'The Nuptuals of Alexander III and Margaret Plantagenet', *Nottingham Medieval Studies*, 30 (1996), 20–45.

directly from the summary of the state of the weather and prosperity of the realm which concluded each year, Paris was hinting at an older tradition that saw the conduct of the king and his court as central to the wellbeing of the realm.'[107]

Kjær turns to the question of the veracity of Paris's description of these rituals.[108] Comparison between Paris's accounts in the *Chronica Majora* and the royal records suggests that here he can generally be trusted, at least as far as the events themselves are concerned. As regards the income of £30 given to Advocatus, for example, we find that he was given the wardship and marriage of the heirs and widow of Robert de Barnevill, which he passed on to the bishop of Carlisle shortly after.[109] Kjær concludes that 'Paris was skilled at crafting narratives of ritualised action but ... did not go so far as to "invent" rituals that had not taken place, nor did he recycle purely literary tropes. What he did do was to take the events of the royal Christmas feasts and present them in a manner that aligned itself with his various authorial agendas'.[110] There is one further point to be made when attempting to assess how far Matthew Paris's writing reflected contemporary opinion. The *Chronica Majora* was written for a monastic audience. As Kjær points out, when Paris came to write the *Historia Anglorum*, which may well have been written with a courtly audience in mind, he excluded material which was likely to give offence.[111] However, the most important point is that if one caustic commentator could see the royal glitter from a refracted perspective, then others could have done so too.

Bjorn Weiler adds some further telling examples, also drawn from Matthew Paris.[112] His account of the Christmas parliament of 1256 'turned an occasion which had been intended to whip up support for the Sicilian Business—in the context of announcing Richard of Cornwall's imminent election to the German throne—into a scathing critique of the king and his policies'. His report on the translation of the relic of the Holy Blood to Westminster in 1247 'undermined the solemnity of the occasion and thwarted the king's act of symbolic representation by recording doubts concerning the authenticity of the relic'.[113] He records the king's prolonged stay at Woodstock in May 1247 to celebrate the marriage between two Provencal ladies and two of his former wards. The festivities caused chagrin, owing to the low standing and obscurity of the chosen spouses.[114] Weiler is much interested in the issue of audience for symbolism and ceremony and the way that the reaction to it could thwart intentions. Thus, the festivities around the translation of Edward the Confessor in 1269 were hijacked by the archbishop of York's

[107] 'Matthew Paris and the Royal Christmas', 149–50.
[108] On this issue see also D. A. Carpenter, 'Matthew Paris and Henry III's Speech at the Exchequer in October 1256', in *The Reign of Henry III*, 137–50.
[109] For the gifts and those that follow, see *CPR 1232–47*, 241; *CR 1227–42*, 145, 257, 264; *CLR 1240–45*, 213.
[110] Kjær, 'Matthew Paris and the Royal Christmas', 154.   [111] Ibid., 147.
[112] Weiler, 'Matthew Paris and the Writing of History', 31–2.
[113] Paris, *CM* iv, 641–4.   [114] Ibid., iv, 628.

36 POLITICS AND SOCIETY IN MID THIRTEENTH-CENTURY ENGLAND

wearing of his pontifical robes and the reaction by the bishops against this and the rival claims of the burgesses of Winchester and London over the service of butler. As Weiler points out, the whole show is indicative of the king's incapacity to inspire fear and respect among his subjects.[115]

In his biography of Henry III David Carpenter furnishes examples of contemptuous ways in which people spoke directly to the king. There is of course the prime example of Simon de Montfort, who told the king on campaign in Poitou that he should be taken and locked up like Charles the Simple, and that at Windsor he should be kept in with iron bars, a reference to the fitting of bars there after an assassination attempt on the king in 1238.[116] This must have really stung a king 'very conscious of his name and fame'.[117] There are numerous others. The king's officials could be treated with contempt. A bailiff of Henry's half-brother, Guy de Lusignan, said that 'he would do no more for the sheriff than he would for the sheriff's daughter', while the Marcher baron, Walter de Clifford, annoyed at the contents of a royal letter, forced the royal messenger to eat it together with its seal.[118] When the 'young and deeply pious' Isabella, countess of Arundel, complained about the king's appropriation of a wardship, Henry was conciliatory. However, she 'silenced Henry with a tirade about his injustices and breaches of Magna Carta'. It was an episode which became widely known, says Carpenter, and 'left a deep mark on the king'. Two years later Henry made another concession to her, but stipulated that she was not to repeat 'the opprobrious things' which she had said at Westminster.[119] On 8 January 1254 Henry wrote an angry letter home from Gascony concerning the northern baron Peter de Maulay, although in the end he did not send it. Peter had tried to persuade others to return to England and had been rude to the king. Apparently, placed in charge of the royal bodyguard of fifty knights he had left Henry alone and in great danger. In fact, Henry soon restored him to favour.[120] Then there is the case of Roger Bigod, who spoke in the parliament of 1255 in favour of a fellow magnate, William de Ros. Henry called him a traitor, which Roger denied, saying that the king could hardly hurt him. Henry replied that he could in fact seize Roger's corn and thresh it. 'Do so', retorted Roger, 'and I will send back your threshers without their heads'.[121] Finally, and perhaps most damning of all, was a story that seems to have been brought to the papal court, where Henry was known for his simplicity. This was of a jester who compared King Henry to Jesus Christ. Why? Because he was as wise as a man as he had been when a little child![122]

---

[115] Weiler, 'Matthew Paris and the Writing of History', 34–8.

[116] Carpenter, *Henry III: 1207–1258*, 262; Maddicott, *Simon de Montfort*, 32; and C. Bémont, *Simon de Montfort* (1st edn., Paris, 1884), 2nd edn. trans. E. F. Jacob (Oxford, 1930), 65 and n. 3.

[117] Carpenter, *Henry III: 1207–1258*, 147.

[118] Ibid., 533, and references given there. Clifford fined for the king's pardon, but Henry's anger did not last and the instalments dwindled.

[119] Ibid., 554; Paris *CM* v, 336–7; *CFR 1253–4*, 510.

[120] Carpenter, *Henry III: 1207–1258*, 581.   [121] See below 73.

[122] Carpenter, *Henry III: 1207–1258*, 632.

Henry's inability to inspire awe may have been partly a matter of physique. Like his father, and unlike his son, Edward, he was not a tall man.[123] He lacked the martial temperament, and he lacked military skill. However, these were not the only qualities Henry was short of. Where was the self-mastery, the self-discipline, and the steadfastness which Simon de Montfort, for example, exhibited in abundance? For Henry, as Simon well knew, his word was not his bond. Simon was in fact the epitome of all that Henry was not. To put the matter another way, Henry's 'cosmic kingship' could not overcome his shortcomings against the most iconic type of masculinity of the day.[124]

These, then, are the characteristics of the English polity and of the kingship of Henry III which provide the context within which the insurrection of 1258 occurred. If we are to begin to explain it, we now need to turn the spotlight upon the nobility and upon how its members were impacted.

Politics and Society in Mid Thirteenth-Century England: The Troubled Realm. Peter Coss, Oxford University Press.
© Peter Coss 2024. DOI: 10.1093/9780198924319.003.0002

---

[123] Ibid., 57. According to Nicholas Trevet, writing in the 1320s, Henry was 'of medium height, compact of body [i.e. sturdy] and with the lid of one eye dropping down over the pupil': Carpenter, *Henry III: 1258–1272*, 632.

[124] See below 203.

3

The Impact of Royal Policy on the Nobility

Patronage, Appeasement, and Privatization

This chapter will examine the effects of Henry's governance upon the landowners, chiefly the higher nobility. It will begin with the issue of patronage, and move on to what one might call his policy of appeasement. It will conclude with the issue of privatization. Henry III's patronage, most particularly of his relatives, has been much studied by recent historians and once again only the outlines need be conveyed here.

Patronage and the Rewards of Service

There can be no doubt that Henry III enjoyed bestowing patronage, even if sometimes he was to regret his liberality. Largesse can so easily slip over into prodigality, and when this occurs there are likely to be serious political consequences. Such was the case for Henry III. At the apex of recipients during Henry's personal rule was his family, as broadly interpreted by the king. Least controversial, and most politic, was the endowment of his brother, Richard. He had been knighted in 1225, given Cornwall during the king's pleasure and the title of count of Poitou. He was subsequently given 1,000 marks and granted Cornwall and the honours of Eye and Wallingford.[1] In 1235 he was granted Knaresborough in hereditary right and the wardship of the lands late of John de Briouze.[2] In 1240 the king gave Richard a gift of 1,000 marks towards his crusade, from the tallage of the Jews.[3] In 1242 he gave him a further £400 and four valuable manors when he agreed to marry Sanchia, the queen's sister, and to go with Henry to Poitou.[4] One or two early glitches aside,[5] Richard was to prove 'a pillar of the regime', even though he differed greatly from Henry in personality, being 'cooler, cleverer, more

---

[1] *CPR 1225–32*, 313; *CR 1227–31*, 287; *CLR 1226–40*, 172; *The Royal Charter Witness Lists of Henry III (1226–72) from the Charter Rolls in the Public Record Office*, ed. M. Morris, List and Index Society nos. 291–2, 2 vols. (2001), i, 84.
[2] *CChR 1226–37*, 89, 191.   [3] *CR 1237–42*, 197.
[4] Carpenter, *Henry III: 1207–1258*, 251.   [5] For the details see ibid., 68–70, 202–3, 264.

THE IMPACT OF ROYAL POLICY ON THE NOBILITY   39

calculating and less pious'.[6] Following the wedding, on 23 November 1243, Richard quitclaimed any right to Gascony and Henry promised the couple and their heirs land worth £500 a year. This land was to come not from the crown's demesne, but from the first escheats that fell in. It was stipulated that no one was to receive escheated land until Richard had been satisfied. Meanwhile, he was to receive 1,000 marks a year, the sum diminishing as land was assigned. Henry did not always keep to what he said, but he was true to his word here, and by 1256 Richard had all the land he had expected.[7]

Another major recipient of Henry's bounty was the 'silver-tongued' Simon de Montfort.[8] In 1229 the young Simon came before Henry III to claim the Montfort half of the earldom of Leicester, resulting from his father's marriage to one of the two heiresses. His elder brother Amaury having transferred his rights to him, Simon paid homage to Henry in August 1231.[9] As Sophie Ambler says, Simon's position was transformed, being admitted into 'England's political elite'.[10] He was now a baron, with lands worth around £500 per annum.[11] He established himself first at Leicester and then at court. Here he was to meet the king's sister, Eleanor. They were married in January 1238 in the king's private chapel at Westminster. The fact that the king had not consulted on this, not even his brother Richard of Cornwall, caused a considerable stir. However, Simon weathered the storm. He was the consummate adventurer.

From her previous marriage to William Marshal, Eleanor possessed dower across southern and south-midland counties worth £534 in 1275. She had given up her dower from Marshal lands in Wales and Ireland for the sum of £400 per annum, agreed between the king and Richard Marshal, though she found this hard to extract from successive Marshal heirs. The king later became surety for it and in 1246 made himself directly responsible for the payment, having then to claim it back from the Marshal family. In 1244 Simon had an overall income of some £1,530, of which £930 was Eleanor's dower. This created problems, the greatest of which was its non-heritability. The Montforts, moreover, were left with two claims against Henry: that the dower of £400 had been inadequate, and that no *maritagium* had been settled on the couple by the king. In May 1244 the king did grant an annual fee of 500 marks, until wardships and escheats of a similar value could be found. In 1245 Montfort was granted the wardship of Gilbert de Umfraville with extensive lands in Northumberland as equivalent to the fee of

---

[6] Ibid., 70, 202. For a biography see N. Denholm-Young, *Richard of Cornwall* (Oxford, 1947). See also N. Vincent, 'Richard, First Earl of Cornwall and King of Germany (1209–1272)', *ODNB*, 46, 702–14.

[7] Ibid., 417.   [8] The phrase is Carpenter's: *Henry III: 1207–1258*, 200.

[9] For a recent discussion of these events, see S. Ambler, *The Song of Simon de Montfort: England's First Revolutionary and the Death of Chivalry* (London, 2019), Ch. 2.

[10] Ibid., 43.

[11] For the details see Maddicott, *Simon de Montfort*, 47–9. What follows is based on Maddicott's discussion of his income thereafter: ibid., 49–59.

40 POLITICS AND SOCIETY IN MID THIRTEENTH-CENTURY ENGLAND

500 marks, the £400 granted in May 1244 for dower losses being allowed to lapse as it was considered to be subsumed in this. Nonetheless, Simon's income in 1246 was £1,860 per annum, putting him among the six wealthiest earls.[12] In 1253 Montfort and Eleanor received Kenilworth Castle, which had earlier been granted to Eleanor for life, with the manor of Odiham which she had previously held during pleasure. New arrangements were made over the *maritagium*. The Umfraville lordship was no longer to be set against the 500-mark fee so that Henry had to find the sum itself; moreover, it was now upped to 600 marks. The arrangements for its payment were extraordinary. It was to be the first charge on the revenues of a number of counties, with the sheriff handing over the money directly to Simon who could distrain on the sheriffs' own property in case of default. 'This was', says John Maddicott, 'one of the most extraordinary financial arrangements ever made between a thirteenth-century king and one of his subjects'.[13]

The most spectacular use of royal patronage in Henry's reign, however, was towards the Savoyards. These were the relatives of Queen Eleanor of Provence, whom Henry III married on 14 January 1236. She was accompanied to England by her uncle, William, bishop-elect of Valence. In April a small council of twelve was formed with William as chief minister, a move not received enthusiastically by the magnates. In the words of David Carpenter, Henry had 'taken on a foreign pilot'.[14] The rewards included the great lordship of Richmond in Yorkshire, giving him an income of baronial size.[15] In 1237 the monks of Durham were pressured into making him their bishop. His elevation, says Carpenter, was 'a portent of what was to come'.[16] In December 1239 William died. In the next few years 'Henry bound himself to the queen's kin as never before'.[17] Three more uncles came, one by one: Thomas, Peter, and Boniface. Thomas of Savoy, count of Flanders, arrived in the summer of 1238. Henry loaned him 1,000 marks and took his homage in return for an annual pension of 500 marks. Carpenter calculates that by the time he died in early 1259, he had received 8,375 marks from the exchequer. Peter of Savoy arrived in December 1240. He was given the honour of Richmond, worth some £1,200 per year in 1261, putting him resource-wise among the greatest barons. In the following year he was given the honour of Pevensey and the custody of the Surrey and Sussex lands of John de Warenne, heir to the earldom of Surrey,

---

[12] See the figures in ibid., 53.

[13] Ibid., 122–3. The counties were: Warwickshire and Leicestershire, Nottinghamshire and Derbyshire, Wiltshire, and Berkshire.

[14] Carpenter, *Henry III: 1207–1258*, 187. Ch. 4 of this work, 'The Years of Success, 1234–41', deals inter alia with the reforms initiated by William. Carpenter points out that the appointment of William 'tells us a great deal about Henry's continuing lack of confidence and his need for a shoulder to lean on'. After William's departure from court, he leant on the papal legate, Otto, whom he himself had requested.

[15] Ibid., 189.   [16] Ibid., 197.   [17] Ibid., 208.

THE IMPACT OF ROYAL POLICY ON THE NOBILITY   41

and then made castellan of Dover.[18] On 1 February 1241 Boniface of Savoy was elected archbishop of Canterbury, although he did not arrive in England until 1244. Meanwhile, in August 1240 the Hereford chapter elected as their bishop Peter of Aigueblanche, a protégé of the bishop-elect of Valence and keeper of the king's wardrobe. For his consecration Henry gave him a jewel-encrusted mitre costing £82. Other Savoyards poured in.

In her impressive biography of Queen Eleanor, Margaret Howell deals in detail with the patronage bestowed on lesser-ranking Savoyards, drawing on the important research of Huw Ridgeway.[19] Over 170 Savoyards 'drank at the fountain of the king's patronage', although more than half were not resident in England. Two thirds were clerks, many of them in the households of Archbishop Boniface and Bishop Peter or in the chapter at Hereford. A few were in the royal household. Others were in the queen's service. Dozens of Savoyards, most of them knights, were granted lands by the king, while others received annual fees. Some of them moved from service with the great Savoyard lords into royal service.[20] Some acquired heiresses and wealthy widows. Peter de Savoy, for example, gained Joan de Somery, widow of the king's steward Godfrey de Crowcombe. Just as these men were gifted wealthy English ladies, so high-born girls related to the house of Savoy married the king's wards. It is little wonder, as Howell points out, that the Petition of the Barons of 1258 complained of the disparagement of women whose marriages were 'in the king's gift' by being bestowed on men 'who were not true-born Englishmen'.[21] There is no doubt that these activities on the marriage market caused considerable resentment among the native aristocracy.

In 1247, Henry 'decided to tie the kingdom to a second group of foreign relatives'.[22] These were the children of his mother, Queen Isabella, by her second husband, Hugh de Lusignan. The Lusignan party, which arrived in April 1247,[23] included Henry's half-sister, Alice, who had come to marry John de Warenne, heir to the earl of Surrey, a royal ward in the king's custody. Another member of the party was the youngest brother, Aymer, who was in England to study at Oxford. The leader of the party, however, was Guy de Lusignan, who was given a pension of 300 marks a year with the usual promise to convert it into land from wardships or escheats. He was given £1,000 as an advance. At the end of the year a further 300-mark pension was given to another brother, Geoffrey de Lusignan,

---

[18] He was later asked to surrender Dover and instead given charge of the castle of Rochester and made warden of the Cinque Ports: *CPR 1232–47*, 265–6.

[19] Howell, *Eleanor of Provence*, 49–54. Details are from H. W. Ridgeway, 'The Politics of the English Royal Court, 1247–65, with Special Reference to the Role of Aliens' (University of Oxford, DPhil thesis, 1983). See also his 'King Henry III and the "Aliens", 1236–72', 81–92, and his 'Foreign Favourites and Henry III's Problems of Patronage, 1247–58', *EHR*, 104/412 (July 1989), 590–610.

[20] For details, see below 130.   [21] *DBM*, nos. 3. 81.

[22] Carpenter, *Henry III: 1207–1258*, 467. Carpenter provides a useful precis of Henry's patronage of the Lusignans, which I have followed here: ibid., 467–74.

[23] See above ...

who, in Carpenter's words, 'had not been of the original party but had hurried to England on hearing the prizes on offer'.[24] Guy and Geoffrey soon returned home but they left yet another brother, William de Valence, who was still in his teens. In June 1247 the death of John de Munchensey, one of the heirs of the Marshal inheritance, leaving his sister Joan as heir, allowed the king to marry her to this William, bringing him Pembroke in Wales and Wexford in Ireland. The marriage took place on 13 August 1247 at Windsor where she was married at the same time as Alice married John de Warenne. Though William gained £703 of land per annum, Henry clearly regarded this as insufficient for a royal brother and promised a further £500 a year to William and his heirs from Alice, first in pension and then in land. Instructively, it was stated that no land was to be given to anyone else, other than Richard of Cornwall, until Valence had been satisfied. A further pension of £500 marks was to be paid for life, and in addition he received two lucrative wardships and a life grant of Hertford Castle. The next year he gained four manors of the 'lands of the Normans', which were not to count against the pensions. Altogether his income reached some £2,300 a year, making him richer than Simon de Montfort.

Although this liberality was much to Henry's desire and taste, it also served a political purpose. Just as the Savoyards had provided the king with valuable international alliances, so his policy towards the Lusignans had a strategic dimension. The Lusignans gave Henry a platform in Poitou, vital to Gascony's defence. The eldest of Henry's half-brothers had become Hugh XI count of Angoulême in 1246 on the death of their mother, but in 1249 he too was given a pension in England of 400 marks, while his daughter Mary (aged 7) was married to Robert de Ferrers, heir to the earldom of Derby (aged 9). When the strategic dimensions have been noted, there were nonetheless familial considerations. Henry seems to have wanted William de Valence at court, and Hertford gave him a base close to Westminster and Windsor.

Henry's elevation of the Lusignans 'did nothing to dull his enthusiasm for the Savoyards'.[25] In 1246 Peter was given the house in London which was to become the Savoy palace. The following year he brought two Savoyard girls to England who were to marry Richard de Burgh and Edmund de Lacy. In 1248 the king made Cheshire part of the queen's dower. Henry's plan was not to exclude native nobles but to draw them into his court by marriage with his kin. They were not necessarily being disparaged, despite comments from Matthew Paris. The Lacy bride was the daughter of the marquess of Saluzzo. Later another daughter married William de Vescy, the Northumberland baron. Henry's policy was accepted by both Richard of Cornwall and Richard de Clare, his greatest earls.

---

[24] Carpenter, *Henry III: 1207–1258*, 467.   [25] Ibid., 170.

THE IMPACT OF ROYAL POLICY ON THE NOBILITY   43

Henry's domestic aim seems to have been to achieve a harmonious court comprising his foreign relatives and the native magnates. For a variety of reasons, this was extremely difficult to achieve. For one thing, divisions opened up between the Lusignans and Savoyards. They became rivals for the king's patronage. In terms of numbers, far fewer Lusignans were established in England. Eight of them received land as opposed to thirty-nine Savoyards. Pensions of 100 marks or more were promised to twenty-eight Lusignans compared to the forty promised to Savoyards. Nonetheless, the extra money needed to be found. Moreover, Henry had committed himself to converting his half-brothers' pensions into land. Furthermore, in addition to finding land for Queen Eleanor, who had become increasingly dissatisfied with support from money alone, he had to endow his son, Lord Edward, with a great estate on his marriage to Eleanor of Castile in 1254. By 1258, less than half of the £500 worth of land promised back in 1247 to William de Valence had been found. Even so, he had done far better than anyone else apart from Richard of Cornwall. And then there was Simon de Montfort. Montfort had every reason to fear that Valence's endowment would push him down the queue in receiving patronage.[26] From 1253 when Simon was expecting the conversion of his annual fee of 500 marks into land, he found himself 'trumped' by Valence. 'The fee question', says Maddicott, 'underlay much of his animus against William de Valence and his brothers, successful rivals for royal patronage, whose removal would leave the way clear for the settlement of Montfort's own claims'.[27] Early in 1257 relations were so strained between Montfort and Valence that Simon brought a particular incident before the court. William had raided one of Simon's manors, and when his steward reclaimed the booty William had flown into a rage and insulted the earl. Matthew Paris recounts the subsequent events at court, with William raving and calling Simon a traitor, 'which is a great insult to knights'.[28] Montfort was so incensed that he threw himself upon William and would have killed him had not the king physically intervened. Henry's favour to foreigners was noticed by the chroniclers, and not just Matthew Paris. Consequently, Carpenter concludes, 'A dangerous gulf was opening up between Henry and his kingdom'.[29]

Henry's problems over patronage were not only on the demand side. Supply became a key issue. The 1250s was a decade of financial difficulty.[30] During the 1230s and 1240s there had been a plentiful supply of escheated land, most of it as we have seen from the 'lands of the Normans'. The 'great mortality' among earls

---

[26] Ibid., 473.

[27] Maddicott, *Simon de Montfort*, 136, where details of the preferential treatment accorded to William are given.

[28] Paris, *CM* v, 634. The incident is related by Ambler, *Song of Simon de Montfort*, 160–1.

[29] Carpenter, *Henry III: 1207–58*, 474.

[30] For what follows see Ridgeway, 'Foreign Favourites and Henry III's Problems of Patronage, 1247–1258', 590–610.

44 POLITICS AND SOCIETY IN MID THIRTEENTH-CENTURY ENGLAND

and magnates had also increased the availability of heiresses and widows to endow his Savoyard household knights.[31] There were also ecclesiastical revenues providing benefices for another Savoyard uncle, the absentee Philip, not to mention Bishop Aigueblanche and Archbishop Boniface. The promises Henry made to convert money fees into land came back later to bite him. As the supply of lands dried up, it was difficult to find the large estates for the Poitevins to match those given to the Savoyards. As Huw Ridgeway says, his favour to the former 'had to be forced through',[32] making them doubly unpopular.

Despite their strategic importance, it became harder to support the Poitevins through Gascon resources, as first Simon de Montfort as lieutenant there and then Lord Edward resisted the king's involvement. The war in Gascony, moreover, considerably worsened the king's financial situation. Henry had relatively little in terms of fall-back positions. After 1237 he had been denied parliamentary taxation. Unable to draw on the many means of increasing income deployed before Magna Carta, his whole *modus operandi* was under strain. The development of the concept of ancient demesne during the 1240s preserved crown lands themselves from alienation. They were particularly significant in terms of revenue in that they could be legitimately tallaged. It is little wonder that by 1257 the councillors' oath contained a promise never to consent to alienation from the ancient demesne.[33] Another feature which reduced the king's freedom of manoeuvre was the development of the concept of inalienability. The idea that certain lands should be declared inseparable from the crown seems to have been prompted by the appanage granted to Lord Edward. With rival pressures crowding in upon him, Henry had to become something of a juggler. He was obliged to devise a list of precedence, with Edward and the queen at the top. By 1251 a 'system of preference' was fully underway.[34] In addition to creating smouldering political tensions at court, the need to find alternative means of providing patronage led the king into arbitrary methods and precarious expedients. For example, in his desire to resume land grants to William de Valence he took back the manor of Dunham in Nottinghamshire from the estate of the late Ralph fitz Nicholas, a royal steward, claiming that it had been given for life and notwithstanding three charters confirming it to him and his heirs. He confiscated Grafton Underwood in Northamptonshire, held by William de Lisle who was on trial for his abuses as sheriff. Anticipating his conviction, the king assigned the land to Geoffrey de Lusignan, who transferred it to Valence.[35] Guy and Geoffrey de Lusignan were assigned considerable Jewish debts. Household knights were found rewards by unusual means. Thus, Guy de Rochford was given custody of a royal castle (Colchester) with its town and hundred, while William de Sancta Ermina was

---

[31] The 'great mortality' was noted in Powicke, *King Henry III and the Lord Edward*, i, 142.
[32] Ridgeway, 'Foreign Favourites', 591.   [33] Ibid., 598 and n. 2.   [34] Ibid., 599.
[35] Ibid., 605–6 and references given there.

given an income from the royal demesne manor of Havering in Essex for the term of seven years. We are reminded that when the various adverse factors have been taken into account, 'in the last analysis, it was the king's own decision after the 1230s to build up such a large circle of royal clients and to rule them with the light rod of patronage, which brought disaster upon himself'.[36]

The rewards given to Henry's foreign-born household knights are also a reminder that there were other dimensions to royal patronage. So far, we have concentrated on the most high-profile recipients. But the king needed to be mindful of the expectations of his baronage as a whole and of the need to reward his own and often native-born servants. This was regarded as a necessity and was dictated by the aristocratic mores of the time. Nonetheless, the perception of extravagant rewards being accorded to them tended to alienate the baronage, given the competition for patronage. One of the less elevated recipients of royal patronage whose career and activities can be reconstructed in some detail is Geoffrey de Langley. Thanks largely to the chancery records on the one hand and the survival of the Langley cartulary on the other, his career and activities can be related in sufficient detail to allow him to stand as an exemplar.[37]

During his long career Langley was inter alia chief justice of the forest, 'guardian' of Henry's daughter, Queen Margaret of Scotland, and steward of Lord Edward's lands. He came under fierce attack from Matthew Paris. Perhaps the most balanced view comes from Margaret Howell: 'Energetic, unscrupulous and acquisitive, but with a knowledge of how to please, Langley found his way into the queen's favour as well as the king's'. 'The queen ... was not so naïve as to be duped as to his real character. She liked his enterprise, his thrust, his firm, clear-cut approach to problems.'[38] Geoffrey de Langley, then, was a particular type of royal servant. Such men were unlikely to be popular outside of court circles. It is not so much Geoffrey's career that is of interest here, however, as the advantages that came his way.

The rewards of royal service were both direct and indirect. The king, like any other lord, would have felt it to be his social duty to reward the men who entered his service. Royal patronage given to those was a matter of custom, expectation, and expediency in that it was designed to guarantee loyalty. In addition to a modest endowment in land, Geoffrey received a whole range of gifts and privileges from 1238 onwards, up to and including royal wardships.

The indirect benefits of royal patronage were principally connections and cash to fund investments. Langley earned considerable sums of money from royal service in both fees and expenses. Payments are noted from time to time on the

---

[36] Ibid., 610.

[37] The details are to be found in P. R. Coss, 'The Langley Cartulary', 2 vols. (University of Birmingham, PhD thesis, 1971), Introduction (i, Ch. 2), and *The Langley Cartulary*, ed. Coss, Dugdale Society, vol. 32 (Stratford-upon-Avon, 1980).

[38] Howell, *Eleanor of Provence*, 1151–6.

46   POLITICS AND SOCIETY IN MID THIRTEENTH-CENTURY ENGLAND

chancery rolls, the details of which would be rather tedious to relate. Suffice it to say that between May 1243 and March 1254, over £737 is recorded in these sources. In March 1250 he was granted 200 marks per annum 'by his own hand' out of the issues of the forest.[39] Investment added to the lands he had inherited, acquired by marriage, and received from the king. A potent factor in bringing land onto the market was indebtedness to the Jews. It was a situation which favoured a royal servant, or indeed anyone with access to ready cash. A number of Geoffrey's acquisitions were, in fact, redemptions of indebted land.[40] As a result of his activities Geoffrey de Langley built particular concentrations in three areas: around Coventry, near Cirencester, and in south-west Warwickshire.

Geoffrey de Langley's activities are likely to have raised aristocratic heckles in a variety of ways, quite apart from the reputation of forest justice and the ire of the marchers.[41] His activities, and those of many another, in the trafficking of indebted estates must have been deeply unpopular in landowning circles. Magnates no doubt tended to look askance at relatively low-born and ambitious men, even if of knightly origins, who behaved as though they were great lords and who looked to the king to sustain them in their pretension. In more practical terms they tended to intrude upon established structures of social power in the counties, as Geoffrey did within the earl of Chester's old honour of Coventry. The ensuing resentment is unlikely to have rebounded to the benefit of Henry's government.

In his career and in his behaviour, Geoffrey de Langley was not atypical of Henry III's servants, and a few additional examples may be given. Paulinus Peyvre had a similar career. In Buckinghamshire the estates of five impoverished knightly families were bought up by him.[42] Paulinus inherited a small estate in Toddington and Chalton in Bedfordshire from his father, the first member of the family who has been traced. He appears in the household of William de Cantilupe, whom he accompanied to Poitou in 1230. From here he moved into the king's service. He was appointed warden of the bishopric of Winchester in 1238, was briefly sheriff of Oxfordshire in 1239, and then sheriff of Bedfordshire and Buckinghamshire. He was a royal councillor and by 1244 a household steward. Matthew Paris described him as an oily character who within a short time of his arrival at court had acquired considerable lands and rents through both licit and illicit means. Beginning, he says, with barely two carucates, he soon possessed

---

[39] CPR 1247–58, 61.

[40] For a more detailed discussion, see P. R. Coss, 'Sir Geoffrey de Langley and the Crisis of the Knightly Class in Thirteenth-Century England', P&P, 68 (1975), 3–37.

[41] See below 166.

[42] See Anne Polden 'A Crisis of the Knightly Class? Inheritance and Office among the Gentry of Thirteenth-Century Buckinghamshire', in P. Fleming, A. Gross, and J. R. Lander (eds.), Regionalism and Revision: The Crown and its Provinces in England 1250–1650 (London, 1998), 41. For Peyvre's career Polden draws on G. H. Fowler (ed.), A Digest of the Charters Preserved in the Cartulary of the Priors of Dunstable, Bedfordshire Historical Record Society, xvii (1935), 316–18.

THE IMPACT OF ROYAL POLICY ON THE NOBILITY   47

over fifty. An insatiable purchaser, he was also an incomparable builder. Pride of place was the house he built at Toddington, for which the king gave him oak trees to construct a chapel and fish to stock its ponds. Paris describes it as a palace with many chambers, stone-built and lead-roofed. In addition to its chapel and its vivaries, there were also orchards. According to Paris it caused astonishment in all who gazed upon it. One can only imagine his self-esteem and his self-congratulation, and the reactions that his swagger provoked.[43] Although he was buried in London, his heart was carried to Toddington, a monument to his achievement. Anne Polden makes the interesting suggestion that Peyvre's acquisition of the caput of the small honour of Lavendon might indicate a 'hankering for baronial status'.[44] Household knights tended to share the same characteristics.[45] At their head were the stewards, whom Carpenter picks out for particular comment.[46]

The stewards were powerful figures with their own entourages. Moreover, they were proficient at promoting their own men. The brother of Ralph fitz Nicholas became sheriff of Hampshire, the nephew of Godfrey de Crowcombe sheriff of Oxfordshire. They were courted by magnates. Gilbert Marshal, earl of Pembroke, for example, gave land to both Ralph fitz Nicholas and Crowcombe. The stewards were employed both in and out of court. They were sheriffs, castellans, and keepers of vacant bishoprics. They were well rewarded. Crowcombe acquired manors in five contiguous counties. With the king's help he developed his estates, setting up markets and fairs, creating parks and fish ponds, and constructing a range of new buildings.[47] Two of Henry's stewards (John fitz Geoffrey and William de Cantilupe II) were of baronial status; most, however, were of knightly background. They tended to enter the household through a connection with an established minister. Until the appointment of the Savoyards, Ebulo de Montibus and Imbert Pugeys, in 1256–7, Henry's stewards were generally English.[48] A famous protégé of Walter de Cantilupe II was his knight, Robert Walerand. Robert served as a sheriff, as a justice, and as a settler of disputes especially in the

---

[43] Paris, CM v, 242 ; Fowler, Priory of Dunstable, 316–18.

[44] Polden 'A Crisis of the Knightly Class?', 41.

[45] For a study of these men see R. F. Walker, The Anglo–Welsh Wars, 1216–67 (University of Oxford D.Phil thesis, 1954), 61–9. See also Ethel Stokes, 'Molis, Nicholas', GEC, ix, 1–4, and Carpenter, Henry III: 1207–1258, 538.

[46] Carpenter, Henry III: 1207–1258, 383–6.

[47] See D. A. Carpenter, 'The Career of Godfrey of Crowcombe: Household Knight of King John and Steward of King Henry III', in C. Given Wilson et al., War, Government and Aristocracy in the British Isles: Essays in Honour of Michael Prestwich (Woodbridge, 2008), 26–54. For other examples see A. Harding, 'Robert Walerand, Administrator', ODNB, 56 (2004), 790–2, and William John Stewart-Parker, 'The Bassets of High Wycombe: Politics, Lordship, Locality and Culture in the Thirteenth Century' (University of London PhD thesis, 2015).

[48] An exception being Amaury de St Amand, who was Norman. It may be that the employment of the Savoyards was felt to threaten the closing of normal access to the stewards. Some of them had earned the praise of Matthew Paris, including Paulinus Peyvre and John de Lexinton for their literacy.

48 POLITICS AND SOCIETY IN MID THIRTEENTH-CENTURY ENGLAND

Welsh Marches.[49] He, too, became a forest justice. He was closely associated with the Sicilian business and high in the king's esteem. Strongly associated with royal policies, he acquired extensive properties through his service. One of these was the castle and manor of Kilpeck, which he was holding by 1259.

The king's lay servants had, of course, ecclesiastical counterparts. The most significant was John Mansel.[50] Said by Matthew Paris to have been the son of priest, Mansel had a long career in royal service, from 1234 at the latest when he was a clerk at the exchequer until his death in 1265. A prominent administrator, royal councillor, and diplomat, he was referred to by Matthew Paris as the king's 'chief' or 'special' advisor. He was much involved in the Sicily enterprise and had crucial dealings with the papal court on Henry's behalf. He played a major part in undermining the baronial regime in 1261-2. In his younger days he had been a successful soldier, in Gascony for instance, notwithstanding his clerical status. By the 1250s he appears to have been the wealthiest of the king's clerical administrators. Such was the opinion of Matthew Paris, who estimated his income as 4,000 marks per year. He accumulated so many ecclesiastical livings that he could afford to be blasé about them. According to the Melrose chronicler, on receiving a living worth £20 per annum he exclaimed that this would provide for his dogs. Among other things he was chancellor of St Paul's Cathedral, where he also held two prebends, provost of Beverley, and later treasurer of York, an extremely rich benefice. He was also much concerned with promoting the interests of his family.

Others include Simon de Walton, Walter de Merton, and Robert Passelewe. Walton, from the West Midlands, was a canon lawyer who became an itinerant justice and was elected bishop of Norwich in 1257.[51] Like Mansel, he was a king's man through and through, and involved in executing the papal bulls absolving barons from their oath to the Provisions of Oxford. He was another accumulator of properties and was involved in the trafficking of Jewish debts. So, too, was Walter de Merton, an ambitious cleric with apparently no scholarly interests at all.[52] He was, however, a founder of ecclesiastical institutions, including famously Merton College, Oxford. He was in royal service by 1240 and became active in the chancery, rising through its ranks and finally becoming chancellor in 1261. The holder of many livings, he was elected bishop of Rochester in 1274. Robert Passelewe we have already met as the predecessor of Geoffrey de Langley as a forest justice.[53] His royal service began at the end of King John's reign under the patronage of Peter des Roches. Changes in regime made his career a spasmodic

[49] Robert C. Stacey, 'Lexinton [Laxton], John of', ODNB, 33, 682-3.
[50] There is a very full discussion of Mansel's career and impact by Robert Stacey in ODNB, 36, 350-3. See also H. Liu, 'Matthew Paris and John Mansel', TCE, xi, 159-73, and her 'John Mansel, Councillor of Henry III: His Life and Career' (University of London PhD thesis, 2004).
[51] A. Harding, 'Walton [Wauton], Simon de', ODNB, 57, 215-16.
[52] G. H. Martin, 'Merton, Walter of', ODNB, 37, 931-3.
[53] Robert C. Stacey, 'Passelewe, Robert', ODNB, 42, 980-1.

THE IMPACT OF ROYAL POLICY ON THE NOBILITY   49

one until 1242 when it really took off. He was appointed archdeacon of Lewes. His role as sheriff and as forest justice hindered his promotion in the church. He was examined by Robert Grosseteste, bishop of Lincoln, and his theology found wanting. Robert refused to institute him to the church of St James, Northampton, but on this occasion he was overruled by the archbishop of Canterbury. He died in 1252, leaving two brothers as his heirs.

Those who served the king received rewards in addition to those of money and land. Scott L. Waugh, looking at respites of knighthood and exemptions from suit of court and from being placed on juries and holding office, that is to say from public service, noted that professional administrators formed a 'significant proportion' of the recipients.[54] 'These officials', he says, 'formed a cohesive group within the royal government and local communities, and they turned royal authority to personal advancement and profit through patronage or corruption'. Although some used them to avoid all public service, 'others used them to avoid only unremunerative, routine service so that they could pursue work which they considered more profitable or prestigious'. It seems that the king granted exemption from jury service and offices to many royal servants as being 'incompatible' with their main duties. Fifty-three of the knights and serjeants who received royal protection in accompanying Henry to Gascony in August 1253 also gained lifetime exemption from juries and assizes. These and the many other privileges granted by the king naturally involved payment, and these are recorded on the fine rolls.[55] Payment was made not only for quittance of being on 'assizes, juries and recognitions' and the like and for respite from distraint to knighthood, but also for writs and judicial procedures, for pardons of various sorts, for the arrangement of terms for payment at the exchequer, for privileges such as free warren and the holding of markets and fairs, for grants of wardships, and for much else besides. The most frequent fine was ½ mark per item, but there were wide variations. An Essex man paid for a charter of free warren with 100 young herons and 100 cormorants.[56] Occasionally we find that grants have been made 'at the instance' of a particular individual, usually members of the royal family, or others close to the king. During the period 1250–58 these include: Aymer de Valance, bishop-elect of Winchester; William de Valence; Peter of Savoy; the Scottish queen; William de Longespée (son and heir of the earl of Salisbury); John Mansel; Stephen Bauzan, knight of Lord Edward; Master Rostand the papal chaplain; the judges Henry de Bath and Philip Lovel; and Simon de Montfort.[57]

---

[54] Scott L. Waugh, 'Reluctant Knights and Jurors: Respites, Exemptions, and Public Obligations in the Reign of Henry III', *Speculum* (October 1983), 937–86, at 971–2.

[55] The fine rolls for the period 1216–72 have been edited under the Fine Roll Project headed by David Carpenter and are available online.

[56] Fine Roll 34 Henry III (1249–50), no. 609.

[57] This last was a pardon to William de la More of Buckinghamshire for the death of a man: Fine Roll 41 Henry III (1256–7), no. 383. Other examples are to be found on the Patent Rolls, which register the grants themselves.

50 POLITICS AND SOCIETY IN MID THIRTEENTH-CENTURY ENGLAND

Among the greatest of prizes were wardships.[58] In the words of Scott Waugh 'feudal wealth given away as patronage' served two purposes: 'ministerial patronage given to officials' and 'political patronage given to favourites or political allies for their loyalty and support', the former being 'by far the more important'. The king gave wardships and marriages of heiresses and widows to officials as 'supplementary benefits'. Moreover, officials, with timely access to information, could put in pre-emptive bids for them. Looking across the period from 1217–1327, Waugh calculates that nearly half of wardships and marriages went to royal ministers and members of the royal family and that courtiers and central administrators used their position to obtain wardships not just for themselves but also for their associates. Henry III, however, gave more wardships to his leading officials than did either of his immediate successors. Twenty-five men received four or more, a total of 152. There were many more among lesser officials, including clerks of the exchequer and chancery and valets in the royal household, who shared in this aspect of patronage. Local officials such as escheators gained too, being present in the localities where the opportunities arose and being involved in the exercise of royal rights. By contrast, relatively few went to magnates or other barons, when compared with royal knights, ministers, and members of the royal family. As Scott Waugh indicates, most of Henry's feudal patronage went to those serving him and magnates were not routinely granted wardships.[59] The actions of Henry III in this respect during the decade 1247 to 1258 caused considerable disquiet, registered by Matthew Paris and surfacing in 1258. Earls and barons who were outside of the court acquired only seven wardships across the entire decade; that is fewer than 4 per cent of all those granted.[60]

Appeasement

There is another dimension, however, to Henry's treatment of his magnates which has been noted by historians, that is his leniency. In his concluding remarks on the king's period of personal rule, Carpenter notes: 'He did not pressurize them to pay their debts. He did not challenge their liberties in the field of local government ... Nor during his personal rule did Henry hold his great men at arms-length when it came to his court and council'.[61] Imagining the situation from Henry's perspective, Carpenter sees the king as conciliatory and his restraint a contributory factor in achieving domestic peace. At numerous points during his

---

[58] For this subject see the wide-ranging study by Scott L. Waugh: *The Lordship of England: Royal Wardships and Marriages in English Society and Politics 1217–1327* (Princeton, 1988). For what follows see especially 180–93, 'Patronage'.

[59] Except, that is, in times of conflict, such as 1258–66, when political considerations surfaced: ibid., 189.

[60] Ibid., 243.   [61] Carpenter, *Henry III: 1207–1258*, 703.

THE IMPACT OF ROYAL POLICY ON THE NOBILITY 51

narrative Carpenter highlights specific instances where concessions were made to individual magnates. In 1248, faced with criticism in parliament, the king made concessions over debts. On his way to Westminster to celebrate Easter he stayed with Roger Bigod at Framlingham, where he respited payment of his debts. He pardoned John de Burgh a debt for the soul of his father, Hubert. John de Warenne and Edmund de Lacy were allowed to succeed to their inheritances while underage.[62] Another case is that of Walter de Cantilupe, bishop of Worcester. He had joined the Gascon expedition and participated in the final negotiation for Lord Edward's marriage. As a reward his lands were largely exempt from the jurisdiction of the local sheriff.[63] The powers given to Simon de Montfort in various counties have already been noted. The encroachment on local government and local courts will be dealt with later. With regards to the judicial system, however, Matthew Paris tells us that in 1256 the king ordered that no writs should be issued that would damage the interests of the earls of Cornwall and Gloucester, Peter of Savoy and the king's half-brothers.[64] This is not verifiable, but the statement is nonetheless indicative. There are known instances, however, of Henry suspending cases in favour of those he supported.[65] This was a dangerous game.

There is an alternative way of looking at these phenomena. They are not so much concessions as appeasement! The policy of appeasement was characteristic of the reign. Hemmed in by Magna Carta, Henry was on the back foot. He was at the mercy of magnate expectations. Only by appeasing their individual wishes could he hope to find a *modus vivendi*. It is against this background that we should see the lack of control exhibited by the Lusignans, who took matters to extremes and in doing so threatened the interests of other magnates. There seems to have been a widespread feeling that it was impossible to secure legal redress against them because they were protected by the king. An example was the action of Aymer de Valence in 1252. In that year, in the words of a jury of presentment, a 'multitude of armed Poitevins from the *familia* of ... the elect of Winchester, William de Valence and their brothers', broke into the archbishop of Canterbury's palace at Lambeth, stole money, jewels, and plate, and dragged his servants off to Aymer's castle at Farnham. Though not all of the property was returned, Aymer escaped any punishment. On oath he disclaimed all knowledge of the incident, and so it was left.[66] Direct evidence of royal interference in the judicial process is rare, but it can be found. One example that has been brought to light concerns Warin de Munchensey, whose daughter Joan had married William de Valence.[67]

---

[62] Ibid., 480.   [63] Ibid., 613.   [64] Paris, *CM* v, 594.

[65] Carpenter, *Henry III: 1207–1258*, 537–8.

[66] Carpenter, 'What Happened in 1258?', in *The Reign of Henry III*, 191, and the references given there.

[67] See Tony Moore, 'The Thorrington Dispute: A Case Study of Henry III's Interference with Judicial Process', Fine of the Month (July 2009), *Fine Roll Project*, online.

52 POLITICS AND SOCIETY IN MID THIRTEENTH-CENTURY ENGLAND

Joan's mother had been one of the five daughters of William Marshal and hence she brought with her a fifth of the Marshal inheritance. Now well connected, Munchensey received marks of royal favour, including interference in the workings of the judicial system. The case concerns the manor of Thorrington (with its advowson) in Essex which Hugh fitz Richard of Elmstead bought for 100 marks in February 1251. It lay within the Munchensey barony of Swanscombe. Munchensey took immediate action and ejected Hugh from the land. Hugh brought, that is to say he paid for, a writ of novel disseisin, the appropriate action in the circumstances. The king replaced the justice first assigned to the case and Hugh withdrew. However, Hugh soon brought another writ, paying more this time, but Munchensey and two codefendants did not appear before this third justice. In fact, they had not been 'attached' to appear, the sheriff claiming that the writ had arrived too late for him to carry this out. The case was respited, that is to say adjourned. In fact, the hearing never took place, because the justice received a royal letter informing him that the assize had been 'superseded'. What now happened was that Hugh fitz Richard sold the manor to Munchensey who later acquired a grant of free warren there and at his neighbouring manor of Great Fordham. Warin de Munchensey and his son were both involved in buying up lands and rents in the area, thus consolidating their presence. The motive must have been partly, at least, to keep Hugh fitz Richard, an 'interloper', out of his fee, using both force and influence to do so. The incident, moreover, does not stand alone. Another plea in which Munchensey was involved was respited in January 1253.[68]

Yet another indicative case was one in 1259 when a Kentish knight protested that he had been unable to obtain justice in the king's court against Roger de Leybourne because of the 'favour' which Roger had enjoyed as one who 'stood' with William de Valence.[69] Cases like this square with the allegation by the barons in 1263 that Henry had broken the terms of Magna Carta over the denial and delay of justice.[70] Perhaps the most famous case is that of Shere in Surrey, where on 1 April 1258 an armed band attacked servants of John fitz Geoffrey, the lord of the manor, and took them to Farnham where one of them died of the wounds inflicted. It was alleged that this had occurred on the orders of Aymer de Valence himself, which was almost certainly the case. It arose from a dispute over the advowson of the local church between the magnate and the abbot of Netley, the bishop-elect taking the abbot's part. This led to a fracas which was out of

---

[68] Most interestingly, in comparing the witness lists to the two charters recording Hugh fitz Richard's purchase and sale of Thorrington, Tony Moore suggests that Munchensey was effectively bypassing the local notables who acknowledged the sale. Carpenter cites an example of the earl of Gloucester securing the termination of an assize by the king: Carpenter, 'Kings, Magnates and Society', 82–3.

[69] Carpenter, 'What Happened in 1258?', 192.   [70] *DBM*, 270–1.

proportion to the case.[71] When parliament opened at Westminster, John fitz Geoffrey complained of the attack and sought justice. Henry, however, 'did not wish to hear him and wholly denied him justice'.[72] This caused fury at the parliament. When the barons subsequently re-established the office of justiciar, it was the first case to be heard.

Privatization

A final area where the king was indulgent or lax, according to one's perspective, in his treatment of his barons and other landowners was over local courts and franchises. What we see is usurpation of royal rights and privatization of local justice and administration. Franchises, as Donald Sutherland said, were 'a miscellaneous lot'.[73] Most of them gave the right to perform a function which belonged to the king and was normally undertaken by his officers, and to take the profits therefrom. Some were major, such as return of writs which excluded the sheriff and other royal officers and allowed the holder of the franchise to carry out all royal orders. Some were quite minor. A common but valuable franchise was view of frankpledge. Twice per annum a sheriff carried out his 'tourn' of all hundreds and wapentakes, calling a full session of the hundred court to review the tithings, ensuring that every adult male (with some allowable exceptions) was included in the peace-keeping system. As Sutherland points out, the name view of frankpledge is deceptive because the sheriff's court did more than that. A jury of presentment reported on recent crimes. Serious ones were recorded by the coroners and held over until the next appearance of the royal justices. Less serious ones, 'the pleas of the sheriff', were dealt with by him. These rights had financial consequences. When a lord had view of frankpledge the sheriff's role was undertaken by his own officials and the profits went into his hands. In other words, the procedures were undertaken at the lord's manor court.[74] From the twelfth century, if not before, lords had held courts for their manorial tenants as a matter of course, where property transfers, agrarian practices, and minor local disputes were dealt with.[75] During the thirteenth century, 'in a process still poorly understood', writes

---

[71] Carpenter, 'What Happened in 1258?', 192–3. See also H. W. Ridgeway, 'The Ecclesiastical Career of Aymer de Lusignan, Bishop Elect of Winchester, 1250–1260', in J. Blair and B. J. Golding (eds.), *The Cloister and the World: Essays in Medieval History in Honour of Barbara Harvey* (Oxford, 1996), 148–77, at 166–7, and S. M. Stewart, 'What Happened at Shere?', *Southern History*, 22 (2000), 1–10.

[72] This was according to the legal record three months later. See also Paris, *CM* v, 708.

[73] Donald W. Sutherland, *Quo Warranto Proceedings in the Reign of Edward I* (Oxford, 1963). For the nature of franchises see Ch. 1, 'Franchises and Legal Theory', especially 2–5.

[74] For what follows see James Masschaele, *Jury State and Society in Medieval England* (New York, 2008), 57–8.

[75] See Mark Bailey, *The English Manor c.1200–c.1500* (Manchester, 2002), 167–240, and K. J. Stocks, 'Manorial Courts in England in the Early Thirteenth Century', in *TCE*, viii (Woodbridge, 2001), 135–42.

54 POLITICS AND SOCIETY IN MID THIRTEENTH-CENTURY ENGLAND

James Masschaele, many lords came to use their manor courts in place of the hundred courts.[76] In doing so they took over the business undertaken by the public court and took the consequent fines. Nor was this all. They also employed the presentment juries to enforce both their manorial and their public rights.

When it comes to franchises, the historian's attention naturally focuses on Edward I's campaign of *quo warranto*, which gave rise to the statute of that name in 1290.[77] The landowners were systematically challenged to show by what right, technically 'by what warrant', they held their franchises. There has been an assumption that the bulk of the usurpation or privatization of these rights had taken place after 1258. Sutherland wrote that Edward I 'must have known that there had been fine opportunities to usurp franchises against the crown during the troubles of the Barons' Wars, and such wrongs he certainly desired to set right'.[78] The issue has recently been reviewed by Andrew Spencer. 'Under Henry III', he tells us, 'and particularly after 1258, ambitious magnates, partly from a desire to increase their local power, partly out of a need to protect their interests at a time when the crown was not strong enough to do so and partly to shore up the loss of their feudal authority, seized new rights and liberties for themselves at the expense of the crown and local societies'.[79] Moreover, 'Edward expressed this sense of loss at his coronation in the additional oath he swore to recover what had been lost under his father'.[80] The Hundred Rolls Inquiry of 1274–5, Spencer points out, 'confirmed that the king's suspicions had been true: the scale of the alleged usurpation contained in them is staggering'.

However, Sutherland himself noted that Henry III and his ministers 'had shown a very similar concern' to that of Edward I.[81] Where revenues normally accountable by the sheriffs were concerned, the barons of the exchequer had the right to challenge the liberties and bring the claimants to court and have them 'allowed' or 'disallowed' by judgement. This practice ceased in 1234, but writs were sent to sheriffs between 1223 and 1244 ordering local inquiries and action.[82] Moreover, during the middle years of Henry's reign the pleas rolls and memoranda rolls of the exchequer 'show a scattering of pleas involving subjects' rights to franchises'.[83] In the 1250s, as Sutherland informs us, a thorough investigation was planned. For the eyres of 1254 there were new articles of inquiry to find

---

[76] Masschaele, *Jury State and Society*, 57.   [77] See below 260.

[78] Sutherland, *Quo Warranto Proceedings*, 19.

[79] A. M. Spencer, *Nobility and Kingship in Medieval England: The Earls and Edward I 1272–1307* (Cambridge, 2014), 71–2.

[80] Citing here M. Prestwich, *Edward I* (London, 1988), 90–1.

[81] Sutherland, *Quo Warranto*, 66–7. See also H. M. Cam, 'The Evolution of the Medieval English Franchise', *Speculum*, 32 (1957), 439, republished in H. M. Cam, *Law-Finders and Law-Makers in Medieval England* (London, 1962; repr. 1967).

[82] Sutherland cites, in particular, writs of 1244: *CR 1242–47*, 242.

[83] Sutherland, *Quo Warranto*, 6 and n. 4. Furthermore, 'others appear in eyre rolls, particularly in the eyre of Devon of 1238'.

THE IMPACT OF ROYAL POLICY ON THE NOBILITY   55

usurpations of franchises,[84] and in the following year an inquest was held throughout the country on the maintenance of the king's rights: the Hundred Rolls of 1255. Jurors were specifically questioned over franchises exercised without warrant. Sutherland considers that writs must have been brought 'in considerable numbers' to test these rights, and indeed the clergy of Canterbury province complained of this in 1257–8. 'In these activities of his father's rule, Edward had ample precedent for investigation and litigation.'[85]

It is necessary to gain a fuller picture. We will proceed by first looking at the evidence from the eyre rolls before turning to the Hundred Rolls of 1255, which will be given particular attention. From 1239 the articles of the eyre instructed juries of presentment to say who had withdrawn suit from the courts of county and hundred without royal authority, although in practice little action seems to have been taken.[86] In the counties visited by Henry of Bath in 1248–9, some men were placed 'in mercy' for usurping liberties and sheriffs were ordered to distrain those who had withdrawn suits.[87] In general, however, the system lacked teeth, and this was largely down to the king. It seems that 'the justices were uncertain of the king's support in taking firm measures'.[88] Carpenter cites the 1257 Norfolk eyre where more than fifty people were summoned to show warrant for their liberties but only one is known to have complied. Telling is the number of times that the word *loquendum* ('to be discussed') appears in the eyres alongside the juries' pronouncements of usurpation. This is to say, the matter was deferred to the king and one can safely assume that in practice little or no action was taken.

The extent of the 'problem' is revealed in the Hundred Rolls of 1255. Before we embark on an enquiry here, we need to note the existence of private hundreds. Helen Cam calculated that when Edward I became king there were something like 628 hundreds in England, of which 270 were royal and 358 in private hands.[89] The phenomenon was by no means new. Cam suggests that by 1066 a hundred or more were already in private hands. Henry II seems to have felt no inconsistency between the expansion of royal jurisdiction on the one hand and the granting out of hundreds, with their courts, to subjects on the other. Cam counts at least fifty-two such grants. Grants by Richard I were frequent, and fifty-five were made by John. Her figure for Henry III is 108. There were wide variations in the conditions by which hundreds were held. They appear to have been regarded as sources of revenue rather than prestige, and could change hands like land. Cam describes

---

[84] Citing Cam, *Studies in the Hundred Rolls*, 23 and Appendix II, 92–5.

[85] Sutherland, *Quo Warrant Proceedings*, 7.

[86] C. A. F. Meekings, *Crown Pleas of the Wiltshire Eyre, 1249*, Wiltshire Archaeological and Natural History Society (Devizes, 1961), 31–2; Cam, *Studies in the Hundred Rolls*, 20–5.

[87] For this and what follows, see Carpenter, 'Kings. Magnates and Society', 87–8, and the references given there.

[88] Ibid., 87.

[89] H. M. Cam, *The Hundred and the Hundred Rolls* (London, 1930; repr. 1963), 137, and for what follows 137–45.

56   POLITICS AND SOCIETY IN MID THIRTEENTH-CENTURY ENGLAND

the lord of a hundred in the majority of cases as 'little more than a sleeping partner', drawing his share of the profits of government but leaving his officials 'very much under the orders of the sheriff in actual governmental work'.

In 1255 the time was ripe for an inquiry into the usurpation of royal rights and liberties of subjects. The surviving returns, however, are fragmentary. They survive for Shropshire, Buckinghamshire, Oxfordshire, Wiltshire, and Rutland. We will take two counties—Shropshire and Buckinghamshire—for detailed examination. Shropshire is in some ways atypical. It was a border county and its society still a relatively militaristic one, home to fiercely independent-minded marcher barons. However, border violence, though endemic, was intermittent and the degree of independence can be exaggerated. It was very much part of the kingdom, with an active sheriff and county and hundred courts. There was, however, no frankpledge system and hence no view. Shropshire, the inquiry tells us, had ten hundreds, all but one of them in the king's hands. However, this does not accurately describe the situation.[90] Of the four lordships on its western border— Oswestry, Clun, Wigmore, and Caus—the first three made no presentation in 1255 and, indeed, were all referred to at some point in the thirteenth or fourteenth centuries as hundreds in their own right. At Oswestry this was first stated in 1241–2. They enjoyed, in effect, judicial immunity from the county and to an extent from the state. This was achieved by the Fitzalans for Oswestry before 1203 and for Clun after 1221. The history of the Mortimer lordship of Wigmore follows these. Caus, as we shall see, came late onto the scene in claiming such immunity. The history of these honours interacted with those of pre-existing hundreds, but they were not coterminous and tended to remain separate. The power of these lords straddled the border, the defence of which lay to a considerable degree in their hands. It was no doubt on the basis of this role that they claimed special privileges in the thirteenth century.

What is striking, looking across the county as a whole, is the degree of withdrawal of suits from the hundred courts.[91] Numerous landowners had done so, from hundred, or from hundred and county. In some hundreds the majority of tenants seem to have withdrawn their suit to the court and sometimes to the county court too. In the hundred of Cound, for example, twelve landholders are listed, all of whom had withdrawn suit 'by unknown warrant'. The same is very largely true of the large hundred of Munslow, where the great majority are said to have withdrawn suit. Again, all are withdrawn 'by unknown warrant' and some from the county as well. In some cases, we are told for how long suit has been withdrawn: two, five, ten, or twenty years. In the hundred of Pimhill, by contrast,

---

[90] For what follows see Max Lieberman, *The Medieval March of Wales: The Creation and Perception of a Frontier, 1066–1283* (Cambridge, 2010), especially Chs. 6–7. The book is a detailed study of the Shropshire–Powys border.
[91] The details which follow are taken from *Hundred Rolls*, ii, 55–86.

THE IMPACT OF ROYAL POLICY ON THE NOBILITY   57

many do suit but some, once again, do not. John de Grey of Ellesmere had with-drawn Ellesmere from both county and hundred twenty-four years before. Two lords had had their suit withdrawn by John de Grey's bailiffs, the implication being that they probably did suit now to Ellesmere rather than the hundred. At Stottesdon hundred most do suit but, nonetheless, there are many who do not. At Stottesdon itself, where John de Plessy was lord, no suit had been done for nine-teen years. At Astley, the abbot of Shrewsbury was said to have the king's warrant for not doing suit, although this is unusual in the roll. One landholder did suit, presumably instead of the hundred, to William Mauduit at Holdgate castle, while another did suit at Montgomery castle. At Preston in Ford hundred the abbot of Lilleshall had received a gift of land there twenty years ago, and had withdrawn suit from the vill from that time on. At Alveley the manor made no suit except for homicide and common summons. Altogether one wonders how the system could have worked efficiently. It is clear that this situation went back twenty years and that it had gradually worsened.

One hundred which did work efficiently was that of Purslow, which was in the hands of John fitz Alan, baron of Clun. As John held the hundred in fee farm, it was in his interests to ensure that no lucrative rights were lost. Twelve tenancies are listed, all owing castle-guard at Clun as well as suit to the hundred.[92] However, Clun and Purslow were administratively separate. Clun was described as a 'town-ship' in 1203 and had a separate burghal court. Only one of the tenants was said to owe suit for afforcement of the court, the others by implication performing regu-lar suit. Another six men still owed suit to the hundred. Only two were laymen, one of them being Thomas Corbet, lord of Caus. The others were the abbots of Haughmond, Wigmore and Buildwas, and the bishop of Hereford. The abbot of Haughmond owed suit from two different landholdings. Of these, only the abbot of Buildwas had withdrawn suit, and only for the past year. Otherwise, John fitz Alan had been able to insist on his rights and, of course, the resultant income and control.

Also interesting is the liberty of Wenlock. We hear that the prior had owed suit for his manor here, and seven appurtenant places, until the time of Richard I. There then follows a list of his tenants owing suit to his court and which of the surrounding hundred court had had their suit withdrawn. There are twenty-two tenants listed, together with another who does not hold directly of him. For the most part, they owe suit when the court requires afforcement rather than for rou-tine business. We hear of suit being withdrawn from the time of Richard I. All of the prior's subtenants are lay, and the majority say that their ancestors had not done suit to the hundred court.

---

[92]   Only Walter de Hopton, who held two fees at Hopton and elsewhere, was a substantial tenant. The others were said to hold a hide or a half hide.

58   POLITICS AND SOCIETY IN MID THIRTEENTH-CENTURY ENGLAND

A particularly informative case is that of Thomas Corbet, whose history encapsulates much of what was going on in this area. We are informed that Caus, the caput of his barony, is not within the hundred of Chirbury but that, nonetheless, he has subtracted pleas belonging to that hundred, that is, those relating to effusion of blood, theft, and the hue and cry, and this for the last five years, to the king's damage of 40s, that is 8s per annum. Moreover, he has withdrawn the manor of Worthen and its members from the eyre since the time of the justice William de Ewerswyke (presumably 1248). Having been separated, it responds by four men and the reeve. Thomas Corbet had also withdrawn suit to the hundred from the vill of Leigh at the time when Hugh Hagar (now a hundred juror) was in his wardship. For the last sixteen years he has taken pleas belonging to the hundred into his own court (no doubt at Caus) to the king's damage of 30s (22d per annum). At the hamlet of 'Ree' in Ford hundred and within the barony of Caus he had withdrawn suit from both county and hundred four years ago. The occasion was the exchange he made with Ralf de Ree for land in Minsterley.

Thomas Corbet was sheriff of Shropshire from 1248–50. The editor of the Shropshire eyre roll of 1256 characterizes him as one of the men who 'represent the worst types of official'.[93] He was head of the family of the Corbets of Caus from 1222 until his death in 1274 (apparently aged 94). His sister had married Gwenwynwyn, prince of Powis, giving him a 'footing on both sides of the border', which 'increased his sense of independence'. At the eyre he asserted his right in accordance with ancient custom to drive cattle taken in distraint from England into Wales, where the processes of English law were 'ineffective'.[94] He was constantly involved in litigation which, according to the antiquary Eyton, shows him 'in his usual character—quarrelsome, crafty, vindictive, the foe of his relations and his own vassals'. To such a man, says Alan Harding, 'the office of sheriff was an additional weapon for use in private quarrels'.[95] At the eyre of 1256, he was fined 20 marks for disseisins, 10 marks for many transgressions, 5 marks for defaults, and 5 marks for failing to produce a man for whom he had stood pledge. Twenty-five years after his term as sheriff, the profits of the county were still owing to the king. In 1252 four justices were appointed to enquire about injuries inflicted on the king and his men in Shropshire, Staffordshire, and the march by Thomas Corbet.

However, this is not the whole of the story. What Corbet was attempting was undoubtedly what the FitzAlans and the Mortimers had already achieved; that is

---

[93] *The Roll of the Shropshire Eyre of 1256*, ed. Alan Harding (Seldon Society, 1981), xxi.

[94] Ibid., nos. 813, 858. For the Corbets more generally, see Melissa Julian-Jones, 'Family Strategy or Personal Principles? The Corbets in the Reign of Henry III', *TCE*, xv (Woodbridge, 2015), 69–79, and 'The Land of the Raven and the Wolf: Family Power and Strategy in the Welsh March c.1199–1300—The Corbets and the Cantilupes' (Cardiff University PhD thesis, 2015).

[95] *Shropshire Eyre*, Harding (ed.), xxi, where he cites R. W. Eyton, *Antiquities of Shropshire*, 12 vols. (London, 1825), vii, 81.

THE IMPACT OF ROYAL POLICY ON THE NOBILITY   59

to create an immunity for Caus, like those at Oswestry, Clun, and Wigmore. His
position as sheriff undoubtedly encouraged him in this endeavour, just as being
virtually hereditary sheriff in the twelfth century had helped the FitzAlans. What
made it difficult for Corbet and provoked a reaction in 1255 was the geographical
position of his lordship. In particular, the hundreds of Chirbury and Ford lay
between his lordship of Caus and the Welsh border.[96] Clearly, he was concerned
with the geographical cohesion of his power, filling the gaps as it were. That he
was a vigorous man and a violent man where his interests were concerned goes
without saying, but this was by no means unusual in the world he inhabited.[97] At
the Shropshire eyre of 1256 the township of Caus was one of three claiming that
they had never been accustomed to appear before the justices.[98] Thomas's own
court was a very active one.[99]

We hear of other liberties. At Corfton we are told that Walter de Clifford has
his liberty by gift of the king, but that the jurors do not know if he has a warrant
for his gallows, for the assize of ale, and for the effusion of blood. In Munslow
hundred six men are listed together as claiming to have liberties and gallows,
pleas of effusion of blood, hue and cry, assize of ale, and writ of right, without
charter. William de Stuteville, we are told, had his liberty from time immemorial
but the jurors do not know by what warrant. In Pimhill hundred some landholders are said to have liberties, but they are not spelled out. There are other anomalies. At Ludstone in Claverley hundred Peter de Rivallis had withdrawn the
amercement of serfs which the king had enjoyed until five years ago. He had also
withdrawn suit to the county over the same timespan.

Let us turn now to Buckinghamshire, where there is abundant evidence for the
private exercise of view of frankpledge.[100] However, we need to put this into context. As we have seen, there were higher franchises, most notably return of writs.[101]
A franchise lying between return of writs and view of frankpledge was *vee de
naam* or *de vetito namii*. This is the royal action of replevin and, in Maitland's
words, 'few lords claim to entertain it'.[102] It concerned the consequences of self-
help. It was an action 'brought against a distrainor, who, though he has now given
back the beasts, has been guilty of detaining them against gage and pledge'.[103] As
we might have expected, the Buckinghamshire rolls indicate that these franchises
were exercised by elevated persons. At the top were Richard earl of Cornwall and
William de Valence, earl of Pembroke. Others include Simon de Montfort, the
earls of Gloucester and Warwick, and the countess of Arundel. Needless to say,

[96] Lieberman, *The Medieval March*, 215–17, 228–32.
[97] For the local activities of Thomas Corbet, see *Shropshire Eyre*, ed. Harding, xx–xxii, xxvii–iii.
[98] Ibid., no. 864.   [99] Ibid., nos. 16, 510, 515–16, 738.
[100] For what follows see *Hundred Rolls*, i, 20–34.
[101] For the spectrum of franchises, see Sutherland, *Quo Warranto Proceedings*, 2–4.
[102] F. W. Maitland, *The History of English Law*, introduced by S. F. C. Milsom, 2 vols. (Cambridge,
1968), i, 587.
[103] Ibid., ii, 524.

60 POLITICS AND SOCIETY IN MID THIRTEENTH-CENTURY ENGLAND

barons held view of frankpledge, where they were joined by many other lay land-owners,[104] as well as religious houses and ecclesiastics.[105]

We come now to the crucial issue of chronology. One immediately startling feature is the number of high franchises as well as views of frankpledge in the hands of the king's relatives, Richard, earl of Cornwall, Simon de Montfort, earl of Leicester, and William de Valence. This can certainly be seen in terms of the king's indulgence towards them. However, in many cases—and certainly with regard to the first two named—the situation almost certainly goes back to Angevin England, in terms of the honours that were given them. In the case of the earl of Cornwall, he was granted St Valery in 1227 and Wallingford in 1231. The former had been confiscated by the crown. Wallingford, however, was in royal hands until granted to the king's brother. In the case of the earl of Leicester, it was believed by jurors of Aylesbury hundred that the liberty of the earl of Leicester went back to the Conquest and that when the earl recovered the land (in 1231) he had its liberties as before. As regards Great Marlow and Hampden, we hear that the earl of Gloucester and his ancestors have always had view of frankpledge and that at [Maids'] Morton the earl's ancestors had held view since time immemorial. There are other clues pointing in the same direction. One is the liberties associated with the honour of Giffard which come up time and time again in the rolls. The honour had escheated to the crown when Walter Giffard III died in 1164. At the beginning of Richard I's reign, it was divided between Richard de Clare, earl of Hertford, and William Marshal. One half simply descended with the Clares. The other half passed to William the Marshal's five sons in turn and then, in 1245, descended to and through his five daughters.[106] Liberties held by ecclesiastical tenants point in the same direction. At Halton the prior of Canterbury holds view of frankpledge from antiquity (*et hec antiquitate*). The jurors of Mursley hundred tell us that at Winslow and Horwood the abbey of St Albans has all liberties, *vee de naam*, and return of writs by charter of King Offa. At Haddenham the king's ancestors had given view to the prior and convent of Rochester by royal charter, while at Stowe the abbot of Oseney is said to be free *ex*

---

[104] They include William de Cantelou, Geoffrey de Mandeville, Sir John de Grey, Peter Carbonel, Sir Hugh Peverel, William de Beauchamp, Hugh de Cressi, John de Trayli, Thomas de Donnington, Sir Luke Passel, Nicholas de Girund, Sir William de Birmingham, Sir Thomas de (le) Mansel, Ralf Harang, Thomas Fitz Bernard, Ralf de Langetot, Robert Boisted, Richard de Kemble, Robert Fitz Nigel, Sir Hugh de Vere, Ralph fitz Nicholas, Warin de Mantek, Sir Henry de Pinkeni, Sir Humbert de Pugeia, as well as royal servants like John Mansel and the heirs of Paulinus Peyvre.

[105] The prior of Canterbury, the abbot of Medmenham, the Templars, the prior of Kenilworth, the bishop elect of Winchester, the prior of St Frideswide, the Hospitallers, the abbot of Woburn, the prior of Newton Longville, the hospital of St John outside eastern gate, Oxford, the prior of Tickford, the prior of Chetwode, and the abbot of Nutley. At Winslow and Horwood, the abbey of St Albans has all liberties, *vee de naam*, and return of writs, and the abbey of Reading *regale*. The abbot of Oseney holds Stowe and is said to be free *ex antiqua tempore*, while the abbot of Westminster holds all liberties and all *regale*.

[106] I. J. Sanders, *English Baronies: A Study of Their Origin and Descent, 1086–1327* (Oxford, 1960), 62–4.

antiqua tempore. At Upper Winchendon the prior of St Frideswide holds of the lord king 'of old enfeoffment' and has view of frankpledge.

But not all liberties were ancient. Some of the juries look back to the time of the sheriff Robert de Braibroc (1204–5) as a vantage point and to 'the war of England'. Thus, at Little Missenden William Longespee has view of frankpledge 'without the sheriff', and this has been the case from the time of Robert de Braibroc 'and before'. At Brokton we hear that the abbot of Missenden has had view of frankpledge from the sheriff's time and before, whereas at Buckland Robert de Vipont, who holds of the bishop of Lincoln, has the same but only from after the time of the same sheriff. At Fawley it is noted that before the war of England the same sheriff had collected the entire dues from the vill. This was so until William the Marshal senior had taken over by means of the liberty of the fee of Giffard, indicating that his exercising of private rights did not go back as far as his tenure of half of the honour. William de Valence now holds the view and all pleas pertaining to the sheriff. As regards Newport Pagnall, we learn that Robert de Braibroc took nothing from the borough.

Some liberties, however, are clearly more recent: at Lillingstone, the jurors tell us William the Marshal junior (d. 1231, eldest son of William the Marshal who died in 1219) drew its suit to himself, that is to say into his court, and held view of frankpledge. The township of Stoke, in Stoke hundred and of the honour of Dudley, was subtracted, we are told, twenty years ago. It is now in the wardship of Sir Humbert de Pugeia, who has view of frankpledge. At Tattenhoe in Mursley hundred Paulinus Peyvre acquired a hide of land from the king, including suit of court and view of frankpledge fourteen years ago. Jarpenvill now holds it of his heirs by exchange, doing suit and paying dues to them. At Morton seven years ago the same Paulinus drew to himself both suit and view of frankpledge. It is now held by Sir John de Grey in wardship. Grey also held an estate at Woolstone in Sedgelaw as part of the same custody. It had paid dues until the time of Paulinus. By a charter of eleven years ago the hospital of St John outside Oxford has withdrawn suit from the county and hundred for Thornborough and exercised view of frankpledge. For the last nine years Richard of Cornwall has taken all that belongs to the king at Thornton, Radclive, and Westbury. It was also nine years ago that he drew suit to himself at Dadford in Stodfold hundred and took view of frankpledge. In some cases the liberties are very recent indeed. At *Chelrey* [Chalvey?] the priory of Morton bought five virgates of land and withdrew them from suit to county and hundred one year ago.

What we are seeing is an ongoing process of privatization, of the withdrawal of suit to county and hundred and the substitution of private views of frankpledge. By both action and lack of action on the part of the king, the system was being steadily subverted. Looking closely, we can see the mechanism by which private courts were being strengthened. Some of it was clearly done through the enterprise of lords themselves, including comparatively lesser barons and minor lords.

62   POLITICS AND SOCIETY IN MID THIRTEENTH-CENTURY ENGLAND

At Ludgershall we hear that Walter de Cauz did suit to the royal manor of Brill for two hides of land. He was followed, however, by his brother, Richard, who held for three years, withdrawing his suit and holding view of frankpledge; he also held the assizes of bread and ale and took money for the pannage of pigs. The estate is now owned by John de Grey who has held it for a further three years, 'deforcing' view of frankpledge. At Mursley Sir Luke Passel holds view of frankpledge, does no suit, and takes scutage. He is an ecclesiastical tenant, of the house of Bradley, itself holding of the Marshal family as of the honour of Giffard. The jurors do not know by what warrant. He had done the same thing at Drayton Parslow. Withdrawal of suit was followed by privatization. An extraordinary case occurs in Sedgelaw hundred, where the jurors say that Sir Hugh de Vere holds a certain 'congregation' annually for those who belong to his view of frankpledge and for those who have been put in his view, but not by the sheriff, and they do not know by what warrant. In many cases all we know is that a lord was holding a view and the jurors did not know by what warrant he held it.

The expansion of the role of private courts was sometimes undertaken by subordinating lesser lords. At Hasley, John Hareg has withdrawn suit to the county and the hundred 'through the liberty of St Valery'. Since the earl of Cornwall has *regale* it seems very likely that John Hareg's suit now goes to Richard's court. There are many villages where there are several lords but with a higher lord holding view of frankpledge. This may well have reduced the taxable capacity of the tenants for other lords. Suit could involve inconvenience. At Addington, Peter Carbunel held four hides, but view of frankpledge was held at Sir John fitz Geoffrey's court at Quarrendon, which required some travel. If the system was not exactly chaotic, it was far from neat. The strength of seigneurial courts in this situation was a matter of power and will.

The incidence of private views of frankpledge, then, was quite high, though the superior franchises were considerably more restricted. Nevertheless, the evidence suggests that the private view was particularly valuable to great landowners. Let us take as an example Earl Richard of Gloucester. The royal inquisition on his death indicates their cumulative value. It is not possible to gain a complete picture as in many instances the liberties exercised are not specified. For Kent there is a list of the views of frankpledge, rents, knights' fees, and advowsons of the honour of Clare. The items are impossible to disaggregate. However, the 4s from the view listed for Hardres is indicative. In Cambridgeshire the view is itemized for Litlington (1 mark), for Meldreth (10s), for Guilden Morden (10s), for Tadlow and Pincote (½ mark), and for Bottisham and Croyrop where pleas and courts render 40s. In Huntingdonshire it is itemized for Great Gransdon (17s), Woolvey (8s), Grafham (2s), Sawtry and Papworth[107] (2s), Folksworth (2s), Walton (2s),

---

[107] *Recte* Cambridgeshire.

from Stilton (2s), and from Southoe where the tenants are specifically said to do suit to Southoe court the value of which is 20s.[108] The yield from such views, taken individually, pales in comparison with honour courts and seigneurial boroughs and their liberties, but cumulatively they were significant in terms of income, prestige, and control.

Moving forwards, the Hundred Rolls of 1274/5 reinforce the impression that with regard to withdrawal of suit to local royal courts and to the privatization of view of frankpledge, the prime period was before 1258. These Hundred Rolls are best known for the attention they give to peculation, corruption, and various misdemeanours by sheriffs and other officials in the localities. However, they are also concerned with royal rights and encroachments upon them. The articles of inquiry include several directly concerned with the usurpation of liberties. The commissioners are asked to inquire of the juries about ancient customs, services, and other items pertaining to the king and his ancestors that have been withdrawn, who has withdrawn them and when, and who has appropriated them, when and by what warrant. Similarly, they are to make inquiry as to who is claiming return of writs, who holds pleas of *vee de naam*, who claims sea wreck, and by what warrant, and who claims other liberties such as gallows, assizes of bread and ale, and other matters pertaining to the crown, and for how long have they done so.

The returns for Buckinghamshire are patchy and survive in two versions.[109] Naturally, they tend to reflect the questions asked. There is no specific mention of view of frankpledge, while private gallows and the assizes of bread and ale are directly voiced. It is partly a consequence of this that the latter figure quite often in the returns, but partly no doubt because of their incidence on the ground. The issues of suit and view of frankpledge continue to occur. In many cases, however, the returns reflect what was reported in 1255, although occasionally they add to the picture. They also supply incidences of withdrawn suit and usurped view of frankpledge not noted in 1255. At Maids' Morton we are told that Paulinus Peyvre appropriated suit and view of frankpledge twenty-six years ago, reflecting the seven years noted in 1255. Both point to 1248. In cases where withdrawal of suit was reported in 1255, we now find lords with gallows and assizes. Thus, in Sedgelaw hundred, William de Valence at Great Linford, the heirs of Roger de Somery at Newport Pagnell, and Reginald de Grey at Eton all had gallows and assizes, as did Hugh de Vere at Stratton. At Eton, John de Grey had been recorded as holding view of frankpledge in 1255. In the hundred of Erle (or Eure?), the abbess of Barking held, at Slapton, gallows, assizes of bread and ale and view of frankpledge, and did no suit to county or hundred. The bishop of Winchester had the same liberties, while the men of the rector of Edlesborough claimed the

---

[108] *CIPM* i, no. 530; TNA, C 132/27/5.   [109] *Hundred Rolls*, i, 35–48.

64   POLITICS AND SOCIETY IN MID THIRTEENTH-CENTURY ENGLAND

assizes of bread and ale from their tenants and have withdrawn them from suit to county and hundred. The township of Marsworth used to present effusion of blood and hue and cry at the hundred twice per annum, but presentation and suit are now made at Wallingford Castle by order of the bailiffs of the earl of Cornwall.

Among those cited frequently for having subtracted suit are Paulinus Peyvre and the earl of Gloucester. Return of writs and other higher franchises remain restricted to the most elevated members of society. In addition to the earl of Cornwall, we find the earl of Leicester, Theobald de Verdon, and Humphrey de Bohun. At [Long] Crendon the countess of Pembroke, holding in dower, claims warren, pleas of *vee de naam*, and whatsoever pertains to the crown (*regale*). Other landowners are said to hold unspecified liberties, in the hundred of Aylesbury for example. One notable feature—partly because it is the subject of a specific article—is the attention given to warrens and parks. The article asks who have newly appropriated free chases or warrens without warrant, who have had these of old by royal grant, and who have extended the metes and boundaries and since what time. There can be no doubt that this article reflects a particular concern and the high degree of encroachment that had been taking place. Reginald de Grey, for example, has a park and warren at Snelston drawn from the woods and lands he and his father bought from the king. John de Tyringham had appropriated warren at Tyringham three years ago. By unknown warrant, say the jurors, is a constant refrain. Free warren was one of those privileges that were frequently being licensed—that is to say sold—by Henry III, as part of his quest for money. It involved not only the exclusive right to hunt specified animals, of less significance than those of the forest or chase, but also the right to hold a court where those who encroached upon the warren could be brought to account. The right to a chase—in effect a private forest—was a different matter, as was the right to impark. We are dealing here with features of what is known to historians now as 'the landscape of lordship'. The private park was a distinctive and increasingly popular feature of local lordship during the middle years of the thirteenth century.[110] There were, of course, other forms of encroachment. William and Ida de Beauchamp, for example, had appropriated the water of *Lavente*, which the men of Newport used to have in common, and held it in severalty. In short, the usurpation of liberties had continued after 1255, with some changes of direction and some shifts in reporting following changes in the inquiries. The Hundred Rolls of 1274/5, however, confirm that this was a continuation of a process that had begun, and probably reached its height of intensity, well before.

The issue of privatization in particular indicates clearly that we cannot explain the revolt of 1258 by means of national politics alone. The perceived weakness of the king and the competition for patronage had a major part to play in

---

[110]   For parks see S. A. Mileson, *Parks in Medieval England* (Oxford, 2009).

heightening tensions and exacerbating rivalry. The Provisions of Oxford were to instal a justiciar who would offer impartial justice, while a baronially appointed chancellor and treasurer could be expected to control royal grants. It is apparent, however, that influence at the centre and power in the provinces were interconnected in a whole variety of ways. In order to comprehend this more fully we need to put magnate power under scrutiny. The next chapter will deal with its major components.

Politics and Society in Mid Thirteenth-Century England: The Troubled Realm. Peter Coss, Oxford University Press.
© Peter Coss 2024. DOI: 10.1093/9780198924319.003.0003

4

Power and Profit in the Provinces

There are arguably three principal dimensions to magnate power in the provinces: one can study their economies and material resources; one can examine their social pre-eminence and its underpinning; and one can look at the institutional framework of their control. All three are of course tightly interconnected. Nevertheless, they are alternative means of approaching local authority. Let us take each of them in turn. We will take two of the magnates of the highest level for detailed consideration: Richard de Clare, earl of Gloucester and Hertford from 1243 until his death in 1262, and Roger Bigod III, earl of Norfolk from 1228 to 1270.[1] This will enable us to take into account the greatest range of resources and expressions of power. Their period of ascendancy, moreover, covers the greater part of the personal rule of Henry III.

Material Resources

A royal ward, Richard de Clare was married to Maud, daughter of John de Lacy, earl of Lincoln, in 1238. His vast inheritance comprised the English honours of Clare, Gloucester, Tonbridge and St Hilary, and half of the honour of Giffard, as well as the great marcher lordships of Glamorgan and Gwynllŵg in south Wales. The partition of the Marshal estates in 1246–7 gave him the additional marcher lordship of Usk and the Anglo–Irish liberty of Kilkenny. In 1258–9, through purchase and exchanges, he acquired two thirds of the Huntingdonshire barony of Southoe Lovetot and some substantial properties in Dorset. At his height he had an annual income of nearly £4,000, making him the richest magnate outside of the royal house. This calculation is based on the inquisitions held on his death and, more fully, on the dower to be assigned to his widow, in 1266–7.[2] The honour of Clare itself was valued at £1,200 and the Gloucester and Giffard lands at £950. The Welsh lordships of Glamorgan and Usk were said to be worth £850, bringing the total to £3,000. However, the Dorset manors are not included, nor the estates appurtenant to the honour of Tonbridge, and nor indeed the lordship of Kilkenny.

---

[1] For an outline of his career, see M. Altschul, 'Clare, Richard de, Sixth Earl of Gloucester and Fifth Earl of Hertford (1222–1262)', *ODNB*, 11, 761–3, and for greater detail the same author's *A Baronial Family in Medieval England: The Clares, 1217–1314* (Baltimore, 1963). For Roger Bigod III, see Marc Morris, *The Bigod Earls of Norfolk in the Thirteenth Century* (Woodbridge, 2005), Chs. 2 and 3.

[2] *CR 1261–4*, 284–93; TNA Rentals and Surveys, General Series, SC 11/610 mm. 1–7.

POWER AND PROFIT IN THE PROVINCES   67

On the basis of the figures available, Michael Altschul estimates the gross annual income at Earl Richard's death to be upwards of £3,700.[3]

Something should be said first of all on the structure of the property in England, our primary concern here. The earls held lands and fees in almost all of the English counties. They included some extremely high-yielding properties.[4] The honour of Gloucester, the greater part of which was located in the western and south-western counties of England, included the Gloucestershire manors, boroughs, and hundreds of Tewkesbury and Thornbury, valued at £169. 2s. 9d. and £131. 9s. 4d., respectively, and the manor of Fairford, valued at £92. 3s. The honour of Clare, centred in East Anglia but with outliers in other counties, included Clare, yielding £126. 11s. 9d, excepting the borough of Bardfield in Essex, valued at £59. 19s., the manor and hundred of Rothwell in Northamptonshire, valued at £130. 3s. 2d., and the manor and borough in Bletchingley in Surrey, worth £52. 7s. 4d. The honour of Tonbridge was held as a serjeanty of the archbishop of Canterbury and included the castle and borough of Tonbridge itself and the manors of Brasted and Hadlow, yielding £10. 8s. 3d., £54. 1s. 10d., and £38. 2s. 8d., respectively, around 1300. For this honour the Clares owed suit at the archiepiscopal court at Otford twice yearly together with ceremonial functions, and gifts in return.

When it comes to the sources of revenue, we have a valuable account given on the Pipe Rolls for the period 2 February–Michaelmas 1243, when the estates were still under royal control, immediately prior to the earl's seisin. This account is important here not only because it was at the beginning of his tenure of the Clare estates, but because it lay near the beginning of our period of particular concern. By this time, moreover, the shift in the mode of exploitation of agrarian resources that had characterized the late twelfth and early thirteenth centuries was largely complete, so that the system of demesne agriculture—whereby lords directly managed their estates through their ministers rather than farming them out—was in full flow. This involved the marshalling of the peasant workforce through villein services, or converting these into cash so that labourers could be hired, and the direct marketing of the produce, beyond what was required for the lord's direct needs.[5] On the manors the greatest source of income was unsurprisingly the sale of grain, accounting for about 45 per cent.[6] Rents, both customary and freehold, constituted the next highest form of income, somewhere in the region of 33 per cent.[7] Then there was the income from boroughs, including Clare, Tonbridge, Tewkesbury, Thornbury, and Cranbourne. As Altschul says, the courts brought a

---

[3] Altschul, *A Baronial Family*, 202–3. Altschul adds that in 1317 the total was closer to £6,000, which tallies with G. A. Holmes, *Estates of the Higher Nobility in Fourteenth Century England* (Cambridge, 1958), 36 and n. 1.

[4] For these figures see Altschul, *A Baronial Family*, Appendix I: Values of Some Clare Estates.

[5] Altschul, *A Baronial Family*, Ch. 7, is devoted to the earls' economy.

[6] That is, over £800 in 1242/3.   [7] About £600 in the same year.

68 POLITICS AND SOCIETY IN MID THIRTEENTH-CENTURY ENGLAND

'small but steady profit', about 5 per cent of the income in 1242–3. Revenue was drawn from burgage rents, from the borough courts, and from seigneurial dues of various kinds, including tolls. Most of this income was clear profit, as the boroughs required little in the way of heavy expenditure in contrast to what was normally needed for the upkeep of manors. The only major expenses were wages to the borough officials themselves. Other income from the estates included the lease of meadow and pastures and of mills and fisheries, the sale of wood, the commutation of villein services, fines from the forests, and the income from manorial courts. The revenue sources at Lakenheath in Suffolk included the fishery of *La Fenne*. At Walsingham in Norfolk, 10s. was garnered from 'stallage at the church', and further income was drawn from the swanneries. The earl held the forests of Malvern and Blakemore with the manor of Hanley in Worcestershire, yielding £54. 6¼d., and the forest of Cors in Gloucestershire 'with all its appurtenances and liberties', yielding £46. 8d.

Of great importance were the revenues derived from 'feudal resources', and from franchise and honourial courts. Let us look in more detail at what these 'feudal resources' comprised. One of them was scutage, a tax in lieu of military service to the king. When a lord served personally, he was allowed to take the scutage of his tenants for his own use. Then there were the so-called feudal incidents of relief, wardship, marriage, and escheat. The first of these was a sum of money paid when a new tenant succeeded, wardship was custody of the person and land of an heir who was underage, marriage was the right to determine the partner of an unmarried heir who was underage, and escheat was the right to the land should no heir exist. These valuable assets had been present since the early days of Norman rule. Another of a lord's rights was to take an aid from his military tenants at certain points in time, that is to say at the knighting of his eldest son, at the marriage of his eldest daughter, and should his own person be in need of being ransomed. Hence David Carpenter, drawing on comments by Malcolm Bean, prefers to describe them with some justice not as 'feudal incidents', as tradition has it, but as 'feudal essentials' and to speak of 'fiscal feudalism' as a vital ingredient in thirteenth-century aristocratic society.[8] As a result, lords tended to take great care in tracking the descent of the knights' fees held of them. Scutage could be lucrative. At the end of the thirteenth century, the Clares were assessed for 495 fees, a total far greater than any other magnates, but they held in fact about 520 in England. When granted, the net profit from scutage, if collected at 40s. per fee, would amount to some £50. In 1251 Earl Richard took an aid of two marks per fee for the marriage of his eldest daughter. As Altschul says, 'In short, if by the thirteenth century feudal relationships were almost entirely financial, still

---

[8] D. A. Carpenter, 'The Second Century of English Feudalism', *P&P*, 168 (August 2000), 30–71, at 43–7; Malcom Bean, *The Decline of English Feudalism 1215–1540* (Manchester, 1968), 1–6.

POWER AND PROFIT IN THE PROVINCES   69

they were valued and tenaciously preserved, precisely for that purpose, and they formed a not insignificant aspect of the total income of the earls of Gloucester.[9]

Information from the inquisitions post mortem and the extents of 1263 indicates the care that was taken over feudal incidents. Some knights' fees are listed under headings: 'fees from which are due marriage and wardship'; 'fees from which wardship and marriage are due with relief'; 'fees held from the earl by those who hold in chief of the king, owing only relief'; 'fees in Suffolk whose tenants hold nothing of the king'; 'fees in Norfolk whose tenants hold nothing of the king'. A certain number of estates would have been held in wardship at any one time. The inquisition post mortem reveals, for example, two in Norfolk, two in Suffolk, and one in Essex, together with one in Glamorgan. They give us the names of the late tenants. We learn, for example, that the earl had the wardship of Joan le Butler, daughter of William le Butler, Richard's nephew. On Joan's death the estate was claimed by Richard's sister and by the two sisters of William. This was, perhaps, something which would be sorted out by the relevant honour court. The inquisition tells us of these, too. At Tewkesbury we hear of the court of the knights and free tenants of the honour of Gloucester to which those of Somerset owe suit. It yields £5. 6s. 8d. per annum. Cumulatively, the profits and perquisites of courts provide a steady income. There are the borough courts, where dues and the implications of trade were profitable, the earl's 'third penny' from county courts (Gloucester, Cambridge, Huntingdon), hundred courts in the earl's hands, and, of course, the many local courts. The court at Southoe, for example, once the caput of a barony, yields £1 per annum. Under many manors the existence of liberties is noted, whereas others refer specifically to view of frankpledge and the income therefrom: a mark; 10s.; 8s.; ½ mark; or 2s. At Great Gransden (Huntingdonshire), view of frankpledge yielded 17s., alongside 8s. 5d. rent of assize. At Botisham and Croyroys (perhaps Quy?) in Cambridgeshire, pleas and courts rendered £2 per annum.

The estates needed, of course, to be administered and officials had to be appointed to the task. The estates were divided into 'bailiwicks', that is to say geographical clusters of manors, courts, and fees that were under the same officials, the honour being, Altschul points out, no longer the fundamental unit of territorial organization.[10] For example, the Marshal and Giffard lands were treated as separate entities only when it came to assessing scutage; otherwise they were administered as parts of larger bailiwicks. Not even the honours of Clare and Gloucester remained as entities. The Clare estates in Kent, Surrey, and Sussex were brought under the honour of Tonbridge in the first half of the thirteenth century. The honour of Clare became another bailiwick comprising the manors

---

[9] Altschul, *A Baronial Family*, 221–2.

[10] Ibid., 222. He cites here Noel Denholm-Young, *Seignorial Administration in England* (Oxford, 1937), 40–41, 93.

70 POLITICS AND SOCIETY IN MID THIRTEENTH-CENTURY ENGLAND

in Norfolk, Suffolk, Essex, and Hertford, along with Southoe in Huntingdonshire and the fees and courts in those counties and in Cambridgeshire. The suitors to the central court came only from Norfolk, Suffolk, and Essex, and on occasion from Cambridgeshire. As far as the honour of Gloucester is concerned, there were probably two or three bailiwicks for financial and judicial purposes. One was centred on Cranbourne, drawing suitors from Dorset and Wiltshire, and probably dealing with Devon and Hampshire, too. Tewkesbury would seem to be the centre of another bailiwick, drawing suitors to its honour court from Gloucestershire, Worcestershire, and Somerset. It seems likely that Rothwell in Northamptonshire served as a third centre encompassing estates and fees in central England, that is in Northamptonshire, Oxfordshire, Buckinghamshire, Berkshire, and Bedfordshire.

In managing their vast estates and, indeed, their household, the earls employed what Altschul calls 'a host of professional salaried officials'.[11] Later evidence shows seneschals who already had royal careers before serving the earls. Thus Hervey de Borham, a close adviser to the earl, 'passed easily between royal and private service and managed an ecclesiastical career in the last years of his life'.[12] In 1259 he was seneschal of Clare for Earl Richard. He was a royal commissioner by 1261, served in the Montfortian government, and was keeper of the peace for Essex and Hertford for Henry III in 1266. In 1267 he acted for Earl Gilbert in negotiations over 'the Disinherited' and in 1268 represented the earl in his dispute with Llewelyn ap Gruffydd over Senghenydd. By the late 1270s he was rector of a number of churches and in 1276 he was dean of St Paul's, when he was also an itinerant justice in Essex. It was not, of course, only clerics who had such careers. Hamo Hautein, seneschal in 1268, had been sheriff of Lincoln in 1259–60, a royal escheator in 1261, sheriff of Lincoln again in 1262, and an official in the king's wardrobe in 1263. Altschul sees these men as professional bureaucrats. Subordinate to them were estate bailiffs. In addition, there were household officers. If a permanent salaried council came later, there was already an informal one in the 1240s, consisting of the earl's prominent knights and officials. In 1245, Richard Siward was described as '*de familia et ... de consilio comitis*'. In 1249, in a dispute with the abbot of Tewkesbury, the earl disallowed the abbot's claim, his counsellors being against it (*per consiliarios suos contrarios*).[13] There were also attorneys, some of whom again had careers in the church. Richard de la Lade, who had been warden (*custos*) of the honours of Gloucester and Clare during Earl Richard's minority, had been an attorney for the first Earl Gilbert (d. 1230), who presented him to the church of Northill in Bedford in 1224.

The presentation to churches, or advowsons, was an important form of patronage and was much valued by the lords. The inquisition post mortem lists nearly a

---

[11] Ibid., 225.   [12] Altschul, *A Baronial Family*, 227.   [13] Ibid., 234.

score of advowsons in the lord's hands, to be precise eighteen plus a half share in another. J. E. Newman made a thorough study of the traffic in advowsons in thirteenth-century Yorkshire.[14] A considerable number had passed into the hands of religious houses through benefaction. Newman found a drying up in the benefaction of advowsons, however, by both barons and greater knights after c.1220–30. Indeed, a reversal followed, so that some barons in particular sought to acquire (or reacquire) them through purchase and litigation.[15] One of these was Richard de Clare. The reason for this development is not hard to find. Clerks played a major part in serving great lords, both in their households and in administering their estates. An advowson was an extremely useful asset when it came to rewarding them. What was needed was a steady supply. Newman pointed to cases where knightly families succeeded in recovering them only for their lords to step in, since it was the tenant's lord who had been responsible for the initial benefaction.[16] By the second quarter of the thirteenth century, a veritable market in advowsons had developed. Barons were not the only purchasers, however; career administrators were also much involved in this traffic. Many livings were in the king's hands, from which he could reward his own clerks. Supply was limited due to the sheer number of livings that had passed to the monasteries.[17] Another phenomenon of the age was the papal reservation of livings, which caused considerable aggravation.[18]

Wardships could also be used in terms of reward, both for clerics and for laymen. Thus in the inquisitions of 1263 it was noted that the knight's fee at Woolvey in Huntingdonshire was in the hands of Hervey de Borham while the heir was in the earl's custody. Some cases where men held an estate for life might also indicate reward for service, as for example the one third fees held at Southoe by John de Mandeville and John de Littlebury and his wife, Mariota.

Social Pre-eminence: Manpower

These examples of reward take us smoothly into the second of the three dimensions to magnate power. Crucial to a lord's social pre-eminence was the quality of the manpower at his command. Here we enter the world of the magnate 'affinity',

---

[14] J. E. Newman, 'Greater and Lesser Landowners and Parochial Patronage: Yorkshire in the Thirteenth Century', *EHR*, 92 (1977), 280–308.

[15] Knights and other lesser landowners sought to reverse their ancestors' benefaction through litigation, but most often unsuccessfully. See Coss, *The Origins of the English Gentry* (Cambridge, 2003), 103, and for a broader treatment of the issue, Coss, *The Foundations of Gentry Life: The Multons of Frampton and their World 1270–1370* (Oxford, 2010), 176–81.

[16] Newman, 'Greater and Lesser Landowners', 292.

[17] Newman calculated that of 419 livings in thirteenth-century Yorkshire, 60 per cent were in monastic hands: 'Greater and Lesser Landowners', 303.

[18] See below 206.

72   POLITICS AND SOCIETY IN MID THIRTEENTH-CENTURY ENGLAND

to use a concept borrowed from K. B. McFarlane and his school, students of late medieval bastard feudalism. Some thirteenth-century 'affinities' have been carefully studied by historians.[19] A particularly useful entrée is that of Roger Bigod III, earl of Norfolk, the earl who led the confrontation with the king in April 1258.[20] Although his father, Hugh II, died in 1225, Roger did not succeed him until 1228, when he was about nineteen years of age. His mother was Maud Marshal, daughter of the great William Marshal, and he was inclined towards the Marshal family and their associates in his early years rather than towards the court. It was a portent of the future, perhaps, that he was at court at Christmas 1245 together with Simon de Montfort and Peter of Savoy, although a great deal of water was to flow under the bridge between then and the debacle of 1258. 1245 was the year when the last of the Marshal brothers died. When Maud also died in 1248, Roger was not only reunited with the third of the Bigod lands she held in dower but also added one third of the Marshal inheritance. This involved major manors in English counties, the town and castle of Chepstow in Wales, and substantial property in Ireland. Once various adjustments had been made, his yearly income, based on Marc Morris's calculations from the various available sources, rose to £1,650. Allowing for under-evaluations, Morris estimates a real income of £2,250, putting him on the same level as Simon de Montfort and William de Valence but way behind 'the top rank of super earls', that is, the late Marshal family, the Clares, and the king's brother, Richard of Cornwall.[21]

Roger was frequently at court during the years 1246–7, but once he had secured his mother's estates 'his attendance dropped off dramatically'. 'No doubt', Morris adds, 'he spent much of his time visiting his new lordships and investigating their potential'.[22] He was not, it seems, a natural courtier. He was, however, a conventional aristocrat. He was a warrior when he felt inclined or called upon—he went to Poitou with the king in 1242, and to Gascony in 1253—and a tourneyer (at Northampton in 1241, for example). In 1256 he entertained the king at Framlingham and participated in the tournament at Blyth. He was also an enthusiastic hunter. In 1251 he was at Chepstow, hunting with his brother-in-law, John fitz Geoffrey. In Yorkshire, during the summer of 1255, as the king was travelling north to Scotland, Roger and his brother, Hugh, joined their cousins, the FitzRanulfs, on a hunting expedition to supply the royal household with deer.[23]

---

[19] Among the earliest studies on these lines were K. J. Stringer, *Earl David of Huntingdon, 1152–1219: A Study in Anglo-Scottish History* (Edinburgh, 1985), Ch. 8, and Grant G. Simpson, 'The *Familia* of Roger de Quincy, Earl of Winchester and Constable of Scotland', in K. Stringer (ed.), *Essays on the Nobility of Medieval Scotland* (Edinburgh, 1985), 102–29. For an earlier retinue, see D. Crouch, *William Marshal: Court, Career and Chivalry in the Angevin Empire 1147–1219* (London and New York, 1990), Ch. 5, 'The Marshal's Men'.

[20] What follows draws on the fine study by Marc Morris, *The Bigod Earls of Norfolk in the Thirteenth Century*, especially Chs. 2–3.

[21] Ibid., 31–42.   [22] Ibid., 43.

[23] 'To judge from the number of animals they caught between them, the hunt was an activity at which the Bigods excelled': ibid., 55.

POWER AND PROFIT IN THE PROVINCES   73

Roger was fervent in support of his rights. He insisted on his inherited prerogatives as 'earl marshal' or 'marshal of England' as he preferred to call himself. These included the right to nominate a deputy as 'marshal of the exchequer' and another as 'marshal of the household', and an entitlement to various—and probably considerable—fees. It also involved duties and privileges in time of war. As most of these rights were customary, they were the subject of tension with the crown. For the most part Henry III tended to accept the Bigods' claims.[24] It was the same with knight's fees, where Roger steadfastly refused to recognize more than his original quota of sixty, even though the Bigods had created 125¼ fees in 1135 and had added another thirty-seven and a half by 1166. For years the exchequer vainly tried to raise the excess from the 'Poitevin' scutage of 1230, but without success.[25] Roger was quick to anger and had several brushes with the king. In 1255, when he intervened in favour of the temporarily disgraced Robert de Ros, Henry called Roger a traitor, leading to a well-known exchange of words reported by Matthew Paris.[26] Henry, characteristically, backed down with regards to Robert de Ros but, equally characteristically, tried to turn the screw over Roger's debts to the exchequer. The St Albans chronicler, Matthew Paris, clearly admired him and his comments collectively form a portrait of the man.[27]

Roger Bigod was firmly focused on his earldom in East Anglia, and principally upon the honour of Framlingham.[28] Here, his ancestor Roger I had built a major castle as well as founding the priory at Thetford in Norfolk, which functioned as the family mausoleum. A second castle lay at Bungay on the border with Norfolk, while Framlingham itself was home to a huge park as well as a seigniorial borough.[29] Framlingham Castle had been massively rebuilt by Roger's grandfather in the latest style, with a curtain wall of stone and thirteen towers. Roger himself, however, was no builder; nor was he a benefactor to the church. This has led to the suggestion that he was by nature parsimonious.[30] Roger must have interpreted his role as preserving what he had inherited and enjoyed.[31] From the outset he was prepared to use violence to protect his interests. In the early 1240s he was in

---

[24] As opposed to Edward I, who was inclined to challenge them: ibid., 31. Morris deals with the Bigods as earls marshal on 26–31.

[25] Ibid., 15–16., The Bigods had not, it seems, reached a compromise with Henry II over the number of knights owed.

[26] Paris, *CM* v, 530. See above 36.

[27] See Morris's summary of the man: *The Bigod Earls*, 184–9.

[28] For a map of the Roger's estates, see Morris, *The Bigod Earls*, 35.

[29] For Framlingham, see John Ridgard (ed.), *Medieval Framlingham*, Suffolk Record Society (Woodbridge, 1985).

[30] All he has to his name are a new chapel at Hamstead Marshal, a new bridge at Chepstow, the gift of a mill to the nuns of Bungay, and gifts to the hospital of St Giles, Norwich, and to the priory which his father had founded at Weybridge: Morris, *The Bigod Earls*, 100, 186.

[31] He was not a great purchaser. In 1232 he and his wife, the Scottish princess, Isabella, bought the manor of Peasenhall, north-east of Framlingham, out of her marriage portion. He gained the manor of Cratfield as the result of a dispute over the honour of Belvoir in Leicestershire. He also bought property with which to endow his brothers.

74 POLITICS AND SOCIETY IN MID THIRTEENTH-CENTURY ENGLAND

contention with the parvenu Peter of Savoy, whose rewards at the king's hands made him a major landowner in East Anglia. A series of disputes between their respective bailiffs was brought to arbitration in 1245.[32] When the jurors were asked whether either of the earls had encouraged their bailiffs, they replied that Bigod was well aware of their activities and, indeed, had given them orders *ex ira*. Roger's behaviour during the years of reform and rebellion adds somewhat to this picture. He held the hundred of Loes in Suffolk, the hundred in which Framlingham lies, and the subject of the unique surviving return from the panels of knights in 1258.[33] It contains complaints about some of his officials, as do the 1275 Hundred Rolls.[34] Although these misdemeanours are relatively slight, and Morris largely exonerates him as a committed reformer, Roger made financial gains from the reform regime, establishing his right to the profits from his brother's special eyre and gaining a wardship. Nonetheless, historians have been happy with his credentials as a genuine reformer. He was to rejoin the king's council at the beginning of 1263. He was absent, however, from the battle of Lewes, as he was to be from Evesham. Indeed, he showed no enthusiasm for the Montfortian regime. Very telling is Montfort's letter to him on 9 June 1265 in which he asked him to put down a rebellion in East Anglia, remarking on his great power there.[35] As Morris remarks, there was probably an element of envy in this, as well as flattery, as Montfort's own power was ebbing away. Nonetheless, there is a strong element of truth here as it indicates where the earl's own priorities lay.[36] His activities after Evesham are equally indicative. He was swift to join the king. He confiscated at least four East Anglian manors from their Montfortian holders.[37] He was one of the magnates who favoured and worked for conciliation, and he played a role in bringing East Anglian men back into the king's peace.[38] His overall concern was undoubtedly his own power in East Anglia.

We can get a little closer to understanding Roger's provincial power by the traditional method of examining the great lord's affinity. The work of Marc Morris allows us to approach that of Roger Bigod with confidence.[39] At the beginning of

---

[32] Ibid., 20–1.

[33] For the text see Jacob, *Studies in the Period of Baronial Reform and Rebellion*, 341–2. For what follows see Morris, *The Bigod Earls*, 77–8.

[34] Ibid., 77.   [35] *CR 1264–8*, 125.   [36] Morris, *The Bigod Earls*, 93.

[37] Ibid., 94. He seized the rent from Sproughton in Norfolk, held by Simon himself, Surlington in Norfolk from Thomas de Moulton, and 'Wyleghby' from William de Evereux: TNA, E159/67, m. 19; *CIM*, i, 250; *Rotuli Selecti*, ed. J. Hunter (*Record Commission*, 1834), 226.

[38] In July 1266 he was given authority to receive those East Anglian rebels who wished to surrender: *CPR 1258–66*, 618. See also *Hundred Rolls* I, 506.

[39] Ibid., 59–60. For Morris's sources and method of reconstruction of the affinity, see *The Bigod Earls*, 59–61. In addition to the thirteen charters there are four 'household lists': the twenty-three individuals who received letters of protection travelling with him to the Council of Lyon in 1245 (*CPR 1232–47*, 454); the *familiares* who hunted with him in Yorkshire on the king's orders in 1255 (*CR 1254–56*, 415); the eighteen *familiares* (where this precise term is used) who were with the earl in London in 1257 and had any pleas against them respited (*CR 1256–9*, 151–2); and those who had quittance of common summons in Norfolk in 1268 (*CR 1264–8*, 500).

POWER AND PROFIT IN THE PROVINCES 75

Roger's time as earl we find five East Anglian knights operating as his close associates.[40] All belonged to families who held of the Bigods, four of them from before 1166. William de Hingham, the exception here, had been enfeoffed by Roger II (1177–1221). Two of them had been seneschals and in the garrison of Framlingham Castle in 1216, one being constable. Such men witnessed his charters, where they were joined by relatives and by others belonging to families who had held of the Bigods since before 1166. An exception was Herbert de Alencon. He was not a tenant but a neighbour. One time sheriff of Norfolk and Suffolk, he held a series of manors north of Framlingham.[41]

These men, as Morris says, were the 'old guard', and by the mid-1240s the affinity had undergone considerable change. The men who had served the two previous earls had been replaced by a younger generation. In the list of men who accompanied Roger III to the Council of Lyon in 1245 we find four knights, one of whom appears as Roger's seneschal between 1245 and 1249. All four were Roger's tenants. Three other men who were less significant in the affinity also appear to have had strong service connections with the Bigods. Another knight, Robert Hovel, who appears in the Bigod 'household lists' but not as a charter witness, seems on the other hand to have had no family or tenurial link to the Bigods. The Hovel family had held at Wyverstone, Norfolk, since the eleventh century. By 1263 they had acquired lands at Istead, Risby, Chediston, and Market Weston, the last being held of the Bigods. However, it is not known how or when this occurred, and it may be that it stems from his service rather than conditioning it. There were other 'new men' in Roger's service who were not knights. One is John Algar, who went to Lyon with the earl. He acquired some property in Loddon, Norfolk, seemingly by marriage, and received life tenure of the manor of Brockley, Suffolk, from Roger. Another is Thomas Lenebaud. He was a clerk and a scholar who was associated with the earl from as early as 1240. He became parson of Framlingham and was later an archdeacon. By 1258 there were some further newcomers. There was Philip de Buckland, a knight with manors in East Suffolk as well as property in Hertfordshire. Roger was to nominate him as marshal of the king's household. Richard de Holbrook, another knight, held manors on the estuary of the Orwell.[42] Other new men were the knight Henry de Rushall and Thomas de Shotford, probably not a knight but nonetheless Roger's steward in East Anglia in 1251. These men were not Roger's tenants but, as Morris points out, most interestingly, they were probably 'drawn into his circle' by the earl's

---

[40] Three of them, together with the prior of Thetford, stood as sureties for him in financial arrangements connected with his inheritance. Morris suggests that they may have been Hugh II's executors. The five laymen extended £100 for Roger's use during his minority.

[41] At Badingham, Colston, Dennington, Brundish, and Tannington.

[42] He held in Suffolk at Bentley, Bucklesham, Foxhall, Freston, Holbrook, Nacton, 'Rushaugh', 'Slich', Sproughton, 'Stubover', Tattingstone, and Wherstead, and in Norfolk at Seething.

76 POLITICS AND SOCIETY IN MID THIRTEENTH-CENTURY ENGLAND

'aggressive expansion' of his interests along the River Waveney.[43] Roger's last affinity included fewer men drawn from his tenantry.[44] Only two—Hugh Tuddenham and Robert de Vaux—were of families with any prior connection with the Bigods.

At this point we can examine what Morris's research has indicated in terms of the characteristics of Roger Bigod III's affinity. The 'household lists' indicate an entourage of about twenty people, plus menial servants like carters, grooms, and porters. There are other men whose names suggest they were household officials: Roger the Butler, Reginald Marshal, William the Cook. Of the twenty-nine household members of the retinue, at least twenty were knights.[45] The charter witness lists suggest five to eight knights serving at any one time. In 1255, when hunting in Yorkshire he had six knights plus Hugh de Tuddenham and his clerk, Thomas Lenebaud. At London for parliament in 1257 he had eighteen men with him, including six knights together with Thomas Lenebaud and John Algar. On his journey to Lyon he had between eight and eleven. Morris concludes that Roger would generally have had about six knights in his household and could double the number for special occasions. His retinue was therefore comparable to contemporaries like William de Valence and Simon de Montfort, but considerably less than Gilbert de Clare and Richard of Cornwall.

At least one third of the earl's *familiares* were drawn from his tenants, which would seem the norm. However, that total may be up to one half, that is, higher than the norm. The most striking feature of the affinity, however, is its 'geographical cohesion'. All of them were East Anglian, and most were from Suffolk. This remained true, despite the earl's share of the Marshal inheritance. It reflects the region from where the greater part of his income was derived. The larger part of his property, including the castles of Framlingham and Bungay, was located south of the river Waveney. Moreover, like the members of his affinity, Roger was firmly rooted in Suffolk. Morris remarks that Roger's *familiares* appear 'lacklustre' compared to the 'high-achievers' who accompanied Simon de Montfort. Similarly, they seem 'superficially less interesting than the courtier knights who trotted after William de Valence'.[46] Roger's affinity, by contrast, was not 'court' but firmly 'country'. On the other hand, many were influential local figures. They were 'the bedrock' of county society. It is unsurprising that we do not see much in the way of royal favours acquired by Roger for members of his affinity. When we do, it tends to be when Roger was in favour with the king, as in 1257, when he was 'deep in the king's counsels'.

---

[43] Henry de Rushall held lands at Rushall and Semer. Thomas de Shotford held land at Thickbroom, Mendham, and probably Shotford itself.

[44] William Malherbe, Philip de Buckland, Henry de Rushall, Thomas de Shotford, Richard de Cransford, Robert Blund, and William de Burgh appear not to have held any land from him.

[45] See the list (Table 3) in Morris, *The Bigod Earls*, 69.   [46] Ibid., 71.

POWER AND PROFIT IN THE PROVINCES   77

Roger Bigod III's affinity and local control is perhaps characteristic of a magnate whose family was well entrenched in a specific region. By way of contrast, the affinity of William de Valence was almost entirely centred on the king's court.[47] William, as we have seen, had come to England with his brothers in 1247 and was well endowed by his half-brother, Henry III. The king found him a prestigious and wealthy wife in Joan de Munchensey, one of the Marshal heiresses, establishing him in Ireland, the Welsh Marches, and elsewhere in England.[48] His income, as of 1272, has been calculated as £2,500 per annum, a little over half of which was in land and the rest in gifts of wardships, transferred debts, and pensions. The estates, however, were not cohesive geographically speaking. Aside from Wexford in Ireland, Pembroke and Goodrich in the Welsh March, the properties he acquired were scattered over many counties, principally in southern England. His main base here was Hertford castle. There was little opportunity to consolidate,[49] and this seems to have affected his ability to develop close ties with his tenants. In fact, Huw Ridgeway finds that the retinue's 'most novel feature' was its 'almost complete freedom from tenurial ties'.[50]

William arrived in England with nine knights, almost none of whom stayed in the country beyond 1251. A total of twenty-seven knights have been associated with him across the period up to 1272, suggesting a normal retinue of about a dozen knights plus a few *valetti*.[51] Very few were foreigners, and only one of the 1247 knights, Imbert Guy, was to stay throughout the period. Englishmen soon predominated, most of them joining him from the king's service. They included Geoffrey Gascelins (of Wiltshire),[52] Robert de Aiguillon (of Surrey, Sussex, and elsewhere), and Roger Leybourne (of Kent), substantial men who had their own sub-retinues.[53] There were also, as one would expect, clerks and administrators. The English estates were supervised by William de Bussay, whom Matthew Paris calls his *'principalis consiliarius'*, with a deputy (William de Kirketon) in the north.[54] Wexford and Pembroke were administered separately, the latter being put under John de Bussay, presumably a relative of William, in 1257. His personal servants seem to have been a mixture of Poitevins and Englishmen, perhaps under the influence of his wife.

---

[47] For what follows see Huw Ridgeway, 'William de Valence and his *Familiares*, 1247–72', *Historical Research*, 45 (October 1992), 239–57.

[48] See above 42.

[49] Ridgeway adds: 'except perhaps in Gloucestershire–Wiltshire, and in Northumberland': ibid., 247.

[50] Ibid., 241.   [51] For *valetti*, see below 146.

[52] See also N. Saul, 'A "Rising" Lord and a "Declining" Esquire: Sir Thomas de Berkeley III and Geoffrey Gascylin of Sheldon', *EHR*, 61 (1988), 345–56.

[53] Ridgeway, 'William de Valence and his *Familiares*', 247–8. Others include Ingram de Villers or Villiers (of Sussex), Robert de Immer (probably of the West Country), and William de Bolleville (of Somerset–Wiltshire).

[54] Ibid., 250; Paris, *CM* v, 726, 738–9.

78 POLITICS AND SOCIETY IN MID THIRTEENTH-CENTURY ENGLAND

Ridgeway speculates that William's familiars were paid by money fees, for they received very little in terms of land. What they did have was access to the king's patronage.[55] Robert de Aiguillon, for example, was permitted to marry another of the Marshal heiresses, Joan de Mohun, and without royal licence. In 1261 he was granted a money fee of forty marks by the king and in 1263 was made steward of the king's household. In addition to Roger Leybourne, whose career seems to have begun with William, Imbert Guy was given the seneschalcy of Perigord, William de Kirketon made keeper of the peace in Holland (Lincolnshire), and Geoffrey de Newbold, one of William's clerks, became chancellor of the exchequer (in 1277). William's followers also gained small land grants, wardships, benefices, and other perquisites.[56] He was also able to protect his men from judicial processes. Even though William clearly wished to establish himself in England, in these years he developed no power base beyond the royal court. This lack of integration into English society must have made it easier for his baronial enemies to force his exile in 1258. As we shall see later, Simon de Montfort provides a significant contrast in this respect.[57]

The Institutional Framework of Control

We come now to the third dimension to magnate power: the institutional framework within which they operated. Here we come face to face with the controversial subject of the honour and the honour court. Scholars are generally agreed that the honour was a vital ingredient of aristocratic society in Anglo–Norman England. There is general agreement, too, that the reforms of Henry II and the advent of the common law were detrimental to the cohesion of the honour and to the operation of the honour court, given that both possession and right were protected by legal remedies that undermined a lord's control over his tenants by military tenure in depriving him of sanctions, above the level that is of distraint by chattels. The problem arises over the timing and pace of the honour's decline. Some scholars have placed this in the twelfth century. Hugh Thomas has argued against Sir James Holt's contention that feudal tenure played an overwhelming role in the rebellion against King John and famously referred to the honour court, by 1216, as 'in an advanced state of senescence as an institution governing the

---

[55] Ibid., 255 and references given there.

[56] They include Geoffrey Gascelins, William de Bussay, Robert de Creppinges, William de Kirketon, Ingram de Vilers, Robert le Blund, and Geoffrey de Newbold. They also gained lands of disinherited rebels after the battle of Evesham.

[57] John Maddicott deals fully with his finances and his affinity: *Simon de Montfort*, Ch. 2, '*Familia* and Fortune'.

POWER AND PROFIT IN THE PROVINCES   79

loyalty and actions of both lords and vassals'.[58] David Crouch is not only in agreement with this interpretation but has added that 'the honor was only part of the framework of twelfth-century political society' and that 'in many cases it cannot have amounted to much in the first place'.[59] Others, including myself, have seen honourial jurisdiction 'waning slowly and unevenly' during the late twelfth and thirteenth centuries, 'the generations from c.1180–c.1230 being transitional', while acknowledging that the honour and its court might continue 'to provide one focus of solidarity in local society even when they were in decline during the first half of the thirteenth century'.[60]

David Carpenter subsequently mounted a powerful rear-guard action in favour of the vitality of feudal tenure and of the honour and its court in the thirteenth century.[61] He begins with Magna Carta, the early chapters of which are centred on the tenurial relationship between the king and his tenants-in-chief, and its consequences. Moreover, the rights accorded the king were also reinforced for his barons in their relationship with their own tenants. Thus the Charter, both in 1215 and in 1217, was concerned to 'protect the authority of the lord within his "fee"'.[62] Carpenter demonstrates how 'feudal' thirteenth-century society remained in its 'structures' and its 'ideas'. As regards the former he demonstrates the role of the fee by reference to the collection of the scutage of 1235 and the royal inquiry into fees in 1242. As regards ideas there can be no doubt that he is correct in that the concept of the fee was ideologically potent. The performance of homage retained great contemporary resonance. We see this in the *Life of William Marshal*, written in the 1220s, and in the romance of *Fouke le Fitz Waryn*, which seems to have originated around 1260.[63] The Dictum of Kenilworth, Carpenter points out, differentiated in terms of leniency between those who had a tenurial obligation to come to their lord, that is Simon de Montfort, at his order and those who joined him in rebellion but did not.[64] With regard to the honour court, he stresses the contemporary significance of suit of court. A royal proclamation of 1234 stipulated that private courts should meet every three weeks.[65] In practice there was a

---

[58] See Hugh M. Thomas, *Vassals, Heiresses, Crusaders and Thugs: The Gentry of Angevin Yorkshire, 1154–1216* (Philadelphia, 1993), especially Ch. 1, 'Vassals, Tenants-in-Chief and the Transformation of the Honor'. The quotation is from page 47.

[59] David Crouch, 'From Stenton to McFarlane: Models of Societies of the Twelfth and Thirteenth Centuries', *TRHS*, sixth ser. v (1995), 179–200. The quotations are from pages 186–7.

[60] P. R. Coss, 'Bastard Feudalism Revised', *P&P*, 125 (November 1989), 27–64.

[61] D. A. Carpenter, 'The Second Century of English Feudalism', *P&P*, 168 (August 2000), 30–71.

[62] Ibid., 37.

[63] *History of William the Marshal*, ed. A. J. Holden (translated by S. Gregory and introduced by D. Crouch), Anglo-Norman Text Society, 3 vols. (London, 2002–6); *Fouke Le Fitz Waryn*, ed. P. T. Rickets et al., Anglo-Norman Text Society (Oxford, 1975).

[64] *DBM*, 332–5. This did not apply, of course, to those who were in arms against the king at Northampton, Lewes, Evesham, and Kenilworth.

[65] *CR 1231–4*, 551. See also Paul Brand, *Kings, Barons and Justices: The Making and Enforcement of Legislation in Thirteenth-Century England* (Cambridge, 2003), 44.

80 POLITICS AND SOCIETY IN MID THIRTEENTH-CENTURY ENGLAND

difference between these regular meetings and the two or three great courts that were held annually. There were disputes between lords and tenants over the level of obligation to attend the regular courts. Carpenter cites the case between Roger de Somery, lord of Dudley, and his most prominent military tenant, William of Birmingham, which came before the justices in eyre in Warwickshire in 1262.[66] It was agreed that henceforth William would do suit only twice yearly, and when it was necessary to afforce the court. With regard to the operation of the honour, Carpenter considers the argument over the shift away from tenure in the construction of affinities as giving an exaggerated impression in that the witness lists to charters do not furnish a complete guide to contemporary relationships and play down tenurial ones. In those days, it was not the greatest tenants who were the mainstays of the honour but the more modest and solidly based ones.[67] They were the men who made up the thirteenth-century honourial community.

'Honours', Carpenter points out, were 'diverse in terms of their tenurial and geographical patterns, continuity of lordship and ability of their individual lords'.[68] This was as true in the thirteenth century as it had been in the twelfth. Naturally, the honours of the greatest lords tended to be among the strongest and the most durable. Carpenter cites, in particular, the honour of Tutbury, held by the Ferrers, earls of Derby.[69] Others include the honour of Coventry in the time of Ranulf III, earl of Chester, Earl Richard of Cornwall's honour of Wallingford, and the earl of Aumale's honour of Holderness.[70] It was not restricted to the greatest lords, however. One thinks of the compact and long-lasting honours on the Welsh borders of Herefordshire and Shropshire, recently studied.[71] At the same time, however, we have to acknowledge—as we have seen in the case of Richard, earl of Gloucester—that widespread estates were no longer being administered in terms of honours. Moreover, as shown in the case of the same lord's inquisition post mortem, major lordships, including boroughs and hundreds, tend to be described in terms of their liberties, that is to say franchises, involving public as well as private jurisdictions. In practice honour and franchisal courts might well be amalgamated, rather than held discretely. When it comes to the durability of the honour court and its relationship to royal courts, an indicative case is that

---

[66] *Warwickshire Feet of Fines i*, ed. E. Stokes et al., Dugdale Society (London, 1932), no. 842.

[67] Carpenter, 'Second Century', 52, 56.   [68] Ibid., 35.

[69] Ibid., 47–55, drawing on P. E. Golob, 'The Ferrers Earls of Derby: A Study of the Honour of Tutbury, 1066–1279', (University of Cambridge PhD thesis, 1984), especially Ch. 5, 'The State of the Honour in the Thirteenth Century'.

[70] B. English, *The Lords of Holderness, 1086–1260: A Study in Feudal Society* (Hull, 1991). For Wallingford see C. Tilly, 'The Honour of Wallingford 1066–1300' (University of London PhD thesis, 2011) and the same author's 'Magna Carta and the Honour of Wallingford', *Historical Research*, 89 (August 2016), 454–69. See also K. S. B. Keats-Rohan, N. Christie, and D. Roffe, *Wallingford: The Castle and the Town in Context*, British Archaeological Reports, no. 621 (2015).

[71] See Brock Holden, *Lords of the Central Marches: English Aristocracy and Frontier Society, 1087–1265* (Oxford, 2008) and Max Lieberman, *The Medieval March of Wales: The Creation and Perception of a Frontier, 1066–1283* (Cambridge, 2010).

POWER AND PROFIT IN THE PROVINCES   81

of Richard Siward against the earl of Gloucester. In 1247 Siward claimed that he could not obtain justice in the earl's own court where the lord of Glamorgan was 'lord and almost king and justice' (*fuit dominus et quasi rex et justiciarius*). For this reason, he had brought his case to the royal court. The courts of even the greatest lords were no longer autonomous.[72]

Some of the proceedings in the Siward case had involved the county court at Cardiff. County courts in England no longer required domination by great lords except, perhaps, where they were hereditary sheriffs, since so much of the business was merely procedural. Even so, their stewards were an ever watchful presence there. The central courts were a different matter. Here it was essential that their interests should be served. This is why they employed professional lawyers. We know from a study by John Maddicott that ecclesiastical lords paid retaining fees to the justices and this was almost certainly true of lay barons, too: it 'presupposed a world in which magnates were such frequent litigants or so frequently in need of favour and professional advice that they found it worthwhile to have justices always on their books'.[73] Much, it seems, depended upon the favour of the king, and here many lords had cause to worry, especially when they found themselves up against the king's favourites. The final locus of institutional power to be considered is the royal court itself. Being in or out of favour here was crucial, and it could impact on power in the provinces.

It was essential for lords to have the capacity and the inclination to fight for their rights against the possibility of erosion. Unless protected, rights had a tendency to lapse. Danger could come from encroachment by other magnates, the intrusion of royal favourites and ministers, from recalcitrant tenants, and from expansive religious houses. It was not just a matter of material resources, but also of prestige within society involving, inter alia, the capacity to keep lesser landowners within one's orbit. Hence the contemporary concern over other lords entering one's fee. We see this graphically when it comes to the alienation of land in mortmain, whereby grantors holding land from their lord subinfeudated it by sale or gift to religious houses or secular ecclesiastics.[74] In the twelfth century it was customary that anyone wishing to do this required the permission of his overlord. The reason is clear. With subinfeudation there was always a danger that the overlord would lose control of the services due to him, that is, wardships, marriages, reliefs, and escheats. There are signs that in King John's reign this rule was breaking down, given that there were incidents of the king being invoked to

---

[72] The full record of the case is contained on the Curia Regis Roll of 31–32 Henry III: KB 26/159 mm. 2, 10–11. The outline is given in Altschul, *A Baronial Family*, 70–3.

[73] J. R. Maddicott, 'Law and Lordship: Royal Justices as Retainers in Thirteenth- and Fourteenth-Century England', *P&P*, supplement no. 4 (1978).

[74] For what follows see Paul Brand, 'The Control of Mortmain Alienation 1200–1300', in J. H. Baker (ed.), *Legal Records and the Historian*, Royal Historical Society (London, 1978), 29–40, republished in Brand, *The Making of the Common Law* (London, 1992), 233–44.

82 POLITICS AND SOCIETY IN MID THIRTEENTH-CENTURY ENGLAND

maintain it. Clause 39 of the 1217 Magna Carta declared that no one was to alienate so much of his tenement that he could no longer perform his services, a clause which seems to have been aimed particularly at alienations in mortmain. Clause 43 countered the practice of grantors to religious houses receiving the property back from them, thus diminishing a lord's control. Nonetheless, during Henry III's personal rule it is clear that this was a cause of contention. In 1228 alienation by tenants-in-chief was forbidden.[75] The legal treatise known under the name of 'Bracton' showed awareness of the legislation but nonetheless championed freedom of alienation, as long as the tenant performed homage and continued to render the services. 'Bracton' indicates that lords were fighting back. One method was to act immediately to prevent seisin taking place, a course of action supported in the courts from 1247. Another was to summon the alienee to the honour court to explain why he had entered the fee without the lord's permission and to his damage. Evident in 1266, this action may well go back earlier. Furthermore, as in the previous reign, we find lords invoking the king. In 1235 a royal charter to Westminster Abbey forbade anyone from entering the abbot's fee without his consent. From 1243 onwards, favoured individuals and religious houses received such royal prohibitions, empowering the local sheriff to act, such encroachments being actionable in the royal courts. A writ of 1256 referred to legislation requiring the lord's assent to any mortmain alienation, but no such legislation has been traced. Much seems to have depended upon the favour of the king.

The maintenance of local power was bound up with the issue of reward. As we have seen, ministers and servants were rewarded with money fees, and the most significant with land, to ensure future loyalty. Men might also be rewarded from a lord's feudal resources. And they might also profit from their lord's access to royal patronage. As Scott Waugh has pointed out, just as the king wanted to protect his servants from 'distracting obligations', so too did baronial landholders. They therefore used their influence with Henry to secure exemptions from juries and offices.[76] For example, the earl of Norfolk acquired acquittance from common summonses before the justices in eyre for seventeen *familiares*, four of whom also received exemptions, while William de Ferrers obtained judicial exemptions for two servants for as long as they were members of his household.[77] In 1256 two men, William Callethorp and Hugh de Caylly, received respites at the request of the bishop of Norwich and acquired exemptions at around the same time.[78] Edmund de Lacy's steward, John de Hoderode, was exempted from assizes while he remained in his service, and the king later added offices as well, at Lacy's

---

[75] *CR 1227–31*, 88. See also Bean, *Decline of English Feudalism*, 58.
[76] Waugh, 'Reluctant Knights and Jurors', 975.
[77] *CR 1256–9*, 151, and *CPR 1247–58*, 219, 578, and 635; *CPR 1232–7*, 242, and *CR 1242–7*, 538.
[78] *CPR 1247–58*, 496, 477.

POWER AND PROFIT IN THE PROVINCES 83

request.[79] In October 1251 Aymer de Valence, bishop of Winchester, was granted exemption from assizes, juries, and recognitions, a grant extended to his entire 'free household', both those who served in his 'inn' and his manorial officials throughout England.[80]

Some ministers, however, gained more than this. In January 1251, for example, the king exempted William de Bussay, steward of William de Valence, from suits of court and from assizes. As we have seen, there was nothing unusual about this. A year later, however, the king granted Bussay a wardship with the right to the marriage of the heir.[81] Similarly, some men were granted respites of knighthood until their lords took up arms, as in 1251-2 when twenty landowners were respited until the earls of Devon, Lincoln, Salisbury, and Surrey, all underage, were knighted.[82] As Scott Waugh says, in words that accord with David Carpenter's, 'Tenurial lordship may have waned by the mid thirteenth century but many landholders still turned to lords for assistance, wealth and prestige'.[83]

However, it was not only great lords who could use their influence in this way. Government officials could also obtain exemptions for friends and relatives. Waugh calculates that at least ninety men who acquired grants on behalf of others were royal officials or favourites. Thus, of around fifty men who witnessed most of the king's charters while he was in Gascony in 1253-4, no less than twenty-three gained exemptions for their friends, family members, or servants, and another twenty-two men who were also there with the king did likewise. For example, Wakelin de Ardern, marshal of the royal household, gained exemption for four others, including Eustace de Watford of Northamptonshire and a relative, John de Ardern.[84] In total, the king exempted more than one hundred men from juries and offices in these years on the advice of fifty-five men. As Scott Waugh points out, there was in existence a community or perhaps a network of such men who exerted a great deal of influence and could grant their own favours in this way. These administrators and their networks must have constituted an alternative locus of local power and could therefore be a nuisance to the great lords.[85]

In this chapter we have examined the bases on which magnate power rested in the provinces, and the actions they needed to take in order to maintain and to nurture it. It is little wonder, therefore, that issues we have discussed in this and

---

[79] TNA, Ancient Deeds DL 25/2/121; *CPR 1232-47*, 56, and *1247-58*, 28.

[80] *CPR 1247-58*, 111.

[81] Valence himself granted Bussay another wardship: *CPR 1232-47*, 84; *1247-58*, 123; TNA, SC 1/7/199.

[82] *CR 1251-3*, 184, 228, 263, 434, 438, 444, 451.

[83] Waugh, 'Reluctant Knights and Jurors', 976.

[84] *CPR 1247-58*, 324, 349; *CLR 1251-60*, 309, 520; *CPR 1232-47*, 370.

[85] For networks see P. Coss, 'How did Thirteenth-Century Knights counter Royal Authority?', *TCE*, xv (Woodbridge, 2015), 3-16.

84 POLITICS AND SOCIETY IN MID THIRTEENTH-CENTURY ENGLAND

the previous chapter should feature in the Petition of the Barons,[86] a compilation that seems to have been drawn up for the Committee of Twenty-Four, established to reform 'the state of the kingdom', which met in June 1258.[87] Clauses 1–3 are concerned with aspects of feudal tenure, including the king's use of prerogative wardship whereby he had custody not only of the lands (and the body) of an heir holding of him, but also of the lands he held of others. Clause 6 concerns the disparagement of ladies by marriage and is explicitly aimed at aliens. Clauses 10 and 11 bring us to the issue of religious houses. The first deals with alienation to them in mortmain without the lord's consent, referring specifically to the loss of wardships, marriages, reliefs, and escheats.[88] The second deals with the king taking custody of religious houses when headships were vacant, thus depriving earls and barons as intermediate lords. The next clause concerns the king granting away the rights of others claiming that they were escheats, and depriving the rightful owners of redress in the courts, while a further clause attacks fines levied against earls and barons for not appearing before justices on eyre on 'the first day of the common summons' in cases where courts were being held simultaneously. Many of the issues raised, then, directly concerned the great lords, sometimes explicitly, while others affected landowners more generally, including their tenants and followers. The trafficking of indebted estates came under fire, for example: 'Jews sometimes transfer their and lands pledged to them to magnates and other powerful persons in the kingdom, who thus enter the lands of lesser men'.[89] Some clauses, most particularly those involving officials, have a wider catchment. Clause 24 deals with new suits to courts, including liberties as well as counties and hundreds. Clause 28 is concerned with acquittances from being put on assizes, juries, and recognitions so that 'in many counties, for lack of knights it is not possible to hold any grand assize, so that pleas of this king remain unfinished, and petitioners never obtain justice'.

We do not know how this petition was put together and, as Paul Brand says, it may have been assembled from various sources and express the concerns of various groups. However, the greater part could quite easily have been derived from within aristocratic ranks, and involved the lords' retinues. It is a reflection, directly and indirectly, of magnate power.

---

[86] *DBM*, no. 3.

[87] Brand, *Kings, Barons and Justices*, 2, and Brand, *The Making of the Common Law*, 326.

[88] According to Paul Brand, 'That the complaint was limited to mortmain alienations to religious houses is evidence that the objection was not just economic or financial in origin, but was also symptomatic of a more general prejudice against the further accumulation of wealth by the old-established religious houses (Brand, 'The Control of Mortmain Alienation', 238). This led to clause 14 of the Provisions of Westminster. It was, however, dropped by the king in his re-enactment of January 1263, no doubt because he needed the support of the church. By contrast, it was cited during the Montfortian regime and indeed after.

[89] *DBM*, no. 3, cl. 25.

The Petition of the Barons is, of course, a set of grievances not enactments. However, it set in motion a process of adjustment to law and administration and many of the clauses are reflected in the Provisions of Westminster and later legislation. The Petition of the Barons has to be contrasted with the Provisions of Oxford, enacted at the Oxford Parliament in June 1258.[90] The latter, as Maddicott says, 'set out a scheme for the wholesale reform of the English polity through the placing of royal government under organised control for the first time.'[91] A council of fifteen was appointed superseding the Committee of Twenty-Four. It was to supervise royal ministers and appoint to the great offices of state, the chancellor, treasurer, and justiciar, the last named being the first since 1234. Parliament was to meet three times per year 'to deal with the common business of the realm and of the king', with twelve representatives of the community of the realm, that is to say twelve barons. Loyal castellans were appointed (and named), and more appropriate sheriffs and escheators were to be installed. The duties of the various officers were spelled out, and great emphasis was placed upon oaths, including a general oath to abide by the Provisions. The justiciar was to travel the country hearing complaints, gathered by four knights in each of the counties. Other reforms were promised, including that of the royal household. As Maddicott points out, 'These innovations came near to putting the Crown into commission.'[92]

It needs to be stressed, nonetheless, that there were two distinct processes at work: one being the seizure of the government from the king and his advisors in favour of the magnates and their associates, and the other being the actual reform of law and administration. Modern commentators tend to elide the two. There is admittedly some overlap, as there is between the Petition of the Barons and the Provisions of Oxford, but the two processes are analytically and for the most part practically distinct. However, the seizure of power and its accompaniments and the reform legislation encapsulated in the Provisions of Westminster have tended to be regarded as in essence a single phenomenon. This is implicit in the title of Treharne's book, *The Baronial Plan of Reform*, and his characterization of the period 1258–67 as one of reform and rebellion, which has become standard in the historiography. In fact, in view of what we now understand from Carpenter and Ridgeway in terms of the genesis of the movement, it would be better to think in terms primarily of revolt, followed by reforms and later by rebellion. The link between the two processes—the seizure of power and the wider reforms—now requires our attention. In the historiography this link has generally been provided by the involvement of 'county knights'. It is to this issue that we shall now turn.

Politics and Society in Mid Thirteenth-Century England: The Troubled Realm. Peter Coss, Oxford University Press.
© Peter Coss 2024. DOI: 10.1093/9780198924319.003.0004

[90] *DBM*, no. 5.   [91] Maddicott, *Simon de Montfort*, 157.   [92] Ibid., 158.

5

Reform and the Knights of 1258

A prominent feature of current historiography is that 'county knights' played a major role in initiating, animating, and sustaining the reform programme of 1258–9, both in their own capacity and as representatives of the county communities. It is often implied, if not directly stated, that these knights were fired up, initially at least, by the desire for a comprehensive reform of law and government. This interpretation stems essentially from the work of R. F. Treharne and has been given further impetus by that of John Maddicott.[1] It has become an integral component in the modern interpretation of the reform movement. In this chapter I intend to show that this interpretation rests on shallow foundations and to offer a more realistic assessment of their role.

Calling on the Knights

Let us first establish the basic facts. The root and branch reforms, as opposed to the actions taken to seize control of the executive, begin with the first clause of the Provisions of Oxford which reads as follows:

> It is provided that from each county four prudent and law-worthy knights (*discreti et legales milites*) shall be chosen (*eligantur*), who, on every day when the county court meets, shall attend to hear all complaints of any trespasses and injuries whatsoever, done to any persons, and to make the attachments arising from these complaints, until the first visit of the chief justiciar to those parts.

There then follow details of the procedure to be followed:

> This they shall do in such a fashion ... that the four knights shall have all the complaints with their attachments, enrolled in order and sequence, separately and severally for each hundred, so that on his first visit the justiciar shall be able to hear and determine the complaints separately for each hundred.

The clause closed with the provision that no knight should be excused on the grounds of a royal quittance from being placed on juries and assizes.[2]

---

[1] See above 4–5.   [2] *DBM*, no. 5, 98–9.

On 4 August 1258 the procedure was modified. Letters were sent out to the counties appointing a commission of four knights in each county to conduct the investigation.[3] They were to swear to do this loyally and truly and to take an oath to that effect at the next shire court, or, if the shire court was not due to be held soon, at a special meeting of the sheriffs and coroners. They were to inquire into 'all the excesses, trespasses, and acts of injustice' committed to anyone and by anyone whatsoever, including royal justices, sheriffs, and bailiffs. The record of this inquisition was to be delivered by the knights, in person, to the council at Westminster on 6 October. The existing sheriffs were exempt from inquiry as regards their actions during the current period of office, but not in respect of earlier terms.[4] Only one of these returns survives.[5] The articles of inquiry were very extensive. As Treharne pointed out, they covered nearly every official in local administration, with the exception of the forests, with no time limit. In his words: 'So vast a field could not possibly be covered, however zealous the commissioners, or however careful the jurors'. Nevertheless, 'the public could not complain of lack of opportunity for stating its wrongs'.[6] It seems to have been understood that the gathering of complaints would take some time. It was therefore decided that the newly appointed justiciar, Hugh Bigod, would undertake a preliminary eyre immediately, and it is generally agreed that he applied himself zealously. The justiciar began his sessions at Oxford and by the end of the year his court had moved in a wide sweep through southern and eastern England.[7] Hugh's judicial circuit was notable for the extended use of the *querela*, a procedure whereby any free person could turn up at court and make an oral complaint, bypassing traditional procedures including those involving the purchase of a writ. Needless to say, the *querela* was genuinely popular and was used by a cross section of people.[8]

It seems, however, that the material that came from the knights was disappointing. It may be that the late harvest that year deterred many likely plaintiffs so that the commissioners either presented incomplete reports or did not attend.[9] However, fifteen counties certainly did report, for writs *de expensis* were issued to

---

[3] *DBM*, no. 6, 112–15.

[4] *CPR 1247–58*, 645, contains an abstract and the list of the knights named. Matthew Paris gives the writ as addressed to the knights of Hertfordshire: Paris, *CM* vi, 396–7. For the list of the surviving texts, see *DBM*, 112. Treharne points out that although the letters were enrolled on 4 August, the letter to the Hertfordshire knights seems to have been sent out on 28 July: Treharne, *Baronial Plan of Reform*, 108n.

[5] That for the hundred of Loes in Suffolk. The text is given in Jacob, *Studies in the Baronial Period of Reform and Rebellion*, 338–44.

[6] Treharne, *Baronial Plan of Reform*, 109–10.

[7] Maddicott, *Simon de Montfort*, 165, citing Jacob, *Studies in the Period of Baronial Reform*, 39–41.

[8] For the cases before Bigod, see *Special Eyre Rolls of Hugh Bigod 1258–60*, 2 vols., ed. and introduced by Andrew Hershey, Selden Society (London, 2021), and A. Hershey (ed.), *The 1258–9 Special Eyre of Surrey and Kent*, Surrey Record Society, no. 38 (Woking, 2004).

[9] Paris, *CM* v, 710.

88 POLITICS AND SOCIETY IN MID THIRTEENTH-CENTURY ENGLAND

the fourteen sheriffs who administered them. The reformers were concerned that not enough was being done, for the letters sent to the counties in the king's name on 20 October, known as The Ordinance of the Sheriffs, opened as follows:

> Since we wish and will that speedy justice be done throughout our realm, no less to the poor than to the rich, we will and command that the wrongs which have been done in our time in your county, no matter who has done them, be reported to the four knights whom we have appointed for this purpose, if they have not already been so reported, and we will have them amended and redressed as fast as we can. But if we cannot accomplish this as fast as we would like and as need may be, both for our sake and for yours, you must not be surprised, for these things have gone amiss for so long, to our loss as well as to yours, that it can by no means be speedily put right: but, from the first corrections which will be made in the first counties into which we shall send our justiciar and other good men of ours for this purpose, you can take sure hope that we shall do the same for you as early as we can.[10]

The reformers may have been aware themselves, as Maddicott has suggested, that they had raised expectations that they could not satisfy.[11] Nonetheless, some wrongs had been addressed: the bailiffs of Brill in Buckinghamshire had been convicted, as had Hugh Manneby, sometime sheriff of Northampton, and William of Ryston, bailiff of Woodstock, who had, amongst his crimes, killed a prisoner by torture and hanged an innocent woman without trial.[12]

The knights of 1258 appear again when it came to the selection of new sheriffs for the year 1258–9. The misdemeanours of the sheriffs had figured from the very beginning of the reform programme. They were complained of in the Petition of the Barons and figured in the Provisions of Oxford.[13] The latter stipulates that:

> Sheriffs shall be appointed who are loyal man and sound landholders (*leus genz et prodes homes et terre tenanz*), so that in each county there shall be as sheriff a vavasour of that same county, who will deal well, loyally, and uprightly with the people of the county. And let him take no payment, and let him not be sheriff for more than one year at a time. And during the year let him render the accounts at the exchequer, and answer for his term. And let the king pay him out of his own revenues, according to his proffer, sufficiently to enable him to administer the

---

[10] *DMB*, no. 8, 118–21.   [11] Maddicott, *Simon de Montfort*, 165.

[12] See Treharne, *Baronial Plan of Reform*, 112–15. See also Ambler, *The Song of Simon de Montfort*, 190–6. For Hugh Bigod's judicial activities as a whole and his surviving records, see also Jacob, *Studies in the Baronial Period of Reform and Rebellion*, Ch. 2, 'Hugh Bigod in the Counties'.

[13] The Petition of the Barons complained of abuses of the sheriff's tourn: *DBM*, no. 3, clauses 17 and 18, 84–5.

county justly. And let him take no bribes neither himself nor his officials, and if they be found guilty, let them be punished.[14]

The proclamation of 20 October 1258, known to historians as The Ordnance of the Sheriffs (the sheriffs forming the greater part of its content), stipulated that each sheriff swear an oath 'that he will do justice in common to all people, according to the power which his office gives him, and that he will not waver in this for love nor for hate, nor for fear of anyone, nor for any greed, but that he will do speedy justice as well and as quickly to the poor as to the rich'. There follows an extraordinarily long list of misdemeanours which the sheriffs will swear not to commit.[15]

The barons were true to their word. Between 23 October and 3 November, the council issued letters patent appointing nineteen sheriffs to twenty-eight counties. The sheriff of Surrey and Sussex, Gerard of Evington, had already been dismissed in August following conviction before the justiciar. As Treharne pointed out, if we include his replacement and the appointment to Lancaster in February 1259, the council provided for thirty-two counties to be held by twenty-one sheriffs during the year 1258-9.[16] Nearly all, he adds, were indeed vavasours of the counties they were to administer, the other three being 'of higher standing'. Vavasours he defines as 'county knights, men of substance and local standing, with knowledge of local conditions and opinion', who seemed likely 'to make better sheriffs than powerful barons, courtly favourites, or greedy and tyrannical speculators'.[17] The usage of vavasour here was not a one-off, and seems to be taken from contemporary parlance. It occurs again in the so-called administrative and political resolutions of the Provisions of Westminster of October 1259, where the projected means of selecting sheriffs for the following year and beyond were outlined. Once again, they were to be vavasours of the counties.[18] In fact this selection never took place, and the sheriffs of 1259-60 continued until the summer of 1261 when they were summarily replaced by the resurgent king.

Before we look in detail at the knights of 1258, who are the main subject of this chapter, there are some terminological issues to be addressed. First, who were the vavasours? Treharne calls them 'the county knights who held of the great barons and other land-owning tenants in chief', although on another occasion he admits that the term is 'indefinite'.[19] The sheriffs, then, were probably intended to be knights of some significance within the counties. Treharne, however, tends to

---

[14] *DBM*, no. 6, clause 17, 108-9. Clause 18 deals with the misdemeanours of the escheators.
[15] *DBM*, no. 8, 118-23.
[16] *CPR 1247-58*, 654-5. For a discussion see Treharne, *Baronial Plan of Reform*, 119-25.
[17] Ibid., 97-8.
[18] *DBM*, no. 12, clause 22, 154-5. The annals of Burton Abbey indicate that this was in fact the case: *Ann. Mon.* i, 148.
[19] Treharne, *Baronial Plan of Reform*, 136 and 263: of the sheriffs of 1261 he writes that few of them 'could reasonably be described as vavassours, indefinite as the term may be': ibid., 263.

90   POLITICS AND SOCIETY IN MID THIRTEENTH-CENTURY ENGLAND

widen its usage so that it becomes a synonym for county knights per se, speaking of 'county vavassour families', of the 'vavassour class', and of the 'local vavassours ... men of the class which formed the characteristic element of the shire court'. We also hear of 'lesser barons and vavassours'. When speaking of the Provisions of Oxford, he stresses that 'Of all the other classes, the county knights were the class with which the baronage was in closest touch and had the greatest natural affinity', adding that 'it was very easy for the magnates to discover the views of the vavassours if they wished to do so, and it was almost impossible to neglect their opinion or to continue for long a policy hostile to their interests'. However, more especially as the reform unfolds, he invokes them in contradistinction to 'the greater barons' and 'the greater landowners', that is, with different interests: 'the class which benefited most was that of the vavasours'; 'strengthening the position of the vavasours against the great barons'; and the 'rules which had been imposed on the king and his bailiffs for regulating their relations with the tenants-in-chief were henceforth to be observed by the barons and their bailiffs towards the vavassours'.[20]

In fact, the term has a history of its own which is quite complex.[21] It is found in romance literature, in legal writings, and in administrative documents. Its meaning was affected by French and Italian usage, and maintained both a fluidity and a capacity to evolve. In romance literature it denotes a relatively modest but significant landowner and has courteous and chivalric overtones. More generally it carries a sense of mediacy, of an *arrière vassal* or a military sub-tenant. According to the treatise known as 'Bracton', which came into the hands of the judge Henry de Bratton in the mid-1230s, vavasour belongs to a hierarchy of social terms: 'But with men, in truth, there is a difference between persons, for there are some of great eminence [who] are placed above others and rule over them ... in temporal matters which pertain to the kingdom, emperors, kings and princes, and under them dukes, earls and barons, magnates or vavasours and knights, also freemen and bondsmen'. 'Bracton' then exemplifies: 'There are other powerful persons under the king who are called barons, that is "belli robur", the strength of war. Others are called vavasours, men of great dignity. A vavasour cannot be better defined than a vessel selected for strength, that is "vas sortitum ad valitudinem". Also under the king are knights, that is, persons chosen for the exercising of military duties ...'. [22] The evidence suggests that it was a term of contemporary

---

[20] Ibid., 85, 88, 89, 137, 162, 163, 170, 184, 191. Treharne's contemporaries thought in similar terms. See, for example, Powicke, *The Thirteenth Century*, 144: 'a sheriff should be a "vavassor" of the shire—that is to say, in general a local man of the knightly class, holding of some barony or baronies'.

[21] What follows is drawn from P. R. Coss, 'Literature and Social Terminology: The Vavasour in England', in T. H. Aston et al. (eds.), *Social Relations and Ideas: Essays in Honour of Rodney Hilton* (Cambridge, 1983), 109–150.

[22] *Bracton de legibus et consuetudinibus Angliae: Bracton on the Laws and Customs of England*, ed. George E. Woodbine, trans. (with revisions and notes) Samuel E. Thorne, 4 vols. (Oxford, 1968–77), ii, 32–3.

parlance, and that the sheriffs were intended to be not just knights but men of some local significance. There are factors which were adding to its fluidity. As we have seen earlier, tenure was becoming of less importance in the mid-thirteenth century. Moreover, the decline in the number of knights in society, especially during the 1220s–40s, must have increased the status of those families which remained knight-bearing. The steady rise of chivalric knighthood tended in the same direction. It seems likely that the reformers intended that the sheriffs should be drawn from among the more (possibly the most) substantial county landowners.

There is another term which historians have held to be of great significance: the *communitas bacheleriae Angliae*, 'the community of the bachelry of England'. To appreciate the context, we need to return to the fortunes of the reform movement from the autumn of 1258. As we have seen, the Ordinance of 20 October 1258 showed concern over the pace at which justice was being done and reveals an anxiety about how the reformers were being perceived in the counties. The letter was issued in Latin, French, and English, together with a letter of two days earlier in which the king ratified what the council had done so far and enjoined all faithful and loyal men to abide by the statutes (*establissements*). They were to be read publicly in the counties several times per year.[23] This began by indicating that the inquiry by the knights was not going as fast as would have been hoped. Some of the knights had not yet reported. This was followed, as we have seen, by detailed regulation of the office of the sheriff. Treharne and Sanders noted that there was no reference in this document to 'feudal officials',[24] perhaps indicating the beginning of the disagreement that was to open up in baronial ranks, although of course the Ordinance did have a particular primary purpose. And so we move to the Candlemas parliament, which opened on 9 February 1259. The Provisions of the Barons of England, probably already drafted in French when parliament opened, defined and restricted a lord's right to demand suit.[25] These and other matters in the same text were to appear in the Provisions of Westminster later in the year. Equally divisive was the Ordinance of the Magnates, which was sent to the counties on 22 February 1259, by which the Council of Fifteen and the Committee of Twelve representing the whole baronage in parliament promised that they would put themselves and their officials under the same scrutiny as the king and his bailiffs.[26] 'Taken together', says Maddicott, 'the Ordinance and the Provisions showed that the impetus of reform was by no means exhausted'.[27] It has been a mainstay of English historiography that these documents both

---

[23] *DBM*, nos. 7 and 8.   [24] *DBM*, 15.

[25] Maddicott, *Simon de Montfort*, 179. The date of this unpublished document has in fact been controversial. It would appear to emanate from debates in the council and there is evidence of legal input. For detailed treatment see Brand, *Kings, Barons and Justices*, 27–30. The document is *DBM*, no. 9.

[26] *DBM*, no. 10.   [27] Maddicott, *Simon de Montfort*, 179.

92 POLITICS AND SOCIETY IN MID THIRTEENTH-CENTURY ENGLAND

reflected and exacerbated a rift between radical and conservative reformers, and there seems little need to question this. It may explain the interval between the issue of the Ordinance and its sanctioning by the king on 28 March. In the end Montfort and Gloucester appear to have sealed it on behalf of the council, 'a tacit recognition', says Maddicott, of their joint leadership of the enterprise.[28] The amending of the original French text to cater for magnate interests suggests a difference of opinion at the parliament.[29] According to Matthew Paris it was Gloucester's reluctance to moved forwards with reform that caused Simon de Montfort to turn on him, saying: 'I do not want to live or have dealings with men so fickle and deceitful. For we have promised and sworn together to do what we are discussing'. Montfort then left England in disgust.[30] Maddicott adds that Montfort's conduct may not have been 'wholly disinterested', given that there was social pressure for these reforms. Impatience over the implementation of reform surfaced at the time of the Westminster parliament of autumn 1259. It was now that the exasperated *communitas bacheleriae Angliae* erupted and complained to Lord Edward and Gloucester that the barons had as yet done nothing for the common good.[31] The bachelors, supported by the prince, seem to have forced the publication of the wide-ranging reforms of the Provisions of Westminster. In accordance with these, a new eyre was set up and new sheriffs were appointed for 1259–60 in accordance with the agreed procedure. The Provisions of Westminster 'marked the zenith of the reforming movement', says Maddicott, while Treharne and Sanders wrote that the Council of Fifteen was now 'at the apex of its power.'[32]

Who were these bachelors? Maddicott's claim that they were 'probably the knights for whose attendance at parliament this is the only evidence' is highly contentious.[33] The consensus hitherto has been that the bachelors were members of magnate retinues.[34] They were similar therefore to the men, whom Treharne calls vavasours, who had very probably had an input into the Petition of the Barons at the beginning of the reform process. The term is open to extension in the same way as vavasour. Helen Cam neatly summarized this line of interpretation in writing of 'the country gentry, the "Bachelry of England"—the vavasours of the shire.'[35] However, as Treharne himself indicated, we need to keep a sense of perspective. He toys with the idea that the bachelors may have been formally reinforced by knights who were present at Westminster for various reasons at the

---

[28] Ibid., 180 and n. 86.

[29] See P. A. Brand, 'The Drafting of Legislation in Mid-Thirteenth Century England', *Parliamentary History*, 9 (1990), 243–85, 260–2.

[30] Paris, *CM* v, 744–5. 'Gloucester was compelled by other magnates to send his steward around his estates to offer redress according to the new reforms': Maddicott, *Simon de Montfort*, 180.

[31] *Ann. Mon.* (Annals of Burton), i, 471–84.   [32] *DBM*, 15.

[33] Maddicott, *Simon de Montfort*, 185.

[34] For an extended discussion, see Treharne, *Baronial Plan of Reform*, 160–4.

[35] H. M. Cam, 'Pedigrees of Villeins and Freemen in the Thirteenth Century', in her *Liberties and Communities in Medieval England* (Cambridge, 1944), 128; repr. from *Genealogists Magazine* (September 1933).

REFORM AND THE KNIGHTS OF 1258   93

time of the October parliament but in the end rejects it: 'A standing organization, or one embracing the entire class of bachelors, seems highly improbable.'[36] One scholar takes the view that the 'question of who the Bachelors were is an insoluble one,'[37] and it may be that it has been given too much credence. The term community of the bachelry of England occurs in only one chronicle, albeit a well-informed one.[38] The impression that pressure from below forced the barons to draw up reforms is false in that the Provisions of Westminster were the product of much debate and work by barons and professionals, from the autumn of 1258 onwards.[39] What appears to have happened is that the same opposition that had surfaced in the spring reappeared now, with conservative nobles voicing antagonism towards enactments which ran contrary to their own narrow interests. In Treharne's words: 'At this stage the *communitas bachelerie*, learning of the danger to reforms designed mainly in the interests of the class to which the "bachelors" belonged, intervened by a remonstrance addressed to the whole Council; Edward supported them, and the reformers in the Council, thus reinforced, were able to gain the day without any open breach with the more conservative element'. 'According to this view', he adds, 'the intervention of the *communitas bacheleriae Angliae* ... was not the reason for the drafting of the Provisions of Westminster, though it assisted in securing their publication.'[40] The use of community in this context clearly echoes the idea of the 'community of the realm'. It may well be that behind the bachelors lay a deliberate move on the part of the reforming wing among the barons to push the conservatives to drop their opposition, a tactic which as we will see was to be used in 1261.

We are now in a position to face the key issue of the role that the counties played in the impetus for reform. For Treharne and his contemporaries, the initiative lay firmly with the baronial opposition to Henry III. In the later twentieth century, however, a shift in emphasis occurred, one particularly associated with John Maddicott. In his interpretation he subtly reverses the concentration up to this point on the faction of the higher nobility who turned on the king. He tells us that the movement for reform 'marked the coalescence of the general and local resentments of clergy, gentry and baronage with the particular and private grievances of some members of the higher nobility',[41] which pointedly reverses the inspiration for reform. It is based partly upon the belief that 'Henry's government came to be increasingly resented by the middling men of the counties: minor barons, knights and major freeholders', which is perhaps hardly to be doubted, and partly on his view of the counties which suggests the presence of a community, and community of interests, stretching from barons to freeholders.[42] This is more

---

[36] Treharne, *Baronial Plan of Reform*, 162.
[37] Michael Prestwich, *Edward I* (London, 1988), 30.
[38] The Burton annalist: *Ann. Mon.* i, 471.   [39] See below 233–7.
[40] Treharne, *Baronial Plan of Reform*, 161.   [41] Maddicott, *Simon de Montfort*, 106.
[42] For Maddicott's view of the counties and county courts, see above 3–5.

94 POLITICS AND SOCIETY IN MID THIRTEENTH-CENTURY ENGLAND

clearly stated when he writes: 'What had begun there as a coup by a small group of disaffected magnates was now transformed into a much broader social movement [sic], directed at the reform of local as well as central government and even at the ways of the magnates themselves'.[43] But were barons and freeholders really partners in a broad social movement? It may be objected that just as there is no substantive evidence of the county court acting as a forum of political debate and discussion,[44] neither is there evidence of revolutionary fervour, as opposed to mere discontent, in the counties in 1258.

How, then, do we explain the attention given by the opposition barons to the reform of local administration? The answer must be that once they had decided not merely to exile their opponents but to take over the reins of government they needed a programme, and a programme based on justice could hardly deny that it should apply to all. However, rhetoric was not enough. They were also quite deliberately seeking wider support in entrenching 'reform'. Moreover, they could hardly be deaf to the interests of those who comprised their retinues. This reaching down reflected the enormity of what they were doing. The magnates, the earls and barons, were appropriating the public authority of the king and aiming to exercise it more effectively and judiciously. Clive Knowles went to the heart of the matter when he wrote that 'concern for these reforms was neither the essential feature of baronial plans nor the exclusive prerogative of the magnates. It was merely another aspect of their assumption of royal responsibilities'.[45]

Another interpretation has surfaced recently. An over-emphasis upon the broadest concerns of the Petition of the Barons has given rise arguably to a rival view of baronial intention. According to Sophie Ambler, 'The barons, then, were seeking to protect lesser folk—from the gentry [sic] to the poorest—from the iniquities of royal justice'. 'But what is remarkable', she adds, 'is how they were determined to protect lesser folk even against baronial interests'.[46] The view that the barons were motivated in quite this way may be questioned, but it does have the virtue of putting the initiative back where it belongs: in the hands of the magnates.

Who Were the Knights of 1258?

How did the barons set about drawing on the counties? The answer is by adopting traditional procedures and exploiting the status of knights as the Angevin system had always done.[47] Knights had long been drawn upon to staff commissions of

[43] Maddicott, *Simon de Montfort*, 156.   [44] See above 23.

[45] Knowles, *Simon de Montfort 1265–1965*, 26.

[46] Ambler, *The Song of Simon de Montfort*, 185. And, again: 'The reformers of 1258...in the Petition of the Barons were setting out their intent to hold themselves to the new standard (ibid., 190).

[47] See above 21.

various kinds and to occupy local offices such as coroner and sub-escheator, as well as for jury service at the grand assize and other judicial tasks. There is every reason to think that the response in 1258 was a traditional one, too, even though men would have been aware that this was an unusual situation. The first question to ask is how they were chosen. It is better to say chosen rather than elected in order to avoid any assumption that there was anything resembling local hustings, let alone rival candidates. Sheriffs had often found it difficult to find the knights to carry out tasks and there are sometimes indications that they chose them themselves. The reformers must have been aware of this possibility since the writ ordering knights to be chosen was addressed not to the sheriff but to the knights of the county, arriving no doubt at the court itself. We cannot be sure that men were always chosen—volunteered, nominated, or pushed forwards—at the county court, but in most cases they may well have been. However, we must be open to the various possibilities. When two of the Devon knights reported sick, the sheriff was ordered to make substitution himself. It may well be indicative that no knight was to be allowed to excuse himself on the grounds of royal quittance. Who, then, were the knights who were called upon to provide the raw material for the chief justiciar's eyre? What were the criteria that governed the choice?

In many cases it is not difficult to show that men who were active in the grand assize were often chosen. In Shropshire, for example, two of the knights—Thomas Costentin and Gilbert de Bucknall—had functioned in that capacity at the 1256 eyre, as had the father of a third knight, Thomas de Roshale.[48] In Northamptonshire all four knights had functioned on the grand assize: Eustace de Watford, Thomas fitz Robert, and Geoffrey de Mara in 1247, 1253, and 1262; John de Weedon in 1253 and 1262.[49] In Bedfordshire Robert de Walton was at the 1247 eyre, Simon de Pattishall and William de Sudbury at the 1262 eyre.[50] In Warwickshire two knights—Adam de Napton and William de Waver—were to so function in the same way at the 1262 eyre.[51] And so on.

Some knights had held offices in the counties. Godfrey de Scudamore had been sheriff of Somerset and Dorset in 1249, while Anketil de Martivas was the current sheriff of Rutland. In Shropshire Gilbert de Bucknall had also been a coroner, as had Thomas de Costentin. In fact, the latter had been fined at the 1256

---

[48] *The Roll of the Shropshire Eyre of 1256*, ed. Alan Harding, Selden Society (London, 1981), nos. 13, 16, 30, 48, 114, 332.

[49] Mario Fernandes, 'The Role of the Midland Knights in the Period of Reform and Rebellion' (University of London PhD thesis, September 2000), Sect. 1.5, 'The Northamptonshire Commissioners of 1258', 81–90.

[50] Katherine S. Naughton, *The Gentry of Bedfordshire in the Thirteenth and Fourteenth Centuries* (Leicester, 1976), 79.

[51] Mario Fernandes, 'The Midland Knights and the Barons' War: The Warwickshire Evidence', in Adrian Jobson (ed.), *Baronial Reform and Revolution in England 1258–1267* (Woodbridge, 2016), 167–82, at 182.

96 POLITICS AND SOCIETY IN MID THIRTEENTH-CENTURY ENGLAND

eyre for sending his clerk to view a body rather than going himself.[52] Simon de Hedon had been coroner in Nottinghamshire and Derbyshire. In Oxfordshire Peter Foliot had been sub-escheator since 1253.[53] In Warwickshire both Adam de Napton and Robert de Waver had been sub-escheators in 1254.[54] In Surrey John de Wauton was actually escheator at the time of Hugh Bigod's special eyre of 1258–9 and was confirmed in office.[55] It seems likely that in some cases at least, knights were chosen who were particularly prominent at the county court, recalling 'Bracton's' *buzones*, those upon whose 'nod' the others depended.[56] Sometimes we can see clearly that the men chosen were senior knights of the county. In some cases, seniority in age and length of service may have been significant. This appears to be the case in Worcestershire, where the knights chosen were Simon de Ribbesford, William Corbet, Inard de Elmbridge, and Richard de Ombersley.[57] Seniority, then, was a factor. If this was one determinant of prestige, however, there were certainly others, including wealth, aristocratic associations, and perhaps antiquity. In Worcestershire the Corbets were a cadet line of the Corbet barons of Caus, the Elmbridge family held of the Stutevilles, and that of Ribbesford was associated with the Mortimers.[58] Elsewhere, too, the knights can be shown to be solidly based. However, this was not always the case. Given that the 'feudal records' do not necessarily give a full picture of county landowning, we have to be careful. Nonetheless, in some cases the knights of 1258 appear to be rather unprepossessing. There are other occasions where we find one or perhaps two knights of significance with others who appear less deeply rooted.

It is extremely difficult for us to penetrate 'county politics', if indeed that is not too grandiose a term, but there are occasions where we seem to perceive the existence of a group. For example, in Surrey we find connections between David

---

[52] *Roll of the Shropshire Eyre of 1256*, ed. Harding, 993.

[53] H. W. Ridgeway, 'Mid Thirteenth-Century Reformers and the Localities: The Sheriffs of the Baronial Regime', in P. Fleming et al. (eds.), *Regionalism and Revision: The Crown and its Provinces in England 1250–1650* (Cambridge, 1998), 59–86, at 68–9.

[54] Coss, *Origins of the English Gentry*, 67.

[55] Some knights had been involved in surveying castles and in raising tallage. Fulk Peyforer had been justice of gaol delivery in Kent: Ridgeway, 'Mid Thirteenth-Century Reformers', 68–9.

[56] G. T. Lapsley, 'Buzones', *EHR*, 47 (1932), 178–93, 546–67; Coss, *Origins of the English Gentry*, 58.

[57] William Corbett was in possession at Chaddesley Corbett in 1235 when he made an agreement with the abbot of Tewkesbury, and was still holding in 1261–2: *VCH Worcestershire* iii, 38, 62. Inard de Elmbridge held in 1242–3: *VCH Worcestershire* iii, 61; *Book of Fees*, 844, 847, 965. Richard de Ombersley descended from Richard son of Maurice de Ombersley, who held of the abbot of Evesham in 1166. At Grafton Flyford he was sued in 1231 by the abbot of Westminster for customs owed: *VCH Worcestershire* iii, 465, and iv, 86, 89. Finally, the eponymous Ribbesford family had held there in unbroken succession since the mid-twelfth century: *VCH Worcestershire* iv, 306–7.

[58] The Ribbesford family had had a long association with the Mortimers. A Simon de Ribbesford had been Roger Mortimer's steward and had held the manor in 1176. Simon succeeded Henry de Ribbesford who had held in 1235–6 and 1242–3. Simon came to an agreement with Roger Mortimer by which he gave up the right to hunt in the wood called 'le Oke' and to pursue deer in Wyre Forest without special leave from Roger, 'save if his hounds chase deer from his own woods into Wyre Forest and follow'. Whether this was considered a trespass would be determined by friends, presumably of both parties: ibid., iv, 306–7; John R. Burton, *History of Bewdley* (London, 1883), 65.

REFORM AND THE KNIGHTS OF 1258   97

Jarpenvill, the man chosen as sheriff, and two of the other knights, John Hansard and John d'Abernon. David Jarpenvill was a tenant of John d'Abernon, while his wife Joan was the widow of Ingram IV d'Abernon. John Hansard was also a tenant of John d'Abernon and Hansards were witnesses to d'Abernon family arrangements.[59] We are left to wonder whether such groups pushed themselves forwards in 1258, or whether they were already exercising an element of control?

The knights appear to have been chosen in accordance with norms either at the county court or by the sheriff, or both. However, it is necessary to ask whether there was any baronial influence in the choice of knights? There is in fact one very clear example. In Shropshire the four men chosen were: Thomas de Roshale, Thomas Costentin, Gilbert de Bucknall, and Hugh de Weston. However, on the patent roll all but the first name are scored through. Against Costentin the name of Walter de Hopton is written 'in his place (*loco eius*)', with Richard Tyrel and Robert de Lacy written against the other two. A note of explanation is added: 'because the other three were not suitable as Peter de Montfort has indicated'.[60] In what sense were they unsuitable? Peter, in addition to being one of the seven confederate barons of April 1258, was also sheriff of Shropshire. Let us look at these original four in the customary way. Thomas de Roshale was clearly a descendant, probably grandson, of the Thomas de Roshale who held one and a half fees of the FitzAlan barony in 1242/3.[61] Thomas and his son Vivian appear together in charters during 1246–53 and in 1250–5. They are found as witnesses for Haughmond Abbey.[62] The heads of the family were all successive witnesses to Shrewsbury Abbey.[63] In 1255 an estate at Alceton in Acton Scott was held by Vivian from his father, Thomas. A later Thomas de Roshale, and no doubt the one under discussion here, held a mesne tenancy at Middleton in 1284/5 and was returned as one of its two lords in 1316. Their chief holding, however, was Rossall, where a John de Roshale was holding in 1346.[64] The 1256 Shropshire eyre has Vivian de Roshale as one of the knights of the grand assize.[65] It looks as though he had been succeeded by Thomas de Roshale by 1258. He made a gift to Haughmond Abbey.[66] Thomas, then, was a solid county knight with a pedigree and a concentrated interest at Rossall. He was not objected to. His profile, however, was little different from at least two of those who were.

Thomas de Costentin was one of the grand assize knights at the 1256 eyre.[67] In 1242/3 either he or a forebear had held a knight's fee, again of the FitzAlan

---

[59] *VCH Surrey* iii, 73–4, and iv, 267; *CIPM* ii, 141.
[60] TNA, C66/72 m. 3: *quia alii tres non fuerunt idonei sicut P. de Monteforti mandavit.* The last word is perhaps ambiguous. Treharne opts for 'sent word', although 'commanded' might be closer to the situation.
[61] *Book of Fees*, 962, 970   [62] For the Roshales see Eyton, *Shropshire*, X, 88–91.
[63] *The Cartulary of Shrewsbury Abbey*, ed. Una Rees, 2 vols. (Aberystwyth, 1975). See index, 486.
[64] *Feudal Aids* iv, 218, 231, 235.
[65] *Roll of the Shropshire Eyre of 1256*, ed. Harding, nos. 13, 16, 30, 43, 114, 332.
[66] Eyton, *Shropshire*, X, 104.   [67] Ibid., nos. 13, 16, 30, 48, 114, 189, 484, 679.

barony, at Eaton and Oldbury, together with a third of a fee of Roger Mortimer at Buswarton.[68] As we have already seen, he was associated with the administration of the county in that he had previously been a coroner. Thomas made a grant to Haughmond Abbey and witnessed a grant with Vivian de Roshale and Walter de Hopton. He also witnessed for Shrewsbury Abbey.[69] Gilbert de Bucknall was a mirror image. In 1242/3 he had held a fee at Bucknell and Purslow.[70] He was a knight of the grand assize in 1256 and had also been a coroner.[71] Hugh de Weston was the one exception in that he fails to figure at the 1256 eyre either as a knight or in any other capacity. Neither he nor anyone with this surname appears in the feudal records for Shropshire. However, he did hold a knight's fee at Weston and Newton of the barony of John FitzAlan in Staffordshire.[72] The tenurial prominence of the FitzAlan barony here is worthy of note.

Why were these men not suitable? They would seem to have been archetypal county knights. They were solidly based, three of them being knights of the grand assize in the county (the fourth belonging to Staffordshire). Could they have been objected to on the grounds that they were 'tainted' with the offices of escheator and coroner? Were they unsympathetic to the role they were being asked to perform? If this had been the case it would hardly be consistent with a county 'seething' and bent on reform! Let us look at the three who replaced them: William de Hopton, Richard Tyrel, and Robert de Lacy.

William de Hopton is rather elusive. There is a William son of John Hopton at the eyre, although he is not a knight, of the assize or otherwise.[73] There is a William who held at Stanton (on Arrow) one estate of the Lacy honour of Weobley of old enfeoffment and another of the honour of Wigmore.[74] In 1284/5 a William occurs as a mesne lord at Scheinton.[75] Is one or the other, or indeed both, of these our man? It would seem more probable that he was related to the Walter de Hopton who was holding two fees at Hopton of the barony of Clun in 1242–3, or even to the Nicholas de Hopton who was holding a fee of the Lacys.[76]

Robert de Lacy was lord of Coolmere. Between 1246 and 1253 he gave a vivary to Haughmond Abbey, a grant witnessed by the Roshales. This was confirmed by

---

[68] *Book of Fees*, 962–3, 971–2. The former was referred to as a half fee at Oldbury and a half fee at Eaton Constantine in 1346: *Feudal Aids* iv, 237, 242.

[69] Eyton, *Shropshire*, X, 298, 379; *Cartulary of Shrewsbury Abbey*, ed. Rees, 96.

[70] *Book of Fees*, 963.   [71] *Roll of the Shropshire Eyre*, ed. Harding, nos. 13, 16, 30, 48, 484, 506.

[72] *Book of Fees*, 969, 972.   [73] *Roll of the Shropshire Eyre*, ed. Harding, nos. 57, 985.

[74] *Book of Fees*, 803, 814.   [75] *Feudal Aids* iv, 215.

[76] In 1284/5 a Walter de Hopton held in right of his wife at Wem. In 1316 a Walter de Hopton held Fittes or Fitz while Buswalton was in the king's hands through the death of Walter. In 1346 another Walter held at Hopton, Schelderton, and Corston: *Feudal Aids* iv, 222, 231, 232, 238. In 1256 a Walter de Hopton was associated with Thomas Costantin. Together they recovered seisin of six virgates at Sutton from the dean and chapter of Shrewsbury, while in 1272 Walter de Hopton figures as a royal justice in Shropshire: *Cartulary of Shrewsbury Abbey*, ed. Rees, 372–3. There are many references to Walter de Hopton in Eyton.

REFORM AND THE KNIGHTS OF 1258   99

Henry III in 1253, suggesting that the grant was closer to the latter year.[77] In 1255 he was said to hold eleven hides at Coolmere as a one-third fee of Bertram de Burgh.[78] There are some additional interesting facts. The manor, it was said, owed suit to the county and hundred and paid 16*d.* for the services of *stretward* and *motfee.* The jurors reported that for the whole of the year Robert de Lacy had withdrawn the said suits. Eyton adds: 'He does not seem to have done so wilfully but by compulsion of bailiffs of Sir John de Grey of Ellesmere who were injuring him with repeated distraints—I suppose to compel him to do suit to Ellesmere manor'. However, on 31 July the king addressed Philip Lovel and Nicholas de Haudlou that 'his beloved Robert de Lacy had complained of the royal bailiff of Ellesmere for exacting from the said Robert other customs and services than his ancestors had been used to perform for their manor of Coolmere'. The justices were ordered to inquire 'that the king may cause justice to be done to de Lacy'. A jury of forty-two persons found in his favour. He had also complained that the king's bailiffs had seized his boat and nets in the mere of Coolmere, a complaint that 'seems to have been recognised as well-founded'.[79] Apart from the insight into his economy (and/or consumption), the whole evidence opens insights into the struggle for suit. Was he perhaps considered to be too inclined towards the king? Eyton tells us, however, that during the civil wars of 1264–5 his loyalty 'did not pass unquestioned'. He clearly held Coolmere in right of his wife and later consigned it to Peter de Montfort.[80] Surprisingly, Robert de Lacy does not figure as a knight of the grand assize in the 1256 eyre.[81] He may be related to the baronial family of Lacy, but this is not clear.

Richard Tyrel appears as yet another coroner in 1256, and he too was fined for a transgression in office. He was also fined for a disseisin of a water mill at Cold Weston. No damages were awarded, interestingly, as he was found to have carried out improvements at the mill.[82] He may have been enterprising, but he was not a knight of the assize. However, he witnessed for Shrewsbury Abbey during 1230–44 when (together with Thomas Costentin) he was specifically designated a knight.[83] We do find a Tyrel in the feudal records, but in Herefordshire. In 1242/3 Roger Tyrel held a fee at Little Marcle of the honour of Weobley of old enfeoff-ment, a half fee of Walter de Lacy at Wormeton, and mesne tenancies of the

---

[77] For Robert de Lacy see Eyton, *Shropshire,* X, 195–6.   [78] *Hundred Rolls,* II, 75.

[79] Eyton, *Shropshire,* X, 195.

[80] Who sold it to Hamo le Strange. At Easter 1271 Amice, widow of Robert de Lacy, receded from the writ de ingress which she had brought against Hamo le Strange with regard to the manor of Coolmere, excepting a messuage and a half virgate. One wonders as to the circumstances in which he parted with it.

[81] However, he and his wife Amice do appear as parties: *Shropshire Eyre,* ed. Harding, nos. 126, 205, 238.

[82] Ibid., nos. 484, 993. He was also fined with eight other men for refusing to undertake a perambu-lation: ibid., no. 43.

[83] *Cartulary of Shrewsbury Abbey,* ed. Rees, 96.

100 POLITICS AND SOCIETY IN MID THIRTEENTH-CENTURY ENGLAND

honour of Weobley at Matham and Evesbatch.[84] In March 1253 both a Roger son of Richard and a Richard Tyrel were given respite from being put on assizes and commissions, and this appears to locate our knight.[85]

All in all, the three replacements do not appear as impressive as the three original Shropshire knights. Why were they a more attractive prospect? It cannot have been because two of the others had held suspect positions, given that Tyrel had also been coroner. The answer must lie in their associations. The original four show heavy association with the FitzAlan barony. John FitzAlan seems to have been something of a waverer, but eventually he sided with the king, becoming a keeper of the peace (*custos pacis*). This is probably part of the answer, but for a full explanation we need to look to Peter de Montfort himself. In 1257 he had been appointed as sheriff of Shropshire, and he was to continue in that office for the next year. Clearly the original knights had not in this case been chosen by their sheriff. Now, however, they were.

This leads us to the question as to whether any of the knights were actually agents of the confederates of 1258. It is possible that one or two of them may have been, although the evidence is not clear. Anketil de Martivas of Leicestershire is an interesting case. He had been reluctant to take up knighthood during the early 1250s and had acquired respites. He had also gained exemption from being placed on juries, assizes, and recognitions, and from being made sheriff.[86] And yet he suddenly appears on the scene. He was in fact the son of a former sheriff (William de Martinwas) and was, as David Crouch says, 'a man of no small income'.[87] He is found in the service of Simon de Montfort. However, the chronology of this service is unclear, and this may not yet have been the case in 1258. He was certainly Simon's steward in 1261.[88] He was also a Montfort tenant, holding the manor of Noseley.[89] He may therefore be an example of magnate interference when it came to the choices made. On the other hand, we cannot discount the possibility that membership of the panel was the origin of his support for his overlord. It is also possible that the Peter le Porter was Simon de Montfort's nominee on the Leicestershire panel.[90] There does not appear to be any evidence of Simon's influence elsewhere in the Montfortian heartlands.

---

[84] *Book of Fees*, 807–8, 811. In 1208/9 a Richard Tirel held a fee of the bishop of Worcester at Crowle, Worcestershire. The Tyrel family had been much involved in the Lacy enterprise in Ireland: Colin Veach, *Lordship in Four Realms: The Lacy Family 1166–1241* (Manchester, 2014), 30, 36, 84, 94, 193.

[85] *CPR 1247–58*, 181.   [86] Maddicott, *Simon de Montfort*, 73; *CPR 1247–58*, 631.

[87] David Crouch, *The Image of Aristocracy in Britain 1000–1300* (London and New York, 1992), 147.

[88] Maddicott, *Simon de Montfort*, 68–9.

[89] See G. F. Farnham and A. H. Thompson, 'The Manor of Noseley', *Leicestershire Archaeological Society*, 12 (1921–2). For the family see also Crouch, *Image of Aristocracy*, 233, 269.

[90] Fernandes, 'Midland Knights', 182. Peter was a member of the affinity of Roger de Quincy, earl of Winchester, until April 1264: Simpson, 'The *Familia* of Roger de Quincy', 115.

REFORM AND THE KNIGHTS OF 1258   101

An obvious place to look for such agency is in East Anglia, given the prominent role taken by the Bigods in 1258. However, neither the panel for Norfolk nor yet the one for Suffolk reveals any obvious connection with Roger Bigod's 'affinity'.[91] It is true that the Norfolk knights Fulk de Kerdiston and William de Stalham did witness a charter for the earl of Norfolk, although the relevant charter is of uncertain date, being between May 1257 and July 1270.[92] In neither county were the chosen knights Bigod tenants. The *Book of Fees* suggests that most of the Norfolk men were in fact minor figures.[93] The one exception was Hamo Hautein, who became the sheriff of Norfolk and Suffolk. Hamo was a Lincolnshire knight of some significance, holding a fee of Gilbert de Gant in Scredington and another half fee there of the earl of Lincoln. He held another property of Gant which included a one fifth at Shillingthorpe, and another half fee of Petronilla de Vaux in Scredington.[94] The evidence for direct involvement of the Bigods in the Norfolk panel seems rather slight. However, that is not the whole story. Sir Fulk de Kerdiston was himself a member of the Committee of Twenty-Four named in the Provisions of Oxford, indicating that he was an active reformer and that a relationship with the Bigods at this stage does seem likely.[95] The Suffolk knights were Robert de Caylly, William son of Reyner, William de Hecham, and Robert de Valognes. The *Book of Fees* is not very forthcoming in pinpointing these men. We find an Adam de Caylly holding a fee of Earl Warenne, but there is no reference to a Hecham in this county.[96] A William son of Reginald appears as a relatively humble character holding by serjeanty with a small demesne and eleven tenants in Plumstead.[97] Robert de Valognes, by contrast, seems to have been holding half of the small barony of Ashfield.[98] It looks as though Suffolk, like Norfolk, may have been represented by one major knight and three other men

Another obvious place to look for agency is Gloucestershire. The four chosen knights—Nicholas Burdun, Adam de Aston, John le Brun, and Henry Muscel—seem relatively unprepossessing. The most prestigious was undoubtedly John le Brun.[99]

---

[91] See Morris, *The Bigod Earls*, Ch. 3.   [92] Ibid., 218.

[93] William de Stalham is returned with one tenth of a knight's fee in Stalham and elsewhere, while Hugh Bird held a half fee in Mendham: *Book of Fees*, 910. The name Kerdiston does not figure there at all.

[94] *Book of Fees*, 1003, 1027, 1003, 1051, 1058–9, 1089.

[95] *DBM*, 104–7. Incidentally, as John Maddicott has pointed out, another member of the twenty-four according to alternative versions was Sir John Oare (Eure or Aller), former sheriff of Somerset and Dorset, a solid member of county society: Maddicott, *Origins of the English Parliament 924–1327*, 245; *VCH Somerset* iii, 63; *Book of Fees*, 844, 847, 882; *Somerset Feet of Fines 1196–1307*, ed. E. Green, Somerset Record Society no. 6 (1892), nos. 104, 117, 190.

[96] *Book of Fees*, 905.   [97] Ibid., 1167.

[98] Sanders, *English Baronies*, 4; *Book of Fees*, 578–9.

[99] John's father, Richard le Brun, married one of the four daughters of Walter II de Cormeilles, who held the barony whose caput was Tarrington in Herefordshire: ibid., 86–7. In 1235/6 John was returned as holding two fees of the honour at Elkestone, and in 1242/3 property in Tarrington, Bullinghope, and Clehonger in Herefordshire. Two fees were also held of him. He died in 1266: *Book*

102   POLITICS AND SOCIETY IN MID THIRTEENTH-CENTURY ENGLAND

Surprisingly, these men had no known connection with the earl of Gloucester.[100] Unusually none of the four men served as sheriff, which may say something of their status. Either none of them was willing to take it on or they were deemed of insufficient weight to do so. We should not exaggerate their relative obscurity, however, for they do appear as knights of the grand assize.[101] The man appointed sheriff was Robert de Meysy. However, this appointment has a curious aftermath. Robert went before the justiciar, treasurer, and the barons of the exchequer exhibiting his charter giving him exemption from being made sheriff against his will. He was ordered to reappear on 2 December after the king and council had been consulted. Meanwhile he was advised to consult the king himself. He must have failed in this for he duly served.[102] Is this perhaps where the earl of Gloucester exerted influence? Robert's family were major and long-standing tenants of the earl of Gloucester, as indicated, in 1212, 1242–3, and 1284–5. Robert held in particular a half fee of the earl at Hampton Meysy.[103] It does seem highly likely that the earl leant on him to become sheriff. Huw Ridgeway adds some information on additional earl of Gloucester links: William Everard (knight of Somerset and appointed sheriff of Somerset and Dorset) is likely to have been the earl's man in 1258 as he was in his service by early 1260; Hamo Hautein (knight of Norfolk and appointed sheriff of Norfolk and Suffolk) and Simon de Pattishall (knight of Bedfordshire and appointed sheriff of Bedfordshire and Buckinghamshire) were both prominent Clare tenants and may also have had links with Richard since we know that later on in the Barons' War they were bachelors in the household of his son, Gilbert de Clare. There is a suggestion that John le Brun had some connection with the earl of Gloucester in 1259. Moreover, Godfrey de Escudamore (knight and appointed sheriff of Wiltshire) was the brother-in-law of the important local magnate John Giffard. This is a feature replicated elsewhere. William de Courtenay was a kinsman, perhaps brother, of John de Courtenay, one of the largest landowners in Devon.

---

of Fees, 440, 809, 815, 819, 1480; *VCH Gloucestershire* vii, 30. Of the others Nicholas Burden also held property in Herefordshire, including a knight's fee of John fitz Alan in 1242/3: *Book of Fees*, 730. Later evidence shows a John Burdon holding a half fee once of Hugh Burdon at Oldbury, Gloucestershire, in 1303. He was also one of five lords at Rodmarton in 1316, and held the vill of Didmarton jointly with John Turpin: *Feudal Aids* ii, 249, 272. No mid-thirteenth-century evidence has yet appeared for Henry Mustel. However, in 1284/5 Hugh Mustel held a half fee at 'Brokemoncote' of William le Poer and he of the abbey of Deerhurst, and in 1303 he held a half fee in Boddington and the manor of Haydon of the abbey of Westminster: *Feudal Aids* ii, 236, 255. Finally, Adam de Aston seems to have belonged to the family who held Eston Somervill, where John de Eston was holding a fee of Ralf Musard: *Feudal Aids* ii, 238.

[100]   Except in that he was the ultimate overlord of Boddington.

[101]   At the 1248 eyre Henry Mustel served on six grand assizes (and on two attaint panels), Roger de Eston on eight, John le Brun on three, John de Eston of Kilcote on three, John de Aston of Somerville on one, and Nicholas Burdon on one: John D. Mullan, 'Landed Society and Locality in Gloucestershire, c.1240–80' (Cardiff University PhD thesis, 1999), 42.

[102]   Treharne, *Baronial Plan of Reform*, 124.

[103]   *Book of Fees*, 75, 706–7, 819; *Feudal Aids* ii, 241.

REFORM AND THE KNIGHTS OF 1258   103

le Butler, 'elected' as sheriff of Lancashire in February 1259 and one of the wealthiest barons of the region, was connected with the earl of Derby.[104]

There is one further county where baronial influence may yet be seen. This is the strategically important county of Kent. The four knights were Simon de Criol, Fulk Peyforer, John de Sandwich, and Geoffrey de Scoland. Two of these can pass with little comment here. Simon de Criol represented one of two main lines of the Criols in 1242/3.[105] John de Sandwich seems to have been the successor to Henry de Sandwich, who was a major tenant of the abbey of St Augustine, Canterbury, and closely associated with it.[106] The two men of direct interest here are Fulk Peyforer and Geoffrey de Scoland. In 1242–3 Fulk held a half fee in Barming of the honour of Clare. He also held the manor of West Peckham of the king in sergeanty, by the service of looking after a goshawk for the king between Michaelmas and the Purification.[107] Whereas Fulk held of the Clares, Geoffrey de Scoland held of Simon de Montfort at Chelsfield in 1242/3, while other properties held of him in the same year were listed under the fees of Simon de Montfort.[108] This must surely be of considerable significance.

This seems to be the sum total of men who may have been baronial nominees. The numbers are relatively small but not necessarily insignificant. There are cases where the knights are predominantly holding of the same honour. In Derbyshire we find: William de Montgomery, Richard de Vernon, Richard de Roffa, and William, son of Herbert. Richard de Roffa does not figure in 1242/3, but the other three were all tenants of the earl of Derby as of the honour of Tutbury.[109] It would be tempting to connect the knights with pressure from the earl, if it were not for

[104] See Ridgeway, 'Mid Thirteenth-Century Reformers', 69–70 and the references given there.
[105] *Book of Fees*, 650, 656, 660. The other line was represented by Bertram de Criol.
[106] In 1242/3 Henry de Sandwich held one fee in Dane Court and another fee in Westgate of the abbot of St Augustine, together with a quarter fee of him in Austen. He also held one fee of the abbot by reason of the wardship of Stephen fitz Hugh in the hundred of Ringeslowe and another fee in Westgate (in Thanet) by reason of the wardship of Robert fitz Robert, in both cases of the said abbot. Henry, then, must have had a close relationship with the abbey: *Book of Fees*, 654. Henry also held one fee at Ham of Robert St John as the heir of Ralf fitz Bernard, a fee at Ripple of Bartholomew de Badlesmere, and a further quarter fee at Wadling Court of Richard, the king's son: ibid., 656–7. In 1284/5 we find Ralph de Sandwich holding one and a quarter fees in the hundred of Ringeslo and one fee of the Badlesmeres in the hundred of 'Quernilowe'. John de Sandwich was holding an eighth and a half fee at 'Cornyle': *Feudal Aids* iii, 53–4. In the same year John de Sandwich and Bertram de Criol were returned as holding the hundred of Folkestone from the king, comprising fifteen and a half fees: ibid., 3.
[107] And another half fee in Lullingstone and 'Jugo' of Hamo de Crevequer, plus a quarter fee of one Arabella: *Book of Fees*, 662–3, 681.
[108] Geoffrey de Scoland is first referenced in 1232/3 when, with Simon de Cokefeud and John de Dyva, he was holding five fees of the honour of Raleigh in Chelsfield, Cliffe, and Strood. He was also one of three men holding five fees in Strood of the honour of Peveril. In 1242/3, in addition to the fee in Chelsfield of Simon de Montfort, he held one and three quarters and one fifth fee of Simon at Horton Kirby: *Book of Fees*, 668–9, 1464.
[109] William de Montgomery held two fees of him at Eckington, a quarter fee at Morton, and three fees plus one third and one tenth fee at Marston Montgomery. He was clearly a substantial figure. Richard de Vernon held one fee of him at Haddon plus a quarter fee of him at Appleby in Leicestershire and one and a quarter fees at Harlaston in Staffordshire. He, too, was clearly of some significance.

104 POLITICS AND SOCIETY IN MID THIRTEENTH-CENTURY ENGLAND

the fact that he was a minor in 1258, Earl William III having died in 1254.[110] The wardship was handed over to Lord Edward who sold it in 1257 to the queen and Peter of Savoy.[111] The county court was separated from that of Nottinghamshire only in 1256.[112] It is difficult to know quite what to make of this. It may, however, indicate that the county court was dominated by the honour of Tutbury, or that these knights had a strong inter-relationship based upon it. Similarly, all four of the Staffordshire knights were tenants of Robert III de Stafford (d. 1261).[113] They are named as Robert de Halcton,[114] Adam de Brymton,[115] William Bagod,[116] and Payn de Wasteneys.[117] Robert de Stafford (d. 1261) appears to have played no part, however, in the reform movement, although his tenants would seem to have dominated the county court, at least in 1258. However, this evidence is not help-ful, to say the least, in affirming reformist fervour.

It looks as though there may have been some magnate interference to get knights chosen who were sympathetic to, or associated with, their cause. However, the evidence does not suggest that this was generally the case. More often the knights appear to be chosen in accordance with local preferences or with per-sonal and collective prestige at the county court. What does seem clear is that there were substantial differences between them. The Hertfordshire knights may be taken as an example. At the top end is Alexander de Andeville, who belonged to a family that stemmed from one Humphrey de Andeville, who was present in

William son of Herbert held three parts of a fee of the earl at *Ash'* plus, in 1235/6, a half fee in Prestwold in Leicestershire of Hugh d'Aubigny: *Book of Fees*, 517, 994.

[110] *GEC* iv, 197.   [111] *CPR 1247–58*, 54, 554.

[112] D. Crook, 'The Establishment of the Derbyshire County Court, 1256', *Journal of the Derbyshire Archaeological and Natural History Society*, 103 (1983), 98–106.

[113] The Stafford family of the Conquest ended in 1193–4 when Robert III died *sine prole*. His sister married Harvey Bagot whose son and heir, Harvey II, took the name Stafford. He was succeeded by Harvey III and he by his brother Robert IV, who died in 1261, leaving Nicholas who came of age in 1276: Sanders, *English Baronies*, 81.

[114] Robert de Haughton is recorded at Haughton, Alstone, Weston Jones in Norbury, Knightley, and Horseley: *VCH Staffordshire* iv, 116, 119, 138, 159. In 1284/5 a Robert de Haughton held one fee at Haughton and another at Horseley of the barony of Stafford. This barony was clearly the key to the family's history. The *Book of Fees* tells us that in 1242–3 Robert de Haughton held three fees in Haughton and Offley of the barony of Stafford and again two fees and two parts of the barony of Robert de Stafford in Haughton, Offley, Weston, and Mere: *Book of Fees*, 967, 974.

[115] The Brintons held an estate at Church Eaton, amounting to three hides, of the Stafford barony. Adam de Brinton had succeeded by 1236 and in 1243 held a fee in Eaton and Orslow, and another in Eaton in 1255. Adam died before 20 June 1275 seised of the manor of Eaton of the barony of Stafford by the service of one knight's fee and two appearances at the court baron of Stafford: *VCH Staffordshire* iv, 93; *Book of Fees*, 967, 974; *CIPM* ii, no. 126, and *Staffordshire Record Society*, 3rd ser., volume for 1911, 162–3.

[116] For William Bagot see below 123–4.

[117] The Wasteneys family were lords of Tixall and Colton in 1316, held by different branches. In 1284–5 Colton was held by John de Wasteneys as one fee of the barony of Stafford, while Walter de Wasteneys had held one fee at Tixall, Hunzard, and Brancote of the same. In 1242–3 William de Wasteneys had held one fee in Colton and Pain de Wasteneys one fee in Tixall, of the barony of Stafford. William also held two fees with Ralf de Mutton in four named places, while Pain held two parts of a fee in Tixall. The two branches clearly existed for a long time: *Feudal Aids* v, 3, 12; *Book of Fees*, 966, 974. The association with the Stafford barony is again clear.

REFORM AND THE KNIGHTS OF 1258   105

the Domesday Book, holding the manors of Knebworth and Everden.[118] Around 1235 Richard de Andeville held Eversden when it was said to consist of five and a half hides, and six knight's fees in Knebworth, Clopton, and Wimple.[119] Robert de Ros or Roos seems to belong to the family who held the manor Rooshall in Sarratt, succeeding Roger son of Alured there. He appears to be the head of a single manor family, although by the nature of our sources we can never be sure.[120] The third knight, Henry de Horwelle as Matthew Paris calls him, or Henry de Holewelle in the patent rolls, is not revealed by the 'feudal records'. However, he was certainly a Hertfordshire knight on a grand assize panel in 1242–3.[121] Thus far we have one major knight and two rather standard knights. The fourth knight, Geoffrey Childwick, seems to have been a different kettle of fish. He held the manor of Childwick. The account in the *Victoria County History* suggests that he held it in the first instance during its seizure by the crown for some reason. He was, however, 'a person of some note at St Albans, who held the office of bailiff there for some time'.[122] He was probably the Geoffrey de Childwick who is described in the middle of the century as an enemy of St Albans. He maltreated the abbot's servants and was excommunicated. However, this charge was withdrawn through the intercession of the king. He seems, therefore, to have had some influence at court. He also hunted on the abbot's lands. Combatting him was reckoned to have cost the monks 2,000 marks. The abbot won a case against him in 1240, but trouble began again in 1248. In this year he was granted free warren there by the king. For the manor itself he paid two quarters of wheat to the convent. Geoffrey, however, was more significant than he seems at first sight and was well connected. He was a household knight and marshal of the king. He was married, moreover, to Clarice, sister of John Mansel.[123] The chances of the abbot gaining a fair hearing were therefore minimal, as the abbot's cellarer and legal expert was well aware.[124]

We should be wary of placing men in arbitrary categories, but clearly the knights of 1258 cover a wide spectrum. There are many substantial men, like

---

[118] *VCH Hertfordshire*, iii, 14; *VCH Cambridgeshire*, v, 60.

[119] *Book of Fees*, 921, 924, 930; *VCH Cambridgeshire*, v, 60. In 1279 it was held by Sir Robert Hoo, whose wife was probably the daughter of Alexander de Andeville: *Placita de Quo Warranto*, 103; *CIPM* ii, 208. The *Book of Fees* tells us that Richard de Andeville had held fees of six knights in Knebworth, Clopton, and Wimple in Cambridgeshire. In 1242/3 he held a fee in Eversden, where it is also said that he held a half fee in Eversden and a half fee in Clopton. In 1279 Wimple was held of the heirs of Alexander de Andevill: *Hundred Rolls* ii, 566.

[120] *VCH Hertfordshire* ii, 439; *Feudal Aids* ii, 426.

[121] *CRR xvii* 1242–3, no. 713. Matthew Paris records the Hertfordshire panel: *CM* vi (*Additamenta*), 396.

[122] For what follows see *VCH Hertfordshire* ii, 397.

[123] Carpenter, *Henry III: 1207–1258*, 538, 541.

[124] Matthew Paris has him exclaim that 'there are certain people in the land like kings against whom it is scarcely or not at all possible to have justice': Paris, GA, I, 340; Carpenter, *Henry III: 1207–1258*, 538.

106   POLITICS AND SOCIETY IN MID THIRTEENTH-CENTURY ENGLAND

Alexander de Andeville in Hertfordshire and Roger Chandos in Herefordshire.[125] There were some who held minor baronies, like the Dorset knights, William Kaynnes and Alured of Lincoln.[126] Some, like the Foliots, had many branches and tentacles across several counties. They are represented in our 1258 panels by Peter Foliot in Oxfordshire and Sampson Foliot in Berkshire.[127] Others had more than one branch in the same county, like the Criols in Kent and the Husseys in Wiltshire, where two cousins, 'Henry Husee' and 'William Hosee', are represented on the Wiltshire panel in 1258.[128] The Wasteneys of Staffordshire also had several branches.[129] Some were descended from royal servants. Some had sheriffs among their recent ancestors, like James son of Baldwin de Paunton of Rutland.[130]

At the lower end we have to be careful too, given that our records are sometimes inadequate. Sometimes a knight does not appear in the county in question—although he must actually have had an interest there—but appears in other counties, such as John de Linguire of the Herefordshire panel whose interests are logged in Oxfordshire.[131] Of the relatively few who do not appear in these records we cannot assume that they were poorly endowed, let alone that they were not knights. The *milituli*, as we noted earlier in this work, had been substantially culled by this stage of the century. At the same time, however, the enterprising, upwardly striving knight Geoffrey of Childwick was not alone, certainly among ecclesiastical tenants. Such men added a dynamic dimension to contemporary knighthood. Another one was Richard de Harlow in Essex. His family's tenure seems to go back to the Conquest when one Geoffrey held a half hide at Harlow of Eustace of Boulogne together with further land there of the manor of Bury St Edmunds.[132] His descendants acquired further property up to the time of Richard, who sought to increase his family's lands still further but was compelled by Abbot Henry of Rushbrook (1235–48) to surrender all claims except to the property that had been held by his father at his death. It looks as though the relatively insecure Richard was trying to increase his standing at the abbey's expense. He seems to have been an enterprising character. He erected a windmill near Church St, Harlow, which was surrendered to the abbot in 1279. It was worth 20s. in 1287.[133] Others were also ecclesiastical tenants but more securely. A good example is William le Moyne, an ecclesiastical tenant of Ramsey Abbey in Huntingdonshire.[134] In Berkshire the Rivers family held Beedon similarly of Abingdon Abbey,[135] and in Kent the Sandwich family held of St Augustine's.

The general relationship of the knights with the ecclesiastical world was naturally a mixed one. Some were minor donors to religious houses. Many families

---

[125] Sanders, *English Baronies*, 79.   [126] Ibid., 99, 146.
[127] *VCH Oxfordshire* v, 9; *VCH Berkshire* iv, 525–6.
[128] For the Husseys see *VCH Wiltshire* vii, 201, and viii, 15, 18.   [129] *Book of Fees*, 46, 49, 50.
[130] *VCH Rutland* ii, 183. The Pauntons appear to have been a classic one manor, one fee family.
[131] *Book of Fees*, 823, 841.   [132] *VCH Essex* viii, 139.
[133] Ibid., 141.   [134] For what follows see *VCH Huntingdonshire* ii, 199, 325, and iii, 51, 204–6.
[135] *VCH Berkshire* iv, 40.

REFORM AND THE KNIGHTS OF 1258   107

held advowsons of local churches, and this was to bring some of them into conflict and litigation with monasteries.[136] Some were genuinely pious and looked after their futures in the afterlife. Indeed, they were encouraged to do so. By contrast, the St Albans chronicles tells us about the behaviour of Ralph Chenduit, who died on 18 November 1243. He had quarrelled with the abbot of St Albans, who excommunicated him. One day, in front of many people at Westminster he jeered: 'Look at the monks of St Albans, just look at them! Why, they have excommunicated me for so long, and so often and so well, that here I am, hale and hearty, and so fat that my saddle will hardly hold me when I ride!' Very soon afterwards, he had a seizure and died, prematurely. According to the chronicler, however, he had repented of his sins and was received back into the church through the special intervention of no less a saint than St Alban himself.[137]

Some of the chosen knights, then, were men seeking to improve their status in the world, and this seems to be true of certain types of ecclesiastical tenants who were relatively poorly endowed. It was also the case with men representing cadet lines of knightly families. A good example is William Bagot or Bagod of the Staffordshire panel.[138] Before 1166 Ulpher granted half of his demesne at Coppenhull in Penkridge to William Bagot. This was the property later known as 'The Hyde'.[139] William Bagot III had succeeded by 1248–9. Meanwhile the Bagot main line had succeeded the Staffords and taken their name. William was described as lord of Coppenhull in 1255, in which year he bought out his undertenancy at Patshull. In 1284–5 he held the manor of 'La Hide' as one fee of the barony of Stafford, a fee at Abbots Bromley of Geoffrey de Gresley, and the manor of Patshull of Nicholas, baron of Stafford. The 1258 panel seems to have opened opportunities for William Bagot, and he made a career as a sheriff.[140]

William Bagot's fortunes may be contrasted with those of Ralph Harengod, whose career was famously dealt with by Eleanor Searle.[141] He, too, belonged to a

---

[136] Adam de Brinton of Staffordshire was heir to a longstanding dispute with Polesworth Abbey over the advowson of Orslow. The dispute went back to the twelfth century and reappeared in the early thirteenth. In 1261 the resulting composition was reaffirmed in the king's court. In 1311 a member of the family was rector: *VCH Staffordshire* iv, 98. In 1254 James de Paunton of Rutland sued the prior of La Lande for the advowson of Glaston, unsuccessfully it seems: *VCH Rutland* ii, 183.

[137] P. D. A. Harvey, *A Medieval Village: Cuxham 1240–1400* (Oxford, 1965), 4–5; Paris, *CM* iv, 262, and i, 319–20.

[138] For William Bagot see Coss, *Lordship, Knighthood and Locality*, 289–90; Ridgeway, 'Mid Thirteenth-Century Reformers', 66 n. 34; and G. Wrottesley, 'A History of the Bagot Family', *William Salt Archaeological Society*, new series, i (1908), 128–37.

[139] It is possible that this may be the same William who was the younger son of Hervey Bagot and received half of Billington from him.

[140] See G. Templeman, 'The Sheriffs of Warwickshire in the Thirteenth Century', *Dugdale Society Occasional Papers*, 7 (Oxford, 1948) 29–30, 37–8, 44.

[141] Eleanor Searle, *Lordship and Community: Battle Abbey and its Banlieu 1066–1538* (Toronto, 1974), 163–5. Ridgeway appears to be incorrect on Ralph's wealth: 'Mid Thirteenth-Century Reformers', 66.

108 POLITICS AND SOCIETY IN MID THIRTEENTH-CENTURY ENGLAND

cadet line.[142] Ralph's father had married Sybilla de Iklesham, benefactress to Battle Abbey. His Sussex inheritance was much diminished, however, by the sales of his pious mother, and by the endowment of his brother, John, as a monk of Battle. Like so many East Sussex lords he found much of his land occupied by free, secure peasants who were thus relatively unexploitable. He tried to impose villeinage upon them. He was employed as leader of a gang to terrorize the tenants of the prior of Hastings, who were equally defending their free status against their lord. Ralph found himself being fined £100. The peasants took the case to court and won. The prior and Ralph were gaoled. Ralph became heavily indebted to the Jews. He died fighting for Simon de Montfort at Evesham.

Indebtedness was shared by a few other 1258 knights. Roger Damory of Buckinghamshire, who held Bucknall in 1243, later mortgaged the manor to Oseney abbey. He managed to pay off his debts in 1271, however, and his manor and documents were returned to him. Stephen Chenduit of Oxfordshire was also indebted,[143] as were Robert de Grendon of Warwickshire and Simon de Lisle of Cambridgeshire.[144] This is unlikely to have been a significant factor in 1258, however. It is also worth asking if any of the knights had suffered personally under Henry III's regime, or had particular grievances? One who may well have done was Philip de Lisle of Cambridgeshire, who lost property to Peter de Chauvent, the courtier, in settlement of debt. As we have seen in Shropshire, Robert de Lacy had endured the effects of rival courts and from the activities of royal bailiffs. Similarly, Inard de Elmbridge in Worcestershire had no perquisites of court, because his tenants did suit to Wychbold from which Elmbridge was held. On the other hand, many of the knights profited from the exercise of 'franchises'. At Glaston in Rutland, for example, the Pauntons held view of frankpledge 'by long prescription.'[145] The d'Abernons in Surrey also held view of frankpledge at Stoke and Fletcham. They were later recorded as having a pillory at Leatherhead, which very probably went back to the thirteenth century. The *quo warranto* proceedings tell us that at Stapleford Tawney the Tanys claimed assize of bread and ale and view of frankpledge but could produce no charter to substantiate this. None of this should surprise us. As we have seen, frankpledge, the assize of bread and ale, and the withdrawal of suit from hundred courts were widespread among landed families. It would be surprising if these knights did not include men who were, once again, using the opportunities offered to improve their lot.

Can we be sure that the knights of 1258 treated their 'appointment' with equal seriousness? Some of them may have carried out their charge in a perfunctory

---

[142] In the rape of Pevensey in 1302–3, a John Heryngaud held of the manor of Chalynton in West Dene, Walderne, Friston, and Sutton three and half fees. In 1316 he was returned as one of six tenants at Hoathley: *Feudal Aids* v, 131, 137.

[143] Polden, 'A Crisis of the Knightly Class?', 29–57, at 48 n. 93; Harvey, *Cuxham*, 5–6.

[144] Coss, *Lordship, Knighthood and Locality*, 289; *VCH Cambridgeshire* ix, 131, 359.

[145] Although they did not claim 'pillory, tumbril or other *judicialia*'.

manner. Some of the commissioners either came in October with incomplete reports or failed to turn up, although at least fifteen panels did actually attend. According to Treharne, 'the returns did not approach the completeness and the details of the articles of inquiry ... and the number of complaints is far smaller than reasonable expectation would allow, nor is there as high a proportion of serious charges as the terms of the enquiry seem to warrant.'[146] Hugh Bigod, it has been remarked, was keen to get moving with his eyre. The speed here may not simply reflect the determination of the justiciar, however. It would seem to indicate that the impetus behind the movement for 'reform' lay squarely, at this point at least, with the baronial confederates and their close supporters.

What, then, can we say about the 1258 knights as a whole? They seem to be a cross-section of contemporary knighthood. At the same time as remaining a vital component of the Angevin system, these men had all the characteristics of a lesser nobility. We can see aspects of their aristocratic lifestyle in our sources, for example their interest in hunting and falconry. The thinning of knightly ranks in the second quarter of the century left the survivors in a more elevated position. The advent of chivalric knighthood and the rise of heraldry raised their status even more.[147] Within the counties their position was a socially significant one, and there are signs that they were beginning to see themselves as collective elites. At this point it is necessary to ask what we mean when we envisage the community of the shire?[148] Historians often write of the knights speaking for the community of knights and freeholders. Their position is surely analogous to that of the barons and the community of the realm. We are now used to understanding that the barons saw their own interests as primary. There is every reason to suppose that this was equally true of knights. With the evolution of the House of Commons in mind, some historians have romanticized the idea of the county community and, arguably, failed to contemplate sufficiently the more mundane and less ideologically charged reality.

Sheriffs and the Royalist Revanche

What was the relationship between the knights appointed in the summer and the sheriffs appointed in October 1258? And does this add anything to our understanding of the motives for involvement? In addition to the nineteen knights

---

[146] Treharne, *Baronial Plan of Reform*, 116.

[147] Although the full effects of this were not to be seen until the end of the century and the early decades of the fourteenth. See Peter Coss, 'Knighthood, Heraldry and Social Exclusion in Edwardian England', in P. Coss and M. Keen (eds.), *Heraldry, Pageantry and Social Display in Medieval England* (Woodbridge, 2002), 39–68.

[148] The medieval county community is a matter of some contention. See below, Chapter 10. For the community of the realm see above, Chapter 1.

110 POLITICS AND SOCIETY IN MID THIRTEENTH-CENTURY ENGLAND

appointed in the autumn, David Jarpenvill had become sheriff of Surrey and Sussex in August 1258.[149] What is striking is that seventeen of the twenty were chosen from the members of the knightly panels from August who were, of course, reporting at parliament. In each case, then, we are talking of one out of the four, or in the case of double shrievalties, one out of eight. This method of appointment was presumably practical because these men were present at Westminster. Anketil de Martival, who was appointed to Warwickshire and Leicestershire, was already sheriff of Rutland in 1257 and was kept in office there. Robert de Meysy in Gloucestershire and Hubert de Montchesney in Essex and Hertfordshire had not been on the panels.[150] On what basis were men chosen? Huw Ridgeway, who has made a study of the sheriffs of 1258–61, explains some of the anomalies.[151] In as many as nine of the existing shrievalties the current sheriff was retained. There was the issue of shrievalties held in fee. The king's brother had held Cornwall since 1225 and Rutland since 1227. Lord Edward had held Chester since 1254, while the Viponts held Westmorland. Not surprisingly, the baronial government did not want to offend high-ranking men. William Beauchamp of Salwarpe, hereditary sheriff of Worcestershire, attended parliament in 1258 in the entourage of the earl of Gloucester.[152] There were also issues of security with regard to the Scottish and Welsh borders. In Cumberland the earl of Aumale, with his castle at Cockermouth, had been sheriff since 1255 and remained so until his death in early 1260. He accounted through an undersheriff—his retainer, Remy de Pocklington. In Yorkshire William Latimer, a man with court connections, had been sheriff since 1254 and remained so until early 1260. There was a tradition of appointing local magnates in the north.[153] In the Welsh marches the threat from Llewelyn had an effect upon who was appointed. Gilbert Talbot, a retainer of Lord Edward and custodian of border castles, was appointed to Herefordshire, though in practice the previous sheriff continued in office.[154] In Shropshire Peter de Montfort had been appointed in 1257 and also continued in office. Other anomalies included Hampshire, where eventually the previous incumbent, James le Sauvage, took over again, and Essex and Hertfordshire, where the elevated incumbent Hubert de Montchesney and 'certainly not a local knight' also continued in office. Huw Ridgeway suggests that it was the presence of Lusignan interests in these counties that determined these particular actions.[155] If in general the

---

[149] *CPR 1247–58*, 649. His predecessor, Gerard of Evingdon, had been convicted before the justiciar. A new sheriff of Lancashire was appointed in February 1259 (*CPR 1247–58*, 122).

[150] Worcestershire does not figure because it was held in fee by William de Beauchamp who accounted in person.

[151] Ridgeway, 'Mid Thirteenth-Century Reformers', 59–86.   [152] *CR 1256–9*, 316.

[153] They were, however, replaced by 'much lesser figures' of Robert de Mulcaster in Cumberland and John de Octon in Yorkshire.

[154] This was Henry de Pembridge who, after six months, was replaced by Richard de Bagingden.

[155] Ridgeway, 'Mid Thirteenth-Century Reformers', 67.

REFORM AND THE KNIGHTS OF 1258   111

reformers were wishing to placate local interests, they were certainly willing to set these aside where other concerns were present.

Outside of these anomalies, however, the reformers were true to their word in choosing vavasours.[156] Moreover, they tended to choose from among the most wealthy and powerful of the knights before them: men like Simon de Pattishall and Hamo Hautein.[157] Furthermore, William Everard, Hamo Hautein, and Simon de Pattishall all had some association with the earl of Gloucester. Everything suggests that the sheriffs were not the choice of the four knights but were chosen by the barons at the exchequer.[158] It seems, moreover, that men were not necessarily queueing up to take on the role of sheriff under the new dispensation, that is to say as custodian rather than farmer and hemmed in by restrictions. On 14 November 1258 the new sheriffs were summoned to the exchequer to take the oath prescribed and to receive custody of their counties. As we have seen, Robert de Meysy of Gloucestershire seems to have been initially unaware of his appointment and was chosen against his will.[159]

The involvement of local knights in the appointment of sheriffs was not a one-off in 1258. The Provisions of Westminster of the autumn of 1259 arranged for the justiciar, the treasurer, the judges Henry of Bath and Roger Thirkelby, and the barons of the exchequer to choose the sheriffs for 1259–60, in each case appointing a vavasour. Accordingly, between 19 November 1259 and 14 January 1260 the exchequer summoned four knights from each county, 'to elect the new sheriff', says Treharne.[160] In fact, the record does not say that. One of the four (for the most part) may have been chosen at the exchequer but probably not by the knights themselves. Treharne is probably right to underline that these, too, were vavasours, but he is almost certainly wrong in suggesting that the panels of knights were those of 1258. In fact, only six of the new sheriffs had been members of the panels in 1258.[161] The evidence which Treharne adduces to the contrary is,

---

[156] Interestingly, Treharne suggested that 'Hubert de Montchesney, Gilbert Talbot and William de Courtenay seem to have been the only sheriffs who may have had a standing higher than vavasours': *Baronial Plan of Reform*, 122 n. 4.

[157] Ridgeway picks out the following as the richer sheriffs: Richard de Bagingden of Hereford, William le Botyler of Lancashire, William de Courtenay of Devon, Godfrey de Escudamore of Wiltshire, Hamo Hautein of Norfolk-Suffolk, David de Jarpenvill of Surrey and Sussex, Robert de Meysy of Gloucestershire, Simon de Patteshull of Bedfordshire and Buckinghamshire, Fulk Peyforer of Kent, Eustace de Watford of Northamptonshire, and John du Plessis of Northumberland: 'Mid Thirteenth-Century Reformers', 68–9.

[158] Ridgeway believes neither that the sheriffs were elected by the four knights nor that the knights themselves were elected in the county court: ibid., 67–8. Perhaps, he suggests, local wishes tended to be taken into account. The argument for his first proposition is much stronger than for the second. I believe that on balance the evidence suggests four knights generally emanated from the county court.

[159] Treharne, *Baronial Plan of Reform*, 124.   [160] Ibid., 350.

[161] Richard de Tany in Essex, John le Brun in Gloucestershire, Geoffrey de Cheetham in Lancashire, Simon de Askleton in Nottinghamshire and Derbyshire, Walter de Rivers in Oxfordshire and Berkshire, and John de Wauton in Surrey and Sussex. Four others elected in 1258 were now moved to neighbouring counties.

112   POLITICS AND SOCIETY IN MID THIRTEENTH-CENTURY ENGLAND

in fact, flawed. Shortly before 5 February it was noted that 'le Butler, Geoffrey Cheetham, William Furness and Alan of Windle, on oath, elected the aforesaid William Butler as sheriff of Lancashire to keep that county in the form provided by the king's council, and the county was committed to the same William after he took the oath, before the barons, of keeping it faithfully as long as it shall please the king'.[162] Another note around the same time says that although Ralph Harengod, sheriff of Hampshire, had been 'chosen' sheriff in the autumn of 1258, he had subsequently fallen ill so that the barons of the exchequer had instructed the sheriff to summon John Launcelence, John de Botley, Thomas de Guisnes, 'and one other of the more discreet knights of the county' to come to the exchequer on 3 February 1259 'to do the king's will'. The three knights came with William of Pakenham and, on oath, the four chose John de St Valery as sheriff.[163] In fact, these panels were deemed appropriate in the above cases precisely because the vacancies were within the year 1258–9, the year for which they were 'responsible'. They are not evidence for 1259–60. Treharne was at pains to show that the four knights were normally elected in the county court and that the four normally chose the new sheriff in the presence of the barons of the exchequer. It looks as though the practice was probably variable, with the barons having a watchful oversight and, if necessary, having the last say. The sheriffs, as Treharne pointed out, are not recorded on the patent rolls except for John of Cobham to Kent (8 December) and Hervey Stanhoe to Norfolk and Suffolk (9 January). The memoranda roll for 1259–60 does contain, however, some incomplete lists, while the names of the new sheriffs can be resurrected, largely from the pipe rolls.[164] All twenty-one sheriffs appointed in 1258 were changed and new men appointed. The decision that no man be appointed for consecutive years was observed, but four were moved to neighbouring counties, suggesting that they were deemed satisfactory. Treharne was probably right to add that the rule that the sheriffs must have land in the county probably stopped them doing more of this.

The Provisions of Westminster go on to spell out how the sheriffs were to be elected for 1260–1. The procedure is clear enough: 'at the last county court before Michaelmas, let four sound and loyal men (*prodes homes e leaus*), who will be useful to the king and the country in that office, be chosen (*esluz*) in full county court, and let them present themselves to the exchequer at Michaelmas; and the *barons* [my italics] will elect those who in their opinion are the most

---

[162] Treharne, *Baronial Plan of Reform*, 205–06, citing Memoranda Rolls of the Lord Treasurer's Remembrancer (TNA, E 368) no. 34, m. 6.

[163] This choice seems to have been ignored in practice and the old sheriff, James le Sauvage, continued: ibid., m. 5.

[164] Treharne, *Baronial Plan of Reform*, 208.

suitable (*plus suffisanz*).[165] This is the fully worked out position at which the reformers arrived; but, because the political situation changed, it was never carried out.

It is noticeable that at every turn Treharne tended to elevate the position of the four knights. In his view, there was:

> already in existence, before 1258, a very important and substantial body of middle-class [sic] landowners practised in co-operating with the chancery, the exchequer, the various kinds of justices, and the sheriffs in matters of all kinds affecting local administration. What the reformers did was to use this skill and experience to assist them in carrying out the various portions of the plan of reform in so far as the plan required co-operation from the communities [sic] of the shire and hundred.[166]

At this point, however, he makes an unwarranted leap:

> The work of the council, as it developed, seemed to be tending to erect the commission of four knights into a permanent supervising, controlling and reporting element in the local administration and in the connection between the localities and the central institutions ... But the most important development of all concerning the four knights of the shire was outlined in another of the clauses of the Provisions of Westminster where it was arranged that in every county four knights should be appointed to act as guardians of the public interest against possible usurpations, exactions, and oppression committed by the sheriffs. These four knights were to be a standing, if not a permanent, commission [another leap] for their duty was to enrol all complaints in which the sheriff refused redress, and to report them at least once a year to the justiciar.[167]

This was never carried out. However, says Treharne:

> Taking this use of the commission of four knights in each shire along with their employment in the selection of sheriffs, we can see that it is no exaggeration to say that the baronial reformers had added a new piece of machinery to the Angevin administrative system, a permanent addition designed to work both in the local administration proper, and in the connection between local and central institutions. In this respect it is at least interesting to note that, in

---

[165] *DBM* no. 12, cl. 22, 154–5.
[166] Treharne, *Baronial Plan of Reform*, 349.   [167] Ibid., 349–50.

114 POLITICS AND SOCIETY IN MID THIRTEENTH-CENTURY ENGLAND

the only cases where we have the names of the commissioners who elected the sheriffs in 1259, they were the same men who conducted the enquiry into grievances in 1258.[168]

This evidence is misleading. It is certainly true that the reformers were happy to make use of panels of knights, but the idea of a standing committee is an unwarranted interpellation, not least because the personnel of the panels was open to frequent change. The most that can be said is that the reformers saw panels as cogs in the machine, and that perhaps they regarded these men as minor members of their regime.

Treharne was led astray again when it comes to the reaction to the king's reassertion of power. Two issues are especially important in this respect: the eyre and the sheriffs. On 24 November 1260 the sheriffs of certain counties were instructed to prepare for the justices coming on 14 January 1261. This was to be an ordinary general eyre, owing nothing to 'the baronial plan of reform'. The eyre was divided into two circuits.[169] The justices visiting Hertford on 2 May 1261 were met by representatives of the barons who informed them that the session could not go ahead on grounds that less than the necessary forty days' notice had been given and that seven years had not elapsed.[170] The justices suspended the eyre to consult the king who stopped it on those grounds and moved them on to Northampton. The session here was unopposed. On the other circuit the justices at Worcester on 1 July found that the seven year 'rule' resulted in no one being willing to plead, or even appear. Moreover, insufficient summons had been given. The *Liber de Antiquis Legibus* says in the autumn that 'up to the present they [the barons] have not allowed the justices who were sent on eyre throughout the realm to do their office'.[171] The reference to the barons here speaks reams, although Treharne is silent on the point! Although, as he says, this cannot mean a complete stoppage in every county (see, for example, Northampton), at Buckingham the objection of insufficient summons was raised in January 1262 and in 1263 the Norfolk session was revoked because insufficient time had elapsed. The real objection in 1261 seems to have been that it was not the promised continuation of the special eyre of 1260. Treharne ends his discussion with: 'Whether the resistance was a purely spontaneous local matter, or the result of an organised and deliberate plan on the part of the reformers, using every opportunity presented by formal irregularities for blocking the eyre, we do not know'.[172] Henry had to give way in the counties

---

[168] Ibid., 350.   [169] Treharne, *Baronial Plan of Reform*, 247.

[170] Ibid., 259, quoting *Flores Historiarum* ii, 468.

[171] *De Antiquis Legibus*, 49. For a translation see 'Chronicles of the Mayors and Sheriffs of London', in H. Rothwell (ed.), *English Historical Documents 1189–1327*, 164.

[172] Although the chronicle cited and its derivatives suggest organized baronial resistance: Treharne, *Baronial Plan of Reform*, 260, n. 2.

REFORM AND THE KNIGHTS OF 1258   115

where law and custom were raised against him. However, he could not be forced to withdraw the eyre itself nor to reinstate the special eyre of the previous year. That there was some dismay at this turn of events is certain. However, the explanation for what transpired seems clear enough. There was no spontaneous opposition in the counties; rather, people followed the baronial lead.

When the eyres took place, in fact, the knights fulfilled their traditional duties, whatever their stance would be when matters subsequently came to armed conflict. In the Northamptonshire eyre roll of 1261, some seventy knights are named as jurors and arbitrators. Seventeen of them were later to be captured as armed Montfortians at the siege of Northampton.[173] Their opposition to Henry clearly did not preclude their participation as normal in the eyre. In Bedfordshire sixteen knights figured in the grand assize at the eyre of 1262.[174] Three of them—Hugh Gubion, Simon de Pattishall, and Robert Crevequer—were later Montfortians. They played their part along with the others. The 1262 Warwickshire eyre has twenty-nine grand assize knights. Mario Fernandes classifies twelve of them as 'contrariants' and five as royalists.[175] Clearly, their future adherence to one side or the other had no bearing on their participation at the eyre.

The second issue which led Treharne astray in discussing Henry's reassertion of power was, once again, that of the sheriffs. By a letter patent of 8–9 July 1261, all twenty-two sheriffs were replaced by men nominated by the king.[176] They were also to have custody of twenty-one royal castles. Nearly all of the earls and many great barons were against the king; 'nor had he reckoned with the strength of the baronial party of reform in the support which it could draw from the country gentlemen [sic]'.[177] According to the *Flores Historiarum*, 'the people were roused throughout England by the institution of new sheriffs by the king, the former sheriffs, to whom the counties had been committed by the barons and by the community of the realm, being removed by him'.[178] An attempt at arbitration was made without result and both parties prepared for war. The fundamental question was who was in control, Henry or his barons. The king exhorted the men of Kent to disregard all seditious and false rumours and on 16 August he issued a general manifesto against baronial agitation,[179] and asserted that his new sheriffs, being powerful magnates, were able to keep the peace and do justice. According

---

[173] TNA, Just 1/455.

[174] K. S. Naughton, *The Gentry of Bedfordshire in the Thirteenth and Fourteenth Centuries*, Department of English Local History, University of Leicester, Occasional Paper no. 2 (Leicester, 1976), 79.

[175] M. Fernandes, 'The Midland Knights and the Barons' War: The Warwickshire Evidence', in Jobson (ed.), *Baronial Reform and Revolution in England*, 167–82.

[176] As Ridgeway says, 'Where rebel sheriffs [had] prevailed, not one of the 1258–61 sheriffs was reappointed': 'Mid Thirteenth-Century Reformers', 78.

[177] Treharne, *Baronial Plan of Reform*, 263–4.

[178] Ibid., 263, quoting *Flores Historiarum* ii, 473.   [179] *Foedera*, 408–9.

116   POLITICS AND SOCIETY IN MID THIRTEENTH-CENTURY ENGLAND

to Treharne, resistance was developing both among individual nobles and 'in the newly-awakened communities of the shire'.[180] Matters then came to a head when the earls of Leicester and Gloucester and the bishop of Worcester summoned three knights from each county to St Albans on 21 September 'to treat with them on the common needs of the realm'.[181] According to Treharne, 'This defiant appeal for the support of the country gentlemen [sic] ... was the most daring and revolutionary step hitherto taken. It shows clearly how the reformers were tending increasingly to the policy of arousing the political sense of the knightly class in the hopes of offsetting the defection of many of the less liberally-minded [sic] of the baronage'.[182] As he says, this was 'a perfectly natural step to take', and it fits squarely with the reaching out that had manifestly occurred in 1258. However, Treharne's impression of a high degree of spontaneous opposition in the counties is highly questionable. Astutely Henry instructed the sheriffs to send the knights to Windsor instead. As Treharne himself suggests, they most probably stayed at home. He was surely close to the truth when he wrote: 'The co-ordination of this move by the baronial leaders is apparent, but spontaneous local feeling was an indispensable ally for the reformers, and whenever it did not emerge, the barons could make no effective defiance of the royal sheriff'.[183] In fact, by the end of October several of the baronial sheriffs were unable to function. In Gloucester William de Tracy was seized in the shire court and mistreated by his royalist rival Matthew Bezil.[184] In other words, if the counties were as incensed as Treharne says, their anger soon abated.[185]

In an addendum to his book,[186] Treharne adds that 'when the king dismissed the council's sheriffs in July 1261 "the angry men of the shires," as Sir Maurice Powicke has called them, soon showed that they would not submit',[187] quoting *King Henry III and the Lord Edward*.[188] However, no such phrase is found there. Powicke says, merely: 'In the meantime the supporters of the Provisions in the shires had begun under the guidance of the baronial leaders to displace the royal sheriffs by their own "wardens of the shires"'.[189] Warden is arguably a better and more accurate term than baronial sheriff.

---

[180] Treharne, *Baronial Plan of Reform*, 265.   [181] Ibid., 266.

[182] Ibid.   [183] Ibid., 267.   [184] For further details see below 163–4.

[185] Ridgeway, although he does refer to the opposition to Henry as an 'uproar', is not convinced by Treharne's interpretation: 'However, this demonstration, much though Treharne made of it, does not necessarily prove that there was a widespread or spontaneous wave of nostalgia in the localities at the passing of the baronial regime': Ridgeway, 'Mid Thirteenth-Century Reformers', 78.

[186] To the 1971 impression of his book Treharne appended his Raleigh lecture of 1954, viz. 'The Personal Rule of Simon de Montfort in the Period of Baronial Reform and Rebellion 1258–65': *Baronial Plan of Reform*, 412–39.

[187] Treharne, *Baronial Plan of Reform*, 429–30.

[188] Powicke, *King Henry III and the Lord Edward*, 424–5.   [189] Ibid., 425.

Who were these wardens? Treharne gives us the following:[190]

Cambridgeshire and Huntingdonshire:	Ralph Pirot[191]
Surrey and Sussex:	John de la Haye and John de Wauton
Kent:	John de la Haye
Bedford and Buckinghamshire:	Ralph Pirot
Suffolk:	William le Blund
Northamptonshire:	William Marshal
Gloucestershire:	William de Tracy
Leicestershire:	Ralph Basset of Sapcote
Derbyshire and Nottinghamshire:	Richard Foliot
Lincolnshire:	Adam de Newmarket
Warwickshire:	Thomas de Astley
Yorkshire:	John d'Eyville

What is immediately striking is that none of the sheriffs of 1258–9, nor the outgoing sheriffs, was involved.[192] In fact, the wardens were men of a rather different kind. They tended to be regional magnates, men who fitted 'Bracton's' more elevated description of vavasours. Some were to be Montfortian henchmen in the years that followed. John d'Eyville was famously the leader of 'the Disinherited', while William le Blund was killed fighting for Montfort at the battle of Lewes. These men were serious warriors. John d'Eyville and Adam de Newmarket were later cited among the rebels 'who were going through the county of York with standards unfurled',[193] while John d'Eyville and John de la Haye were among those who held out at Ely with Simon de Montfort junior. Thomas de Astley was one of Simon de Montfort's own affinity. It has been noted already that this affinity contained a great proportion of higher-ranking knights than was the norm.[194] It was arguably a characteristic of the reform period and of the Montfortian rebellion that the higher reaches of society were seen in a hierarchical manner: earls and greater barons, regional magnates, vavasours (in the 1258 sense), lesser knights, and then freeholders. Up to 1261, and indeed beyond, county knights played their part largely as directed.

On 18 October 1261 Henry summoned nearly 150 tenants-in-chief to come to London with their entire service and any additional service they could bring 'for urgent matters specially affecting our realm and person', and thirty-seven abbots and priors were also ordered to send the military service they owed.[195] The king

---

[190] For the list see Treharne, *Baronial Plan of Reform*, 268.

[191] Treharne says that 'Giles of Erdington was accused at first', the same being the case of John fitz John in Bedfordshire and Buckinghamshire, and John d' Abernon in Surrey. D'Abernon, for one, strongly denied receiving any monies due to the king: TNA, E159/36 m. 11d.

[192] Admittedly, two men from the 1258 panels were involved for Surrey, but their role is unclear.

[193] Jacob, *Studies in the Period of Baronial Reform and Rebellion*, 270.

[194] See above 140–3.   [195] *CR 1259–71*, 497–9.

118 POLITICS AND SOCIETY IN MID THIRTEENTH-CENTURY ENGLAND

also made arrangements to bring in foreign mercenaries. Henry was preparing for an all-out military struggle. Richard of Gloucester now deserted to the king and Simon left England in disgust. On 20 October safe conducts were issued to barons coming to the meeting at Kingston to treat for peace.[196] Although matters are often frequently reported in terms of Gloucester versus Leicester, it certainly looks as though the baronage had no real appetite for armed conflict with the king. The treaty at Kingston tackled the issue of the sheriffs. It provided that each of those counties which had rejected Henry's sheriffs could send four knights to the exchequer at epiphany when Henry would choose one.[197] All future appointments were to be made by an arbitration process. In other words, the concession was a grudging one, applicable only in cases where counties might be determined to hold out. Early in 1262 the sheriffs were appointed at the king's will.

Studies of the period from 1258–65/7 tend to make a break in 1263 when real hostilities opened. However, there is a case for seeing a sea change in 1261 when the king's belligerent actions and military preparations changed the climate and brought different men to the fore. It is interesting in this context that Huw Ridgeway, examining the texts of the king's grievances against this council in March 1261, reports the sources as indicating that 'Henry exerted maximum pressure on the magnates and that there was deadlock and, perhaps, threat of war.'[198]

The baronial 'reformers' continued to reach out to 'the counties', as they had done since 1258. Clearly, they were after capturing the local elites, knights, and major freeholders, who were not members of aristocratic affinities. The instrument was the county—what else could it be?—but to put the accent on 'county communities' distorts the perspective. That the reformers aimed to channel discontent is clear. The accent on the conduct of sheriffs alone shows this. Moreover, as Ridgeway has pointed out, the reformers did have some success in improving the conduct of sheriffs. For one thing the terms on which the custodial sheriffs took office reduced the pressure on localities. The lower increments introduced in 1259 stayed at this level for the remainder of Henry III's reign. However, the exchequer could still drive a hard bargain and the reduction in the financial pressure was variable. Some sheriffs still behaved worse than others, but in general their conduct did improve.[199] However, there is really no evidence that the 1258 panels reflected counties burning for reform. Membership of these panels rarely carried through into direct opposition to the crown. If we look, for example, at the sixteen men known to have functioned as baronial keepers in 1261 in opposition to Henry III's sheriffs, only one—John de Wauton of Surrey—had figured among the 'knights of 1258'. This is not altogether surprising. As we have noted, the keepers were for the most part men of higher status, indicative of the much different conditions when

---

[196] CPR 1258–66, 179.   [197] Royal Letters ii, 197–8.

[198] Huw Ridgeway, 'King Henry III's Grievances against the Council in 1261: A New Version and a Letter describing Political Events', Historical Research, 61/145 (1988), 235.

[199] Ridgeway, 'Mid Thirteenth-Century Reformers', 74–9.

REFORM AND THE KNIGHTS OF 1258   119

the king's resurgence and willingness to physically confront his opposition barons brought a different kind of man to the fore. Although it was avoided at this juncture, the conditions were now present that would lead to civil war.

Montfortian, Royalist, and Neutral Knights

The knights of 1258 played a minor role, if any, in temporarily resisting the king in 1261. How many of them subsequently joined or supported the Montfortian regime? Of the 153 knights named in the commissions of 1258, only seven appear in Clive Knowles's list of 214 who fought on the Montfortian side at Northampton, Lewes, Kenilworth, or Evesham.[200] Baldwin de Drayton, Eustace de Watford, Simon de Pattishall, William Everard, and Roger de Wauton were captured at Northampton, Ralf Haringod was killed at Lewes and Ralf de Normanvill at Evesham. This is a tiny number.[201] To construct a full list of Montfortians is wellnigh impossible, but there are sources we can call upon. Our first port of call is the returns of the commissions appointed in September 1265. After Evesham there had been a veritable scramble for rebel lands, and at the Winchester parliament, on 14 September 1265, these were declared forfeited. On 21 September two knights were appointed from each county to act with the sheriff in taking into the king's hands all lands and tenements of rebels and of those who adhered to them. The returns were to be brought to Westminster at the feast of St Edward (13 October). The lands were to be extended by the oaths of true and faithful men of the king. They were also to assign two collectors for each hundred who would receive the Michaelmas rent from the rebel's manors. It was an attempt to bring order to the situation, although the *seisitores* could hardly take land back from the likes of Mortimer and Gloucester. The returns are inadequate and not all counties are included in the commissions or returns. However, they provide a useful starting point. One who lost land at this point was Simon de Pattishall. Knight for Bedfordshire in 1258 and appointed sheriff of Bedfordshire and Buckinghamshire, he had fought at Northampton and Kenilworth.[202] He had been appointed sheriff of the two counties again in June 1264. Land had been taken from him in Bedfordshire, Dorset, Essex, and Suffolk. Hamo Hautein, knight of Norfolk in 1258, was made sheriff of Norfolk and Suffolk with the castle of Norwich. Hamo lost his land, water mill, and fishery at Oxnead. His brother was with him against

[200] C. H. Knowles, 'The Disinherited 1265–1280: A Political and Social Study of the Supporters of Simon de Montfort after the Barons' War (University of Wales PhD thesis, 1959), Appendix 1. The list was provisional and there were caveats. In some cases, the sources indicate that they were present, not that they fought. I have retained the three replaced Shropshire knights in the 1258 list. All counties had four knights except Yorkshire, for which there were six.

[201] A few others share surnames with 1258 knights and two share patronymics.

[202] P. Brand, 'Pattishall, Sir Simon', *ODNB* 43, 110–11. See also Ridgeway, 'Mid Thirteenth-Century Reformers', 80 n. 99.

120 POLITICS AND SOCIETY IN MID THIRTEENTH-CENTURY ENGLAND

the king and lost 120 acres at Heydon. Hamo had been appointed justice of the Jews in 1265 and joined Gloucester's revolt as a knight bachelor.[203] Perhaps these two had been among the most strident reformers among the knights of 1258? Another rebel was John de Sandwich, '1258 knight' of Kent, whose manor of Preston was seized by the king. One of the six knights appointed for Yorkshire in 1258 was Mauger le Vavasour. Described as a rebel and robber of John le Vavasour at Aldingham, his two-carucate demesne at 'Woolaston' worth 100s. was seized, as was his land in Drafton. A less serious case was the Warwickshire knight William Waver. It was said that he was taken at Northampton but that afterwards 'he bore no arms against the king'. Another example appears to be that of Richard de Tany, who was a knight of Essex in 1258. His manor of Chignal Tany had been seized by Sir John Rivers. A further five can be added from this source, making a running title of twelve.

The holding of shrievalties under the Montfortian regime would seem to suggest Montfortian sympathies. Simon de Gousle in Lincoln was sheriff from midsummer 1264, as was Eustace de Watford in Northamptonshire; in Somerset William de Staunton was appointed on 27 June 1264, as was John Abernon in Surrey. John de Botley was made sheriff of Hampshire. Eustace de Watford was pardoned in 1268 for any trespasses charged against him during the recent disturbances, in return for his long service.[204] Similarly, Anketil de Martival was reconciled with the king, and remained sheriff of Rutland for Richard of Cornwall until 1272.

Similarly, we can look at the men appointed wardens of the peace by the Montfortian regime between December 1263 and June 1264. Of the sixty-four men named, nine figure among the knights of 1258. They are William le Moyne, now acting in Huntingdonshire and Cambridgeshire, John de Morevill of Westmorland, John de Plessy of Northumberland, Richard de Tany, acting for Essex and Hertford, Geoffrey de Scudamore in Wiltshire, John de Aller (Aure) of Somerset, acting in Somerset and Dorset, Fulk Peyforer in Kent,[205] John de Wauton in Surrey, and William Butler in Lancashire.[206] That is to say 14 per cent of the wardens were drawn from the knights of 1258. Our total of 1258 knights now runs to twenty-five. Another rebel was Bernard de Brus of Exton in Rutland,[207] taking us to twenty-six. A few more can be added from the chancery rolls. Richard de Vernon, John de Weedon, Peter le Poterne (alias Peter le Porter?), and Stephen de Chenduit all had lands confiscated, while Eustace de Folleville received

---

[203] See also ibid., 80 n. 101.   [204] CPR 1266–72, 248, 621.

[205] For Fulk Peyforer, who had been appointed sheriff of Kent in 1258, see Richard Cassidy, 'Fulk Peyforer's Wages', Fine Rolls Project, online.

[206] In addition, there was Oliver Dinham in Devon, probably the successor to the Geoffrey Dynot of 1258: CPR 1258–66, 327–8; Foedera, 442.

[207] VCH Rutland i, 173, and ii, 128; Hunter, Rotuli Selecti, 253; CIPM i, no. 262.

REFORM AND THE KNIGHTS OF 1258   121

remission of the king's anger.[208] This brings the figure to thirty-one, around one fifth of the 1258 knights. It should be regarded as a minimum figure given that we are dependent upon the names that figure in our sources. It may be said to give a false impression because some of the 153 knights had died in the meantime. Ralph de Normanvill of Rutland, for example, died at some point during 1259–60. Peter Foliot died in 1261, as did Richard Filliol of Essex, while Simon of Aslacton died in the mid-1260s.[209] Also, of course, the political world of 1258–9 was rather different from that of 1263–5, and it is possible to argue that men who were reformist in the first instance may have baulked when it came to rebellion against the king. Nonetheless, the low proportion of 1258 knights that can be shown to have been involved in the Montfortian enterprise is surely significant.

There is another source which we can bring into play which allows us to understand somewhat better what was happening on the ground. This is the special eyre of 1267–72. The surviving rolls reveal the situation to be rather more complex than appears at first sight. In Cambridgeshire, for example, one of the four 1258 knights was William de Boxworth. In March 1267 he received protection for standing trial before the king, which implies at least a suspicion of guilt.[210] And yet the special eyre has him a victim of spoliation.[211] Another 1258 Cambridgeshire knight was Thomas de Lavenham. He does not appear to have been a rebel, but his son, William, was. It was presented by the jury that he was with the earl of Oxford and 'of the counsel' of the earl of Leicester. He was captured at Kenilworth. He had a carucate of land at Saxton which he held at farm from Thomas his father for twenty marks per annum. It was valued at twenty-five marks per annum. He was made to pay the extra five marks to the king. William came before the court and said that he did not have a free tenement but held from his father on an annual basis. The jury backed him, and he recovered seisin.[212] The war, then, might divide father and son.

It worked the other way around with the Tanys.[213] Richard de Tany the elder was a knight of 1258 and sheriff of Hertfordshire and Essex in 1258–9. Marriage brought him the manors of Stapleford Tawney and Latton Hall (or Latton Tany).

---

[208] *Close Rolls (Supplementary) of the Reign of Henry III, 1244–66*, ed. Ann Morton, nos. 342, 395, 414, 417; *CPR 1266–72*, 149.

[209] Ridgeway, 'Mid Thirteenth-Century Reformers', n. 96.   [210] *CPR 1266–72*, 50.

[211] Just 1/83, m. 17d. Sir William de Boxford and Robert de Boxford also appear on the roll as jurors: ibid., m. 34d. I have utilized here the University of Manchester MA theses by Charles C. Bayley and Kathleen H. Holden (1929).

[212] TNA, Just 1/83, m. 27d.

[213] For what follows see *VCH Essex* viii, 188, 191, 277, and Jacob, *Studies in the Period of Reform and Rebellion*, 199–201, 376–81. It is not clear whether Richard was related to Gilbert de Tany, who married one of the heiresses of the honour of Aveley whose lands were partitioned on his death in 1221 (he clearly had no sons), or to Peter de Tany, who was sheriff of Essex and Hertfordshire in 1236. A Richard de Tany held two fees of the honour of Bourne, at Eastwick and 'Beningeho' in 1212: *RBE*, 505.

122 POLITICS AND SOCIETY IN MID THIRTEENTH-CENTURY ENGLAND

On 15 April 1253 he received a royal charter granting him the right to have eight harriers and twenty brachets to hunt the hare, fox, and badger as well as the cat in the king's forest of Essex. In 1253 as Richard de Tany of Latton Hall he was licensed to cut timber.[214] In 1264 he had licence to enclose wood at Stapleton Tawney within the bounds of the forest. He died around 1270, leaving his son Richard.

Richard de Tany senior and Richard de Tany junior took opposing sides in the civil war. The former's manor of Chignal Tany had been seized by Sir John Rivers. It was stated that Sir Richard Tany the younger had received the Michaelmas rents. In Hertfordshire the manor of Estwick, which had belonged to Richard de Tany the elder, was restored to Richard de Tany the younger. The patent rolls add some details. In February 1266 Richard de Tany the elder was given safe conduct to come to the king to treat for peace. This was repeated in July. In September 1266 he received remission of the king's rancour, as the rolls put it, providing he stand trial. In February 1267 he was pardoned providing he stand to the *Dictum of Kenilworth*. Tany, then, had been one of 'the Disinherited' who continued to fight after Evesham and its immediate consequences. It is the Essex special eyre roll, however, which gives us some clues as to what was happening on the ground.[215] We find that Richard de Tany senior went to John Mansel's manor of East Tilbury and took a considerable number of livestock. He was accompanied by Richard of Gloucester and William of Gloucester. Afterwards Humphrey de Bohun junior came and seized the manor. Finding corn reaped in the field he took it and had it carried to London. It was worth twenty marks.

Richard de Tany the younger, however, being on the other side, swiftly seized the manor of Theydon Mount from the rebel Robert de Sutton after the battle of Evesham and proceeded to take the Michaelmas rent of 7.s 2d.[216] He was also accused, with three others, of robbery against John of Colchester. Nonetheless Richard de Tany the younger must have done valuable service to the crown. Around the time his father was returning to the king's peace, Richard received a grant of £20 per annum from the exchequer, until he could be found the equivalent in land. He was warden of the peace for Essex and Hertfordshire for the post-Evesham royal government. Something of the man is shown by the subsequent history of the manor of Theydon Mount. In October 1265 the king gave the manor to Robert de Briwes, who had a claim to it. However, matters did not end there. Richard de Tany, presumably the younger, who held the adjacent manor to Theydon (that is, Stapleford Tawney) put out Robert de Briwes, producing a charter which preceded Robert's by three days and 'contrived to have it entered on the Charter Roll'. Apparently, he had said to a chancery official: 'Theydon is a pretty manor and lies next to mine at Stapleford; it would just do for me'.

---

[214] In 1301 Latton, with other parishes in Harlow Hundred, was excluded from the forest.

[215] TNA, Just 1/237 m. 3.

[216] See also Jacobs, *Studies in the Period of Baronial Reform and Rebellion*, 199–201.

REFORM AND THE KNIGHTS OF 1258   123

The official complied. However, Robert de Briwes declared the charter to be a forgery and proved it before the justices *coram rege*.[217]

One wonders why father and son were on different sides. Was the decision tactical perhaps? Another case of divided loyalties comes from Rutland. In 1250 Hasculf de Neville and his wife, Christine, held land in Rutland. Hasculf was probably a cadet of the Nevilles of Raby. He and Christine had four sons: Robert, Thomas, Peter, and Stephen. Stephen was one of the Rutland knights of 1258. Robert, the eldest, sided with the baronial party and after Evesham his land at Stoke Dry was seized. However, it was restored to him in the same year. He settled his land on Thomas, presumably his son, and his heirs, with remainder to his brother Thomas. The fourth brother, Stephen, initially took the same stance as his eldest brother but changed sides with Gilbert de Clare and John Giffard.[218] In 1265 we find that the Neville holding in Bisbrooke had been held by Stephen and that during the war Stephen's land had been seized by his brother, Sir Peter, but was restored in 1265, presumably after Evesham, suggesting that Peter was a rebel. This is, in fact, shown by his appearance in the chancery rolls as one of those in receipt of remission of the king's anger.[219] Are we seeing here an example of a family with numerous sons hedging its bets?

Some of the knights definitely tended to the other side. A few of them were among the king's commissioners in 1265, who were ordered to take the lands of named rebels into the king's hands. These are William Bagot and Robert de Grendon in Warwickshire, John de Wauton in Surrey, William Everard in Lincoln (although he was a knight of Somerset in 1258), John Vautort of Middlesex, John Strode of Dorset, William de Montgomery of Nottinghamshire and Derbyshire, Richard de Harlow of Essex and Hertfordshire, and James de Paunton of Rutland.[220] William Bagot, as we have seen, was a knight of Staffordshire in 1258 and became sheriff of Staffordshire and Shropshire later in the year. The following year, 1259–60, he was sheriff of Warwickshire and Leicestershire. The king's recovery did not dampen his enthusiasm for the shrievalty. In October 1262 he was appointed again to Warwickshire and Leicestershire, and yet again in September 1265. Robert de Grendon of Warwickshire in 1258 was similarly appointed sheriff of Staffordshire and Shropshire in February 1265. These men clearly gravitated towards the royalist side. John de Wauton, knight of Surrey in 1258, seems to have been associated with the baronial keeper in 1261. If so, he quickly moved on for he was appointed in July to the shrievalty of the county as substitute for the ailing William de la Zouche. William Everard, knight of Somerset in 1258, had been appointed sheriff of Somerset and Dorset. He was later a royalist. William de Hecham, knight of Suffolk in 1258, became sheriff of Norfolk and Suffolk in 1262. Simon de Heddon was made sheriff of Nottinghamshire. The Berkshire knight

---

[217] In 1274 the manor comprised 200 acres of arable, twenty-one of meadow, fifty-one of pasture, a windmill, woodland, and £4. 5s. 61/2. rent of assize.

[218] TNA, Just1/59, m. 5.   [219] *CPR 1266–72*, 149.   [220] *CPR 1258–66*, 490.

124   POLITICS AND SOCIETY IN MID THIRTEENTH-CENTURY ENGLAND

Sampson Foliot was sheriff in 1267, suggesting at least a non-Montfortian position. The assize roll for Essex suggests that Richard de Harlow, Tany's colleague on the 1258 panel, was a royalist. Others were counted among the royalist wardens of the peace during 1265–7. In addition to Richard de Tany the younger, we find Ralf de Sanzavar of Sussex, Stephen Chenduit of Oxfordshire (despite his past), and Gilbert de St Laud of Lincolnshire. Some royalists figure almost incidentally in the records. When the royalist castle of Scarborough surrendered to Simon de Montfort's regime in December 1264, the 1258 knight Richard de Neuton was among the garrison.[221] Around seventeen of the 1258 knights are found, ultimately at least, to have been royalists, that is half of the number of those logged as Montfortians. These are no doubt underestimates. It must be significant, however, that over two thirds remain unaccounted for. The conclusion would seem to be that the great majority remained neutral during the time of the civil war.[222]

Mario Fernandes, looking at the knights of the Warwickshire eyre of 1262, it will be recalled, classified twelve of the twenty-nine as 'contrariants' and five as royalists, leaving the remaining twelve as 'unrecorded'. In other words, wherever their sympathies may have lain, if indeed they had any, they were effectively neutral. Even in the Montfortian heartland only two fifths of the eyre knights were prepared to actively support the baronial cause. Wherever wc look, it does seem that the majority of the knights had no reforming passion, or if they did it did not induce them to bear arms or actively participate against the king. Perhaps they took the safest option.

Compatible results were obtained by Huw Ridgeway in his study of the thirty-nine sheriffs appointed by the baronial regime of 1258–61. Leaving aside the six who had died and six for whom there is little evidence of political activity,[223] he finds that only four or five[224] of the sheriffs can be considered Montfortians during the Barons' Wars, while six supported the king's cause.[225] He adds that the 'Montfortians were certainly some of the wealthiest and best-connected of the group, more barons than knights'. There were others, he says, who were lukewarm: thirteen were 'trimmers to varying degrees', and three were 'apparently royalists'. He has a very strict definition of Montfortian and royalist which

---

[221] CPR 1258–66, 391; Maddicott, Simon de Montfort, 308.

[222] For further comments on neutrality see below, Chapter 9.

[223] H. Ridgeway, 'Mid Thirteenth-Century Reformers and the Localities: The Sheriffs of the Baronial Regime, 1258–61', in Fleming, Gross, and Lander, (eds.), Regionalism and Revision, 59–86. Those for whom evidence is lacking are John le Brun, William de Courtney, Geoffrey de Cheetham, Thomas fitz Michael, Walter de Riviere, and Philip de Cerne. At the same time Ridgeway quotes evidence to suggest that John le Brun may have been a Montfortian (CR 1264–68, 127) and that Walter de la Riviere may have been a royalist (CR 1261–4, 380).

[224] All but John de Cobham of Kent were among the knights of 1258. The others were: William le Botyler, Simon de Patteshull, Hamo Hauteyn, and Richard de Tany. William le Botyler, he thinks, may have been with Robert de Ferrers at Chesterfield. However, he submitted shortly afterwards, and his lands were redeemed under the Dictum, which does seem strong evidence.

[225] The royalists were William Bagot, Simon de Hedon, William le Moigne, John de Oketon, and William le Latymer.

REFORM AND THE KNIGHTS OF 1258   125

seems to be confined to those who were involved in the military forces. There were three others who did the king good service.[226] These are set alongside 'the large and interesting group of "trimmers".' This seems to be a rather unjust appellation, in that it supposes that each man's duty was to choose one side or the other. As Ridgeway says, five of the 'trimmers' had been sheriffs again in 1264–5.[227] Three others had been among Simon de Montfort's keepers of the peace.[228] Two of the latter group, John de Wauton and Geoffrey de Scudamore, were followers of John Giffard and were therefore royalist in 1265, though rebels earlier. John de Wauton and two others (Peyforer of Kent and Bagingden of Hereford) were among those seizing rebel lands in 1265. Hervey de Stanho was later regarded as having been 'a rebel sheriff', while Eustace de Watford was pardoned in 1268. Anketil de Martival was another who was reconciled with the king. Taking a wider lens we could probably add another three to the tally of royalists and another nine as rebel sympathizers.[229] Even then, the total who were inclined to one side or another is only twenty, half of the thirty-nine sheriffs. Since we could expect those who functioned as sheriffs to be among the most active knights, it is significant that one third or more showed no sign of allegiance one way or the other and only a quarter were fully committed.

Ridgeway concludes that the careers of the sheriffs of the baronial regime reveal political attitudes in the 'Period of Baronial Reform' which were 'more ambiguous than past commentators have allowed' and that to 'describe them as tepid might not be unjust'. On this basis he argues that the assumption that Montfort had lost magnate support by 1263 but retained that of the knights is untenable. On the contrary, 'the ambivalent attitudes of the knightly class must have played their part in precipitating the downfall of Simon de Montfort in 1265'.[230]

Several further points should be underlined. One is that the 'knightly class', if we wish to use that term, was not homogeneous. Those who took on the task of sheriff are likely to have been of a particular type. In some cases, at least, it was the prospect of 'getting on' in the world and furthering their own, their family's, and sometimes their lord's interests that motivated them. Some sheriffs probably welcomed office. The barons in 1264 spoke as if some had competed for shrievalties, obtaining in their cause 'the support of the courtiers by prayer and price'.[231] One such may have been William de Lisle, 'who from being rich was desirous of becoming richer', and who was said by Matthew Paris to have

---

[226] William Everard, William de Caverswall, and Robert de Mulcaster.

[227] Richard de Bagingden, Fulk Peyforer, Eustace de Watford, John de Scalariis, and Harvey de Stanho.

[228] John de Walton, Geoffrey de Scudamore, and John du Plessis.

[229] Perhaps the closest to a trimmer was Richard de Bagingden: Ridgeway, 'Mid Thirteenth-Century Reformers', 83, where reference is made to his 'convoluted experience'.

[230] Ibid., 84. The view expressed here runs counter to that of Claire Valente who believes that over 60 per cent of the knights active in the country were rebels: *The Theory and Practice of Revolt in Medieval England* (Aldershot, 2002), 95.

[231] *DBM* no. 37C, 276–7.

126 POLITICS AND SOCIETY IN MID THIRTEENTH-CENTURY ENGLAND

procured his own appointment as sheriff of Northumberland and to have run the county with notorious oppressiveness.[232] His standing as a local knight showed that native birth was no guarantee of upright behaviour. Many, on the other hand, were averse to official roles as the many exemptions granted to them indicate, even if the main benefit of such a licence was to allow them to choose with what and when they would comply. At the same time involvement in commissions and in a judicial capacity was strongly connected to the traditional status of being a knight. In this sense those who were not active Montfortians were *ipso facto* part of the status quo. This made them in practical terms royalist.

Towards the end of his famous essay 'Magna Carta and the Local Community', John Maddicott writes:

> The assertiveness of local opinion was not merely a reaction to pressure from above. It possessed an internal dynamic of its own, derived largely from the strength of local community and from the leadership provided by a powerful knightly class ... Although knightly opinion on matters such as the forest was often shared by a wider class of gentry [sic] and barons, it was usually the knights who took the lead in demanding reform. They had local weight, deriving from both wealth and residence, which barons, holding lands in many counties and only represented by their stewards, were seldom able to match; and they shared with the substantial freeholders of their counties, from whom some are likely to have been recruited by ways of distraint, a close identification with the local community and its needs.[233]

Although there is truth in this, especially in terms of knightly status, its judgement needs to be tempered in light of the above survey of 1258 knights. Angevin knights performed many judicial duties, as we know, where their status was required, and these continued throughout the reign of Henry III. In addition, many of them, and particularly those who were especially trusted, performed a variety of administrative roles for the crown. They were generally responsive to central government whenever the king called for information, help, or even, perhaps one could say, for advice. It was therefore perfectly normal that they, and indeed the sheriffs of 1258–9, should respond as they did. Many knights must have seen themselves as part of a natural and established order, identifying with the operation of the state and its rulers. To regard them as instinctive proponents of radical reform is unjustified.

Politics and Society in Mid Thirteenth-Century England: The Troubled Realm. Peter Coss, Oxford University Press.
© Peter Coss 2024. DOI: 10.1093/9780198924319.003.0005

---

[232] Paris, *CM* v, 577.
[233] Maddicott, 'Magna Carta and the Local Community', 63–4.

6
Faction, Party, and Affinity

We are now in a position to examine in more detail how aristocratic society was articulated, and the bearing this has upon the interpretation of events between 1258 and 1267. How did the various political entities come about, how were they constructed, and how were they sustained up to the point of fighting a civil war? In considering power within the provinces, we have already introduced the 'affinity' and examples of its study by historians of the thirteenth century.[1] We will now turn to national politics and to the study of first 'faction' and then 'party', before making some further observations on the affinity and its significance.

Factions

Since the pioneering work of Huw Ridgeway and David Carpenter, historians have become much more aware of the prominence of faction and of self-interest in the politics of the period.[2] Although Ridgeway has gone so far as to say that this research has shown the 'baronial movement of reform' to be a 'misnomer', there remains an ambivalence in the way the phenomenon has been interpreted. Margaret Howell has expressed the situation clearly in writing that '"1258" was a reform movement with its roots in the grievances of the community of the realm, but it was also a palace revolution and the relationship between the two has been a vexed question in recent historical writing.'[3] For John Maddicott, 'What had begun ... as a coup by a small number of disaffected magnates was now transformed into a much broader social movement, directed at the reform of local as well as central government and even at the ways of the magnates themselves.'[4] Suffice it to say at this point that a major part in the unfolding of these events, not only in 1258 but thereafter, was played by the prevalence of aristocratic faction.

Faction may be endemic within aristocratic society. Derived from the Latin *factio*, it refers to a group, sometimes within a larger organization, acting in concert for shared ends, and often carries opprobrious connotations. In a medieval context it tends to arise when there are benefits to be gained from a central

---

[1] See above, Chapter 4.
[2] Ridgeway, 'The Lord Edward', 90, citing his thesis 'The Politics of the English Court 1247–65', 247–314, and Carpenter, 'What Happened in 1258?', 106–19.
[3] Howell, *Eleanor of Provence*, 140–1.   [4] Maddicott, *Simon de Montfort*, 156.

128   POLITICS AND SOCIETY IN MID THIRTEENTH-CENTURY ENGLAND

authority in terms of wealth and power. Faction played a major part in the reign of Henry III, during his minority and during the years of his personal rule. Weak kingship, growth in available rewards, and the need felt by magnates for personal gain and for rewards for their followers all played their part. The height of Henry's power saw the dominance of the two alien factions of the Lusignans and the Savoyards. A faction, however, may also centre on a collective desire for security as well as for gain. The confederation of the seven magnates in 1258 was the heart of a new faction, or perhaps one might say counter-faction, aimed at ending the domination of the Lusignans. This confederation, however, proved to be a rather uneasy coalition, which later unravelled. We perceive a division within the ranks, the conservative wing being led by Richard, earl of Gloucester. Then we see the re-emergence of the Savoyards as a royalist faction, with Peter of Savoy a leading figure. Another group formed around Lord Edward, the king's eldest adult son being a traditional focus for the formation of a faction rivalling the royal court.[5] The period from 1260–3 is usually treated in terms of royal machinations and the retreat of the reform programme. Although this is a perfectly valid standpoint, there is another way of looking at the period, that is in terms of noble behaviour and interests, and, most particularly, aristocratic faction. The 'marchers' were later to emerge as another faction. Then, of course, there was a faction around Simon de Montfort. No doubt there were others. The existence of factions makes the politics of the period of reform and rebellion seem somewhat kaleidoscopic. It is partly to see through this that historians tend to concentrate on the main actors or personalities. Here, however, we will make the faction itself the centre of our enquiry.

The Savoyards and the Lusignans

To understand the full force of faction in Henry III's England it is necessary to step back to the period of his 'personal rule'. The most longstanding faction was the Savoyards, the relatives of Queen Eleanor of Provence whom Henry III married on 14 January 1236. For details of the activities of the Savoyards as a faction in England we have Margaret Howell's biography of Queen Eleanor herself, who with Peter of Savoy became joint leader of the faction.[6] At the feast of St Edward in January 1241, Peter had been knighted by the king with fifteen other young noblemen. In the months that followed Peter was endowed with lands, honours, and influential positions.[7] The patronage bestowed on the Savoyards has been

---

[5] One thinks, for example, of Robert, duke of Normandy, William the Conqueror's eldest son, and the Young Henry, son of Henry II. See W. M. Aird, *Robert Curthose, Duke of Normandy* (Woodbridge, 2008) and M. Strickland, *Henry the Young King* (New Haven and London, 2016).

[6] Howell, *Eleanor of Provence*.

[7] Ibid., 31. For the family more generally, see E. L. Cox, *The Eagles of Savoy: The House of Savoy in Thirteenth-Century Europe* (Princeton, 1974).

FACTION, PARTY, AND AFFINITY 129

dealt with above and little more needs to be added here on that score.[8] Howell makes two particularly pertinent comments, however, a propos the house of Savoy. The first is that the Savoyard brothers were adept in unobtrusively supporting one another in their apparently independent policies. The second is that Eleanor provides a 'supreme example' of how a wife could continue to be sustained by her natal family after her marriage.[9] Her contacts therefore reached out beyond England. Some of the men she supported moved from service with the Savoyard lords into royal service. Some are especially noteworthy. Imbert de Montferrand, for example, was in the entourage of Bishop Peter of Aigueblanche, while Bernard of Savoy became constable of Windsor and keeper of the lands destined for Lord Edward. Imbert Pugeys, steward of the king's household and keeper of the Tower of London, had come with the queen herself. Many were associated with Peter of Savoy, who worked in close collaboration with the queen. She maintained contacts abroad, including the papal court, while Peter had his own ambitions in Savoy. The king's patronage was extremely useful to him. Members of the Savoyard families of Chauvent, Grandson, de Montibus, and Joinville were in Peter's 'affinity'.[10] The Joinvilles, brothers of King Louis IX's biographer, were also half-brothers to Peter's wife, Agnes de Faicigny. The queen forged her own relationships with members of the Joinville family, including William de Salines, one of her clerks, and Geoffrey, who was granted the marriage of Maud de Lacy by the king in 1252. In addition to considerable land in Meath, she was heiress to Ludlow Castle and other property in the Welsh march. As we have seen, male Savoyards acquired wealthy English ladies, while Savoyard girls married the king's wards. The queen was very much involved in these negotiations, and in 1257 she apparently persuaded no less a person than Richard, earl of Gloucester, to allow the marriage of his eldest daughter to her kinsman, the marquis of Montferrant.[11]

Howell designates the Savoyards as the queen's men, in contrast to the king's men, who formed a rival faction following the arrival of Henry's Poitevin half-brothers in 1247.[12] The two factions soon found themselves in competition for royal patronage. There was no longer enough to go around. The gravy train of the 1240s slowed down spectacularly during the 1250s as, for various reasons, the king no longer had the resources to satisfy his need to bestow upon his relatives adequate rewards, as he and they saw it.[13] The Savoyards had certain clear advantages. The queen's access to the king was like no other. Moreover, she and Peter of Savoy 'kept a firm and controlling hand on the household and affairs of her eldest

---

[8] See above, Chapter 3.   [9] Howell, *Eleanor of Provence*, 47–8.

[10] Howell cites here in particular G. E. Watson, 'The Families of Lacy, Geneva, Joinville and La Marche', *The Genealogist*, new series 21 (1904); Howell, *Eleanor of Provence*, 51.

[11] Howell, *Eleanor of Provence*, 54.   [12] For the arrival of the Lusignans, see above 41–2.

[13] The issue is thoroughly explored in Ridgeway, 'Foreign Favourites and Henry III's Problems of Patronage, 1247–58'.

130 POLITICS AND SOCIETY IN MID THIRTEENTH-CENTURY ENGLAND

son, Edward'.[14] The Gascon expedition of 1253–4, however, put the Lusignans in the ascendant. Not only was the king inordinately fond of his half-brothers, but he was reliant on their support in France. In consequence the king 'squeezed his dwindling patronage resources' to reward them for their military support, drawing closer to them and protecting them in 'their most unlawful acts'.[15] Nonetheless, the house of Savoy continued to profit. In 1253 Peter of Savoy was promised 10,000 marks, half of it being handed over immediately in cash and wardships, and during the years 1256–8 the king had to find over £700 in wardships for the queen to maintain her income level.[16] Further down, Savoyards felt the pinch rather more. For example, in 1252 a wardship was taken from Stephen de Salines and given to Alice de Lusignan, while Ebulo de Montibus and Geoffrey de Joinville also lost out to Lusignan claims.[17] Edward's entourage was to a great extent in the hands of the Savoyards, while the queen adroitly kept on good terms with many men who were prominent at court, including Simon de Montfort, as well as with royal officials like John Mansel. One of the clerks of her chapel was Hugh de la Penne, who became keeper of her wardrobe. He was a protégé of Henry of Wingham, keeper of the king's seal. The queen was busily constructing a power base at court. At the same time 'the Savoyard network' was penetrating deeply into society, and at its heart lay the queen.[18] Her regency from August 1253 to May 1254, the king being in Gascony, increased her power and prestige even more.

Meanwhile, at the end of 1252 there had been an open breach between the two factions, when a dispute over the appointment to the post of prior of the hospital at St Thomas at Southwark led to Aymer de Valence, bishop-elect of Winchester, sending an armed band to Archbishop Boniface of Savoy's manor of Maidstone, ransacking and then setting fire to it, and seriously manhandling the archbishop's official. A more serious conflagration was averted with difficulty in the New Year. This incident came at the end of a difficult year in which the king and queen had quarrelled bitterly over the presentation to the church of Flamstead and the king had imprisoned one of Eleanor's clerks on a charge of corruption. Matthew Paris regarded the quarrel as essentially one between the Poitevins and the Savoyards, between the two alien factions at the royal court.[19] There were further tussles in the years that followed, often involving control over Lord Edward and his lands.[20] Then came the momentous events of 1258 in which the struggle between the Savoyards and the Lusignans was a contributary factor.

---

[14] Howell, *Eleanor of Provence*, 55.   [15] Ibid., 141.

[16] *CPR 1247–58*, 188–9; Ridgeway, 'Foreign Favourites', 600; M. Howell, 'The Resources of Eleanor of Provence as Queen Consort', *EHR*, 102 (1987), at 386. In 1256, 1,000 marks were handed over to Beatrice of Savoy, Eleanor's mother, in political subsidy, and over 5,000 marks were given towards the ransom of Thomas of Savoy, paid to the cities of Asti and Turin: Ridgeway, 'Foreign Favourites', 600.

[17] Ridgeway, 'Foreign Favourites', 603.   [18] Howell, *Eleanor of Provence*, 57–8.

[19] Howell, *Eleanor of Provence*, 68; Paris, *CM* v, 352.   [20] See below 159.

The immediate object of the Savoyards in 1258 was no doubt to destroy the rising power of the Lusignans. 'What concerned the queen', writes Howell, 'was not constitutional and administrative reform but the expulsion of the Lusignans from England'.[21] Peter of Savoy was one of the seven confederates who bound themselves to act in concert in the face of any armed challenge from them. But Peter and the queen were inevitably concerned to maintain their own influence and power. They and Archbishop Boniface all took the oath to the Provisions of Oxford. Inevitably there were some losses. When the castles were taken from the Lusignans, the Savoyards Imbert Pugeys and Ebulo of Geneva lost their control of the Tower of London and Hadleigh respectively, although the queen's steward Matthias Bezill retained Gloucester. There was hostility to Peter d'Aigueblanche, bishop of Hereford, but he survived nonetheless. The resolutions of the October parliament which were later to form part of the Provisions of Westminster hurt them. The sale of wardships falling to the king was to be placed in the hands of a committee of five—the justiciar, treasurer, and three others—who were also to 'determine and decree in what matters queen's gold shall be paid'.[22] This was raised on feudal reliefs and constituted an important part of her income.[23] The queen had certainly not modified her expectations. On the eve of her departure with the king for France on 14 November 1259, a royal mandate said that, for his service to the king and the queen, her steward, Matthias Bezill, was to be granted the first available wardship of between £40 and £60 per year, with the marriage of the heirs and with no reservations. The Patent Rolls tell us that the writ was authorized by Hugh Bigod and John Mansel 'at the instance of the queen'. In other words, 'the official committee of five had apparently been by-passed'.[24]

Simon de Montfort and Richard, Earl of Gloucester, as Leaders of Factions

Famously a split occurred within the ranks of the confederates, focused upon Simon de Montfort and Richard, earl of Gloucester. Can they be seen as the leaders of factions? Let us begin with Michael Altschul's assessment of why the king was able to draw Richard back to his side in 1260.[25] He notes Richard's dislike of Simon de Montfort's rigidity over the Provisions, the speed with which he was prepared to take up arms, and his willingness to exclude the king from active involvement in government. He notes, too, Richard's unwillingness to participate in the mundane tasks of ruling and his feeling that championing the interests of

---

[21] Howell, *Eleanor of Provence*, 156.   [22] Ibid., 164.

[23] Howell, 'The Resources of Eleanor of Provence', 374–9.

[24] Howell, *Eleanor of Provence*, 164; *CPR 1258–66*, 63.

[25] For what follows see Michael Altschul, *A Baronial Family in Medieval England: The Clares, 1217–1314* (Baltimore, 1965), 89–90.

132 POLITICS AND SOCIETY IN MID THIRTEENTH-CENTURY ENGLAND

freeholders 'constituted a direct threat to his control over his own estates and franchises'. Altschul suggests that Richard's support for the king may have been conditional on the further extension of his jurisdictional powers: on 18 March 1260 Henry of Bath was appointed 'to make inquiry of the counties of Norfolk, Suffolk, Cambridge, Huntingdon, Essex, Hertford, Kent, Surrey and Sussex, how much the king would lose of the farm of those counties if he granted Richard de Clare, earl of Gloucester and Hertford, the return of all the king's writs, and the execution thereof in all his fees of the honor of Clare in those counties'.[26] Altschul adds that there is 'no need ... to characterize Richard's actions as mere reactionary jealousy and hatred of the selfless idealism of Simon de Montfort', and concludes poignantly that Richard's 'apparent inconsistency is characteristic of most of the great baronial leaders, who either championed or opposed their own program, not on a basis of some vague commitment to some even vaguer principles of constitutional government, but rather on the basis of whether or not it contributed to their own personal power, influence and interests'. 'Earl Richard', he concludes, 'is perhaps the prime example of such a man.'[27] There is good reason to believe that the split in the baronial ranks goes back to the previous year. Gloucester's joining of the confederacy had much to do with the king's failure to deal with the rise of Llewelyn ap Gruffydd and the serious threat he posed to the earl's regional interests. Nonetheless, there is consensus among historians that Gloucester was firmly against the extension of restraints to encompass baronial officials and the crown's transformation into what Altschul has called 'a kind of open-ended receivership'.[28]

According to Matthew Paris, Richard's reluctance to implement reform in the spring of 1259 led to Simon de Montfort's eruption against him when he declared, 'I do not want to live or have dealings with men so fickle and deceitful. For we have promised and sworn together to do what we are doing'.[29] Simon left the country, and Richard had to back down. The continuing distrust between the two men is well attested, and each had most probably taken the measure of the other.[30] The disagreement transcends the clash of personalities, however. The tardiness in implementing reform and its watering down in the interests of magnates does surely point to disagreement within the council, and Gloucester, the wealthiest and most powerful man in England outside of the royal family, was undoubtedly the leader of its conservative wing. Where he went others would be likely to

---

[26] *CPR 1258–66*, 99.   [27] Altschul, *A Baronial Family*, 93.

[28] M. Altschul, 'Clare, Richard de, Sixth Earl of Gloucester and Fifth Earl of Hertford 1222–1262', *ODNB* 11, 761–3.

[29] Paris, *CM* v, 744–5; *Flores Historiarum* ii, 424–5. See Maddicott, *Simon de Montfort*, 80; Jobson, *The First English Revolution*, 32–3.

[30] Montfort's tactics in holding up ratification of the Treaty of Paris over his wife's rights caused Gloucester to accuse him of greed in a quarrel which led to both men being physically restrained: Jobson, *The First English Revolution*, 36, quoting Carpenter, 'Montfort', 247–8, and Treharne, *Baronial Plan of Reform*, 141.

FACTION, PARTY, AND AFFINITY   133

follow. The king's excesses, however, in particular the publication of the papal bulls condemning the Provisions, led to Richard and Simon coming together as joint leaders of a new opposition, perhaps one might say the recoalescing of the factions, only for this to break up once again as the king bought men off during the autumn. Apart from the earl of Gloucester, we find Roger Clifford and Humphrey de Bohun earl of Hereford among the defectors. Another was Hugh Bigod. This led to Simon de Montfort leaving once again for France, declaring that 'he would rather die landless than depart from the truth and be perjured'.[31] Although Gloucester's leadership of the conservatives seems clear, it is not easy to delineate his 'faction'.

The Royalist Faction

Not surprisingly, Eleanor and Peter's views were more in line with Gloucester's than with Montfort's, and they began to distance themselves from the latter. It is indicative that on 16 March 1259 Simon refused to stand as a surety for a bond for 3,000 marks to pay arrears of exchequer fees to members of the house of Savoy, while the council's agreement to the conversion of his £4,000 annual fee from the king into lands involved taking property from Savoyards who had previously been granted it by the monarch.[32] There was also an issue arising from the marriage of the Lady Beatrice to the son of the duke of Brittany, given that the duke had a claim to the earldom of Richmond. Peter wanted the duke to be compensated elsewhere, while the council, including Montfort, disagreed.[33] In other words, there was considerable distrust. Montfort was to secure Peter's removal from the council early in 1260.[34]

Peter of Savoy was abroad for most of 1260, returning in November. At the end of the year a 'close-knit group of advisors was forming around the king ... that devised and engineered the plan for the revival of royal power'.[35] It comprised the queen and Peter of Savoy, John Mansel, and Robert Walerand, supported by the Savoyards Ebulo de Montibus and Imbert de Montferrand. The Savoyards per se were now embedded in a new faction of ultra-royalists who were working to destroy the Provisions and to restore the status quo ante. The Savoyards were also involved in building up military support abroad, ready for deployment in England. The queen herself played an important role in this. As early as December 1260, knights of the Savoyard connection, men with military experience, were receiving robes from the king. They included Simon de Joinville, Baldwin de

---

[31] Jobson, *The First English Revolution*, 70–1, citing *CPR 1258–66*, 178, 192–3, and *Ann. Mon.* iii (Annals of Dunstable), 217; Maddicott, *Simon de Montfort*, 214; Carpenter, *Struggle for Mastery*, 374.
[32] Howell, *Eleanor of Provence*, 160–1; Ridgeway, 'Politics', 330–1.
[33] Howell, *Eleanor of Provence*, 161–2; Ridgeway, 'Politics', 357.   [34] *DBM*, 206–7.
[35] Howell, *Eleanor of Provence*, 176.

134 POLITICS AND SOCIETY IN MID THIRTEENTH-CENTURY ENGLAND

Villa, and Baldwin de Fiennes.[36] After a difficult year of ups and downs, the royalist revanche continued through 1262. It was now that the Savoyards came to be designated specifically as 'aliens'. When Peter of Savoy went abroad in June 1262, the queen and his Savoyard steward, Guichard de Charron, oversaw his affairs in England. Other Savoyards were present in the royal counsels.[37] Among those closely associated with the queen were Ebulo de Montibus, steward of the king's household from February 1262, while Henry of Ghent, a long-term servant of the Savoyards, became keeper of the king's wardrobe in July 1261. Imbert de Montferrand, one of the king's marshals and at one point keeper of the king's seal, later joined the queen's household. After the king and queen had crossed to France in July 1262, the Savoyards dominated the court. Key figures included Ebulo de Montibus, Henry of Ghent, Imbert de Montferrand, Imbert Pugeys, and the queen's steward Matthias Bezill, alongside John Mansel, Robert Walerand, and Ingram de Fiennes. The few outsiders included William de Valence and Henry of Almain. Various grants were made to Savoyards, and the queen herself received a very favourable dower settlement.[38]

Lord Edward and the 'Marchers'

Not surprisingly the royalist faction came under attack when 'the marchers' erupted in 1263. In June the Savoyard bishop of Hereford was seized in his cathedral and with some of his canons was imprisoned in Roger Clifford's castle of Eardisley. The 'marchers' attacked Mathias Bezill in Gloucester Castle and he, too, was imprisoned at Eardisley. The lands of Robert Walerand, including his castle at Kilpeck, were plundered, as were the East Anglian estates of Peter of Savoy, the lands of Ebulo de Montibus in Cambridgeshire, the estates of Ingram de Fiennes, the midland estates of Geoffrey de Langley, and the lands of John Mansel and the royalist bishop of Norwich. After the king submitted, the great offices of state were placed in the hands of Montfortian supporters and aliens were purged from the households of the king and queen.

To provide a more rounded picture of the role of faction, we need to look more closely at the part played by Lord Edward. In 1254, aged 15, he was knighted and married to Eleanor, daughter of Alphonse X of Castile. An appanage was conferred upon him, comprising: Ireland, with some exceptions; royal conquests in the north of Wales together with numerous Welsh castles including the Three Castles in the south once held by Hubert de Burgh; Gascony, the Isle of Oléron, and the Channel Islands; the earldom of Chester; Bristol; Stamford and Grantham in Lincolnshire; the manor of Freemantle in Hampshire; and the

---

[36] Ridgeway, 'Politics', 378. [37] Ibid., 390–4. [38] Ibid., 189–90.

lands once held by the count of Eu.[39] Although this looks impressive, Edward had very little independent power. As Robin Studd showed, in the years that followed the king constantly interfered in Edward's affairs.[40] In Gascony the king and Edward were at odds, while in north Wales Edward's officials, led by his steward Geoffrey de Langley, appointed by the king and queen, behaved harshly, introducing new exactions and attempting to make local government conform to English models. The result was the rising of 'the Four Cantreds' in 1256.[41] Llewelyn ap Gruffydd not only won a remarkable victory in the north but advanced into mid Wales where he took land from Roger Mortimer and in 1257 discomforted other marcher lords, including the earl of Gloucester. In the summer Edward was defeated in the Towy valley and a royal campaign in the north fizzled out. There can be little doubt that Edward was frustrated in these years. For one thing, his financial resources were inadequate. His officials were largely appointed by his parents. Moreover, he was strongly under the influence, if not the control, of the queen and the Savoyard faction. Howell points out that four of the six men who took seisin of his possessions had close contacts with the queen,[42] while Peter of Savoy was clearly regarded by the king as 'the appropriate man to play a guiding role in the conduct of Edward's affairs'.[43] He and the queen were 'jealous guardians' of Edward's interests. They kept the king's brother, Richard of Cornwall, in check, and they played a major part in securing Edward's marriage to Eleanor of Castile and King Alfonso's renunciation of his claim to Gascony.[44] John fitz Geoffrey, Edward's chief counsellor, was a curial ally of Peter and the queen, while Michael de Fiennes, Edward's first chancellor, was a kinsman of the Savoyards.[45] Edward was bound to chafe. By 1257 he was beginning to recruit his own men, non-courtiers like the marcher lords Roger Clifford and Hamo Lestrange, others of his own generation like Earl Warenne and John de Vaux, and Robert Burnell, who was one day to become his chancellor. Particularly galling for the Savoyard faction was that in 1258 Edward began to link himself to the Lusignans.

Much light on this is shed by Huw Ridgeway in an essay significantly subtitled 'A Study in Faction'. Edward's opposition to the magnates at the Oxford parliament and his support of his four Lusignan uncles put him 'at odds' with those who had served him since 1254.[46] Peter of Savoy, John fitz Geoffrey, and Peter de

---

[39] For Edward's early years see Prestwich, *Edward I*, Ch. 1.

[40] J. R. Studd, 'The Lord Edward and Henry III', *BIHR*, 50/121 (1977), 4–19.

[41] See J. R. Studd, 'The Lord Edward's Lordship of Chester, 1254–72', *Transactions of the Historic Society of Lancashire and Cheshire*, 127 (1979), 1–25. For Geoffrey de Langley see above, Chapter 3.

[42] Howell, *Eleanor of Provence*, 125. They were: Geoffrey de Langley, Ralph Dunion, Bartholomew Pecche, and Stephen Bauzan.

[43] Howell, *Eleanor of Provence*, 145.

[44] H. W. Ridgeway, 'The Lord Edward and the Provisions of Oxford (1258): A Study in Faction', *TCE*, i (Woodbridge, 1986), 89–99, at 91–2.

[45] His council also included Peter de Montfort and Robert Walerand.

[46] Ridgeway, 'A Study in Faction', 93.

136 POLITICS AND SOCIETY IN MID THIRTEENTH-CENTURY ENGLAND

Montfort, to take the most prominent, were among the seven confederate magnates in April 1258 and were subsequently elected to the ruling council of fifteen. Edward appears to have acted on his own initiative in moving towards the Lusignans. By April 1258 they had begun to witness his charters. Around the same time, he had begun mortgaging manors to them for loans to fight the Welsh. Ridgeway suggests that there were three factors in this rapprochement. One was his drawing close to William de Valence, conditioned by their 'mutual frustration' at the king's failure to contain the Welsh revolt of 1256–8 which threatened their lands, and their quarrels with Richard de Clare. A second was his need for money and his finding it from the Lusignans. The third was over the 'inseparability' of Edward's appanage from the crown.[47] Edward wished to be free from this, one manifestation being his desire to appoint and reward the Lusignans. As far as the Savoyards were concerned, the fact that their factional rivals were allying themselves with the prince was the 'last straw'. Some of those Edward recruited around him, as Ridgeway points out, were already connected with William de Valence: Roger de Leybourne had been a knight in his service and John de Warenne was his brother-in-law. Within Edward's circle was his cousin, Henry of Almain, who, like John de Warenne, earl of Surrey, was closer to his own age. Other members were Roger de Clifford, Hamo l'Estrange, John de Vaux, and Roger de Leybourne. These men were 'the very antithesis of well-established courtiers'.[48] Moreover, they were of similar outlook to Edward. They were devotees of the tournament, which was not much favoured at court. The group comprised the men who dominated Edward's service before his accession to the throne, who fought with him at Lewes, and who were to go on crusade with him.[49] Edward rewarded their devotion between 1259 and 1264 with large grants of land, often of £100 per annum or more. Meanwhile, the reformers of 1258 had taken action to bring him under control. At the end of July they wrote to the pope complaining that the Lusignans were 'infatuating' Edward and that Aymer de Valence was misdirecting him to oppose the Provisions. The 'veteran courtiers' shackled him with 'men of the old type', imposing four councillors upon him,[50] and putting royal castles out of his control. It would not be long before Edward began to manoeuvre to free himself from these shackles, exploiting divisions within the new royal council.[51]

The origins of Edward's faction are not difficult to explain. On the one hand, he represented the future and for that reason he was worth cultivating as a man who would one day possess considerable authority and dispense great patronage. On the other, Edward was bound to be in search of his own role and security.

---

[47] For further discussion of this concept, see below 272.

[48] Ridgeway, 'A Study in Faction', 97.

[49] See S. D. Lloyd, 'The Lord Edward's Crusade: Its Setting and Significance', in Gillingham and Holt (eds.), *War and Government in the Middle Ages*.

[50] John Balliol, Roger de Mohaut, John de Grey, and Stephen Longespee.

[51] Ridgeway, 'The Lord Edward and the Provisions of Oxford', 89, 98.

FACTION, PARTY, AND AFFINITY   137

This explains, in part at least, the treaty of alliance which he and Richard de Clare, earl of Gloucester, drew up in March 1259. Gloucester and his 'friends' promised to assist Edward and his supporters in all matters, especially in the recovery of Edward's lands, castles, and rights in England and elsewhere.[52] As Treharne remarked, it is uncertain what Richard got out of it, 'but it seems probable that Gloucester could count on Edward's support in opposing further reforms'. 'If so', he adds, 'a formidable obstacle was presented to the reformers'.[53] It may have served to plaster over the bad feeling between the two men, centring on Bristol, considered by the earl to be his by right but included in Edward's appanage. What we seem to have presented to us is two sets of supporters, as of this point in time. If they had not yet crystallized into factions, on Edward's side at least it was certainly tending in that direction. Edward's supporters were Henry of Almain, John de Warenne, Baldwin de Lisle, Philip Basset, Stephen Longespee, Robert Walerand, Roger Clifford, Roger Leybourne, John de Vaux, Warin de Bassingbourne, Hamo l'Estrange, and William la Zouche.[54] Roger Leybourne, a Kentish landowner, succeeded William de Wilton as Edward's steward. Roger Clifford had been bailiff of the Three Castles. Warin de Bassingbourne, like Hamo, was a tourneyer and close associate of Edward. William la Zouche, who was in Edward's service, was the brother of Alan la Zouche, justiciar of Chester (1250–6) and then of Ireland (1256–8). Henry of Almain, John de Warenne, and Roger Leybourne were shortly to be described as Edward's *amis*. Of the councillors imposed on Edward, only Longespee survived. Robert Walerand, however, had been a royal steward, and in August 1259 Edward had not been allowed to dismiss him as castellan of Bristol. Philip Basset was of the ruling council, but his allegiance was a shifting one, and in 1261 he was to become the king's justiciar. As Michael Prestwich pointed out, the group was a 'heterogeneous' one, but its members were to show a striking loyalty to Edward when it came to civil war. He clearly had the power to inspire loyalty.[55]

The agreement with Gloucester did not last long, and on 15 October 1259 Edward swore to give aid and counsel to Simon de Montfort, a seeming reversal of his earlier position.[56] It was indeed a political *volte face*. Edward swore to aid and counsel Simon, his heirs, and his English friends (*tous ses amis de Angleterre*), in their need against all, and was held 'to maintain the enterprise (*l'emprise*) made

---

[52] The text is published in *Historical Manuscripts Commission Reports*, no. 69, Middleton Manuscripts (London, 1911), 67–9. It is discussed by Treharne: *Baronial Plan of Reform*, 139–40. The language employed is discussed by Carpenter in 'The Lord Edward's Oath to Aid and Counsel Simon de Montfort'. See also Prestwich, *Edward I*, 27–8, for some important observations.

[53] Treharne, *Baronial Plan of Reform*, 139–40.

[54] Gloucester's group included: the justiciar and the earl marshal; the earl of Albermarle; Henry de Percy; Roger de Somery; Robert de Bruce; Richard de Montfichet; William de Say; William de Braose; John d'Eyville.

[55] Prestwich, *Edward I*, 28.

[56] The text of this is the subject of the essay by Carpenter noted above, *BIHR*, 58 (1985), repr. in *The Reign of Henry III* (London, 1996), 241–52. The text is reproduced there in full.

138 POLITICS AND SOCIETY IN MID THIRTEENTH-CENTURY ENGLAND

by the barons of the land', and not to make war on anyone involved in it. This has been seen by historians as binding Edward to the reform of the realm which he had hitherto accepted very reluctantly. The counterpart is not extant but presumably, as Carpenter suggests, it focused on freeing Edward's hands, most especially from control by the council of fifteen over his appointments.[57] The letters were sealed by Edward and by *nos chers amis*, Sir Henry, son of the king of Germany, Sir John, earl of Warenne, and Sir Roger de Leybourne. All three, as we have seen, had been of Edward's party in the agreement with Richard de Clare in March 1259. It was in October, too, that Edward supported the mysterious community of the bachelors of England in demanding the publication of the reforms known as the Provisions of Westminster. Edward was now firmly in the reformist camp.

Edward remained broadly in this camp during 1260, leaving in November to tourney on the continent with the likes of Henry of Almain, John de Warenne, William la Zouche, and Warin de Bassingbourne.[58] The overthrow of the Provisions in 1261 brought him back in his father's camp, not least because of his precarious financial state, and he found himself once again in a subordinate position. The Savoyards and their allies were back at the centre of affairs. At Michaelmas 1261 the king ordered an audit of the accounts of Edward's bailiffs, and Leybourne and Clifford were among those in the firing line. In 1262 the queen secured the disgrace of Roger de Leybourne and his expulsion from court. Roger de Clifford went with him, with John de Vaux and Hamo l'Estrange following soon after. They were to join Simon de Montfort and 'spearheaded his rebellion in 1263'.[59] Henry of Almain, John de Warenne, and William de Valence were all in varying degrees marginalized. Edward had lost his faction. This did not mean, however, that the group had disbanded. A list of Simon de Montfort's supporters early in 1263, given by the Dunstable annalist, included Almain, Warenne, Clifford, John de Vaux, and Hamo Lestrange.[60] According to Prestwich, this strongly suggests that it would be wrong to see Edward as the clear leader, and this role may well have been taken by Henry of Almain or John de Warenne.[61] What this faction wanted was to be back at the centre and to regain Edward's favour. As Howell puts it, Leybourne 'and his friends were not reformers; they were not even Montfortians; they had once been the Lord Edward's men and it was to the service of the Lord Edward that they wanted to return'.[62] He was able to bring them back to his, and now the royalist, cause in the autumn of 1263, with disastrous consequences, ultimately, for Simon de Montfort. Let us now turn to the issue of 'party'.

---

[57] Ibid., 249 and n. 46.   [58] *CPR 1258–66*, 126, 181.
[59] Ridgeway, 'The Lord Edward', 98.   [60] *Ann. Mon.* iii (Annals of Dunstable), 222.
[61] Prestwich, *Edward I*, 38.   [62] Howell, *Eleanor of Provence*, 140–1.

Party

In one of his famous essays David Carpenter portrays Simon de Montfort as the first leader of a political movement in English history, concentrating on the qualities and on the circumstances which fitted him to lead such a movement.[63] He does not write in terms of a political party, except to say that in 1263, 'when the blunders of the king and his son had created *a new party of dissidents* [my italics], it was natural for them to turn to Simon'.[64] It is necessary to ask, however, whether Simon de Montfort should be considered as the leader of a political party and, if so, how such a party was constructed. It may be suggested, as a first approximation, that a party consisted of a combination of a faction and an affinity, or affinities, the one supplying horizontal and the other vertical relationships.

As a first step let us deal briefly with Simon de Montfort's affinity, to which John Maddicott devotes important pages.[65] Its members provided the basis on which his leadership in the community/territory rested. Some of his followers were recruited from his tenants. One is Thomas de Astley, whose base at Astley in Warwickshire was held of the earls of Warwick. However, he had larger holdings in Leicestershire held from its earls, whom his family had previously served. Thomas first occurs as a charter witness in 1240. He went with Simon to Gascony in 1248 and occurs as his steward. Ralph Basset of Sapcote appeared around the same time and also followed Simon to Gascony. He held his main Leicestershire manor, Sapcote, of the earl. Another, but more substantial, man was Richard de Grey of Codnore in Derbyshire, who held one and a half fees from the earl in Northamptonshire and was lord of Alvington in Leicestershire. He witnessed no charter until 1259, and Maddicott believes that his association with Montfort was due more to his political leanings than to tenure.

However, as Maddicott points out, echoing Daniel Williams, Simon was able to take advantage of the fact that rivals for local supremacy were lacking. Roger de Quincy, earl of Winchester, was more concerned with Scotland, while the earldom of Chester had been divided, leaving its estates in Warwickshire and Leicestershire without strong direction. Moreover, the earl of Warwick had died without heir in 1242.[66] The majority of Simon's followers were not tenants but neighbours. In Maddicott's words, Simon was 'the one remaining magnate who could offer patronage and leadership to the minor baronage and gentry of the *patria*'.[67] From the entourage of Ranulf, earl of Chester, came the Segraves

---

[63] D. A. Carpenter, 'Simon de Montfort: The First Leader of a Political Movement in English History', *History*, 76 (1991), 3–23; republished in Carpenter, *The Reign of Henry III* (London, 1996), 219–39.

[64] Ibid., 222.   [65] Maddicott, *Simon de Montfort*, 59–76.

[66] D. Williams, 'Simon de Montfort and his Adherents', in W. M. Ormrod (ed.), *England in the Thirteenth Century: Proceedings of the 1984 Harlaxton Symposium* (Grantham, 1985), 174–6.

[67] Maddicott, *Simon de Montfort*, 62.

140   POLITICS AND SOCIETY IN MID THIRTEENTH-CENTURY ENGLAND

(Stephen, Gilbert, and Nicholas in succession), of Seagrave in Leicestershire, and the Despensers of Loughborough. Hugh Despenser was later to become the baronial justiciar. Of less weight were the knights from the Quincy lordship who became a major element in Simon's affinity. Thomas Menill, who held part of a fee at Hemington (Leicestershire), was Montfort's steward as early as 1231–2. The two Arnolds du Bois, father and son, of Thorpe Arnold were both prominent in his service. Other members of the Quincy affinity—Saer de Harcourt, Peter le Porter, and Saher of St Andrews—also figure in Montfort's entourage. Through this assimilation Simon de Montfort was able to put down roots. It was a slow process at first. In the 1240s, however, he 'became more firmly fixed in the social landscape of the English midlands'.[68] This association was deepened by Simon's growing interest in Warwickshire, following his custody of Kenilworth Castle in 1244, extended for life in 1248, and facilitated by the death of the last Newburgh earl of Warwick. Into Simon's ken came Peter de Montfort of Beaudesert and Whitchurch, a major local figure related to the Cantilupes, who also went to Gascony with the earl. Warwickshire and Leicestershire constituted 'the homeland' of almost all of Simon de Montfort's leading supporters.[69]

It is worth dwelling for a moment on what his affinity's association with erstwhile lordships actually signified. It was not just a matter of cherry-picking men, or choosing those with whom he was most comfortable. It meant that he was heir, to some degree at least, to the several networks of association which pre-existed. The honour of Coventry, for example, had been a cohesive lordship. Twelve men belonged to Simon's inner circle, but only six to eight at any one time. Roger de Quincy, who was poorer than Simon, had a larger following, as indeed did William de Valence.[70] However, this was not 'the full tally of Montfort's followers'. There was an outer circle, including Anketin de Martival, called Simon's steward in 1261, William Trussell, who once figured as his attorney, and an obscure knight called William Basset. Moreover, as Maddicott puts it, 'Montfort's affinity had a weightiness that was out of proportion to its size'.[71] Indeed, some of his men were substantial figures, minor barons rather than knights: in addition to Gilbert de

---

[68] Ibid., 65.

[69] Only two of his familiars, Maddicott points out, 'stood slightly apart from this connection'. John de la Haye held manors in Lincolnshire, Sussex, and Kent. However, he did hold 1½ fees of the honour of Leicester in Northamptonshire and was married to Margaret, daughter of Richard de Harcourt, a follower of Roger de Quincy. He, too, went to Gascony. Further apart from the mainstream was Richard de Havering, the earl's steward. He first appears in the service of Eleanor in a legal case in 1234 and was bailiff of Newbury and Hungerford in 1241. He witnessed more of Simon's charters than any other man and came to be called 'steward of Leicester' and 'steward of the earl of Leicester'. He clearly had oversight of all of his estates, and appears to have been his general factotum. He probably inherited some land at Havering in Essex and was able to build up an estate centred on Simon's Dorset manor of Shapwick.

[70] Simpson, 'The *Familia* of Roger de Quincy', 107; Ridgeway, 'William de Valence and His *Familiares*', 245.

[71] Maddicott, *Simon de Montfort*, 70.

FACTION, PARTY, AND AFFINITY   141

Seagrave and Hugh Despenser, men like Thomas de Astley, Ralph Basset of Sapcote, and the formidable Peter de Montfort. They were a cohesive group whose cohesion rested not only on their service to the earl but upon neighbourhood and marriage ties. Some of the men received land from Simon.[72] Richard de Havering, for example, gained a small estate in Shapwick, while Peter de Montfort received £40 worth of land at Ilmington with a manor house and another Warwickshire estate. Thomas Menill received the Leicestershire manors of Bagworth and Thornton until £30 of land was found for him elsewhere. Gilbert de Segrave received various properties. There were a few gains from royal favour. John de la Haye received royal license to lease a manor, at Montfort's instance, and Anketin Martival escaped knighthood for a time and the civil obligations associated with his rank. Maddicott suggests that should these men have sought material gain they would have been better to look to Richard of Cornwall or to Peter Savoy. He concludes rather that 'Their fidelity, like that of the bishops, is a sign of the respect and perfection in which this hard and uncompromising man was held and of his ability to identify his men with his own interests. It is some tribute to Montfort's qualities that in these last years the affinity transcended its local background and became instead a party to a cause'.[73]

There are some further observations to be made. Why exactly did Simon recruit such locally powerful men as Peter de Montfort when it came to his own entourage? There are indications that Simon looked at the world in terms of hierarchies, and sought the support of men who were powerful knights or minor barons, that is to say *vavasours*, as 'Bracton' defined them.[74] Such men, moreover, were likely to be warriors like himself, devotees of the chivalric approach to life. A second question is how the aforementioned affinity gave way in 1263 to widespread regional support for the Montfortian cause and to rebellion against the king. Rather than springing up overnight it seems likely that Simon's regional power and influence was already greater than the narrow concept of the magnate affinity would suggest. There were other tenants of the earldom of Chester who were Montfortians. John de Bracebridge, for example, who held at Kingsbury in Warwickshire, as well as Bracebridge in Lincolnshire. He was one of the many men captured at Northampton. The Warwickshire knight, Robert de Hartshill, similarly held of the honour of Chester. He died at Evesham. The great warrior Henry de Hastings, although he held widespread lands, held Allesley near Coventry whose Franciscan Friary, founded by the earl of Chester, housed his family mausoleum. Henry was captured at Evesham. Also of Warwickshire, but holding of the earldom of Warwick, were the Amundevilles, one of whom died at Evesham, and several Ardens, including Thomas, who was captured there. Two Trussells were also killed at Evesham. And then there is William de Birmingham,

---

[72] Ibid., 72–3.   [73] Ibid., 74. And see below, Chapter 8.   [74] See above 89–91.

142 POLITICS AND SOCIETY IN MID THIRTEENTH-CENTURY ENGLAND

who held of the royalist lord of Dudley, Roger de Somery, and also perished at Evesham. The Dudley tenants as a whole seem to have sided with Simon. The configuration of Simon's affinity helps to explain the later formation of a Montfortian 'party'.[75]

Mario Fernandes has studied the motivations of knights in joining the rebel side in four Midland counties:[76] tenurial links, familial connections, service to great lords, grievances and debts, and neighbourhood, the last being the singular most important factor. This is an instructive way of looking at the evidence and one which yields valuable results. There is another approach one might take, however, which puts less emphasis upon individual choices, whether freely made or not, and more on the way that society is articulated, a significant aspect of which being the power and prestige a great lord might wield within local society. The difficulty for the historian in this particular context is that our evidence comes largely from the civil war, or more accurately from post-war courts and commissions which relate to events that transpired during the time of conflict. As we shall see later, cases arising from the civil war have a great deal to impart about the workings of mid-thirteenth-century society. In the meantime, as the work of Fernandes shows clearly, we can see Montfort's lieutenants playing a considerable part in leading local responses. One example is Ralph Basset of Drayton, a Montfortian lieutenant active in Staffordshire.[77] Ralph's Staffordshire estates were at Drayton Basset and Pattingham; he also held at Dunton in Leicestershire and Colston Basset in Nottinghamshire. Complaints about Basset's men are recorded in the Warwickshire Eyre Roll of 1262, demonstrating, as Fernandes puts it, 'both the powerful force that he could attract and the chaos it could bring to the locality'. His position was apparently such that 'his men could flout the law and ignore it'.

Indicative is a poaching case of 1271 which refers back to events in 1263. It was reported that a number of Basset's adherents had been 'customary malefactors of the king's venison' in Cannock Forest, but because they were under their lord's protection no one dared to attach (that is, arrest) them while he was alive. On one poaching expedition Robert de Standon took sixteen beasts and transported them to Ralph Basset's house. Another member of the group was Robert de Knightley. Both men were closely associated with Basset and, as we shall see, probably belonged to his retinue. Hunting and feasting were social activities greatly prized by this sector of society and were important ways of cementing

---

[75] See below 156.

[76] Fernandes, 'The Role of the Midlands Knights'. The counties are Cambridgeshire, Northamptonshire, Staffordshire, and Warwickshire. For the motivations of rebels in the thirteenth century, see also A. Jobson, 'The Rebel's Four Dilemmas in the Long Thirteenth Century', *TCE*, xvi (Woodbridge, 2017), 89–111.

[77] For what follows see Fernandes, 'The Role of the Midlands Knights', 246, 267, 293–4, 305–7. See also John Hunt, 'Families at War: Royalists and Montfortians in the West Midlands', *Midland History*, 22 (1997), 1–34, where further details are given.

FACTION, PARTY, AND AFFINITY 143

social bonds.[78] On 29 May 1264 a large force descended on Philip Marmion's manor of Norbury and caused considerable destruction.[79] This was undoubtedly inspired by Ralph Basset, Marmion's enemy, and among the perpetrators were Robert de Standon, Robert de Knightley, and his brother William. Marmion, a royalist, brought a case against them in October 1268. A similar case was brought by Odo de Hodinet, who claimed that eighteen named men had despoiled his manor of Hodnet during the time of disturbance.[80] Among them was Robert de Standon, as well as three men who are named elsewhere as members of Basset's retinue: Hugh de Weston, Philip de Mitten, and Henry de Verdun. The first two served with Basset defending Stafford Castle against the royalists, while Henry de Verdun was involved in Basset's own depredations, as was Richard de Loges, another of the eighteen who attacked Hodnet. Richard stated in court in 1272 that he had served Basset 'all his life'. It seems that he had led Basset's forces in attacks across Shropshire, that is at Bridgenorth, Radnor, and Shrewsbury.[81] He was taken to court by the royalist Thomas Corbet. Many of the men charged with him were also known adherents of Basset. When his land was given to Corbet after the war, two other men were included in the same mandate: Hugh de Weston and Thomas de Gresley.[82] The latter was no doubt related to Geoffrey de Gresley, rebel, who was one of those who had attacked Philip Marmion's manor of Norbury. These men were members of Basset's own affinity. They were not his tenants. Rather they were all landowners in western Staffordshire.[83] Charter witness lists show that during the mid-thirteenth century Basset and Loges had links with members of the Parles and Birmingham families, tenants of the honour of Dudley.[84] William de Parles of Handsworth and William de Birmingham were both rebels, like other members of the Dudley lordship, and like those of Basset's affinity. William de Birmingham was a substantial knight with, no doubt, his own drawing power. Locality was certainly a dimension in creating Montfortian associations, but underlying networks were important, and the role of middling aristocrats like Ralph Basset of Drayton was vital.

In Warwickshire a number of rebels were associated with Peter de Montfort, lord of Beaudesert, the site of his sizeable castle, and of Wellesbourne and Whitchurch.[85] Like many of the rebels Peter was a tenant of the earl of Warwick but was, of course, in the retinue of Simon de Montfort. Robert Hastang held

[78] G. Wrottesley (ed.), *Pleas of the Forest in Staffordshire, temp. Henry III and Edward I*, Staffordshire Historical Collections V, I (1884), 145–6, 153.

[79] G. Wrottesley (ed.), *Extracts from the Plea Rolls 1272–1294*, Staffordshire Historical Collections VI, I (1885), 169, 173.

[80] Ibid., 49.   [81] Ibid., 57.   [82] *Supplementary Close Rolls, 1244–66*, no. 375.

[83] Hunt, 'Families at War', 14, has a very useful map, showing the locations of these estates.

[84] For Loges see Coss, *Lordship, Knighthood and Locality*, especially Ch. 5. For the honour of Dudley, see J. R. Hunt, *Lordship and the Landscape: A Documentary and Archaeological Study of the Honor of Dudley c.1066–1322*, British Archaeological Reports, 264 (1997).

[85] Fernandes, 'The Role of the Midland Knights', 126–7, 179–81, 184–5.

144 POLITICS AND SOCIETY IN MID THIRTEENTH-CENTURY ENGLAND

Nuthurst, located close to Beaudesert. He and four other rebels—William de Bereford, John de Bracebridge, Thomas de Clinton, and Robert de Verdon—had contacts with Peter. All five, plus the rebel Henry Huband, held estates within five miles of one another. Fernandes suggests that these men belonged to Peter's retinue.

Another county with a high number of rebels was Northamptonshire. Here Fernandes has calculated that of fifty-eight knights he identified in grand assizes in the Northamptonshire Eyre Roll of 1261–2, no less than thirty-nine were rebels (or as he says 'contrariants').[86] Among the substantial figures operating in the county we find not only Henry de Hastings[87] and Stephen de Seagrave,[88] but others of the same ilk, like Ralph Camoys, who held six fees of the abbot of Peterborough,[89] and Baldwin Wake, lord of Blisworth, whose interests stretched northwards into Derbyshire, Nottinghamshire, and Lincolnshire. Both were to be strong Montfortians. There were also substantial knights like Adam de Cockfield, Humphrey de Bassingbourne, Hugh Gubion, and Reginald de Waterville, all of the same persuasion. Nonetheless, Northamptonshire may not have had the same strictly Montfortian underpinning as Warwickshire or Leicestershire. Simon de Montfort, although he had a large number of tenants (twenty-seven), had no demesne in the county. Both Hastings and Seagrave were very young and their lands had been in wardship. They had not had long to make their mark. Others held of the earl of Gloucester, who had Rothwell in demesne, of the earl of Derby, who held Higham Ferrers, of the earl of Winchester, and the abbot of Peterborough, which helps to explain why the county may have had 'reformist' inclinations.

Moreover, in 1258 Ralph Basset of Sapcote became constable of Northampton Castle, while in 1259 Simon de Pattishall, the earl of Gloucester's man, became sheriff. In early April 1263, the first engagement of the war took place, with disastrous consequences for the rebels. The town of Northampton was taken through subterfuge and the garrison surrendered. Fernandes calculates that twenty-two of the rebel knights in his sample took part in the action and were captured.[90] Nine days later, the sheriff of Leicestershire and Warwickshire was ordered to take the lands of eleven men into his hands. In addition to Simon de Montfort the elder and Simon de Montfort the younger, these included Hugh le Despenser, Henry de Hastings, Stephen de Seagrave, Ralph Basset of Sapcote, Ralph Basset of

[86] For the Northamptonshire context, see ibid., 36–122, especially 36–42, 67–8.
[87] Henry held many properties in Wylmersley Hundred, including Yardley Hastings and Great Houghton.
[88] His chief estate in Northamptonshire was Raunds.
[89] See Edmund King, *Peterborough Abbey 1086–1310: A Study in the Land Market* (Cambridge, 1973), 39.
[90] For the battle see R. F. Treharne, 'The Battle of Northampton', *Northamptonshire Past and Present*, 2/2 (1955), 73–90, repr. in E. B. Fryde (ed.), *Simon de Montfort and Baronial Reform: Thirteenth Century Essays* (London, 1986).

FACTION, PARTY, AND AFFINITY   145

Drayton, Peter de Montfort, and Simon the elder's steward, Anketil de Martival.[91] The main contours of the rebel organization seem clear enough.

When it comes to the Montfortian party outside of its heartland it is more difficult to get one's bearings. It is well known that Simon had agents of various sorts,[92] but this does not take us very close to how his 'party' was formed. Our sources do not give sufficient direct insight. However, much can be gained by examining the social and political influence of Gilbert de Clare, earl of Gloucester, more particularly the underpinning of his challenge to the crown in 1267. On 30 June 1267 Simon de Pattishall, bachelor of the earl, received a 'formal remission of the king's rancour and indignation against him' as a result of recent events, a remission extended to William de Plessetis, the earl's knight, Walter de Coleville, another of his bachelors, and Henry de Leyton, his clerk. The next entry on the patent rolls, dated four days later, extended the remission to a longer list of the earl's men.[93] It seems likely that they were all directly connected with Gilbert's occupation of London, although the entries on the roll indicate this specifically in a few cases only. There were fifty-eight men in total, twenty-five of whom were described as knight or bachelor, seventeen as *valetti*, and two as esquires or men-at-arms (*armigeri*).[94] In contemporary parlance the word *valetti* referred to men who were not yet knights but belonged to families that had traditionally produced knights. It also has strong service, including household, connotations.[95] Two men were clerks, one was a bailiff, and one a citizen of London. Others lack designations. Historians have described the 1267 list as the earl's *familia*, or even as a 'partial list' of his household.[96] The term *valetti* is certainly suggestive, as is the presence of clerks, although there seem to be an abnormally large number of the former, and few of the latter. At the same time, however, the list, with its knights, also resembles a magnate retinue, although the numbers involved are excessive compared to the 'affinities' we have described earlier. Was this, then, an 'affinity' on a war footing? In fact, neither institution, household nor retinue, *familia* nor *societas*, seems to quite fit the size and nature of the list. For the moment it would be safer to say that these men constituted some of the earl's 'adherents'.

Nonetheless, it is important to ask what this list actually represents. There are some immediate clues. Of the knights/bachelors, the majority are referred to as 'the earl's'. One of them was Hamo Hautein, described as one of the earl's seneschals in 1268.[97] Hamo had had a prior career. He had been sheriff of Lincoln in

---

[91] TNA, C60/61 m. 4.   [92] See below, Chapter 7.   [93] *CPR 1266–72*, 145–7.

[94] The calendar translated *valetti* anachronistically as yeomen. Moreover, on two occasions the calendar gives 'yeoman' in the singular not the plural, thereby reducing the number of men described as *valetti* to twelve: TNA, C66/85 m. 14d.

[95] See P. Coss, 'Knights, Esquires and the Origins of Social Gradation in England', *TRHS*, 6th ser. v (1995), 155–78, repr. in Coss, *The Origins of the English Gentry* (Cambridge, 2003), 216–38.

[96] Altschul, *A Baronial Family*, 112.   [97] Ibid., 228.

146   POLITICS AND SOCIETY IN MID THIRTEENTH-CENTURY ENGLAND

1259–60, a royal escheator in 1261, and sheriff again in 1262. His interests lay in eastern England. Another of the earl's bachelors was the clearly related Bartholomew Hautein. Yet another was Laurence Whytepens, 'baron of Sandwich'. A few are the earl's tenants. One is John Trayly, who held four fees in Bedfordshire of the earl at 'Hineldon and 'Chelfiston'.[98] Another is perhaps Robert Penifader (or Payforer), who belonged to a family who were tenants of the earl in Kent. These knights and the two men who were esquires of the earl would seem to constitute the earl's military retinue, or at least its core, at this point in time. Other men who are known to have been major tenants and/or known associates of the earl do not, however, figure here. Whatever we have here appears some way from reflecting Gilbert's 'normal' retinue. Some of the knights are not recognizable from the government's feudal records relating to the counties, which suggests that they were stipendiary knights.[99]

What of the *valetti*? They are all described as 'the earl's'. Their activities were evidently not confined to the household. The Buckinghamshire assize roll[100] shows two of them acting for the earl of Gloucester during the civil war. These are Thomas de St Andrew and Thomas de Bragenham. Their activities here resemble those of John de Trayly bachelor, Robert de Noers bachelor, and Henry de Leyton clerk. Thomas de St Andrew, who was admitted to the peace with the rebel Geoffrey de Lucy at Gloucester Castle, was said to have been in the earl's retinue.[101] Thomas of Bragenham,[102] involved in plundering Earl Warenne, was said to be a *valettus* of the earl of Gloucester.[103] In fact, the roll contains a letter from the earl defending Thomas de Bragenham, *wallettus noster*, together with a royal letter accepting this.[104] The same was true in the case of John de Trayly, while Robert de Noers, *bachelor* of the earl of Gloucester, was pardoned in July 1270.[105] Finally, Master Henry de Leyton, enemy of the king, was pardoned as a clerk of the earl of Gloucester in June 1267.[106] The links between the household and local power are also suggested by the presence on the list of Bartholomew de la More, bailiff of the earl.

Particularly interesting are those who appear to have no formal service (or indeed tenurial) connection with the earl, and in most cases no designation whatsoever. They seem a motley crew, ranging from the powerful baron John fitz John

---

[98]   *CR 1261–4*, 288. He also held at Brill and Ludgershall.
[99]   The group beginning with Robert Mainard and ending with Peter de la Bataille looks 'suspicious' in this respect.
[100]   See below, Chapter 7.   [101]   Buckinghamshire special eyre (TNA, Just 1/59), mm. 12, 19.
[102]   For Bradenham?   [103]   Buckinghamshire special eyre (TNA, Just 1/59), m. 12.
[104]   Ibid., m. 8.   [105]   Ibid., m. 4.
[106]   Ibid., m. 12; *CPR 1266–72*, 146. He held land in Linslade (*Hundred Rolls* I, 43). There are other letters on the roll. Geoffrey de Worminghall, plunderer of Roger de Seyton, calls to warrant the earl of Gloucester by letters patent, while Stephen de Neville was with the earl of Gloucester and shows letters patent (m. 19). He is probably related to the John de Neville who is on the 1267 list.

FACTION, PARTY, AND AFFINITY   147

to Robert de Linton, citizen of London, who had functioned in 1264 as a buyer for the royal wardrobe.[107] John fitz John, the son of one of the leaders of 1258, was constable of Windsor Castle for Montfort. An ally of the earl of Gloucester at Lewes and an enemy at Evesham, he later became closely associated with the earl. On 4 June 1267 he headed a six-man delegation (another being Hamo Hautein) who were given safe conduct for a day coming with their households to bring a message from the earl to the king.[108] He was to be a member of the earl's company (*comitiva*) in the Welsh War of 1282.[109] Other adherents include William Bannister of Finchamstead in Berkshire, and his brother Richard.[110] The brothers were members of the Windsor garrison under John fitz John. They had been active in eastern Berkshire where they plundered in the company of Henry, parson of Shottesbrook, the warlike cleric who was also on the list of Gloucester's 1267 adherents. Another was Robert de Hardres, a military tenant of the earl of Gloucester in Kent.[111] There appears to have been a Worcestershire contingent. John de Churchill and his brother, Thomas, of Churchill and Peopleton, were fairly minor landowners.[112] On 9 February 1266 John was in prison when, at the instance of the queen and the countess of Aumale, his wife was given extra land to sustain her as her portion of Churchill and Peopleton was insufficient. Another Worcestershire man, John le Waleys, was probably the tenant of that name who was lord of Shelsay Walsh in 1242–3.[113] Some of these men, like the earl's bachelors, are known to have participated in the civil war. Adam le Despenser, for example, was taken at Northampton, while Ralph fitz Fulk was captured at Kenilworth.[114] Michael Altschul has some instructive comments on the 1267 'adherents'.[115] It includes, he points out, a number of men who had adhered to Simon de Montfort but 'were back with' Gilbert. He names Simon de Pattishall, the Hautein brothers, Roger Taillard, John de Bruton (that is Bretun), Brian de Gouiz, and John de Neville, and suggests that there were 'doubtless many others'.[116] One way or another, however, Gilbert de Clare, earl of Gloucester, had his tentacles well and truly into many of the counties.

Some further light on this can be shown by examining Gilbert de Clare's actions when it came to the seizure of lands after the battle of Evesham. Considerable evidence for this phenomenon is provided by the inquisitions ordered by the

---

[107] *CPR 1258–1266*, 329, 385.   [108] *CPR 1266–1272*, 143.
[109] *CPR 1266–1272*, 236.   [110] *Book of Fees*, 845, 849, and 855.
[111] *CR 1261–4*, 291. He held one knight's fee. See also *Feudal Aids*, iii, 22, 51.
[112] *VCH Worcestershire* iii, 298.
[113] *Book of Fees*, 527, 960. John also shared a half fee in Hampshire via two mesne tenants of the earl of Gloucester: ibid., 766. Richard de Aston, who is associated with these men, may have belonged to the family who held of Thomas Corbett at Aston in Shropshire: ibid., 966, 972.
[114] *CPR 1258–66*, 359, 425, 469, 526.   [115] Altschul, *A Baronial Family*, 113–14.
[116] Ibid., 113.

148 POLITICS AND SOCIETY IN MID THIRTEENTH-CENTURY ENGLAND

crown in 1266.[117] For various reasons they do not provide a complete picture, but, nonetheless, they are immensely informative. They give us an insight into the earl's attitude and motives. In many ways he reacted to the situation like any other magnate, although he did not behave in the rampant land-hungry way that some of the royalists did. As one would expect, the earl acted to intensify his holdings in areas where he had a strong interest. This can be seen in a defensive as much as an aggressive light, as he strove to prevent others gaining footholds in areas which he needed to dominate. We see this clearly when it comes to rebel properties in and around the honour of Clare.[118] The earl's officers and agents can be found seizing property the length and breadth of the country, although naturally in some areas their activities are more prominent than in others.[119] With the exception of William de Stobinton,[120] who was active on the earl's behalf in Kent, none of these agents appear among the 'adherents' of 1267, not even the stewards Walter de la Hyde and Roger de Merlawe,[121] or Hugh Cheval who is described as having other bailiffs under him. These three, at least, were probably members of the earl's *familia*. Hugh le Cheval, however, had been active on his behalf during the civil war. Accused of plundering John Peyvre of £20 worth of goods at Woolstone, Buckinghamshire, it transpired that he was a bailiff of the earl of Gloucester and rendered his account to him.[122] Household officers could certainly be involved in coordinating raids, as reported of Earl Ferrers' chamberlain in the Berkshire roll.[123]

In most cases the property seized by the earl of Gloucester was later handed to the king, and sometimes the record explicitly says that the earl did so himself, implying that this was voluntary. The king generally gave the land to loyal supporters. In some cases, though, the supporter in question was actually the earl, as was the case of the manors of John fitz John. There are, however, other dimensions to the earl's seizures that are particularly significant in the present context. On the one hand we find him seizing manors belonging to his own tenants and to men who were associated with him, as officers, members of his retinue, or, as we shall see, of his 'friendship group'. On the other hand, we find him restoring lands to their original owners, among them, once again, men with whom he can be shown to have had a former association. Neither phenomenon is unique to the earl of Gloucester, but they are prominent

---

[117] They are published in volume one of the *Calendar of Inquisitions Miscellaneous*.

[118] For Essex we have a surviving assize roll which deals with key events in the county during and after the civil war.

[119] Ten stewards and bailiffs are named, together with twelve others plus 'the men of Sir William de Say', acting 'to the use of the earl': *CIM*, i, nos. 610, 629, 632, 662, 656, 666, 658, 711–12, 719, 723, 726, 729, 730, 753, 758, 762, 764–5, 807, 878, 925.

[120] Stubbesdon in the text. [121] Presumably Marlow.

[122] Buckinghamshire special eyre, m. 7. [123] TNA, Just 1/142, mm. 2, 3d.

FACTION, PARTY, AND AFFINITY   149

features of his post-Evesham activity. Among those whose property he seized were the following:

Fig. 1 Seizure of Property by the Earl of Gloucester from his Adherents

---

From: Simon de Pattishull, of a messuage in Little Crawley, Bedfordshire (*CIM*, no. 632).

John fitz John, of land at Addington, Buckinghamshire (634), and at East Tilbury, Essex (659), and of rent at Massingham, Norfolk (816), and at Spelho and Moulton, Northamptonshire (843).

Robert de Merk, of a manor at Dunsmow, Essex (664).

John the Chamberlain, at Sturmer, Essex (665).

Dame Joan de Basinges of London, of manor at Reydon, Essex (666).

John Brito (alias le Breton), of lands at Wormingford and Boxted, Essex (667).

Sir William de Monteneie (that is Montchensey), the earl's knight, of land in Hertfordshire (714).

Sir W. de Criol, of land at Shoulden, Kent (730).

William Marshal, of land at Banham, Norfolk, seized as escheat (William being dead) (818).

Sir Hamo Hautein, property at Oxnead, and land and rent at Hellesdon, Norfolk (828–9).

Sir Walter de Coleville, land and rent in (Barrow) Berkshire and Thistleton, Rutland (856).

John la Warr (that is de la Ware), of manor of Brislington 'of the honour of the earl of Gloucester', Somerset (858).

John de Churchill, of Peopleton, Worcestershire (934).[124]

As the reader will have noticed, these men include some of those in the 1267 list: Sir Simon de Pattishall, Sir John fitz John, Sir Hamo Hautein, Sir Walter de Coleville, John de Churchill, and John le Bretun. We also learn here that the Bartholomew Hautein of the 1267 list was Hamo's brother. Robert de Meysy and John de la Ware were Clare tenants. The others, however, do not seem to have been connected in these ways.[125]

---

[124] He held a carucate of land at Churchill, Worcestershire.

[125] *CR 1261–4*, 286, 288. Another action that was probably connected with these was the seizing of the rent at Stones (Buckinghamshire), held by Sir William de Montchesney (636).

150 POLITICS AND SOCIETY IN MID THIRTEENTH-CENTURY ENGLAND

Fig. 2 Restorations by the Earl of Gloucester to Pre-Evesham Incumbents

Manor of Willingale Doe (*Willingehale Rokele*) in Dunmow hundred, Essex, seized by the earl and later restored to its lord (663).

Manor of Beckenham, Kent, taken by the earl and restored to Richard de la Rokele (727).

Lands of Sir William Breouse at Wickham and Lukedale (in Well), Kent, originally seized by Roger de Leybourne, later taken by the earl of Gloucester and demised to Sir William de Breouse (731).

Land of Sir Robert de Crevequer at Chatham, Kent, seized by the earl himself and later restored to him (736).

Tenements of Thomas Malemayns and Theodore de Stokes in the hundred of Ho, Kent (738).

Land of Sir Geoffrey de Lucy in Newenden, Kent (747).

Manor of Hunton, Kent, belonging to Nicholas de Lenham, seized by Sir William de Say but later taken by the earl of Gloucester and restored to Nicholas 'without fine' (759).

Land of Simon fitz Simon at Brampton, Northamptonshire, seized by the earl's bailiffs 'on account of the war', and later restored to him (835).

Manor of Shutford, Oxfordshire, seized by the earl's bailiffs with the goods found there which had belonged to Sir William de Birmingham, who was killed at Evesham. The earl restored the manor to Maud de Gatecombe 'by way of dower', and she received the Michaelmas rent (852).

As regards the restoring of lands to their pre-Evesham incumbents, however, we find that only Geoffrey de Lucy is readily identifiable as a tenant.[126] Clearly, we need to take care how we interpret these events. There are indications that the man who seized the land sometimes levied a fine for restoring it. In the case of Nicholas de Lenham noted above, we are explicitly told that no fine was levied. The implication is that they often were. In Buckinghamshire, for example, John Giffard seized the land of Geoffrey le Mortimer who 'made fine' with him.[127] There were occasions for private initiative. We learn of a 'certain cook who was with the earl' who seized the land in Kent late of Thomas de Suthese until his wife and his heirs made a fine of eight seams of wheat.[128] Moreover, the timing of restorations was significant. If it were after Michaelmas, it is likely that the disseisor,

---

[126] *CR 1261–4*, 285. [127] *CIM*, no. 727.

[128] *CIM*, no. 719. In Warwickshire we find that James de Audley seized the land of Ralph de Audley of Hardwick, imprisoned him, and carried off his goods to the value of thirty marks. The inquisition tells us that James still has him in prison and demands a ransom of thirty marks: no. 855.

FACTION, PARTY, AND AFFINITY   151

whatever his actions later, had helped himself to the autumn rents. In many cases it is made clear that the earl restored the property before this; but not always. The manor of Beckenham, Kent, which the earl took from Richard de la Rokebi, was not restored until after Michaelmas.[129] Nonetheless, it does look to be the case that the earl was exercising his patronage for favoured individuals.

We also see the earl reacting to seizures by others. An interesting case occurred at Blackmanstowe, Kent, with regard to the property belonging to Thomas de Quarines. It was seized by Guncelin de Badlesmere, a knight of William de Valence, who kept it for only eight days when it was seized by the earl of Gloucester's men. However, Guncelin later restored it to Thomas de Quarines, who, says the inquisition, was not a rebel.[130] In another case, this time in Middlesex, Maurice de Berkeley seized the manor of Robert de Crevequer at Halliford, 'whereupon' the earl of Gloucester took the manor 'and still holds it'.[131] There are occasions when the earl behaved less altruistically. John 'called le Moyne' had the manor of Westcliff, Kent, on lease from the monks of Canterbury. Seisin was taken on behalf of the earl of Gloucester, the corn threshed and sold.[132] There are also occasions when the earl passed the property on to someone else. For example, the land of John de St Helens at Wittenham, Berkshire, was passed on by the earl to Aimery de St Amand.[133] In Suffolk the earl seized the manor of Lidgate, Suffolk, which had belonged to Sir Henry de Hastings, and gave it to his brother, Sir Thomas de Clare.[134]

The earl was also prepared to take preventative action. For example, the earl's bailiffs would not allow seisin to be taken of the land of his man, Simon de Pattishall, at Nailsea, Suffolk. Similarly, when the earl claimed the land of the late rebel William Marshal at Banham in Norfolk, the earl's servant, John the Clerk, would not allow it to be extended. Again, when the earl seized Sir Henry de Hastings' manor of Lidgate, Kent, and gave it to his brother Thomas, the jurors were prevented from making any further extent.[135] A variety of local political considerations were involved, then, when it came to the seizure of land, but when all is said and done it does look as though the earl of Gloucester was fully prepared

---

[129] *CIM*, no. 727. The *Chancery Rolls* contain further interventions, including the acquiring of pardons, by the earl. The men who benefitted were: Richard de Hanred, Robert de Munteny, 'brother of the sometime Arnold de Munteny, who was taken with the king's enemies at Northampton', Richard de Hemington, Thomas Gulafre, Geoffrey de Sancto Leodegario, William Harangod, William de Tracy, William de Appleford knight of the earl, Robert de la More, the earl's *valettus*, Geoffrey Chaumpeneys, of his household (in 1270), Richard le Brun, of his household (in 1272), Geoffrey de Dunham, Thomas de Poulton, and [Nicholas] de Gimeges: *CPR 1258–66; CR 1264–8*.

[130] *CIM*, no. 762.

[131] *CIM* no. 809. There were other interventions. Sir William de Aldrefeld seized the land of Sir Nicholas de Cres whom he led to Tonbridge Castle where he was detained until released after an enquiry ordered by the earl of Gloucester. The inquisition confirms that he did not bear arms against the king and he was re-seised (753).

[132] *CIM*, no. 753.   [133] *CIM*, no. 625.   [134] *CIM*, no. 895.

[135] *CIM*, nos. 818, 888, 895.

152 POLITICS AND SOCIETY IN MID THIRTEENTH-CENTURY ENGLAND

to extend his help to those whom he considered to be in one way or another his 'clients'.

Before moving on from these sources it is worth pointing out that they sometimes allow us an insight into the sub-retinues of Montfortians who were active militarily on Simon's behalf within the counties. Sir Brian de Gouiz is a case in point. As we have seen, some of the earl of Gloucester's 'adherents' were clearly quite minor figures. This is also true of members of sub-retinues. Brian de Gouiz held the manor of Kingsdon in Somerset worth £30 per annum. He held it of William de 'Gowyz', who was presumably a relative. He regained seisin before 29 August 1265, through the action of the earl of Gloucester and Sir John Giffard.[136] He was active in the county of Somerset, we are told, because the earl of Leicester had made him a knight.[137] He and Adam Gurdon are named respectively as keepers of the castles of Sherborne (Dorset) and Dunster and both are described as 'open rebels'.[138] He also had a hide of land at Tatton (Dorset) which the earl took into his own hands. The following members of his retinue are named:

Fig. 3 Members of the Sub-Retinue of Brian de Gouiz

Sir William de Ortiary, holding one carucate in Lopen, Somerset, as his wife's dower, worth £10 per annum. His land was restored to him by the bailiffs of Sir John Giffard.

William de Lyt, holding one carucate at Tuckscary, Somerset, worth 40s. per annum.

John le Norreys, holding one carucate at Bridgehampton, Somerset.

Richard de Gouiz, Brian's son.

William Haket, who was 'in the company of Sir Brian', holding a virgate in Hescombe, Somerset.

Peter le Rus of Preston, holding two carucates at Preston, Somerset, worth 60s. per annum.

Andrew de Tatton, who 'followed Brian as his servant' (or serjeant), held land in Tatton, Dorset, in right of his wife, worth ½ mark per annum. (Land in Tatton was taken into the hands of the earl of Gloucester.)

Philip la War, holding a virgate in West Corscombe, Dorset, worth 4s. per annum.

Richard de Gussich, holding a half carucate in Broughton, Hampshire, worth 40s.[139]

---

[136] *CIM*, no. 877.   [137] *CIM*, no. 871.

[138] *CIM*, no. 653. Adam Gurdon's retinue can also be constructed from the inquisitions.

[139] *CIM*, nos. 656, 700, 872, 875, 877.

FACTION, PARTY, AND AFFINITY 153

None of these men held of the earl or indeed of the Gouiz family. They may of course have held additional property, but on the face of it they seem to be of little significance. We have an insight into how some minor individuals participated in the Montfortian cause.

Further understanding of Gilbert de Clare's wider associations is provided by entries in the assize roll for Essex in 1268. Robert de Merk brought a case against William de Leybourne, who had received his lands from the king after the disorder in the realm and which were to be restored according to the Dictum of Kenilworth. Robert's attorney said that redemption ought not to apply here because although Robert had been at the battle of Lewes and elsewhere and against the king, he had always been an adherent of the earl of Gloucester and the king had pardoned the earl and all his adherents. His attorney argued that he did not need to redeem his lands because he was both an adherent and of the *amicisia* of the earl.[140] A man, then, may be an adherent (*adherens, adherens se*) of the earl and/or a member of his *amicitia*, translatable perhaps as something like 'friendship group'. This suggests an association that was real, but informal not institutional. A 'friendship group' is evidently not the same as a retinue. The Buckinghamshire special eyre roll tells us that Thomas de St Andrew, who was admitted to the peace with the rebel Geoffrey de Lucy at Gloucester Castle, was of the friendship (*amicitia*) of the earl of Gloucester in London and in the society (*societate*), that is retinue, of the earl.[141] This, I suggest, shows both the distinction between a retinue (*societas*) and a 'friendship group' while at the same time pointing to their interpenetration.

The Merk case does not stand alone. It is followed by that of Bartholomew Bigod. Bartholomew brought a case against John de Mandeville that he and others on 12 March 1264 came to his manor of Alveriston in the parish of Dunmow and despoiled it to the value of £1,000. John de Mandeville, through his attorney, proffered a charter of the earl of Gloucester saying that he was of the earl's *amicissia* and an adherent in the time of disorder and did not need to respond, for the reason given above. The attorney was then questioned by the justice as to whether this *amiciscia* was really the case. He replied that he did not want to acknowledge this precisely and had nothing more to say. Bartholomew was awarded damages and John was in mercy.[142] The concept of *amicitia* and its implications in this context appear to have been well understood in the courts.

---

[140] Hunter, *Rotuli Selecti*, 124. A day was given to the parties at Ipswich for judgement to be heard.
[141] TNA, Just 1/59, mm. 12, 19.
[142] Et Hunter, *Rotuli Selecti*, 124 attorn' requisitus per justic' 'si factum predictum confiteri voluerit sicut se de amiciscia predicti com' advocavit per quam inde quietus esse debebat & Hunter, *Rotuli Selecti*, 124 attornat' dicit precise quod factum illum confiteri nolebat nec aliquid aliud inde respondere. He was pardoned the amercement at the instance of Lord Edward, and paid a fine of two marks to Bartholomew: Hunter, *Rotuli Selecti*, 124.

154 POLITICS AND SOCIETY IN MID THIRTEENTH-CENTURY ENGLAND

A case on the Northamptonshire assize roll of the same year deepens our understanding of what is meant here. John de Warenne was the guardian (*custos*) of Isabel, daughter and heir of Stephen de Ashby and heir of David de Ashby, whose lands and tenements had been given to Imbert Guy. Warenne sought to redeem them for Isabel, presumably because he had been awarded her wardship and marriage.[143] Imbert, a Poitevin, could not be found, but, given that he had demised the property to Alan la Zouche, the court summoned the latter. When the issue was finally heard, John de Warenne brought letters of the king witnessing that Stephen and David had been helpers (*adjutores*) of the earl of Gloucester when the latter had aided the king against his enemies and therefore shared in his pardon. He petitioned that consequently Isabel's property should be restored to her. Alan la Zouche immediately countered with his own royal letters testifying that although David de Ashby did not do anything *against* the earl, he did not assist or adhere to him[144] wherefore Isabel should redeem the lands under the Dictum. Because one set of royal letters witnessed that David and Stephen were of the earls' *amicitia* and another set said the opposite, the matter was to be brought before the king. The clear implication, however, is that members of a great lord's 'friendship group' were to aid him when called upon, that is to say the relationship was reciprocal.

Faction, Party, and Affinity

In this context it is difficult not to think of K. B. McFarlane's essay on 'bastard feudalism' and in particular his finding that a great lord's indentured retinue was only 'the hard core' of his affinity, and that many others (he calls them 'a swarm of hangers-on') were not bound to do him exclusive service but were in receipt of his bounty.[145] Historians of the thirteenth century have borrowed the concept of affinity but have tended to apply it only to this hardcore, while historians of later times have used it rather differently. G. A. Holmes, referring to the same phenomenon, wrote of 'a sea of varying relationships,'[146] while others have seen an affinity as a series of concentric circles.[147] Christine Carpenter in her analysis of the actual workings of an affinity spoke of the inner and outer circles, with some members of the latter apparently holding no office, and 'a more indefinite circle of well-wishers and personal connections, whose existence can usually only

---

[143] Hunter, *Rotuli Selecti*, 150–1.
[144] The roll is slightly defective at this point.
[145] K. B. McFarlane, 'Bastard Feudalism', in G. L. Harriss (ed.), *England in the Fifteenth Century: Collected Essays* (London, 1981), 32. Reprinted from *BIHR*, 20 (1945), 161–80.
[146] G. A. Holmes, *The Estates of the Higher Nobility in Fourteenth-Century England* (Cambridge, 1957), 79.
[147] See Harriss, *England in the Fifteenth Century*, xi.

FACTION, PARTY, AND AFFINITY   155

be inferred'. The outer circles included minor estate officials and others receiving annuities but performing no office, and beyond them 'a more indefinite circle of well-wishers and personal connections, whose existence can usually only be inferred ... but is sometimes confirmed by their appearance as co-defendants or fellow-plaintiffs with the earl'.[148] These observations have some significance, it would seem, in relation to the thirteenth century. A further dimension is supplied by an important essay by Scott L. Waugh showing in some detail that the reign of Henry III saw the beginnings of contractual arrangements between lords and clients with an action of annuity added to Common Law legal remedies by the 1240s.[149] The majority of ensuing cases indicate that contracts tended to be with administrators and legal experts as lords recruited the necessary manpower to administer their estates, and indeed household, as a consequence of the revolution in estate management.[150] At this point in time, they were not as yet recruiting warriors or lesser landowners as such in this way. Nonetheless, the later evidence highlights the same general phenomenon, that is, the need by great lords to dominate particular areas and to have 'friends' within the lesser aristocracy, and the need among lesser men to belong to a wider affinity, to serve, and to be protected. *Mutatis mutandis*, there does seem evidence to suppose the existence of wider affinities, at least in some instances, during the thirteenth century.

To return, after this rather long excursus, to the Montfortian 'party', the concept of a 'friendship group' helps us to understand how it was articulated outside of its heartland. The party may be said to have three components. The first is the 'swollen' affinity, much—but not all of it—arising out of the heartlands themselves. This affinity extends downwards by means of service at several levels, seen not only in the case of henchmen like Ralph Basset of Drayton and Peter de Montfort, but also in the sub-retinue of Brian de Gouiz. It also incorporates associations by kin and by neighbourhood. The second component is the faction. Here we can examine its core by looking at the 'lords' who received an individual summons to the parliament of January 1265. Leaving aside the few earls who were summoned—Gloucester, Norfolk, Oxford, and Derby—we are left with eighteen men. Among them were many we have already met in this chapter: Ralph de Camoys, Hugh le Despenser, Nicholas de Segrave, Ralph Basset of Drayton, Ralph Basset of Sapcote, and Henry de Hastings. What is striking is that most of the others are men of similar station and proclivity to these, but from various parts of the country. The faction is similar to Montfort's own narrow 'affinity' in the prevalence of warlike members of the intermediate aristocracy, men with

[148] Christine Carpenter, 'The Beauchamp Affinity: A Study of Bastard Feudalism at Work', *EHR*, 95 (1980), 514–32, at 515–16.
[149] Scott L. Waugh, 'Tenure to Contract: Lordship and Clientage in Thirteenth-Century England', *EHR*, 101 (1986), 811–39.
[150] For this phenomenon, see above 70.

156 POLITICS AND SOCIETY IN MID THIRTEENTH-CENTURY ENGLAND

strong regional presence.[151] But these two components will not account for the ninety-six men (excepting his son Simon junior) who were on the Montfortian side at the battle of Northampton. And then there are the agents, 'procurers', fund raisers, and members of sub-retinues who are much in evidence on the Montfortian side in the post-war records. The evidence suggests a considerable organization at work and orchestration of their activities. There is, then, a third component: a network, which we may call a 'friendship group', a component of a wider affinity, and which again both involves important men and drills down quite deeply into the counties. Although these components are distinct both analytically and indeed in origin, they may be said to have merged to form a 'party' and to provide much of the manpower that sustained Montfort's provincial strength.

There are, of course, further components to the Montfortian party—from within the clergy and in the towns—but these can be more fruitfully analysed when we come to consider the details of the civil war in the following chapter. In the meantime, the foregoing analysis of faction, party, affinity, and 'friendship group' has reinforced the interpretation of the revolt and the subsequent rebellion as fundamentally aristocratic in inspiration.

Politics and Society in Mid Thirteenth-Century England: The Troubled Realm. Peter Coss, Oxford University Press.
© Peter Coss 2024. DOI: 10.1093/9780198924319.003.0006

---

[151] The others are: Roger de St John, John fitz John, William de Montchesney, John de Vescy, Geoffrey de Lucy, Robert de Ros, John d'Eyvill, Adam de Newmarket, Walter de Coleville, William Marmion, Roger Bertram, and Gilbert de Gaunt. Robert de Ros of Wark, Roger Bertram of Mitford, and John de Vescy of Alnwick were prominent Monfortians in the far north. See Fergus Oakes, 'The Barons' War in the North of England, 1264–5', in Jobson (ed.), *Baronial Reform and Revolution 1258–1267*, 199–217. John d'Eyville was a Yorkshire knight, with estates at Egmanton, Kilburn, and Adlingfleet.

7

Civil War

The civil war was a power struggle between the Montfortian party on the one hand and the royal family and its supporters on the other. For Montfort and his adherents, the measures to control the king, encapsulated in the Provisions of Oxford, were the essence of the matter. For the royalists the objective was to break open the straitjacket within which the baronial opponents strove persistently to confine the king and to return to the status quo ante. It was manifestly not about the implementation of the detailed legal and administrative reforms of the Provisions of Westminster, even if the king reaffirmed them twice in 1263 in an effort to secure support.[1] Faction played an important role in the events that led up to the armed struggle, as indeed it was to do again in determining the course of the war. The struggle between Simon de Montfort and the king had numerous dimensions. On the diplomatic side it involved, among others, the popes and their agents and the French royal family. In terms of national politics, it involved innumerable negotiations, with the advantage switching from one side to another. Armed action, when it occurred, involved despoliation and sieges, the normal constituents of medieval warfare, rather than pitched battles. There were occasional surrenders, spectacularly the so-called Battle of Northampton in April 1264, when the town was taken by royalists, the garrison surrendered, and ninety Montfortians were taken prisoner. The two major battles were, of course, at Lewes in May 1264, when Montfort's (flawed) triumph put power firmly in his hands, and the 'murder of Evesham' on 4 August 1265, where he met his death.

The Genesis of the War

Before dealing with the war in more detail, however, it is necessary to establish the national context.[2] Adrian Jobson characterizes the period from November 1261 to April 1263, that is, from the drawing up of the Treaty of Kingston to the revolt of 'the marchers', as a period of uneasy truce. The resurgence of royal power was accompanied by the re-emergence of many of Henry's normative policies.

---

[1] In January and again in June.
[2] The narrative history is handled very effectively by Jobson, *First English Revolution*, Chs. 4–5. See also Maddicott's deeply insightful *Simon de Montfort*, and Treharne, *The Baronial Plan of Reform*. Jobson also draws on Howell, *Eleanor of Provence*, and Marc Morris, *A Great and Terrible King: Edward I and the Forging of Britain* (London, 2008).

158 POLITICS AND SOCIETY IN MID THIRTEENTH-CENTURY ENGLAND

It also saw the renewed prominence of the Savoyard faction, most notably the queen herself, Peter of Savoy, Eubulo de Montibus, now steward of the king's household, and Imbert de Montferrand, royal chamberlain. The Savoyards now supplanted the Poitevins as the baronial movement's 'bogeymen'.[3] Not surprisingly, they turned their fire on their rivals for influence over Lord Edward: Roger Leybourne and 'the marcher lords'. To the queen these had been the cause of Edward's alienation, as well as being responsible for his extravagant lifestyle, with his tournaments and his largesse to his followers. In the autumn of 1261, his parents set up an inquiry into his financial situation. The result was a foregone conclusion. The blame lay with Edward's retinue, most especially with Leybourne, the chief culprit. He was ordered to repay £1,820.[4] Roger Clifford was another among those targeted. Edward's erstwhile companions were now deprived of his patronage. Having already lost their offices in May 1260, many of these men were seething with resentment.

There is little doubt that Montfort was intent on sowing distrust. Hence his sudden appearance at the Michaelmas parliament of 1262 brandishing a papal bull confirming the Provisions of Oxford and annulling the hostile bulls, and his sudden disappearance thereafter. The episode is related solely by the Kentish chronicler, but it has the ring of truth about it.[5] He adds, most presciently, that Simon quietly retired to France leaving behind him many 'associates and supporters' to forward his business.[6] It is likely, then, that he was already planning his return to prominence both diplomatically and in the provinces. The flash point, however, was the marches where Roger Mortimer and John fitz Alan were already engaged in action with Llewelyn ap Gruffydd, notwithstanding the existing truce between the Welsh prince and the king. Welsh tenants, beginning with those of Roger Mortimer, were soon in revolt and Llewelyn was pushing deep into Herefordshire. By the end of 1262 the situation was desperate, and worse was to follow. Roger Leybourne began ravaging in Kent, while it had become clear that a major campaign now needed to be fought against the Welsh. Into this situation stepped Simon de Montfort, around 25 April 1263. According to the chronicler of Merton Priory, he had been invited back by Lord Edward's disgruntled former followers.[7] Whether this was strictly true or not, Simon clearly assumed leadership of the 'reform movement'. It was a fateful decision, but one he had undoubtedly been preparing for.

The members of what was in effect a 'coalition' met first at Oxford, appropriately, and were joined by other supporters of reform, including the new earl of

---

[3] Jobson, *First English Revolution*, 77.
[4] Edward also revoked his grant to Leybourne of Eltham in Kent.
[5] Maddicott, *Simon de Montfort*, 219. The chronicle is a continuation of Gervase of Canterbury: *The Historical Works of Gervase of Canterbury*, ed. W. Stubbs, 2 vols., Rolls Series (London, 1879–80), ii, 217.
[6] ... *multos post ipsum in Anglia relinquens complices et fautores ad propositum suum prosequendum.*
[7] Maddicott, *Simon de Montfort*, 223; *Flores Historiarum* ii, 479.

CIVIL WAR 159

Gloucester, Gilbert de Clare. Here they demanded that the king adhere to the Provisions. The king remained defiant. Meanwhile Lord Edward launched a campaign in Wales. It was a failure, not least because the 'marchers' refused to fight with Edward's foreign mercenaries, unsurprisingly given that they had been replaced in his service. The king now marshalled for a larger campaign. His domestic opponents, however, had other ideas. On 7 June the forces of John Giffard, Roger de Vaux, Roger Clifford, and Roger Leybourne attacked Hereford, their target being its Savoyard bishop, Peter of Aigueblanche. Violating sanctuary, they placed him in Clifford's castle at Eardisley. Robert Walerand's castle at Kilpeck was seized and all of the major towns along the line of the River Severn fell to them. It was all clearly planned, and very probably orchestrated by Simon de Montfort at Kenilworth. Despite the king taking various preventative actions elsewhere, this turned into a wider rebellion. The lands of prominent royalists were ravaged. They included those of the bishop of Norwich, Simon de Walton, who took sanctuary at Bury St Edmunds,[8] John Mansel, who had played a leading part in the papal absolution, Robert Walerand, whose manors in fifteen counties were occupied, Peter of Savoy, and Geoffrey de Langley, whose most recent activities had included being one of the auditors of Edward's accounts. The spoliation was celebrated in a contemporary ballad in French, surviving sadly in a fragmentary state and known as *The Song of the Barons*.[9] The men praised for their action, in addition to Montfort himself, are the earl of Warenne, Sir John Giffard, Sir John D'Eyville, Sir Roger Leybourne, and Sir Roger Clifford. The last named was praised for his attack on Langley, in which every item of property was taken away: 'Cursed be he who complains of it (*Deheis eit que l'en pleine*)'.[10] A letter from the northern royalist Robert de Neville requested help.[11] The king retreated to the Tower of London, and negotiations followed. Three bishops drew up a 'form of peace' (the *Forma Pacis*). In London, short of money with which to fight, Edward raided the New Temple and stole its treasure. This provoked a rising in the capital and a new regime there, led by its mayor Thomas fitz Thomas. Meanwhile, Montfort moved into Kent, taking the Cinque Ports and Canterbury, and bringing more knights under his banner. Henry finally gave in to the demands.

Simon de Montfort was now in control. Among his actions were appointments to offices and to castles, and rewards for his supporters. Roger Leybourne now

---

[8] The bishop had been singled out partly at least because he had been involved in the papal bulls absolving prelates and magnates from their oaths to the Provisions: Jobson, *First English Revolution*, 89.

[9] *Thomas Wright's Political Songs of England*, new edn. introduced by Peter Coss (*RHS*, Cambridge, 1996), 59–63.

[10] The same was done to Matthew Bezil. Other named victims were the bishop of Hereford, the bishop of Norwich—'the shepherd who devours his own sheep'—and Sir John de Grey.

[11] *Royal Letters* ii, no. 612; *Diplomatic Documents Preserved in the Public Record Office* i, ed. P. Chaplais (HMSO, 1964), no. 387.

160 POLITICS AND SOCIETY IN MID THIRTEENTH-CENTURY ENGLAND

became one of the king's household stewards. Gilbert de Clare gained control of his entire inheritance, which the king had been denying him.[12] Peter de Montfort was given custody of John Mansel's manor and castle of Sedgewick, Surrey, while the rest of Mansel's extensive estates were granted to Montfort's younger son, Simon.[13] To keep order in the counties, keepers of the peace (*custodes pacis*) were appointed to act alongside the sheriffs.[14] All those who opposed the Provisions were to be considered 'mortal enemies'.[15]

Once the king had given in, however, things began to move in another direction. As Jobson puts it, 'the fragile ties of self-interest holding the factions together quickly began to unravel'.[16] The 'marchers', in particular, who had no genuine commitment to the Provisions and had achieved their objectives—undermining the Savoyard faction and ridding the country of Edward's foreign knights—were soon reconciled with the crown. By August, Roger Clifford, Roger Leybourne, Hamo Lestrange, and others were back with Edward, agreeing 'to be his friends in all his affairs'.[17] Others changed sides, including Henry of Almain, John de Warenne, and the earl of Norfolk, with Richard of Cornwall now, once again, beside his brother. The 'judicious use of royal patronage' was also a factor, with Leybourne, for example, regaining Elham.[18] Much of the attention now switched to France, from where both parties hoped for succour. They agreed to put their quarrel to the arbitration of King Louis IX at Amiens on 8 January 1264. Meanwhile Queen Eleanor was busy assembling a mercenary army across the Channel. Before setting out for France Henry promised to abide by both sets of Provisions and appointed (on 24 December) new keepers in twenty-two counties. Both parties presented their cases at Amiens, although Simon himself had been unable to travel, having broken his leg. When the French king reached his decision, on 23 January 1264, it was for Henry. Needless to say, this was unacceptable to Montfort and the Montfortians, and a clash of arms seemed almost inevitable. The war began officially when the king raised his standard at Oxford on 3 April. In reality the country had been subject to armed violence since the middle of 1263. The 'Battle of Northampton' opened hostilities two to three days later. On 14 May 1264, Simon de Montfort won his great victory at Lewes.[19] A second period of intense spoliation now followed, with wholesale attacks upon, and confiscation of, royalists' lands. As to who was responsible for the drift to civil war, it seems that the honours should probably be shared. On the one hand, the royal

---

[12] On 8 July the king had finally given him his English lands for a fine of £1,000. In August he gained his lands in Wales: *CFR 1262–3*, no. 727; Altschul, *A Baronial Family*, 99–100.

[13] *CPR 1258–66*, 269, 273.   [14] Ibid., 271–2.

[15] *Ann. Mon.* iii (Annals of Dunstable), 221.   [16] Jobson, *First English Revolution*, 100.

[17] Maddicott, *Simon de Montfort*, 244.

[18] Jobson, *First English Revolution*, 102; *CPR 1258–66*, 278; Ann. Mon. iii (Annals of Dunstable), 225.

[19] For the battle see, in particular, D. Carpenter, *The Battles of Lewes and Evesham, 1264/5* (Keele, 1987).

CIVIL WAR 161

family had shown itself ever ready to employ foreign mercenary forces to subdue their subjects. On the other hand, 'the marchers' lived in a world where military action was second nature and Simon de Montfort was always inclined to use force in support of a cause.

The 'marchers' belonged to a warrior caste, and subscribed to the chivalric code where prowess, a mixture of military skill and courage, was highly prized. The concept of honour made them swift to anger, while their idea of politics revolved around personal and dynastic self-interest. To maintain the integrity of their estates was a minimum requirement, to extend them optimal. An entrée into their mode of thought is provided by the romance of Fulk fitz Warin.[20] These men were fierce and formidable, some of them ferocious. But these qualities were not confined to 'the marchers'. They were shared by many of the leading Montfortians. Men like John D'Eyville, the Montfortian lieutenant in the north who later led the 'Disinherited' at Ely, and Henry de Hastings, who was to hold out for so long at Kenilworth, were of the same mould.[21] Henry sent a royal messenger back whence he came minus his hands.[22] John fitz John, who led the attack on the Jews in London in 1264, is said to have strangled Kok son of Abraham, with his bare hands.[23] The priorities of Henry de Hastings are perhaps shown in the tableau which remained until the dissolution of the monasteries in the chapel he founded at Greyfriars, Coventry. Buried close to him was Robert de Shottesbrook, described as 'most valiant esquire and sometime standard-bearer of the same Henry and afterwards his steward'.[24] This seems to encapsulate Henry's values.

It is hardly surprising that the major events of the civil war, as related by the chronicles, were dominated by the nobility. There are echoes of romance literature, especially in the rhyming chronicle written in English by Robert of Gloucester, with its emphasis upon aristocratic *mores*.[25] It is worth looking closely at this chronicle in order to grasp something of the nature and spirit of the war as seen from the perspective of one who was sympathetic to the aristocratic perception and experience of the world. Since the seventeenth century there has been an assumption that Robert was a monk at St Peter's, Gloucester. The indirect evidence for this is not convincing, and it seems on balance unlikely. It is more probable that he was a secular clerk, possibly connected to the knight Warin de

[20] *Fouke Le Fitz Waryn*, ed. E. J. Hathaway et al., Anglo-Norman Text Society (Oxford, 1975).

[21] For D'Eyville see Oscar De Ville, 'Deyville [Daiville], Sir John de', *ODNB* 16, 11–12, and O. De Ville, 'John Deyville: A Neglected Rebel', *Northern History*, 34 (1988), 17–40.

[22] P. Coss, *The Foundations of Gentry Life: The Multons of Frampton and their World, 1270–1370* (Oxford, 2010), 156.

[23] D. A. Carpenter, 'John, Sir, *fitz* John, Baronial Leader', *ODNB* 30, 192–3.

[24] *Robertus de Shotesbroke armiger strenuissimus, & ejusdem domini Henrici quondam vexillator, et postea Senescallus*: W. Dugdale, *The Antiquities of Warwickshire*, 2 vols, revised by W. Thomas (London, 1730), i, 182–3; Coss, *Foundations of Gentry Life*, 156.

[25] *The Metrical Chronicle of Robert of Gloucester*, ed. W. A. Wright, 2 vols., Rolls Series (London, 1887).

162   POLITICS AND SOCIETY IN MID THIRTEENTH-CENTURY ENGLAND

Bassingbourne.[26] Bassingbourne is heavily praised, and his role unduly emphasized in the text. But the author could also have been a layman. Lay society in the localities was more literate and more engaged with literature than historians have previously thought.[27] Although the existing text appears to be late thirteenth century, and was written before King Louis IX was canonized in 1297, the section on the civil war was clearly contemporary. Robert tells us that the darkening of the world at the time of the battle of Evesham was experienced for thirty miles around and that he was 'sore afraid'. The content has a strong regional bias with a great deal of local colour and incident. The struggle for the city and castle of Gloucester is told in detail, and the author has topographical knowledge of the city itself.[28] Its language also reflects the area.

The chronicle is secular in tone and content. Some of its episodes seem to be straight out of romance. Among the most famous are two involving the Lord Edward. One was the attempt to rescue Edward from captivity at Wallingford.[29] At the queen's instigation a group of royalist knights who were gathered at Bristol set out to rescue him and valiantly breached the outer walls, only to be confronted by the garrison who threatened to throw him out from a mangonel. Edward himself appeared on the battlements, instructing them to retreat 'other he was ded'. Four of the knights are named, including Warin de Bassingbourne. Warin is described in the text as a 'man of gret los', that is, renown. When Simon de Montfort heard of this, he lodged his royal prisoners more securely at Kenilworth. From here, however, Edward escaped by a ruse. Trading on Simon de Montfort's 'reverence' for him, he gained permission to leave the town in company (presumably under a lax guard) to try the mettle of some horses. Managing to tire several out before taking the strongest, he then fled and found his way to Roger Mortimer's stronghold at Wigmore.[30]

A more local episode was the contest between the baronial 'warden' and the recently appointed royalist sheriff of Gloucester in the autumn of 1261.[31] The appointment of Matthias Bezil (here Sir Maci de Besile) as both sheriff and constable was against the Provisions (the *pourveance*), as Robert reminds us, and was mirrored in other counties. The barons 'through common counsel' appointed 'a knight of the country' called Sir William Tracy, who 'put out' Sir Maci. However, this was not the end of the matter. William was holding the shire court on a Monday when Sir Maci came armed 'with power sent from the [royal] court'.

---

[26] As suggested by Antonia Gransden in her *Historical Writing in England c.550 to c.1307* (London, 1974), 432–38, where there is a full discussion of the chronicle. Curiously, having raised the possibility of a Bassingbourne connection, Gransden dismisses it in favour of Robert being a monk.

[27] For a survey of literacy and the literature in the local secular world, see Coss, *Foundations of Gentry Life*, Chs. 11–12.

[28] He was also clearly acquainted with Oxford, which may reinforce the impression that he was a clerk.

[29] *Metrical Chronicle*, lines 11,416–41.   [30] Ibid., lines 11,546–68.

[31] For the context, see above Chapter 5.

CIVIL WAR   163

While the county court was sitting, he and his men arrived armed at the end of town. With drawn swords and maces they cleared their way until they got to the dais. They seized William by the top of the head and threw him to the ground. They then dragged him into the street, giving him many strong blows as they went, slung him into a puddle, and drove their horses over him. They did the same to a squire. They then took William through the town to the castle and flung him into prison.[32] It was a violent demonstration, intended to cause the maximum humiliation. The barons were later to take their revenge. When they took Gloucester, they led Bezil away to the castle at Eardisley and held him prisoner with his fellow alien, the bishop of Hereford.

A participant in this attack was Sir John Giffard of Brimpsfield, whose swashbuckling activities are much dwelt on by Robert of Gloucester. He relates that when Roger Clifford, John's former ally, and other 'marchers', had changed sides and joined Lord Edward, he first ensured that his castle at Brimpsfield was well stocked—by taking provisions from his neighbours through the actions of 'the most stalwart men he could find'—and then moved into action. He was summoned by the constable of Gloucester to attend a hundred court at Quedgley which he was holding 'with a great many folk and honour' (*mid gret folk & onour*), meaning that Sir John was to do suit to the court. John's answer was to essoin himself, that is to say to send an excuse. His essoin was not, however, of the normal kind, for his 'essoiners' were armed men from Brimpsfield who promptly wielded their swords. Some of the officials were killed, while others fled to the church. The constable barely escaped with his life. Robert adds that the evil bailiffs who brought frequent harm to poor men were repaid in kind, and that he would like Giffard's essoin to be brought more often:

> These luther bailiffs that poueremen. so gret wo dith ilome.
> Suich giffardes asoyne. icholds hom ofte come.

This is the only reference in the chronicle to the king's regime as it affected the exercise of public authority.[33]

Another of Giffard's escapades is better known, and once again involves Gloucester. With the town now in Roger Clifford's hands, Giffard and a fellow knight, John de Balun, rode over the bridge to the west gate. Riding on woolpacks as though they were chapmen selling their wares and dressed in 'Welsh mantles', they persuaded the porters to let them in. Having gained entry, they jumped down from their horses and threw off their cloaks. When the frightened porters saw that they were armed from head to toe they promptly threw down the keys. The Montfortians now entered from across the bridge and took the town, though not in fact the castle. When Edward's forces retook the town, Roger Clifford had

---

[32] *Metrical Chronicle*, lines 11,061–83.   [33] Ibid., lines 11,148–63.

164 POLITICS AND SOCIETY IN MID THIRTEENTH-CENTURY ENGLAND

the hapless porters hanged over the west gate, the scene of their 'crime'. This scenario tells us much about the nature of the war and the social attitudes displayed. There is a similar occurrence when Clifford and Giffard had first attacked Gloucester castle. A squire of Giffard's was killed by a crossbow bolt as they attacked, which greatly upset Sir John. When the castle was taken the killer was identified as a carpenter. He was taken to high spot on the tower and made to jump to the ground. Not surprisingly, he died a short while after.[34]

Giffard clearly liked a good fight. He was at the battle of Lewes, but he also enjoyed pillaging and burning. After the disastrous engagement, for the Montfortians, at Northampton and before Lewes, for example, when men were burning each other's courts, Giffard, Robert tells us, was not the last into the fray, burning around Oxford during Easter week.[35] He was not only into creating havoc. He also took advantage of situations to take or plunder the lands of his enemies. After Matthias Bezil was captured and taken into the marches, Giffard raided his manor at Sherstone in Wiltshire, rustling his cattle and taking whatever he could find of his possessions.[36] It can hardly be doubted that John Giffard had one eye on his own profit. Robert tells us that he was the first of the barons to break with Montfort in 1265. This, he says, was because Simon would not allow him to keep the prisoners he had taken at the battle of Lewes, and no doubt hold them to ransom.[37] Robert paints a romantic picture of Sir John with his men high upon a hill called Erdland (near Gloucester) where his fires 'of wode & of sprai' and his revelry could be seen from afar at night, even by his foes in Gloucester. The reality is that Giffard, after several years of manoeuvring between Simon de Montfort and Gloucester, had finally thrown in his lot with the latter earl, that is to say he had joined Gloucester's retinue and was now of his party. This was not simply an alliance. Giffard had joined the earl's retinue and was rewarded with Burford in Oxfordshire and Badgeworth in Gloucestershire.[38] This was a typical aristocratic relationship, at the same time affective—for Gloucester was now his lord—and involving reward. Such was the cement of aristocratic society. It made perfect sense for Giffard to choose Gilbert de Clare at this juncture, for he was now the prime political force in his area, while Simon de Montfort's power was beginning to look rather shaky. John Giffard, it is no surprise to learn, was a frequenter of tournaments and a prodigious huntsman.[39] All in all he was the

---

[34] Ibid., lines 11,100–105.   [35] Ibid., lines 11,339–43. See also lines 11,254–7.
[36] Ibid., lines 11,108–9.   [37] Ibid., lines 11,470–2.
[38] Ibid., lines 11,489–92. What he gained in fact was the manor of Badgeworth and £30 rent from the borough of Burford for life. For this and for the details of Giffard's political manoeuvrings between Simon and Edward, see David Crouch, 'Giffard, John, First Lord Giffard (1232–1299)' *ODNB* 22, 126–7.
[39] J. Birrell, 'A Great Thirteenth-Century Hunter: John Giffard of Brimpsfield', *Medieval Prosopography*, 15 (1994), 37–66.

epitome of the thirteenth-century aristocrat and a paradigm through whom we can perceive aristocratic behaviour during the civil war.

Robert of Gloucester was clearly fascinated by the aristocracy, 'heiemen' as he called them, although he did not necessarily approve of their actions. He was interested not only in those who were known in his area and/or were powerful in the marches, but also in the names of the men who were present at the various engagements, in those who were with Lord Edward at his tournaments in 1260, and in those who held with the king in 1264–5. He was also interested in aristocratic personalities. Henry de Montfort, Simon's eldest son, he twice calls a gentle knight (*Sir Henri the hende*), while his brother was known for his overweening pride and extravagant self-belief. Simon de Montfort was a wise man who was let down by his 'reverence' for Edward. The latter was a good knight but cunning and treacherous. In what follows we will follow Robert of Gloucester, not in the narrating of the major engagements and the roles of the central participants, nor indeed in the romance, but in the attention given to what was happening during the civil war on the ground and in the localities.

The War in Berkshire

Court records following the end of hostilities enable us to enter into people's experiences in some of the counties. What we see is a continuous struggle for dominance. These records allow us considerable insight into the nature of the struggle and the forces at work in the provinces, and to appreciate how a greater number of people actually experienced the strife. We will concentrate on the rolls dealing with cases heard before the special eyre held between 1267 and 1272. The eyre was commissioned as part of the pacification process following the wars and was occasioned by the peace made by the king and the earl of Gloucester in June 1267. Gloucester had championed the cause of the Disinherited, those landowners who had suffered seizure or confiscation after the Battle of Evesham and who had consequently decided to fight on.[40] The justices received their first commissions on 17 September 1267.[41] The proceedings of the eyre survive for a number of counties, including three of the four Midland counties whose cases were heard before Nicholas de Yattendon and his fellow justices.[42] The cases that came before the justices were essentially of two kinds, one dealing with the record of lands granted or seized from rebels and considered redeemable under the Dictum of Kenilworth of 1266, and the other with presentments and complaints of offences

---

[40] Jacob discusses these records in *Studies in the Period of Reform and Rebellion*, 156–66.
[41] *CPR 1266–72*, 160.
[42] Nicholas himself had been added to the panel by 18 December 1267: ibid., 276.

166 POLITICS AND SOCIETY IN MID THIRTEENTH-CENTURY ENGLAND

committed during the whole period of disturbance in the realm. It is the latter with which we will be principally concerned here.[43] Our interest is the light the records shed on the actions of rebels in the localities during the period 1263–5. They do not deal with those of royalists, at least not for the most part, because incidents of plundering of 'enemies of the king' were considered to have been justifiable and therefore beyond the remit. Also within the court's jurisdiction was participation in Gloucester's rebellion of 1267 when the king was at Stratford. At the same time, the actions taken by the court were tempered in this respect by the cognizance it was required to take of the pardons granted to members of the retinues of the earl of Gloucester and his associates. I will begin with a detailed study of Berkshire, which lay outside of the Montfortian heartland and can be expected to have been contested territory.[44]

The Role of Sub-Retinues

In his *Studies in the Period of Baronial Reform and Rebellion*, E. F. Jacob drew attention to the high incidence of 'manorial spoliation' that took place during the period of the Barons' Wars. Although he emphasized the wanton pillaging of the lands of royalists by 'men of neighbouring vills or townships' and the widespread settling of 'grudges' that took place between the battles of Lewes and Evesham, he was also struck by the thorough and systematic way in which the attacks on the properties of prominent royalists, officials, and 'special councillors' were undertaken. He explained this in terms of 'emissaries ... passing to and fro the country encouraging both communities and individuals to attack the estates of royalists.'[45] What I want to do here is to look further at the deployment of physical force and intimidation by the rebels during the period of upheaval, with a view to assessing how organized and targeted it actually was. The Berkshire roll allows us to look in some detail at three interrelated phenomena: the operation of retinues or, more correctly, sub-retinues; the role of *procuratores* or agents; and the actions of the castle garrisons of Windsor and Wallingford.[46]

---

[43] For the pleas *de terris datis*, see Susan Stewart, 'The Eyre *de terris datis*, 1267–72', *TCE*, x (2005), 69–79. This essay gives details of pleas relating to land and to trespasses in the roll relating to Surrey (Just 1/1207). For details of the fifteen chapters of the eyre and for the types of cases under trespass, see Jacob, *Studies in the Period of Baronial Reform and Rebellion*, 183–201.

[44] What follows is adopted from my essay 'Retinues, Agents and Garrisons during the Barons' Wars', in Jobson (ed.), *Baronial Reform and Revolution in England*, 183–98.

[45] Jacob, *Studies in the Period of Reform and Rebellion*, 222–39.

[46] The Berkshire roll is TNA JUST 1/42. I what follows I have cited the individual cases by membrane. Yattendon's rolls for the counties of Northamptonshire and Buckinghamshire also survive. The one for Oxfordshire is sadly lost. As Jacob pointed out, the presentments of the juries and individual complaints are rather intermingled in the rolls, which he suggests tends to reflect Yattendon's manner of proceeding. The counties were not dealt with *seriatim*; rather Yattendon and his fellows travelled to and fro. Jacob's study contains considerable information and extracts from the rolls, although Berkshire is barely represented. The roll for Essex and portions of those for Northamptonshire, Cambridgeshire, and Suffolk were published by Joseph Hunter in *Rotuli Selecti* (London, 1834).

CIVIL WAR 167

The hearing of Berkshire cases opened at Wallingford on 15 September 1268.[47] The rolls are vague as to chronology when it comes to the cases concerned, and unlike those of the central courts *coram rege* they do not give even the regnal year involved. Although there are occasional references to the battles of Lewes and Evesham, generally we hear only that this or that case occurred during the time of disturbance (*tempore disturbationis*). One's first impression on reading the rolls is of considerable disorder and despoliation. A closer inspection does not dispel this impression, but it does also suggest that the attacks are less indiscriminate and more thought through than one might have initially supposed. If so, we ought to be thinking less about the wanton behaviour of impassioned activists and more about the actions of structured groups. Our first and obvious port of call is therefore with the baronial retinues themselves. Where the chief perpetrator named in the roll is a baron, there can hardly be any question that the action was undertaken by his armed retinue, or at least a component of the same. We learn for example that the *curia* of the royal justice, Sir Nicholas de Yattenden, at Up Lambourn was itself 'despoiled by Sir John Giffard'. It is no surprise to discover that this attack was planned from Sir John's headquarters at Brimpsfield.[48]

Another retinue that was active in West Berkshire was that of Robert de Ferrers, earl of Derby. Andrew Badking was found by jurors to have been present when men of Earl Ferrers plundered the livestock of William de Valence at Farnham (Surrey). He had himself taken a bull, a cow, twenty-seven sheep, and five lambs, and seems to have pastured them in the park at Stanford in the Vale, on the manor that is of the earl of Derby. He attempted to deflect his responsibility by claiming that William the Chamberlain, the earl's bailiff, had taken them from him.[49] This had clearly been a major operation. William the Chamberlain was quite an active figure in the area. Some of the incidents cited are relatively minor. On one occasion, for example, he and 'his fellows' are reported to have despoiled the church at Hanney of wool and bacon.[50] A much more significant episode occurred when William and 'other malefactors' arrived at the house of John Bagpuize at Kingston, stole four horses together with pigs, oxen, and other items and threshed his corn. The animals were driven to the house of his lord, Earl Ferrers, presumably at Stanford.[51] A defendant in this matter, William de la Grave, called the earl to warrant. We learn elsewhere in the roll that the manor was in fact 'seized for the use of the earl of Derby' on Monday after the Battle of Lewes.[52] The *seisitores*—William de Warmington and Reginald son of the priest—took the manor into his possession, as they said, on the orders of William the

---

[47] I have made use of the transcripts and supporting material submitted by Ellen Roberts and Alys Lydia Gregory for the degree of MA at the University of Manchester in 1927. These and other theses were part of a project to publish all surviving rolls of the special eyre. Sadly, this did not happen.

[48] Just 1/42 m. 2d   [49] Ibid., m. 2   [50] Ibid., m 2.
[51] Ibid., m. 7d.   [52] Ibid., mm. 9,11.

168   POLITICS AND SOCIETY IN MID THIRTEENTH-CENTURY ENGLAND

Chamberlain. The relationship between these men is revealed by a case brought by John Bagpuize against Walter de la Grave 'of Wantage',[53] Henry de Copeshull 'of the same', Reginald son of the priest 'of Stanford', Thomas the vicar of Stanford, and William de Warminster, accusing them 'of many robberies'.[54] The group (or at least some of the group) that had attacked Kingston is revealed. William the Chamberlain is no doubt identical with the William de Camera who was reported as calling himself bailiff of Earl 'Ferrers'[55] in another case where two defendants switched the blame for a robbery onto him. They were William de Warminster and 'the son of a priest'. Bailiff is a generic term, and William seems to have been the earl's chamberlain, coordinating the operation against Kingston from that office. Household and retinue (*familia* and *societas* in the roll) were naturally interconnected and must often have acted in concert. We have our first identification of a sub-retinue in operation, in this case one attached to the earl of Derby.

Sub-retinues, I would argue, are key to understanding the perpetration of political violence on the ground. I use the term to describe relatively small units or bands that are capable of operating independently but tend to be associated with, or affiliated to, full-scale retinues.[56] For the most part, however, the eyre rolls do not express themselves in such a way as to reveal the contours of these armed bands. Frequently we are told the name of only the principal despoiler, often accompanied by the tell-tale phrase 'with other malefactors'. There are occasions, however, when it is possible to reconstruct the membership of such groups. One of these is the retinue operating in an area of West Berkshire under the leadership of John Tregoz. One Robert de Bicester brought a case against him for robbery.[57] More revealing, however, is a complaint the same Robert made against John de Norton, describing him as the steward of John Tregoz, that on the orders of his said lord he went to Lyford and despoiled Robert of oxen, cows, sheep, and other 'goods' to the value of fifty marks.[58] The case was resolved by the current steward making peace with Robert on behalf of his lord and by John de Norton, Walter de Canning, and John de Marsh paying reparations. Three other men acted as pledges that the money would be handed over at Robert's house in Oxford. They were Ralph de Hadley, William de Paveley, and Nicholas Giffard. The significance of these men will be revealed shortly.

Meanwhile we learn of another action involving John de Norton when he and John Marsh, one of his associates in despoiling Robert de Bicester while laden with plunder from Lambourn, came across a William de Brythmere and imprisoned him.[59] However, John de Marsh was not the only associate of John de

---

[53] Presumably of Grove near Wantage.   [54] Just 1/42 m. 7.
[55] The reading here is uncertain due to damage to the edge of the roll.
[56] Sub-retinues are more readily identifiable through the records surrounding the national wars fought by Edward I and his successors. See, in particular, David Simpkin, *The English Aristocracy at War: From the Welsh Wars of Edward I to the Battle of Bannockburn* (Woodbridge, 2008), 64–5.
[57] Just 1/42 m. 7.   [58] Ibid., m. 1.   [59] Ibid., m. 6.

CIVIL WAR   169

Norton to be involved in further despoliation. A Ralph de Greenham brought a complaint against John Tregoz, Nicholas Giffard of Winterbourne, and Thomas Danvers.[60] Nicholas Giffard, it will be recalled, was one of the pledges for the reparation to be paid to Robert de Bicester on behalf of John Tregoz and the others in the first case mentioned. Another of the pledges was Ralph de Hadley. Ralph was accused that with other malefactors he had plundered a cart travelling from Southampton, taking two horses and 8s. from the carter. Ralph's testimony included the statement that he was on his way to Winchester to meet John Tregoz. He knew the name of the actual perpetrator, who had in fact taken the horse because his own was exhausted, and later returned it. Ralph knew nothing, he said, of the 8s. The jury believed him. His loyalty, however, was questionable, at least in some quarters. We know that he suffered after Evesham in that his lands were seized and conferred on John de Monmouth. A Berkshire jury reported that Ralph was innocent of any enmity towards the king, but that Adam de Mathine, clerk of Sir John Giffard, hated him and had arranged for John de Monmouth to seize his lands.[61]

John Tregoz appears to have been a common denominator in these cases. There is more to say where he is concerned. Two men, Richard Page and William Trenchemele, were charged with having plundered the home of John de la Strode. They replied that they were men of John Tregoz and called him to warranty. Two others, Henry Walcote and Ralph Strapel, also accused, acknowledged that John Tregoz was their lord and that they were present at the robbery, but took nothing. They were there, they said, through John's coercion.[62] William de Trenchemele and Richard Page were also accused of leading William de Brythmere, who was on his way to Wantage, into the hands of John de Norton and John de Marsh who plundered him. They were acquitted in this instance. Nonetheless, the implication is clear. What is revealed is a company under the leadership of John Tregoz, responsible for a series of depredations perpetrated in West Berkshire. The centre of operations was probably Lambourn, where John Tregoz held a manor. To the south-east lay Chieveley where, at Winterbourne, lay the manor of Thomas Danvers and from where Nicholas Giffard of Winterbourne took his name. To the north of Lambourn is Wantage, where the Paveleys held a manor.

Did these men have any other association in common? The answer appears to be yes, and a quite startling one. On 26 April 1269 six men received royal letters of pardon for the part they had played during the civil war. Five of them were: John Tregoz, John de Norton, Nicholas Giffard, Thomas Danvers, and John de Marsh.[63] They received their pardon by the testimony of the marcher baron,

---

[60] Ibid., m. 4d.   [61] Ibid., m. 1.   [62] Ibid., m. 2.

[63] *CIM*, no. 823. The other was Richard de Newton. *CPR 1266–72*, 378, gives: John Tregoz of Norton, Richard de Newenton, Nicholas Giffard, Thomas Danvers, John de Marsh, and Richard de Burton.

170   POLITICS AND SOCIETY IN MID THIRTEENTH-CENTURY ENGLAND

Roger de Clifford. In March of the previous year William de Paveley had received a similar pardon by Clifford's testimony.[64] Paveley was described as having been at the time in the *familia et societate* of Roger de Clifford, a phrase which can be taken to mean that he belonged both to Roger's household and his retinue. These, and another group of six men who were pardoned at Clifford's instance, had their pardons registered at our itinerant court.[65] The Paveleys were longstanding tenants of the Cliffords at Charlton in Wantage.[66] The Tregoz family, fellow marchers, were related to the Cliffords by marriage.[67] John de Norton also enjoyed a strong relationship with Clifford. By 1265 he was no longer in the service of John Tregoz but of Clifford himself. The prior of Poughley (in Chaddleworth, Berkshire) complained that John de Norton came to his sheepcote on the Friday after the battle of Evesham and plundered ninety sheep to the value of ten marks. John explained to the court that he was in the service of Sir Roger de Clifford at the time and called him to warrant his action. He explained further that he was given to understand that the sheep had belonged to the late rebel Gilbert de Elsfield, and although in the custody of the prior, had passed to John de St Helens, an enemy of the king. The point is that such action would then have been justified and not actionable. To the prior's response that they belonged to Beatrice de St Helens who was not the king's enemy, John de Norton replied that she was indeed an enemy and had sheltered her son and others of the king's enemies; consequently, she had deserved to be plundered.[68]

It would be possible to construct an argument that what we have been seeing is a sub-retinue under John de Tregoz that was ultimately responsible to that of Roger de Clifford. If this interpretation were correct, it would suggest that many of these incidents took place in 1263 rather than in the period between the battles of Lewes and Evesham, for in August 1263 Clifford had changed sides and returned to the royalist fold. He remained on the king's side thereafter. Although the war was deemed to have begun on 4 April 1264, those who had committed atrocities from June 1263 'under guise of war' were also liable.[69] However, the series of events reported in our roll would seem to be better located during the period 1264–5, when the circle of those despoiled had widened considerably from merely the most prominent and despised royal servants. The chronology is uncertain, and the roll fails us in this respect.

The key figure in the episodes described above is clearly John Tregoz. Who exactly was he? During the time of the special eyre he was the head of the Tregoz family. However, he had only recently been elevated to this position. His father, Robert de Tregoz, had died fighting with Simon de Montfort

---

[64]   *CIM*, no. 822 and *CPR 1266–72*, 222.

[65]   The other group comprised: Robert de Meysy, Robert his son, Philip de Stapleton, Walter de Chadfield, and John de Eton: no. 824.

[66]   *VCH Berkshire* iv, 325; *Book of Fees*, 846.   [67]   Sanders, *English Baronies*, 43.

[68]   Just 1/42 m. 11.   [69]   See Carpenter, *Henry III: 1258–1272*, 578.

CIVIL WAR   171

at Evesham.[70] The family had extensive lands. The inquisition post mortem of John Tregoz himself in 1300 reveals their extent. They include manors at Ewyas Harold and Eaton Tregose in Herefordshire, Albrighton in Shropshire, Great Doddington in Northamptonshire, Lydiard Tregoze, Allington and East Kennett in Wiltshire, and Burnham and Chelwood in Somerset.[71] These widely dispersed lands had long been enjoyed by the family. However, they had little tradition of landholding in Berkshire. The Berkshire interest had come through John's marriage to Mabel, daughter of Fulk fitz Warin, with whom he acquired the manor of Chipping Lambourn (otherwise known as Grandisons) and which he clearly held in his father's lifetime.[72] He was, therefore, well placed to be running an operation in this part of Berkshire.

Of the men attached to him, Thomas Danvers of Winterborne would appear to have been the most significant.[73] Nicholas Giffard came from the same settlement, although his precise interest there is not evident. John Marsh is very probably the John le Mareys who held a quarter fee at Eastbury, south of Lambourn, in right of his wife, Agnes, one of the heiresses of Ralph the Welshman (*Walens*); she later married Ralph de Hadley.[74] John de Norton, who was clearly a career steward, probably originated at Norton in Wiltshire, a Tregoz property, while Walter de Canning may perhaps have come from Bishop's Cannings near Allington in the same county.[75] These men are likely to have seen the possibility of advancement through association with the rebel cause. That the father of John Tregoz was a rebel elsewhere adds weight to the probability that John's own retinue had links further up the Montfortian chain. John's band was playing a role in helping to secure this part of Berkshire for the rebel cause. This did not directly involve the royalist Roger de Clifford. He did, however, play the role of good lord to William de Paveley, John Tregoz and his associates, and his new steward, John de Norton. Berkshire was away from his own spheres of major concern, but he did have an interest there, both at Wantage and at Kingston Bagpuise, where a family called Kingston appears to have held of him.[76] He very likely maintained this interest by keeping his distance during the time of disturbance, allowing his tenants freedom to operate as they saw fit. The relationship between national and local politics was not perhaps as straightforward as one might assume.

The sub-retinue led by John Tregoz was only one of the many that were active in Berkshire. Among the leading 'malefactors' active in the county were: Adam Gurdon, Robert de Whitfield, William Franceys, William le Savage, Henry Terry

---

[70] *VCH Wiltshire* ix, 78–9. Robert's land at Witham in Essex had been confiscated after Evesham: *CIM*, no. 674.

[71] *CIPM* iii, no. 603. John and his wife, Mabel, were granted free warren in many of these manors in 1285.

[72] *VCH Berkshire* iv, 254.   [73] Ibid., 64.   [74] *CPR 1258–66*, 448; *CIPM* i, no. 1.

[75] John Tregoz was also known as John Tregoz of Norton: *CPR 1258–66*, 378. In 1293 a manor at Norton was held of Sir John Tregoz by Peter de Scudamore: *CIPM* iii, no. 74.

[76] *VCH Berkshire* iv, 325; *Book of Fees*, 844, 846.

172   POLITICS AND SOCIETY IN MID THIRTEENTH-CENTURY ENGLAND

of Henley, Gilbert de Elsfield, and John de Musgrave. In West Berkshire the manors of William de Beauchamp at Compton, Geoffrey Foliot at Ashbury, and Reginald fitz Peter at Leckhampstead were despoiled, together with the property of many other landowners, large and small. Adam Fettiplace, Nicholas de Moeles, the Lisles, and the Pecches were among the sufferers. Sometimes actions involved more than a single retinue.[77] Although Giffard's men would seem to have been primarily responsible for the despoliation of Yattenden's property at Up Lambourn, others were involved too. A curious case was brought against two men, Robert the Tailor and Richard son of Ralph Tralbe, that they took a bee-hive with its resident bees from Up Lambourn when Yattendon's *curia* was plundered by Sir John Giffard.[78] The defendants explained that the bees were, in fact, their own and that they had swarmed into the court of Sir Nicholas; they merely retrieved them. The jury agreed.

Instigators

Members of sub-retinues did not act alone. Ralph de Hadley, for instance, is not the only member of his family who appears in the roll. Reginald de Hadley, its head and a minor landowner in Lambourn,[79] was involved in a number of incidents. He was charged with instigating men to despoil the property of the royal justice, Nicholas de Yattendon, at Lambourn. The jury found him guilty of procuring malefactors. He was convicted of the same offence against John Godde of Lambourn, the jurors finding that he was not a despoiler but an instigator.[80] For Reginald this sort of activity seems to have been a normal part of his life at this time. He was also charged with receiving two men who had plundered the chapel of John Mansel, at Froxfield, just over the border in Wiltshire;[81] Mansel's corn ended up at Reginald's house. Nor was this all. John Godde complained that after the Montfortian victory at Lewes, Reginald had seized, bound, and imprisoned him until he paid a ransom. He also took two tunics, a supertunic, and a cloak from him. This incident did not stand alone. Stephen Marshal complained that Reginald had procured the men of Sir John Giffard to seize and imprison him, carrying away to Lambourn a horse worth 40s., a robe, and a tabard. Stephen was forced to hand over £10. These were at heart acts of reprisal against loyalists, but at the same time they were undoubtedly profitable.

Yet another Hadley, John, was accused of involvement in the attack on the property of Sir Nicholas de Yattendon, and specifically of burning his sheepcote. The role of the Hadleys in relation to the strongly orchestrated attack on the

---

[77] Just 1/42 mm. 1–18.   [78] Ibid., m. 2d.
[79] He held the manor of Hadley: *VCH Berkshire* iv, 260.   [80] Just 1/42 mm. 1d, 2.
[81] Ibid., m. 2d.

CIVIL WAR 173

property of Justice Yattendon opens up another dimension. Reginald de Hadley procured one Richard Coppers to go to Brimpsfield, the headquarters of the warlike John Giffard, to tell the garrison (*castellani*) what property Yattendon had at Lambourn, information that must have greatly aided the plunderers. The jury found that Richard had complied because he 'wanted to have Sir John Giffard as his lord'.[82] Orchestrated action like the attack on Up Lambourn required men like Reginald de Hadley operating at a lower level as much as it did the actual 'despoilers'. It also provided opportunities for employment in aristocratic service.

West Berkshire was an area which saw a good deal of action of this kind. As E. F. Jacob pointed out, men like Reginald de Hadley, described as *procuratores*, were not uncommon in the rolls. In addition to Simon de Montfort's bailiffs and stewards and those involved in raising financial contributions (that is to say, taxation) for his cause, Jacob noted occasional references to *cursores*, men like Sir Brian de Gouiz in Somerset, 'who "ran" or were "out" against the king'. Such men acted effectively as agents of the rebel cause but *pace* Jacob they were not necessarily connected directly to the earl.[83] Although *procurator* means in general agent or proctor, it carries here the additional connotation of 'instigator', perhaps one might say 'procurer'. Such men were guilty of acts of procurement (*procuratio*). Their role was often multipurpose and included acting as receivers of 'malefactors' and committing acts of extortion to help fund rebel operations. These agents of one sort or another were vital to the rebel cause. One of those operating in West Berkshire, Richard de Heydon, seems to have specialized in harassing clergy. The hundred jurors of Compton charged him with being 'a plunderer of the king's faithful', and said that he went to the church of West Ilsley, despoiled it, and held it until the parson paid an enormous fine of £20. He protested that since then he had been a faithful man of the king.[84] Another jury, however, charged him that together with the men of Ardington he had despoiled the prior of Steventon. We hear that he ordered these men to the prior's house from where, on Monday 18 August 1264, they took 10 horses, a bull, and 16 cows, together with 56 oxen, 240 sheep, 97 pigs, and 100 quarters of wheat and barley. Seven men are named, including the reeve of Ardington, strongly suggesting that the raiding party comprised its tenants. This was a large robbery and was undoubtedly orchestrated from above.[85]

The Activities of Castle Garrisons

Not surprisingly we learn a good deal about the violent side of rebel operations from the activities of the castle garrisons at Wallingford and Windsor. Wallingford

[82] Ibid.   [83] Simon's minister John Godman was certainly active in Berkshire (nos. 564, 593).
[84] Just 1/42 m. 1d.   [85] Ibid., m. 1d.

174   POLITICS AND SOCIETY IN MID THIRTEENTH-CENTURY ENGLAND

seems to have been taken by Simon de Montfort in the spring of 1263 as he moved down the Thames valley towards London. After the battle of Lewes, he deposited his most important prisoners there: Richard of Cornwall, his son Edmund, and Lord Edward himself. As we have seen, the chronicler Robert of Gloucester tells us of the attempt to rescue Edward. Consequently, Simon removed his royal prisoners to his stronghold at Kenilworth, at the same time strengthening the garrisons at Wallingford and Windsor.[86] Not surprisingly, the incident is referred to in our roll. Hugh Plucknet, arrested for robbery against Margery de Bulcheth, argued that 'if' he had plundered her it was as an enemy of the king and as a receiver of Gilbert de Elsfield, the Montfortian stalwart who was subsequently killed at Chesterfield. Hugh said that he had been one of those who went to Wallingford with the Bristol garrison to rescue the Lord Edward. When he got there, he found Margery's men in the castle. The sheriff was ordered to bring her into court to respond.[87]

Among those accused of being in the garrison at Wallingford was John Musson. In defence he claimed that he was a man of the earl of Leicester and that he had been distrained and then physically seized to compel him to join in the depredation against his will. The jury found, to the contrary, that he went to the castle voluntarily and that, in particular, he had robbed Walter de Merton and Aimery de Pecche of horses at Cumnor.[88] In addition to actual membership, the main issues coming before the court from garrison activity were appropriation and intimidation. The supply of horses is likely to have been a particular problem. Richard de Beenham complained that William de le Garston had taken a warhorse from him. The case turned out to be more complicated. William responded that Henry, parson of Shottesbrook, took him and led him to Wallingford as his prisoner and he 'in fear of ransom and of dire incarceration' handed over the horse. Later, at Reading Abbey, William recognized his horse and asked for it back; the abbot complied. Richard now claimed, however, that William had given the horse freely to Parson Henry and not through extortion, and that he, Richard, had bought the horse from him in good faith. The jury found that Henry had indeed extorted the horse from William in ransom. In a twist to the tale, William was acquitted, and Richard charged with buying the proceeds of a robbery.[89]

In another case, Thomas son of Geoffrey the chaplain was charged with plundering the corn of the parson of St Helens and taking it to the garrison. He responded that he did so under compulsion. He said that Philip the Welshman (le Waleys) and other malefactors took both the corn and him to Wallingford where he was incarcerated for eight days. The jury agreed with him.[90] An intervention in a dispute over tithes introduces us to the constable Richard de Havering;

---

[86] *Metrical Chronicle*, lines 11,424–11,445.   [87] Just 1/42 m. 8.   [88] Ibid., m. 1d.
[89] Although the court ruled that he could prosecute the seller if he wished (m. 10d).
[90] Ibid., m. 8d.

CIVIL WAR   175

his action here will undoubtedly have resulted in the contents of the tithe barns reaching the garrison.[91] Three other members of the garrison—William le Franceys, Baldwin de Cuserigg, and Matthew de Chieveley—sent men from the vills of Kintbury and Hungerford to the royalist castle at Marlborough, where they launched an assault and killed many men.[92] The jury sustained the general thrust of the defence and noted that some of those sent fled when they got there and 'did nothing evil'. The men were dealt with differentially. Those from Hungerford, being men of the earl of Leicester, and presumably therefore less able to refuse, were fined. Those from Kintbury and Holt, not being the earl's men, had to redeem their lands at a year's valuation.[93]

These men were clearly intimidated into actions in support of the rebel cause. Cases involving intimidation, however, were not necessarily clear cut. William de Rivers was charged with receiving Sir William de Berkeley and other enemies of the king, sending his squire with armour to the Wallingford garrison, and sustaining the king's enemies with money. Once again, the defendant gave a contrary account. This time he said that Sir William de Berkeley came to his house uninvited with horses and arms, then took him and led him to Sir Reginald fitz Peter's park (at Leckhampstead) against his will. The jury agreed with what Walter said and added that because he tried to escape, Sir William had knocked him off his palfrey three times. Nonetheless, they found that, although uninvited, he did participate with William in taking animals from the park.[94] A John Streg' complained that three men came 'along with the garrison of Wallingford' to his houses at Burghfield after the battle of Lewes and burned them. He said that they were 'in counsel and aid' with the garrison. Although the jury found them not guilty, the implication that the garrison had accomplices and supporters on the outside is clear enough.[95]

The cases involving the Windsor garrison are even more instructive. Windsor surrendered to Simon de Montfort in July 1263, and Lord Edward's alien garrison was allowed to depart freely on condition that they did not return. Its constable during the crucial period between the battles of Lewes and Evesham was the baronial leader John fitz John. He held substantial lands in Buckinghamshire. He was to fight at Evesham where his life was in fact saved by the intervention of Roger de Clifford, who had married his niece.[96] A major issue before the court was identifying who was with him at Windsor, and in what capacity. One man charged and imprisoned had been there as a crossbowman.[97] William Atwell was convicted of being there and being a plunderer.[98] William the Marshal was

[91] Ibid., m. 10.
[92] This case is noted by Jacob, *Studies in the Period of Reform and Rebellion*, as is the case relating to the vills of Cookham and Bray mentioned below, 234–5.
[93] Just 1/42 m. 3.   [94] Ibid., m. 12.   [95] Ibid., m. 13.
[96] See Carpenter, 'John, Sir, *fitz* John, Baronial Leader', 192–3.
[97] Just 1/42 m. 10.   [98] Ibid., m. 10d.

176 POLITICS AND SOCIETY IN MID THIRTEENTH-CENTURY ENGLAND

charged with being in the castle and of going on plundering raids with John fitz John, with some examples of his particular robberies given. He was found guilty of being in the castle of his own free will and at wages.[99] Various others who were charged with being in John fitz John's garrison claimed to have been taken there by force, including Thomas Upnor of Windsor, Robert de la More, and Thomas Burnel.[100] With regard to the first of these the jury found that Richard de la Vache and others of the castle had taken him there 'bodily' and by force, but that he did no robberies. The outcome in the other two cases is not known. Philip Burnel, John de Molins, and his brother Nicholas were also charged with being in the garrison, and pleaded the same defence. The jury said that they had indeed been taken by force, but that afterwards they left and then returned voluntarily, taking up residence there 'for fear of their kin (*propter timorem parentum suorum*)', an interesting slant. However, they did not plunder.[101]

Further light is shone by the testimony of Hugh David who said that Thomas Burnel and Robert del la More took him there by force 'for the keeping of the castle (*ad conservandum castrum*)'. He seems to have committed no robbery 'except for the doors and windows he took to the castle'. William de Warwick, John Pedami, and John de Odiham pleaded the usual defence. Of William, the jury said that he was there for pay and 'right willingly'; however, he did no robbery, and the same was true of John Pedami. Of John de Odiham they said that he went out on robberies and was guilty of appropriation. Nicholas Tonney on the other hand was found not guilty either of being in the garrison or of committing robbery. His defence was that in the time of Drew de Barentine (the royalist constable) he was in the king's pay and still was. He said that when John fitz John took custody he left and stayed in Windsor itself for a long time. On a certain day John's ministers sent for him to join them, he having taken an oath (presumably as a member of the previous royal garrison). He said that he had no wish to take another oath unless it were for the support of the king and his sons. He therefore refused. Richard Banaster (of Sulhamstead and Finchamstead) was another man charged with being in the Windsor garrison, together with his brother William. The latter said that he was there for six weeks as a result of force and menaces but that he was not involved in plunder. This was to be inquired into. Meanwhile the jury said that Richard was in the castle armed of his own free will and on pay like others of the garrison.[102] The Banaster brothers were later involved in the revolt led by the earl of Gloucester in London in 1267 on behalf of the 'Disinherited'. Another member of the Windsor garrison, Henry Atwell, had the same history.[103]

The garrison needed manpower and was prepared to coerce additional men to join it. Some were there unwillingly, others willingly and on contract. An interesting insight is provided when five men from the vill of Cookham were charged

---

[99] Ibid.   [100] Ibid., m. 15.   [101] This and the following cases are on m. 15.
[102] Ibid., m. 5.   [103] Ibid., m. 10d.

with being in the garrison. Four of them argued in their defence that when Drew de Barentine was keeper of the castle he had called the men of the vills of Cookham and Bray together and asked for six from each of them to serve for forty days at the cost of those vills. They were chosen for Cookham but dwelt there unwillingly. When John fitz John took over he held a similar inquiry and had them in the garrison by distraint and by strong threats. The case was put in respite until the justices could consult the king's counsel. Meanwhile the fifth man was acquitted because, although forced to join the garrison with his equipment, he had escaped at the first opportunity, after having been there for eight days. Six men from Bray were accused of the same offence and their case put in respite 'until the said parliament'.[104] An extraordinary insight into John fitz John's need for manpower is provided by the defence offered by three men accused of the robbery of John le Fleming.[105] They said they were neifs of the knight, John fitz John, and had been sent there through distraint by his bailiff. Although they claimed to have appropriated nothing, they each received a sheep from the robbery as wages.

The court distinguished, however, between those who were merely members of the garrison and those who participated in the raids. Three men—Henry the Crossbowman, Nicholas Herlewin, and Reginald the Carpenter—were charged with being in the garrison in the pay of John fitz John and being 'chief plunderers'. Henry and Nicholas said that they were in the castle as serjeants (*servientes*) of the king and were not plunderers. Reginald said that he was once in the castle with Richard de la Vache but was not armed. The jury found Nicholas and Reginald guilty as charged. Henry was found to have been in the castle willingly working, just as he had been in the king's time, but was not a plunderer.[106] Others were charged with being in the castle in other capacities, such as a master carpenter, a master mason, and a smith, who were charged with being there in the time of Fitz John 'working and making machines'.[107] Another man said in defence to the charge of being in the castle that he had taken a rick of corn there and followed into the castle to get his money but was detained there against his will and committed no robberies. Yet another had been a miller in the castle before then and had been held there unwillingly. Both were acquitted.[108]

The abbot of Chertsey was accused of helping the garrison with carts, horses, and men when they were out seeking wood, corn, and other necessities for the castle. The abbot denied this, saying that if there had been any such accommodation it was by his tenants who owed the annual service of carrying hay to the

---

[104] Ibid., m. 16d.
[105] The robbery took place in Wiltshire, but they were received at East Garton, Berkshire.
[106] Ibid., m. 6d.
[107] The roll is damaged and the meaning unclear, but they appear to have been ejected by John fitz John and were found not guilty.
[108] Ibid., m. 14d.

178   POLITICS AND SOCIETY IN MID THIRTEENTH-CENTURY ENGLAND

castle.[109] More fundamental was the help provided by the abbot of Abingdon. The charges against him were multifaceted. He was a procurer for Simon de Montfort, and he had received the king's enemies, that is, John de St Helens and others.[110] Furthermore, the abbot was accused of supplying aid to the earl and of sending money to him. He compelled his knights 'by great distraint', it was said, to go to Windsor castle and hold it with John fitz John against the king. As one would have expected he denied the charges, acknowledging only that through distraint by the constable, who had shown him 'letters of the lord king', he had closed his barns and cellars so that neither he nor his convent could have victuals and that he owed service to the castle in the form of thirty knights' fees.[111]

John fitz John was heavily involved in selling off royal assets. Robert Ruddock, charged with buying the king's wood, admitted the charge, saying that it was proclaimed at the market at Windsor by John's bailiff.[112] Seven others were accused of the same.[113] John's erstwhile servants were also under attack. Alexander the Parker was accused by the justices of being a minister of John fitz John, 'a seller of the wood he should have guarded', and a receiver of money for John's use. His defence that he was under compulsion was upheld by the jury, who said that he was an unwilling participant and under physical constraint from the actual sellers, Adam de Meopham and William Mot.[114] Thomas Burnel was charged that he was a 'minister of the king's enemies', was in the castle, and was a seller of its park. He replied that he was taken to the park unwillingly and 'did not know what they wanted him to do'. He claimed that he made no sale or appropriation from the park. As soon as he saw an opportunity he escaped from the office and from the retinue of those enemies (*de ipsorum officio ac societate*). He went into Buckinghamshire, where he resided until the bailiffs of John fitz John came after him, took him to London, and imprisoned him for four days and nights until he paid John 70s. Numerous men were charged with receiving wood from the sell-off from the park[115] and indeed from the sale of the king's wood at Binfield.[116] More generally, Adam de Binfield was charged with being the bailiff and minister of John fitz John for seven hundreds, and in that capacity arresting and plundering the king's faithful men. He, too, pleaded that he did so unwillingly.[117]

A similar set of accusations was made with regard to robbery from Roger Mortimer's park at Stratfield Mortimer. Five men were convicted of buying his wood.[118] One man bought sheep from Maude de Chieveley, one of the plunderers, not knowing that they had been stolen.[119] Another man said that he did not know that the timber he had bought for his carts came from this source.[120] Ecclesiastics were accused of being receivers too. The abbot of Oseney was

---

[109] Ibid., m. 15d.
[110] John was, in fact, a tenant of the abbey and his family long associated with it.
[111] Just 1/42 m. 8d.   [112] Ibid., m. 14d.   [113] Ibid., m. 15d.   [114] Ibid., m. 15d.
[115] Ibid., m. 15.   [116] Ibid., m. 15d.   [117] Ibid., m. 16d.
[118] Ibid., m. 5.   [119] Ibid., m. 10.   [120] Ibid., m. 3d.

CIVIL WAR 179

accused of buying wood from Mortimer's house at Stratfield and then carrying it in carts to his manors. The abbot claimed that he had bought it from a named individual in the market at Reading. Mortimer and the abbot settled out of court.[121] One of the accusations made against the abbot of Reading was that he, too, had bought Mortimer's wood and that members of his household had carried it away in his carts.[122]

Throughout the roll we find individuals charged with receiving the proceeds of robberies, most of them the result of raids by members of the garrisons of Wallingford and Windsor and by similar groups. The garrisons were clearly a base from which some of the sub-retinues operated. Indeed, we may well suspect that some of these bands were directly affiliated to John fitz John. But they were by no means confined to the garrisons. Richard and William Banaster, who as we have seen were part of John fitz John's garrison, were also active more widely in East Berkshire. They were indicted of plundering John de Binfield at his house, in the *societas* of Henry, parson of Shottesbrooke.[123] Thomas Banaster was convicted of robbery with the same Henry de Shottesbrooke, in particular of stealing items of armour.[124] Henry was deprived of his living after the Battle of Evesham. He was also with the earl of Gloucester in London in June 1267, as were all three of the Banasters. There can be no doubt that this war-like cleric was heading his own retinue or sub-retinue, as the word *societas* must undoubtedly indicate. Incidentally, Alice Banaster, the mother of Thomas, was accused of receiving her son, but pleaded that she was unaware that he was a plunderer and enemy of the king.[125] She was not alone among knightly mothers accused of giving shelter and succour to Montfortian sons. Another Montfortian activist was Adam Gurdon. Robert de Uffington was accused of receiving Adam and David de Uffington at his house. He denied the charge but acknowledged that they came to his house at Beenham and fed themselves against his will. The jury found that they did indeed come to his house in the way he said, early in the morning, breakfasted, and took him away with them. Afterwards, however, he left them.[126] It looks as though they were attempting to pressgang him into their cause. Another Montfortian stalwart was William Franceys, whom we have met in the garrison at Wallingford. Peter Heartlove, accused of receiving a plundered horse, said that Franceys and others of the king's enemies came uninvited to his house, dined there, and left him the horse.[127] The men of Gilbert de Elsfield arrived similarly at the house of William Alyn, took food and drink, and left him six sheep and a lamb from the plunder of Reginald fitz Peter. Men variously described as plunderers and malefactors came to the house of Thomas Favus uninvited, dined, and left him a mare. The jury found that the value of the food and drink was of greater value than the horse,

[121] Ibid., m. 5.   [122] Ibid., m. 10.   [123] Ibid., m. 5.
[124] He was also in London with the earl of Gloucester of his own free will when the king was at Stratford.
[125] Just 1/42 m. 4d.   [126] Ibid., m. 10.   [127] This and the following cases are on m. 12d.

180 POLITICS AND SOCIETY IN MID THIRTEENTH-CENTURY ENGLAND

and so he was pardoned. Something similar happened to John de Basing. Plunderers entered his houses and left him an infirm horse, which had subsequently died. He was, nonetheless, found guilty of receiving. Some of these acts of intimidation must have been designed to 'neutralize' men, or even to bring them on side.

Jacob pointed to actions by communities and by landowners that were motivated, in part at least, by local antagonisms which helped to nourish the Montfortian regime.[128] The sending of the reeve and villagers by Richard de Heydon was one example of community action in this context, while the conflict between the royalist Peter de Anesy and the rebel Richard de Vernon over the Berkshire manor of Basildon provides an excellent instance of the working through of a pre-existing grudge. Peter's land was seized by Richard de Vernon after Lewes,[129] with Peter securing the Vernon manors of Basildon and Ashampstead after Evesham.[130] However, it is the organized nature of the physical violence and intimidation that is most apparent from a close examination of the Berkshire roll. The actions of the sub-retinues were quite clearly targeted, and they were underpinned by the activities of agents or procurers. These played a major logistical role in identifying targets, major and minor, real and personal. They acted as receivers of rebels and of plunder, and they were involved in acts of extortion which helped to fund the various enterprises. Those who were bailiffs and the like helped with the marketing of plunder. The components of castle garrisons and their supporters were involved in identical enterprises, fuelled by the added needs for manpower, horses, and provisions. Maintaining the rebel cause on the ground must have required considerable organization, vigilance, and determination. If the rolls convey a certain drive, a dynamism even, in the quest to control disputed territory, there is also a sense of urgency, perhaps a hint of desperation in their actions. Some might argue that these records convey a one-sided, even a distorted, picture. By their very nature they place a heavy emphasis upon physical force and intimidation, and they are not equipped to convey any principles or ideals that may have motivated the rebel cause. Be that as it may, the very least that can be said in this respect is that their actions on the ground were hardly likely to win hearts and minds.

The War in Buckinghamshire

The impression gained from the Berkshire record can be broadened by taking another county for which a roll from the special eyre survives. Buckinghamshire

---

[128] Jacob, *Studies in the Period of Reform and Rebellion*, 224–5.   [129] Just 1/42 m. 3d.
[130] *CIM*, 190. Richard sought to redeem his lands in 1272 under the Dictum of Kenilworth: *CPR 1266–72*, 687. For the history of the manor and Peter's claims, see *VCH Berkshire* iii, 459.

CIVIL WAR 181

was a county dominated by lesser landowners, and for that reason it is particularly interesting from the perspective of this chapter. Nonetheless, there was a magnate presence and estates held by politically significant figures. The roll gives us details of the attacks on some high- status victims as well as the perpetrators.[131] The victims include Queen Eleanor at Wingrave, Hugh de la Penne at Passenham (Oxfordshire), John de Grey at Eton, William de Wykewan, chancellor of York, the parson of Ivinghoe, Thomas Basset of Adstock, Gilbert de Woodham, Ingram de Fiennes, John Peyvre, and Lawrence del Brok (at Finmere, Oxfordshire). All were royalists, and some of them Savoyards.[132] The Fiennes family were favourites with the queen and were distantly related to her. Ingram was one of the party of alien knights who came to England in 1260. He had interests on both sides of the channel. He frustrated the attempt by Henry of Almain, then a supporter of Earl Simon, to prevent John Mansel taking the ladies of the court across the sea to safety in 1263, imprisoning Henry at Boulogne.[133] Hugh de la Penne was keeper of the queen's wardrobe between 1257 and 1272. He held a prebend at Salisbury and had been a clerk of her chapel. In the early summer of 1260, she gave him stone to build the chancel of his church at Stanton Harcourt in Oxfordshire.[134]

The Plunderers

Among the perpetrators, three prominent agents can be identified: Richard de la Vache, Robert fitz Nigel (or Robert Finel), and William de Lay. Richard de la Vache was in the garrison at Windsor under the constable John fitz John, from whence he no doubt operated. He was spoken of as the steward of Walton, suggesting that he had a background in local office.[135] Both he and Robert fitz Nigel were heavily involved in the attack on the queen's manor of Wingrave.[136] Something of their modus operandi is revealed by the roll. Two men responded on behalf of their dead relatives over the accusation that they took part in the raid on Wingrave. They were Gilbert, brother and heir of Herbert Bolebec, and John, son and heir of Geoffrey Neyrnuit. The raid on Wingrave was certainly a major event in that Geoffrey Neyrnuit was accused of participating in the raiding to the value of £100. Their defence was that, faced with a refusal to participate, Richard de la Vache and Robert fitz Nigel had come to their houses, taken them prisoner, and led them to Wingrave. Geoffrey is said to have escaped later and joined the

[131] This is TNA Just 1/159. I have used the transcripts and supporting material submitted by two Manchester MA students, John Lunn and Margery L. Hoyle, in 1928.
[132] Margaret Howell assigns the attacks on the estates of the Savoyards to the summer of 1263: *Eleanor of Provence*, 193.
[133] Ibid., 195.
[134] The chancel still survives. See J. Sherwood and N. Pevsner, *The Buildings of Oxfordshire* (London, 1974), 778–9.
[135] Just 1/159 m. 11d.   [136] Ibid., m.1.

182 POLITICS AND SOCIETY IN MID THIRTEENTH-CENTURY ENGLAND

king's party. The jury concurred that Geoffrey had been sent for and had been unwilling. He was made to arm himself and was taken both to Wingrave and to the raid on Ivinghoe, a manor lying to its east. There he plundered and took his share of the proceeds, although he did leave when he was able.[137] By implication, the career of Herbert Bolebec must have been similar. Although these men were clearly guilty as charged, their defence was a common one and sometimes prevailed. It was plausible because it reflected how the Montfortian agents, or to use contemporary parlance 'procurers', functioned.

Vache was inclined to use the well-known procedure of distraint to enforce compliance. William Angevin, accused of plundering the township of Walton, explained that he held his tenement for carrying out the orders of the steward (*ad faciendum preceptum senescalli*) when it came to making distraints.[138] The steward was, of course, Vache himself. The jury agreed. William Angevin was no innocent, however. He was accused of breaking into the church at Aylesbury, forcing open a chest, and carrying off a considerable amount of money.[139] One can imagine its destiny. There were several other cases where distraint was used. On one occasion the jury said that far from being distrained the man in question had actually been Vache's bailiff.[140] But Vache, as we have seen, was equally involved in the more direct method of recruitment. Ralf de Verney told the court that Vache had come to his home and taken him naked (*nudum*, by which he probably meant unarmed) to take part in the plundering of the royal estate of Piddington in Oxfordshire.[141] He claimed that he escaped at the first opportunity (*quando horam vidit ad recendum de ipsis*).

In addition to Wingrave, Vache's fellow operative, Robert fitz Nigel, was heavily involved in the raid at Piddington, the roll calling him a chief plunderer (*principalis predo*).[142] The third agent was William de Lay, whose activities in Buckinghamshire can be outlined from the roll. Four men of Chilton were charged with being with him at the despoliation of John de Grey.[143] The jury says that William de Lay beat and bound them (*quosdem ligavit quosdem verberavit*) 'so that they went with him'. They were nonetheless convicted of being there.[144] In the case of Henry de Grenville, the jury told the court that William de Lay came to his father's house and threatened to kill him unless he sent his son. Although the jury said that they did not actually participate, they were all convicted of being there.[145] Another man found to have been there was Walter de Burg. He was accused of being a fellow (*socius*) of William de Lay and of being involved in many robberies in the neighbourhood (*patria*) against loyal men, and of being a receiver, sending and procuring man against the king and his party. Walter

---

[137] Ibid., m. 15d.   [138] Ibid., m. 11d.   [139] Ibid.   [140] Ibid., m. 15d.

[141] This case was noticed by Jacob, *Studies in the Period of Reform and Rebellion*, 186.

[142] Just 1/159 m. 14d.

[143] The following case names a fifth Chilton man, William Cay, for a robbery with William de Lay.

[144] Ibid., m. 18.   [145] Ibid., m. 19.

CIVIL WAR 183

mounted the usual defence, asserting that William de Lay came to his home, threatening to burn his houses and hang him from the gate unless he participated. Walter was not actually present, being at the abbey of Notley at the time. He sent a groom to discover whether William actually intended to carry this out. Having ascertained that he did not, he returned to his master, having appropriated nothing.[146] This may be a case where the jury was saving the accused from five years' redemption.[147]

John fitz John himself made the occasional sally from Windsor Castle. The township of Wendover, accused of pillage, said that John had taken the vill into his own hands and that he and his bailiffs had held the courts taking the pleas and the amercements. None of this could they resist.[148] Henry de la Hulle of Wendover was accused of carrying away ten cartloads of wood from the robbery of Ingram de Fiennes.[149] He explained that when John fitz John was at Wendover with his dogs his men carried the wood to Henry's house for the baking of bread for the dogs. He was given some of the wood. Ingram's corn was carried to Weston and Henry had done this for fourteen days, again receiving a share. Altogether, fourteen men were indicted for receiving wood.[150]

What do we know of these men? John fitz John, the constable of Windsor, is of course a major Montfortian figure. Richard de la Vache seems to have originated at 'The Vache' in Chalfont St Giles, where he held a half fee.[151] Anne Polden in her study of Buckinghamshire knights tells us that the de la Vaches were very minor tenants of the Wolverton barony at Chalfont St Giles in the twelfth century and little is known about them until the mid-1260s, when Richard de la Vache was steward of the honour of Lewes.[152] He held land at Shenley of the earl of Arundel.[153] He was in Windsor castle with John fitz John, and was pardoned in 1265.[154] He was probably a man seeking a way up in the world. In this respect he offers a contrast to Robert fitz Nigel. His family were minor knights in the early thirteenth century with a manor at Kimble.[155] However, in 1252 Robert inherited the lands of his elder brother, Richard, at Beauchampton, Mursley, Salden, and Iffley in Oxfordshire.[156] He also seems to have held land at Buckland and La Hyde, and a house in London.[157] He was killed at Evesham. There is a suggestion that he may have been in the Despenser household.[158] The third major agent,

[146] Ibid.   [147] *CIM*, nos. 163, 841.   [148] Just 1/159 m. 17.
[149] Ibid., m. 16.   [150] Ibid.   [151] *VCH Buckinghamshire*, iii, 187; *CIM*, no. 628.
[152] Polden, 'A Crisis of the Knightly Class?', at 44.   [153] *Hundred Rolls*, ii, 34.
[154] *CPR 1258–66*, 46.
[155] Anne Polden, 'The Social Networks of the Buckinghamshire Gentry in the Thirteenth Century', *JMH*, 32 (2006), 371–94, at 278 and references given there.
[156] Polden, 'A Crisis of the Knightly Class', 46, n. 85; *VCH Oxfordshire* v, 191–2; *Luffield Priory Charters* Part II, ed. G. R. Elvey, Buckinghamshire and Northamptonshire Record Societies (1975), lxvii–lxviii.
[157] *CPR 1266–72*, 166–7.
[158] *FitzNells Cartulary: A Calendar of Bodleian Library MS. Rawlinson B 430*, ed. C. A. F. Meekings and P. Shearman, Surrey Record Society, vol. xxvi (Guildford, 1968), xci; *CPR 1258–66*, 428.

184   POLITICS AND SOCIETY IN MID THIRTEENTH-CENTURY ENGLAND

William de Lay, apparently held land in Caldecote in Warwickshire of the honour of Chester and a manor at Great Paxton, of the honour of Huntingdon, for half a knight's fee.[159] He was obviously a minor figure, very probably sub-knightly. One would dearly like to know to whom he was attached.

Of the other plunderers named, some were Buckinghamshire knights. Geoffrey Neyrnuit and Herbert Bolbec were longstanding members of Buckinghamshire society. Geoffrey Neyrnuit held at Morton, Lillyfee, Pitstone Lee, Blechgrove, Grove, and Risborough, as well as Kingston and Clifton in Oxfordshire.[160] There is no doubt that the family was committed to the Montfortian side. Other rebels include Geoffrey son of Geoffrey Neyrnuit, bastard, who was involved in plundering the prior of Newton Longueville.[161] Walter Neyrnuit, the parson of Pitstone (clearly a Neyrnuit living), was accused of plundering and of receiving the king's enemies. It is not difficult to envisage who these may have been. His defence was that through dread of war, an interesting enough statement in itself, he went to Oxford and then to Berkhampstead, where he stayed with men who were faithful to the king. The jury found him not guilty.[162] The Bolbecs held Kingsey and Little Kimble. At Kimble they were neighbours of the FitzNigels. The Bolbecs had once held the honour of Whitchurch, held of the Giffards. Where Buckinghamshire knights are concerned, Anne Polden considers neighbourhood to have been a major factor in their lives and presumably, therefore, in Monfortian recruitment.[163]

However, a cross-section of lay society can be perceived in the plundering. There were lesser manorial lords, and others of similar status, among the plunderers, as well as men from well below this level of society. William of Olney (with land at both Olney and Lillingstone)[164] was an enemy of the king who was with the Disinherited at the Isle of Ely. Hugh le Cheval of Bow Brickhill plundered John Pevre at Woolstone and Weston and was also present when a group plundered the parson of Hachecote.[165] As we know he was active as a bailiff of the earl of Gloucester. William Popping, who was one of those who plundered John de Grey, held land in the hundred of Mursley,[166] while William le Noble, who held a virgate of the abbot of Woburn in Drayton, was one of the (very many) who received Sir John's wood.[167] Another was Robert the Smith of Mursley, who held one virgate.[168] Richard Cosin of Stoke was charged with robbery of the faithful. He held one fifth of a knight's fee in Sutton.[169]

Some men are difficult to identify socially. One of these is William Capel, who despoiled Laurence del Brok at Finmere (Oxfordshire, near Tingewick), as well

---

[159] *CIM*, no. 928; *Hundred Rolls*, ii, 687; *Feudal Aids* ii, 372.
[160] The family were tenants of the honour of Wallingford (held by Richard of Cornwall) at Hitcham, Pitstone Neirenuit, and Fleet Marston: Polden, 'Social Networks', 384.
[161] Just 1/159 m. 16.   [162] Ibid., m. 13.
[163] Polden, 'Social Networks', 76–9. She lists another ten knights who were against the king.
[164] *Hundred Rolls*, i, 30, 44.   [165] Ibid., 41–2; Just 1/159, m. 7.   [166] *Hundred Rolls*, 334.
[167] Ibid., 337.   [168] Ibid., 356.   [169] *Book of Fees*, 250.

CIVIL WAR   185

as Simon le Kane at Sherington and Ralf Donjon, the steward of the abbot of St Katherine, Rouen, at Drayton. Capel was also accused by Thomas le Marshal of being *procurator principalior totius comitatus*. The jury agreed, associating him with the party of the earl of Leicester.[170]

Plundering was certainly undertaken by men who were associated in terms of locality. Four men, including Henry de Grenville, of Chilton were with William de Lay at the robbery of John de Grey.[171] Hugh de la Penne accused nineteen men of plundering his manor of Passenham in Northamptonshire.[172] Of these nineteen, five or six appear in 1279 as tenants at nearby Hanslope just across the county border, while three other 1279 tenants bear the surnames of other perpetrators.[173] Unfortunately, there is no indication of who instigated this raid, although the fact that Hugh was attached to the queen's party suggests that more than local issues were involved.[174]

Once again, the roll identifies men who were in castle garrisons: at Windsor,[175] Wallingford,[176] and Kenilworth.[177] We also learn more of networks of association and their consequences. As we have seen, Walter de Burg, a bailiff of Earl Simon, is described as a fellow (*socius*) of William de Lay. Henry of Okeburn, accused of plundering, called to warrant William de Derneford, who says that John Giffard has quittance for himself and all his men.[178] Gilbert de Morton, who supported Robert fitz Nigel and sent his men to aid him, was the steward of Osbert Giffard, an adherent of Earl Simon.[179] William de Stokes was charged with being a bailiff and minster of the earl of Leicester and despoiling the area (*patria*) of Aylesbury and elsewhere. He said that he had been in the service of the earl for twelve years before the war and that he was 'with the earl'.[180] He had been sent to the land of Richard de Seyton the royal justice, with letters from the earl for levying a rent. He said, however, that he appropriated nothing and had committed no hostile

---

[170] Just 1/179 m.6d.

[171] The location of Chilton suggests that the target here was Grey's manor of Ludgershall, not Eton or Bletchley.

[172] Just 1/179 m. 2d.   [173] *Hundred Rolls*, ii, 344. Did Hugh perhaps hold the living there?

[174] Hugh was perhaps related to John de la Penne, who held the manor of La Penne in Burnham Hundred: *VCH Buckinghamshire* iii, 237.

[175] The following are revealed as members of the Windsor garrison with John fitz John: Walter de Rudham, Richard de la Vache, Jordan de Saukevill, Adam Nutting and Michael Benechose (there *ad vadia*, m. 17d.), Nicholas Herlwyne, convicted of plundering £12 worth of goods, and said that he left Windsor Castle with Jordan de Saukervill, Simon Russel of Datchet (who was charged with being a constable guarding his hundred by day and night), and John de St Helens.

[176] William de Tulhuse, who held two hides at Ludgershall and land in Hanslope and Crendon, was said to have been there, as was Robert Ravel, 'a plunderer'.

[177] At Kenilworth were Stephen de Holewell (who was killed there), Anketil de Burton, Richard Borre, John le Franc of Great Harwood, Ralf Marmion (with Stephen de Holewell), and John de Esse (in the party of William de Beauchampton and later taken to Ely by Gerard de Insula).

[178] Just 1/179 m. 17d. Giffard held at Little Missenden and Tyringham.

[179] Just 1/179 m. 6d. He was pardoned for his role as sheriff at the siege of Kenilworth and at Evesham.

[180] He also held land of the fee of Leicester.

186 POLITICS AND SOCIETY IN MID THIRTEENTH-CENTURY ENGLAND

act.[181] The Montfortians seem to have been perennially short of money. Peter de la Chaumbre, 'a plunderer', said that he was sent by the bailiff of Newport hundred under the sheriff, Simon de Pattishall, to make a levy under the green wax. Henry de Crandon, described as a *lindraper*, recruited a man for Wallingford Castle. He said he held land of the earl of Leicester and was distrained to do it by the earl's bailiff. The jury agreed, but he was nonetheless convicted.[182] Shortage of manpower was clearly another, and quite serious, problem. Robert de Dodinton, *juvenis*, was charged with being constable of Doddington and taking slings and slingers to Northampton to defend it against the king. He was in the retinue (*societate*) of Nicholas de la Champayne. We also learn that James de Appleby was in the service of Nicholas de Segrave, that Hugh Peche was steward of Henry de Hastings, that Geoffrey Mortimer was of the *familia* of Baldwin Wake and was captured at Northampton with horses and arms, that Sir John Bordon was of the household of John Giffard, as well as of the many men who were associated with the earl of Gloucester.[183]

Towns and Clergy

It is difficult to pass a verdict on where Buckinghamshire stood overall. That the society was divided is clear enough. This is shown in the case of the towns. Wendover, despite being in the hands of John fitz John and his bailiffs and having to submit 'by force and distraint' to his collection of aid, was found not guilty of participating in any acts of robbery.[184] Brill, on the other hand, summoned to execute the Dictum, refused and Wycombe in 1269 was fined £10 for its double contempt (*pro dupplici contemptu*).[185] Amersham and Marlow were in mercy for the same, and the former was fined 40s. as late as November 1270 for failing to make any presentations.[186] They do not appear to have been characteristic of the whole county, however. Aylesbury, Walton, and Borton all claimed that they had been of the king's party and that they had given hospitality to the king's faithful men (*fideles*).[187] Furthermore, they had letters patent of Lord Edward showing that they were among his friends and were faithful to the king (*de amicitia sua et fideles domini Regi*). All three towns were found to be innocent of any misdeeds.

The same division is found among the clergy. The possessions of foreign ecclesiastics were marked out for plunder. The parson of Ivinghoe comes up repeatedly as the victim of robbery.[188] He is not named, but the advowson of the church belonged to the see of Winchester and Aylmer de Valence invariably instituted foreigners. Aylmer's manor of West Wycombe was also the object of attack.

---

[181] Just 1/179 m. 16. [182] Ibid., m. 18d. [183] See above 146–9.
[184] Just 1/179 m. 17. [185] Ibid., m. 2d. [186] Ibid. [187] Ibid., m. 11d.
[188] Ibid., mm. 9, 13, 15d

CIVIL WAR 187

Naturally, the property of foreign monasteries was also targeted. The manor of Tingewick, belonging to the abbot of Mount S. Katherine at Rouen, was plundered, as was the property of the French abbot of Grestein and that of Peter, the prior of Newington Longueville, an alien Cluniac house.[189] Naturally, these were royalist, as was the abbot of Thame (Oxfordshire). Unsurprisingly, though, as in Berkshire there were regular clergy who aided the Montfortians. The abbot of St Albans was attached for sending men to the assistance of the earl of Leicester (*de missione hominum suorum ad Marchiam comitis Leyc'*). The abbot's attorney brandished a writ remitting him of all trespasses 'during the time of tumult' for the sum of 300 marks.[190] The abbot of Notley was charged with receiving enemies of the king, namely Simon himself, his steward Richard de Havering, and others of his party.[191] The abbot responded that his predecessor, deceased, had indeed done so but instructed the court that the house had been founded by 'the Marshals of England' whose heiress Simon had married. The house was therefore unable to resist, and duly received them. He insisted, however, that his predecessor had not been an enemy of the king. The abbot of Woburn (Bedfordshire) had taken corn from Master Robert of Edgcott, while Brother Nicholas, a canon of the Premonstratensian house of Lavendon, had purchased corn belonging to John de Grey. The master of the hospital of Hogshaw had done likewise.[192] The prior of Luffield was in mercy for not allowing his men of Thornborough to attend the royal court, while the abbot of Missenden was asked why he had held his own court when he had been prohibited from doing so. He replied that he was not aware of this prohibition and that he had not done so in contempt of the king.[193]

As one would expect, members of the secular clergy were found on both sides. Many were plundered. There were others, however, who were with the rebels. Indeed, they were thicker on the ground than plundered royalists. A serious case was that of Master Henry de Luton', the principal plunderer accused of burning and plundering against the royalist, Roger de Molis, and others (*depredator principalis, ardendo depredando*).[194] He was sentenced to five years redemption of his property. This is the man otherwise known as Master Henry de Leytton, 'king's enemy', whose land the sheriff was ordered to seize and who was later an adherent of the earl of Gloucester in 1267. Roger the chaplain of Hertwell plundered John le Waleys of 120 sheep and 4 pigs.[195] He was found to be a *consiliarius* and *procurator* against the king. Walter Neyrnuit, parson of Pitstone (Yardley), was accused of plundering and receiving the king's enemies but found not guilty.[196] As Walter, parson of Pitstone, he was also accused of plundering hay. Then there was Miles, parson of Drayton, otherwise known as Miles de Beauchamp, accused of

---

[189] Ibid., mm. 6, 18, 19.   [190] Ibid., m. 18d.   [191] Ibid., m. 19d.
[192] Ibid., mm. 6, 6d, 12.   [193] Ibid., m. 2d.   [194] Ibid., m. 11d.
[195] Ibid., m. 15d.   [196] Ibid., m. 13.

188   POLITICS AND SOCIETY IN MID THIRTEENTH-CENTURY ENGLAND

plundering John Russel and others.[197] The last two cases seem to indicate clearly that clerical brethren of rebels often adhered to the same side as lay members of their families. One Master Roger was accused of vilely slandering Lord Edward at Oxford and of being an enemy of the king, but was found not guilty.[198] He probably belonged to the university.

An interesting case is that of Alan de Somery, not because he was plundered but because he is described as neutral (*ex neutral parte fuit*).[199] Alan had been thought 'to stand with' the rebel Robert fitz Nigel, but the jury found this to be untrue. In being neutral, Alan was not alone. Hugh de Plessis, son of the late earl of Warwick, was asked why he had plundered William de Chalgrave, presumably after Evesham, who was neutral (*qui fuit ex neutra parte*).[200] Similarly, John de Verdon was asked to respond with regard to his robbery of Geoffrey de Clivedon, who also took a neutral stance (*qui se ex neutra parte habuit*).[201] One would have expected royal courts to have stressed the indivisibility of fidelity to the king, that is to say you were either for him or a rebel. However, the concept of neutrality probably better matches the situation on the ground, as we saw when we examined the stances taken by 'county knights' in general.[202]

Another sidelight is shone by Henry de la Merke, who was charged inter alia with preaching against the king's peace.[203] In this he was far from being alone. One thinks especially of the gathering at Cow Meadow below Northampton where William Marshal organized preaching in favour of the earl of Leicester.[204] Back in August 1262, John Mansel had written that the royalists would be in a better position if they had preachers on their side of the calibre of those working for the opposition.[205] It is no coincidence that in the same year the king ordered the arrest of anyone who 'presumes to persuade the people or who preaches against us and our honour'.[206] The highly intellectual *Song of Lewes*, written in the wake of the battle and probably written by a Montfortian friar, seems to indicate the content of such sermons. It seems possible, as Sophie Ambler suggests, that the Montfortian bishops were involved in a wholesale preaching campaign, supported by friars and other members of the clergy.[207] As she says, the *Song of Lewes* 'set out the basis for revolution', explaining how the system of government could be changed.[208] In her view, the potential audience was vast. It needed to be: 'To

---

[197] Ibid. John Russel held at Grafton (Huntingdonshire) and Papworth (Cambridgeshire). He was on the royalist side at Evesham.

[198] Just 1/179 m. 18d.   [199] Ibid., m. 16.   [200] Ibid., m. 16d.   [201] Ibid., m. 17.

[202] See above 125–6.   [203] Just 1/179 m. 17d.   [204] Hunter, *Rotuli Selecti*, 194–5.

[205] Maddicott, *Simon de Montfort*, 221, citing *Royal Letters*, ii, 157–8. The date of the letter was established by Denholm-Young, *Richard of Cornwall*, 172–3.

[206] *CR 1261–4*, 123.

[207] For the role of the *Song of Lewes* in this context, see S. T. Ambler, *Bishops in the Political Community of England 1213–1272* (Oxford, 2017), 169–78. See also J. R. Maddicott, 'Politics and the People in Thirteenth-Century England', in *TCE*, xiv, 1–13.

[208] Ambler, *Bishops in the Political Community*, 171.

CIVIL WAR 189

ensure the survival of the new regime ... required nothing less than the mobilization of the broadest constituency'.[209]

The overriding impression from the special eyre rolls is that the years 1264–5 were characterized by a bitter and desperate struggle between the partisans of the two parties. It may well be, though, that these parties were outnumbered by those who preferred, insofar as they could, to remain neutral. Although a cross-section of lay society was drawn on, it is clear that numbers were inadequate and efforts were made, some of them violent, to recruit others. Some saw the possibility of social advancement through joining the cause.

The Outcome

In the meantime, the struggle on the ground was matched by the conflict that was dominating national politics.[210] It seems certain that the victory at the Battle of Lewes produced a wave of euphoria throughout the Montfortian party, and that Montfort was feted, at least hypothetically.[211] In the Mise of Lewes that underscored the king's humiliation, Henry promised to abide thoroughly by the Provisions of Oxford and to exclude all traitors from his council.[212] The Montfortians taken at Northampton were to be released, while the royalists captured at Lewes were to be ransomed. Lord Edward and Henry of Almain were taken as hostages to ensure the king's compliance. The issue of whether the Provisions of Oxford required 'correction' and the search for a permanent peace were both to be put to arbitration, involving high-ranking Frenchmen.[213] As part of the deal, ominously, the captured marcher barons were to be set free. This was to cause major problems for Montfort. In the meantime, however, he had full control of the government, even if the king was its nominal head.

There were, however, two major problems facing the Montfortian government. The first was the military threat, from 'the marchers' and the royalists in the north on the one hand and from the invasion force which the queen was soon putting together on the continent on the other. The second problem was the lack of legitimacy. To help with this the June parliament agreed to a constitution, known as the *Ordinatio* (or Ordinance).[214] Three men were to elect nine councillors, the three being Simon de Montfort, Gilbert de Clare, and the bishop of Chichester.

---

[209] Ibid., 178.

[210] For the narrative see again Jobson, *First English Revolution*, Ch. 5, and Maddicott, *Simon de Montfort*, Ch. 7.

[211] Maddicott, *Simon de Montfort*, 274; Carpenter, *Lewes and Evesham*, 37.

[212] For discussion of the Mise of Lewes (of which no original survives), see J. R. Maddicott, 'The Mise of Lewes, 1264', *EHR*, 98 (July 1983), 588–603; D. A. Carpenter, 'Simon de Montfort and the Mise of Lewes', *BIHR*, 58 (1985), 1–11, repr. in *The Reign of Henry III*, 281–91; Maddicott, *Simon de Montfort*, 272–8.

[213] Maddicott, 'The Mise of Lewes, 1264'.   [214] For which see *DBM*, 224–5.

190 POLITICS AND SOCIETY IN MID THIRTEENTH-CENTURY ENGLAND

They were where power actually lay. To oppose the serious military threat from the continent, in early July Simon called out the feudal host and assembled a huge army of peasants on Barham Downs. With a hostile papal legate seeking to enter England, armed with the power of excommunication and interdict, and a desperate need to win over Louis IX of France, the Peace of Canterbury was published, an enhanced version of the *Ordinatio*. Louis, however, totally refused to endorse it. On 20 October 1264, the legate finally pronounced the excommunication and interdict, from Artois. Although published abroad, this did cause consternation, especially within the church where the recent spoliation of its lands had made the country vulnerable to papal sanctions. The invasion force had eventually to disperse, but the 'marchers' remained a problem, necessitating a military campaign. The Peace of Worcester of 12 December 1264 imposed harsh conditions on them, including exile in Ireland and the final release of the Northampton prisoners. However, they had no intention of complying.

For a period of four months Simon was in full control. The regime, however, still had problems. A major one, as ever, was the exercise of patronage, given that the greatest benefits went to Simon himself and his sons. There were other worrying signs. Alan la Zouche was arrested for uttering threats against Montfort. More disturbing was the arrest and trial of the earl of Derby, who had been involved in a longstanding dispute with Lord Edward over the Peveril inheritance; he had seized the castle of the Peak, causing devastation around, notwithstanding the fact that it was now officially in Simon's hands. He was imprisoned in the Tower. Montfort's aim was strategic control of the north Midlands rather than personal gain as such, but his action led directly to the defection of Gilbert de Clare, who probably wondered if he would be next. Moreover, the increasing prominence of Simon's sons and his own declining influence must have severely tried him. Gilbert retreated to his estates in the marches where he was joined by John Giffard of Brimpsfeld. The earl was soon in contact with William de Valence and John de Warenne, who had landed in Pembrokeshire with 120 men. On 28 May Edward escaped from custody and joined Simon's enemy Roger Mortimer to be entertained by Roger and his wife, Maud, at Wigmore Castle. Clare now made common cause with Edward against Simon, after having extracted a promise that he would rule only through native-born Englishmen. The remainder of the story has been told many times. Montfort was trapped west of the River Severn, but managed to cross at Kempsey from where he quickly moved to Evesham, expecting to be joined there by Simon the Younger with his additional forces. Lord Edward, however, surprised these as they were camped outside Kenilworth, and many were taken prisoner. Montfort himself was left to face impossible odds against the forces of Edward, Clare, and Mortimer at what a contemporary chronicler called the 'murder of Evesham'.[215]

---

[215] For the battle, see below 224–7.

CIVIL WAR   191

Simon's death sent shock waves across the country. In reality, however, his position had been deteriorating for some time. The defection of Gloucester, followed by his contact with Mortimer and 'the marchers', had been a serious blow. Not only did the whole of the marches, from Chester to Gloucester, fall into Edward's hands, but his agents, and indeed Gloucester's, became active across much of the country. In an invaluable section of his thesis on the Disinherited, Clive Knowles sketched the state of the country.[216] His findings are important. In central England, as one would suspect, Simon's keepers of the peace, stalwarts of the regime, held firm and were loyally supported by their sheriffs, although in Huntingdonshire the keeper, Henry Engaine, seems to have gone over to the royalists, while in Northamptonshire, where the keeper, William Marshal, had died during the year, the loyalty of the sheriff, Eustace de Watford, was dubious. One of the men who went over to Gloucester's steward—who was given a commission to draw men back to the king's peace—was David de Ashby, a tenant of Henry de Hastings, who was offered horses, arms, and money. In the south-east, where the presence of Countess Eleanor at Dover was an important focus, there were, nonetheless, some defectors, including very probably the sheriff of Surrey and Sussex. In the south-west the picture was mixed. In Gloucestershire, both the sheriff, Reginald de Acle, and the keeper, William de Tracy, went over. In Somerset and Dorset the Montfortians seemed to hold firm, while in Devon the sheriff was unable to prevent the fall of Launceston Castle. In Shropshire and Herefordshire the sheriffs changed sides, notwithstanding the keeper being Ralph Basset of Drayton. In East Anglia the loyalty of some of the keepers was uncertain, the only clear case of unmitigated support being Richard de Tany in Essex and Hertford, although of the sheriff, Nicholas le Spigurnel, it was later said that 'he never withdrew from his fealty to the king and Edward his son'.[217] In fact, he was reappointed sheriff after the Battle of Evesham. Although the keepers in Yorkshire, Nottinghamshire, Derbyshire, and Lincolnshire remained firm, the sheriff of the last, Giles de Gousle, went over. Here Thomas de Boulton, Edward's sergeant, accepted pledges of allegiance from former Montfortians who, Knowles tells us, felt that a loyalist victory was 'imminent'.[218] In the far north there was a steady swing in favour of Edward where his representatives had a great deal of success in bringing men back into the peace. In Westmorland thirty-three men came back on 28 June, while in Lancashire the sheriff deserted.

Knowles concludes that with Montfort isolated from the rest of England and the royalists gaining ground, Simon's local administration began to crumble everywhere. It seems that a large number of the sheriffs appointed after Lewes

---

[216] C. H. Knowles, 'The Disinherited, 1265–80: A Political and Social Study of the Supporters of Simon de Montfort and the Resettlememt after the Barons' War' (University of Wales PhD thesis, 1959), Part I, Ch. 1. This contains a great deal more detail than is conveyed here.

[217] *CPR 1258–66*, 442, 446; Knowles, 'The Disinherited', Part I, Ch. 1, 13.

[218] Ibid., 12.

192 POLITICS AND SOCIETY IN MID THIRTEENTH-CENTURY ENGLAND

had cooperated with Montfort without being committed to his programme. They were therefore able to transfer their loyalties to Edward without any difficulty. Even among the keepers of the peace, whom one would have expected to have been Montfort's strongest supporters, there were those who either deserted or waited on events. In short, Montfort lost much of his hold on the country during the summer of 1265. 'Everywhere men who had formally supported the earl or had acquiesced to his rule were forced to re-examine their allegiance, and many of them joined the loyalists as an insurance against the fate which would surely overtake the supporters of Montfort if he was defeated'.[219]

In this they were not wrong. Just as Edward, Clare, and Mortimer had been unwilling or unable to stop the orgy of killing that immediately followed the fighting at Evesham, so the king made no attempt to prevent the wholesale seizure of rebel lands after the battle; on the contrary he encouraged it.[220] In fact, in Buckinghamshire and Oxfordshire confiscations began the very next day, followed by Bedfordshire and Berkshire the day after and Leicestershire and Kent on the 7th. By mid-August they had reached Devon. Within a few weeks of Evesham more than a thousand estates and properties had been seized or looted by loyalists in a whirlwind of reprisals and vengeance.[221] This was all very well, but it must soon have become clear to the king and his advisors that an official settlement had to be made, and a parliament was consequently called at Winchester in early September.[222] On 17 September Robert Walerand pronounced the verdict. All supporters of Simon de Montfort were to forfeit their lands to the king, and all the property seized after Evesham was to pass into the king's hands. A national survey was ordered which would list the names and holding of the Montfortians. Two knights were appointed in each county, or contiguous counties, to help the sheriffs in making extents.[223] Those who had seized the Michaelmas rents were to restore them. The information gathered by the *seisitores* was to be available on 13 October at Westminster and parliament was prorogued until then. Meanwhile severe reprisals were taken against London and its citizens. At the adjourned parliament the disherison of the rebels was publicly proclaimed, and the official distribution of rebel lands began. In the words of Clive Knowles, 'The king was surrounded by a jostling throng of followers all demanding rewards for their loyalty'.[224]

---

[219] Ibid., 16.

[220] The classic account is again by Clive Knowles in 'The Resettlement of England after the Barons' War, 1264–7', *TRHS*, 32 (1982), 25–41. More detail is given in his thesis, 'The Disinherited', especially Part III, Ch. 1, 'The Seizures after the Battle of Evesham', which is also drawn on here.

[221] Ibid., 2.

[222] For what follows see Knowles, 'The Disinherited', Part III, Ch. 2, 'Disherison and the Territorial Revolution'.

[223] The surviving returns are collected in *Calendar of Inquisitions Miscellaneous Preserved in the Public Record Office*, Vol. I (London, HMSO, 1916), nos. 608–944.

[224] Knowles, 'The Disinherited', Part III, Ch. 2, 15.

CIVIL WAR 193

The redistribution was more organized than the original seizures, but still 'far from orderly'. Grants were unevenly spread, and local men often 'passed over'. The main roll of grants shows the lands of 316 rebels being given to 133 royalists. However, looking more closely, the estates of 254 rebels were 'conferred on a specially favoured group of only 71 supporters of the king'.[225] Pre-eminent were members of the royal family: Edward, Edmund, Queen Eleanor (whose share included the estates of the northern magnate John D'Eyville), and Eleanor of Castile.[226] Next came household knights and royal officials.[227] Among baronial supporters, however, only Roger Mortimer was particularly favoured (gaining inter alia the lands of the earl of Oxford). Of the other 'marchers', and in addition to Mortimer's wife, Maud, who gained £100 land in her own right, Roger de Clifford did particularly well.[228] Some, arguably, were inadequately rewarded, primarily the earl of Gloucester. The 'territorial revolution', as Knowles calls it, created a new power structure on the ruins of the old. Land was concentrated in fewer hands. Even the loyalist sympathizer Thomas Wykes was shocked at 'the reckless way' in which the king's followers had distributed the lands of the rebels *sine personarum discretione*.[229]

Consequently, as Knowles also says, they created 'social dislocation and misery on an unparalleled scale'.[230] Hundreds of men faced ruin and turned to guerrilla tactics. The result was two more years of warfare until the king and the 'Disinherited' finally came to terms.[231] This ought not to have happened, given that the Montfortian position had largely collapsed after Evesham, as shown by the surrender of many key castles. However, the harshness of the 'territorial revolution' encouraged Simon de Montfort junior to open a new centre of resistance in the Isle of Axholme, where he was joined by John D'Eyville, Baldwin Wake, and others. However, they were forced to come to terms in December at Bycarrs Dyke, and in February 1266 Simon junior left for the continent and the resistance of the Cinque Ports collapsed. By the early summer the rebels were in reduced circumstances, with resistance more or less centred on Kenilworth,

---

[225] Knowles, 'The Resettlement of England', 26. See Hunter, *Rotuli Selecti*, 247–58, and Jacob, *Studies in the Period of Reform and Rebellion*, 153–5.

[226] Edmund's allocation of the estates of Simon de Montfort and Nicholas de Segrave was in compensation for the cancellation of the Sicilian enterprise. This made him a very large landowner in the midlands, especially in Leicestershire. His acquisition of the estates of the earl of Derby strengthened his regional power even further.

[227] They were headed by Robert Walerand, who substantially increased his holding in Somerset and Dorset, as well as in Essex and East Anglia.

[228] He acquired various manors of William de Birmingham, Walter de Baskerville, Ralf Basset of Drayton, John de Bracebridge, and Thomas de Clinton, mainly in Herefordshire, Gloucestershire, and Warwickshire.

[229] Chronicon vulgo dictum Chronicon Thomae Wykes, 1066–1288, Annales Monastici, ed. H. R. Luard, Vol. iv, Rolls Series (1869), 183.

[230] Knowles, 'The Resettlement of England', 27.

[231] What follows is drawn from Knowles, 'The Disinherited', Part I, Ch. 2, 'The War of the Disinherited'.

194 POLITICS AND SOCIETY IN MID THIRTEENTH-CENTURY ENGLAND

Derbyshire, and Essex. However, they were beginning to reform, and in May they gathered at Baldwin Wake's manor of Chesterfield. In the same month there was a Montfortian riot in London. Once the rebels had been defeated at Chesterfield, in the north and in Essex and East Anglia, however, the way was open for an attack on Kenilworth.[232]

Although a stream of rebels had come into the king's peace during the first half of 1266, the war was far from over. In August D'Eyville led the occupation of the Isle of Ely, opening a new locus of resistance. With moderate opinion pressing for compromise, a procedure was established to create a settlement. The result was the Dictum of Kenilworth, published 31 October 1266. Disherison was now to be replaced by redemption. The followers of Montfort were to recover their estates by paying fines on a scale based on the annual value of their lands and the degree of their involvement in the rebellion. Whatever hopes the king and his advisors may have had, this did not bring an end to the war. The hard core of rebels found the terms unacceptable, although there were probably other factors too.[233] Although the Kenilworth garrison, in dire straits and exhausted, finally surrendered in December 1266, and men had been coming to terms since November, the hard core was irreconcilable. Moreover, the Isle of Ely was a greater threat than Kenilworth had ever been, given the support from the countryside and the ability of the rebels to raise money both from Cambridge burgesses and from the resident Jews. The town jury of Cambridge later admitted that 'in very truth the whole province sold the rebels the necessities of life, which they took back to the island'.[234]

It was now that the earl of Gloucester entered the fray, demanding the removal of aliens from the king's council and acceptance of the Provisions of Oxford.[235] To these he later added the restoration of the rebels' lands prior to acceptance of the Dictum. With negotiations a failure and plans for a siege of the island in preparation, Gloucester decided to attack, in concert with D'Eyville and the Ely rebels, and to march on London. On 20 April the *minutus populus* rose, overthrew the ruling oligarchy of merchants, and replaced the aldermen by keepers. Two new bailiffs were appointed, and above them stood Gloucester's own high bailiff, Hugh de Coleworth. However, with the military balance swinging in favour of the king, Gloucester came to terms. John D'Eyville and his companions followed suit. The king agreed to exhort those who held the rebels' lands to restore seisin,

---

[232] The East Anglians were heavily defeated at Alton in Hampshire.

[233] *DBM*, no. 44. Knowles suggests that they objected to the Dictum's declaration of the invalidity of Simon's acts and to the attempts to suppress his popular veneration as a saint: 'The Disinherited', Part I, Ch. 3, 31.

[234] Jacob, *Studies in the Period of Reform and Rebellion*, 236–7. The assize roll for Cambridgeshire, moreover, reveals a chaotic situation: Hunter, *Rotuli Selecti*, 231–46, and Jacob, *Studies in the Period of Reform and Rebellion*, 395–406.

[235] For a detailed discussion see Knowles, 'The Disinherited', Part I, Chs. 4 and 5. See also Altschul, *A Baronial Family*, 110–21.

while the papal legate promised some financial help. On 1 July 1267 John D'Eyville and others had their pardons enrolled. Even then the struggle was not quite finished. The intransigent Henry de Hastings held out until the loyalists entered the Isle on 13 July. The war was finally over.

In the words of Clive Knowles: 'In the years 1265–7 the individual rebel was confronted, not so much with the question of the advisability of baronial reform and the fundamental rights of kingship, but with the more squalid, if agonizingly personal problem of confiscation and disherison'.[236] He clearly envisaged a radical shift in the character of the war. It can be seriously doubted, however, whether the struggle had ever really been about principles. In the pages above we have learned a great deal about the exercise of local power and influence. Many men sought to protect and/or improve their positions. Some saw the possibility of social advancement and availed themselves of the opportunities offered. After Evesham royalists helped themselves to estates and were later rewarded with the receipt of substantial redemption fines. Conflicts must often have antedated the war, as in the case of the struggle between Peter de Anesley and John de Vernon over the manor of Basildon. In south-east Staffordshire, middling aristocrats vied for control. In the words of their historian, John Hunt, 'Those who were suitably placed—men like Philip Marmion, Roger de Somery and Ralph Basset of Drayton, pursued opportunities presented by the disruption of civil war to enhance their local position and resources—as did those upon whom they relied in the locality'.[237] We are in the world of retinues, service, loyalty, and reward, and of the affective relations that these involved. In all of this, however, it is rather difficult to feel anything much of the idealism which some historians of the period are fond of asserting.

Politics and Society in Mid Thirteenth-Century England: The Troubled Realm. Peter Coss, Oxford University Press.
© Peter Coss 2024. DOI: 10.1093/9780198924319.003.0007

---

[236] Knowles, 'The Disinherited', Part I, Ch. 5, 69.   [237] Hunt, 'Families at War', 21.

8

Simon de Montfort and His Support

And so, inevitably, we come to Simon de Montfort. There has been a tendency in the past to see the actions of Simon de Montfort—the supposed founder of parliament and pioneer of popular representation—as so extraordinary as to be historically transcendent. This view was bequeathed by nineteenth-century scholars and espoused by others into the second half of the twentieth century. These days most professional historians tend to be more circumspect. Many do still regard him, however, as effectively *sui generis*. One can hardly pick up a modern book on Simon de Montfort without being confronted by the claim that he is in fact an 'enigma'.[1] The words may differ, but the idea is the same. Thus, Margaret Wade Labarge wrote in 1962: 'The paradoxes and contradictions of his character perplexed his contemporaries, as they have confused later generations of students';[2] and John Maddicott in 1984: 'his participation ... was by no means an unambivalent matter, for it was distorted by appetites, greed and grievances which cast a shadow over his motives and which raise for any historian the most difficult questions about his ultimate ambitions'.[3] More recent writers have tended to be of the same mind. Adrian Jobson wrote of a complex mixture of 'idealism' and 'manipulation of the "machinery of reform" in furtherance of his private interests',[4] while according to Darren Baker this 'improbable mix of idealism and self-interest is what makes Simon de Montfort such an intriguing figure'.[5] The apparent dichotomy between public and private interests lies at the heart of the matter. There are, however, other dimensions, such as the foreign-born noble who urged strong action against aliens, and the man whose essentially secular ambitions had fanatically religious overtones. But are these 'contradictions' overstated? And do they, in fact, rely over-much on modern rather than contemporary standards? What I want to do in this chapter is to put Simon de Montfort back into context, while at the same time deploying modern concepts in trying to pin down his role and significance in an attempt to understand the Montfortian regime. I will look in particular at the support he commanded and his own actions in engendering it. It will end, as did he, with the Battle of Evesham.

---

[1] In what follows I have drawn on my essay 'Ugolino of the Gherardesca and the "Enigma" of Simon de Montfort', *TCE*, xviii (Woodbridge, 2023), 71–88.

[2] Labarge, *Simon de Montfort*, 276. For Victorian and early to mid-twentieth-century views, see Knowles, *Simon de Montfort 1265–1965*. Knowles himself was more sceptical than most of his forbears.

[3] Maddicott, *Simon de Montfort*, xiv.   [4] Jobson, *First English Revolution*, 21.

[5] Darren Baker, *Simon de Montfort and the Rise of the English Nation* (Stroud, 2015).

SIMON DE MONTFORT AND HIS SUPPORT   197

If we are looking for the roots of the Montfortian 'enigma', however, we can hardly do better than to concentrate on the dichotomy between the man of principle and the seeker after personal advantage on which most scholars comment. Simon, as we know, lost no opportunity to bring his material grievances, most specifically those concerning his wife's dower, into play.[6] On 5 May 1258, only three days after the king had formally agreed to a committee of reform, he was pressed into agreeing that he would accept the committee's decision on assigning land to Simon and on the payment of the king's debts to him.[7] Famously, he and Countess Eleanor held up the negotiations and the ratification of the Treaty of Paris over this issue. As we have seen, Simon and his sons profited considerably from the Montfortian regime. Not surprisingly, the opprobrium directed at Simon their father in some quarters extended to his sons. One of them, Henry, died at Evesham, and another, Guy, was lucky to have survived it.

It is not just a question of the nuclear family, however, but of the lineage. It was a matter of aristocratic lore that a man was in effect a custodian of his family's position and that it was his duty to maintain and, if possible, extend its interests during his tenure. People were conscious of their family's prestige as well as its material concerns, and this was felt to lie across past, present, and future. Simon, as is well known, was deeply conscious of his father's role as an exemplar. Sophie Ambler has recently put great emphasis on this aspect of his thinking.[8] He was born to rule and to fight in God's cause. As Ambler says, 'to be a Montfort is to be a knight, is to be a crusader'.[9] If there is a dichotomy here it is a general one to which aristocrats were prone. It seems unlikely that these men felt any conflict of principle between fighting for one's own and one's family interests on the one hand and fighting for the interests of the collective on the other. One principle, or perhaps one should say behavioural norm, could be accommodated within the other: the interests of the family could be accented within the interests of the collective. Moreover, the aristocracy was by nature expansive, and a spirit of adventurism was inherent among its membership. This often led to conquests, to the winning of heiresses, and to upwards mobility in position and status. There is something of the knight errant about Simon de Montfort, the high-born knight who wins a heiress and conquers by the sword to become an effective and praised ruler. It was normal aristocratic practice, moreover, to seek to profit from what the Germans call *königsnehe*, closeness to the king. The ultimate prize was a throne. Contemporary aristocrats understood this very well, not least the members of the royal family. Henry III clearly felt at times in danger of being deposed, perhaps in favour of his son. Edward also had much to fear. Montfort was not, of course, of

---

[6] This is a leitmotif in the biographies; see especially those of Labarge and Maddicott.

[7] *CPR 1247–58*, 267.

[8] 'Simon, as his son and namesake, bore the air of his celebrity': Ambler, *The Song of Simon de Montfort*, 40. See also her account of Simon de Montfort in Gascony: ibid., especially 111, 122.

[9] Ibid., 29.

198   POLITICS AND SOCIETY IN MID THIRTEENTH-CENTURY ENGLAND

royal blood and could barely aspire to the throne, but his sons, being nephews of
the current king, certainly could.

Charisma

Clearly, there was an extra dimension to Simon de Montfort. It comes as no
surprise to find that he has been, and still is, considered charismatic.[10] Darren
Baker calls him 'an inspiring and charismatic leader' and 'a charismatic Anglo-
French nobleman'.[11] The strongest statement comes from Simon's most recent
biographer, Sophie Ambler: 'The revolution required an uncommon leader, possessed of uncommon traits: above all, monumental audacity and charisma. This
is charisma not in the quotidian sense, but in the sense that describes the belief of
Simon's followers that he was superhuman, even sent by God'. 'Charisma', she
adds, 'is one of the few forces powerful enough to change the world'.[12] Is his
'charisma', then, yet another dimension to the 'enigma' of Simon de Montfort?

Is 'charisma', in fact, a viable concept when it comes to understanding the
thirteenth-century aristocracy? If so, in what sense or senses of the word does it
help us? In general, medievalists have tended to apply the concept more to
churchmen than to secular lords.[13] There are good reasons for this. In origin the
word applied to a spiritual gift enjoyed by the early Christians, and it was
employed in this sense by Paul of Tarsus. Consequently, charisma was an issue of
debate amongst nineteenth-century theologians. As is well known, however, the
concept was reinvented by the early twentieth-century sociologist Max Weber.[14]
For Weber charisma is an innate quality which sets some people apart and draws
others magnetically to them, and charismatic authority is a form of leadership
exercised by those who possess this extraordinary but rather elusive quality. In
this, perhaps primary, sense, charisma is more or less synonymous with animal
magnetism and with mesmerism, in the sense of a spellbinding appeal reflecting

[10] See, for example, Daniel Williams, 'Simon de Montfort and his Adherents', in Ormrod (ed.),
England in the Thirteenth Century, 166–77, at 171 and 176, and Ambler, *Bishops in the Political
Community*, 129 and 136.

[11] Baker, *Simon de Montfort*, 21 and 210.

[12] Ambler, *Song of Simon de Montfort*, 5–6. See also her comments on 280 and on the meaning of
charisma in Ambler, *Bishops in the Political Community*, 29.

[13] See, for example, William M. Aird, 'Saint Anselm of Canterbury and Charismatic Authority',
Religions, 5 (2014), 90–108. I have drawn on this essay both for its content and for its citations. For
'the charisma of the episcopal office', see Ambler, *Bishops in the Political Community*, 7. See also
D. L. d'Avray, *Medieval Religious Rationalities: A Weberian Analysis* (Cambridge, 2010).

[14] See, especially, John Potts, *A History of Charisma* (Basingstoke, 2009). Weber's *Wirtschaft und
Gesellschaft* was published in 1922. Part One was translated by R. A. Henderson and edited by Talcott
Parsons as *Theory of Social Organisation* (New York) in 1947 and the entirety as *Economy and Society:
An Outline of Interpretative Sociology*, ed. G. Roth and C. Wittich, trans. E. Fischoff et al. (New York,
1968). See also *From Max Weber: Essays in Sociology*, trans., edited, and introduced by H. H. Gerth
and C. Wright Mills (London, 1947).

SIMON DE MONTFORT AND HIS SUPPORT 199

such magnetism. However, Weber spoke also of the 'charisma of office', a product as he saw it of the 'routinization of charisma', as officeholders inherited it from a primary possessor.[15]

In which of these senses, then, is charisma applicable to Simon de Montfort? Daniel Williams refers to his 'charismatic spell' as leader, while Sophie Ambler speaks of his 'magnetic power'.[16] He certainly seems to have had the capacity to draw men to him.[17] Such 'magnetic power' must have been an invaluable ingredient in the leadership of any lord when it came to running his affinity, most especially in times of war when men might be called upon, if necessary, to die alongside him. This magnetic quality, moreover, seems to have allowed Simon to reach out beyond his own affinity to enthuse, if not captivate, other, especially younger, barons.[18]

But what of the religious dimension, which Ambler emphasizes? Simon de Montfort was, of course, popularly venerated as a saint, and sainthood is not entirely divorced from spiritual charisma.[19] In England it had become peculiarly attached to those who had suffered political martyrdom.[20] Moreover, Simon had, as Claire Valente puts it, 'many characteristics typical of saints: piety, single-mindedness, self-righteousness, and a noble cause given by God'.[21] André Vauchez speaks of the 'charismatic sanctity', and, in fact, of the 'charismatic and functional sainthood', of kings and bishops. Interestingly, and in contrast, the Papal *Curia* had become increasingly wary by this time of 'charismatic' claims to sainthood.[22]

Many scholars, however, add another dimension to Simon's appeal: an extraordinary piety and a close association with high-minded churchmen. Our starting point here must be John Maddicott's splendidly nuanced portrait.[23] Maddicott admits that, when all else has been said, Simon's piety had 'a deeply conventional side': 'Montfort's affection for the religious, the value he placed on monastic

[15] It was an idea which Weber borrowed from Rudolf Sohm, who used it of the early church: R. Sohm, *Outlines of Church History*, trans. M. Sinclair (London, 2013; first pub. 1895).

[16] Williams, 'Simon de Montfort and his Adherents', 176; Ambler, *Song of Simon de Montfort*, 280.

[17] According to Ambler, 'Montfort's charisma was the compelling force that drew the bishops to him and his cause': *Bishops in the Political Community*, 136.

[18] See the summary in Williams, 'Simon de Montfort and his Adherents', 171.

[19] See, especially, C. Valente, 'Simon de Montfort, Earl of Leicester, and the Utility of Sanctity in Thirteenth-Century England', *Journal of Medieval History*, 21 (1995), 27–49.

[20] A. Vauchez, *Sainthood in the Later Middle Ages* (Cambridge, 1997), 155, 170. Vauchez also points out that elsewhere 'popular martyred saints were relatively rare in the medieval world'. See also J. C. Russell, 'The Canonization of Opposition to the King in Angevin England', in Charles H. Taylor and John L. La Monte (eds.), *Haskins Anniversary Essays* (New York, 1929), 280–98. This is not to say that martyrdom was a necessary ingredient. We need to set against it the bishop–saints of thirteenth-century England, although they were in a sense part of the Becket tradition.

[21] Valente, 'Simon de Montfort, Earl of Leicester', 48.

[22] Vauchez, *Sainthood*, 159, 307, 391, 418. One may well speak of 'charismatic kingship', given its sacral quality: Ambler, *Bishops in the Political Community*, 7. Weber spoke of charismatic kingship as the exercise of a form of hereditary charisma.

[23] Maddicott, *Simon de Montfort*, Ch. 3, 'Religion and Virtue'.

200 POLITICS AND SOCIETY IN MID THIRTEENTH-CENTURY ENGLAND

prayer, and his desire for "fraternal association" ... are undoubted."[24] Moreover, the central place he accorded the crusades was by no means untypical of high-placed noblemen of the thirteenth century, just as had been the case in the twelfth. There were facets of his piety, however, that were very much a product of his times. He was a child of the Fourth Lateran Council, which stressed the need for regular confession, frequent participation in the eucharist, and receptivity to the teaching of the clergy. Like others, he was strongly supportive of the friars, especially of the Franciscans and their mission. None of this marks Simon out.

What does mark him out, however, is the strength of his convictions. He seems to have had what Ambler calls 'a holy war mindset', which governed his behaviour and beliefs.[25] This lay, she believes, at the heart of the 'pure charisma' which, after his God-given victory at Lewes, transformed or even 'transfigured' him in the eyes of his followers into 'something almost superhuman.'[26] She draws substantially here on the so-called *Song of Lewes*, written by a highly learned supporter.[27] This interpretation of Simon's appeal, and the mental outlook that underpinned it, is reinforced by his famous friendship with high-ranking churchmen, the most prominent being Robert Grosseteste, bishop of Lincoln, the Franciscan Adam Marsh, Eudes Rigaud, archbishop of Rouen, and Walter de Cantilupe, bishop of Worcester.[28] Such men were not of the common stock of thirteenth-century ecclesiastics.[29] They were high-minded, disciplined, harsh if necessary, and rather uncompromising zealots, whose passion was to make the world conform to their ideals. There was a mutuality here, and it seems clear that they saw themselves as working through Simon, just as he drew succour from them. An indicative episode comes from very early in his career in England. One of his first acts in his newly acquired lordship in Leicester was to expel the Jewish inhabitants of the town. They responded, not unreasonably, by translocating to the other half of the lordship held by Margaret de Quincy, countess of Winchester. She promptly found herself in receipt of a stern rebuke from Robert Grosseteste, at that time archdeacon of Leicester. He not only endorsed Simon's action but reinforced it with theological justification.[30] It was from Robert Grosseteste, moreover, that Simon absorbed the Aristotelian concept of tyranny, as found among medieval kings.[31] There is an interesting contrast to be made, as Maddicott has pointed out,

---

[24] Ibid., 104–5.   [25] Ambler, *Song of Simon de Montfort*, 28–9, 235, 420.   [26] Ibid., 280.

[27] *The Song of Lewes*, ed. and trans. C. L. Kingsford (Oxford, 1963).

[28] The relationships are neatly captured in Maddicott, *Simon de Montfort*, 77–84.

[29] The standard of thirteenth-century bishops, however, was high. For an elegant and incisive appreciation of their political role, see Ambler, *Bishops in the Political Community*.

[30] For Simon's charter see Maddicott, *Simon de Montfort*, 15, and for Robert's letter *Roberti Grosseteste Episcopi Lincolniensis 1235–53, Epistolae*, ed. H. R. Luard (London: Rolls Series, 1861), no. 5. For a translation see F. A. C. Mantello and J. Goering (eds.), *The Letters of Robert Grosseteste* (Toronto, 2010), no. 5. For a full discussion of the episode see Ambler, *Song of Simon de Montfort*, 44–9.

[31] See S. T. Ambler, 'On Kingship and Tyranny: Grosseteste's Memorandum and its Place in the Baronial Reform Movement', *TCE*, xiv, *Proceedings of the Aberystwyth and Lampeter Conference 2011*, ed. J. Burton, P. Schofield, and B. K. Weiler (Woodbridge, 2013), 115–28.

between Simon's friendship and partnership with these men and the lack of a strong clerical component in his own household.[32] His behaviour was rather unconventional here. Simon's ecclesiastical contacts were decidedly high-powered ones, and it could be said that his relationship with these men earns him the title of 'honorary churchman'.

As far as Simon's 'charisma' is concerned, however, we may be in danger of placing too much emphasis on the religious component, as opposed to the underlying animal magnetism of the man. In this context I would like to return to Weber's concept of the 'routinization of charisma'. I would suggest that we can detect this in the lay world and that in this period a form of 'secular charisma' was coming to the fore, that is to say that it was beginning to adhere to some high-ranking noblemen as opposed to clerics. How might this have occurred? The intensifying prestige attached to knighthood from the late twelfth century onwards and the new emphasis upon nobility with which it was intimately associated were undoubtedly contributing factors, predicated as they were upon a spirit of social exclusion.[33] A corollary of this was an increasing demand for social deference, as David Crouch has recently emphasized.[34] Another factor was the visibility of wealth and social superiority, reflecting the increased spending power of the higher echelons of the nobility in particular. Some of the reaction to this is conveyed to us by moralists. Adam Marsh castigated Simon's countess, Eleanor, for her 'superfluous adornment', referring specifically to the painting of the face and plaited hair, and to jewellery and 'courtly attire', an accusation which gains some support from her surviving household roll.[35]

Wealth, prestige, and deference, combined with a strong sense of lineage, must have helped to create a sort of aristocratic hauteur, reinforced in the case of men like Simon with an over-weaning sense of self-belief. That he could be haughty in manner is evident enough. The Franciscan Adam Marsh says as much in a

[32] Maddicott, *Simon de Montfort*, 70.

[33] For nobility and knighthood in Italy and England, see Peter Coss, *The Aristocracy in England and Tuscany, 1000–1250* (Oxford, 2019), Ch. 8 and 418–28. The most recent monograph on chivalry is David Crouch, *The Chivalric Turn: Conduct and Hegemony in Europe before 1300* (Oxford, 2019). For the historiography, see Peter Coss, 'The Origins and Diffusion of Chivalry', in Robert W. Jones and Peter Coss (eds.), *A Companion to Chivalry* (Woodbridge, 2019), 7–38.

[34] Crouch, *The Chivalric Turn*, 272, 305. For Crouch, chivalry may be defined as 'a conjunction of hypermoral excellence and social hegemony situated in the knight': ibid., 300.

[35] Maddicott, *Simon de Montfort*, 42 and 92–3, citing *Monumenta Franciscana*, ed. J. S. Brewer and R. Howlett, 2 vols., Rolls Series (London), I, 1858–82, 294–6, 299, and *Manners and Household Expenses in Thirteenth and Fifteenth Centuries*, ed. T. H. Turner (Roxburghe Club, 1841), 25. See also *The Letters of Adam Marsh*, ed. and trans. C. H. Lawrence, 2 vols. (Oxford, 2006–10), ii, nos. 157, 160. For Eleanor's household, see L. J. Wilkinson, *Eleanor de Montfort: A Rebel Countess in Medieval England* (London, 2012), and for the roll L. J. Wilkinson, *The Household Roll of Eleanor de Montfort, Countess of Leicester and Pembroke, 1265*, Pipe Roll Society, n.s. 63 (Woodbridge, 2020). Simon's tastes are more uncertain. Two chroniclers write of his frugality and moderation in dress, and of his wearing of a hair shirt. For the details see Maddicott, *Simon de Montfort*, 87–90, who gives credence to both writers. However, they are relatively late and may be considered hagiographical. Even if we take this at face value, it would refer only to the last years of Simon's life.

202 POLITICS AND SOCIETY IN MID THIRTEENTH-CENTURY ENGLAND

famous letter to Simon, in which he advises him to 'govern the utterance of his tongue' for 'lack of restraint causes offence'.[36] Simon could be condescending, notably in cases where it was especially impolitic, as in his treatment of the young Gilbert de Clare. At the same time, though, he could be courteous and certainly persuasive in speech.[37]

Fundamental to any secular charisma must have been the image of the fearless, feared, and successful warrior. Simon de Montfort had developed such a reputation long before he reached the height of his career. But it was not just a question of warrior reputation. What is especially important in this context is that his reputation was gained in the service of the community. Finally, crucially but contentiously, there is the holding of offices that were very largely reserved for noblemen. Simon held such offices—seneschal of Gascony and steward of England, for example—and was famously offered others.[38] I say this 'characteristic' is contentious because it is an inversion of Weber, for whom as we have seen the charisma of office was derived from 'routinization'. Here I am suggesting that the holding of secular office by high-ranking noblemen was combined with a primary magnetic charisma in a manner which served to reinforce it. Finally, we should not neglect Weber's belief that charismatic leaders tend to arise at moments of distress or crisis, a feature which certainly applies to Simon.

These elements, it could be argued, were combining to produce a secular 'charisma'. Perhaps Simon de Montfort, with his cult of sanctity, represents a halfway house between religious and secular charisma. Danny Williams wrote appositely of his 'chivalric charisma', and this concept is perhaps significant.[39] Tim Reuter once suggested that the turn of the thirteenth century marked the end of traditional charismatic politics based on spiritual qualities. This observation, we might argue, is a little anachronistic, and that charisma not only persisted but also changed its locus.[40] There is, however, another way of looking at Simon de Montfort's striking persona. It is one given to us by the historians of masculinity. I have looked earlier at the significance of homosocial bonds, as witnessed characteristically in retinues and in looser affective relations.[41] The qualities Montfort encapsulated were clearly those of the hegemonic masculinity of his day, and were very different from those which emanated from the king, reliant as he was on the 'cosmic' dimension to his rank.[42] To borrow yet another concept,

---

[36] *Letters of Adam Marsh*, ed. and trans. C. H. Lawrence (Oxford, 2006–10), vol. ii, no. 141.

[37] Ibid., 350–1, quoting the chronicler William Rishanger.

[38] In 1241 he was said to have been chosen as regent of Jerusalem, while in 1253 members of the French nobility had wanted him as guardian of the crown and realm: Maddicott, *Simon de Montfort*, 30, 76, 121; Ambler, *Song of Simon de Montfort*, 89, 142–4, and Plate 15.

[39] Williams, 'Simon de Montfort and his Adherents', 170.

[40] See the arguments put forwards in Ambler, *Bishops in the Political Community*, 5–6, and the references given there.

[41] See above 154–5.   [42] See above 37.

SIMON DE MONTFORT AND HIS SUPPORT   203

Montfort's masculinity was iconic.[43] It embodied and propagated the contemporary ideal of manliness, involving physical courage and prowess, steadfastness, loyalty, and control. But whether we talk about charisma or iconic masculinity, men who personify these ideals—these avatars who inspire devotion—can also incite negative reactions: jealousy, envy, and vicious spite. There is no doubt that Simon earned the hatred of both king and queen and instilled fear in Lord Edward, a one-time devotee. This is not surprising. The conditions for Edward's release from Simon's custody in January 1265 raised the possibility of his disherison should he bring in aliens, and in any case there was the possibility of Simon's rule continuing into his reign.[44] His actions sowed resentment in some, as in the case of Gilbert de Clare, and hatred in others, quintessentially Roger de Mortimer and his wife, Maud.[45] We must be careful, however, not to see all behaviour in such terms. For others, perhaps, Simon de Montfort and his fanatical addiction to the Provisions of Oxford just simply got in the way.

Support Within the Church

Simon, as we know, had a body of support from among the lesser aristocracy, though this was numerically smaller than has sometimes been supposed, and another within the church, most spectacularly from a group of bishops. His support in general, however, was rather eclectic.[46] Nothing shows this more clearly than the backing he received from some of the towns. Let us look at these two areas of support in turn. First of all, the church. To understand this support we need to take a long view. The writers of monastic chronicles and annals are extremely revealing about how Henry III and Simon de Montfort were perceived, not only by the regular clergy but also by the church as a whole. They measured Henry against their own image of what kingship should be, and found him wanting.[47] Naturally, they

---

[43] For this concept see Simon Yarrow, 'Masculinity as a World Historical Category of Analysis', in John H. Arnold and Sean Brady (eds.), *What is Masculinity? Historical Dynamics from Antiquity to the Contemporary World* (London and New York, 2011), 114–38.

[44] *DBM*, no. 40; Maddicott, *Simon de Montfort*, 319.

[45] See, especially, David Carpenter, 'A Noble in Politics: Roger Mortimer in the Period of Baronial Reform and Rebellion, 1258–65', in A. J. Duggan (ed.), *Nobles and Nobility in Medieval Europe: Concepts, Origins, Transformations* (Woodbridge, 2000), 183–203. The problem arose over Montfort receiving a royal grant of the manors of Lugwardine, Marden, and Dilwyn, located 'in the middle of Roger's sphere of rule' (199), and the king's later grant of them to Roger in December 1263. Simon's sons wasted Roger's lands and sacked the castles of Wigmore and Radnor early in 1264. Maud was probably resident in one of them.

[46] For a recent review of the support for Simon de Montfort, see Carpenter, *Henry III: 1258–1272*, Ch. 10, 'Montfort's Kingdom', where greater emphasis is placed on the rhetoric of the community of the realm and of 'the cause' than is given here (348, 357, 406).

[47] For what follows I have drawn on Barbara Gray Eldridge, 'Religious Commentary on the Barons' Wars' (University of Virginia, PhD thesis, 1983), using a copy acquired by Dr Clive Knowles from University Microfilms International, Anna Arbor, Michigan, 1987. Among the chroniclers most used in her analysis are Matthew Paris, John of Oxenedes, and those of Lanercost and Melrose.

204   POLITICS AND SOCIETY IN MID THIRTEENTH-CENTURY ENGLAND

saw the world in moral rather than political terms, at least in our sense of the word. The king was lacking in his Christian duty as a king and in moral fibre. His reliance on, and inordinate support for, foreign favourites and worldly courtiers were symptomatic of his failures. Henry was corrupted by them, but this did not absolve him of responsibility. For all his piety, Henry was not a friend to the church. In fact, he corrupted it with the appointment of worldly men. He was avaricious and allied himself with popes in mulcting the church. These clerical writers were operating not only in the wake of the Gregorian reform movement in general, but more specifically in that of Thomas Becket. The king's lack of moral leadership, moreover, was contrasted with the behaviour of contemporary holy men, like St Edmund, archbishop of Canterbury (d. 1240), Robert Grosseteste, bishop of Lincoln (d. 1253), and the Franciscan Adam Marsh (d. 1259), who were not afraid to speak truth to power. The episcopal reform circle in general was highly esteemed within the church. Baronial attempts to bring the king under control were treated sympathetically, and ecclesiastical writers generally maintained what Barbara Eldridge calls 'the legend of Magna Carta': 'Throughout the reign', she says, clerics 'presented the barons as a class in a very sympathetic light'.[48] Although they were seldom interested in the details of secular reform, most of the clerical writers supported the shackling of the king. As many of the magnates eventually recoiled, Simon was left silhouetted as the true saviour, and was accepted by many churchmen as a genuine secular leader. He had a reputation already, as a warrior and crusader. Writers supported him when the king brought him to trial over his record in Gascony. His friendship with Grosseteste, Marsh, and Walter de Cantilupe made him readily believable as 'an enthusiast for spiritual causes'.[49] His mind, said Adam Marsh, 'was fixed on penance'.[50] Above all, perhaps, they were attracted by his resolution and constancy. There seems little doubt that in these circles he was held in a degree of awe.

But there were other, more mundane, reasons why the clergy were increasingly antagonistic towards Henry III and were drawn to the Montfortian 'party'. High on the list was the level of taxation they had suffered. They were exasperated at the king's failure to protect them from papal taxes. This problem began early in the reign, when the church was expected to help finance the pope's war against the emperor Frederick II, and reached crisis point during the years 1242–7 when the king 'was torn and tormented by how to react'.[51] Between 1244 and 1247, seven parliaments debated the pope's exactions. The king seemed to stand up for his kingdom, under internal pressure, but then drew back. The next decade saw taxation for the king's intended crusade, followed by the cost of the Sicilian adventure

---

[48]   Ibid., 184, 206.   [49]   Ibid., 246.

[50]   *Letters of Adam Marsh*, ed. J. S. Brewer, Rolls Series (London, 1858), 169.

[51]   Carpenter, *Henry III: 1207–1258*, 443.

SIMON DE MONTFORT AND HIS SUPPORT   205

which soon 'swept all other projects from Henry's mind'.[52] The clergy drew up a
schedule of objections mirroring one presented by the magnates.[53] Archbishop
Boniface now intervened, calling an assembly of the bishops and clergy of the
Canterbury province, hoping to settle the financial demands with a lump sum in
return for the settlement of grievances. A whole series of complaints followed,
including the subjection of the clergy to secular justice, the king's manipulation of
ecclesiastical elections, and the financial exploitation of vacancies.[54]

An area where clergy and laity were equally incensed was that of papal provisions.
As long ago as 1231 there had been attacks on foreign clerks who were increasingly being provided to livings in England, much to the king's embarrassment.[55]
In 1232 a Yorkshire knight had led violent protests against the phenomenon. The
sum of 60,000 marks, it was argued, was being taken out of the country by
Italians. When the papal clerk Master Martin came to England in 1244, he had
permission to appoint to positions including cathedral prebends, which meant a
further influx of Italians. Cathedrals, monasteries, lay patrons, and lesser clergy,
including royal clerks, were all threatened. It was an issue on which Robert
Grossesteste, the reformist bishop of Lincoln, felt very strongly, in his case for its
effect upon the cure of souls. There were other areas, too, where the grievances of
clergy and laity overlapped. One was over the issue of lords having to appear
before the justices in eyre on the first day of their proceedings. But they were not
always in step. An area of direct disagreement was alienation in mortmain, which
figured in the Petition of the Barons.[56] The most important point is that from the
1230s onwards the history of the English clergy in the thirteenth century was one
characterized by complaint against the crown, and centring on ecclesiastical
liberties.

The period 1257–61 was one of particularly intense complaint, beginning with
the grievances (*gravamina*) put forwards by the assemblies called by Archbishop
Boniface. These resulted in a set of ordinances in 1258 which became the statutes
of the council held by Boniface at Lambeth in May 1261. The role of the church
during the reform period has recently been reviewed by Philippa Hoskin.[57]
The ordinances/statutes, although belonging to the same political environment,
were not, Hoskin tells us, 'consciously complementary to the baronial provisions,
nor ... integrated into the documentation of the rebellion'. Rather, they were 'part
of a long process of ecclesiastical complaint and protest in the thirteenth century,

---

[52] Ibid., 588.   [53] Ibid., 645–6.

[54] Ibid., 649–50; *Ann. Mon.* I (Annals of Burton), 401–7; *C & S ii*, 530–48; Philippa Hoskin, 'The
Church and the King: Canon Law and Kingship in England', in D. Crook and L. J. Wilkinson (eds.),
The Growth of Royal Government under Henry III (Woodbridge, 2015), 196–211, at 197–8.

[55] Ibid., 119, 216, 444, citing *The Letters and Charters of Cardinal Guala Bicchieri, Papal Legate in
England, 1216–1218*, ed. N. Vincent, Canterbury and York Society, 83 (1996), lxvii–xxiv, and Vincent,
Peter des Roches, 303–7.

[56] See Brand, *Kings, Barons and Justice*, 57–62. For mortmain see also below 259–60.

[57] P. Hoskin, 'The Church and the King', 196–211.

206   POLITICS AND SOCIETY IN MID THIRTEENTH-CENTURY ENGLAND

starting in the 1230s'.[58] Some overlap notwithstanding, their aims were not the same as those of the barons. Nonetheless, the church councils did add to the atmosphere of exasperation with the king's behaviour, and the 1261 Statutes were an enabling factor when it came to the Montfortian rebellion. With Boniface now out of the country, and unwilling to return given that his estates had been attacked as those of a hostile foreigner, leadership passed to Walter de Cantilupe, the elder statesman of the church and a close friend of Simon de Montfort. His guidance of the southern province placed the church largely behind the rebels in 1264. The belief 'that the king could and should be brought under the law ... provided an ideological link with the baronial rebellion which enabled episcopal support for Simon de Montfort in the mid-1260s'.[59]

In her recent study of the role of bishops in the reign of Henry III, Sophie Ambler emphasizes the growth of episcopal unity and its breakdown during the early 1260s.[60] Particular episodes illustrate this unity being forged. In 1252 Henry ordered the prelates of the province of York to assemble separately, but was frustrated by the archbishop of York. When, in 1253, a tenth was agreed in return for confirmation of Magna Carta, a famous ceremony ensued which involved the symbolic throwing down of candles.[61] Then came the Sicilian business and the king's new financial commitments. Clerics complained that they had never consented to the Sicilian enterprise. When it came to taxation, the issues for senior clerics were consent and necessity. The church was trapped in a 'pincer movement' of king and pope and decided to defend itself. As we have seen, a series of councils ensued. As a result, 'the senior clergy were forged into a genuine unit, with a vigorous identity', and Archbishop Boniface could present himself as 'the champion of English ecclesiastical unity and Becket's successor'.[62]

When it comes to the 'Revolution of 1258', Ambler shows that although some prelates involved themselves in the events, the English episcopate 'as a whole' remained detached from the baronial reform. In her view this was because divesting the king of his power and putting it into the hands of the reforming council was far too radical a move.[63] Fulk Basset, bishop of London, and Walter de Cantilupe, bishop of Worcester, did take part, but as councillors as well as bishops. It must be remembered that they were also secular lords, effectively heads of baronial families. They had, in fact, only recently returned to the council, having been sacked in 1255 for opposing the Sicilian business. According to Matthew Paris, they had declared that they would die before the English Church was subjected to ruin.[64] At the Westminster parliament, however, the prelates withdrew as a whole, in the words of the Tewkesbury annalist, 'lest they incur the anger of

---

[58] Ibid., 201.   [59] Ibid., 210.   [60] Ambler, *Bishops in the Political Community.*
[61] See D. Carpenter, 'Magna Carta 1253: The Ambitions of the Church and the Divisions within the Realm', *Historical Journal*, 86 (May 2013), 179–90.
[62] Ambler, *Bishops in the Political Community*, 98–9.   [63] Ibid., 108.
[64] Paris, *CM* V, 525.

SIMON DE MONTFORT AND HIS SUPPORT   207

the king'.[65] It seems probable that they wanted to distance themselves from the meeting of magnates that was about to take place at Oxford. The royal charter lists show only Basset and Cantilupe among the bishops witnessing them at this point. After examining the evidence, Ambler concludes that the episcopate 'did not endorse' the reforming council in 1258.[66]

Most bishops followed Boniface in remaining aloof from the baronial actions. Why did they refuse to join the reformers? In answering this Ambler tackles the views of Powicke and Treharne, before offering her own. It was not, she says, because of the king's alliance with the pope, nor that they were 'timid and peace-loving'.[67] It was not because the king had managed to appoint bishops of his own liking.[68] Neither was it that they had lost interest in the affairs of the kingdom. In fact, in October 1259 they had pronounced excommunication on those contravening the Provisions of Westminster. In 1258 they could find no justification for taking 'the reins of government from the king's hands'. The Provisions of Westminster of 1259 were different in that they did not threaten Henry's power. Moreover, he endorsed them. What is 'remarkable', in Ambler's view, is not that the bishops failed to back the opposition in 1258, but that they did not intervene to stop the conflict escalating.[69]

Why did their position change when it came to the Montfortian regime? In 1266 five English bishops were excommunicated as confederates of Simon de Montfort. They and three others were sued at king's bench for having repudiated their loyalty to the king and joined the revolutionary party. Why did they make this choice? Ambler finds the answer in the charisma of Simon de Montfort rather than, as one might have expected, along the lines of Grosseteste's view of kingship and the king's manifest failures. Moreover, the king's behaviour after his resumption of power in 1261–2 had demonstrated that he had learned nothing through his tribulations. Either way, the effect was to shatter the unity of the episcopate. Only two bishops were strong supporters of the king: Peter of Aigueblanche of Hereford and Simon de Walton of Norwich. Two others, those of Carlisle and Exeter, leaned towards the king's side, while Walter Giffard of Bath and Roger Meuland of Coventry and Lichfield were regarded as royal supporters after Evesham. The Montfortians regarded the bishop of Rochester as another royal sympathizer. The archbishop of York was apparently neutral, while Boniface was out of the country. This was against eight active Montfortians. Ambler argues, surely correctly, that what we are seeing are personal decisions. After Lewes, Walter de Cantilupe kept the papal legate, charged with bringing peace and tranquillity, out of England. The bishops helped the regime financially from their

---

[65] *Ann. Mon.* i (Tewkesbury), 163.   [66] Ibid., 112.

[67] Powicke, *Henry III and the Lord Edward*, vol. 1, 382, n. 1; Treharne, *Baronial Plan of Reform*, 57–8.

[68] Katherine Harvey has shown that the thirteenth century was a 'golden age of electoral freedom' in England: *Episcopal Appointments in England, c.1214–1344* (Aldershot, 2014).

[69] Ambler, *Bishops in the Political Community*, 123.

208 POLITICS AND SOCIETY IN MID THIRTEENTH-CENTURY ENGLAND

own resources, and by a tax of a tenth of spiritual income in the summer of 1264 for the defence of the kingdom against invasion. This was granted by the greater and lesser clergy of both provinces. They also participated at the muster on Barham Down. In short, the Montfortian churchmen were 'not only apologists for the new regime ... but active participants in it'.[70] The *Forma Pacis* of August 1263 set up a new council to rule England. One of the three electors was Stephen Berksted, bishop of Chichester, the other two being Simon and Gilbert de Clare. Of the nine councillors, one was the bishop of London and another the prestigious cleric Thomas de Cantilupe, a learned doctor of canon law who, together with Peter de Montfort and Adam de Newmarket, was charged with making the baronial case at Amiens. It was Thomas who set out the case.[71]

As we know reformist bishops were key members of the Montfortian party. The leading figure was Walter de Cantilupe, bishop of Worcester since 1236, and he, in particular, saw eye to eye with Simon de Montfort.[72] The support Simon received from some ecclesiastics, both religious and secular, was therefore considerable and was found on all sides, from abbots and priors, from senior secular clergy and parish priests. If in practice the bishops were free to choose their allegiance, then so were all manner of clerics. Their activities run parallel to those of laymen, and they emerge out of the same provincial societies. Various modes of interaction between clergy and laity must have conditioned choices, and the Montfortian party was thereby considerably enhanced. Among the abbots was Robert de Sutton, who, like ten of his fourteen military tenants, was a rebel. His land at Collingham, Nottinghamshire, was seized because 'the abbot's servants were found to be at Kenilworth with Simon de Montfort the younger'. He was charged a post-war redemption fine of 500 marks.[73] Henry parson of Shottesworth was so involved in the Montfortian cause that he headed his own military retinue.

Support Within the Towns

The other area which needs to be examined is that of the towns. As is well known, the Montfortian parliament which met in January 1265 included representatives from towns, although we do not know which ones, except for London, York, Lincoln, and the Cinque Ports. Unfortunately, as Jacob pointed out, the part played by the larger cities and towns in 'the rising' is not well illustrated by the legal records. London, by contrast, is well provided for, and being *sui generis*

---

[70] Ibid., 145.

[71] See Ambler, *Bishops in the Political Community*, Ch. 7, and also see S. T. Ambler, 'The Montfortian Bishops and the Baronial Gravamina of 1263-4', *TCE*, iii, 137-50.

[72] See P. Hoskin, 'Cantilupe's Crusade: Walter de Cantilupe, Bishop of Worcester, and the Baronial Rebellion', *Transactions of the Worcestershire Archaeological Society*, 23 (2012), 91-102.

[73] Fernandes, 'The Role of the Midland Knights', 110; *CIM*, 851; *CR 1264-8*, 160.

must be dealt with first. In particular we have the chronicle of the 'staunch patrician' Arnold fitz Thedmar, who, according to Jacob, 'represents his opponents as a mere faction and inveighs against Thomas fitz Thomas the mayor for his democratic leanings and pernicious practice of superseding the authority of the aldermen by that of the populace'.[74]

London politics in this period are still best approached through the pioneering work of Gwyn Alf Williams,[75] although his analysis has been criticized for being overly systematic in its identification of discreet social levels and groupings.[76] The key to understanding its history in the thirteenth century is to appreciate that the 'commune was essentially an oligarchical conception', and that 'London politics were patrician politics and the politics of the patriciate were largely personal'.[77] Political stances were shared by members of rival groups, and tended to centre on support for, or opposition to, the king. This produced feuds and alliances. Naturally, the oligarchy aroused resentment from those on the outside, particularly over differential taxation. What disturbed politics more, though, were external threats to the city's liberties, and the threat here came principally from the crown. Henry III had confirmed the city's privileges in 1227. Over the next thirty years, however, he repeatedly sought to control the city's sheriffs and took heavy tallages from its citizens. The aldermen resisted and the king suspended the city's liberties on ten different occasions between 1239 and 1257. The privileges accorded to Westminster Abbey infuriated the aldermen even more, as these deprived them of much of their jurisdiction in Middlesex.[78] The king's actions in 1258, however, changed the character of this conflict. In January he announced that a petition from London citizens had accused aldermen of fraud and corruption, and set up a commission of enquiry led by John Mansel. The aldermen tried to boycott it, but the tables were turned when Mansel summoned a 'folkmoot', where the Londoners were ordered to elect juries from the wards. On their sworn testimony, the mayor and five aldermen were deposed. A further confrontation led to the deposition of the entire body and fresh elections being called. As

---

[74] Jacob, *Studies in the Period of Baronial Reform and Rebellion*, 281. This is supplemented now by David Carpenter's account in *Henry III: 1258–1272*, 385–90.

[75] Gwyn A. Williams, *Medieval London: From Commune to Capital* (London, 1963).

[76] See Derek Keene, 'London From the Post-Roman Period to 1300', in D. M. Palliser (ed.), *The Cambridge Urban History of Britain, Volume I, 600–1540* (Cambridge, 2000), 210: 'The lively account in Williams, *Medieval London* ... forces the recorded events into a preconceived pattern'. Susan Reynolds criticized the work for its use of the concept 'patriciate', its belief in the existence of 'patrician dynasties' in the early thirteenth century, and its argument that this 'mercantile patriciate' was transformed during the century: *An Introduction to the History of English Medieval Towns* (Oxford, 1977), 78, 137. She admitted, however, that 'What his account graphically shows is the multifarious interests of the rich, their domination of the city in their own interests, and the jealous preoccupation of all citizens with the trading rights of citizenship, often attained through craft apprenticeship'. For a broad account of London's institutions and social structure, see Caroline M. Barron, *London in the Middle Ages: Government and People* (Oxford, 2004). See also Elspeth Veale, 'The "Great Twelve": Mystery and Fraternity in Thirteenth-Century London', *Historical Research*, 64 (Oct. 1991), 237–63.

[77] Williams, *Medieval London*, 196, 202.   [78] Knowles, 'The Disinherited', Part II, 87–8.

210 POLITICS AND SOCIETY IN MID THIRTEENTH-CENTURY ENGLAND

Williams puts it, 'the exasperation of the *populares* had at last found an outlet', and the events of spring 1258 'shook the aldermanic regime to its foundations'.[79]

National events then came into play. In July 1258 Montfort, Roger Bigod, and other members of the baronial council entered the city, demanding that the Londoners affix their seal to the Provisions of Oxford. When the aldermen procrastinated, they too invoked the *populares* and the deed was done, 'saving the liberties of London'.[80] Then, in December came Hugh Bigod's eyre, which fundamentally challenged the city's liberties by allowing oral complaints or *querelae*. The traditional court, the Husting, was set aside. Events in the city tended to follow the national trend. When the king reasserted power, London's rulers gravitated towards him once again. In October 1261 a new mayor, Thomas fitz Thomas, came into office, a choice which was to have startling consequences. Montfort's reappearance in 1263 led to the restoration of the Provisions and London was in turmoil.

What tipped the balance against the royalists was Lord Edward's attack on the Temple—a naked and mendacious money grab—on 26 June 1263. Londoners flooded on to the streets and houses were wrecked or pillaged, including that of Simon Passelew. John de Grey's mansion near the Temple was in flames. The aldermen sent delegates to Montfort to seal an alliance, and on 16 July Henry capitulated. The queen, by contrast, famously set out on the Thames in an attempt to join Edward at Windsor. She was stopped at the bridge by hostile crowds who repulsed and insulted her. In the brief struggle for power which ensued, says Williams, a radical faction among the old patriciate joined forces with 'rising merchants and entrepreneurs', and a new personality appeared in the form of Master Thomas Puleston, a royal administrator from a Shropshire family. The mayor, Thomas fitz Thomas, went over to the rebels, proclaiming himself leader of the *populares*. 'Aldermanic resistance collapsed and the commune disintegrated', power passing to 'the sworn confederacy of the commons'.[81] Under Fitz Thomas and Puleston, the Londoners organized themselves into a militia. The folkmoot was rejuvenated, and crafts were liberated from control. The liberties claimed by Westminster Abbey were denied. London now belonged to Simon de Montfort. In October, Edward and the king moved to Windsor where they rallied their supporters, and Montfort took the Tower. Fitz Thomas was re-elected mayor 'by mass acclamation'.[82]

There was one dangerous moment for Montfort. In December 1263, when returning to the city with a small force, he found the city gates barred to him. This royalist plot left him at the mercy of the king and Lord Edward, who were approaching with a larger armed force. Montfort was in dire straits. However, the plot was revealed and the excited *populares* battered open their own gates. When

---

[79] Williams, *Medieval London*, 211.　　[80] *De Antiquis Legibus*, 38–9; Paris, *CM* v, 704.
[81] Williams, *Medieval London*, 221–2.　　[82] Ibid., 223.

SIMON DE MONTFORT AND HIS SUPPORT   211

the news came of King Louis's verdict at Amiens, riots broke out again. Moreover, according to Arnold fitz Thedmar, nearly all the middle order of people in England rejected it.[83] The Londoners now made a formal alliance with Simon.[84] In March the armed militia moved out against the enemies. Richard of Cornwall's mansion at Westminster and his manor in Isleworth were destroyed, as was Peter of Savoy's manor at Cheshunt and Walter de Merton's property at Merton. The lands of William de Valence and Philip Basset were also attacked. In London itself 500 Jews were killed in an antisemitic riot. At the battle of Lewes the London militia were on the left wing of the baronial army and broke before the onslaught from Lord Edward and his cavalry. As is well known, Edward pursued the Londoners in an orgy of slaughter only to return to find the battle lost. However, the survivors could return to London in victory, certain of the continuance of their regime. There followed what Williams called 'the first successful displacement of aldermanic power' which 'broke the bonds of oligarchy'.[85] Newer social interests found expression and ordinances were granted to crafts. The handful of patrician leaders apart, most of the others were *mediocres*. In short, Williams tells us, the revolt of 1263 was 'evidently a revolt of middle class citizens'.[86]

Needless to say, for the popular leaders the Battle of Evesham was a disaster. On 3 October, when the mayor and leading citizens presented themselves at Windsor in surrender they were imprisoned. Confiscations began two days later. Apparently, over a third of the men who were despoiled had actually been loyal to the king. Everywhere Londoners were at the mercy of royalist despoilers.[87] Naturally, the liberties of Westminster Abbey were restored. Finally, on 5 December the king declared that Londoners were no longer to be under attack, and on 10 January 1266 he issued a formal pardon. For this the citizens were charged a fine of 20,000 marks. Moreover, Londoners were excluded from the terms of the Dictum of Kenilworth, although some restitutions were made. Early in 1270 the city, by a special letter, pledged absolute fidelity to the king.[88]

With regard to the behaviour of English provincial towns during the Montfortian period, the fullest survey is by Clive Knowles.[89] He points first of all to the achievement of corporate self-government. Northampton, Norwich, Oxford, and Lincoln, among others, had acquired privileges modelled on those of London. Many were governed by mayors and councils, while by the start of

---

[83] *De Antiquis Legibus*, 61.

[84] See I. Stone, 'The Rebel Barons of 1264 and the Commune of London: An Oath of Mutual Aid', *EHR*, 129 (2014), 1–18.

[85] Williams, *Medieval London*, 227.   [86] Ibid., 228, 230.

[87] However, 'Offence—a Londoner', cited by Jacob and Williams supposedly from the Surrey special eyre, is in fact apocryphal, being an interpellation: Jacob, *Studies in the Period of Baronial Reform and Rebellion*, 325; Williams, *Medieval London*, 227.

[88] The history of London in these years was intricate, and only the bare bones of Williams's full analysis has been given here.

[89] Knowles, 'The Disinherited', Part II, 86–106. Once again, this is supplemented now by the account in Carpenter, *Henry III: 1258–1272*, 378–85.

212   POLITICS AND SOCIETY IN MID THIRTEENTH-CENTURY ENGLAND

Henry's reign twenty-three towns were answering to the exchequer for their farms.[90] The king's financial needs extended this 'constitutional advance' during the middle years of the thirteenth century. An alternative type of development occurred in the south-east, where the Cinque Ports were forming themselves into a federation. They lacked 'a formal constitution' but were collectively important given their strategic position.[91]

The towns of mid-thirteenth-century England, Knowles pointed out, were in a 'ferment of unrest'. This was partly due to a continual struggle against powerful lords who denied them any effective self-government. A particular case was that of the monastic boroughs. At Bury St Edmunds, for example, the Benedictine abbey and its officials held considerable power, notwithstanding the existence of aldermen, since these had to be approved by the abbot. Another grievance, apparently, was the citizens' lack of control over the opening and closing of the town gates.[92] Disputes led to riots, as in the case of Dunstable and its Augustinian canons.[93] More widespread were dissensions within the body of citizens themselves. By the mid-thirteenth century the towns were dominated by 'small, highly privileged, oligarchies of rich men', largely but by no means exclusively merchants. Some were property owners, as was the case in Cambridge and York.[94] Members of these oligarchies intermarried and tended to monopolize local office. At Oxford, the town bailiffs were drawn from the ruling body of fifteen 'jurats', and the same men can be seen holding office repeatedly during the years 1240–60.[95] At Northampton, ten or more of the twenty-four ruling burgesses in 1260 had previously been mayor or bailiff of the town.[96]

As in London, this domination was not unchallenged. The grievances of 'the lower community' of Oxford were presented to the king in 1253. They included not only their exclusion from power but also unequal taxation and purprestures.[97] The same or similar issues were to be found in other towns: in Winchester, Lincoln, York, Carlisle, Northampton, and Bristol.[98] 'This urban discontent',

---

[90]   Citing A. Ballard, *British Borough Charters, 1042–1216* (Cambridge, 1913), xvii–xxxiii.

[91]   Citing F. W. Brooks, 'The Cinque Ports', *Mariners Mirror*, 15 (1929), 142–91. See now A. Jobson, 'The Maritime Theatre, 1258–67', in Jobson (ed.), *Baronial Reform and Revolution in England*, 218–36.

[92]   M. D. Lobel, *The Borough of Bury St Edmunds* (Oxford, 1935), 120.

[93]   N. M. Trenholme, *The English Monastic Boroughs*, University of Missouri Studies (Columbia, 1927), 16–17.

[94]   For Cambridge he cites H. M. Cam, 'The Early Burgesses of Cambridge in Relation to the Surrounding Countryside', in her *Liberties and Communities in Medieval England* (Cambridge, 1944), 19–26, and for York, E. Miller, 'Rulers of Thirteenth Century Towns: The Cases of York and Newcastle upon Tyne', *TCE*, i (1986), 128–41.

[95]   Citing *Snappe's Formulary and Other Records*, ed. H. E. Salter, Oxford Historical Society, lxxx (Oxford, 1924), 272–80.

[96]   *VCH Northamptonshire* iii, 6.

[97]   C. I. Hammer, 'Complaints of the Lesser Commune: Oligarchic Rule and Baronial Reform in Thirteenth-Century Oxford', *HR*, 85 (August 2012), 353–71.

[98]   To these issues should be added rigging the market. See A. H. Hershey, 'Baronial Reform, the Justiciar's Court and Commercial Legislation: The Case of Grimsby', in Jobson (ed.), *Baronial Reform and Rebellion*, 43–55, and Carpenter, *Henry III: 1258–1272*, 379.

SIMON DE MONTFORT AND HIS SUPPORT   213

Knowles suggests, 'seemed to require only a favourable opportunity to break out in communal revolution', although there is no record of this around 1258–9.[99] The royalist chronicler Wykes tells us that the London revolt of 1263 had repercussions throughout the English towns. Conspiracies of low-fellows (*ribaldi*) calling themselves bachelors sprang up to oppress the more important men in every town and city.[100] Although the chronicler's claim was certainly exaggerated, Knowles pointed to two towns which 'seem to lend colour to this assertion'.[101] One is Bury St Edmunds where, before the Battle of Lewes, young men of the town formed a gild of youth (*gilda juvenum*) and overthrew the town government. Not only did they appoint their own aldermen, but they used a horn to summon men to the moot. All those who were opposed to their new government were to be treated as 'public enemies'. At Oxford, an inquisition of 1266 showed that Simon de Montfort junior had imprisoned Adam de Feteplace, a rich burgess and former mayor, until his son Philip had purchased his release with ten marks rent in the town.[102] Given that Adam was one of the men accused in 1253 of trespasses against the burgesses of the 'lower commune', Jacob suggested that the baronial disturbances may have encouraged 'the smaller burgesses' to take revenge against their oppressors.[103] However, Knowles was sceptical over the connection between many of these disturbances and events in London. He had good reason to be. A re-examination by Carl Hammer, moreover, has shown that there was indeed serious social friction in mid thirteenth-century Oxford, as indicated by the petition of the lesser commune (*minor comunia*) in 1253, but that Simon de Montfort's 'prominent local partisans' came from 'factions within the merchant oligarchy opposed to one another for whatever reasons, personal and public, and to Adam Feteplace's local domination'.[104] The troubles in Bury St Edmunds were distinctly local, not national, in character. For one thing the gild of youth was aimed not at the leading burgesses, but at the control the abbot exercised over the town.[105] For another, both the abbot and the burgesses were implicated in the rebellion against the king. In the case of Oxford, the situation is difficult to read, but the existence of a popular revolt is doubtful. The mayor during the Montfortian period was Nicholas de Stockwell. Not only had he been mayor in 1247–9, but he was also one of the leading citizens accused in 1253. After Evesham the burgesses as a body agreed to a fine of 500 marks to Edward for remission of 'the indignation

---

[99] Knowles, 'The Disinherited', 92. As he says there, 'The history of the towns during the opening years of the baronial period is very obscure'.

[100] Wykes, 138.   [101] Knowles, 'The Disinherited', 94.   [102] *CIM*, 294.

[103] Jacob, *Studies in the Period of Reform and Rebellion*, 288–9.

[104] Hammer, 'Complaints of the Lesser Commune', 367.

[105] 'Indeed, for a time the burgesses actively encouraged the malcontents, but when the abbot laid the dispute before the king towards the end of 1264, they became thoroughly alarmed. They feared that the abbot's action night jeopardize their liberties and so they anticipated legal proceedings by reaching an agreement with the abbot by which he agreed to respect the liberties of the alderman and the community in return for the suppression of the gild of youth': Lobel, *Borough of Bury St Edmunds*, 127–8. See also *CPR 1258–66*, 375.

214 POLITICS AND SOCIETY IN MID THIRTEENTH-CENTURY ENGLAND

and rancour of mind which he had conceived against them because in the disturbance of the realm they were said to have adhered to the enemies of the king and
himself'. It looks as though the oligarchy retained control throughout the
disturbances.[106]

There were certainly cases where burgesses did support the rebels. The rebels
who occupied Ely in 1266, for example, were allowed to keep their booty in the
town. For this and other trespasses the burgesses made fine with the king for
200 marks in June 1266.[107] The abbot had already been fined £266. 13s. 4d. for his
disloyalty in December 1265, and this sum may not include the eighty marks he
was fined for assisting Montfort to defend the sea coast against the anticipated
invasion in 1264.[108] In Northampton, the 'patriciate' constituted the core of
Montfortian sympathizers. At least four of the twenty-four burgesses of the town
appointed by Montfort in June 1264 to protect the Jewish community held the
office of mayor at some time.[109] One of the commissioners, Ralph fitz Ralph, paid
a personal fine of forty marks on 13 April 1264, 'for persisting with the king's
adversaries in the town of Northampton in the assault which happened lately
between the king and his said adversaries'.[110] The citizens of Lincoln were clearly
implicated in the rebellion. Henry imposed a fine of 1,000 marks on them, which
was increased to £1,000 due to their tardiness in paying.[111] The composition of the
commission of twenty-four appointed in May 1265 to protect the Jews indicates
that here, too, the ruling oligarchy had remained in power during the disturbances. Almost all the commissioners were of the ruling families, and at least nine
had held the office of mayor.[112] In the north, the burgesses of Beverley, Yorkshire,
were fined £80 for trespasses committed during the war, and one of them paid a
special fine of 100 marks.[113] At Hereford the citizens strongly resisted a royalist
attack and after Evesham were fined 600 marks for their disloyalty.[114] A heavy fine
was also imposed on the citizens of Norwich, while Bristol paid a fine for its
transgressions.[115] The Cinque Ports supported Montfort and, indeed, continued
to resist against the king, but escaped being fined.

There are another two towns which may have had leanings towards the rebels:
Cambridge and King's Lynn. The evidence for Cambridge, Knowles pointed out,
is inconclusive. The citizens certainly sold provisions to the rebels who were

[106] See Powicke, *King Henry III and the Lord Edward*, ii, 785–6, where the allegiance of the Oxford
students is examined. This is corrected by C. H. Lawrence, 'The University of Oxford and the
Chronicle of the Barons' Wars', *EHR*, 95/374 (1980), 99–113. Carpenter takes a different view from the
one expressed here: *Henry III: 1258–1272*, 381–2.

[107] *CPR 1258–66*, 129, 604; Jacob, *Studies in the Period of Reform and Rebellion*, 238, 295.

[108] *CPR 1258–66*, 575; W. Blaauw, *The Barons' War* (2nd edn., London, 1971), 235, n. 2.

[109] For the details see Knowles, 'The Disinherited', 96–7.

[110] *CPR 1258–66*, 311. See also *VCH Northamptonshire* iii, 10.

[111] *CPR 1266–72*, 28, 34, 152. See also J. W. F. Hill, *Medieval Lincoln* (Cambridge, 1948), 210–11.

[112] Ibid., 295.   [113] *CPR 1258–66*, 499, 571.

[114] *CIM*, 291, and *CPR 1258–66*, 548.   [115] *CPR 1258–66*, 510, and *CPR 1266–72*, 451.

SIMON DE MONTFORT AND HIS SUPPORT   215

occupying Ely in 1266, and they were so close to the Isle that they had no option but to cooperate with them. Even so, the citizens only saved the town from destruction by paying the impecunious rebels a heavy fine.[116] At Lynn there was a struggle for power between two groups of leading citizens, and it seems to have contained a body of rebel sympathizers. The town temporarily forfeited its liberties after Evesham.[117]

There were, by contrast, a few towns which were definitely royalist in the civil war, although some of these contained individual Montfortians. As one would expect, the seaports of East Anglia and south-western England supported the king in opposition to the Cinque Ports.[118] Dunwich was loyal, and one of the townsmen, Peter son of John of Dunwich, was a member of the household of John de Warenne.[119] Ipswich supported the king and sent 200 men to the siege of Ely.[120] The bailiffs of Southampton received the king's thanks in October 1263 for refusing Montfort the money which they had been forced to collect for him from the townspeople, while in the following year the bailiffs had obstructed the sergeants of John fitz John when they had tried to seize the goods of foreign merchants at the port.[121] Portsmouth was punished for its loyalty to the king by a punitive raid from the Cinque Ports in November 1265.[122] Shrewsbury and Bridgnorth were bastions of royal support in the marches. After Evesham, the citizens were rewarded for their loyalty with acquittances from their annual farm.[123] Even so, a member of a leading family was a Montfortian.[124] At Shrewsbury the citizens had arrested the men of Ralph Basset of Drayton, keeper of the peace, and after Evesham the king compensated the town for its losses during the war.[125] Even here, however, at least one important burgess, Hugh Vylayn, bailiff in 1261–2, was considered a Montfortian.[126] Finally, Winchester favoured the king. The composition of the commission of twenty-four citizens appointed in June 1264 to protect the Jewish community again indicates that the old oligarchy remained in control, and although it cooperated with Montfort from time to time

---

[116] See *VCH Cambridgeshire* iii, 5. The 'Disinherited' used Cambridge as a supply base, sold their loot there, occupied Barnwell Priory, and took 300 marks from the town.

[117] *CPR 1266–72*, 36–7, 48–9, 449, 473; Rishanger, 44–5.

[118] F. W. Brooks, 'The Cinque Ports' Feud with Yarmouth in the Thirteenth Century', *Mariners' Mirror*, 19 (1933), 27–51.

[119] Jacob, *Studies in the Period of Reform and Rebellion*, 316.

[120] Knowles, 'The Disinherited', Part II, 100; *CIM*, no. 881.   [121] *CPR 1258–66*, 291, 388.

[122] *CPR 1258–66*, 539. Southampton, by contrast, managed to avoid this. Here, as elsewhere, there were certainly individual Montfortians. One such was John Fortin, former bailiff and a member of a prominent family, who was in the service of Simon de Montfort, the younger. See Colin Platt, *Medieval Southampton* (London and Boston, 1973), 38.

[123] Eyton, *Shropshire*, i, 285, 308–9.

[124] This was Walter le Palmer, brother of William la Palmer, one of the two bailiffs of the town in March 1265. After the war Walter paid 40s. to avoid redeeming his lands: Eyton, *Shropshire*, i, 316, 369–73.

[125] *CPR 1258–66*, 45; Lord Treasurer's Remembrancer's Memoranda Rolls: TNA, E 368/40, m. 1d.

[126] *CPR 1258–66*, 625; J. Morris, 'The Provosts and Bailiffs of Shrewsbury', *Transactions of the Shropshire Archaeological Society*, 3rd ser. vol. 1 (1901), 12, 158.

216 POLITICS AND SOCIETY IN MID THIRTEENTH-CENTURY ENGLAND

it declared for the king in the summer of 1265. Simon de Montfort junior stormed the city when making his way to join his father in the west.[127] After Evesham one of the burgesses, Simon le Draper, mayor in 1266, was granted the lands of Richard de Halliwell for his loyalty.[128] Montfort, however, did have at least one supporter in the town. This was the prior of St Swithun's, Ralph Russell, who was in contention with the citizens of Winchester over the town gates which he considered to be his responsibility. On 4 May 1264 there was a riot in which several members of the priory were killed by the townspeople. The agreement ending this dispute in 1266 seems to imply that Ralph enabled Montfort's successful attack in the previous year by purposefully neglecting to repair the gates. Moreover, the king imposed a fine of 500 marks on the prior and convent for disloyalty.[129]

The conclusions reached by Clive Knowles are as follows.[130] The first is that London was exceptional and that the towns which supported Montfort did so not against but through the oligarchs that ruled them. Secondly, and as a corollary of the first, the reasons for their support were particular. The Cinque Ports, for example, had their own agenda which included their longstanding feud with the seaports of East Anglia and elsewhere, while at Lincoln the burgesses had long been opposed to Peter of Savoy, who had been taking heavy tolls from their out-port of Boston. Thirdly, the leading burgesses were concerned, primarily, to prevent communal uprisings on the one hand and the loss of their liberties on the other in the circumstances of civil war. Fourthly, and perhaps most importantly from the current perspective, Montfort was entirely flexible with regard to urban governance. He summoned representatives of a number of English towns to the parliament of 1265 not from any democratic principle whatsoever, but purely because their support was important to his cause.

We might add some further summary observations. One is that, in addition to those already discussed, there seem to have been members of the urban oligarchies who were broadly speaking members of the Montfortian party, although how they were recruited and how they were managed seem irrecoverable. Another is that Clive Knowles was dealing in this discussion with major towns. As far as minor towns are concerned, it seems from what we know, from Berkshire and Buckinghamshire in particular, that they tended to follow their lords.[131]

Simon de Montfort was well aware that he needed to reach out to maximize his support. When a faction was engaged in a wholesale bid to take or to maintain

---

[127] For the details see Knowles, 'The Disinherited', Part I, 17.
[128] Knowles, 'The Disinherited', Part II, 102.
[129] Carpenter, *Henry III: 1258–1272*, 381; *VCH Hampshire* v, 34; *CPR 1258–66*, 558.
[130] Knowles, 'The Disinherited', Part II, 104–6.
[131] See above 87–8.

power, it must often have been tempting to look beyond aristocratic ranks for support. This is essentially what the opposition barons had done in their desperate struggle against King John, a strategy reflected in the clauses of Magna Carta. It is what the seven confederates and their allies did in the summer of 1258 when they reached out to what was effectively a minor nobility in the counties, the knights, and to other major free tenants. They looked beyond their retinues, and in doing so made use of the traditional administrative mechanism of Angevin and post-Angevin England: the county court. As we have seen, four knights were nominated in each county to receive complaints and to bring them to the Michaelmas parliament.[132] Most of the sheriffs who took office for 1258–9 were chosen from among these men. Moreover, a special judicial eyre was instituted to try complaints. The legislation which ensued was in many respects a product of this 'reaching out'. It also led, as we know, to disagreements over how far reform should go, that is, how far the interests of the higher nobility themselves could be compromised.[133] The same strategy of reaching out was deployed by the Montfortians when it widened the membership of parliament: four knights from the counties in 1264, burgesses from the towns as well as knights in 1265.[134]

Nor was the strategy confined to the level of knights and prominent townsmen. It was implicit in the reform programme that a wide constituency of stakeholders had much to gain from its implementation, and the fallout from a famous incident at Peatling Magna in Leicestershire in 1265 shows clearly that villagers understood what was meant by 'the common enterprise'.[135] As David Carpenter has written: 'Peasants ... had some reason for thinking "the barons" were working for "the welfare of the community of the realm", a community of which, in significant respects, the peasantry of thirteenth-century England were part'.[136] Although the implications of this have tended to be exaggerated, there was a strong element of populism in the anti-alien stance taken by the Montfortians from 1263 onwards. It was, of course, a paradox that Simon, himself of foreign birth, should put himself at the head of such a movement, but this was lost in the politics and the propaganda.[137]

---

[132] *DBM*, no. 6. The procedure was, in fact, modified. The original intention had been for the complaints to be received directly by the justiciar.

[133] For a recent discussion of the events of these years, see Jobson, *First English Revolution*, Ch. 2. The legislation is dealt with thoroughly in Brand, *Kings, Barons and Justices*.

[134] This was not the first time that townsmen had been present in parliaments, however. They seem to have attended the taxation parliament of 1237: Maddicott, *The Origins of the English Parliament*, 202. The parliaments of 1258–65 are discussed in Ch. 5 of this important work.

[135] See Carpenter, 'English Peasants in Politics', 309–48.   [136] Ibid., 348.

[137] There were also safeguards. Aliens were allowed to stay if 'the faithful men of the realm' were to accept them; in other words, Simon himself was perfectly safe in this respect. For the political construction of identity, see also Lucy Hemmings, 'Simon de Montfort and the Ambiguity of Ethnicity in Thirteenth-Century Politics', *TCE*, xvi, ed. A. M. Spencer and C. Watkins (Woodbridge, 2017), 137–52.

218 POLITICS AND SOCIETY IN MID THIRTEENTH-CENTURY ENGLAND

Xenophobia and Populism

To truly understand the anti-alienism and xenophobia of Monfortian England, we need to broaden the perspective. Historians are generally agreed that thirteenth-century England saw a rise in national feeling.[138] Greater emphasis was put on being native-born (*naturalis*), even among the higher nobility after the loss of Normandy in 1204. There was increasing territorial definition between England on the one hand and Scotland and Wales on the other. A sense of national cohesion displayed itself against the French and against the internationalism of the papacy, with practical manifestation in terms of taxation and papal provision. A strong suspicion of foreigners was manifest among monastic chroniclers, pre-eminently the two St Albans writers Roger of Wendover and Matthew Paris. In the words of Michael Clanchy: 'Although medieval nations cannot be equated in terms of political power with the sovereign states of modern Europe, national identity was already in the thirteenth century an important element in a ruler's authority over his own subjects and in the assertion of power over his neighbours.'[139]

There was, of course, an anti-alien dimension to the faction fighting which triggered the events of 1258 and again when the royalist revanche brought the Savoyards into the frame, supplemented as they were by the return of the Poitevins. As we have seen earlier, the coalition between the Montfortians and 'the marchers' saw assaults on alien landowners.[140] In a characteristically perceptive re-examination of the sources, David Carpenter has shown that the Montfortian 'statute' against aliens, condemned by King Louis IX at Amiens in January 1264, belonged to July 1263. In essence, the evidence is this. Around 24 June 1263, a letter, sealed by Simon de Montfort, was sent to the citizens of London asking if they intended to observe the ordinances and statutes made at Oxford. To this was added a petition of the barons (*Petitio Baronum*) which included a demand that the realm be governed solely by native born men.[141] On or before 29 June, a document known as the form of peace (*Forma Pacis*) was sent to the king and Lord Edward on the barons' behalf for their acceptance. It included the above provision but added another to the effect that all aliens were to be permanently expelled from the realm, except those whose stay was agreed unanimously by its faithful men.[142] This acceptance was finally proclaimed by

---

[138] See, for example, M. T. Clanchy, *England and its Rulers 1066–1307* (3rd edn., London, 2006), Ch. 12. See also Carpenter, *The Reign of Henry III*, 261, n. 4.

[139] Clanchy, *England and its Rulers*, 241.   [140] See above 160.

[141] *De Antiquis Legibus*, 54: ... *petunt quod regnum de cetero per indigenas fideles et utiles sub Domino Rege gubernetur.*

[142] ... *quod exeant alienigae a regno ulterius non reversuri exceptis illis quorum moram fideles regni unanimi assensu acceptarent.* See D. A. Carpenter, 'King Henry III's "Statute" against Aliens: July 1263', *EHR*, 107 (1992), 721–52, repr. in Carpenter, *The Reign of Henry III*, 261–80.

letters patent on 16 July 1263. 'It marked', says Carpenter, 'the decision of the Montfortians to sanction and exploit the popular tide of xenophobia in the hope of winning wide support for their clause'.[143]

How is this development to be explained? It is understandable, Carpenter tells us, because the years between 1258 and 1263 had seen 'anti-alien feeling' rapidly become 'both less discriminating and more intense'.[144] In Carpenter's words, 'The statute against the aliens ... was promulgated in July 1263, events over the previous three years having magnified hatred of foreigners many times over'.[145] Even in 1267, he says, the country 'was still awash with anti-alien sentiment'.[146] Although he is perfectly aware of the Montfortian propaganda, Carpenter concludes that 'What gave the issue such potency was that it appealed across the classes and divisions of English society. More than anything else, anti-alien feelings solidified his movement and broadened its popular appeal'.[147]

But did aristocratic resentment against alien landholders and recipients of patronage on the one hand and popular xenophobia on the other really merge? Nicholas Vincent's observations in his fine biography of Bishop Peter des Roches, Henry III's old tutor, must give us pause.[148] Peter famously lost out to Hubert de Burgh in the struggle to control the king and hence direct policy during his minority, but returned to power, though not to office, in 1232–4. Vincent writes: 'Much has been written of the growing xenophobia of thirteenth-century England. Yet "xenophobia" is a misleading term. Outbursts of anti-alien feeling were the result not so much of indiscriminate hatred of foreigners, as of a highly politicized, highly selective attack upon particular aliens in a particular set of political circumstances'. He reminds us that there were prominent figures who 'played upon such sentiments for political gain'.[149] The revolt of Richard Marshal in 1233–4 also had an anti-alien dimension, which seems to have centred on property and patronage.[150] There is mileage, too, in Vincent's comment that, notwithstanding the English chronicles, the aliens were a heterogeneous group lacking cohesion. This is, of course, less the case with the Lusignans and Savoyards of mid-century, who, as we have seen, can genuinely be referred to as factions. At the same time, however, as Vincent points out, we should not lightly dismiss the power of labels, both positively and negatively.[151] He notes the parallel with the term 'Northerners' by which the chroniclers designate the rebel barons of 1215, noted by J. C. Holt as 'the first use in English history of a party-political label'.[152]

---

[143] Carpenter, *The Reign of Henry III*, 272.   [144] Ibid., 268.   [145] Ibid., 272.
[146] Ibid., 278.   [147] Ibid.
[148] For what follows see N. Vincent, *Peter des Roches: An Alien in English Politics, 1205–1238* (Cambridge, 1996), 37. See also 156–63 on the position of aliens and the patronage of them exercised by Peter de Roches.
[149] In this case Stephen Langton, Hubert de Burgh, and Richard Marshal.
[150] Vincent, *Peter des Roches*, 393.
[151] Ibid., 40.   [152] J. C. Holt, *The Northerners* (2nd edn., Oxford, 1992), xv.

220 POLITICS AND SOCIETY IN MID THIRTEENTH-CENTURY ENGLAND

Even the attacks against alien clergy and their estates, which began in December 1231 and lasted through the first half of 1232, were not quite what they might seem.[153] Some of these were led by the Yorkshire knight Robert de Thweng, who called himself William Wither (William the Angry). He had a particular grievance, however, in that the pope had appointed to the living at the church of Kirkleatham, which Robert and his wife had only recently recovered through legal action. It seems likely, moreover, that anti-alien feeling was being stirred up at the centre by Hubert de Burgh, whose influence was now declining. 'Once again', writes Vincent, 'it appears that what has been taken to be a spontaneous outburst of popular xenophobia, may in fact have been a carefully orchestrated political ploy, organized from within the court'. Moreover, 'we should beware of accepting outward appearances, or of reading back into the 1230s, nationalist sentiments which are more appropriate to the nineteenth century'.[154]

What, if anything, was different in 1258–63? Carpenter cites Huw Ridgeway in support of his contention that xenophobia grew exponentially in these years.[155] Ridgeway, however, puts the emphasis on the years 1258–9, on the propaganda against the Lusignans, and on the justiciar's inquiries into seigneurial abuses. Within English provincial society, he says, xenophobia 'had begun to be fired' in 1258. There can be no doubt that the continuing presence of the Savoyards and Lusignans within court politics sustained an anti-alien stance within the aristocratic world. Indeed, their perceived monopolization of position and patronage poisoned opposition opinion throughout 'the period of reform and rebellion'. One need only think of the attitude and behaviour of the marcher lords. The issue was still figuring in negotiations between the king and the earl of Gloucester and between the king and the Disinherited in 1266–7.[156] Carpenter points to the introduction of foreign mercenaries, which 'enabled the king's opponents to play on the fear of foreign invasion and conquest, just as the young king himself had done when faced by Prince Louis and his Frenchmen in 1216–17'.[157] In August 1261, Henry sought to distil such fears by means of a proclamation, an indication in itself that the presence of mercenaries could turn minds.[158] As far as the general populace is concerned, however, Ridgeway emphasizes the effects of Hugh Bigod's judicial eyre. The problem here is that it is impossible to measure the general effects of this when it comes to attitudes towards aliens in general. The same is true with regard to the Provisions of Westminster and the expectations they raised. Were the events of 1258–9 sufficient to arouse widespread xenophobia?

---

[153] Vincent, *Peter des Roches*, 303–7. See also H. Mackenzie, 'The Anti-Foreign Movement in England, 1231–1232', in C. H. Taylor and J. L. La Monte (eds.), *Anniversary Essays in Medieval History by Students of Charles Homer Haskins* (Boston, 1929), 183–203.

[154] Vincent, *Peter des Roches*, 305.   [155] Ridgeway, 'Henry III and the "Aliens"', 90–1.

[156] See Carpenter, *The Reign of Henry III*, 278, and Knowles, 'The Disinherited', Part I, 40, 46.

[157] Carpenter, *The Reign of Henry III*, 270.

[158] *DBM*, 209–11.

SIMON DE MONTFORT AND HIS SUPPORT   221

A clue as to what was actually going on lies in the negotiation post-Lewes, that is to say in the 'Canterbury Peace' of August 1264. Here Simon de Montfort actually modified his position with regard to aliens. The ban on foreigners playing any part in government, by office or otherwise, was maintained in line with Montfortian aristocratic opinion, but the blanket ban on the presence of aliens within the country was dropped.[159] It was neither a practical nor an essential component of the Montfortian programme. It is difficult to envisage widespread xenophobia as a spontaneous phenomenon, outside of the monasteries at least and perhaps London. There was, no doubt, an underlying resentment against alien clerics and Cahorsin money lenders, and these were brought to the surface during 1263. But xenophobia was either generated by Simon de Montfort and the Montfortians or, at the very least, exacerbated by them.

What is certain is that Simon de Montfort was a master at propaganda. We have already seen his agents at work in the counties. Simon's propaganda was accompanied by self-projection and an acute use of symbolism. For one thing he used the sign of the cross, *crucesignatus*, to raise his military campaign to the status of holy war. In December 1263 when he found himself shut out of London, between the city gates and the king's oncoming forces, he called his men to arms and had them all signed with the mark of the holy cross front and back.[160] Later, at Lewes, greatly aided by Walter de Cantilupe, he instilled in his troops a spirit of piety and self-sacrifice and then addressed them with a rallying cry that identified the state of the kingdom of England with God's cause. He made reference, too, to the belt of knighthood, yet another ideological component of his projection, one which identifies him with the aristocracy in general and points to the exclusive approach of his social thinking.[161]

But Montfort knew well enough that the support of knights, 'the flower of England' as the *Song of Lewes* calls them, was not enough, given that in reality he was supported by only a minority of them. Even with a vocal Montfortian party in the church and the adherence of London and other towns, Simon's position was not as strong as it might have been, especially when faced with the prospect of invasion. His response to this threat in the summer of 1264 was masterly. He summoned an army the likes of which had not been seen in England since the Norman Conquest.[162] To Sophie Ambler, the 'earl's call to arms was a demagogic masterpiece'. Through royal letters to the counties he spoke of 'a great horde of aliens' ready to invade and disinherit everyone.[163] The result was phenomenal.

---

[159] *DBM*, 218–19.

[160] According to Gervase of Canterbury, 230–1. See Maddicott, *Simon de Montfort*, 247.

[161] See Ambler, *Bishops in the Political Community*, 134–5, quoting *Rishanger*, 30 and *Chronica Johannis de Oxenede*, ed. H. Ellis, Rolls Series (London, 1859), 222.

[162] Maddicott, *Simon de Montfort*, 290.

[163] *Foedera* i, 444; Maddicott, *Simon de Montfort*, 291; Ambler, *Bishops in the Political Community*, 144.

222 POLITICS AND SOCIETY IN MID THIRTEENTH-CENTURY ENGLAND

At Barham Down, said one chronicle, 'such a multitude gathered together against the aliens that you would not have believed so many men equipped for war existed in England'.[164] The supportive bishops sent letters to their clergy in favour of a tax of a tenth in which they echoed Montfort's stance.[165] They sent levies to Barham, as did monastic prelates. At Montfort's side on the shores of Kent, in August 1264, stood four bishops. In the words of Sophie Ambler: 'The experience must have been electrifying: watching as their God-given leader walked amongst his army, girding the men of the kingdom to defend their homes and the lives of their families'.[166]

Ambler has also taken a detailed look at the parliament of January 1265.[167] More than 120 prelates—bishops, abbots, and priors—were summoned together with two knights from each county, two townsmen from each of the major towns, four from the Cinque Ports, and perhaps four from London. Ten bishops were present, plus representatives from the Templars and Hospitallers and probably some friars. The only other earl present was Gilbert de Clare, this being before his fatal quarrel with Montfort. There was a total of twenty-three Montfortian barons. The assembly, therefore, must have been quite different, as Ambler points out, from earlier parliaments. The apparent purpose was to secure the release of Lord Edward and Henry of Almain, as well as to discuss the security of the realm and reform of central and local government. Given that there was no request for taxation, the summoning of knights was unusual and the invitation of both these and the townsmen 'acknowledged the longing of local knights and of the rising urban elite for a greater voice'.[168] The most important point, however, in the present context, is this: 'It also gave the Montfortians a major opportunity to cascade a carefully crafted image of the regime throughout the kingdom, for the parliament would expose leading figures from the shires and towns to the charismatic presence of Montfort, and provide a platform on which the regime could advertise its credentials'.[169] It was aimed, says Ambler, at a specific audience, one which would have appreciated the confirmation of Magna Carta and the Charter of the Forests. This was repeated on 11 March at the parliament's dramatic climax, involving a ceremony with candles (once again) and the excommunication of all who would violate the Charter of Liberties, the Form of Peace, or the Provisions of Westminster. 'It was a spectacular piece of theatre, designed to awaken the senses and impress itself upon the memory', whose 'intended effect was to imbue

---

[164] *Flores Historiarum*, ii, 499.

[165] *C & S*, 695, 698; Ambler, *Bishops in the Political Community*, 144.

[166] Ibid., 144. Perhaps, she suggests, Walter de Cantilupe preached to the troops, as he had done at Lewes, while friars may also have been there.

[167] Ambler, *Bishop in the Political Community*, 178–83. See also S. T. Ambler, 'Magna Carta: Its Confirmation at Simon de Montfort's Parliament of 1265', *EHR*, 130 (2015), 801–30.

[168] Ambler, *Bishops in the Political Community*, 178–9. See also Maddicott, *Origins of the English Parliament*, 259–60.

[169] Ambler, *Bishops in the Political Community*, 179.

SIMON DE MONTFORT AND HIS SUPPORT   223

a radical movement with the comforting aura of an ancient and valued tradition'.[170] Letters were sent to every county, to be kept safely in the courts by trustworthy men and their contents 'to be read aloud in full county court at least twice a year'.[171] At the heart of the operation was Thomas de Cantilupe, now chancellor, 'who can be counted as the Montfortian spin doctor'.[172]

And yet, it is doubtful that the attendees were all fervent supporters and equally doubtful that the Montfortians really did speak for the majority of the nation. Although it was famously said by the London chronicler Arnold fitz Thedmar that they had the support of 'almost all the middling people of the kingdom',[173] this was written in a particular context (the news of King Louis's decision at Amiens) and from a London perspective. It was clearly an exaggeration. The reality is that Simon de Montfort was not so much the first popular leader as the first *populist* leader in English history. As we have seen, the support for Simon was in reality patchy and inchoate. Moreover, the somewhat beleaguered Montfortians were prone to employ not only persuasion but also coercion in support of their cause. In the last analysis, whatever fervour Simon generated was insufficient to sustain him.

Martyrdom

For months Simon ruled effectively. The triumvirate and the council of nine functioned efficiently. The regime, however, had problems. A major one, as ever, was the exercise of patronage. Among measures taken was the relief of Jewish debts owed by his supporters.[174] The greatest benefits bestowed, however, went to Simon himself and his sons. Under the terms of the Peace of Worcester he took control of the Chester lordship, rendering him nearly £1,400 per annum. Land was confiscated from men who were against him at Lewes, and he took eighteen baronies into his custody. Probably even worse in terms of impact were the gains made by his sons. Property was being heaped on his heir, Henry, while Simon the Younger, who had already gained Mansel's estates, now received those of Earl Warenne in Sussex. Guy de Montfort acquired Richard of Cornwall's property in the south-west peninsula, including the tin mines, while Aimery gained further livings in the church, including the treasureship of York. In some quarters at least there was a mounting atmosphere of tension and insecurity.

For the dénouement at Evesham we are reliant upon the chroniclers, that is to say for the most part upon the Montfortian supporters within the church. By their nature chronicles tend to be mutually inconsistent and variably informed.

---

[170] Ibid., 180–1.   [171] *DBM*, 308–15.
[172] Ambler, *Bishops in the Political Community*, 183.   [173] Maddicott, *Simon de Montfort*, 263.
[174] Knowles, 'The Disinherited', Part II, 52–4; *CFR 1264–5*, nos. 54–5.

224 POLITICS AND SOCIETY IN MID THIRTEENTH-CENTURY ENGLAND

They can be based on eyewitness accounts at one extreme or third-hand information at the other. It is little wonder that historians have varied considerably in their interpretation of the battle.[175] The discovery of 'a new account', contemporary or near contemporary, from Evesham has clarified important aspects of the conflict, and produced a good deal of consensus.[176] We now know for sure, for example, how the loyalist forces were aligned, to the north of the town. One of the features that stands out in the chronicles is the air of doom and pessimism they portray on the Montfortian side before the battle. The atmosphere was heavy with premonition. The bishop of Worcester, who took Simon's confession and gave him communion, is portrayed leaving Montfort in tears. The splintering of the spear holding the banner on the abbey gate by Guy de Balliol, the earl's standard bearer, as they rode out to battle was reportedly perceived as a bad omen. A curious feature of the preparations for battle was the decision by Humphrey de Bohun, who was assigned command of the foot soldiers, to draw back and form them up as a rear-guard. Simon is reported to have said: 'Sir Humphrey, Sir Humphrey, that is no way to conduct a battle, putting the foot soldiers in the rear. I know well how this will turn out'.[177] He meant presumably that the soldiers would flee. Most striking of all is the reporting of the storm that took place before the battle and the degree to which the sky darkened. This has religious and possibly Christological connotations and seems to indicate that heaven itself was displeased. What is being reported is the prelude to martyrdom. Indeed, the Annals of Waverley say as much: 'Alas! A glorious martyr for the peace of the land, and for the redemption of the realm and of mother church'.[178] Indeed, all the ingredients were there. It was a bloody death, deliberate and politically motivated, in the tradition of Thomas Becket. There seems no doubt that a decision was made on the royalist side that Montfort should die. We learn from the 'new account' that Edward and Gloucester selected twelve of the strongest men,[179] whose role was to kill him. This went against all the contemporary conventions of chivalric war, according to which knights were to be saved whenever possible and ransomed after the conflict. These twelve were to 'penetrate the host forcefully and rapidly in such a way that they would look at no-one nor let anyone come between them until they reached the person of the

---

[175] See D. C. Cox, *The Battle of Evesham: A New Account* (Evesham, 1988); Carpenter, *The Battles of Lewes and Evesham 1264/5*; David Snowden, '1265: The Murder of Evesham', *The Lion*, Simon de Montfort Society (2020).

[176] Olivier de Laborderie, J. R. Maddicott, and D. A. Carpenter, 'The Last Hours of Simon de Montfort: A New Account', *EHR*, 115/461 (April 2000), 378–412.

[177] *Sire Humfrai, sire Humfrai, n'est par la manere de bataille a mettere la pedaille derere. Bien sai coment la chose se prenda*: Laborderie, Maddicott, and Carpenter, 'The Last Hours of Simon de Montfort', 408.

[178] *Ann. Mon.* ii (Annals of Waverley), 365; quoted by Snowden, 'The Murder of Evesham', 49.

[179] Curiously called *serjans* in the text.

SIMON DE MONTFORT AND HIS SUPPORT   225

earl'.[180] Although these details may or may not be true, the decision itself is clear enough, and explains why the death toll was so high on the baronial side as the royalists hacked their way through to the earl, slaughtering his crack troops. And it is why the chronicler, Robert of Gloucester, called it no battle but 'the murder of Evesham'.[181]

In addition to this unnecessary killing on the battlefield we are told of the slaughter of a large, but untold, number of fleeing men, largely no doubt foot soldiers, in the fields, at the river, and in the town. The abbey church, even to the altar, was a scene of bloodshed, adding sacrilege to the royalist sins. The emphasis on blood, moreover, adds to the air of martyrdom. And, despite Henry III's best efforts, Simon *was* popularly venerated as a saint and miracles performed at his tomb.[182] There was a posthumous cult embracing not only chronicles, but also poems and songs, and liturgical offices.[183] One hundred and ninety-six miracles are recorded, mostly involving the sick and the lame. The pilgrims were socially diverse, from Letitia Lamede, who was pushed by her devoted husband in a wheelbarrow from London, a journey of ten weeks' duration, and who was promptly cured, to the countesses of Gloucester and Aumale. Particularly interesting in the present context are Geoffrey de Say, an elderly and seemingly pro-Montfortian knight from Essex, the earl of Oxford, who journeyed there in 1273 and lived another twenty-three years, and Sir Simon de Pattishall, baronial sheriff and one of the 'Disinherited', who lived only one.[184] As John Maddicott says, 'The distinctiveness of Montfort's cult partly rests on the unusual number of these upper-class adherents whom it attracted'.[185]

This begs the question as to whether Simon himself sought martyrdom. Simon was a high-ranking crusader, the leading representative of a crusader lineage, and martyrdom in battle was the ultimate sacrifice for the cause that a warrior could make. It seems more likely, however, that despite the odds, at least as far as he could see them, Simon did have a strategy. We have to consider the dreadful situation he was in, surprised by the nearness of Lord Edward and

[180] ... *e vivement e atasement percereient l'ost, issi qe nulli regardasent ne suffrisent entre eaus venir deskes il venissent al corps le conte:* Laborderie, Maddicott, and Carpenter, 'The Last Hours of Simon de Montfort', 408.

[181] *Swiche was the morthere of Eivesham; vor bataile non it was: Metrical Chronicle,* ii, 765 (l. 11, 736).

[182] The Dictum of Kenilworth forbade any talk of 'the vain and fatuous miracles' told of Simon de Montfort: *DBM*, 322–5.

[183] See Maddicott, *Simon de Montfort,* 347, and his 'Follower, Leader, Pilgrim: Robert de Vere, Earl of Oxford at the Shrine of Simon de Montfort, 1273', *EHR,* 109 (1994), 641–53.

[184] Three abbots, three priors, and two university masters were also among the pilgrims.

[185] Ibid., 653. The miracles are recorded in *Miracula* [Simonis de Montfort] in *The Chronicle of William de Rishanger of the Barons' Wars,* ed. J. O. Halliwell (Camden Society, 1840), 67–110. For discussion of the miracles and their context, see R. C. Finucane, *Miracles and Pilgrims* (London, 1997), 131–5, and Cox, *The Battle of Evesham,* 24–6, as well as D. W. Burton, 'Politics, Propaganda and Public Opinion in the Reigns of Henry III and Edward I' (University of Oxford, DPhil thesis, 1985).

226 POLITICS AND SOCIETY IN MID THIRTEENTH-CENTURY ENGLAND

lacking the expected reinforcements from his son, Simon de Montfort junior. He was, in fact, trapped in Evesham. Although it is clear that the three components of the royal army were all situated on the north side of the town, it is hard to believe that retreat via the bridge, located on the other side of the town, was a viable possibility. Even if it was not covered by at least a small royalist force, which is surely probable,[186] it soon would have been. Montfort would have been unable to get the bulk of his men out, even if he and some of his knights could have made it. Flight in this fashion would surely have been considered dishonourable. Theoretically at least, Montfort had four alternatives: he could flee, putting personal safety first; he could stay put in the abbey and wait for reinforcements to arrive and try to relieve the inevitable siege that would follow; he could open negotiations, which would inevitably mean surrender; or he could fight. He chose the fourth and, in the event, disastrous option. The 'new account', written in Anglo–Norman, contains a good deal of reconstructed dialogue in the abbey before Simon and his knights rode out. Taking the words presented by chroniclers as an accurate account of what was said, either literally or in essence, is always a dangerous procedure. In this case, however, we have grounds for putting at least some degree of trust in what is reported. This is partly because of the circumstantial evidence provided by the account as a whole and partly because, in John Maddicott's view, it captures Simon's 'forceful and sometimes almost epigrammatic way of speaking, a facility for which he was well known'.[187] The writer may even have been an eyewitness. Surrender was not an option, since it would inevitably see the end of the enterprise and Simon is likely to have found the idea dishonourable and repugnant. As to staying put and waiting upon events, this was apparently put to him by one of his followers, arguing that the army was exhausted and hungry and needed time to build up its strength. Moreover, the church and its tower were defensible. Simon, with bravado, replied: 'No, fair friend, no. One ought to seek knights on the battlefield and chaplains in churches'.[188] He may also have considered this option impractical.[189] The Oseney chronicler tells us that this was urged upon him by his followers, while several sources have him urging flight on others. In the 'new account' Simon addresses his troops as they leave the town, suggesting to the younger members with their wives and children and their lives ahead of them that they should cross the bridge and 'escape from the peril that is to come'. To Hugh le Despenser, in particular, he urged that he save himself, given that he had so much still to give the country and that after him there would

---

[186] In this I am in agreement with David Snowden: 'The Murder of Evesham', 133, 159.

[187] Maddicott, in 'A New Account', 394.

[188] 'Noun, beaus amis, noun, mes hommes doit quere chivalers en champs e chapileins a mousters': Laborderie, Maddicott, and Carpenter, 'The Last Hours of Simon de Montfort', 408.

[189] Ibid., 404.

scarcely be anyone of such loyalty and worth. The answer was predictable: 'My lord. My lord, let it be. Today we shall all drink from one cup, just as we have long since done'.[190]

The difficulty is that these are tropes. They are what men of honour and pride would have been expected to say. The reactions of the lord are mirrored by those of his followers. Here we have neatly laid before us the glue that held the affinity together. Simon was a warrior, and he and his knights held to the ideals of the warrior band. The fact that this 'new account' seems to come from a knightly milieu sharpens its value in reflecting the thinking of Simon de Montfort and his men. Simon's last stand was indeed heroic, and it is hard not to be moved by it. His strategy was to break the line between Edward's and Clare's forces, advancing most probably at speed in a wedge-like formation. At first, he succeeded in precisely this until Warin de Bassingbourne rallied Mortimer's troops, they being in the rear of the other two formations. It is quite possible that Simon was ignorant of the size of this force, since the topography of Greenhill meant they were hidden from him at the outset of the battle. From his perspective and with God's help, it seemed possible that the Montfortian cavalry could break through or that Simon the Younger would appear in the nick of time. If not, martyrdom would have been his second choice.

And so, martyrdom it was and likely death for most of his closest followers. We know the names of thirty-six men who died with him, thirty-seven if we include Sir Humphrey de Bohun who later died in captivity, presumably from the effects of his wounds. We know of sixteen others who were taken prisoner.[191] These fifty-three were very probably a large proportion of the knights Simon had with him, many of them members of his old Midland affinity. Finally, the 'new account' tells us, it was Roger Mortimer who killed Simon, striking him with his lance through the neck. Although this contradicts other accounts that say he was killed with a dagger, not to mention the story of the twelve stout men, it would help to explain a longstanding puzzle, which is why Roger's wife, Maud, was sent Simon's head after the battle, although it still does not explain why she also received his testicles. The narrator of the 'new account' is at pains to say that the men of worth (*la gent de value*) turned away from the mutilating of Simon's body that followed his death. At this point, presumably, there was a brief lull in the fighting on the hill, as the remaining knights were allowed to surrender.

The accounts of the battle are significant in terms of the myth and legend of Simon de Montfort. His supporters in the church did him one last service in glorifying his death. In so doing they have greatly influenced modern historians.

---

[190] '*Sire, sire, lessez ester. Touz beveroms hui de un hanap, come pieça avoms fet*': Laborderie, Maddicott, and Carpenter, 'The Last Hours of Simon de Montfort', 408.

[191] These men are listed in Appendices 5 and 6 of Cox, *The Battle of Evesham*.

However one sees him—adventurer, zealot, hegemonic male, charismatic warrior and crusader, populist and propagandist, the epitome of aristocratic values, or whatever—it would be churlish to deny his heroism or that he was capable of attracting support from many directions and melding it into a (perhaps rather unstable) whole.

Politics and Society in Mid Thirteenth-Century England: The Troubled Realm. Peter Coss, Oxford University Press. © Peter Coss 2024. DOI: 10.1093/9780198924319.003.0008

9

Public Authority and the Provisions of Westminster

Mutatis mutandis the revolt of 1258 can be seen as a rerun of the aristocratic rebellion against King John. The main players were the magnates and barons together with some of the knights, both in their own capacity as members of the aristocracy and as followers of greater lords. At the heart of the revolt, as we have seen, was a move against the Lusignan faction and the desperate need for a more equitable monarchy, at least from an aristocratic point of view. A key issue was therefore the direction of royal patronage. The revolt itself was orchestrated in, or at least through, parliament and backed by naked force, notwithstanding Roger Bigod's reassurances that Henry was not to be in the magnates' power. In current historiography, as we have seen, the monopolization of patronage and the generally unruly behaviour of the Lusignans, both of which are in themselves undeniable, have replaced the need to save the country from the chaos created by Henry's pursuance of his Sicilian ambitions as the trigger for the revolt.

Paul Brand, however, has raised an important question. Precisely why did the magnates seek to reform 'the state of the kingdom?' Why was it not enough to simply drive out the Lusignans? 'There was perhaps', he suggests, 'already some kind of commonly understood linkage between reform of the *status regni* through the remedying of general grievances and abuses and the granting of taxation by the *communitas regni*, of a kind that is certainly observable in later parliamentary practice. The magnates may have warned the king that there was no chance of getting the *communitas regni* to agree to the subsidy he was seeking unless he agreed to some such arrangement'. Brand, moreover, makes the thought-provoking suggestion that 'the magnates may well not themselves have had any particular grievances or abuses in mind when they made the demand but may simply have been pointing out to the king that the remedying of grievances was a *sine qua non* for getting the county representatives to agree to taxation'.[1] These suggestions seem inherently more plausible than the idea that the baronial opposition was seeking to engage a wider political community in the debates over kingship and tyranny, good rulership and public utility, which had been

---

[1] Brand, *Kings, Barons and Justices*, 18.

230 POLITICS AND SOCIETY IN MID THIRTEENTH-CENTURY ENGLAND

exercising the intellectual and cultural elite and which had filtered down to the likes of Simon de Montfort.[2]

There is, however, another dimension. Hatred was running high against the detested faction and there was always the prospect of an armed return. It should not be forgotten that the confederation of April 1258 had had as its stated purpose mutual protection against just such an eventuality. Beyond any immediate consideration was the prospect of future action by a fickle and slippery king who had consistently failed to rule in a manner that suited the higher nobility. There appeared no alternative to the magnate opposition but to bring him under control. The core of the Provisions of Oxford was aimed precisely at this issue. The primary enactments were, therefore, the imposition of a ruling council, the revitalization of the major offices of state, the appointment of appropriate castellans—so necessary when it came to the exercise of physical force—and the king's primary representatives in the shires, the sheriffs. Reform at a lower level, affecting a wider spectrum of the population, was in contrast a secondary matter.

Why, then, was it necessary? No doubt there was a realization that to succeed in taking power away from the king, his family, and his supporters, it was important to gain wider support. The magnates' retainers would certainly have informed them of that. Whether the country was actually seething with discontent, let alone subject to revolutionary fervour, is questionable. But there can be no doubt of the corruption and malpractice that was present in the operation of the law and local government, and there is every reason to think that this caused widespread disquiet. The plea rolls of 1250–60 certainly indicate this.[3] It was well known that by contrast King Louis of France had instigated inquiries into the actions of his officials and had encouraged complainants to bring matters to his attention. Henry III was failing in his public duty. As Clive Knowles perceptively pointed out, the magnates were stepping into the space effectively vacated by the king.[4] Here was the justification for usurping his role, most especially as much of the king's failure could be laid at the door of his relatives and favourites. The position taken by the magnates was therefore symbolic as well as practical.

There can be no doubt but that the king understood perfectly well that he was the custodian of the public interest.[5] That he was aware of the obligations involved is evident in the lecture he gave to his sheriffs in October 1250. Their duties included observing the liberties of the church and delivering justice to minors, orphans, and widows, arresting for blasphemy, protecting rustics from being

---

[2] As seems to be suggested in Laura Slater, *Art and Political Thought in Medieval England c.1150–1350* (Woodbridge, 2018), 125, a stimulating discussion of twelfth- and thirteenth-century expressions of this culture.

[3] It is noticeable that many cases were brought against lords and their officials, reflecting the operation and the extension of their courts. See Carpenter, *Henry III: 1258–1272*, Ch. 2, 'Henry and His People'. For the cases themselves, see *Special Eyre Rolls of Hugh Bigod 1258–60*, ed. and introduced by Andrew Hershey, 2 vols. (Selden Society 131 and 133, 2021), and Hershey (ed.), *The 1259 Eyre of Surrey and Kent* (Surrey Record Society 38, 2004).

[4] Knowles, *Simon de Montfort*, 26.   [5] See above 30–1.

PUBLIC AUTHORITY 231

made responsible for their lords' debts, refraining from putting hundreds and other bailiwicks out to farm for profit, countering unauthorized markets, and so on. There is no doubt, too, that contemporaries understood the Aristotelian concept of 'public good'. Learned men knew the Roman concept of *res publica*. As Gerald Harriss showed, the idea of common utility was bound up with the power of the *princeps* to call upon the military and financial resources of the realm.[6] In fact, as Harriss pointed out, the increased power of the Angevin rulers 'forced subjects to seek safeguards for their rights in custom and legal doctrine and to evolve, as a counterpoise to the public authority of the King, a political identity as a *communitas*'.[7] The concepts involved here are neatly encapsulated by the early thirteenth-century London interpolator of the *Leges Edwardi Confessoris* when he argues that all free men should keep arms for the protection of the realm (*ad tuitionem regni*) while shire levies *pro commune utilitate* should be prepared to serve for the honour and utility of the crown (*ad honorem et ad utilitatem coronem regni*).[8] Public power and right rule were much thought about in the twelfth and thirteenth centuries,[9] and as Ian Forrest says: 'The public was newly prominent in government ideology ... and we see this in the importance that rulers placed upon new legal and theological discourses celebrating their purpose and usefulness'.[10] It is quite clear from Matthew Paris that in monastic circles at least men thought Henry was deficient in this respect.[11] The truth is, as Maddicott says, that 'his public conscience' was 'selective in its targets'.[12] He seemed to believe, moreover, that public authority was a matter for the crown, and the crown alone.[13]

The Process of Reform

Three questions have to be broached before we can assess the role and significance of the legislation that resulted. Who was advocating it? Who provided it? And, who supported it? To gain a handle on this we must first examine the

[6] G. L. Harriss, *King, Parliament and Public Finance in Medieval England to 1369* (Oxford, 1975), 3–9.

[7] Ibid., 4.

[8] Ibid., 9, citing *Die Gesetze der Angelsachsen I*, ed. F. Liebermann (Halle, 1903), 655–6, and Liebermann, *Über die Leges Anglorum saeculo xiii ineunte Londoniis collectae* (Halle, 1894). See also J. E. A. Jolliffe, *Angevin Kingship* (London, 1955), 323. On the famous occasion in the autumn of 1259 when Lord Edward aligned himself with 'the community of the bachelry of England', the Burton annalist has both him and them express themselves in terms of the *utilitas respublicae*: *Ann. Mon.* i (Annals of Burton), 471. According to Roger of Wendover, the *Statute of Merton* of 1236 was 'for the common utility of the realm': Wendover, iii, 49.

[9] J. Sabapathy, *Officers and Accountability in Medieval England 1170–1300* (Oxford, 2014), 237, citing Beryl Smalley, *The Becket Conflict and the Schools: A Study of Intellectuals in Politics* (Oxford, 1973), 228–9, 231, 239–40.

[10] I. Forrest, *Trustworthy Men: How Inequality and Faith made the Medieval Church* (Princeton and Oxford, 2018), 98.

[11] See, for example, Paris, *CM* iii, 410.

[12] Maddicott, 'Magna Carta and the Local Community', 60.

[13] Maddicott, *Origins of the English Parliament*, 231.

232 POLITICS AND SOCIETY IN MID THIRTEENTH-CENTURY ENGLAND

process of reform, even if this involves retracing our steps a little. Here we cannot do better than follow the magisterial study of Paul Brand.[14] On 2 May 1258 the king issued letters patent announcing that he had promised the magnates on oath that the state of the kingdom would be 'put in order, corrected and reformed' by a Committee of Twenty-Four (comprising twelve baronial and twelve royal nominees). A second letter, issued on the same day, put this into context. The king explained that he had summoned his magnates to parliament to ask for financial assistance to pay for the Sicilian business.[15] This had been held at London in early April. Eventually they had promised to support a request for money which he would submit to the 'community of the realm', an expression which seems to refer here to 'a body which included representatives from the counties'. There were two provisos. One was that the pope would have to agree to modify his demands.[16] The other was that the king must assent to the Committee of Twenty-Four reforming the state of the realm. The committee duly met at Oxford in June to where parliament had been adjourned. It proceeded to make rapid changes in the machinery of government: the revival of the office of justiciar; the replacement of the king's council with an entirely new body elected by members of the Twenty-Four, to which body the principal officers of state would be responsible; and thrice-yearly parliaments to be attended by the councillors and by twelve men representing the wider community of the realm (*communitas regni*). The sheriffs were now to be vavasours of their counties, to serve for one year only, and to be on expenses (that is, they were no longer to be farmers). The castellans of royal castles were replaced by men chosen by the Twenty-Four. Four knights in each county were to receive complaints against sheriffs, bailiffs, and other officers, and these were to be heard by the justiciar as he visited the counties. The committee appears to have noted down other areas where administrative reforms were needed.[17] They may also have considered legal reforms, to judge from items in the document known to historians as the Petition of the Barons. This appears to have been drawn up for the meeting of the Twenty-Four in Oxford, to have been read out publicly and probably made available for copying.[18] Some of the complaints are said explicitly to derive from the earls and barons, or just the barons. However, others do not, and seem rather to represent different voices. Clause 25, for example, complains that certain magnates and powerful men (*magnates et potentiores regni*) acquire Jewish debts and then refuse to accept payment from the creditors, called here lesser men (*minores*).[19] Brand concludes that the Petition of the Barons is a collation of complaints put together from a variety of sources and reflecting the interests and grievances of a variety of different groups, including

---

[14] Brand, *Kings, Barons and Justices*.   [15] *DBM*, nos. 1–2.

[16] For the implications of this see Brand, *Kings, Barons and Justices*, 17–18.   [17] Ibid., 20.

[18] See also Paul Brand, 'The Drafting of Legislation in Mid Thirteenth-Century England', in P. A. Brand, *The Making of the Common Law* (London, 1992), 326.

[19] And see Coss, 'Sir Geoffrey de Langley', 29.

PUBLIC AUTHORITY   233

less powerful ones.[20] What sources they were is, of course, unknowable, but it may well be that we need look no further than the magnates' own followers.

Brand's illuminating discussion of the process of reform following the Oxford parliament divides it into five stages. The first stage takes us to the Michaelmas parliament of 1258. The four knights who were to receive complaints in each county do not appear to have been appointed until late June or early August, and the procedure was changed. They were now to hold enquiries and to bring a record to parliament in early October. In the meantime, however, the justiciar, Hugh Bigod, had already begun hearing complaints, an earnest of intent on his part.[21] Preparations for legal and administrative reform seem to be already underway, as according to the London chronicle of Arnold fitz Thedmar some of the Twenty-Four were holding daily discussions in the city on the usages and customs of the realm.[22] Among the work undertaken at this point was the production of a detailed code of conduct for the sheriffs, all of whom were to take an oath to observe it. What was done at the parliament itself is unclear, but a document was sent out in the king's name on 18 October ordering all subjects to take an oath swearing to observe and maintain the provisions (*establissements*) made thus far and those that would be made by the council in the future.[23] This document indicates that the council understood 'the need to manipulate public opinion in the counties'.[24] Another document, known as the Ordinance of the Sheriffs, was issued on 20 October apologizing for the delay in addressing grievances and informing his subjects that the justices would make amendments in the counties as they visited them, reinforcing the impression that the council was attempting 'to gain favour with lesser men in the localities'. Brand suggests that it was at this parliament that the decision recorded in the 'Coke' roll was reached: that justices and other wise men (*autres sages homes*) were to be summoned between then and the next parliament to make changes in the law.[25] This indicates that legal experts were not only involved from early on in drafting the future legislation but also participated in determining its content.[26] The point is an extremely important one. They may have been expected, as Brand says, to draw on the complaints brought by the knights, although there is no evidence for it and less than half of the panels had actually sent their returns. This, incidentally, should give us pause when assessing the appetite for reform within the localities.[27]

---

[20] Brand, *Kings, Barons and Justices*, 24.

[21] See A. H. Hershey, 'Success or Failure? Hugh Bigod and Judicial Reform during the Baronial Movement of Reform and Rebellion, June 1258–February 1259', in *TCE*, v, 65–97.

[22] *Liber de Antiquis Legibus*, 38–9; Brand, *Kings, Barons and Justices*, 25.   [23] *DBM*, 116–17.

[24] Brand, *Kings, Barons and Justices*, 26.

[25] The 'Coke' roll is discussed in H. G. Richardson and G. O. Sayles, 'The Provisions of Oxford: A Forgotten Document and Some Comments', *Bulletin of the John Rylands Library*, 17 (1933), 291–321.

[26] Brand, *Kings, Barons and Justices*, 27.

[27] On the other hand, Brand adds quite reasonably: 'It is difficult to see why arrangements should have been made to bring the complaints to the meeting of parliament unless it was envisaged that some use would be made of them': ibid., 27.

234 POLITICS AND SOCIETY IN MID THIRTEENTH-CENTURY ENGLAND

The second stage runs from the Michaelmas parliament of 1258 to the Candlemas parliament of 1259. During this period Hugh Bigod dealt with the presentments from Surrey and Kent and held sessions in London. It was now that the main work was probably done on the Provisions of the English Barons (*Providencia Baronum*),[28] nine of its eleven clauses being later included in the Provisions of Westminster of October 1259. It is clear that the drafters were doing far more than simply turning the grievances and remedies listed in the Petition of the Barons into legislation. On the contrary, this latter document was seen as only a starting point. In some cases, such as suit of court and the sheriff's tourn, they took the issues further. Two clauses in particular 'relate to technical improvements of the kind we might expect to have been suggested by the judges and other legal experts consulted on matters in need of reform'.[29]

The third stage is the Candlemas parliament itself and its aftermath. There seems to have been discussion here of the draft legislation, and detailed changes were made to the *Providencia Baronum*, seen in the revised text published in March 1259. These concerned attendance at the tourn, *beaupleader*, and charters of exemption from jury service. Other matters, including suit of court, were under discussion. Letters patent issued on 22 February put the members of the council on the back foot in terms of extending the matters the king had addressed to their own tenants, that is to say that they were being told to put their own houses in order along the lines demanded of the king. An appeal was being made 'over their heads to the wider world of the *communitas regni* for support against the magnates'.[30] Although these letters were sealed on 22 February, they were not published until 28 March when a covering letter from the king ordered their reading out in every county and hundred court. The Latin text of the *Providencia Baronum* belongs to the end of March, being translated from the French after the parliaments. This, too, was only a draft, but it was clearly circulated.

The fourth stage ran from March to October 1259. A further draft of the *Providencia Baronum* was probably discussed at the June parliament before a penultimate draft of the Provisions as a whole was produced for approval at the Michaelmas parliament. In this there are sixteen 'new clauses', six of which relate to grievances and demands that were present in the Petition of the Barons. All but one of them go beyond the original suggestions. Surprisingly, four clauses of this draft assert royal rights and royal justice, suggesting that the king and others supporting him were having a major input into the legislation. Some clauses were watered down while others seem to indicate that members of the judiciary were actually involved in the drafting process. Thus, for example, clause no. 8 allowed for the overriding of charters of exemption in assizes (not just the grand assize) and 'whenever the royal justices thought it necessary'.

---

[28] *DBM*, no. 9.   [29] Brand, *Kings, Barons and Justices*, 30.   [30] Ibid., 31.

PUBLIC AUTHORITY 235

The fifth stage was the Michaelmas parliament of 1259 itself and the promulgation of the Provisions of Westminster. Changes were made again, and two clauses were omitted. After the final amendments the legislation was translated into the official Latin of legislation and read out in public in Westminster Hall on 24 October 1259. It was decided that in future two or three of the lesser men (*mesne gent*) of the council would be chosen at each parliament to be in continual attendance upon the king, presumably to deal with routine business. Several committees were established, indicating that the 'reforming impulse' was not 'exhausted'.[31]

This was not the end of the matter. Far from it. Henry III returned to England in December 1262 to face a general Welsh rising, discontent from those members of Edward's retinue who had been dismissed in the summer, and widespread local disaffection. Brand sees the reissuing of the Provisions of Westminster as a 'conciliatory gesture' on the king's part towards the more moderate of his opponents: 'This marked his own personal acceptance and approval of the legislation but at the same time put his own distinctive stamp upon it'.[32] This reissue was based on an official Latin text of the Provisions as issued in October 1259. It incorporated a new preamble, some of its phrasing being taken up in the covering writs sent to the justices in eyre and to the barons of the exchequer. Only one clause was omitted. The original Provisions had been, it was said, 'made by king and magnates by the common counsel and consent of the king and magnates'. The corresponding clause in 1263 has the king acting with the advice not of his magnates but of his 'lieges', giving advice as loyal subjects. No one is required to consent and the king is acting on his own free will. The legislation is also described as 'constitutions (*constitutiones*)' rather than 'provisions'. The legislation was issued for the reform and improvement of the realm (*ad reformationem et melioracionem regni sui Anglie*), and its publication was undertaken by the king on his own authority. There is no reference to the earlier text.[33] The following year brought the armed clash at Lewes. It is important to stress, in line with Brand, that they were fighting for control of the government and not for the Provisions of Westminster. Although both sides claimed to stand by these, it was not what the conflict was essentially about.[34] Nonetheless, the Provisions were reissued in December 1264. The text was that of 1263, the difference being the preamble. It was cast in terms of the problem of non-observance and the need therefore for republication. This message was reinforced in the concluding clause with the provision that the sheriffs should have it published monthly in their county courts and in hundreds and wapentake courts as well as in courts baron. No mention was made of the central courts, local enforcement being thought to be the key.[35]

---

[31] Ibid., 41. [32] Ibid., 140. A second reissue followed later in the year.
[33] For the details of the changes, see Brand, *Kings, Barons and Justices*, Ch. 5. [34] Ibid., 161.
[35] For the enforcement see Brand, *Kings, Barons and Justices*, Ch. 6.

236 POLITICS AND SOCIETY IN MID THIRTEENTH-CENTURY ENGLAND

After the civil war the clauses of the Dictum of Kenilworth reaffirmed in a fulsome manner not only the king's authority but also his right to total obedience and the respect due to his royal dignity. He was reverently requested to appoint suitable men to provide justice according to the laws and customs of the realm, thus strengthening the throne and royal majesty. He was also pressed to uphold the liberties of the church and observe Magna Carta and the Charter of the Forest. It was recommended furthermore that the king should observe those 'concessions' which he has made 'spontaneously and without coercion', and that he should confirm on a permanent basis other necessary measures devised by his men, with his agreement.[36] What the committee seems to have been recommending was a further issue and confirmation of the Provisions, and this appears to have led to the Statute of Marlborough in November 1267, which saw some further modification of clauses. There was a new preamble and eight new clauses sandwiched between the preamble and the reissued clauses. Brand points out, astutely, that the preamble here emphasizes the king's role 'without the almost neurotic emphasis of the 1263 preamble on the king's free will'.[37] It again talks of the king's 'lieges' and of a meeting between the king and the 'wiser men of the kingdom, both the great men and the lesser men'. It justifies the legislation at great length, beginning by mentioning the 'amelioration' of the kingdom and 'the king's duty to secure the better administration of justice'.

In Brand's view, the Provisions of Westminster of 1259 was one of the most significant achievements of the baronial council which took power in the summer of 1258. At least seven out of the twenty-four clauses of the Provisions of Westminster, he points out, were 'drafted and enacted in response to the grievances of his subjects against the king, his justices or his local officials'. What is more striking and impressive about the legislation, though, is just how little it reflects the specifically magnate domination of the king's council in 1258–9.[38] In fact, there is no reason why it should have done. This takes us back to the earlier point that there were two distinct dimensions to the process of reform: control of the executive on the one hand and the reform of the legal and administrative system on the other. The king and the magnates were both keen to take credit for the Provisions of Westminster.

Some of the clauses in the Petition of the Barons seem to have acted as a starting point for the drafting of legislation and led to more consideration and discussion.[39] It could be that the discussion was further influenced by the returns made by the knights and by complaints made to the justiciar, Hugh Bigod, although there is no

---

[36] *DBM*, no. 44, clauses 1–4.

[37] The full text of the statute is given, and a translation provided, in Brand, *Kings, Barons and Justices*, Ch. 5, Appendix 3.

[38] Ibid., 90.

[39] He suggests, moreover, that the clauses on suit of court and amercement for default of common summons may have been suggested by complaints made at a clerical council: ibid., 393.

evidence for this. However, as Brand legitimately asks, why would they have diverted these to parliament unless some use was expected to be made of them? The subsequent discussion allowed for differences of opinion. As to who the participants in the discussion were, the evidence is rather dark. There is some evidence of councillors taking part, but also clear indications that members of the judiciary and other legal experts participated. The king's reissue also reveals the hand of legal experts. Some of the changes were to make the operation of the law more efficient and to plug gaps in provision. There was also some lobbying from major religious houses, most particularly (although not solely) in dropping the need for a lord's consent when land was to be given in mortmain.

The ultimate issue of the reforms as the Statute of Marlborough in 1267 gave sole responsibility once again to the king.[40] The statute reinforced traditional royal ideology while at the same time reclaiming public authority. Having laid claim to their broad responsibility, Henry and Edward could hardly retract it. The genie could not be returned to the bottle, and legislation to meet public concerns, as well as enforcing royal rights, became once again a characteristic of the crown. The first half of the thirteenth century had not been a period of large-scale legislative reform of the common law. In contrast, the Provisions of Westminster and the Statute of Marlborough effectively created the idea of large-scale legislative reform and acted as a 'curtain-raiser' for the legislative activity associated with the reign of Edward I. These statutes were pioneering in another respect, being the first legislation to deliberately alter existing procedures in the king's courts.[41]

Reform and the Deep State

We began the discussion of the role and significance of the legislative reform with three questions. Who was advocating it? Who provided it? And, who supported it? We have gone some way towards answering the first two. The third question is more difficult. It has tended to be confused with designating who was and who was not Montfortian. This is understandable because the evidence offers more of an answer to the latter. An important question is who was the propaganda trying to reach? [42] It may be thought useful to begin with the Dictum of Kenilworth.[43]

---

[40] 'It seems plain that the drafters decided that there needed to be a grand restatement about the place of the king's courts and royal justice in the English polity': ibid., 395.

[41] 'The end result of the co-operative efforts of barons, justices and the king in the legislative process between 1259 and 1267 was to produce genuinely innovative legislation and to create an impressive model of large-scale legislative improvement in the common law': ibid., 410.

[42] For a broad discussion of propaganda and the king's failure until late to reach out to the realm, see D. W. Burton, *Politics, Propaganda and Public Opinion in the Reigns of Henry III and Edward I* (University of Oxford, DPhil thesis, 1985).

[43] For what follows see *DBM*, no. 44, clauses 22, 26, 32.

238   POLITICS AND SOCIETY IN MID THIRTEENTH-CENTURY ENGLAND

Here those 'laymen who openly supported the earl [Simon de Montfort] and his accomplices, drawing men to their party by lies and falsehoods, and drawing them away from the royal party' were to be punished by ransoming their lands.[44] Those, on the other hand, 'who aided the king and faithfully stood by him' were to be rewarded from the ransom payments. There appears, however, to have been a third category, for no ransom was to be paid by those who were not against the king: *qui in nullo fuerunt contra regem*. This does not seem to be ideologically sound, at least from the crown's point of view, since all faithful subjects should be with the king and only the faithless against. It was a matter, however, of practicalities. Neutrality was recognized, too, in the Buckinghamshire special eyre roll. Hugh de Plessiz was accused of plundering the Berkshire landowner William de Chalegrove *qui fuit ex neutra parte*, while John de Verdon, a royalist, was accused of robbing Geoffrey de Clivedon *qui se ex neutra parte habuit*. Walter de Geyton was charged with plundering a priest, Alan de Somery, who was neutral (*ex neutra parte fuit*).[45] As we have noted earlier, a study of the knights of Warwickshire takes those twenty-nine who figured in the grand assize at the 1262 eyre in the county and classifies twelve as 'contrariants', five as royalist, and twelve as 'unrecorded'.[46] The terms are deliberately cautious ones. The actual balance reflects the fact that Warwickshire was in the Montfortian heartland. Nonetheless, the fact that twelve are classified as 'unrecorded' is very significant. The majority of these must have been effectively neutral, putting further flesh on the bones of a skeletal 'neutral party'.

But, of course, it was not only knights who were involved. By comparing the rolls of the special eyre with the Hundred Rolls of 1279 we can identify some of the other people who were active as Montfortian sympathizers or as royalist victims during the period of civil war. Many of them, as one would expect, were lesser landowners and major freeholders, though not all. Many lesser men were charged with being receivers, men like Robert the Smith and William de Fonte, each of whom held a mere virgate of land at Mursley, Buckinghamshire.[47] They were accused of receiving wood from the robbery of Sir John de Grey and were found guilty by the jurors.[48] We can also identify members of the hundred juries who were involved. A study of Cambridgeshire jurors identifies thirty-seven of the 379 who figure on the eyre roll for the county in 1261 or the roll of the special eyre of 1268 who were accused as supporters of the baronial opposition, and

---

[44] *Laici manifeste procurantes negocia domini comitis et complicium suorum, attrahendo homines per mendacia, per falsitates insidiando partem comitis et complicium suorum, et detrahendo partem domini regis et filii sui, puniantur quantum valet terra eorum ...'*

[45] TNA, Just 1/59, mm. 16, 16d, 17.

[46] Fernandes, 'The Midland Knights and the Barons' War', 167–82.

[47] *Hundred Rolls*, ii, 336: Richard the Smith held a virgate for 12s. per annum and suit of court of John Passelew, while William de Fonte held a virgate of Robert fitz Nigel for 12s. plus services including suit of court. A fellow perpetrator was also said to be from Mursley.

[48] TNA, Just 1/59, m. 14d.

thirteen who were themselves injured as royalist sympathizers.[49] Naturally this is likely to underestimate the degree of Montfortian sympathy in the counties. The failure of some jurors, and some juries, to take part in the inquiries into civil war activities may well indicate a degree of antipathy to the weighted proceedings. Nevertheless, it seems highly likely that many free tenants, very probably the majority, would have been of the neutral party. This being so, it is hardly surprising that both sides in the conflict seem to have worked hard in delivering their message, either through the established administrative procedure of the county and hundred courts or by alternative methods of disseminating their cause: through preaching, through agents, and the like. In the other words there appears to have been a rather desperate propaganda war.

However, as has been pointed out, the civil war was not fought over the Provisions of Westminster. Hence the evidence gleaned from judicial proceedings relating to the war years does not tell us very much about enthusiasm for reform during the years 1258–9. We still have to broach the question of how far the wider populace pushed for reform and how they reacted to it. Some certainly took advantage of the justiciar's eyres to raise their complaints and grievances at the activities of sheriffs, bailiffs, and others, reinforcing known criticisms of the system. There are clear links between such grievances and the subsequent legislation. However, this gives us only one perspective. Rural inhabitants and their urban counterparts were not just victims. Although by no means as high profile as knights, sub-knightly landowners and free tenants also functioned ubiquitously within the Angevin system as its rank-and-file jurors in sworn inquests.[50] This was increasingly so in the thirteenth century. One thinks of surveys, like those which produced the Hundred Rolls of 1255, 1274–5, and 1279–80. There were other inquisitions like those of postmortem, *ad quod damnum*, and the category classified in the national archives as 'miscellaneous'. There were many inquiries to furnish information for the crown, while inquests were also used locally. Then, beginning with the jury of presentment introduced by Henry II, there was the constantly expanding use of juries in courts. These included the juries in the ever popular petty assizes. There were also coroners' juries, and of course trial juries. The special eyre after the civil war, the rolls of which we have much utilized in this study, used both presentment and trial juries. The question as to who staffed juries has been debated. At the end of our period two statutes dealt with the matter. Chapter 38 of the second Statute of Westminster in 1285 specified that jurors should generally have an annual income of 20*s*., while in the statute of 1293, later known as the 'statute of those who ought to be put on juries', this was raised to 40*s*. Both statutes raised the

---

[49] Keizo Asaji, 'The Barons' War and the Hundred Jurors in Cambridgeshire', *JMH*, 21 (1995), 153–65.
[50] On this subject see, especially, James Masschaele, *Jury, State and Society in Medieval England* (New York, 2008).

240 POLITICS AND SOCIETY IN MID THIRTEENTH-CENTURY ENGLAND

threshold (to 40s. and 100s., respectively) for those juries whose verdicts were given outside of their county, including Westminster. These statutes reflected concerns that the ever expanding need for juries meant that sheriffs and others were empanelling lesser men. The sheriffs had encountered problems resulting directly from the king's issuing of lifetime exemptions from being put on 'juries, assizes and recognitions' against one's will. Officials, moreover, took bribes from men not to call on them. Nonetheless, James Masschaele's thorough study of juries indicates that their membership generally ranged from knights down to villagers but that the majority were minor landowners, substantial freeholders, and solidly based peasants, or their urban equivalents. There was a tendency for the status of jurors to match the perceived status of the jury, and men of higher status were inclined to draw away from the routine and more localized types of jury in favour of more elevated ones such as those responsible for perambulating boundaries or hearing appeals of verdicts returned by lower juries.[51] Here the jurors aped the knights who formed the juries of the grand assize, dealing with the issue of right. These were also the men who tended to be called on as coroners, sub-escheators, tax assessors, purveyors, and so on.

Historians have concentrated on the burdensome nature of jury service,[52] and have concentrated on licences to avoid it and the bribery of officials. At the same time, however, the jury system was very popular with litigants, and many of the more substantial men must have felt that their status was enhanced through their participation in the local components of the Angevin system, so that they had a vested interest in its continuation. It may be useful here to adapt the concept of the 'deep state', not in a conspiratorial sense but in the sense of networks of people who had a stake in the status quo. Such networks did not function on the basis of a particular political programme, but on that of shared interests, values, and attitudes.[53] The 'deep state' was a good deal shallower than in modern times, but it was, I would maintain, a factor to be taken into account in understanding the socio-politics of the thirteenth century. Some of the terminology used at the time reinforces this picture. Jurors in the petty assizes had long been called *legales homines*, or *libri et legales homines*, and there can be no doubt that these words were taken seriously.[54] In short, jurors needed to have public standing, meaning essentially that they were considered to be of good reputation. In general, this would have reflected their social status. There were other terms also which indicated both legal and a social standing. Among them was *probi homines*, the

---

[51] Ibid., 154–5.

[52] 'There can be little doubt that medieval people saw jury service as difficult, burdensome and even potentially dangerous': ibid., 204.

[53] For an example of networks in action, see Peter Coss, 'How Did Thirteenth-Century Knights Counter Royal Authority?', *TCE*, xv (Woodbridge, 2015), 3–16.

[54] Masschaele discusses this issue at length, in Ch. 4 of his study. 'Both the adjectives and the noun in the phrase were ripe with meaning': ibid., 128.

equivalent of *boni homines* used, for example, in Italy.[55] What was most at issue for such men was the proper exercise of public authority. Many are likely to have favoured moves against corruption and more generally supported modification and improvement of the system under which they lived without necessarily being strident or diehard about it.

Such men were involved, too, as plaintiffs and indeed defendants in the courts of county and hundred, and increasingly in the central courts. Many took the opportunity of bringing cases before the justiciar as they had long done when opportunities for complaint or redress had been offered them. Their role in the reforms was essentially that of interested consumers. This does not, of course, show that they reacted in an idealistic way to the prospect of reform and legislation; indeed, many may have taken the rhetoric with a large pinch of salt. This fits with the emphasis upon reform rather than radical change which characterized the movement of 1258–9. The only point of fundamental challenge lay at the apex of the system. The crucial issue for the opposition magnates and their supporters was who was to run the post-Angevin polity.

It has been suggested by Susan Stewart, editor of the 1263 Surrey eyre, that the leading freeholders in each case constituted a hundredal community on the model of the community of the shire and that where men held wider interests they would have belonged to several such communities.[56] Although we should be careful not to romanticize the idea of community, this has some basis in reality in that the jurors were often experienced men of some local importance and with some knowledge of the operation of the Angevin system at this level. They were constituents of the Angevin system and had a vested interest in the status that participation conveyed. In Stewart's view, 'men such as these made up the community of the realm to whom the baronial council appealed in the programme of reform'. Even if true, this does not justify her argument that the evidence that was brought forwards in 1258–9 through the instances given to the knights and the cases brought before Bigod's eyre 'were more than just a catalogue of petty complaints; they were political statements in support of the programme of reform'.[57]

What is true, though, is that this was an increasingly sophisticated society. We have noted advances in record keeping and administration, both royal and seigneurial, and in the content and application of the law.[58] It was also a society characterized by growing commercialization, with all that that involved.[59] There were other dimensions too. One thinks, for example, of all those of the 'great

---

[55] For a discussion of these terms see Forrest, *Trustworthy Men*, 100–5.

[56] For what follows see S. Stewart (ed.), *The 1263 Surrey Eyre*, vol. 40 (Surrey Record Society, 2006), cxxxiii–cxlv, 'Was There a Hundredal Community?'

[57] Ibid., cxliv.

[58] For record keeping in general, see M. Clanchy, *From Memory to Written Record: England 1066–1307* (London, 1979; 3rd edn. 2012).

[59] See R. H. Britnell, *The Commercialisation of English Society 1000–1500* (Cambridge, 1993).

242   POLITICS AND SOCIETY IN MID THIRTEENTH-CENTURY ENGLAND

middling group (*mediocres*)' and their delegated officials whom John Sabapathy evokes in his study of the growth of accountability in late twelfth- and thirteenth-century England, a growth that was coterminous with the developing idea of 'public good'.[60] One thinks also of Ian Forrest's study of the trustworthy men (*fidedigni*) of the parishes, who were increasingly important to the bishops as jurors, and as witnesses in inquests, visitations, and like matters.[61] These were men of status with their own concerns and interests, belonging to what Forrest calls the 'social church'.[62] What we are seeing in such studies is a 'new' institutional or administrative history which focuses upon agency, on people's involvement and their relationships within given structures. Such involvement gave rise to 'political thinking' as opposed to 'political thought'.[63] Emphasis upon 'community' and 'representation' alone fails to capture the rich vein of obligations, values, and personal motivations that are manifested in such roles.

What we are seeing in the legislation, arguably, is the working out of some of the consequences latent within the Angevin reforms themselves, as they became increasingly entrenched. It was an age of increasing knowledge of the law.[64] This was due partly to the use of juries and of expanding legislation, but it was also due to the expansion of the legal profession itself.[65] During the mature years of Henry III, we are on the cusp of a major expansion in legal training and legal education.[66] It was to lead to, and indeed reflect, the age of the administrator–lawyer and of the diffusion of knowledge of the law and legal procedure among the population. Even lawyers who practised in the central courts were nevertheless rooted in local societies; apart from other considerations they belonged themselves to networks and even to affinities.[67] This is not to say that lawyers were necessarily perceived as among the angels, and for many, no doubt, they were to be bracketed with sheriffs, bailiffs, and the like in their tendency to practise extortion. The important point is that people were increasingly aware that corruption could be countered.[68]

It follows that people did not necessarily care, by 1263 at least, who was claiming the initiative in legislating for reform. A great number were very probably of the 'neutral party'. This is one reason why the propaganda was so strong. It is not

---

[60] Sabapathy, *Officers and Accountability*.

[61] 'As the thirteenth century wore on, the *fidedignus* became entrenched as a figure in the English church's administration of financial relationships, material interests, and justice': Forrest, *Trustworthy Men*, 109.

[62] Ibid., 4–5.   [63] See Sabapathy, *Officers and Accountability*, 10–24.

[64] For what follows see especially A. Musson, *Medieval Law in Context: The Growth of Legal Consciousness from Magna Carta to the Peasants' Revolt* (Manchester, 2001).

[65] See Brand, *The Origins of the English Legal Profession*.

[66] P. Brand, 'Courtroom and Schoolroom: The Education of Lawyers in England Prior to 1400', *Historical Research*, 60 (1987), 147–65; repr. in Brand, *The Making of the Common Law*, as Ch. 3.

[67] Musson, *Medieval Law in Context*.

[68] The Statute of Westminster I (1275) was the first legislation to regulate the behaviour of the legal profession.

at all surprising that the peasants of Peatling Magna should have been aware of national events and to have capitalized upon them, or that we should find peasants involved in the Montfortian rebellion.[69] There seems no doubt, however, that people generally acquiesced in the longstanding public authority of the crown, and we must be careful not to overstate the degree to which the antagonism manifested during the years 1258–67 reflected a truly national movement. There seems no reason to doubt, too, that people in general preferred the system to be run more efficiently and with greater integrity. It is probable that there was a degree of politicization arising from the barrage of propaganda and the preaching campaign. But it does not follow from this that we should speak in exaggerated terms of a national movement for reform, and doubts need to be expressed about historians' use of the terminology of revolution. As we have seen, the baronial leaders were by no means indifferent to the reactions of the broader populace and were prepared to act upon their grievances. Nevertheless, I would argue, enough evidence has been presented in the previous pages to show that both the revolt and reform of 1258–9 and the Montfortian enterprise which followed were born of an aristocratic revolt at the heart of which was a naked struggle for power between factions.

Politics and Society in Mid Thirteenth-Century England: The Troubled Realm. Peter Coss, Oxford University Press. © Peter Coss 2024. DOI: 10.1093/9780198924319.003.0009

---

[69] Carpenter, 'English Peasants in Politics', 3–42.

10

Resolution and Equilibrium, 1267–90

In examining the aftermath of 'the period of reform and rebellion' it is necessary to take a long or at least a medium view, covering the last years of the reign of Henry III and the first half of the reign of his successor. After all, the effects of such a deep crisis within the body politic can hardly be expected to have been 'overcome' or its challenges fully 'resolved' in a short space of time. It is essential to conduct such an examination not only in its own right, but also in order to complete our understanding of the nature of the conflict and of the society from which it emerged.

The initial task facing Henry III after the Battle of Evesham was, however, the restoration of his government. The task was made more difficult by past and ongoing disruption to the workings of the several departments and the continuation of pockets of resistance.[1] Some departments, pre-eminently the chancery, were back in operation 'within a matter of weeks'. Others found the 'restoration process more challenging', the law courts taking two years to become 'fully operational'. For the exchequer it took fully five years to restore its processes to where they had been before.[2] Over and above these considerations, however, the king and his supporters faced the formidable challenge of restabilizing political society. Edward I, on the other hand, famously pledged himself to the restoration of royal rights, and his historians have tended to place their emphasis here. While in no way denying the validity of this perspective, the present study requires us to concentrate on the process or resolution, within which the restoration of royal rights may be subsumed. Resolution may be said to have three principal dimensions—reconciliation, the restoration of harmony, and reform—dimensions which are at least implicit in work on Edward's earlier years. Having examined each of these in turn, I will turn to an alternative focus, that is to say the recreation of political and social equilibrium. We will conclude with some reflections on the characteristics of the English polity in 1290. The chapter is not to be understood, however, as a study of the first half of the reign of Edward I per se,[3]

---

[1] For an assessment and for the various contributions to our knowledge here, see Adrian Jobson, 'Royal Government and Administration in Post-Evesham Government', in D. Crook and L. Wilkinson (eds.), *The Growth of Royal Government under Henry III* (Woodbridge, 2015), 179–95.

[2] Ibid., 195.

[3] For recent work on the reign of Edward I, see, in addition to the books cited below, A. King and A. M. Spencer (eds.), *Edward I: New Interpretations* (York, 2020), and K. B. Neal, *The Letters of Edward I: Political Communication in the Thirteenth Century* (Woodbridge, 2021).

RESOLUTION AND EQUILIBRIUM, 1267–90   245

but rather as an exploration of what precisely had and had not changed as a result
of the crisis of the years 1258–67.

Reconciliation

The first and primary 'need' was for reconciliation. Here we enter the territory
that was dominated by Clive Knowles, who neatly outlined what he called the
resettlement of England after the Barons' War.[4] Of the confiscation and redistribution of lands after Evesham he writes: 'Such was the magnitude and violence of the social upheaval that even after the general surrender of the rebels
in the summer of 1267 had brought organized resistance to an end, the country
was still tense and uneasy.'[5] In August 1270 Henry III abandoned his intention
of accompanying his son to the Holy Land because 'the prelates, magnates and
community of the realm consider it neither expedient nor safe that both of us
should leave the kingdom.'[6] By the time Edward returned to England in August
1274, however, the great majority of Montfort's supporters were back in possession of their lands and were in the process of being 're-assimilated into the
political community'.[7]

The problem had been a very considerable one. As Knowles wrote, the seizures
after Evesham were 'like an irresistible wave spreading outwards from the battlefield'; by mid-August it had reached Devon. Some of those who were dispossessed
had played no part in the war. Within weeks of the battle over a thousand estates
and properties had been taken or despoiled in 'an orgy of vengeance'.[8] At a parliament held at Winchester in mid-September, the king compounded the situation
by ordering the confiscation of the lands of opponents and beginning to redis-
tribute them. This was more organized than the original seizures had been, but
by no means orderly. The grants were unevenly distributed, and local men were
often passed over. In the main roll of grants the lands of 316 rebels were given to
133 royalists. However, on a closer look the estates of 254 rebels were 'conferred
on a specially favoured group' of only seventy-one supporters of the king.[9] The
leading recipients comprised a narrow range of the king's followers. Particularly
prominent were members of the royal family itself: Lord Edward, Lord Edmund,
Queen Eleanor (whose share included the estates of the northern magnate John
d'Eyvill), and Eleanor of Castile. Next came household knights and royal officials, led by Robert Walerand. Among baronial supporters, by contrast, only

---

[4] Knowles, 'The Resettlement', 25–41.   [5] Ibid., 25.
[6] Quoted in Powicke, *Henry III and the Lord Edward*, 582.
[7] Knowles, 'The Resettlement', 25.
[8] Ibid., 25–6. See also Jacob, *Studies in the Period of Reform and Rebellion*, Part II, Ch. 1, and
Knowles, 'The Disinherited', Part III.
[9] Knowles, 'The Resettlement', 26.

246   POLITICS AND SOCIETY IN MID THIRTEENTH-CENTURY ENGLAND

Roger Mortimer was particularly favoured.[10] The king had helped to create a new power structure on the ruins of the old. He also created, in the words of Knowles, 'social dislocation and misery on an unparalleled scale'.[11] Hundreds of men were faced with ruin. Not surprisingly, they turned to guerilla warfare.

Another feature noted by Knowles, however, was the existence of some points of mitigation. He cites the king's sympathy towards family claims. Among the examples is the bestowal of Richard de Tany's lands upon his son.[12] Increasing efforts were made to protect the wives and widows of rebels. The first such grants were made at pleasure, but before February 1266 an ordinance had made systematic provision. A short essay by Knowles discusses this in more detail.[13] Among the issues was that of wardship. Chief lords tended to insist on their rights here, even though it meant paying redemption fines which might not be recouped for many years. A good example is the wardship of the son and heir of William de Birmingham, who was killed at Evesham. Following the Dictum of Kenilworth, his lord, Roger de Somery, sought to redeem the manor of Birmingham from the grantee, Roger de Clifford, because the son was underage. Clifford simply ignored this and exploited the estate. Finally, in February 1268, the justices of the special eyre were ordered to extend the land or to refer the matter to the king. Later in the year Somery was able to redeem the manor, but he was not reimbursed until after the son reached his majority in 1283. The rights of the chief lords were so ingrained that they could not be denied. On the issue of the women, Knowles asked why it was that the wives and widows were treated so generously. The obvious explanation lies in the blood and marriage ties that bound the loyalists and rebels closely together. He gives the examples of Roger de Somery's stepson, Nicholas de Segrave, and his son-in-law, Ralph Basset of Drayton, who were both rebels, and of Philip Basset's sons-in-law, who fought for Montfort at Evesham.[14] Knowles pointed out that the Montfortians had equally protected the womenfolk after Lewes. He suggests also that 'the special solicitude' of the king Henry III himself may have been a factor.[15] The plain fact, however, is that the wholesale confiscations were against the grain of contemporary behaviour and belief.

The policy of disinheriting the rebels was also modified when it came to specially favoured rebels who were permitted to redeem their lands from the grantees. Such cases, says Knowles, reflect a realization that the resistance of The 'Disinherited' could not be crushed by force, and that provision had to be made for them to recover their lands. There were some high-placed royalists who were actually opposed to the policy of disherison, and they were supported by the

---

[10] His gains included the lands of the earl of Oxford.   [11] Knowles, 'The Resettlement', 27.
[12] *CIM*, nos. 661, 706.
[13] C. H. Knowles, 'Provision for the Families of the Montfortians Disinherited after the Battle of Evesham', in *TCE*, i (Woodbridge, 1986), 124–7.
[14] For further details see Hunt, 'Families at War'.
[15] Knowles, 'Provision for the Families', 127.

RESOLUTION AND EQUILIBRIUM, 1267–90 247

papal legate, Cardinal Ottobuono, from his arrival in November 1265. Consequently, at the end of August 1266 the king set up a committee of bishops and magnates to 'procure what they understand to be necessary for the reformation of the peace of the land'.[16] Their recommendations were published on 31 October 1266, with the provision for arbitration by the legate and Henry of Almain.[17]

The means of redemption are well known. The rebels were permitted to recover their lands from the grantees in return for fines on a graduated scale— between one and seven times their annual value—according to their culpability. As Knowles pointed out, this favoured those who had played a less significant role or who had been forced to join the rebel side, and it certainly encouraged these to return to the king's peace.[18] Within two or three years the great majority of significant Montfortians had agreed to the redemption payments. Some whose complicity in the rebellion was contestable took their cases to the court of king's bench,[19] but most of those who were under suspicion waited until the special eyre that had been constituted reached their area. The eyre, comprising four circuits, was established in September 1267 and continued in operation until 1272. Knowles considered the Dictum to have been applied with 'general liberality and flexibility' and with little evidence of vindictiveness.[20] Sometimes lower penalties than were strictly warranted were laid down. The great majority of the 'Disinherited' did recover their lands. Seventeen of the twenty-three earls, barons, and magnates who had been summoned to the Montfortian parliament of January 1265 were disinherited, but only two families were irretrievably damaged (Montfort and Ferrers).[21] Other evidence comes from the 1275 inquiries in Kent, Surrey, and Sussex into whose lands had not been seized after Evesham and who held them now. Surviving returns from Kent show that of fifty-two properties belonging to forty-four reputed rebels, twenty-five had not, in fact, been confiscated and of those that had been taken twenty-two were back in the hands of their original owners or their heirs. Nine or more had been recovered after redemption payments, while a mere five properties had been lost as a result of the resettlement.[22]

Although most of the 'Disinherited' eventually recovered their lands, this was often at considerable cost. The result was greatly increased indebtedness. In

[16] *CPR 1258–67*, 672.   [17] *DBM*, no. 44, 317–37.
[18] Knowles, 'The Resettlement', 29–30.
[19] G. O. Sayles (ed.), *Select Cases in the Court of King's Bench*, vol. 2, Selden Society no. 57 (London, 1938), cxxii.
[20] Knowles, 'The Resettlement', 33.
[21] The other fifteen are: Robert de Vere, Ralph Basset of Drayton, Ralph Basset of Sapcote, Walter de Coleville, Hugh Despenser, John d'Eyvill, Gilbert de Gaunt, Henry de Hastings, John fitz John, William Marmion, William de Muntchesney, Adam de Newmarket, Roger de St John, Nicholas de Segrave, and John de Vescy.
[22] Knowles, 'The Resettlement', 34.

248 POLITICS AND SOCIETY IN MID THIRTEENTH-CENTURY ENGLAND

actual fact there were many Montfortians who were already in financial difficulties before the rebellion, and Simon had arranged for the relief of their Jewish debts.[23] The revocation of these grants after Evesham and the imposition of heavy redemption fines placed a severe strain on the financial resources of many former rebels. Some lost lands as a result. The activities of Walter de Merton are indicative here. He acquired estates from Saer de Harcourt, a household knight of Simon de Montfort, and three other insolvent rebels. Eleanor of Castile also acquired land through Jewish creditors, gaining the lands of twelve of them; only three of these, however, had been involved in the rebellion. However, relatively few 'new or appreciably enlarged estates' were built up out of lands of financially encumbered rebels.[24]

As Knowles emphasized, however, the general recovery of lands by the 'Disinherited' was followed by their gradual re-entry into public life.[25] This is not, of course, to underestimate the legacy left by the civil war, although it is impossible for us to gauge or even appreciate it from the sources we have. Something of the mood, however, can be seen in the activities of Simon de Pattishall. Simon, whom we have met many times during the course of this study, was a stalwart Montfortian and as such had no choice but to redeem his lands. The gainer was no less a figure than John Giffard, from whom Simon was obliged to redeem his property at a cost of £900 in 1268. Five years later he believed he had recovered from illness through an object which had touched the relics of Simon de Montfort. He later made a pilgrimage to Evesham to make an offering for the cure. Nonetheless, memories would inevitably fade and anger pass. A process of social reabsorption was inevitable given that a sizeable section of the landed community was involved and their permanent exclusion from public life unthinkable. In 1271, during a redemption trial *coram rege*, it was claimed that the whole of Staffordshire had been on the rebel side during the war so that a viable jury had to be put together from neighbouring Warwickshire and Worcestershire.[26] The complaint was exaggerated but, as Knowles suggested, it indicates the problems that would have occurred should all Montfortians have been excluded from royal service, leaving England with insufficient fighting men, experienced officials, and knights to perform their various roles.[27] When Edward was preparing to invade Wales in 1276, a feudal summons went out to nearly 180 earls, barons, and knights. One tenth of these men had been in rebellion against his father a decade before. Many officials were also rehabilitated.

However, we must be careful not to offer too functional an explanation. As has already been indicated, the prevailing social mores need to be taken into consideration. The underlying beliefs of the aristocracy a propos inheritance and

---

[23] The evidence is on the fine rolls. See Coss, 'Sir Geoffrey de Langley', 31–2.
[24] Knowles, 'The Resettlement', 36. [25] Ibid., 37. [26] TNA, KB 26/205 m. 8.
[27] Knowles, 'The Resettlement', 38.

RESOLUTION AND EQUILIBRIUM, 1267–90   249

lineage must also have been a vital ingredient, as were pre-existing social networks. Men will have made their own arrangements locally to defuse tensions.

The Restoration of Harmony

The second dimension to resolution was the restoration of harmony, or at least relative harmony, between the crown and the nobility. A critical factor was naturally the character, personality, and proclivities of the king. The death of the old king and the succession of Edward I was bound to have a profound effect. Edward, unlike his father, was every inch an aristocrat of the traditional type. He was fundamentally a warrior. This was shown quite early on in his taste for the tournament and for other quasi-martial activities.[28] Edward went on crusade in 1270 despite the unsettled nature of the country, the age of his father, the fact that it would take out of the country the realm's 'most doughty warriors and efficient administrators',[29] and the protestations of king and pope. It is likely that Edward's decision was prompted by the papal legate, Ottobuono, and that he was influenced by Louis IX. Although the crusade was not a success militarily, by fulfilling his crusader vow Edward gained an international reputation, an enviable position to be in at the outset of his reign. On 24 June 1268 at the parliament of Northampton, Lords Edward and Edmund, Henry of Almain, Gilbert de Clare, John de Warenne, William de Valence, and others took their crusade vows.[30] The majority of those who contracted with Edward for the crusade were men whom he had come to know and trust. Some were his followers; others were his friends and kinsmen. He had campaigned with most in the turbulent days of 1263–7 and acted in affairs of state with others. Three were great lords in their own right: Edmund, Valence, and Almain. Walter de Percy was one of Edmund's knights and had been in Henry III's household. Adam de Montalt, Hamo l'Estrange, Brian de Brampton, and William de Huntercombe were prominent royal servants. Robert de Munteny had been a knight of Gilbert de Clare. Of the rest, Robert Tiptoft, Richard de la Rochelle, Thomas de Clare, and Roger de Leybourne definitely appear as being in Edward's close circle before the crusade, while Payn de Chaworth, Adam de Gesemue, William fitz Warin, and Roger de Clifford were closely associated with both Henry III and his son. It was entirely natural that Edward should turn to such men for support. With Edmund went the marcher knight, Robert de Turberville. At the centre of the English crusade of 1270–2, then, lay a group of important lords intimately connected to the royal house, tied to Edward through contracts and serving with their own squadrons of knights

---

[28] For what follows see S. D. Lloyd, 'The Lord Edward's Crusade, 1270–2: Its Setting and Significance', in Gillingham and Holt (eds.), *War and Government in the Middle Ages*, 120–33.
[29] Ibid., 122.   [30] Although Gilbert de Clare and Henry of Almain did not ultimately set out.

250   POLITICS AND SOCIETY IN MID THIRTEENTH-CENTURY ENGLAND

raised for the crusade. They were accompanied by a large group of crusaders, men who were in the service of Henry III, his sons, and their respective wives, either as household members or in administrative and military positions. A number of reasonably well-defined circles can be identified. Needless to say, this was an important episode in the king's development and in many ways set the tone of his reign. Naturally, there were few Montfortians, although there were some. The crusade was not, therefore, in itself a major step towards reconciliation.

A real step forwards in terms of the king's relations with his nobility was the war for Wales, even if it appealed most notably to 'the marchers'. Nine earls participated in the campaign of 1277 and eight in that of 1282–3.[31] The point is that the king took his nobility into a successful war in which he demonstrated considerable military skill, and one that was popular with them. The end of the Montfortian era had seen Llewelyn ap Gruffudd in the ascendant, despite the difficulties that might lie ahead for him in consolidating his position.[32] On 22 June 1265, 'the king' granted him the principality to be held by himself and his heirs, and the lordship of all its magnates. His seisin of the lands he held, including his most recent acquisitions, was acknowledged and confirmed. He was addressed, moreover, as prince of Wales. All of this was given in return for a grant of £20,000 and for a promise of military aid against 'the marchers'. The situation was, of course, precarious as the Montfortian government was in a desperate situation. Ten days after Evesham, Lord Edward regained the earldom of Chester, putting the north-east of Llewelyn's dominions once again in uncertain territory. Marcher lords were no doubt already looking askance at Llewelyn's accretion of power. When it came to a formal settlement in 1267, however, it was obvious that the prince would not budge from what he had achieved under Montfort. Given the general need for pacification it was also clear that he would get his way. The papal legate, Ottobuono, presided over the negotiations, which produced a very similar result. Llewelyn did homage and swore fealty, and agreed to pay 25,000 marks at a rate of £200 per annum for eighty years.[33] He secured lordship of Powys and Deheubarth, and particular mention was made of the much-contested Four Cantreds of Perfeddwlad. The 'marchers' had been forced to cede territories granted to him. It was especially galling for Gilbert de Clare and Roger Mortimer, given the prominence they had acquired. These two, plus Humphrey de Bohun, were soon to give him problems along his borders. There were lesser lords, too, like John Giffard and Payn de Chaworth, who were to add to his difficulties, not to mention his internal enemies.

---

[31] Andrew M. Spencer, *Nobility and Kingship in Medieval England: The Earls and Edward I 1272–1307* (Cambridge, 2014), 207. For the Welsh Wars see Prestwich, *Edward I*, Ch. 7. For aristocratic participation in Edward I's wars, see now Simpkin, *The English Aristocracy at War*.

[32] For what follows I have drawn liberally on J. Beverley Smith, *Llewelyn ap Gruffudd, Prince of Wales* (Cardiff, 1998).

[33] A further 5,000 marks was to be paid if the king were ever to grant the homage of Maredudd ap Rhys Gryg.

RESOLUTION AND EQUILIBRIUM, 1267–90   251

The departure of Edward on crusade was not good news either, as it left Llewelyn open to encroachments. Roger Mortimer, furthermore, was one of the guardians of Edward's property while he was away. When Edward finally returned as king, having first prioritized a visit to Gascony, he was met by complaints that the prince had failed to keep up payments and to swear fealty. It now became a question of homage. Matters went from bad to worse for Llewelyn: a conspiracy to murder him, Edward's harbouring of the conspirators, the king's hostile reaction to his decision to marry Eleanor de Montfort, and her capture, along with that of Amaury de Montfort. Llewelyn refused to pay homage while the king harboured his enemies. He was formally condemned in November 1276, and three commanders were appointed and 'charged with dismembering the principality': the earl of Warwick operating from Chester, Roger Mortimer from Montgomery, and Payn de Chaworth from Carmarthen.[34] By the end of May 1277 they had been successful, and Llewelyn's supremacy had been destroyed. The king was all set on an invasion of Gwynedd itself, although it was proving difficult. In the event, Llewelyn submitted. Although his principality had been destroyed, he was allowed to keep the title of prince. It was the future of Gwynedd that was at issue now, not Wales. By the Treaty of Aberconway the Four Cantreds were given up. Now at last Llewelyn performed homage. Restricted to Snowdonia, he was no longer in contention with Mortimer, Bohun, and Clare. He and Eleanor were married at the cathedral church of Worcester.

This story did not, of course, end well. A Welsh rebellion began on Palm Sunday 1282 at Hawarden, though it was not initiated by Llewelyn. Once again, the behaviour of royal officials had caused considerable disaffection, among them Reginald de Grey, justiciar of Chester. However, the king was soon at war with Llewelyn and his brother Dafydd. There were complex issues over the operation of rival systems of law, but behind it all lay the struggle between king and prince. Gwynedd was now invested by sea. Llewelyn meanwhile took a large army south to Builth where he was matched by substantial forces and some of the king's most important commanders: Roger Lestrange, Edmund Mortimer, Roger Mortimer, Gruffudd ap Gwenwynwyn, Peter Corbet, Reginald fitz Peter, and John Giffard, constable of Builth. Llewelyn appears to have died ingloriously in a skirmish, while his brother Dafydd was later captured and horribly executed as a traitor by the merciless king. By the Statute of Rhuddlan of 1284, the principality passed to English rule. It was the end of an era.

Evidence suggests that Edward had wide support for his wars in Wales. Assemblies were held early in 1283 in response to the king's request for aid. The laity conceded and the clergy, although they were concerned about the shedding of Christian blood, offered a reduced sum. Moreover, the condemnation of Dafydd was agreed after the king had proclaimed that the treacherous prince had

[34] Smith, *Llewelyn ap Gruffudd*, 414.

252 POLITICS AND SOCIETY IN MID THIRTEENTH-CENTURY ENGLAND

been captured by men of his own nation (*per homines lingue sue*).[35] The king had himself successfully played the nationality card.

Edward's earls were conspicuous in their support for his military designs. This subtly changed the nature of the relationship between crown and nobility, drawing them closer to each other and integrating the nobility more closely into the military apparatus of the crown. It was naturally of great benefit to the king that his pleasures and pastimes were essentially the aristocratic ones of hunting, falconry, and the tournament. Examining the king's relationship with his twelve earls, Andrew Spencer shows how the king treated these men as companions, natural advisers, and governmental aides, notwithstanding the fact that royal rights and interests were kept firmly at the centre of his mind.[36] The value he placed on their 'camaraderie' helped to create political harmony. The royal witness lists show the earls much more in attendance upon Edward I than had been the case with his father or was to be with his son.[37] His marriage 'policy' brought the occupants of the earldoms closer to the crown. However, stability was greatly aided by the fact that between 1275 and 1295 not one earl died, creating an unusual sense of continuity at the apex of society.

A key issue in the relationship between the crown and the nobility was, of course, patronage, and it had been a particularly divisive one during the reign of Henry III, as has been amply demonstrated. Recent historians of the reign of Edward I have consequently paid the issue some attention. In the opening volume of the conferences on thirteenth-century England, Michael Prestwich published his findings on the matter.[38] As he pointed out, patronage was 'an essential lubricant of political society', while emphasizing its relatively limited deployment by the new king.[39] Characteristic is his treatment of Roger Leybourne and Roger Clifford. In addition to obtaining land from former rebels, they were granted the marriages of the heiresses of Robert de Vipont for their sons, so acquiring major interests in the north-west. The considerable build-up of Clifford power there, although founded upon royal patronage, owed little thereafter to the king's generosity. The Cliffords and the Leybournes were families of some standing, and it is not perhaps surprising that royal patronage in such cases was of a limited and cautious character. A concern for his own family, including Amadeus of Savoy, was certainly a major element in the king's patronage policies. Edward was also generous to John of Brittany, second son of Duke John of Brittany. It should be noted, though, that while Edward was generous to a man whom he treated almost

---

[35] Ibid., 572–3, 578.

[36] Spencer, *Nobility and Kingship in Medieval England*. See especially Part One, 'The King and the Earls', where he quarrels with traditional historiography (that is to say, K. B. McFarlane and T. F. Tout).

[37] Spencer argues further that 'Edward was using the prestige and authority they possessed, and demonstrating that they, like everyone else, were expected to start shouldering their share of the burden for maintaining the king's governance where necessary': ibid., 63.

[38] M. Prestwich, 'Royal Patronage under Edward I', *TCE*, i (Woodbridge, 1986), 41–52.

[39] Ibid., 41.

RESOLUTION AND EQUILIBRIUM, 1267–90   253

as his own son, he nevertheless did not diminish the crown's stock of lands by granting any royal estates in perpetuity to him.

Examination of Edward's relations with his magnates and his treatment of his household knights brings out the limited scale of patronage in this period. The great men were certainly rewarded for service in Wales, and more so later in Scotland, with grants of lands, but the king was careful not to make hereditary grants of estates in England. Even those household knights who rose from relatively humble origins in the course of the reign received relatively little from the crown, though they were obviously able to profit very considerably from their position to build up their own estates. Prestwich makes the point that patronage 'on an extensive scale' was only possible if the crown had an ample supply of lands to grant out. This Edward certainly had. At the same time, however, there were constraints upon him. He had apparently promised at his coronation that he would recover for the crown all that his father had lost, and there was on his part a clear desire to increase the landed endowments of the crown rather than a readiness to dissipate it. Even with regard to the famous acquisitions discussed by K. B. McFarlane, very little was granted out in perpetuity.[40] Edward was much more prepared to make grants of lands in his overseas dominions, Wales, and Scotland than he was in England.[41] In Wales, the conclusion of the second Welsh War was marked by grants to some of the leading magnates. The main beneficiaries were the earl of Lincoln, Earl Warenne, and Reginald de Grey, with some rewards going to the Mortimers and to John Giffard of Brimpsfield. The bulk of the knights of the household and others who fought in the king's armies received no grants in Wales, though Lincoln and other beneficiaries of the king's generosity naturally brought their own followers into their new marcher estates.

In terms of other gifts from the king there is 'certainly no impression of great generosity on Edward's behalf'.[42] The most substantial presents were given for diplomatic purposes. The bulk of the payments for gifts do not suggest any systematic patronage policy, but rather the giving of ad hoc rewards for special services. The great men at court do not appear to have received royal gifts on any scale. The typical acts of generosity were those to the relatively humble. As for the magnates, they seem to have found it necessary to give the king himself presents. The accounts of *dona* suggest that Edward I did not rely on largesse to any great extent to get his way.

How did Edward I employ the windfalls from feudal incidents? An essay by Scott Waugh provides an answer. 'In the period down to 1296 he allocated most of them as patronage while simultaneously improving the efficiency of his

---

[40] K. B. McFarlane, 'Had Edward I a "Policy" towards the Earls?', *History*, 50 (1965), 145–59; repr. in McFarlane, *The Nobility of Later Medieval England*, 248–67.

[41] Prestwich notes Thomas Clare in Ireland and Otto de Grandson, the Savoyard, who was given lands in Ireland and custody of the Channel Islands.

[42] Prestwich, 'Royal Patronage', 44.

254 POLITICS AND SOCIETY IN MID THIRTEENTH-CENTURY ENGLAND

administration to increase the cash receipts from feudal lordship'.[43] His policy differed in important respects from that of his father. While profiting from minor wardships, by sales and leases or by direct receipts, he used major wardships largely as rewards for service from lords, knights, and officials. There was also a new drive to enforce the king's prohibition on alienation by tenants-in-chief without royal license, replacing Henry III's rather relaxed policy.

The one area where royal patronage was considerably extended under Edward I was that of the church. There was a substantial increase in the number of livings granted by the king, and it appears that clerks in royal service gained much more than laymen did. The hard-headed and ambitious clerks in the royal administration were the obvious chief beneficiaries of the king's policy to exploit appointments to livings wherever possible and, indeed, probably the authors of it. In many cases Edward himself took no part: just as his officials were given discretion to sell small wardships, so the chancellor was fully empowered to act without consultation in the case of livings worth less than twenty marks. He also developed corrodies from monasteries, replacing Henry III's practice of using exchequer pensions to reward his servants.

The impetus for many grants came from below, not from above. The granting of commissions of *oyer* and *terminer* for example. Prestwich cites the case of Margaret de Hartshill, who wrote to John Langton the chancellor to say she did not want Hengham to act as justice in a case she had against Philip Marmion, and suggested other names. It may be the case that Edward had a certain disdain for the whole business of patronage. He cites also the letter from Katherine Paynel, who died in 1296, to John de Langton about placing her son in the royal household, 'where he could learn good sense and manners'. This failed, indicating how hard it was to get places at court.[44]

Andrew Spencer sees the dispensation of patronage by the king rather differently. Spencer praises Edward for his treatment of the earls, in knowing when to come down hard and when to be lenient.[45] On the question of reward he argues that Edward 'handled patronage in a way that was very much in line with contemporary expectations in that patronage was a reward not an inducement for good service'.[46] Against Prestwich's view that he failed to make substantial grants of land in England outside of the royal family, he points out that the relative internal peace of Edward I's reign meant that there were barely any lands to be confiscated and regranted, and that he could hardly dip into the royal demesne. The king used what Spencer calls 'negative' patronage, largely the remission of debt.

[43] S. L. Waugh, 'The Fiscal Uses of Royal Wardship in the Reign of Edward I', *TCE*, i (1986), 53–60.

[44] Prestwich, 'Royal Patronage', 49–50. There were other means by which the king's servants could increase their wealth, for example by use of statute merchant, of which someone like Walter Langton was a master. See A. Beardwood, 'The Trial of Walter Langton, Bishop of Lichfield, 1307–12', *Transactions of the American Philosophical Society*, n.s. (1914).

[45] Spencer, *Nobility and Kingship*, Ch. 3, 'Justice, Franchise, War and Reward'. [46] Ibid., 89.

RESOLUTION AND EQUILIBRIUM, 1267–90   255

He concludes that Edward's use of patronage was judicious and targeted and many earldoms came out of the reign better than they went in. In other words, the king steered a middle course between prodigality and avarice. Wherever one puts the emphasis, the overarching point is that royal patronage ceased in these years to be the destabilizing factor that had dogged the mid-thirteenth-century polity. Yet there were dangers in Edward's policies. His lack of generosity towards his magnates was a contributory factor in the crisis of 1297. His failure to reward those Welsh and Scots who supported him had grave consequences. However, such considerations take us beyond our time frame.

Reform

The third dimension to the resolution was to accommodate the desire for reform. A start was made in the immediate aftermath of war with the Statute of Marlborough, which re-enacted the Provisions of Westminster. In a context where the reaffirmation of royal power was paramount, this action was necessary and unavoidable. It was the new king's return to England in 1274, however, which inaugurated a period of more deliberate action from the centre. This was thoroughly analysed by John Maddicott in a closely argued and justly famous essay.[47] Maddicott sees the period essentially in terms of Edward I learning from the mistakes of his father. He begins with the tense years at the end of Henry's reign, but adds that there are signs that the Statute of Marlborough, which had seemed to perpetuate much of the reformers' work, was not widely observed. The statute, it seems, represented the 'limits of conciliation' and, in reality, not much changed. The sheriffs, for example, were a mixed group, often *curiales* and professional administrators. After 1265 they had once again to pay increments, generally at the figure fixed in 1241. The results are seen in the complaints found in the Hundred Rolls.[48] Systematic reform had to await Edward's return. Meanwhile, the prolonged absence of the ruler had encouraged further encroachment on royal rights, not least by the earl of Gloucester.

Once in England the new king took immediate action. To restore the standing of the crown he needed both to re-establish royal rights and to root out the corruption among local officials which had for long been a subject of grievance. Thus, within two months of the coronation the escheators had been ordered to repossess all lands wrongfully alienated from the royal demesne since the civil war, new sheriffs had been appointed in thirty-two counties, and enquiries had

---

[47] J. R. Maddicott, 'Edward I and the Lessons of Baronial Reform: Local Government, 1258–80', *TCE*, i (1986), 1–30.

[48] In Essex and elsewhere complaints against recent and illicit exactions of the murdrum fine, the *beaupleader* fine, and the sheriff's misuse of the tourn were all common in the Hundred Rolls enquiries of 1274–5, although the statute had regulated all these matters.

256 POLITICS AND SOCIETY IN MID THIRTEENTH-CENTURY ENGLAND

been begun into both royal rights and the behaviour of local officials. The sequence of events, as Maddicott points out, was essentially that of 1258: local enquiry and the reception of complaints; national legislation; and a return to the localities to address old grievances and enforce new laws through the eyre. The abuses found in the Hundred Rolls enquiries were legislated against in the first Statute of Westminster published in the parliament of April 1275. The intended eyre was delayed because of the Welsh War, but was commissioned in 1278. Maddicott highlights three aspects of the Hundred Rolls enquiries which he deems important: the articles of the inquiry, the *querelae* or plaints, and the occasional use of juries of knights. The articles put to the hundred juries were designed to reveal official misdeeds, to ascertain the king's rights, both feudal and landed, and to disclose their usurpation. They were applied not just to royal officials but also to 'the lords and bailiffs of liberties whatsoever'. The profession of impartial justice, Maddicott stresses, was to be one of the props of the new regime. In 1274, however, the matter of the crown's rights predominated over the redress offered to subjects. In some counties the commissioners are known to have received *querelae*. Edward was preparing the way for the much wider use of these over the next few years. In at least one of the circuits use was made of juries of knights to present evidence. The articles of the eyre of 1278 incorporated those of 1274–5 and justices were empowered to hear *querelae*. Henceforth plaints began to be included as separate sections in the eyre rolls. Between 1281 and 1289, knightly juries of presentment feature in eyre rolls for six counties, reporting most frequently on cases involving great men or their servants. In all these ways the eyre of 1278 adopted on a more general scale some of the precedents set in 1274 and in 1258–60.

There can be little doubt that the reforms of local government brought the crown popularity. The first Statute of Westminster was promulgated in Edward's first parliament and in the presence of numerous representatives of shires and boroughs: four knights from each county and six burgesses from every city, borough, and market town. Maddicott points out that it has usually been asserted that the reason for the high representation was the imposition of new customs on wool and hides. In his view, however, their presence was probably intended to allow the reforms the widest possible audience. The statute was given considerable publicity and was to be kept by 'two or four of the more faithful and worthy knights of the county'.[49] Although Maddicott's view that the statutes 'bound the hearts of the people' to the king 'with an inestimable love' is surely an exaggeration, it is difficult to deny his assertion that the Statute of Westminster, promulgated in the crowded Easter parliament of 1275, marked the growing importance of that assembly as a focal point for reform and for contact between king and subjects. From this time onwards it normally met twice per year, at Easter and

[49] Ibid., 15.

RESOLUTION AND EQUILIBRIUM, 1267–90   257

Michaelmas. The presence of the commons, apparently only occasional, may have been more frequent, he suggests, than the records allow us to detect. Parliament was now a forum for legislation and royal acta which took on board wider interests. Conciliatory measures were taken up again at the Easter parliament of 1276, though no official records survive. In this parliament Edward confirmed Magna Carta and the Charter of the Forests. In March of the following year confirmation of the forest charter was followed by orders for the perambulation of the forests. Edward was seeking to appease local grievances.

At the same time, however, the king's overriding interest was in the restoration of royal rights. The massive usurpation of these was not of course the result of civil war alone but resulted from the ineffectiveness of the sheriffs who before and after 1258 had been complaisant before magnate power. In 1274 a new oath was imposed on the incoming sheriffs, indicating that the king's primary consideration at this point was to protect royal rights rather than to conciliate local interests. The crown's rights took precedence. He also changed the escheators.[50] From the mid-1270s Edward was placing increasing reliance on the plaint. Plaints were received by the Hundred Roll commissioners, the stewards, in common pleas, in king's bench, and at the eyre. What was lacking, however, was a means of complaining at the centre. From 1275 parliament became the venue for the delivery of petitions to the king.[51] The abruptness of this innovation, Maddicott points out, suggests that an invitation to deliver *querelae* was sent out to the counties before the parliament and that some of the representatives actually brought petitions from their constituents with them. In these ways local opinion could be harnessed against local officials. The thinking, he suggests, was that encouraging complaint would help to improve the conduct of the sheriffs. In addition, franchises now came under attack. The Statute of Gloucester of 1278 gave the justices the power to try claims to franchises in the counties at the forthcoming eyre. The resultant Quo Warranto proceedings indicated that the magnates could no longer appropriate royal rights seemingly at will. In short, the 'heyday of the expanding franchise was over'.[52]

These developments lay behind the significant changes in the shrievalties once again in the autumn of 1278. Sixteen sheriffs were replaced in twenty-three counties. As the Dunstable chronicler says: 'The king removed all the sheriffs, namely clerks and foreigners, and replaced them with knights from their own counties'.[53] After a long period of experiment, local men were once again given the shrievalties; this time permanently. Edward's reforms helped restore confidence in royal government. The large and steady increase in the monies paid by the sheriffs into

---

[50] An experiment was conducted whereby three stewards were given responsibility for wards and escheats: ibid., 21–3.

[51] Ibid., 24.   [52] Maddicott, 'Edward I and the Lessons of Baronial Reform', 26.

[53] *Ann. Mon.* iii (Dunstable), 279.

258 POLITICS AND SOCIETY IN MID THIRTEENTH-CENTURY ENGLAND

the exchequer between 1274 and 1287 suggests a comparable success in reasserting crown control over local officials and royal rights.[54]

It is important, however, to avoid the temptation to become starry eyed when it comes to the policies of Edward I in relation to his subjects in a manner that evokes Bishop Stubbs. We 'can scarcely doubt', he wrote:

> that Edward had a definite idea of government before his eyes, or that that idea was successful because it approved itself to the genius and grew out of the habits of the people. Edward saw, in fact, what the nation was capable of, and adapted his constitutional reforms to that capacity.[55]

To this he adds:

> But the design was not ... imposed on an unwilling or unprepared people ... The nation, on whom and by whom he was working, had now become a consolidated people, aroused by the lessons of his father's reign to the intelligent appreciation of their own condition, and attached to their own laws and customs with a steady though not unreasoning affection, jealous of their privileges, their charters, their local customs, unwilling that the laws of England should be changed.[56]

It is necessary to quote Stubbs in order to ensure that we do not follow him in taking the king's policies out of their time. If Edward had a model of kingship in his mind, it was undoubtedly not something peculiarly English but that of St Louis. The king, that is, would brook no opposition to his rule, but his subjects had every right to invoke him in search of redress and should indeed be encouraged to do so. In other words, the king should take serious account of the obligations inherent in his public authority. What comes across, above all, from Maddicott's observations is that the resurrection and exercise of royal power was paramount. We see this wherever we look. At the same time, Stubbs was quite correct that it was not a one-way traffic and we should be wary of looking too much from the top down, that is to say in taking too much of a king-centred approach. Edward I had too much political intelligence to be unaware that the crown had to take due account of the interests and attitudes that were current in his state.

Equilibrium

Another way of looking at the early Edwardian polity, as I have suggested, is to see it in terms of the restoration of equilibrium. A striking feature of Maddicott's

---

[54] Ibid., 27.
[55] William Stubbs, *The Constitutional History of England*, vol. 2 (Oxford, 1880), 315.
[56] Ibid., 317.

RESOLUTION AND EQUILIBRIUM, 1267–90   259

analysis is the degree of bargaining, implicit or explicit, that was present in Edward's rule. In a sense the whole of the king's 'reform programme' was a bargain between the crown and those of his subjects who were to some degree or another politically active or cognizant. Especially important in this respect is once again the king's relations with the higher nobility. A significant example of concerted action between them is the Statute of Mortmain of Michaelmas 1279.[57] Mortmain was the sale or gift of property by laymen to religious houses or holders of ecclesiastical benefices in perpetuity. During the twelfth century such a grant had required the lord's consent. By the early thirteenth century, however, this control was in jeopardy as another by-product of the Angevin legal reforms and this lay behind two clauses in the second 1217 reissue of Magna Carta. The problem for lords lay in the diminution of their control leading to the potential loss of services and the feudal incidents of wardship, marriage, relief, and escheat. It became a serious issue during the reign of Henry III with lords, including ecclesiastical lords, complaining of religious houses entering their fees and seeking remedies against this. Clause no. 10 of the Petition of the Barons of 1258 complained precisely about the lack of consent and of the losses involved, and led directly to such consent being imposed by the Provisions of Westminster. It was omitted, however, from the king's reissue in January 1263, since the king needed the support of the church, and from the subsequent reissues and the Statute of Marlborough of 1267. The result was a degree of confusion in the royal courts, a confusion that was still present at the Yorkshire eyre of 1279.

The Statute of Mortmain banned all future alienations in mortmain under pain of forfeiture of the land either to the lord (or to a superior lord) or to the crown if no such action were taken. The total ban was soon superseded by a system of licences, after inquisition *ad quod damnum* and consideration by the king and council. The legislation was the result of cooperation between the king and his magnates, giving both an element of control of the phenomenon. In addition to listening to the laments of the lords, the king may have been concerned over the loss of military service as well as being aware of a strong feeling that too much property had been passing to already very rich religious houses. It plausible, moreover, as Brand has pointed out, that the statute's origins lay in a debate in council over the confused situation as revealed in the 1279 eyre.[58]

The services due to lords were also threatened more generally by the process of subinfeudation, where tenants granted away part or all of their property, creating a chain. The Statute of Quia Emptores was duly passed, it was said, at the request of the great men of the realm. The statute reaffirmed the right of every free man to

---

[57] For what follows see P. Brand, 'The Control of Mortmain Legislation', in J. H. Baker (ed.), *Legal Records and the Historian*, Royal Historical Society (London, 1978), 29–40, repr. in Brand, *The Making of the Common Law*, 233–44, and Brand, *Kings, Barons and Justices*, 58–62, 279–81. See also S. Raban, *Mortmain Legislation and the English Church, 1279–1500* (Cambridge, 1982).

[58] Brand, *Kings, Barons and Justices*, 279–80.

260   POLITICS AND SOCIETY IN MID THIRTEENTH-CENTURY ENGLAND

make grants but by substitution not subinfeudation, so that in doing so he dropped out of the chain. The new tenant would hold directly from the overlord. Yet this statute was also in the nature of a compromise, in that the same freedom was not accorded to tenants-in-chief whose right to alienate remained under the control of the crown.[59]

An issue that is crucial to our understanding is that of *quo warranto*. Andrew Spencer has recently argued that Edward demonstrated throughout his reign that those close to him could not infringe the crown's rights with impunity, as had occurred so often under his father. Warenne and Gloucester were targeted during the campaign as notorious usurpers of royal rights and examples were made of both men.[60] The king meanwhile did not want to see an end to marcher privilege in particular, recognizing that any attempt would be doomed to failure, but what he wanted was definition of their status vis à vis the crown and to uphold and extend royal rights in the marches. On usurpation of franchises in general, Spencer writes that the Hundred Roll inquiry of 1274–5 confirmed that the king's suspicion had been true: the scale of alleged usurpation contained in them is 'staggering'.[61] Judged against the rhetoric, however, the *quo warranto* proceedings were a failure, both in prosecution and in conclusion. The Statute of Quo Warranto of 1290 was essentially a climb down, and 'long user' was accepted as 'custom'. However, as Spencer affirms, the statute 'stopped dead in its tracks an alternative theory about the nature of power and authority within England',[62] that is, the conquest theory. The earls had actually been treated much more leniently by the *quo warranto* pleaders and judges than were their non-titled neighbours, when, for example, they claimed by prescriptive right.[63] Spencer argues, justifiably, that in the last instance Edward's behaviour was 'pragmatic'.

A balance was created between the interests of the higher nobility and those of the king. The restoration of equilibrium can be seen not only in the relations between the nobility and the king, however, but also within aristocratic society itself. The king's reforms may have taken some of the tension out of social and political relations, but they did not fundamentally alter the structure of society nor the manner in which power was articulated; they were not intended to. At this point we need to return briefly to the vantage point of the higher nobility. Studies of magnate 'affinities' indicate that relatively little had changed in the way power was exercised. Let us take the Bigod earls of Norfolk as one example. Roger Bigod IV succeeded his uncle in 1268.[64] A charter of his dating from 1271–6 is witnessed by four knights and the steward of Norfolk. Two of the knights had

---

[59] Prestwich, *Edward I*, 274, and references given there.

[60] Spencer, *Nobility and Kingship*, 67. Note 15 gives the references for the list of usurpations by each man.

[61] Spencer puts the onus on post 1258. But see above 60–2.

[62] Spencer, *Nobility and Kingship*, 73.   [63] Ibid., 75.

[64] For what follows see Morris, *The Bigod Earls of Norfolk*, Ch. 5.

served his uncle and remained prominent in his service. Another was Thomas Weyland, knight and royal justice, who was described in 1289 as Roger's chief counsellor, having been long in his service. Thomas became chief justice of common pleas and fell from grace following a scandal in 1289. Four others who had served the uncle and were constituted his executors quarrelled with Roger IV and did not serve him, new men taking their place. With one exception these new men were once again from East Anglia. During the late 1280s there are references to Roger's council, of which Thomas Weyland, the clerk Geoffrey de Aspall, and, no doubt, the prominent household knights formed part. His estate stewards were a separate group from the household knights but were of similar status. They tended to receive substantial money fees, as opposed to the lesser fees received by minor officials such as constables and foresters. There are others, however, who received larger fees but lacked clear administrative roles. Marc Morris estimates that 'in normal circumstances' the earl retained fifteen to twenty men, around half of whom would have been with him at any one time. On special occasions the retinue would have been inflated, as was also the case when the earl went to war in Wales.

A second indicative affinity from the early years of Edward's reign is that of William de Beauchamp, who became earl of Warwick in 1268, dying in 1298.[65] The study of his charters reveals ten men acting three to four times, another ten five to nine times, and five acting fourteen times or more. Caroline Burt suggests that the first ten should be considered an outer circle. The second ten were all men with a meaningful association with the earl. What is especially noticeable is that they are nearly all based in Warwickshire and Worcestershire. Six of them were Warwickshire landowners, while three of the other four were Worcestershire men, one being undersheriff of the county for the earl.[66] The most prominent of the witnesses comprised one Warwickshire and four Worcestershire men, including the earl's uncle. 'In other words, this was at its heart a Worcestershire following/affinity.'[67] Once again we find that comital officials—stewards, undersheriffs, constables—tend to have been a different category of men. Another very noticeable feature is the heavy predominance of the earl's own tenants.[68]

Andrew Spencer has recently extended the range by looking at the affinities of Edmund earl of Lancaster, Edmund earl of Cornwall, and Henry de Lacy, earl of Lincoln.[69] The affinity of the earl of Lancaster is reminiscent of that of William de

---

[65] What follows is from Caroline Burt, 'A "Bastard Feudal" Affinity in the Making? The Followings of William and Guy de Beauchamp, Earls of Warwick, 1268–1315', *Midland History*, 34 (2009), 156–80.

[66] The one exception was Richard de Rokele, whose lands were in Essex and Norfolk.

[67] Burt, 'A "Bastard Feudal" Affinity in the Making?', 169.

[68] In striking contrast to the affinity of his son and successor, Guy de Beauchamp. This has particular relevance to debates over the origins of bastard feudalism, but is not pertinent here.

[69] Spencer, *Nobility and Kingship*, Ch. 5, 'The Creation of Comital Followings'. Spencer's discussion is dominated by his concern to contrast these 'followings' with the 'bastard-feudal' affinities of the later fourteenth and fifteenth centuries.

262   POLITICS AND SOCIETY IN MID THIRTEENTH-CENTURY ENGLAND

Valence, being court-centred rather than regionally based as befitting the king's brother, and lacking as it did a history of personal service to an ancient honour or honours. That of Henry de Lacy was more normative, with a hard core of feudal tenants and others from the counties where the earl was a prominent landowner, some of these men being quite substantial figures. Around 1280 there were ten knights who were strongly attached to him.[70] The affinity of the earl of Cornwall, the son of Henry III's famous brother, was not dissimilar. Overall, there appears to have been an increase in the use of temporary and life grants, but there were still outright grants in perpetuity to followers, whether traditional tenants or new men. Spencer finds some evidence of Edward I's earls obtaining royal favours for their followers but laments that 'influence is an invisible agent', as we have noted so often before.[71]

Naturally, great lords remained as concerned as ever with maintaining their zones of prominence and keeping others at bay. Useful case studies are the earl of Lincoln's control over his honour of Pontefract and Earl John de Warenne's long-standing struggle to keep the 'interloper' Sir Robert Aguillon[72] at bay within his rape of Sussex.[73] The extent of the great lords' control over local justice, and indeed that of very many lesser lords, was revealed by the Hundred Rolls of 1274–5 and by the *quo warranto* cases which ensued. As we have seen, in practical terms the king was ultimately to back down. Lords needed to be increasingly active when it came to containing the central courts, which continued to burgeon. Maddicott showed that ties between the nobility and professional judges are evidenced in the reign of Edward I,[74] and Andrew Spencer has recently provided an overview. Associations between royal justices and the earls in Edward's reign were, as he says, 'ubiquitous'.[75] Edmund of Lancaster had 'very close links' with Roger Brabazon (who became chief justice of the king's bench) and Walter de Helyun, both members of his council, while the earl of Lincoln was associated with no less than five justices. The earl of Gloucester was associated with Hervey de Borham, Geoffrey de Lewknor, and Gilbert de Thornton. Others judges were associated with the earl of Hereford and the earl of Cornwall. In the latter's case, William de Bereford, justice of the common bench from 1292, was one of his executors. On one level these relationships reflect the professionalization of English justice and, indeed, administration.[76] The implications, however, for the impartiality of the legal system are obvious. As we have seen, Thomas Weyland was closely associated with, and on the payroll of, Roger Bigod IV, earl of Norfolk. When Weyland fell from power and petitions against him were encouraged,

---

[70] Ibid. ,129 and n. 86, where they are named.   [71] Ibid., 132.
[72] A late household steward of Henry III.   [73] Spencer, *Nobility and Kingship*, 152–70.
[74] Maddicott, 'Law and Lordship', 16–17.   [75] Spencer, *Nobility and Kingship*, 148.
[76] See, in particular, Brand, *The Origins of the Legal Profession*, and Brand, 'The Professionalisation of Lawyers in England', *Zeitschrift Für Neure Rechtsgeschichte*, 28 (2006).

RESOLUTION AND EQUILIBRIUM, 1267–90   263

accusations of biased judgement in favour of the earl soon surfaced.[77] These interconnections must have resulted in many cases not reaching the central courts. As Spencer has pointed out, the 'influence of feed justices' may explain why the earls 'appear so infrequently in royal legal records'.[78] There were other ways, moreover, by which the powerful could manipulate justice. There were, for example, commissions of *oyer* and *terminer*. Much used in Edward I's reign, these were appointed centrally to deal with individual cases and allowed the plaintiff to nominate the judges who would hear the case.[79]

The predominant trend during the first decades of Edward I's reign, both in terms of relations between crown and nobility and within the nobility itself, was one of reconciliation and the recreation of equilibrium, as aristocratic society rebalanced itself. Royal power and the power of the nobility continued to intermesh as they had done before, with the latter striving to tame the system where their own interests were concerned.

The English Polity in 1290

What then can we say of the English polity in 1290? How should it be characterized? The England of Edward I has been described, with some justification, as 'a parliamentary state', or more specifically as 'a tax-based parliamentary state'.[80] Through parliament the king inaugurated new sources of revenue that placed the royal finances on a much more stable foundation, successfully tapping the wealth of English society. The tax on movables granted in 1275 was followed by others in 1283, 1290, and thereafter. The 1275 parliament also granted customs duty on the export of wool, henceforth a permanent feature of royal finances. Parliament was also 'the forum which held Edward's realm together'.[81] Here the king and his council, including his judges and officials, met with magnates and others who received a personal summons as and when required, primarily for taxation, with representatives from the counties and from boroughs. It is necessary to emphasize, however, in order to maintain a sense of perspective, that the majority of the king's early parliaments were of what Carpenter describes as 'the old-style magnate type'. John Maddicott tells us that of the thirty parliaments held between 1274 and 1294, only two involved knights and burgesses while two others involved

---

[77] For an objective assessment see P. A. Brand, 'Chief Justice and Felon: The Career of Thomas Weyland', in R. Eales and D. Sullivan (eds.), *The Political Context of Law* (London, 1987), 26–47; repr. in Brand, *The Making of the Common Law*, 113–33.

[78] Spencer, *Nobility and Kingship*, 149.

[79] The standard treatment is R. W. Kaeuper, 'Law and Order in Fourteenth-Century England: The Evidence of Special Commissions of Oyer and Terminer', *Speculum*, 54 (1979), 734–84.

[80] By Carpenter in *Struggle for Mastery*, Ch. 15, 'King Edward I: The Parliamentary State'. This chapter provides a masterly and illuminating sketch of the character of Edward's domestic kingship.

[81] Ibid., 484.

264 POLITICS AND SOCIETY IN MID THIRTEENTH-CENTURY ENGLAND

knights alone. To add to these however, we might include two other assemblies, one during the king's absence in January 1273 and another in January 1283, which though not called parliaments had 'parliamentary characteristics'.[82]

Nonetheless, for Maddicott parliament was 'central' to Edward's 'mode of kingship'.[83] In his authoritative study he describes its characteristics during the early years of the reign.[84] The king valued the giving of counsel and the receipt of consent. Although the representatives were present only spasmodically, they were not, he stresses, mere 'ciphers' but participated in the expression of views. At the same time the king valued parliamentary theatre as an instrument of power. He also valued the two-way traffic of information, publicity for his actions on the one hand and petitions from his subjects on the other. The former had always been a major concern for thirteenth-century governments, while the latter was part and parcel of the king's reputation as the dispenser of justice, complementing the increasing recourse to royal courts by his free subjects. In Maddicott's words it was a means of 'creating a warmer climate of acceptance' for his monarchy.[85] In these years the king had considerable success in taking his people with him. The decision to go to war with Wales was made in parliament at Michaelmas 1276, while Dafydd of Wales was tried and condemned at the parliament at Shrewsbury in 1283, giving 'a national institution a more sharply nationalistic edge'.[86]

With these characteristics in mind let us conclude our examination of the 'reformed' polity of Edward I by looking more closely at the parliament of Easter 1290.[87] This parliament was the second of three to be held that year. The Hilary parliament had been the first to be called after the king's return to England from his three-year sojourn abroad. It was required to deal with various matters that had arisen during the king's absence, and only magnates were summoned. The same is true of the Michaelmas parliament, where it is known that it was attended by three bishops plus the chancellor, six earls, and several magnates. The Easter parliament was a much larger affair altogether. Its immediate context was the desperate state of the king's finances after his return from his three years in Gascony and the need to obtain a grant of a fifteenth. For this he was prepared to make a series of concessions to his subjects which included a resolution of magnate grievances over the *quo warranto* proceedings, the enactment of the Statute of *Quia Emptores*, again in response to magnate demands, various measures responding to ecclesiastical grievances, and the expulsion of the Jewish community from England. The meeting of parliament was also timed to coincide with various celebrations: the marriage of the king's daughter, Joan of Acre, to the earl of Gloucester; the translation of the body of Henry III to a new burial place in

---

[82] Maddicott, *Origins of the English Parliament*, 287–8.   [83] Ibid., 279.
[84] Ibid., 277–99.   [85] Ibid., 296.   [86] Ibid., 298.
[87] For what follows see *The Parliament Rolls of Medieval England 1275–1504*, vol. 1, ed. P. Brand (London, 2005), 49–50.

Westminster Abbey; and the wedding of the king's daughter, Margaret, to John son of the duke of Brabant. Only at the end of the parliament was it decided to summon representatives from the counties. Writs were issued on 14 June for two or three knights from each county to come by the week beginning 15 June at the latest, and the surviving returns give the names of those elected for twenty-eight counties. Evidence from Lincolnshire and Essex shows us that knights of the shire were not necessarily anxious to attend parliament. As regards the former shire, three knights were elected in full county court and two of them, John Dyne and John of Holland, were enrolled and returned to the king. The third knight, Gilbert de Neville, was not in Lincolnshire, and no one was willing to stand surety for his appearance. The seneschals and suitors would not elect anyone in his place. In Essex four knights were elected, of whom only two were present; the other two had to be distrained to appear at Westminster.

An important essay by Robert Stacey sees the measures passed in this parliament as 'connected elements in an evolving political bargain, the ultimate shape of which could not have been foreseen when the negotiations began'.[88] It was a lengthy parliamentary session that mixed 'religious ceremony, royal occasion, chivalric celebration and hard-nosed bargaining'.[89] The ceremonial and symbolic side of kingship was as operative in this reign as in that of his predecessor. Stacey argues that the expulsion of the Jews, decreed by the king on 18 July 1290 and carried into effect by 1 November, was conceded specifically to the shire knights in parliament in return for their consent to a tax for which Edward had already been negotiating with his magnates for some weeks. The representatives of the commons had consistently demanded legislation against Jews and Jewish lending as the price for their consent to royal taxation in almost every parliamentary session since 1268. Between 1268 and 1290 the only taxation not accompanied by anti-Jewish legislation was the 1283 tax to support the conquest of Wales. It is clear that the expulsion arose suddenly, in the final weeks of the parliamentary session, after the outline of the king's bargain with his magnates had already been determined, and that it was pronounced only after the commons' representatives had assembled specifically in return for the parliament's grant of taxation to the king.

The king was desperate for taxation. On 12 August 1289 Edward returned to a realm that had become disgruntled by his absence. In February 1288 his request for a subsidy for his expenses in Gascony was turned down by the magnates, following Gloucester's lead in asserting that they would consider no taxation until the king returned. The king banned tournaments after problems at Boston. In 1289 open warfare took place in the marches between the earls of Hereford and

---

[88] Robert C. Stacey, 'Parliamentary Negotiation and the Expulsion of the Jews from England', *TCE*, vi (1997), 77–101. The quotation comes from page 77.

[89] Ibid., 77.

266 POLITICS AND SOCIETY IN MID THIRTEENTH-CENTURY ENGLAND

Gloucester, while in the south-east war had also broken out between the men of Yarmouth and those of the Cinque Ports. These disputes were occurring against a background of grievances against the government. These grievances had been developing over the previous decade but came to a head during his absence, not least as a result of the judicial eyre of 1286–9. Taken together they affected a very sizeable proportion of the 'political nation'. The bishops remained very critical of the crown's encroachments on the liberties of the church. The 1279 Statute of Mortmain was a continual irritant, having seriously restricted ecclesiastical land acquisitions. Licences of exemption could be sought, but not while the king was out of the country. Equally aggravating were the king's efforts of 1285–6 to challenge the jurisdiction of ecclesiastical courts and the abuse of writs of prohibition by defendants. At the same time, laymen felt that not enough had been done to curb ecclesiastical justice. The men of London had particular grievances. The king had taken its governance into his own hands in 1285, and it was still controlled by the king's bailiffs. The king's policy towards London was characteristic of his attitude to urban liberties during the 1280s. As Prestwich has said, 'Urban judicial privileges and rights of self-government did not accord well with the king's concepts of his authority'.[90] There had been the Statute of Acton Burnell (1283) and the Statute of Merchants (1285), designed to aid the collection of commercial debts and hence benefit the mercantile community. However, the most obvious beneficiaries of the aid to collecting debts were, in fact, the king's own officials, a sizeable number of whom were now lending money by statute merchant recognizances.[91] The trafficking in Jewish debts was still rife, led by Queen Eleanor and Edmund of Lancaster.[92] The queen's acquisitions gave rise to doggerel verse: 'The king desires to get our gold; the queen, our manors fair to hold'.[93]

We have, of course, been here before. If the king had made a bargain with his people before, he now had to make it over again. That is to say, what was required was yet another resolution. The king's problem was that he had not fought a war in Gascony, and so there was no obvious justification for taxation. To secure a tax he was going to have to bargain with his subjects in parliament. The measures he took in 1289–90 to restore confidence in his government and secure consent to a subsidy are strikingly similar to those he took in 1274–5. However, the king was in a much stronger position than he had been then. Complaints about Adam de Stratton, a chamberlain of the exchequer, had reached him in Gascony, while Chief Justice Weyland's indictment and flight into sanctuary had followed hard upon his return. As Paul Brand has shown, the king's initial intention in

[90] Prestwich, *Edward I*, 264.
[91] See R. H. Bowers, 'From Rolls to Riches: King's Clerks and Moneylending in Thirteenth-Century England', *Speculum*, 58 (1983), 60–71.
[92] See J. C. Parsons, *Eleanor of Castile: Queen and Society in Thirteenth-Century England* (New York, 1995).
[93] Ibid., 2.

RESOLUTION AND EQUILIBRIUM, 1267–90   267

appointing auditors to hear *querelae* was not to solicit complaints against Weyland, Stratton, and other victims of the so-called state trails of 1289–90, but rather by the proclamation of 13 October to uncover abuses by the king's local officials.[94] Like the similar proclamation in 1274, it was intended to improve the king's image in the countryside in preparing for the parliamentary negotiations over taxation; and perhaps also to produce a modest amount of money. In 1289, however, the public response to the *auditores querelarum* was unenthusiastic. It was not until the Hilary parliament met, and Edward's justices and clerks began to fall, that complaints against royal officials at every level began to arrive at Westminster. Although it was not actually true, in the view of the countryside the *querelae* were seen as having led to the downfall of a corrupt and dishonest judiciary. The seven-week session of this parliament was largely taken up with matters pertaining to the trials of the justices and of Adam de Stratton. The resolution of the various conflicts was postponed until the Easter parliament.

Although Edward had been able to present himself as a determined opponent of official corruption and had also provided himself with a windfall of fines and confiscation, nothing had been done to secure the taxation he needed to pay off his debts. He had no choice but to negotiate on *quo warranto*. More than 250 cases had now been adjourned to the exchequer from the 1286–9 eyres alone, and a stream of petitions was arriving in chancery in which petitioners sought replevin of lands and liberties they had lost through *quo warranto* proceedings.

The Easter parliament had begun with festivities. It continued until 20 or 21 June when there was a wedding between Roger Bigod and Alice, daughter of John d'Avesnes. There was a recess from 20 June to 8 July when there was yet another royal wedding. On 8 July or soon after, *Quia Emptores* was enrolled, and the magnates were now prepared to recommend to the commons that they grant the king his tax. The representatives now demanded the expulsion of the Jews as their price, and this was secured very quickly. On 18 July expulsion orders were issued to the sheriffs.

Finally, before leaving parliament, we need to discuss the petitions presented there. Just as the study of parliament, a traditional focus of British historiography, has been given new life recently by the new edition of the Parliament Rolls, that of parliamentary petitions has been the subject of considerable research in recent years as a result of the Ancient Petitions project.[95] It was the reign of Edward I which saw the submission of written petitions to parliament as a regular practice,

---

[94] See P. Brand, 'Edward I and the Judges: The "State Trials" of 1289–93', *TCE*, i (Woodbridge, 1986), and Brand, 'Chief Justice and Felon', both repr. in P. Brand, *The Making of the Common Law* (London, 1992).

[95] *The Parliament Rolls of Medieval England* (henceforth *PROME*), ed. C. Given-Wilson et al., CD ROM version (Leicester, 2005), and 'Medieval Petitions: A Catalogue of the "Ancient Petitions" in the Public Record Office' [now The National Archives], directed by W. M. Ormrod and G. Dodd in 2003–7 and funded by the Arts and Humanities Research Council.

268   POLITICS AND SOCIETY IN MID THIRTEENTH-CENTURY ENGLAND

although not all petitions to the king and council were presented there. The fragmentary evidence and the details of the process at this time have been carefully analysed by Paul Brand.[96] Petitions have come down to us, sometimes through tortuous routes, for some of the parliaments. From 1290 onwards, however, they are to be found often in summary fashion on specific rolls.[97] Much seems to have depended upon the king's desire to receive them. Although it is not until 1305 that we learn about the actual arrangements being made for inviting petitions from the king's subjects during sessions of parliament, it is known that receivers had been appointed to receive them as early as 1280, when an ordinance arranged for the sorting of petitions into four groups: those seeking action by the chancery; those relating to the exchequer; those relating 'to justices or the law of the land'; and those concerning the jewry. These were to go to the officers concerned, who answered many of them themselves but set aside for the king and his council those matters that they deemed to be of greater significance or to require the king's discretionary power.[98] Petitioning, however, needs to be put into perspective. Dealing with them was not a prime purpose of parliament, and if the king felt it was his duty to answer petitioners this could not be expected to displace the matters of state for which parliament was called. Nonetheless, it does seem that from the beginning the receiving of petitions was a deliberate policy designed to make the crown more accessible.

Paul Brand has also offered a preliminary analysis of the contents of the petitions presented to the parliaments of Edward I.[99] Some were for grants that he was in a position to make. These could be for property of various kinds, for privileges, or for franchises. They could be for pardons for criminal offences or for money owed to the king. They could also be for licences of various types. Other petitions reflect the king's overall control of the judicial system. Thus petitioners being held without trial asked for trial to take place. Others asked for release on bail. Yet others were asking for justice from the king himself against unjustified action or for failure to take action, such as the honouring of debts. Since one could not ordinarily complain against the king in his own courts, petitioning was the obvious answer. A major category comprised petitions against wrongs, either those committed by the king's officials, or 'wrongs for which no regular remedy was available from Chancery or where in the particular circumstances they [the petitioners] would be

---

[96] For what follows see P. Brand, 'Petitions and Parliament in the Reign of Edward I', *Parliamentary History*, 23 (2004), 14–38.

[97] For details see P. Brand, 'Petitions, 1275–1340', in *PROME*, vol. 1, 7–9.

[98] The system was subsequently modified and in 1293 those destined for the king and council were decided at the outset, presumably by the receivers: Brand, 'Petitions and Parliament', 37.

[99] P. Brand, 'Understanding Early Petitions: An Analysis of the Content of Petitions to Parliament in the Reign of Edward I', in W. M. Ormrod, Gwilym Dodd, and A. Musson (eds.), *Medieval Petitions: Grace and Grievance* (York, 2009), 99–119. He draws on 62 petitions mainly from 1278, 20 from 1283, almost 300 from 1290, around 300 from 1305, and 86 from 1307.

RESOLUTION AND EQUILIBRIUM, 1267–90   269

unlikely to succeed in any action they did bring in the courts'.[100] Finally, there are petitions concerning the welfare of the king's subjects.[101]

The parliamentary petition had antecedents and was essentially the successor to the legal procedure of plaint which had come to be used effectively in the eyres.[102] The king was acutely aware of the well of grievance that was present in the country, of the perennial problem of corrupt royal officials, and of the need to increase and preserve the reputation of the crown.[103] Pressure was being placed upon the king but in a way that was acceptable to the parties concerned, while from the king's point of view the petition was an important safety net. Who, then, were the petitioners? For the most part they were named individuals. A significant minority, however, were submitted in the name of groups or of communities, most often the communities of counties or cities.[104] We also find 'the community of the kingdom of England' or 'the community of the land'. Brand points out that there is no clear division between these 'communities' on the one hand and groups which, although broad, do not define themselves in such terms on the other. It is noticeable that poverty is sometimes pleaded by communities. Thus we find petitions from the 'poor men of Lincoln' and the 'poor burgesses of the town of Newcastle on Tyne'. As Brand says, the initiative in such cases must have come from individuals or small groups who claimed to be speaking on behalf of the collective concerned. Community is such a predominant part of thirteenth-century thinking that we should be wary of turning it into a quasi-technical term and of reifying county communities in particular, as some historians have tended to do.

Let us look more closely at the petitions of 1290. We have 285 of them. The great majority are from people with property. Over thirty are from heads of religious houses, not to mention the master of the Temple and two from the Cistercian abbots as a group.[105] There are twenty-five requests for licence to grant property in mortmain. One of the lay petitioners was of the highest possible status; the king's brother Edmund. They also include the Northumberland

---

[100]   Brand, 'Understanding Early Petitions', 117.

[101]   One example given by Brand explains how the sea had washed away the road from Bridlington to Hull causing general inconvenience, including access to markets, and landowners refused to allow people to pass further inland. The petition asked for a new road (*PROME*, Original Documents: Edward 1 Parliaments, Roll 12 no. 29).

[102]   See Alan Harding, 'Plaints and Bills in the History of the English Law, Mainly in the Period 1250–1350', in D. Jenkin (ed.), *Legal History Studies, 1972* (Cardiff, 1975), 65–86, and Harding, ed., *Roll of the Shropshire Eyre of 1256*, Selden Society, 96 (London, 1981), xlii–xliii. See also G. Dodd, *Justice and Grace: Private Petitioning and the English Parliament in the Late Middle Ages* (Oxford, 2007), 29–31.

[103]   For a discussion of the king's motives and the pressures upon him see Dodd, *Justice and Grace*, 25–37. See also the classic study by Maddicott, 'Edward I and the Lessons of Baronial Reform', 1–30.

[104]   Brand, 'Petitions and Parliament', 31–2.

[105]   Bishops barely figure in the petitions. The bishops of Exeter and Ely submit one petition each. There are a few from friars and more from hospitals. There is one from the nuns of Cheshunt, one from a warden, one from a parson, one from an archdeacon, and one from a clerk of the Roman curia.

270 POLITICS AND SOCIETY IN MID THIRTEENTH-CENTURY ENGLAND

tenant-in-chief, Gilbert de Umfraville, and county knights and other landowners, like the Shropshire men Walter de Hopton and Roger Tyrel. A dozen petitions concern the tenure of entire manors and another dozen or more relate to substantial lands and rents. Others concern ladies and their dower. Yet others are on matters of direct concern to landowners and their estates. These included knights' fees, scutage (payment in lieu of military service), ransom, seisin (that is, possession), marriage and disparagement thereby, franchises including wreck, treasure trove, debt, and a propos a landowner who was *non compos mentis* when he made an enfeoffment. Many petitions deal with the aftereffects of the fall of the king's justices in 1289 and the dismissal of Adam de Stratton and of Master Henry de Bray, escheator south of the Trent. Much of this, too, concerns land and other property as well as injustice.

What of those further down the social scale? A notable feature of the petitions is once again the references to the poor and to poverty, although the incidences cannot necessarily be taken at face value. The problem with poverty is, of course, that it is relative. It can also be used rhetorically and to add a degree of piquancy to a request or complaint. The men of Appleby, besides asking the king to build them a watermill, claimed that they were also impoverished because they no longer had return of writs and other franchises. The citizens of London claimed that they were impoverished while alien merchants were getting rich and asked for the situation to be remedied. The king was unmoved. Poor women were likely to get a more sympathetic response, as when the two daughters of Richard de Gilmonby, described as *pauperes*, asked for an attaint to reverse the verdict of a jury in the court of king's bench.

Not all petitions were successful by any means. Whereas those requesting favours could be granted or not as long as they lay within the king's power, complaints needed to be dealt with according to the law and according to legal and administrative processes. Petitioning seems to have been naturally, and in some respects institutionally, biased towards those with substantial interests, even though it remains true that petitioning the king did encompass broad sectors of society, including some people of relatively small means, that poverty was expected to invoke a response, and that there was a genuine communitarian dimension to many petitions.

The same was true of parliamentary representation. Chosen in the counties, in theory at least at meetings of the county court, the members of parliament elected in the shires saw themselves as representing the community of the county (or perhaps collectively of the communities of the counties), just as the magnates represented the community of the realm. It is important to remember, however, just how exclusive an elite the knights of the late thirteenth and early fourteenth centuries actually were.[106] The so-called Parliamentary Roll of Arms from early in

---

[106] For what follows see Coss, 'Knighthood, Heraldry and Social Exclusion in Edwardian England', 39–68. See also P. Coss, *The Knight in Medieval England* (Stroud, 1993).

Edward II's reign lists 1,100 names nationally, this being a high proportion of the knights active at the time.[107] In their chivalric culture, beliefs, and way of life they were much closer to the baronage than to those beneath them in the social order. The ubiquitous external expression of this elitism was heraldry, found in so many artistic media of the time. The knights cherished their social relationships within a highly aristocratic elite. They constituted in effect a minor nobility, and we should not be seduced by later history into seeing them at this point in time as the highest grade of the gentry. The representatives drawn from the cities and towns were also, though to a lesser degree, high flyers. They were the leading figures in their communities, as property-holding officials and richer merchants. The references to the 'barons' of the Cinque Ports helps to put them in perspective.

We have examined the years 1267–90 in terms of the resolution of issues and conflicts and of the restoration of stability and equilibrium in politics and society. There were certainly shifts within the polity. A resurgent monarchy under Edward I commanded more authority, and the king was prepared to legislate, to bargain with his subjects, and to make the crown more accessible via parliament. The idea of representation grew stronger, and a more elevated and consistent role for knights here was becoming normalized, although their deployment and their status in society was multifaceted. We must be careful not to exaggerate the degree or pace of change, and there were no really fundamental shifts as yet within the social fabric. It is undeniable that these years lie at the beginning of a dynamic era in the history of parliament. This is a different perspective, however, from the one adopted here. It is true that institutions are 'path dependent' in that they tend to develop in ways that are conditioned by their underlying structures and values.[108] The linear history of institutions, however, is marred by hindsight and can very easily spill over into teleology. There are always exogenous factors that come into play. Furthermore, equilibrium is by nature transient and the English polity, for a variety of reasons, would soon once again destabilize.

Politics and Society in Mid Thirteenth-Century England: The Troubled Realm. Peter Coss, Oxford University Press.
© Peter Coss 2024. DOI: 10.1093/9780198924319.003.0010

---

[107] Based on this source, N. Denholm-Young estimated that there were 1,250 functioning knights in contemporary England: 'Feudal Society in the Thirteenth Century: The Knights', in *Collected Papers of N. Denholm-Young* (Cardiff, 1969), 86.

[108] For path dependency see J. Mahoney, 'Path Dependence in Historical Sociology', *Theory and Society*, 29/4 (2000), 507–48.

11

Conclusion

Once we acknowledge the primacy of the revolt of the higher nobility in 1258 and abandon the idea that reform emanated essentially from county communities, the events of the years 1258–67 became easier to interpret. The weakness of Henry III's kingship and the ambitions and thwarted expectations of some of his leading magnates provide one level of interpretation. Beneath the clash of personalities and personal aims lay differing approaches to the contemporary polity and, indeed, to the institution of kingship. The relationship between the crown and the nobility is a complex one, embodying both past relationships and contemporary requirements.

On the one side lay the king whose exercise of power, though circumscribed in many ways, rested fundamentally on the king's will and self-perception, on the initiative of himself and his advisers, and on the running of an evolving system of government, an edifice founded upon command, loyalty, and reward. On the other side lay the dynamics of aristocratic society, a society prone to the formation of factions and peopled by men and women who sought advantages and openings for themselves and their lineages, not to mention their relatives and supporters, while desiring a relatively stable and basically supportive order in which they could satisfy their needs. The nobility, and especially the magnates, lay at the apex of a social structure in which they commanded respect and loyalty and channelled the expectations of a wider aristocracy, would-be aristocrats, and others, who shared their culture, assumptions, and social values. Needless to say, this was not a straightforward dichotomy, given the interaction between the two sets of institutions. The royal family was in many ways a noble one writ large, while men made complementary careers in serving one or the other, and sometimes both. Nonetheless, differences in how the contemporary polity was appreciated and how people were individually positioned in relation to the crown and members of the nobility explains a great deal about the myriad individual and collective actions that were taken subsequently.

In conceptual terms, the historian needs to make some clear distinctions. For example, the king, the crown, and the state cannot be understood as synonymous. The crown is a personification and has perceptible interests that do not necessarily synchronize with the desires of the individual king and may indeed transcend them. It is an idea as well as an institution and may command loyalty in its own right.[1]

---

[1] Henry III seems to have understood the distinction when he granted Lord Edward the lands of his appanage on the condition that they were not to be alienated from the English crown: *CPR 1247–58*, 382; Prestwich, *Edward I*, 11.

CONCLUSION   273

More significant, arguably, is the distinction between the king and the crown on the one hand and the state on the other. The state is a totality: the structure of administration, of courts, and of law and custom, and the ideas that underpin them.[2] It embodies, among other things, the public interest of which the king is the guardian. The state and the king interact and interlock, primarily because the legislative and executive powers are his, but they are not identical. This is why it was possible for the 'reformist' barons to usurp his position in effectively managing the state. A state may be considered strong or weak, according to what political scientists have termed 'state capacity'.[3] Thus an individual king may be a weak ruler, while the apparatus of the state may be strong. This, it can well be argued, is precisely the situation in mid-thirteenth-century England. Henry III can be regarded as lax in his treatment of his magnates, if less than even-handed and somewhat petulant, while they felt the need to contain encroachments by the state. This, in my view, is the explanation for their moves to bend the public courts to their will, by privatizing jurisdictions in the provinces and 'corrupting' the central courts. These reactions to state power are the beginnings of the phenomenon which historians have labelled 'bastard feudalism'.[4]

It has been argued that every political entity has a constitution, whether written or not, whether defined or not, that is to say 'political and governmental structures, and the beliefs of those who participate in them about how those structures should operate'.[5] It could be argued, too, and indeed it is often assumed, that the core of the constitution in thirteenth-century England was the relationship between the king and the nobility, and that it developed progressively from this. However, in my view it is better not to understand the mid-century struggle in these terms. The English nobility were not constitutionalists and had no conscious agency in that direction. Moreover, in view of the later history of constitutionalism and its ideological undercurrents, it would be better to avoid any in-built anachronism and to adopt the more neutral term 'polity' when talking of the political structure of thirteenth-century England. It is certainly the case, as has been demonstrated, that this polity widened somewhat during the power struggle as the opposition barons reached out to bring the interests of a wider section of society into play. At the same time, this should not be taken too far. As we have seen, the civil war was not fought over the Provisions of Westminster, but over power. Moreover, the detailed examination of the nature and characteristics of the war has evidenced a great deal of self-interest, at high and low levels, but very little of the idealism much trumpeted by historians.

[2] I discuss the English state in *The Aristocracy in England and Tuscany*, 273–6.
[3] I owe my understanding of this concept to Deborah Boucoyannis, *Kings as Judges: Power, Justice and the Origins of Parliament* (Cambridge, 2021).
[4] Coss, 'Bastard Feudalism Revised', 27–64.
[5] Christine Carpenter, 'Political and Constitutional History: Before and After McFarlane', in R. H. Britnell and A. J. Pollard (eds.), *The McFarlane Legacy: Studies in Late Medieval Politics and Society* (Stroud, 1995), 176.

274   POLITICS AND SOCIETY IN MID THIRTEENTH-CENTURY ENGLAND

This brings us inevitably to the question of Simon de Montfort. Enough has been said to show that he cannot be perceived as anything like the world-historical figure in the Hegelian sense that earlier historians and English tradition have posited. He was not the creator of new institutions, nor was he armed with a prescient vision of how society might be reformed. He was, by contrast, the epitome of the thirteenth-century nobleman, charismatic no doubt and single-minded, perhaps to an extraordinary degree in his own day. There is no doubt that in fighting his cause he reached out and down, and in so doing tapped quite deliberately into the anti-alienism and xenophobia of his day. It is unwarranted to regard him on this slender basis as the leader of a national revolution.

Indeed, it is questionable whether it is appropriate to describe the events of 1258–67 as a revolution at all, most especially if this involves linking them to the events of seventeenth-century England. The leap here is remarkable, and fundamentally ideological. Since David Carpenter and other commentators on the thirteenth-century struggle have not defined what they mean by revolution, it is necessary for us to ask what is generally meant by the term. Online definitions drawn from political science include the following:

> A revolution (*revolutio* = 'a turn around') is a fundamental and relatively sudden change in political power and political organization which occurs when the population revolts against the government, typically due to perceived oppression ... ,

and

> As a historical process, 'revolution' refers to a movement, often violent, to overthrow an old regime and effect complete change in the fundamental institutions of society.

Carpenter's usage may fit the first of these definitions, though whether it fits the second definition is, perhaps, more debateable. Did clipping the king's wings and up-fronting parliament really amount to overthrowing 'the old regime' and totally changing 'the fundamental institutions of society'? There is another definition commonly used by social scientists, viz:

> A revolution is a fundamental change in a society. It involves a shift in power in a society. Revolution seeks to overthrow the whole system. Revolution occurs when a number of people in a society feel discontent with the current order and agree that change is necessary. Revolution can be about important social, political and economic changes.

A shift in the exercise of power from the king to representatives of the nobility acting on behalf of the king hardly constitutes a fundamental change in society, nor does it overthrow a system. It would be safer to see the events of 1258–67 as fundamentally a crisis in the relationship between the king and the higher nobility. Here, the *Oxford English Dictionary* comes to our aid. Crisis is defined as:

> A vitally important or decisive stage in the process of anything; a turning-point; also, a state of affairs in which a decisive change for better or worse is imminent; now applied especially to times of difficulty, insecurity, and suspense in politics or commerce.

This, I would contend, better fits the years 1258–67.

Historians are in the business of identifying and explaining developments over time. There are, however, obvious dangers in linear history, and it is hardly necessary to rehearse them again. As a counterweight to the epistemological dangers of the grand narrative with its teleology and its essentialism, the linear approach needs to be juxtaposed with Meinecke's historicism which endeavours to understand the society of a given time and place as an entity in itself.

Politics and Society in Mid Thirteenth-Century England: The Troubled Realm. Peter Coss, Oxford University Press.
© Peter Coss 2024. DOI: 10.1093/9780198924319.003.0011

Bibliography

Unpublished Sources in The National Archives

Chancery:

C 60   Fine Rolls
C 61   Gascon Rolls
C 66   Patent Rolls
C 132   Inquisitions Post Mortem

Exchequer:

E 159   Memoranda Rolls (King's Remembrancer)
E 368   Memoranda Rolls (Lord Treasurer's Remembrancer)

Judicial Records:

KB 26   Curia Regis Rolls, Henry III
Just 1   Eyre Rolls

Duchy of Lancaster:

D. L. 25   Deeds, Series L

Special Collections:

SC 1   Ancient Correspondence
SC 11   Rentals and Surveys, General Series

Published Sources

Annales Monastici, ed. H. R. Luard, 5 vols., Rolls Series (London, 1864–69). Annals of Burton (vol. i.); Annals of Dunstable (vol. iii.); Annals of Tewkesbury (vol. i.); Annals of Waverley (vol. ii.).

British Borough Charters, 1042–1216, ed. A. Ballard (Cambridge, 1913).

The Book of Fees (Liber feodorum), commonly called Testa de Nevill, 3 vols. (London, 1920–32).

Calendar of Ancient Deeds, 6 vols., HMSO (London, 1890–1915).

Calendar of Charter Rolls, vol. i, 1226–57, HMSO (London, 1903).

Calendar of Inquisitions Miscellaneous, vol. i, 1219–307, HMSO (London, 1916).

Calendar of Inquisitions Post Mortem, vols. i–iii, HMSO (London, 1904–12).

Calendar of the Fine Rolls of the Reign of Henry III, 1216–1242, ed. P. Dryburgh and B. Hartland, 3 vols. (Woodbridge, 2007–9). Publications of Fine Roll Project headed by D. Carpenter, available at https://finerollshenry3.org.uk/home.html.

Calendar of Liberate Rolls, 6 vols., 1226–72, HMSO (London, 1916–64).

Calendar of Patent Rolls, 1232–72, 4 vols. HMSO (London, 1906–13).

Cartulary of Oseney Abbey, v, ed. H. E. Salter, Oxford Historical Series, vol. xcviii (Oxford, 1935).

The Cartulary of Shrewsbury Abbey, ed. Una Rees, 2 vols. (Aberystwyth, 1975).

Chronica Johannis de Oxenede, ed. H. Ellis, Rolls Series (London, 1859).

The Chronicle of Melrose, ed. and trans. A. O. and M. O. Anderson (London, 1961).

The Chronicle of William de Rishanger of the Barons' Wars, ed. J. O. Halliwell, Camden Society (London, 1840).

Chronicon vulgo dictum Chronicon Thomae Wykes, 1066–1288, Annales Monastici, ed. H. R. Luard, vol. iv, Rolls Series (1869).

278 BIBLIOGRAPHY

Complete Peerage, ed. G. E. Cokayne, revised by V. Gibbs and others (London, 1910–57).
Close Rolls, 1227–1272, 14 vols., HMSO (London, 1905–38).
Close Rolls (Supplementary) of the Reign of Henry III, 1244–66, ed. Ann Morton, HMSO (London, 1975).
Councils & Synods with Other Documents Relating to the English Church, vol. ii, 1205–313, eds. F. M. Powicke and C. R. Cheney (Oxford, 1964).
Crown Pleas of the Wiltshire Eyre, 1249, ed. C. A. F. Meekings, Wiltshire Archaeological and Natural History Society (Devizes, 1961).
Curia Regis Rolls, vol. xvii, 1242–3, ed. A. Nicol, HMSO (London, 1991).
De Antiquis Legibus Liber: Cronica Maiorum et Vicecomitum Londiniarum, ed. T. Stapleton, Camden Society (London, 1846).
De Legibus et Consuetudinibus Angliae, ed. G. E. Woodbine/*Bracton on the Laws and Customs of England*, trans. S. E. Thorne, 4 vols. (Cambridge, Mass, 1968).
A Digest of the Charters Preserved in the Cartulary of the Priors of Dunstable, ed. G. H. Fowler, Bedfordshire Historical Record Society, xvii (1935).
Diplomatic Documents Preserved in the Public Record Office, vol. i, ed. P. Chaplais, HMSO (London, 1964).
Documents of the Period of Reform and Rebellion, 1258–67, ed. R. F. Treharne and I. J. Sanders, Oxford Medieval Texts (Oxford, 1973).
English Historical Documents 1189–1327, ed. H. Rothwell (London, 1975).
Extracts from the Plea Rolls 1272–1294, ed. G. Wrottesley, Staffordshire Historical Collections 6, Part I, William Salt Archaeological Society (London, 1885).
Eyton, R. W., *Antiquities of Shropshire*, 12 vols. (London, 1854–60).
Feet of Fines for Essex, vol. i, ed. R. E. G. Kirk, Essex Archaeological Society (Colchester, 1899–1910).
Feudal Aids, 6 vols., HMSO (London, 1899–1920).
FitzNells Cartulary: A Calendar of Bodleian Library MS. Rawlinson B 430, ed. C. A. F. Meekings and P. Shearman, Surrey Record Society, vol. xxvi (Guildford, 1968).
Flores Historiarum, ed. H. R. Luard, 3 vols., Rolls Series (London, 1890).
A Feodary of Glastonbury Abbey, 1342, ed. F. W. Weaver, with introduction by C. H. Mayo, Somerset Record Society, vol. 26 (1909).
Foedera, Conventiones, Litterae et Acta Publica, ed. T. Rymer, new edn., ed. A. Clark and F. Holbrooke, Record Commission (London, 1816), vol. i.
The Flowers of History by Roger of Wendover, ed. H. G. Hewlett, 3 vols., Rolls Series (London, 1886–9).
Fouke Le Fitz Waryn, ed. P. T. Rickets et al., Anglo-Norman Text Society (Oxford, 1975).
Gesta Abbatum Monasterii Sancti Albani, ed. H. T. Riley, 3 vols., Rolls Series (London, 1867–9).
The Historical Works of Gervase of Canterbury, ed. W. Stubbs, 2 vols., Rolls Series (London, 1879–80).
History of William the Marshal, ed. A. J. Holden, translated by S. Gregory and introduced by D. Crouch, 3 vols., Anglo-Norman Text Society (London, 2002–6).
Historical Manuscripts Commission Reports, no. 69, Middleton Manuscripts (London, 1911).
The Household Rolls of Eleanor de Montfort, Countess of Leicester and Pembroke, 1265, ed. and trans. Louise J. Wilkinson, Pipe Rolls Society (Woodbridge, 2020).
The Langley Cartulary, ed. P. R. Coss, Dugdale Society, vol. xxxii (Stratford-upon-Avon, 1980).
The *Opusculum de nobili Simone de Montforti*.
The Letters of Adam Marsh, ed. J. S. Brewer, Rolls Series (London, 1858).
The Letters of Adam Marsh, ed. and trans. C. H. Lawrence, 2 vols. (Oxford, 2006–10).
The Letters of Robert Grosseteste, ed. F. A. C. Mantello and J. Goering (Toronto, 2010).
Liebermann, F., *Über die Leges Anglorum saeculo xiii ineunte Londoniis collectae* (Halle, 1894).
Liebermann, F., *Die Gesetze der Angelsachsen I*, ed. F. Liebermann (Halle, 1903).
Luffield Priory Charters Part II, ed. G. R. Elvey, Buckinghamshire and Northamptonshire Record Societies (1975).

BIBLIOGRAPHY   279

Magna Carta Project: magnacartaresearch.org.

Manners and Household Expenses in Thirteenth and Fifteenth Centuries, ed. T. H. Turner (Roxburghe Club, 1841).

Matthaei Parisiensis, Monachi Sancti Albani, Chronica Majora, ed. H. R. Luard, 7 vols., Rolls Series (London, 1872–83).

Medieval Petitions: A Catalogue of the 'Ancient Petitions' in the Public Record Office [now The National Archives]; project directed by W. M. Ormrod and G. Dodd (2003–7).

The Metrical Chronicle of Robert of Gloucester, ed. W. A. Wright, 2 vols., Rolls Series (London, 1887).

Miracula [Simonis de Montfort] in *The Chronicle of William de Rishanger of the Barons' Wars,* ed. J. O. Halliwell (Camden Society, 1840), 67–110.

Monumenta Franciscana, ed. J. S. Brewer and R. Howlett, 2 vols., Rolls Series (London), vol. i, 1858–82.

Opusculum de nobili Simone de Montforti, in J. Stevenson, Bannantyne Club (Edinburgh, 1835), and *The Chronicle of Melrose,* intro. A. O. and M. O. Anderson (London, 1936).

The Parliament Rolls of Medieval England (PROME), ed. C. Given-Wilson et al., CD ROM version (Leicester, 2005).

The Parliament Rolls of Medieval England 1275–1504, vol. i, ed. P. Brand (London, 2005).

Placita de Quo Warranto, Record Commission (London, 1818).

Pleas of the Forest in Staffordshire, temp. Henry III and Edward I, ed. G. Wrottesley, Staffordshire Historical Collections 5, Part I, William Salt Archaeological Society (London, 1884).

The Red Book of the Exchequer, ed. H. Hall, 3 vols., Rolls Series (London,1896).

The Register of Thomas de Cantilupe, Bishop of Hereford (1275–1282), ed. R. G. Griffiths and W. W. Capes, Canterbury and York Society (1907).

Roberti Grossetesti Epistolae, ed. H. R. Luard, Rolls Series (London, 1861).

The Roll and Writ File of the Berkshire Eyre of 1248, ed. M. T. Clanchy, Selden Society, xc (1973).

The Roll of the Shropshire Eyre of 1256, ed. A. Harding, Seldon Society (1981).

Rotuli Hundredorum, ed. W. Illingworth, 2 vols., Record Commission (London, 1812–18).

Rotuli Ricardi Gravesendi Diocisis Lincolniensis, ed. F. N. Davis, Canterbury and York Society (Oxford, 1925).

Rotuli Selecti, ed. J. Hunter, Record Commission (London, 1834).

Royal and Other Historical Letters Illustrative of the Reign of Henry III, ed. W. W, Shirley, Rolls Series (London, 1866).

The Royal Charter Witness Lists of Henry III, ed. M. Morris, 2 vols., List and Index Society (London, 2001).

Select Cases in the Court of King's Bench, vol. ii, ed. G. O. Sayles, Selden Society no. 57 (London, 1938).

Select Pleas of the Forest, ed. G. J. Turner, Selden Society, vol. 15 (1899).

Snappe's Formulary and Other Records, ed. H. E. Salter, Oxford Historical Society, lxxx (Oxford, 1924).

Somerset Feet of Fines 1196–1307, ed. E. Green, Somerset Record Society, no. 6 (1892).

The Song of Lewes, ed. and trans. C. L. Kingsford (Oxford, 1963).

Special Eyre Rolls of Hugh Bigod 1258–60, ed. and introduced by Andrew Hershey, 2 vols., Selden Society (London, 2021).

The 1258–9 Special Eyre of Surrey and Kent, ed. A. Hershey, Surrey Record Society, no. 38 (Woking, 2004).

The 1263 Surrey Eyre, ed. S. Stewart, Surrey Record Society, vol. 40 (2006).

Thomas Wright's Political Songs of England, new edn. introduced by P. Coss, Royal Historical Society (Cambridge, 1996).

Three Early Assize Rolls for the County of Northumberland, ed. W. Page, Surtees Society lxxxviii (1891).

Warwickshire Feet of Fines, vol. i, ed. E. Stokes and F. C. Wellstood, Dugdale Society (London, 1932).

280 BIBLIOGRAPHY

Secondary Sources

Aird, W. M., *Robert Curthose, Duke of Normandy* (Woodbridge, 2008).

Aird, W. M., 'Saint Anselm of Canterbury and Charismatic Authority', *Religions*, 5 (2014), 90–108.

Althoff, G., *Spielregeln der Politik in Mittelalter. Kommunikation in Frieden unde Fehde* (Darmstadt, 1997).

Althoff, G., 'Zur Bedeutung symbolischer Kommunikation für das Verständnis des Mittelalters', in *Frühmittelalters Studien*, 31 (1997), 370–89.

Altschul, M., *A Baronial Family in Medieval England: The Clares, 1217–1314* (Baltimore, 1963).

Altschul, M., 'Clare, Richard de, Sixth Earl of Gloucester and Fifth Earl of Hertford 1222–1262', *ODNB* 11 (2004), 761–3.

Ambler, S. T., 'The Montfortian Bishops and the Baronial Gravamina of 1263–4', in P. R. Coss and S. D. Lloyd (eds.), *TCE*, iii (Newcastle, 1991), 137–50.

Ambler, S. T., *Bishops in the Political Community of England 1213–1272* (Oxford, 2017).

Ambler, S. T., *The Song of Simon de Montfort: England's First Revolutionary and the Death of Chivalry* (London, 2019).

Arlidge, A., and Judge, I., *Magna Carta Uncovered* (Oxford and Portland, 2015).

Asaji, K., 'The Barons' War and the Hundred Jurors in Cambridgeshire', *JMH*, 21 (1995), 153–65.

Bailey, M., *The English Manor c.1200–c.1500* (Manchester, 2002).

Baker, D., *Simon de Montfort and the Rise of the English Nation* (Stroud, 2015).

Barratt, N., 'The Revenues of King John', *I*, 111 (1996), 835–55.

Barratt, N., 'The English Revenue of Richard I', *EHR*, 116 (2001), 635–56.

Barratt, N., 'Finance on a Shoestring: The Exchequer in the Thirteenth Century', in A. Jobson (ed.), *English Government in the Thirteenth Century* (Woodbridge, 2004), 71–86.

Barron, C. M., *London in the Middle Ages: Government and People* (Oxford, 2004).

Bayley, Charles C., 'Judicial Investigations under the Dictum of Kenilworth, Cambridgeshire' (University of Manchester, MA thesis, 1929).

Beam, C. (ed.), *The Royal Minorities of Medieval and Early Modern England* (New York, 2008).

Bean, M., *The Decline of English Feudalism 1215–1540* (Manchester, 1968).

Beardwood, A., 'The Trial of Walter Langton, Bishop of Lichfield, 1307–12', *Transactions of the American Philosophical Society*, n.s. liv, Part 3 (Philadelphia, 1964).

Bémont, C., *Simon de Montfort* (1st edn. Paris, 1884; 2nd edn. trans. E. F. Jacob, Oxford, 1930).

Beverley Smith, J., *Llewelyn ap Gruffudd, Prince of Wales* (Cardiff, 1998).

Binski, P., *Westminster Abbey and the Plantagenets: Kingship and the Representations of Power, 1200–1400* (New Haven and London, 1995).

Birrell, J., 'A Great Thirteenth-Century Hunter: John Giffard of Brimpsfield', *Medieval Prosopography*, 15 (1994), 37–66.

Blaauw, W. *The Barons' War* (2nd edn., London, 1871).

Blaauw, W., *The Barons' War* (2nd edn., London, 1971).

Boucoyannis, D., *Kings and Judges: Power, Justice and the Origins of Parliament* (Cambridge, 2021).

Bowers, R. H., 'From Rolls to Riches: Clerks and Moneylending in Thirteenth-Century England', *Speculum*, 58 (1983), 60–71.

Brand, P. A., 'The Control of Mortmain Alienation 1200–1300', in J. H. Baker (ed.), *Legal Records and the Historian*, Royal Historical Society (London, 1978), 29–40, repr. in Brand, *The Making of the Common Law*, 233–44.

Brand, P. A., 'Edward I and the Judges: The "State Trials" of 1289–93', in P. R. Coss and S. D. Lloyd (eds.), *TCE*, i (Woodbridge, 1986).

Brand, P. A., 'Chief Justice and Felon: The Career of Thomas Weyland', in R. Eales and D. Sullivan (eds.), *The Political Context of Law* (London, 1987), 26–47; repr. in Brand, *The Making of the Common Law*, 113–33.

Brand, P. A., 'Courtroom and Schoolroom: The Education of Lawyers in England Prior to 1400', *Historical Research*, 60 (1987), 147–65; repr. in Brand, *The Making of the Common Law*, 57–75.

Brand, P. A., 'The Drafting of Legislation in Mid-Thirteenth Century England', *Parliamentary History*, 9 (1990), 243–85, 260–2.

Brand, P. A., *The Making of the Common Law* (London, 1992).

BIBLIOGRAPHY   281

Brand, P. A., *The Origins of the English Legal Profession* (London, 1992).

Brand, P. A., *Kings, Barons and Justices: The Making and Enforcement of Legislation in Thirteenth-Century England* (Cambridge, 2003).

Brand, P. A., 'Pattishall, Sir Simon', *ODNB* 43 (2004), 110–11.

Brand, P. A., 'Petitions and Parliament in the Reign of Edward I', *Parliamentary History*, 23 (2004), 14–38.

Brand, P. A., 'Petitions, 1275–1340', in *PROME*, i (2005).

Brand, P. A., 'The Professionalisation of Lawyers in England', *Zeitschrift Für Neure Rechtsgeschichte*, 28 (2006).

Brand, P. A., 'Understanding Early Petitions: An Analysis of the Content of Petitions to Parliament in the Reign of Edward I', in W. M. Ormrod, G. Dodd, and A. Musson (eds.), *Medieval Petitions: Grace and Grievance* (York, 2009), 99–119.

Britnell, R. H., *The Commercialisation of English Society 1000–1500* (Cambridge, 1993).

Brooks, F. W., 'The Cinque Ports', *Mariners Mirror*, 15 (1929), 142–91.

Brooks, F. W., 'The Cinque Ports' Feud with Yarmouth in the Thirteenth Century', *Mariners' Mirror*, 19 (1933), 27–51.

Buc, P., *The Dangers of Ritual* (Princeton, 2001).

Burt, C., 'A "Bastard Feudal" Affinity in the Making? The Followings of William and Guy de Beauchamp, Earls of Warwick, 1268–1315', *Midland History*, 34 (2009), 156–80.

Burton, D. W., 'Politics, Propaganda and Public Opinion in the Reigns of Henry III and Edward I' (University of Oxford, DPhil thesis, 1985).

Burton, John R., *History of Bewdley* (London, 1883).

Butterfield, Herbert, *The Whig Interpretation of History* (Penguin edition, Harmondsworth, 1973; first published 1931).

Cam, H. M. *Studies in the Hundred Rolls: Some Aspects of Thirteenth-Century Administration* (Oxford Studies in Social and Legal History, 1921).

Cam, H. M., *The Hundred and the Hundred Rolls* (London, 1930; repr. 1963).

Cam, H. M., 'The Early Burgesses of Cambridge in Relation to the Surrounding Countryside', in H. M. Cam, *Liberties and Communities in Medieval England: Collected Studies in Local Administration and Topography* (Cambridge, 1944; repr. London, 1963), 19–26.

Cam, H. M., *Liberties and Communities in Medieval England: Collected Studies in Local Administration and Topography* (Cambridge, 1944; repr. London, 1963).

Cam, H. M., 'The Evolution of the Medieval English Franchise', *Speculum*, 32 (1957), 439, repr. in Cam, *Law-Finders and Law-Makers in Medieval England*.

Cam, H. M., *Law-Finders and Law-Makers in Medieval England* (London, 1962; repr. 1967).

Carpenter, C., 'The Beauchamp Affinity: A Study of Bastard Feudalism at Work', *EHR*, 95 (1980), 514–32.

Carpenter, C., 'Political and Constitutional History: Before and After McFarlane', in R. H. Britnell and A. J. Pollard (eds.), *The McFarlane Legacy: Studies in Late Medieval Politics and Society* (Stroud, 1995), 176.

Carpenter, D. A., 'The Decline of the Curial Sheriff in England, 1194–1258', *EHR*, 101 (1976), 1–32; repr. in *The Reign of Henry III*, 151–82.

Carpenter, D. A., 'King Henry III's "Statute" against the Aliens: July 1263', in *EHR*, 95 (1980), 925–44; repr. in *The Reign of Henry III*, 261–80.

Carpenter, D. A., 'What Happened in 1258?', in J. Gillingham and J. C. Holt (eds.), *War and Government in the Middle Ages: Essays in Honour of J. O. Prestwich* (Woodbridge, 1984), 106–119; repr. in *The Reign of Henry III*, 183–98.

Carpenter, D. A., 'King, Magnates and Society: The Personal Rule of King Henry III, 1234–1258', *Speculum*, 60 (1985), 39–70; repr. in *The Reign of Henry III*, 75–106.

Carpenter, D. A., 'Simon de Montfort and the Mise of Lewes', *BIHR*, 58 (1985), 1–11; repr. in *The Reign of Henry III*, 281–91.

Carpenter, D. A., 'The Lord Edward's Oath to Aid and Counsel Simon de Montfort', *BIHR*, 58 (1985) 226–37; repr. in *The Reign of Henry III*, 241–52.

Carpenter, D. A., 'The Gold Treasure of King Henry III', in P. R. Coss and S. D. Lloyd (eds.), *TCE*, i (Woodbridge, 1986), 61–88; repr. in *The Reign of Henry III*, 107–36.

282 BIBLIOGRAPHY

Carpenter, D. A., *The Battles of Lewes and Evesham, 1264/5* (Keele, 1987).

Carpenter, D. A., *The Minority of Henry III* (London, 1990).

Carpenter, D. A., 'Simon de Montfort: The First Leader of a Political Movement in English History', *History*, 76 (1991), 3–23; repr. *The Reign of Henry III*, 219–39.

Carpenter, D. A., 'English Peasants in Politics, 1258–1267', *P&P*, 136 (1992), 3–22; repr. in *The Reign of Henry III*, 309–48.

Carpenter, D. A., 'King Henry III's "Statute" against Aliens: July 1263', *EHR*, 107 (1992), 721–52; repr. in *The Reign of Henry III*, 261–80.

Carpenter, D. A., 'The Burial of King Henry III, the Regalia and Royal Ideology', in D. A. Carpenter, *The Reign of Henry III* (London, 1996), 28–54.

Carpenter, D. A., 'Matthew Paris and Henry III's Speech at the Exchequer in October 1256', in D. A. Carpenter, *The Reign of Henry III* (London, 1996), 137–50.

Carpenter, D. A., *The Reign of Henry III* (London, 1996).

Carpenter, D. A., 'A Noble in Politics: Roger Mortimer in the Period of Baronial Reform and Rebellion, 1258–65', in A. J. Duggan (ed.), *Nobles and Nobility in Medieval Europe: Concepts, Origins, Transformations* (Woodbridge, 2000), 183–203.

Carpenter, D. A., 'The Second Century of English Feudalism', *P&P*, 168 (August 2000), 30–71.

Carpenter, D. A., *The Struggle for Mastery: Britain 1066–1284* (Oxford, 2003).

Carpenter, D. A., 'The English Chancery in the Thirteenth Century', in A. Jobson (ed.), *English Government in the Thirteenth Century* (Woodbridge, 2004), 49–69.

Carpenter, D. A., 'Introduction', to *Calendar of the Fine Rolls of the Reign of Henry III*, vol. i, 1216–24, ed. P. Dryburgh and B. Hartland (Woodbridge and National Archives, 2007).

Carpenter, D. A., 'The Household Rolls of King Henry III of England (1216–72)', *HR*, 86 (2007).

Carpenter, D. A., 'The Career of Godfrey of Crowcombe: Household Knight of King John and Steward of King Henry III', in C. Given Wilson et al. (eds.), *War, Government and Aristocracy in the British Isles: Essays in Honour of Michael Prestwich* (Woodbridge, 2008), 26–54.

Carpenter, D. A., 'Magna Carta 1253: The Ambitions of the Church and the Divisions within the Realm', *Historical Journal*, 86 (May 2013), 179–90.

Carpenter, D. A., *Magna Carta* (London, 2015).

Carpenter, D. A., *Henry III: Reform, Rebellion, Civil War, Settlement* (New Haven and London, 2023).

Carpenter, D. A., 'John, Sir, fitz John, Baronial Leader', *ODNB*, 30.

Cassidy, R., 'William Heron, "Hammer of the Poor, Persecutor of the Religious", Sheriff of Northumberland, 1246–58', *Northern History*, 50 (2013), 9–19.

Cassidy, R., 'Bad Sheriffs, Custodial Sheriffs and Control of the Counties', in Janet Burton, Phillipp Schofield, and Bjorn Weiler (eds.), *TCE*, xv (Woodbridge, 2015), 35–49.

Cassidy, R., 'Fulk Peyforer's Wages', Fine Rolls Project, online.

Church, S., *King John: England, Magna Carta and the Making of a Tyrant* (London, 2015).

Clanchy, M. T., 'Did Henry III Have a Policy', *History*, 53/178 (1968), 203–16.

Clanchy, M. T., *From Memory to Written Record: England 1066–1307* (London, 1979; 3rd edn. 2012).

Clanchy, M. T., *England and its Rulers, 1066–1272* (Glasgow, 1983; 3rd edn. London, 2006).

Colvin, H. M., Brown, R. A., and Taylor, A. J., *The History of the King's Works*, vol. 1 (London, 1963).

Coss, P. R., 'The Langley Cartulary', 2 vols. (University of Birmingham, PhD thesis, 1971).

Coss, P. R., 'Sir Geoffrey de Langley and the Crisis of the Knightly Class in Thirteenth-Century England', *P&P*, 68 (1975), 3–37; repr. in Aston (ed.), *Landlords, Peasants and Politics in Medieval England*, 166–202.

Coss, P. R., 'Literature and Social Terminology: The Vavasour in England', in T. H. Aston et al. (eds.), *Social Relations and Ideas: Essays in Honour of Rodney Hilton* (Cambridge, 1983), 109–50.

Coss, P. R., 'Knighthood and the Early Thirteenth Century County Court', in P. R. Coss and S. D. Lloyd (eds.), *TCE*, ii (Woodbridge, 1988), 45–57.

Coss, P. R., 'Bastard Feudalism Revised', *P&P*, 125 (November 1989), 27–64.

BIBLIOGRAPHY 283

Coss, P. R., *Lordship, Knighthood and Locality: A Study in English Society c.1180–c.1280* (Cambridge, 1991).

Coss, P. R., *The. Knight in Medieval England* (Stroud, 1993).

Coss, P. R., 'Knighthood, Heraldry and Social Exclusion in Edwardian England', in P. Coss and M. Keen (eds.), *Heraldry, Pageantry and Social Display in Medieval England* (Woodbridge, 2002), 39–68.

Coss, P. R., *The Origins of the Gentry* (Cambridge, 2003).

Coss, P. R., *The Foundations of Gentry Life: The Multons of Frampton and their World 1270–1370* (Oxford, 2010).

Coss, P. R., 'How Did Thirteenth-Century Knights counter Royal Authority?', in Janet Burton, Phillipp Schofield, and Björn Weiler (eds.), *TCE*, xv (Woodbridge, 2015), 3–16.

Coss, P. R., 'Retinues, Agents and Garrisons during the Barons' Wars', in A. Jobson (ed.), *Baronial Reform and Revolution in England* (Woodbridge, 2016), 183–98.

Coss, P. R, 'Presentism and the "Myth" of Magna Carta', *P&P*, 234 (February 2017), 227–36.

Coss, P. R., 'Ugolino of the Gherardesca and the "Enigma" of Simon de Montfort', in Andrew M. Spencer and Carl Watkins (eds.), *TCE*, xviii (Woodbridge, 2023), 71–88.

Cox, D. C., *The Battle of Evesham: A New Account* (Evesham, 1988).

Cox, E. L., *The Eagles of Savoy: The House of Savoy in Thirteenth-Century Europe* (Princeton, 1974).

Crook, D., 'The Establishment of the Derbyshire County Court, 1256', *Journal of the Derbyshire Archaeological and Natural History Society*, 103 (1983),

Crouch, D., *William Marshal: Court, Career and Chivalry in the Angevin Empire 1147–1219* (London and New York, 1990).

Crouch, D., *The Image of Aristocracy in Britain 1000–1300* (London and New York, 1992).

Crouch, D., 'From Stenton to McFarlane: Models of Societies of the Twelfth and Thirteenth Centuries', *TRHS* sixth ser. V (1995), 179–200.

Crouch, D., 'Giffard, John, First Lord Giffard (1232–1299)', *ODNB* 22 (2004), 126–7.

Davies, R. G., and Denton, J. H. (eds.), *The English Parliament in the Middle Ages* (Manchester, 1981).

D'Avray, D. L., *Medieval Religious Rationalities: A Weberian Analysis* (Cambridge, 2010).

Dejoux, M., *Les Enquêtes de Saint Louis: Gouverner et Sauvor son Âme* (Paris, 2014).

Denholm-Young, N., 'Feudal Society in the Thirteenth Century: The Knights', in *Collected Papers of N. Denholm-Young* (Cardiff, 1969), 83–94.

Denholm-Young, N., *Seignorial Administration in England* (Oxford, 1937).

Denholm-Young, N., *Richard of Cornwall* (Oxford, 1947).

De Ville, O., 'John Deyville: A Neglected Rebel', *Northern History*, 34 (1988), 17–40.

De Ville, O., 'Deyville [Daiville], Sir John de', *ODNB* 16 (2004), 11–12.

Dixon-Smith, S., 'The Image and Reality of Alms-giving in the Great Halls of Henry III', *Journal of the British Archaeological Association*, 152 (1999), 79–96.

Dodd, G., *Justice and Grace: Private Petitioning and the English Parliament in the Late Middle Ages* (Oxford, 2007).

Dugdale, W., *The Antiquities of Warwickshire*, 2 vols. Revised by W. Thomas (London, 1730).

Eldridge, B. G., 'Religious Commentary on the Barons' Wars' (University of Virginia, PhD thesis, 1983); University Microfilms International, Anna Arbor, Michigan, 1987.

English, B., *The Lords of Holderness, 1086–1260: A Study in Feudal Society* (Hull, 1991).

Eyton, R. W., *Antiquities of Shropshire*, 12 vols. (London, 1825).

Farnham, G. F., and Thompson, A. H., 'The Manor of Noseley', *Leicestershire Archaeological Society*, 12 (1921–2).

Fernandes, M., 'The Role of the Midland Knights in the Period of Reform and Rebellion' (University of London, PhD thesis, September 2000).

Fernandes, M., 'The Midland Knights and the Barons' War: The Warwickshire Evidence', in A. Jobson (ed.), *Baronial Reform and Revolution in England 1258–1267* (Woodbridge, 2016), 167–82.

Finucane, R. C., *Miracles and Pilgrims* (London, 1997).

284 BIBLIOGRAPHY

Forrest, I., *Trustworthy Men: How Inequality and Faith made the Medieval Church* (Princeton and Oxford, 2018).

Gerth, H. H., and Wright Mills, C. (eds.), *From Max Weber: Essays in Sociology* (London, 1947).

Golob, P. E., 'The Ferrers Earls of Derby: A Study of the Honour of Tutbury, 1066–1279' (University of Cambridge, PhD thesis, 1984).

Gransden, A., *Historical Writing in England c.550–c.1307* (London, 1974).

Gregory, A. L., 'Judicial Proceedings under the Dictum of Kenilworth, East Berkshire' (University of Manchester, MA thesis, 1927).

Hammer, Carl I., 'Complaints of the Lesser Commune, Oligarchic Rule and Baronial Reform in Thirteenth-Century Oxford', *Historical Research*, 85 (August 2012), 353–71.

Harding, A., 'Plaints and Bills in the History of the English Law, Mainly in the Period 1250–1350', in D. Jenkin (ed.), *Legal History Studies 1972* (Cardiff, 1975), 65–86.

Harding, A., 'Robert Walerand, Administrator', *ODNB* 56 (2004), 790–2.

Harding, A., 'Walton [Wauton], Simon de', *ODNB* 57 (2004), 215–16.

Harriss, G. L., *King, Parliament, and Public Finance in Medieval England to 1369* (Oxford, 1975).

Harriss, G. L., 'Introduction', in K. B. McFarlane (ed.), *England in the Fifteenth Century: Collected Essays* (London, 1981).

Harvey, K., *Episcopal Appointments in England, c.1214–1344* (Aldershot, 2014).

Harvey, P. D. A., *A Medieval Village: Cuxham 1240–1400* (Oxford, 1965).

Hemmings, L., 'Simon de Montfort and the Ambiguity of Ethnicity in Thirteenth-Century Politics', in A. M. Spencer and C. Watkins (eds.), *TCE*, xvi (Woodbridge, 2017), 137–52.

Hershey, A. H., 'Success or Failure? Hugh Bigod and Judicial Reform during the Baronial Movement of Reform and Rebellion, June 1258–February 1259', in P. R. Coss and S. D. Lloyd (eds.), *TCE*, v (Woodbridge, 1995), 65–97.

Hershey, A. H., 'Baronial Reform, the Justiciar's Court and Commercial Legislation: The Case of Grimsby', in A. Jobson (ed.), *Baronial Reform and Rebellion* (Woodbridge, 2016), 43–55.

Hill, J. W. F., *Medieval Lincoln* (Cambridge, 1948).

Hillen, C., and Wiswall, F., 'The Minority of Henry III in the Context of Europe', in C. Beam (ed.), *The Royal Minorities of Medieval and Early Modern England* (New York, 2008), 17–66.

Holden, B., *Lords of the Central Marches: English Aristocracy and Frontier Society, 1087–1265* (Oxford, 2008).

Holden, K. H., 'Judicial Proceedings in Cambridgeshire under the Dictum of Kenilworth', (University of Manchester, MA thesis, 1929).

Holmes, G. A., *Estates of the Higher Nobility in Fourteenth Century England* (Cambridge, 1958).

Holt, J. C. *The Northerners* (2nd edn., Oxford, 1992).

Hoskin, P., 'Cantilupe's Crusade: Walter de Cantilupe, Bishop of Worcester, and the Baronial Rebellion', *Transactions of the Worcestershire Archaeological Society*, 23 (2012), 91–102.

Howell, M., 'The Resources of Eleanor of Provence as Queen Consort', *EHR*, 102 (1987).

Howell, M., *Eleanor of Provence: Queenship in Thirteenth-Century England* (Oxford, 1998).

Hoyle, M. L., 'Judicial Proceedings under the Dictum of Kenilworth, Buckinghamshire' (University of Manchester, MA thesis 1928).

Hunt, J. R., 'Families at War: Royalists and Montfortians in the West Midlands', *Midland History*, 22 (1997), 1–34.

Hunt, J. R., 'Lordship and the Landscape: A Documentary and Archaeological Study of the Honor of Dudley c.1066–1322', *British Archaeological Reports*, 264 (1997).

Jacob, E. F, 'Studies in the Period of Baronial Reform and Rebellion, 1258–67', *Oxford Studies in Social and Legal History*, vol. 8 (Oxford, 1925).

Jobson, A., *English Government in the Thirteenth Century* (Woodbridge, 2004).

Jobson, A., 'Introduction', in A. Jobson, *English Government in the Thirteenth Century* (Woodbridge, 2004).

Jobson, A., *The First English Revolution: Simon de Montfort, Henry III and the Barons' War* (London, 2012).

Jobson, A., 'Royal Government and Administration in Post-Evesham Government', in D. Crook and L. Wilkinson (eds.), *The Growth of Royal Government under Henry III* (Woodbridge, 2015), 179–95.

BIBLIOGRAPHY   285

Jobson, A., 'The Rebel's Four Dilemmas in the Long Thirteenth Century', in A. M. Spencer and C. Watkins (eds.), *TCE*, xvi (Woodbridge, 2017), 89–111.

Jolliffe, J. E. A., *Angevin Kingship* (London, 1955).

Julian-Jones, Melissa, 'Family Strategy or Personal Principles? The Corbets in the Reign of Henry III', in Janet Burton, Phillipp Schofield, and Bjorn Weiler (eds.), *TCE*, xv (Woodbridge, 2015), 69–79.

Julian-Jones, Melissa, 'The Land of the Raven and the Wolf: Family Power and Strategy in the Welsh March c.1199–1300—The Corbets and the Cantilupes' (Cardiff University PhD. Thesis, 2015).

Kaeuper, R. W., 'Law and Order in Fourteenth-Century England: The Evidence of Special Commissions of Oyer and Terminer', *Speculum*, 54 (1979), 734–84.

Keats-Rohan, K. S. B., Christie, N., and Roffe, D., 'Wallingford: The Castle and the Town in Context', *British Archaeological Reports*, 21 (2015).

Keene, Derek, 'London from the post-Roman period to 1300', in D. M. Palliser (ed.), *The Cambridge Urban History of Britain, Volume I, 600–1540* (Cambridge, 2000), 187–216.

King, A., and Spencer, A. M. (eds.), *Edward I: New Interpretations* (York, 2020).

King, Edmund, *Peterborough Abbey 1086–1310: A Study in the Land Market* (Cambridge, 1973).

Kjær, Lars, 'Matthew Paris and the Royal Christmas: Ritualised Communication in Text and Practice', in Janet Burton, Phillipp Schofield, and Björn Weiler (eds.), *TCE*, xi (Woodbridge, 2013), 141–54.

Knowles, C. H., 'The Disinherited 1265–1280: A Political and Social Study of the Supporters of Simon de Montfort after the Barons' War' (University of Wales, PhD thesis, 1959).

Knowles, C. H., *Simon de Montfort*, Historical Association Pamphlet (London, 1965).

Knowles, C. H., 'The Resettlement of England after the Barons' War, 1264–7', *TRHS*, 32 (1982), 25–41.

Knowles, C. H., 'Provision for the Families of the Montfortians Disinherited after the Battle of Evesham', in P. R. Coss and S. D. Lloyd (eds.), *TCE*, i (Woodbridge, 1986), 124–7.

Koziol, G., 'England, France and the Problem of Sacrality in Twelfth-Century Ritual', in T. N. Bisson (ed.), *Cultures of Power, Lordship, Status and Process in Twelfth-Century Europe* (Philadelphia, 1995), 124–48.

Labarge, Margaret Wade, *Simon de Montfort* (London, 1962).

de Laborderie, O., Maddicott, J. R., and Carpenter, D. A., 'The Last Hours of Simon de Montfort: A New Account', *EHR*, 115/461 (April 2000), 378–412.

Lapsley, G., 'Buzones', *EHR*, 47 (1932), 178–93, 546–67.

Lawrence, C. H., 'The University of Oxford and the Chronicle of the Barons' Wars', *EHR*, 95/374 (1980), 99–113.

Lieberman, M., *The Medieval March of Wales: The Creation and Perception of a Frontier, 1066–1283* (Cambridge, 2010).

Liu, H., 'John Mansel, Councillor of Henry III: His Life and Career' (University of London PhD thesis, 2004).

Liu, H., 'Matthew Paris and John Mansel', in Björn Weiler, Janet Burton, Phillipp Schofield, and Karten Stöber (eds.), *TCE*, xi (Woodbridge, 2007), 159–73.

Lloyd, S. D., 'The Lord Edward's Crusade, 1270–2: Its Setting and Significance', in J. Gillingham and J. C. Holt (eds.), *War and Government in the Middle Ages: Essays in Honour of J. O. Prestwich* (Cambridge, 1984), 120–33.

Lobel, M. D., *The Borough of Bury St Edmunds* (Oxford, 1935).

Lunn, J., 'Judicial Proceedings under the Dictum of Kenilworth, Buckinghamshire' (University of Manchester, MA thesis 1928).

Lunt, W. E., 'Financial Relations of the Papacy with England' (University of Cambridge, MA thesis, 1939).

Mackenzie, H., 'The Anti-Foreign Movement in England, 1231–1232', in C. H. Taylor and J. L. La Monte (eds.), *Anniversary Essays in Mediaeval History by Students of Charles Homer Haskins* (Boston, 1929), 183–203.

Maddicott, J. R., 'The County Community and the Making of Public Opinion in Fourteenth Century England', *TRHS* 5th ser., 28 (1978), 27–43.

286 BIBLIOGRAPHY

Maddicott, J. R., 'Law and Lordship: Royal Justices as Retainers in Thirteenth- and Fourteenth-Century England', *P&P* supplement no. 4 (1978).

Maddicott, J. R., 'Parliament and the Constituencies, 1272-1377', in R. G. Davies and J. Denton (eds.), *The English Parliament in the Middle Ages* (Manchester, 1981), 61-87.

Maddicott, J. R., 'Magna Carta and the Local Community 1215-1259', *P&P*, 102 (February 1984), 25-65.

Maddicott, J. R., 'Edward I and the Lessons of Baronial Reform: Local Government, 1258-80', in P. R. Coss and S. D. Lloyd (eds.), *TCE*, i (Woodbridge, 1986), 1-30.

Maddicott, J. R., 'Follower, Leader, Pilgrim: Robert de Vere, Earl of Oxford at the Shrine of Simon de Montfort, 1273', *EHR*, 109 (1994), 641-53.

Maddicott, J. R., *Simon de Montfort* (Cambridge, 1994).

Maddicott, J. R., *The Origins of the English Parliament 924-1327* (Oxford, 2010).

Mahoney, J., 'Path Dependence in Historical Sociology', *Theory and Society*, 29/4 (2000), 507-48.

Maitland, F. W., *The History of English Law*, introduced by S. F. C. Milsom, 2 vols. (Cambridge, 1968).

Martin, G. H., 'Merton, Walter of', *ODNB* 37 (2004), 931-3.

Masschaele, James, *Jury, State and Society in Medieval England* (New York, 2008).

Matthew, C., and Harrison, B. (eds.), *Oxford Dictionary of National Biography*, 60 vols. (Oxford, 2004).

McFarlane, K. B., 'Had Edward I a "Policy" towards the Earls?', *History*, 50 (1965), 145-59; repr. in McFarlane, *The Nobility of Later Medieval England*, 248-67.

McFarlane, K. B., *The Nobility of Later Medieval England* (Oxford, 1973).

McFarlane, K. B., 'Bastard Feudalism', in G. L. Harriss (ed.), *England in the Fifteenth Century: Collected Essays* (London, 1981), 32. Reprinted from *BIHR*, 20 (1945), 161-80.

Mileson, S. A., *Parks in Medieval England* (Oxford, 2009).

Miller, E., 'Rulers of Thirteenth Century Towns: The Cases of York and Newcastle upon Tyne', in P. R. Coss and S. D. Lloyd (eds.), *TCE*, i (Woodbridge, 1986), 128-41.

Mills, M. H., 'Experiments in Exchequer Procedures (1200-1232)', *TRHS*, 4th ser. vii (1925).

Mills, M. H., 'The Reforms of the Exchequer (1232-42)', *TRHS*, 4th ser., x (1927), 111-13.

Moore, T. K., 'Government and Locality in Essex in the Reign of Henry III' (University of Cambridge, PhD thesis, 2006).

Moore, T. K., 'The Thorrington Dispute: A Case Study of Henry III's Interference with Judicial Process', Fine of the Month (July 2009), Fine Roll Project, online.

Moore, T. K., 'The Fine Rolls as Evidence of Royal Justice during the Reign of Henry III', in D. Crook and L. Wilkinson (eds.), *The Growth of Royal Government under Henry III* (Woodbridge, 2015).

Morris, J., 'The Provosts and Bailiffs of Shrewsbury', *Transactions of the Shropshire Archaeological Society*, 3rd ser. I (1901).

Morris, M., *The Bigod Earls of Norfolk in the Thirteenth Century* (Woodbridge, 2005).

Morris, M., *A Great and Terrible King: Edward I and the Forging of Britain* (London, 2008).

Morris, M., *King John: Treachery, Tyranny and the Road to Magna Carta* (London, 2015).

Mullan, J. D., 'Landed Society and Locality in Gloucestershire, c.1240-80' (Cardiff University, PhD thesis, 1999).

Musson, A., *Medieval Law in Context: The Growth of Legal Consciousness from Magna Carta to the Peasants' Revolt* (Manchester, 2001).

Naughton, K. S., *The Gentry of Bedfordshire in the Thirteenth and Fourteenth Centuries* (Leicester, 1976).

Neal, K. B., *The Letters of Edward I: Political Communication in the Thirteenth Century* (Woodbridge, 2021).

Newman, J. E., 'Greater and Lesser Landowners and Parochial Patronage: Yorkshire in the Thirteenth Century', *EHR*, 92 (1977), 280-308.

Oakes, Fergus, 'The Barons' War in the North of England, 1264-5', in A. Jobson (ed.), *Baronial Reform and Revolution 1258-1267* (Woodbridge, 2016), 199-217.

Parsons, J. C., *Eleanor of Castile: Queen and Society in Thirteenth-Century England* (New York, 1995).

BIBLIOGRAPHY   287

Parsons, T. (ed.), *Theory of Social Organisation* (New York, 1947), part one of Max Weber, *Wirtschaft und Gesellschaft,* trans. R. A. Henderson.

Platt, C., *Medieval Southampton* (London and Boston, 1973).

Prestwich, M., *English Politics in the Thirteenth Century* (London, 1990).

Polden, A., 'A Crisis of the Knightly Class? Inheritance and Office among the Gentry of Thirteenth-Century Buckinghamshire', in P. Fleming, A. Gross, and J. R. Lander, (eds.), *Regionalism and Revision: The Crown and its Provinces in England 1250–1650* (London, 1998), 30–57.

Polden, A., 'The Social Networks of the Buckinghamshire Gentry in the Thirteenth Century', *JMH*, 32 (2006), 371–94.

Potts, John, *A History of Charisma* (Basingstoke, 2009).

Powicke, F. M., *King Henry III and the Lord Edward*, 2 vols. (Oxford, 1947).

Powicke, F. M., *The Thirteenth Century, 1216–1307* (Oxford, 1953).

Prestwich, M., *Edward I* (London, 1988).

Prestwich, M., *English Politics in the Thirteenth Century* (London, 1990).

Prestwich, M., 'Royal Patronage under Edward I', in P. R. Coss and S. D. Lloyd (eds.), *TCE*, i (Woodbridge, 1986), 41–52.

Raban, S., *Mortmain Legislation and the English Church, 1279–1500* (Cambridge, 1982).

Reuter, T., 'Velle Sibi Fier in forma hac. Symbolisches Handeln im Beckestreit', in G. Althoff (ed.), *Formen und Funktionen öffentlicher Kommunikation im Mittelalter, Vortäge und Forschungen* 51 (Stuttgart, 2001), 201–25.

Reynolds, Susan, *An Introduction to the History of English Medieval Towns* (Oxford, 1977).

Reynolds, Susan, *Kingdoms and Communities in Western Europe 900–1300* (Oxford, 1984 and 1997).

Richardson, H. G., and Sayles, G. O., 'The Provisions of Oxford: A Forgotten Document and Some Comments', *Bulletin of the John Rylands Library*, 17 (1933), 291–321.

Ridgard, John (ed.), *Medieval Framlingham*, Suffolk Record Society (Woodbridge, 1985).

Ridgeway, H. W., 'The Politics of the English Royal Court, 1247–65, with Special Reference to the Role of Aliens' (University of Oxford, D Phil. thesis, 1983).

Ridgeway, H. W., 'The Lord Edward and the Provisions of Oxford (1258): A Study in Faction', in P. R. Coss and S. D. Lloyd (eds.), *TCE*, i (Woodbridge, 1986), 89–99.

Ridgeway, H. W., 'King Henry III and the "Aliens" 1236–72', in P. R. Coss and S. D. Lloyd (eds.), *TCE*, ii (Woodbridge, 1988), 81–92.

Ridgeway, H. W., 'King Henry III's Grievances against the Council in 1261: A New Version and a Letter Describing Political Events', *Historical Research*, 6/145 (1988), 227–42.

Ridgeway, H. W., 'Foreign Favourites and Henry III's Problems of Patronage, 1247–1258', *EHR*, 104 (1989), 590–610.

Ridgeway, H. W., 'William de Valence and his *Familiares*, 1247–72', *Historical Research*, 45 (October 1992), 239–57.

Ridgeway, H. W., 'The Ecclesiastical Career of Aymer de Lusignan, Bishop Elect of Winchester, 1250–1260', in J. Blair and B. J. Golding (eds.), *The Cloister and the World: Essays in Medieval History in Honour of Barbara Harvey* (Oxford, 1996), 148–77.

Ridgeway, H. W., 'Mid Thirteenth-Century Reformers and the Localities: The Sheriffs of the Baronial Regime', in P. Fleming et al. (eds.), *Regionalism and Revision: The Crown and its Provinces in England 1250–1650* (Cambridge, 1998), 59–86.

Roberts, E., 'The Judicial Proceedings under the Dictum of Kenilworth, West Berkshire' (University of Manchester, MA thesis, 1927).

Roderick, A., J., '"The Four Cantreds": A Study in Administration', *Bulletin of the Board of Celtic Studies*, 10 (1939–41), 246–56.

Roth, G., and Wittich, C. (eds.), *Economy and Society: An Outline of Interpretative Sociology* (New York, 1968), of Max Weber, *Wirtschaft und Gesellschaft,* trans. R. A. Henderson.

Russell, J. C., 'The Canonization of Opposition to the King in Angevin England', in Charles H. Taylor and John L. La Monte (eds.), *Haskins Anniversary* (New York, 1929), 280–98.

Sabathapy, J., *Officers and Accountability in Medieval England 1170–1300* (Oxford, 2014).

Sanders, I. J., *English Baronies: A Study of Their Origin and Descent, 1086–1327* (Oxford, 1960).

288 BIBLIOGRAPHY

Saul, N., 'A "Rising" Lord and a "Declining" Esquire: Sir Thomas de Berkeley III and Geoffrey Gascylin of Sheldon', *EHR*, 61 (1988), 345–56.

Searle, Eleanor, *Lordship and Community: Battle Abbey and its Banlieu 1066–1538* (Toronto, 1974).

Sherwood, J., and Pevsner, N., *The Buildings of Oxfordshire* (London, 1974).

Simpkin, David, *The English Aristocracy at War: From the Welsh Wars of Edward I to the Battle of Bannockburn* (Woodbridge, 2008).

Simpson, Grant G., 'The *Familia* of Roger de Quincy, Earl of Winchester and Constable of Scotland', in K. Stringer (ed.), *Essays on the Nobility of Medieval Scotland* (Edinburgh, 1985).

Smalley, Beryl, *The Becket Conflict and the Schools: A Study of Intellectuals in Politics* (Oxford, 1973).

Snowden, David, '1265: The Murder of Evesham', *The Lion*, Simon de Montfort Society (2020).

Sohm, R., *Outlines of Church History*, trans. M. Sinclair (London, 2013; first pub. 1895).

Spencer, A. M., *Nobility and Kingship in Medieval England: The Earls and Edward I 1272–1307* (Cambridge, 2014).

Spencer, A. M., 'Dealing with Inadequate Kingship: Uncertain Reponses from Magna Carta to Deposition', in A. M. Spencer and C. Watkins (eds.), *TCE*, xvi (Woodbridge, 2017), 71–87.

Stacey, R. C., 'Agricultural Investment and the Management of the Royal Demesne Manors, 1236–1240', *Journal of Economic History*, 46 (1986), 919–34.

Stacey, R. C., *Politics, Policy and Finance under Henry III, 1216–45* (Oxford, 1987).

Stacey, R. C., '"1240–60": A Watershed in Anglo-Jewish relations?', *Historical Research*, 61 (1988), 135–50.

Stacey, R. C., 'Parliamentary Negotiation and the Expulsion of the Jews from England', in M. Prestwich, R. H. Britnell, and R. Frame (eds.,), *TCE*, vi (Woodbridge, 1997), 77–101.

Stacey, R. C., 'Lexinton [Laxton], John of', *ODNB* 33 (2004), 682–3.

Stacey, R. C., 'Mansel, John', *ODNB* 36 (2004), 350–3.

Stacey, R. F., 'Passelewe, Robert', *ODNB* 42 (2004), 980–1.

Staniland, K., 'The Nuptuals of Alexander III and Margaret Plantagenet', *Nottingham Medieval Studies*, 30 (1996), 20–45.

Stewart-Parker, William John, 'The Bassets of High Wycombe: Politics, Lordship, Locality and Culture in the Thirteenth Century' (University of London, PhD thesis, 2015).

Stewart, S. M., 'What Happened at Shere?', *Southern History*, 22 (2000), 1–10.

Stewart, S. M., 'The Eyre *de terris datis*, 1267–72', in M. Prestwich, R. Britnell, and R. Frame (eds.), *TCE*, x (Woodbridge, 2005), 69–79.

Stewart, S. M, 'Was There a Hundredal Community?', in S. M. Stewart (ed.), *The 1263 Surrey Eyre*, Surrey Record Society, vol. 40 (2006), cxxxiii–cxlv.

Stewart, S. M. (ed.), *The 1263 Surrey Eyre*, Surrey Record Society, vol. 40 (2006).

Stocks, K. J., 'Manorial Courts in England in the Early Thirteenth Century', in M. Prestwich, R. Britnell, and R. Frame (eds.), *TCE*, viii (Woodbridge, 2001), 135–42.

Stone, I., 'The Rebel Barons of 1264 and the Commune of London: An Oath of Mutual Aid', *EHR*, 129 (2014), 1–18.

Storey, R. L., 'The First Convocation, 1257?', in P. R. Coss and S. D. Lloyd (eds.), *TCE*, iii (Woodbridge, 1991), 151–9.

Strickland, M., *Henry the Young King* (New Haven and London, 2016).

Stringer, K. J., *Earl David of Huntingdon, 1152–1219: A Study in Anglo-Scottish History* (Edinburgh, 1985).

Stubbs, W., *The Constitutional History of England*, vol. 2 (Oxford, 1880).

Studd, J. R., 'A Catalogue of the Acts of the Lord Edward, 1254–1272' (University of Leeds, PhD thesis, 1971).

Studd, J. R., 'The Lord Edward and Henry III', *BIHR*, 50/121 (1977), 4–19.

Studd, J. R., 'The Lord Edward's Lordship of Chester, 1254–72', *Transactions of the Historic Society of Lancashire and Cheshire*, 127 (1979), 1–25.

Sutherland, Donald W., *Quo Warranto Proceedings in the Reign of Edward I* (Oxford, 1963).

Templeman, G., 'The Sheriffs of Warwickshire in the Thirteenth Century', *Dugdale Society Occasional Papers* no. 7 (Oxford, 1948).

BIBLIOGRAPHY   289

Thomas, H. M., *Vassals, Heiresses, Crusaders and Thugs: The Gentry of Angevin Yorkshire, 1154–1216* (Philadelphia, 1993).

Thomas, H. M., *The English and the Normans: Ethnic Hostility, Assimilation and Identity 1066–c.1220* (Oxford, 2003).

Tilly, C., 'The Honour of Wallingford 1066–1300' (University of London, PhD thesis, 2011).

Tilly, C., 'Magna Carta and the Honour of Wallingford', *Historical Research*, 89 (August 2016), 454–69.

Treharne, R. F., *The Baronial Plan of Reform, 1258–63* (Manchester, 1932).

Treharne, R. F., 'The Knights in the Period of Reform and Rebellion, 1258–67: A Critical Phase in the Rise of a New Social Class', *BIHR*, 21 (1946–8), 1–12.

Treharne, R. F., 'The Battle of Northampton', *Northamptonshire Past and Present*, 2/2 (1995), repr. in Fryde (ed.), *Simon de Montfort and Baronial Reform: Thirteenth Century Essays*.

Treharne, R. F., 'The Personal Rule of Simon de Montfort in the Period of Reform and Rebellion 1258–65', Raleigh Lecture 1954, appended to *The Baronial Plan of Reform*, 412–39.

Trenholme, N. M., *The English Monastic Boroughs*, University of Missouri Studies (Columbia, 1927).

Turner, R. V., *The English Justiciary in the Age of Glanvill and Bracton, c.1176–1239* (Cambridge, 1985).

Turner, T. H. (ed.), *Manners and Household Expenses in the Thirteenth and Fifteenth Centuries* (Roxburghe Club, 1841).

Valente, C., 'Simon de Montfort, Earl of Leicester, and the Utility of Sanctity in Thirteenth-Century England', *Journal of Medieval History*, 21 (1995), 27–49.

Valente, C., *The Theory and Practice of Revolt in Medieval England* (Aldershot, 2003).

Vauchez, A., *Sainthood in the Later Middle Ages* (Cambridge, 1997).

Vaughan, R., *Matthew Paris* (Cambridge, 1958).

Veach, Colin, *Lordship in Four Realms: The Lacy Family 1166–1241* (Manchester, 2014).

Veale, Elspeth, 'The "Great Twelve": Mystery and Fraternity in Thirteenth-Century London', *Historical Research*, 64 (October 1991), 237–63.

Victoria History of the Counties of England (1901–): Berkshire vols. iii and iv; Buckinghamshire vol. iii; Cambridgeshire vols. iii, v, and ix; Essex vol. viii; Gloucestershire vol. vii; Hampshire vol. v; Hertfordshire vols. ii and iii; Huntingdonshire vols. ii and iii; Oxfordshire vol. v; Middlesex vol. iii; Northamptonshire vol. iii; Rutland vols. i and ii; Somerset vol. iii; Staffordshire vol. iv; Surrey vols. iii and iv; Wiltshire vols. vii, viii, and ix; Worcestershire vols. iii, and iv.

Vincent, N., *Peter des Roches: An Alien in English Politics, 1205–1238* (Cambridge, 1996).

Vincent, N., *The Holy Blood: King Henry III and the Westminster Blood Relic* (Cambridge, 2001.

Vincent, N., 'The Pilgrimages of the Angevin kings of England, 1154–1272', in C. Morris and P. Roberts (eds.), *Pilgrimage: The English Experience from Becket to Bunyan*, (Cambridge, 2002), 31–45.

Wait, H. A., 'The Household and Resources of the Lord Edward, 1239–1272' (University of Oxford, DPhil thesis, 1988).

Walker, R. F., 'The Anglo–Welsh Wars, 1216–67' (University of Oxford, DPhil thesis, 1954).

Ward, E. J., *Royal Childhood and Child Kingship* (Cambridge, 2022).

Ward, E. J., '"A Star Lit by God": Boy Kings, Childish Innocence, and English Exceptionalism during Henry III's Minority, c.1216–c.1227', in Andrew M. Spencer and Carl Watkins (eds.), *TCE*, xviii (Woodbridge, 2023), 125–46.

Watson, G. E., 'The Families of Lacy, Geneva, Joinville and La Marche', *The Geneaologist* new series, 21 (1904).

Waugh, S. L. 'Reluctant Knights and Jurors: Respites, Exemptions, and Public Obligations in the Reign of Henry III', *Speculum* (October 1983), 937–86.

Waugh, S. L. 'The Fiscal Uses of Royal Wardship in the Reign of Edward I', in P. R. Coss and S. D. Lloyd (eds.), *TCE*, i (Woodbridge, 1986), 53–60.

Waugh, S. L., 'Tenure to Contract: Lordship and Clientage in Thirteenth-Century England', *EHR*, 101 (1986), 811–39.

Waugh, S. L., *The Lordship of England: Royal Wardships and Marriages in English Society and Politics 1217–1327* (Princeton, 1988).

290 BIBLIOGRAPHY

Weiler, B., 'Symbolism and Politics in the Reign of Henry III', in M. Prestwich, R. Britnell, and R. Frame (eds.), *TCE*, ix (Woodbridge, 2003), 15–41.

Weiler, B., *Henry III of England and the Staufen Empire, 1216–1272* (Woodbridge, 2006).

Weiler, B., 'Knighting, Homage, and the Meaning of Ritual: The Kings of England and Their Neighbours in the Thirteenth Century', *Viator*, 37 (2006), 275–99.

Weiler, B., 'Matthew Paris and the Writing of History', *JMH*, 35 (2009), 254–78.

Weiler, B., and Maclean, S. (eds.), *Representations of Power in Medieval Germany, 800–1500* (Turnhout, 2006).

White, A. B., *Self-Government at the King's Command* (Minneapolis, 1933; repr. Westport, CT, 1974).

Wild, B., 'A Gift Inventory from the Reign of Henry III', *EHR*, 125 (2010), 529–69.

Wild, B., 'Secrecy, Splendour and Statecraft: The Jewel Accounts of King Henry III of England, 1216–72', *Historical Research*, 83 (2010), 409–30.

Wilkinson, L. J., *Eleanor de Montfort: A Rebel Countess in Medieval England* (London, 2012).

Williams, D., 'Simon de Montfort and his Adherents', in W. M. Ormrod (ed.), *England in the Thirteenth Century: Proceedings of the 1984 Harlaxton Symposium* (Grantham, 1985).

Williams, Gwyn A., *Medieval London: From Commune to Capital* (London, 1963).

Wrottesley, G., 'A History of the Bagot Family', *William Salt Archaeological Society*, new series i (1908), 128–37.

Yarrow, Simon, 'Masculinity as a World Historical Category of Analysis', in John H. Arnold and Sean Brady (eds.), *What is Masculinity? Historical Dynamics from Antiquity to the Contemporary World* (London and New York, 2011), 114–38.

Index

Since the index has been created to work across multiple formats, indexed terms for which a page range is given (e.g., 52–53, 66–70, etc.) may occasionally appear only on some, but not all of the pages within the range.

abbeys 60 n.105, 225–7
  Abingdon 106, 177–8
  Battle 107–8
  Buildwas 57
  Burton 89 n.18
  Bury St Edmunds 212
  Chertsey 177–8
  Deerhurst 102 n.100
  Evesham 96 n.57
  Grestein 186–7
  Haughmond 57, 97–9
  Missenden 61, 186–7
  Notley 182–3, 186–7
  Osney 60–1, 108, 178–9
  Peterborough 144
  Polesworth 107 n.137
  Ramsey 106, 178–9
  Reading 60 n.105, 174, 178–9
  Shrewsbury 57, 97–100, 98 n.76
  St Albans 60–1, 106–7, 186–7
  St Augustine 103, 103 n.107, 106
  Tewkesbury 70, 96 n.57
  Thame 186–7
  Waverley 223–5
  Westminster 27–8, 32–3, 81–2, 102 n.100, 209–11, 264–5
  Wigmore 57
  Woburn 60 n.105, 184, 187–8
  see also priories
abbots 52–3, 56–7, 60–1, 70, 81–2, 96 n.57, 103 n.107, 104–7, 117–18, 144, 174, 177–9, 184–7, 208, 212–14, 222–3, 225 n.184, 269–70, *see also* priors
Abbots Bromley 107
Aberconway 251
Abingdon Abbey 106, 177–8
Acle, Reginald de 191
Acton Scott 97
Addington 62, 149
administration 18, 22–3, 53–4, 85, 87, 94, 97–8, 113, 191–2, 241–2, 242 n.61, 253–4, 262–3, 272–3
  documents 90–1
  mechanism 216–17
  positions 249–50

  procedure 238–9
  processes 270
  reforms 28 n.71, 131, 157, 231–3
  resolutions 89
  roles 126, 260–1
  separation 57
  system 14, 21–2, 113–14, 236
administrators 21–2, 48–50, 70–1, 77, 83, 154–5, 210, 242, 249–50, 255
Adstock 180–1
Advocatus 33–5
advowsons 51–3, 62–3, 70–1, 106–7, 186–7
affinity 13–14, 71–2, 74–7, 78 n.57, 79–80, 89–90, 100, 117–19, 127–56, 199, 227, 242, 260–2
agency 10–12, 101, 241–2, 273
agents 18, 100, 145, 147–8, 155–7, 166, 173, 180–4, 191, 221, 238–9, 261–2
Aigueblanche, Peter of 40–1, 43–4, 128–9, 131, 158–9, 207–8
Aiguillon, Robert de 77–8
Albermarle, earl of 137 n.54
Albrighton 170–1
Alceton 97
aldermen 194–5, 208–14
Aldingham 119–20
Aldrefeld, William de 151 n.131
Alencon, Herbert de 74–5
Alexander III, King 34
Alexander the Parker 178
Algar, John 75–6
alienation 18 n.12, 44–5, 81–4, 205, 253–6, 259–60, 272 n.1
aliens 8, 27–8, 83–4, 133–4, 162–3, 186–7, 194–6, 202–3, 217 n.137, 219–22
  clergy 220
  clerics 221
  factions 127–8, 130
  garrison 175–6
  kinsmen 2
  knights 180–1
  landholders 219
  landowners 218–19
  merchants 270
  see also anti-alienism, foreigners, xenophobia

292   INDEX

Aller (Aure, Eure), John de 101 n.96, 120–1
Allesley 141–2
alliances 16, 42, 50, 136–8, 164–5, 203–4, 207,
    209–11, 216–17
Allington 170–1
Almain, Henry of 133–8, 160–1, 180–1, 189,
    222–3, 246–7, 249–50
Alnwick 156 n.151
Alphonse X of Castile 134–5
Alstone 104 n.115
Altschul, Michael 66 n.1, 66–70, 67 n.4, 81 n.72,
    131–2, 146–7
Alveley 56–7
Alvington 139
Alyn, William 179–80
Ambler, Sophie 39, 43 n.28, 94, 188–9, 197–201,
    202 n.40, 206–8, 221–3
Amersham 186
Amiens 32, 160–1, 207–8, 210–11, 218–19, 223
Amundevilles 141–2
Andeville, Alexander de 104–6
Andeville, Humphrey de 104–5
Andeville, Richard de 104–5
Anesley, Peter de 195
Anesy, Peter de 180
Angevin
    administrative system 21–2, 113–14
    England 21–2, 60–1, 216–17
    knights 126
    legacy 13, 15–37
    norm 18
    polity 241
    reforms 9, 258–9
    rulers 230–1
    system 24, 94–5, 109, 239–42
Angevin, William 182
Anglo-French noblemen 198
Anglo-Irish liberty 66–7
Anglo-Norman England 78–9
Anglo-Norman language 225–7
Anglo-Welsh relations 26–7
annalists 20, 93 n.38, 138, 206–7, 231 n.8, see also
    chroniclers
annals 89 n.18, 203–4, 223–5, see also chronicles
anti-alienism 8, 217–20, 274, see also aliens,
    foreigners, xenophobia
appeasement 13, 38–65, 256–7
Appleby 104 n.110, 270
Appleby, James de 185–6
Appleford, William de 151 n.129
archbishops 19–20, 41
    Boniface of Savoy 40–1, 43–4, 130–1, 204–8
    Canterbury 16, 25–6, 40–1, 48–9, 51–2,
        67, 203–4

Rouen 200–1
York 35–6, 206–8
Ardern, John de 83
Ardern, Wakelin de 83
Ardington 173
aristocracy/aristocrats 10–11, 19–20, 33–4, 41,
    72–3, 142–3, 154–6, 195, 198–9, 203–4,
    220–1, 248–50
    affinities 118–19
    associations 95–6
    behaviour 164–5
    elite 270–1
    expectations 21
    factions 127–8
    hauteur 201–2
    lifestyle 109
    mores 45, 161–2
    nature of the constitution 2
    opinion 221
    opposition 8–9
    participation 250 n.31
    pastimes 252
    perception 161–2
    personalities 165
    practice 197–8
    ranks 84, 216–17
    rebellion/revolt 156, 229, 242–3
    resentment 219
    service 172–3
    society 13–14, 68–9, 78–9, 127–8, 164–5,
        260–1, 263, 272
    values 13–14, 227–8
    see also nobility/nobles
Ashampstead 180
Ashbury 171–2
Ashby, David de 154, 191
Ashby, Isabel de 154
Ashby, Stephen de 154
Askleton (Aslacton), Simon de 112 n.162, 120–1
Aspall, Geoffrey de 260–1
assizes 23–4, 49, 51–2, 52 n.68, 69, 82–3, 86,
    98–100, 123 n.218
    ale 59, 62–4, 108
    arms 3
    bread 62–4, 108
    grand assizes 24, 83–4, 94–5, 97–9, 102–5, 115,
        144, 234, 237–40
    petty assizes 239–41
    see also chancery, courts, eyres, judges, juries
assize rolls 123–4, 146, 148 n.118, 153–4,
    194 n.235
Asti 130 n.16
Astley 56–7
Astley, Thomas de 117, 139–41

INDEX   293

Aston 147 n.113
Aston, Adam de 101
Aston, John de 102 n.102
Aston, Richard de 147 n.113
attorneys 23, 70, 140, 153, 187
    lawyers 7, 9, 81
Atwell, Henry 176
Atwell, William 175–6
Audley, James de 150 n.128
Audley, Ralph de 150 n.128
Aumale, countess of 146–7, 225
Aumale, earl of 80–1, 109–11
Austen 103 n.107
Aveley 122 n.214
Aylesbury 60–1, 64, 182, 185–6

bachelors 91–3, 102–3, 119–20, 145–7
bachelry of England (communitas bacheleriae
    Angliae) 91–4, 137–8, 231 n.8
Badingham 75 n.41
Badking, Andrew 167–8
Badlesmere, Bartholomew de 103 n.107
Badlesmere, Guncelin de 151
Bagingden, Richard de 110 n.155, 111 n.158,
    124–5, 125 n.228
Bagot, Harvey 104 n.114, 107 n.140
Bagot, Harvey II 104 n.114
Bagot, Harvey III 104 n.114
Bagot, Nicholas 104 n.114
Bagot, Robert IV 104 n.114
Bagot, William 103–4, 107–8, 123–4,
    125 n.226
Bagot, William III 103–4, 107
Bagpuize, John 167–8
Bagworth 140–1
bailiffs 36, 56–7, 63–4, 70, 73–4, 87–92, 98–9,
    104–5, 108, 136–8, 140 n.69, 145–8, 148 n.119,
    150–2, 163, 167–8, 173, 176–8, 180, 182–6,
    194–5, 212, 215–16, 231–3, 239–40, 242,
    255–6, 265–6
bailiwicks 69–70, 230–1
Baker, Darren 196, 198
Balliol, Guy de 223–5
Balliol, John 136 n.50
Balun, John de 163–4
Banaster, Alice 179–80
Banaster, Richard 146–7, 176, 179–80
Banaster, Thomas 179–80
Banaster, William 146–7, 176, 179–80
Banham 149, 151–2
Bardfield 67
Barentine, Drew de 176–7
Barham Downs 189–90, 207–8, 222–3
Barnevill, Robert de 35

baronage/barony 1–3, 7, 16, 45, 51–2, 58, 66–7, 69,
    89–94, 97–8, 100–1, 102 n.100, 104 nn.115–116,
    107, 115–18, 140–1, 183–4, 270–1
baronial reform 12–13, 113–14, 125, 166, 195,
    206–7, see also reformers, reform movement
Barons' Wars 54, 103, 124–5, 166, 245
Barron, Caroline M. 209 n.76
Basildon 180, 195
Basinges, Dame Joan de 149
Basing, John de 179–80
Basset, Fulk 206–7
Basset, Gilbert 17–19
Basset, Philip 136–7, 210–11, 246
Basset, Ralph (of Drayton) 142–5, 155–6,
    193 n.229, 195, 215–16, 246, 247 n.20
Basset, Ralph (of Sapcote) 117, 139–41, 144–5,
    155–6, 191, 247 n.20
Basset, Thomas 18–19, 180–1
Basset, William 140–1
Bassingbourne, Humphrey de 144
Bassingbourne, Warin de 136–8, 161–2, 227
bastard feudalism 71–2, 154–5, 261 n.68, 272–3
Bath 207–8
Bath, Henry de 49, 55, 111–12, 131–2
Battle Abbey 107–8
battles
    Bedford 16–17
    Evesham 2–3, 9–10, 13–14, 32, 73–4, 78 n.56,
        107–8, 119–20, 122–3, 141–2, 146–51, 157,
        161–2, 165–6, 168–71, 175–6, 179–80, 183–4,
        188, 188 n.198, 190–7, 207–8, 211–16, 223–7,
        244–8, 250
    Kenilworth 79 n.64, 119–21, 146–7, 158–9,
        185 nn.178, 180, 190, 193–4
    Lewes 73–4, 79 n.64, 117, 119–20, 135–6, 146–7,
        153, 157, 160–1, 164–8, 170, 172–6, 180, 188–9,
        191–2, 200–1, 207–8, 210–14, 221, 222 n.166,
        223, 235, 246
    Northampton 115, 155–7, 160–1
Bauzan, Stephen 49, 135 n.42
Bayonne 16–17
Beauchamp, Guy de 261 n.68
Beauchamp, Ida de 64
Beauchamp, Miles de 187–8
Beauchampton 183–4
Beauchampton, William de 185 n.178
Beauchamp, William de 60 n.104, 64, 109–11,
    171–2, 261
Beaudesert 139–40, 143–4
Beckenham 150–1
Becket, Thomas 20, 199 n.20, 203–4, 206, 223–5
Bedford 16–17, 70, 117, see also battles
Bedfordshire 46–7, 69–70, 95, 102–3, 111 n.158,
    115, 117 n.193, 119–20, 145–6, 149, 186–7, 192

294 INDEX

Beedon 106
Beenham 179–80
Beenham, Richard de 174
Belvoir 73 n.31
Benechose, Michael 185 n.176
Bentley 75 n.42
Bereford, William de 143–4, 262–3
Berkeley, Maurice de 151
Berkeley, William de 175
Berkhampstead 184
Berkshire 40 n.13, 69–70, 105–6, 112 n.162,
 123–4, 146–9, 151, 165–73, 177 n.105, 179–81,
 186–7, 192, 216, 237–8
Berksted, August 207–8
Bernard, Ralf fitz 103 n.107
Bernard, Thomas fitz 60 n.104
Bertram, Roger 156 n.151
Beverley 48, 214
Bezill, Matthias (Matthew) 115–16, 131, 133–4,
 159 n.10, 162–5
Bicester, Robert de 168–9
Bigod, Bartholomew 153
Bigod, Hugh 87, 88 n.12, 95–6, 108–9, 131–3, 210,
 220, 233–4, 236–7
Bigod, Hugh II 71–2, 75 n.40
Bigod, Isabella 73 n.31
Bigod, Roger 36, 50–1, 72–5, 101, 210, 229, 267
Bigod, Roger I 73–4
Bigod, Roger III 66, 71–2, 76–7
Bigod, Roger IV 260–3
Billington 107 n.140
Binfield 178
Binfield, Adam de 178
Binfield, John de 179–80
Birmingham 246
Birmingham, William de 60 n.104, 79–80, 141–3,
 150, 193 n.229, 246
bishops 19–20, 33, 49, 52–3, 128–9, 207,
 219, 258
 Carlisle 35, 207–8
 Chichester 189–90, 207–8
 Coventry 32–3
 Ely 269 n.105
 Exeter 207–8, 269 n.105
 Hereford 57, 131, 134, 159 n.10, 162–3
 Lincoln 48–9, 61, 200–1, 203–5
 London 206–8
 Norwich 48–9, 82–3, 134, 158–9
 Rochester 48–9, 207–8
 Winchester 60 n.105, 63–4, 82–3, 130
 Worcester 50–1, 100 n.85, 115–16, 200–1,
 206–8, 223–5
Bishop's Cannings 171
Blakemore 67–8

Blechgrove 184
Bletchingley 67
Bletchley 185 n.172
Blisworth 144
Blund, Robert 76 n.44, 78 n.56
Blund, William le 117
Blyth 72–3
Boddington 102 nn.100, 101
Bohun, Humphrey de 64, 132–3, 223–5,
 227, 250–1
Bohun, Humphrey de (the younger) 122
Bois, Arnold du 139–40
Boisted, Robert 60 n.104
Bolebec, Gilbert 181–2
Bolebec, Herbert 181–2, 184
Bordeaux 16–17
Bordon, John 185–6
Borham, Hervey de 70–1, 262–3
boroughs 5, 61–3, 67–9, 73–4, 80–1, 139–40,
 164 n.38, 212, 256–7, 263–4
Borre, Richard 185 n.178
Borton 186
Botisham 69
Botley, John de 111–12, 120
Bottisham 62–3
Boulogne 180–1
Boulogne, Eustace of 106
Boulton, Thomas de 191
Bourne 122 n.214
Bow Brickhill 184
Boxted 149
Boxworth, William de 121
Bracebridge 141–2
Bracebridge, John de 141–4
Bracton 6, 31–3, 31 n.88, 81–2, 90–1, 95–6,
 117, 141–2
Bradley 61–2
Bragenham, Thomas de 146
Braibroc, Robert de 61
Brampton 150
Brampton, Brian de 249–50
Brancote 105 n.118
Brand, Paul 22, 29, 84, 84 n.88, 215 n.122,
 229–33, 235–7, 259, 266–9, 269 n.101
Braose, Maud de 190
Braose, William de 137 n.54
Brasted 67
Bratton, Henry de 90–1
Bray 175 n.92, 176–7
Bray, Henry de 269–70
Bréauté, Falkes de 16, 18–19
Bréauté, William de 18–19
Breouse, William de 150
Breton campaign 26–7

INDEX 295

Bretun, John le 146–7, 149
bribes 28–9, 88–9, 239–41, *see also* corruption, extortion
Bricheville, William de 18–19
Bridgehampton 152
Bridgnorth 142–3, 215–16
Brill 61–2, 88, 145 n.97, 186
Brimpsfield 163, 167, 172–3, 253
Briouze, John de 38–9
Brislington 149
Bristol 134–7, 162, 212–14
Brito (le Breton), John 149
Brittany 17
Brittany, John of 133, 252–3
Briwes, Robert de 122–3
Brockley 75–6
Brok, Laurence del 180–1, 184–5
Brokton 61
Broughton 152
Bruce, Robert de 137 n.54
Brundish 75 n.41
Brun, John le 97 n.59, 101–3, 102 n.102, 112 n.162, 124 n.224
Brun, Richard le 102 n.100, 151 n.129
Brus, Bernard de 120–1
Bruton, John de 146–7
Brymton, Adam de 103–4
Brythmere, William de 168–9
Buckingham 114–15
Buckinghamshire 46–7, 49 n.57, 56, 59–60, 63–4, 69–70, 88, 102–3, 108, 111 n.158, 117, 117 n.192, 119–20, 146–51, 153, 166 n.46, 175–6, 178, 180–4, 186, 192, 216, 237–9
Buckland 61, 183–4
Buckland, Philip de 75–6
Bucklesham 75 n.42
Bucknall 97–8, 108
Bucknall, Gilbert de 95–8
Buildwas Abbey 57
Builth 251
Bulcheth, Margery de 173–4
Bullinghope 102 n.100
Bungay 73–4, 76
Burdon, Hugh 102 n.100
Burdon, John 102 n.100
Burdun, Nicholas 101, 102 nn.100, 102
Burg, Walter de 182–3, 185–6
burgesses 5–6, 9–10, 35–6, 194, 212–17, 256–7, 263–4, 269
Burgh, Bertram de 98–9
Burghfield 175
Burgh, Hubert de 6–7, 15–20, 24–5, 42, 134–5, 219–20

Burgh, John de 50–1
Burgh, Richard de 42
Burgh, William de 76 n.44
Burnell, Robert 134–5
Burnel, Philip 175–6
Burnel, Thomas 175–6, 178
Burnham 170–1, 185 n.175
Burt, Caroline 261
Burton Abbey 89 n.18
Burton, Anketil de 185 n.178
Burton annalist/annals 89 n.18, 93 n.38, 231 n.8
Burton, Richard de 169 n.63
Bury St Edmunds 106, 158–9, 212–14
Bury St Edmunds Abbey 212
Bussay, William de 77, 83
Buswarton 97–8
Butler, Joan le 69
Butler, Roger the 76
Butler, William le 69, 102–3, 111–12, 111 n.158, 120–1, 124 n.225
Butterfield, Herbert 10–12

Caldecote 183–4
Callethorp, William 82–3
Cambridge 69, 131–2, 194, 212, 214–15
Cambridgeshire 62–3, 69–70, 97 n.59, 105 n.120, 108, 117, 120–1, 134, 142 n.76, 166 n.46, 188 n.198, 194 n.235, 238–9
Camera, William de 167–8
Cam, Helen 55–6, 92–3
Camoys, Ralph de 144, 155–6
Candlemas parliament 91–2, 234
Canning, Walter de 168, 171
Cannock Forest 142–3
Canterbury 55, 60–1, 103, 151, 158–9, 204–5, *see also* archbishops, Gervase of Canterbury, Peace of Canterbury
Cantilupe, Thomas de 207–8, 222–3
Cantilupe, Walter de 200–1, 207–8, 221
Cantilupe, William de 24, 46–7, 60 n.104
Cantilupe, William II de 47–8
Capel, William 184–5
Capetian dynasty 26–7, 31–2, 33 n.97
Carbonel, Peter 60 n.104, 62
Cardiff 81
Carlisle 212–14, *see also* bishops
Carmarthen 251
Carpenter, Christine 154–5
Carpenter, David 6–9, 12–13, 15–21, 22 nn.33, 38, 23 n.42, 24–5, 26 n.58, 28–31, 33–4, 36, 40–3, 46–7, 49 n.55, 50–1, 52 n.68, 55, 68–9, 79–81, 83, 85, 127, 137 n.52, 137–9, 203 n.46, 214 n.106, 217–20, 263–4, 274

296 INDEX

Cassidy, Richard 29, 120 n.206
castellans 16–18, 28–9, 40–1, 47–8, 85, 136–7,
    172–3, 230–3, *see also* constables
castles 12–13, 28–9, 96 n.55, 115–16, 131, 134–7,
    143–4, 173–80, 193–4, 231–3
  Bedford 16
  Brimpsfield 163
  Bungay 73–4, 76
  Chepstow 71–2
  Clun 57
  Cockermouth 109–11
  Colchester 44–5
  Eardisley 134, 158–9, 162–3
  Farnham 51–2
  Framlingham 73–6
  Gloucester 134, 146, 153, 163–4, 200–1
  Hertford 42, 77
  Holdgate 56–7
  Kenilworth 39–40, 139–41
  Kilpeck 47–8, 134, 158–9
  Launceston 191
  Ludlow 128–9
  Marlborough 174–5
  Montgomery 56–7
  Northampton 144–5
  Norwich 119–20
  Radnor 203 n.45
  Rochester 41 n.18
  Scarborough 123–4
  Sedgwick 159–60
  Sherborne 152
  Stafford 142–3
  Tonbridge 67, 151 n.131
  Wallingford 63–4, 185–6
  Wigmore 190, 203 n.45
  Windsor 146–7, 166, 175–6, 183–6
cathedrals 205
  Hereford 134
  St Paul's 48, 70
  Winchester 32 n.95
  Worcester 251
  see also chapels, churches, religious houses
Caus 56–9, 95–6
Cauz, Walter de 61–2
Caverswall, William de 125 n.227
Caylly, Adam de 101
Caylly, Hugh de 82–3
Caylly, Robert de 101
Cay, William 182 n.144
Cerne, Philip de 124 n.224
Chaddesley Corbett 96 n.57
Chaddleworth 169–70
Chadfield, Walter de 170 n.65
Chalfont St Giles 183–4

Chalgrave, William de 188
Chalton 46–7
Chalvey 61
Chalynton 108 n.143
Chamberlain, John the 149
chamberlains 147–8, 157–8, 266–7
Chamberlain, William the 167–8
Champayne, Nicholas de la 185–6
chancellor 5, 27–8, 48–9, 64–5, 78, 85, 134–5,
    180–3, 222–3, 254, 264–5
chancery 21–2, 32–3, 45, 48–50, 113, 122–3,
    244–5, 267–9, *see also* assizes, courts, eyres,
    judges, juries
chancery rolls 45–6, 120–1, 123, 151 n.129
Chandos, Roger 105–6
Channel Islands 134–5, 253 n.41
chapels 24–5, 39, 46–7, 73 n.30, 129–30, 161, 172,
    180–1, *see also* cathedrals, churches,
    religious houses
charisma 13–14, 198–203, 207–8, 222–3,
    227–8, 274
Charles I, King 7
Charles the Simple 36
Charron, Guichard de 133–4
Charter of Liberties 222–3
Charter of the Forest 4, 16–17, 19–20, 222–3,
    236, 256–7
charters 8–9, 17, 21–2, 27–31, 44–5, 49, 52 n.68,
    59–61, 74–6, 79–83, 97, 101–3, 108, 121–3,
    135–6, 139, 140 n.69, 142–3, 153, 200 n.30,
    206–7, 234, 258, 260–1, *see also*
    Magna Carta
Chatham 150
Chaumbre, Peter de la 185–6
Chaumpeneys, Geoffrey 151 n.129
Chauvent, Peter de 108, 128–9, 249–51
Chediston 75–6
Cheetham, Geoffrey de 111–12, 124 n.224
Chelsfield 103
Chelwood 170–1
Chenduit, Ralph 106–7
Chenduit, Stephen 108, 120–1, 123–4
Chepstow 71–3, 73 n.30
Chertsey Abbey 177–8
Cheshunt 210–11, 269 n.105
Chester 46, 109–11, 136–7, 183–4, 191, 223, 251
Chester, earl of 80–1, 139–42
Chester, earldom of 134–5, 139–42, 250
Chesterfield 124 n.225, 173–4, 193–4
Chetwode 60 n.105
Cheval, Hugh le 147–8, 184
Chieveley 169
Chieveley, Matthew de 174–5
Chieveley, Maude de 178–9

INDEX   297

Chignal Tany 119–20, 122
Childwick 104–5
Childwick, Geoffrey de 104–6
Chilton 182–3, 185
Chipping Lambourn 170–1
Chirbury 58–9
Christmas 20–1, 34–5, 71–2
    courts 20
    feasts/festivities 25–6, 33–5
    parliament 35–6
chroniclers 2–3, 8, 20–1, 25–6, 33–4, 43, 48,
    72–3, 106–7, 158, 173–4, 190, 201 n.35,
    202 n.37, 203 n.47, 212–14, 218–19, 223–7,
    258, *see also* annalists
chronicles 92–3, 106–7, 115 n.173, 158 n.5, 161–3,
    203–4, 208–9, 219, 221–5, 233, *see also* annals
church 11–12, 25–6, 48–9, 70, 84 n.88, 106–7, 182,
    189–90, 199 n.15, 203–8, 221–5, 227–8,
    230–1, 236, 254, 258–9, 265–6
Church Eaton 104 n.116
churches 32–3, 48–9, 52–3, 67–8, 70–1, 73–4,
    106–7, 130, 163, 167–8, 173, 180–2, 186–7,
    220, 225–7, 251, *see also* cathedrals, chapels,
    religious houses
Churchill 146–7
Churchill, John de 146–7, 149
Churchill, Thomas de 146–7
Church, Stephen 10
Cigogné, Engelard de 17–18
Cinque Ports 41 n.18, 158–9, 193–4, 208–9,
    211–12, 214–16, 222–3, 265–6, 270–1
Cirencester 45–6
citizens 145–7, 192, 209–16, 218–19, 270
civil war 1, 8, 13–14, 18–19, 21–2, 98–9, 118–19,
    122–4, 127, 136–7, 142, 146–8, 156–95,
    215–16, 236, 238–40, 248, 255–7, 273
Clanchy, Michael 21–2, 29–33, 31 nn.86, 88, 218
Clare 62–3, 66–70, 103, 131–2, 147–9
Clare, Gilbert de 76, 102–3, 123, 145–8, 153,
    158–60, 164–5, 189–90, 192, 201–3, 207–8,
    222–3, 227, 249–51
Clare, Richard de 42, 60–1, 66–7, 70–1,
    131–2, 135–8
Clare, Thomas de 151, 249–50, 253 n.41
Clarice Mansel 104–5
Claverley 59
Clehonger 102 n.100
clergy/clerics/churchmen 5–6, 32–3, 48–9, 70–1,
    146–7, 179–80, 186–9, 198–201, 203–8, 221,
    236 n.39
clerks 41, 48, 50, 70–1, 75–8, 95–6, 128–30,
    145–6, 161–2, 168–9, 180–1, 205, 254, 257–8,
    260–1, 266–7, 269 n.105
Cliffe 103 n.109

Clifford, Roger de 132–8, 157–61, 163–4, 169–71,
    175–6, 193, 246, 249–50, 252–3
Clifford, Walter de 36, 59
Clifton 184
Clinton, Thomas de 143–4, 193 n.229
Clopton 104–5
Clun 56–9, 98
Cobham, John de 111–12, 124 n.225
Cockermouth 109–11
Cockfield, Adam de 144
Coke roll 233
Cokefeud, Simon de 103 n.109
Colchester 44–5
Colchester, John of 122–3
Cold Weston 99–100
Coleville, Walter de 145, 149, 156 n.151, 247 n.21
Coleworth, Hugh de 194–5
Colston 75 n.41
Colston Basset 142
Colton 105 n.118
Committee of Twenty-Four 83–5, 101, 231–3
committees 91–2, 114, 131, 197, 236, 246–7
common law 9–11, 21–2, 22 n.38, 78–9,
    154–5, 237
commons 4–5, 109, 210, 256–7, 265, 267
communes 3, 209–10, 212–14
community of the realm (*communitas regni*) 3,
    5–6, 33, 85, 92–3, 109, 115–16, 127, 203 n.46,
    217, 229–34, 241, 245, 270–1
Compton 171–3
constables 74–5, 128–9, 144–7, 162–3, 174–8,
    181–6, 185 n.176, 251, 260–1, *see also*
    castellans
constitution 2, 7, 10–12, 19–20, 27–8, 131–2,
    189–90, 211–12, 235, 258, 273
constitutionalism 6, 11–12, 273
Cookham 175 n.92, 176–7
Coolmere 98–9
Copeshull, Henry de 167–8
Coppenhull 107
Coppers, Richard 172–3
Corbet, Peter 251
Corbet, Thomas 57–9, 142–3, 147 n.113
Corbet, William 95–6
Corfton 59
Cormailles 97 n.59
Cormeilles, Walter II de 102 n.100
Cornwall 38–9, 109–11
Cornwall, earl of 50–1, 59–64, 261–3
Cornwall, Richard of 24–7, 35–6, 38–9, 41–3,
    59–61, 71–2, 76, 80–1, 120, 134–5, 140–1,
    160–1, 173–4, 184 n.161, 210–11, 223
coronations 15–16, 20, 25–6, 29–32, 54,
    253, 255–6

298 INDEX

coroners 23–4, 53–4, 87, 94–100, 239–40
corruption 28–9, 49, 63, 130, 203–4, 209–10, 230,
    240–2, 255–6, 266–7, 269, 272–3, *see also*
    bribes, extortion
Cosin, Richard 184
Costentin, Thomas de 95–100
councillors 18, 27–9, 31–2, 44–8, 135–7, 166,
    189–90, 206–8, 231–3, 236–7
councils 6, 16–17, 19–20, 24, 32, 40–1, 50–1, 70,
    73–4, 85, 87, 89, 91–3, 102–3, 111–13, 116, 118,
    132–8, 189, 194–5, 199–200, 205–8, 210–12,
    223, 230–6, 236 n.39, 241, 259–64, 267–8
  Council of Lyon 74 n.39, 75–6
  Fourth Lateran Council 199–200
counsel 2, 6, 9–10, 19–21, 27–8, 33–4, 76, 121,
    133–4, 137–8, 162–3, 175–7, 235, 264
counsellors 24, 70, 134–5, 260–1
Courtenay, John de 102–3
Courtenay, William de 102–3, 111 nn.157–158,
    124 n.224
courts 9–10, 18–22, 43, 49–51, 54–6, 58–9, 61, 64,
    83–4, 107–8, 121, 142–3, 153, 164–6, 173–9,
    182–3, 186–7, 230 n.3, 234, 239–40, 244–5,
    247, 268–70
  archiepiscopal 67
  borough 67–8
  burghal 57
  central 23, 69–70, 81, 167, 235, 241–2,
    262–3, 272–3
  Christmas 20
  county 23, 55–7, 69, 81, 86, 93–7, 103–5,
    111–13, 162–3, 216–17, 222–3, 235, 241,
    264–5, 270–1
  ecclesiastical 265–6
  franchisal 80–1
  honour 62–3, 68–70, 78–82
  hundred 23–4, 29, 53–7, 69, 108, 111 n.159, 163,
    234, 238–9, 241
  itinerant 169–70
  king's 4, 12–13, 22–3, 52–3, 237
  local 53–4, 63, 69
  manorial 53–4, 67–8
  Northampton 20
  private 61–2, 79–80
  royal 21–3, 63, 78, 80–2, 188, 258–9, 264
  sheriff's 53–4
  shire 87, 89–90, 112–13, 162–3
  wapentake 235
  see also assizes, chancery, eyres, judges, juries
Coventry 45–6, 80–1, 140–2, 161, 207–8,
    see also bishops
Cranbourne 67–70
Crandon, Henry de 185–6
Cransford, Richard de 76 n.44

Cres, Nicholas de 151 n.131
Cressi, Hugh de 60 n.104
Crevequer, Hamo de 103 n.108
Crevequer, Robert de 115, 150–1
Criol, Bertram de 103, 103 nn.106–107
Criols 105–6
Criol, Simon de 103
Criol, William de 149
Crouch, David 78–9, 100, 164 n.38, 201
Crowcombe, Godfrey de 24, 41, 47–8
Croyrop 62–3
crusades/crusaders 38–9, 135–6, 197–200, 203–5,
    225–8, 249–51
Cumberland 109–11
Cumnor 174
Cuserigg, Baldwin de 174–5

d'Abernon, Ingram IV 96–7
d'Abernon, John 117 n.192, 120
d'Abernons 108
Dadford 61
Dafydd ap Gruffydd 251–2, 264
Dafydd ap Llywelyn 26–7
Damory, Roger 108
Dane Court 103 n.107
Danvers, Thomas 168–71
Datchet 185 n.176
d'Aubigny, Hugh 104 n.110
d'Avesnes, Alice 267
d'Avesnes, John 267
David, Hugh 176
Deerhurst Abbey 102 n.100
demesne 101, 107, 119–20, 144
  agriculture 67–8
  ancient 44–5
  crown 38–9
  royal 18, 23–4, 254–6
Dennington 75 n.41
Derby, earl of 42, 80–1, 102–4, 144, 155–6, 167–8,
    190, 193 n.227
Derbyshire 40 n.13, 95–6, 103–4, 112 n.162, 117,
    123–4, 139, 144, 191, 193–4
Derneford, William de 185–6
Despenser, Adam le 146–7
Despenser, Hugh le 139–41, 144–5, 155–6, 225–7,
    247 n.21
Despensers 139–40, 184
Devon 54 n.83, 69–70, 83, 94–5, 102–3, 111 n.158,
    120 n.207, 191–2, 245–6
d'Eyville, John 117, 137 n.54, 156 n.151, 158–9, 161,
    193–5, 245–6, 247 n.21
Dictum of Kenilworth 31–2, 79–80, 122, 124 n.225,
    153–4, 165–6, 181 n.131, 186, 194–5, 211,
    225 n.182, 236–8, 246–7

Didmarton 102 n.100
Dilwyn 203 n.45
Dinham, Oliver 120 n.207
disherison 192, 194–5, 202–3, 246–7
Disinherited 70, 78 n.56, 117, 122, 161, 165–6, 176, 184, 191, 193–4, 220, 225, 246–8
Dodinton, Robert de 185–6
Donjon, Ralf 184–5
Donnington, Thomas de 60 n.104
Dorset 66–7, 69–70, 95–6, 101 n.96, 102–3, 105–6, 119–21, 123–4, 140 n.69, 152, 191
Dover 40–1, 191
dowers 39–40, 42, 64, 66–7, 71–2, 133–4, 150, 152, 197, 269–70
Drafton 119–20
Draper, Simon le 215–16
Drayton, Baldwin de 119–20
Drayton Basset 142–5, 155–6, 184–5, 187–8, 191, 193 n.229, 195, 215–16, 246, 247 n.21
Drayton Parslow 61–2
Dudley 61, 79–80, 141–3
Dunham 44–5
Dunham, Geoffrey de 151 n.129
Dunmow 149–50, 153
Dunstable 212
Dunstable annalist 20, 138
Dunstable chronicler 257–8
Dunster 152
Dunton 142
Dunwich 215–16
Dunwich, John of 215–16
Dunwich, Peter of 215–16
Durham 40–1
Dyne, John 264–5
Dynot, Geoffrey 120 n.207
Dyva, John de 103 n.109

Eardisley 134, 158–9, 162–3
East Anglia 67, 75–6, 101, 191, 193–4, 193 n.228, 215–16, 260–1
   estates 134
   knights 74–5
   manors 73–4
   rebels 74 n.38
Eastbury 171
Easter 50–1, 99 n.81, 164–5
Easter parliament 256–7, 264–7
East Garton 177 n.105
East Kennett 170–1
East Tilbury 122, 149
Eastwick 122 n.214
Eaton 97–8, 104 n.116
Eaton Constantine 98 n.69
Eaton Tregose 170–1

ecclesiastical
   affairs 32–3
   benefices 258–9
   career 70
   complaint 205–6
   contacts 200–1
   courts 265–6
   elections 204–5
   garment 33
   grievances 264–5
   institutions 48–9
   justice 265–6
   land 265–6
   liberties 205
   livings 48
   lords 81, 258–9
   revenues 43–4
   tenants 61–2, 106–7
   unity 206
   world 5–6, 106–7
   writers 203–4
ecclesiastics 59–60, 81–2, 186–7, 200–1, 208
Eckington 104 n.110
Edgcott, Robert of 186–7
Edlesborough 63–4
Edmund, younger son of Henry III 12–13, 26–8, 173–4, 193, 245–6, 249–50, 261–3, 265–6
Edward I, King (Lord Edward) 14, 26–8, 37, 43–5, 49–51, 54–6, 73 n.24, 91–3, 103–4, 109–11, 127–30, 134–8, 153 n.142, 157–65, 168 n.56, 173–6, 186–93, 197–8, 202–3, 210–14, 218–19, 222–7, 231 n.8, 235, 237, 244–6, 248–69, 271, 272 n.1
Edward II, King 270–1
Edward the Confessor 32–3, 35–6
Eldridge, Barbara 203–4
Eleanor of Castile, Queen 25–6, 43, 134–5, 193, 245–8
Eleanor of Provence, Queen 25–7, 40–1, 43, 128–30, 133, 140 n.69, 160–1, 180–1, 193, 245–6, 265–6
Eleanor, Countess 39–40, 191, 197, 201
Elham 160–1
Elkestone 102 n.100
Ellesmere 56–7, 98–9
Elmbridge family 95–6
Elmbridge, Inard de 95–6, 108
Elsfield, Gilbert de 169–74, 179–80
Ely 117, 161, 184, 185 n.178, 194–5, 214–16, see also bishops
Engaine, Henry 191
Erdington, Giles of 117 n.192
Escudamore, Godfrey de 95–6, 102–3, 111 n.158. See also Scudamore

300   INDEX

Esse, John de 185 n.178
Essex 44–5, 49, 51–2, 67, 69–70, 106, 109–11,
    112 n.162, 119–24, 131–2, 140 n.69, 148 n.118,
    149–50, 153, 166 n.46, 171 n.70, 191, 193–4,
    193 n.228, 225, 255 n.48, 261 n.66, 264–5
Eston, John de 102 nn.100, 102
Eston, Roger de 102 n.102
Eston Somervill 102 n.100
Estwick 122
Eton 63–4, 180–1, 185 n.172
Eton, John de 170 n.65
Eu, Robert of 134–5
Everard, William 102–3, 111, 119–20, 123–4,
    125 n.227
Eversden 104–5
Evesbatch 99–100
Evesham, *see* battles
Evesham Abbey 96 n.57
Evington, Gerard of 89
Ewerswyke, William de 58
Ewyas Harold 170–1
exchequer 21–4, 28–9, 40–1, 48–50, 72–3, 78,
    88–9, 102–3, 109–13, 117–19, 122–3, 133,
    211–12, 235, 244–5, 254, 257–8, 266–8
    memoranda rolls 29–31, 54–5, 111–12
    see also finances, income, money, revenues,
    taxation/tallage, treasurers
excommunication 12–13, 25–6, 32–3, 104–7,
    189–90, 207–8, 222–3
Exton 120–1
extortion 29, 173–4, 180, 242, *see also* bribes,
    corruption
Eye 38–9
eyre rolls 54 n.83, 55, 58, 115, 122, 142, 144, 153,
    168, 189, 237–9, 255–6
eyres 4, 21–4, 22 n.38, 29, 54–5, 58–9, 73–4,
    79–80, 82–4, 87, 91–2, 94–9, 102 n.102,
    114–15, 121–2, 124, 144, 165–6, 168, 170–1,
    180–1, 205, 210, 211 n.87, 216–17, 220, 235,
    237–41, 246–7, 255–9, 265–7, 269, *see also*
    assizes, courts, chancery, judges, juries
Eyton, R. W. 58, 98–9

Faber, Richard 238 n.47
factions 13–14, 17–18, 93–4, 127–58, 160–1,
    208–10, 212–14, 216–19, 229–30, 242–3, 272
Faicigny, Agnes de 128–9
Fairford 67
Farnham 51–3, 167–8
Favus, Thomas 179–80
Fawley 61
Fernandes, Mario 115, 124, 142–5
Ferrers, earl 80–1, 147–8, 167–8, 247
Ferrers, Robert de 42, 124 n.225, 167–8

Ferrers, William de 82–3
Feteplace, Adam de 212–14
feudal
    authority 54
    essentials 68–9
    host 189–90
    incidents 68–9, 258–9
    lordship 253–4
    officials 91–2
    patronage 50
    records 97–100, 104–5, 145–6
    relationships 68–9
    reliefs 131
    resources 27–8, 68–9, 82–3
    rights 255–6
    society 79–80
    summons 248
    tenants 261–2
    tenure 78–80, 83–4
    wealth 50
    see also bastard feudalism
Fiennes, Baldwin de 133–4
Fiennes, Ingram de 133–4, 180–1, 183
Fiennes, Michael 134–5
Filliol, Richard 120–1
finances 16, 19–22, 27–9, 78 n.57, 204–5, 263–5,
    see also exchequer, income, money,
    revenues, taxation/tallage, treasurers
Finchamstead 146–7, 176
fine rolls 21–2, 22 n.38, 23 n.42, 49, 49 n.55, 248 n.23
fines 22 n.33, 23 n.42, 27–9, 53–4, 67–8, 83–4,
    89, 186, 194–5, 246–8, 267
Finmere 180–1, 184–5
FitzAlan, John 57, 97–8, 100, 102 n.100, 158
FitzAlans 56, 58–9
Flanders 40–1
Fleming, John le 176–7
Fletcham 108
Foliot, Geoffrey 171–2
Foliot, Peter 95–6, 105–6, 120–1
Foliot, Richard 117
Foliot, Sampson 105–6, 123–4
Folkestone 103 n.107
Folksworth 62–3
Folleville, Eustace de 120–1
Fonte, William de 238–9
Ford 56–9
foreign
    clerks 205
    ecclesiastics 186–7
    favourites 203–4
    invasion 220
    knights 45, 160–1
    mercenaries 117–18, 158–61, 220

INDEX 301

merchants 215–16
monasteries 186–7
noble 196
policy 2
relatives 41–3
soldiers 16
foreigners 33–4, 43, 77, 186–7, 205–6, 218–19,
  221, 257–8, *see also* aliens, anti-alienism,
  xenophobia
forest justices 24, 45–9
forests 29, 45–6, 64, 67–8, 87, 96 n.58, 121–2, 126,
  142–3, 222–3, 236, 256–7, *see also* Charter of
  the Forest
Forrest, Ian 230–1, 241–2, 241 n.55
Fortin, John 215 n.122
Four Cantreds 134–5, 250–1
Foxhall 75 n.42
Framlingham 50–1, 72–6
France/French 20–1, 129–34, 158–9, 186–7, 218
  language 90–2, 234
  monarchy 3, 10, 16–17, 26–7, 31–2, 157, 160–1,
    189–90, 220, 230
  nobility 198, 202 n.38
Franceys, William le 171–2, 174–5, 179–80
franchises 53–5, 59–64, 68–9, 80–1, 108, 131–2,
  257, 260, 268–70
Franc, John le 185 n.178
frankpledge 53–4, 56, 59–64, 69, 108
Frederick II, Emperor 26–7, 31 n.88, 204–5
freeholders 4, 23, 93–4, 109, 117–19, 126,
  131–2, 238–41
Freemantle 134–5
Freston 75 n.42
friendship group 148–9, 153–6
Friston 108 n.143
Froxfield 172
Fulk, Ralph fitz 146–7
Furness, William 111–12

garrisons 74–5, 123–4, 144–7, 157, 162, 166,
  172–82, 185–6, 185 n.176, 194
Garston, William de le 174
Gascelins, Geoffrey 77, 78 n.56
Gascon expedition 50–1, 129–30
Gascony 16–17, 25–8, 36, 38–9, 42, 44–5, 48–9,
  72–3, 83, 129–30, 134–5, 139–40, 197 n.8,
  202–4, 251, 264–7
Gatecombe, Maud de 150
Gaunt, Gilbert de 101, 156 n.151, 247 n.21
Geneva, Ebulo of 131
Geoffrey, John fitz 47–8, 52–3, 62, 72–3, 134–6
Germany 25–7, 35–6, 137–8, 197–8
Gervase of Canterbury 158 n.5, 221 n.160
Gesemue, Adam de 249–50

Geyton, Walter de 237–8
Ghent, Henry of 133–4
Giffard 61–2, 66–7, 69–70
Giffard, honour of
Giffard, John 102–3, 123–5, 150–2, 158–9, 163–5,
  167–9, 171–3, 184–6, 191, 248, 250–1, 253
Giffard, Nicholas 168–71
Giffard, Osbert 185–6
Giffard, Walter 207–8
Giffard, Walter III 60–1
Gimeges, Nicholas de 151 n.129
Girund, Nicholas de 60 n.104
Glamorgan 66–7, 69, 80–1
Glaston 107 n.137, 108
Glorious Revolution 7
Gloucester 66–7, 69–70, 131, 134, 146, 153, 161–5, 257
Gloucester, countess of 225
Gloucester, earl of 50–1, 52 n.68, 59–61, 64, 66,
  80–1, 89, 102–3, 109–11, 115–16, 136–7,
  144–56, 158–9, 165–6, 176, 182–8, 191, 193–5,
  220, 223–5, 255, 260, 262–6
Gloucester, Richard of 62–3, 91–2, 117–20, 122,
  127–9, 131–3
Gloucester, Robert of 137–8, 161–3, 165, 173–4
Gloucester, William of 122
Gloucestershire 67–70, 77 n.49, 97 n.59, 101,
  102 nn.100, 102, 109–11, 111 n.158, 117, 164–5,
  191, 193 n.229
Godde, John 172
Godman, John 173 n.83
Gouiz, Brian de 146–7, 152–3, 155–6, 173
Gouiz, Richard de 152
Gousle, Giles de 191
Gousle, Simon de 120
governance 13, 32, 38, 216, 252 n.37, 265–6
government 2, 4–7, 9–13, 17, 18 n.12, 19–24, 29,
  32–3, 46, 49–51, 55–6, 70, 83, 85–6, 93–4,
  109–11, 126–7, 131–2, 134–5, 145–6, 188–9,
  207, 211–14, 221–3, 230–3, 235, 244–5, 250,
  252, 256–8, 264–7, 272–4
Grafton 188 n.198
Grafton Flyford 96 n.57
Grafton Underwood 44–5
Grandson, Otto de 128–9, 253 n.41
Grantham 134–5
Grave, Walter de la 167–8
Great Doddington 170–1, 185–6
Great Gransden 62–3, 69
Great Harwood 185 n.178
Great Houghton 144 n.87
Great Linford 63–4
Great Marlow 60–1
great mortality of magnates 43–4
Great Paxton 183–4

302 INDEX

Greenham, Ralph de 168–9
Grendon, Robert de 108, 123–4
Grenville, Henry de 182–3, 185
Gresley, Geoffrey de 107, 142–3
Gresley, Thomas de 142–3
Grestein Abbey 186–7
Grey, John de 56–7, 60 n.104, 61–4, 98–9,
  136 n.50, 159 n.10, 180–7, 210, 238–9
Grey, Reginald de 63–4, 251, 253
Grey, Richard de 139
grievances 4–8, 28 n.71, 32, 85, 93–4, 108, 113–14,
  118, 127, 142, 196–7, 204–6, 212–14, 220,
  229–34, 236, 239–40, 242–3, 255–7,
  264–6, 269
Grosseteste, Robert 33, 48–9, 200–1, 203–4,
  207–8
Gryffudd ap Gwenwynwyn 58, 251
Gubion, Hugh 115, 144
Guilden Morden 62–3
Guisnes, Thomas de 111–12
Gulafre, Thomas 151 n.129
Gurdon, Adam 152, 171–2, 179–80
Gussich, Richard de 152
Guy, Imbert 77–8, 154
Gwynedd 251
Gwynllŵg 66–7

Hachecote 184
Haddenham 60–1
Haddon 104 n.110
Hadleigh 131
Hadley, John 172–3
Hadley, Ralph de 168–9, 171–2
Hadley, Reginald de 172–3
Hadlow 67
Hagar, Hugh 58
Haket, William 152
Halcton, Robert de 103–4
Halliford 151
Halton 46–7, 60–1
Ham 103 n.107
Hampden 60–1
Hampshire 47–8, 69–70, 97 n.59, 109–12, 120,
  134–5, 147 n.113, 152, 194 n.233
Hampton Meysy 102–3
Hamstead Marshal 73 n.30
Handsworth 142–3
Hanley 67–8
Hanred, Richard de 151 n.129
Hansard, John 96–7
Hanslope 185, 185 n.177
Harangod, William 151 n.129
Harang, Ralf 60 n.104
Harcourt, Margaret de 140 n.69

Harcourt, Richard de 140 n.69
Harcourt, Saer de 139–40, 247–8
Harding, Alan 58
Hardwick 150 n.128
Hareg, John 62
Haringod, Ralph 107–8, 111–12, 119–20
Harlaston 104 n.110
Harlow 106, 122 n.215
Harlow, Richard de 106, 123–4
Hartshill, Margaret de 254
Hartshill, Robert de 141–2
Hasley 62
Hastang, Robert 143–4
Hastings 107–8
Hastings, Henry de 141–2, 144–5, 151–2, 155–6,
  161, 185–6, 191, 194–5, 247 n.21
Hastings, Thomas de 151–2
Haudlou, Nicholas de 98–9
Haughmond 57
Haughmond Abbey 57, 97–9
Haughton 104 n.115
Haughton, Robert de 104 n.115
Hautein, Bartholomew 145–6, 149
Hautein, Hamo 70, 101–3, 111, 111 n.158, 119–20,
  124 n.225, 145–7, 149
Havering 44–5
Havering, Richard de 140–1, 140 n.69,
  174–5, 186–7
Hawarden 251
Haydon 102 n.100
Haye, John de la 117, 140–1, 140 n.69
Heartlove, Peter 179–80
Hecham, William de 101, 123–4
Hedon, Simon de 95–6, 123–4, 125 n.226
Hellesdon 149
Hemington 139–40
Hemington, Richard de 151 n.129
Henley 171–2
Henry II, King 3, 23–4, 55–6, 73 n.25, 78–9,
  127 n.4, 239–40
Henry III, King 3, 7–8, 10–39, 46–7, 50, 54–6,
  64, 66, 70, 72–3, 77, 81–2, 93–4, 98–9, 108,
  118–19, 126, 154–5, 158–9, 197–8, 203–6,
  209–10, 225, 230, 235, 244–6, 249–50,
  252–4, 258–9, 261–2, 272–3
  burial 264–5
  coronation 15–16, 20
  coronation oath 29–32
  kingship 2, 13, 15–37, 127–8, 203–4, 272
  last years 244
  marriage 40–1, 128–9
  mature years 242
  middle years 5–6, 54–5
  minority 2, 6, 9–10, 13, 15–21, 24, 127–8, 219

INDEX 303

Henry the Crossbowman 177
Hereford 40–1, 57, 111 n.158, 124–5, 132–3, 158–9,
  207–8, 214, 262–3, 265–6, *see also* bishops
Herefordshire 80–1, 99–100, 102 n.100, 105–6,
  109–11, 158, 170–1, 191, 193 n.228
Herlwyne, Nicholas 177, 185 n.176
Heron, William 29
Hertford 41–2, 60–1, 66, 69–70, 77, 114–15, 120–1,
  131–2, 191
Hertfordshire 75–6, 87 n.4, 104–6, 109–11,
  121–4, 149
Hertwell 187–8
Heryngaud, John 108 n.143
Hescombe 152
Heydon 119–20
Heydon, Richard de 173, 180
Higham Ferrers 144
Hingham, William de 74–5
Ho 150
Hoderode, John de 82–3
Hodnet 142–3
Hogshaw 186–7
Hoketide Parliament 2–3
Holbrook 75 n.42
Holbrook, Richard de 75–6
Holderness 80–1
Holdgate 56–7
Holewelle, Henry de 104–5
Holewell, Stephen de 185 n.178
Holland 78
Holland, John of 264–5
Holmes, G. A. 67 n.3, 154–5
Holt 174–5
Holt, James C. 78–9, 219
Holy Blood 25–6, 35–6
Holy Land 245
Hoo, Robert 105 n.120
Hopton 57 n.92
Hopton, John 98
Hopton, Nicholas de 98
Hopton, Walter de 57 n.92, 97–8, 269–70
Hopton, William de 98
Horseley 104 n.115
Horton Kirby 103 n.109
Horwood 60–1, 60 n.105
Hoskin, Philippa 205–6
Hospitallers 60 n.105, 222–3
House of Commons 109
Hovel, Robert 75–6
Howell, Margaret 25 n.53, 41, 45, 127–31, 134–5,
  138, 181 n.133
Huband, Henry 143–4
Hugh XI of Angouleme 42
Hugh, Stephen fitz 103 n.107

Hulle, Henry de la 183
Hundred Rolls 29, 54–6, 56 n.91, 59 n.100, 63–4,
  73–4, 238–40, 255–7, 262–3
Hungerford 140 n.69, 174–5
Huntercombe, William de 249–50
Huntingdon 69, 131–2, 183–4
Huntingdonshire 62–3, 66–7, 69–71, 106, 117,
  120–1, 188 n.198, 191
Hunt, John R. 195
Hunton 150
Hunzard 105 n.118
Husseys 105–6
Hyde, Walter de la 147–8, 183–4

Iffley 183–4
Iklesham, Sybilla de 107–8
Ilmington 140–1
income 20–1, 24, 28–9, 33–5, 39–42, 44–5, 48, 57,
  62–3, 66–9, 71–2, 76–7, 100, 129–31, 207–8,
  239–40, *see also* exchequer, finances, money,
  revenues, taxation/tallage, treasurers
inquisitions 62–3, 66–7, 69–71, 80–1, 87, 147–8,
  150 n.128, 151, 151 n.131, 170–1, 212–14,
  239–40, 259
Insula, Gerard de 185 n.178
Ireland 39–42, 66–7, 71–2, 77, 100 n.85, 134–7,
  189–90, 253 n.41
Isabella of Angouleme 16–17, 26–7, 41–2
Isabella of Arundel 26–7, 36, 59–60
Isle of Axholme 193–4
Isle of Oléron 134–5
Istead 75–6
italy/Italian 90–1, 201 n.33, 205, 240–1
Ivinghoe 180–2, 186–7

Jacob, E. F. 3, 6–7, 74 n.33, 87 n.5, 88 n.12,
  122 n.214, 165 n.40, 173, 175 n.92, 180, 208–9,
  211 n.87, 212–14
  *Studies in the Period of Baronial Reform and
  Rebellion* 166
Jarpenvill, David de 96–7, 109–11, 111 n.158
Jarpenvill 61
Jewish
  community 214–16, 264–5
  creditors 247–8
  debts 44–5, 48–9, 223, 231–3, 247–8, 265–6
  inhabitants 200–1
  legislation 265
  lending 265
Jews 28–9, 38–9, 45–6, 83–4, 107–8, 119–20, 161,
  194, 210–11, 267
Jobson, Adrian 21 n.29, 132 n.30, 142 n.76, 157–8,
  160–1, 189 n.211, 196, 217 n.133, 244 n.1
  The First English Revolution 7

304　INDEX

John, John fitz 117 n.192, 146–9, 156 n.151,
　175–84, 185 n.176, 186, 215–16, 247 n.21
John, King 2–3, 8–10, 15–17, 48–9, 78–9, 81–2,
　216–17, 229
Joinville family 128–9
Joinville, Geoffrey de 129–30
Joinville, Simon de 133–4
judges 22–3, 49, 90–1, 111–12, 234, 260, 262–4
juries 21–2, 24, 49, 51–6, 61, 63, 82–4, 94–5,
　98–100, 121, 166 n.46, 168–9, 171–86, 188,
　194, 209–10, 234, 238–42, 248, 255–6, 270,
　see also assizes, chancery, courts, eyres
jurors 58–62, 64, 73–4, 87, 98–9, 115, 151–2,
　167–8, 172–3, 238–42
justiciars 6–7, 13–16, 19–20, 27–8, 52–3, 64–5,
　85–9, 94–5, 102–3, 108–9, 110 n.150, 111–13,
　131, 136–7, 139–40, 217 n.132, 220, 231–3,
　236–7, 239–41, 251

Kane, Simon le 184–5
Kaynnes, William 105–6
Kemble, Richard de 60 n.104
Kenilworth 39–40, 60 n.105, 139–40, 161–2,
　173–4, 185–6, 208, see also battles, Dictum
　of Kenilworth
Kent 52–3, 62–3, 69–70, 77, 96 n.55, 103, 105–6,
　111–12, 111 n.158, 115–17, 119–21, 124–5, 131–2,
　136–7, 140 n.69, 145–52, 158–9, 192, 221–2,
　234, 248
Kentish chronicler 158
Kerdiston, Fulk de 101
Kilcote 102 n.102
Kilkenny 66–7
Kilkenny, William of 33 n.98
Kilpeck 47–8, 134, 158–9
King's Lynn 214–15
Kingsbury 141–2
Kingsdon 152
Kingsey 184
Kingston 117–18, 157–8, 167–8, 184
Kingston Bagpuise 171
Kintbury 174–5
Kirketon, William de 77–8
Kirtlington 18–19
Kjaer, Lars 33–5
Knaresborough 38–9
Knebworth 104–5
knighthood 49, 83, 90–1, 100, 106, 109, 140–1,
　201, 221
Knightley 104 n.115
Knightley, Robert de 142–3
Knightley, William de 142–3
Knowles, Clive 12–13, 94, 119–20, 191–5, 196 n.2,
　203 n.47, 211–16, 230, 245–8
Koziol, G. 33 n.97

Labarge, Margaret W. 12–13, 196, 197 n.6
Lacy, Edmund de 42, 50–1, 82–3
Lacy, Henry de 261–2
Lacy, John de 66–7
Lacy, Maud de 66–7, 128–9
Lacy, Robert de 97–9, 108
Lacy, Walter de 99–100
Lade, Richard de la 70
Lakenheath 67–8
Lambeth 51–2, 205–6
Lambourn 167–9, 171–3
Lamede, Letitia 225
Lancashire 102–3, 111 n.158
Lancaster 89
Lancaster, earl of 261–3, 265–6
landowners 38, 53–7, 62–4, 71 n.15, 73–4, 81–4,
　89–91, 102–3, 113, 136–7, 142–3, 146–7, 154–5,
　165–6, 171–2, 180–1, 193 n.227, 218–19,
　237–40, 261–2, 269 n.101, 269–70
Lanercost 203 n.47
Langetot, Ralf de 60 n.104
Langley, Geoffrey de 45–9, 134–5, 158–9
Langton, John de 254
Langton, Stephen 16
Latimer, William 109–11
Latton Hall (Latton Tany) 121–2
Latymer, William le 125 n.226
Launcelence, John 111–12
Launceston Castle 191
Lavendon 46–7, 186–7
Lavenham, Thomas de 121
lawyers, see attorneys/lawyers
Lay, William de 181–6
Leatherhead 108
Leckhampstead 171–2, 175
Leicester 39, 60–1, 140 n.69, 186 n.181, 200–1
Leicester, earl of 39, 60–1, 64, 115–18, 121, 152,
　174–5, 184–9
Leicestershire 40 n.13, 73 n.31, 100, 104 n.110,
　109–11, 117, 123–4, 139–45, 192,
　193 n.227, 217
Lenebaud, Thomas 75–6
Lenham, Nicholas de 150–1
Lestrange, Hamo 134–8, 160–1, 249–50
Lestrange, Roger 251
Lewes 48–9, 183–4
　Mise of Lewes 189
　Song of Lewes 188–9, 200–1, 221–2
　see also battles
Lewknor, Geoffrey de 262–3
Lexinton, John de 31 n.88, 47 n.48
Leybourne, Roger de 52–3, 77–8, 135–8, 150,
　157–61, 249–50, 252–3
Leybourne, William de 153
Leyton, Henry de 145–6, 187–8

liberties 9–10, 31–3, 50–1, 54–6, 59–64, 67–9,
80–1, 83–4, 205, 209–11, 213 n.105, 214–16,
222–3, 230–1, 236, 255–6, 265–7
Lidgate 151–2
Lilleshall 56–7
Lillingstone 61, 184
Lillyfee 184
Lincoln 70, 83, 101, 105–6, 120, 123–4, 145–6,
208–9, 211–14, 216, 253, 261–3, 269,
see also bishops
Lincoln, Alured of 105–6
Lincolnshire 78, 101, 117, 123–4, 134–5, 140 n.69,
141–2, 144, 191, 264–5
Linguire, John de 106
Linslade 146 n.106
Linton, Robert de 146–7
Lisle, Baldwin de 136–7
Lisle, Brian de 17–18
Lisle, Philip de 108
Lisle, Simon de 108
Lisle, William de 44–5, 125–6
Litlington 62–3
Little Crawley 149
Little Kimble 99–100, 184
Littlebury, John de 71
Llewelyn ap Gruffudd 70, 109–11, 131–2, 134–5,
158, 250–1
Llewelyn the Great 26–7
Loes 73–4, 87 n.5
Loges, Richard de 142–3
London 18–19, 25–6, 35–6, 42, 46–7, 74 n.39, 76,
117–18, 122, 145–7, 149, 153, 161, 173–4, 176,
178–80, 183–4, 192–5, 208–14, 209 n.76,
211 n.88, 216, 218–19, 221–3, 225, 230–4,
265–6, 270
chronicle/chronicler 223, 233
Tower of London 128–9, 131, 158–9, 210
see also bishops
Londoners 209–11
Long Crendon 64
Longespée, Stephen 136 n.50, 136–7
Longespée, William 49, 61
Lopen 152
Lord Edward, *see* Edward I
lordships 39–41, 56, 58–9, 64, 66–7, 72–3, 80–1,
83, 139–41, 200–1, 223, 250, 253–4
Loughborough 139–40
Louis VIII, King 16–17
Louis IX, King 3, 29–31, 34–5, 128–9, 160–2,
189–90, 210–11, 218–20, 223, 230,
249–50, 258
Lovel, Philip 49, 98–9
Lucy, Geoffrey de 146, 150–1, 153, 156 n.151
Ludgershall 61–2, 145 n.97, 185 nn.172, 177
Ludlow Castle 128–9

Ludstone 59
Lugwardine 203 n.45
Lukedale 150
Lullingstone 103 n.108
Lusignan, Alice de 41–2, 129–30
Lusignan, Aymer de 41–2, 53 n.71
Lusignan, Geoffrey de 41–2, 44–5
Lusignan, Guy de 36, 41–2, 44–5
Lusignan, Hugh de 16–17, 26–7, 41–2
Lusignans 12–13, 41 n.22, 42–3, 51–2, 109–11,
127–31, 134–6, 220, 229–30
Luton, Henry de 187–8
Lydiard Tregoze 170–1
Lyford 168
Lyon 74 n.39, 75–6
Lyt, William de 152

Macauley, Thomas Babington 7
Maddicott, John 3–6, 12–13, 23, 27–8, 39–40, 43,
78 n.57, 81, 85–6, 88, 91–4, 101 n.96, 127,
139–41, 196, 197 n.6, 199–201, 202 n.38,
225–7, 230–1, 255–9, 262–4, 269 n.103
Ford Lectures 5
'Magna Carta and the Local Community' 126
Magna Carta 2–6, 8–11, 15–23, 25–31, 36, 44–5,
51–3, 79–82, 126, 203–4, 206, 216–17, 222–3,
236, 256–9
magnate power 13, 64–6, 71–2, 78–9, 83–4, 257
magnates 3, 5–6, 12–13, 18–20, 22–3, 27–31, 36,
40–1, 43–4, 46–8, 50–4, 66–9, 73–4, 77,
81–2, 84–5, 89–92, 94, 100, 102–5, 109–11,
115–18, 125, 127–8, 132–3, 135–6, 139–42,
145, 147–8, 159 n.8, 180–1, 193, 203–7,
229–36, 241, 245–7, 250, 253–5, 259–61,
263–7, 270–3
Maidstone 130
Maitland, F. W. 59–60
Malemayns, Thomas 150
Malherbe, William 76 n.44
Malvern 67–8
Mandeville, Geoffrey de 60 n.104
Mandeville, John de 153
Manneby, Hugh 88
Mansel, John 48–9, 60 n.104, 104–5, 122, 129–31,
133–4, 158–60, 172, 180–1, 188–9,
209–10, 223
Mansel, Thomas de 60 n.104
Mantek, Warin de 60 n.104
marcher
barons 36, 56, 169–70, 189
estates 253
knight 249–50
lords 134–5, 157–8, 220, 250
lordships 66–7
privilege 260

306 INDEX

marchers 46, 127–8, 134–8, 158–61, 163, 189–91, 193, 218–19, 250
marches 47–8, 58–9, 77, 109–11, 158, 164–5, 190–1, 215–16, 260, 265–6
Marden 203 n.45
Margaret, duchess of Brabant 264–5
Margaret, Queen of Scotland 34, 45
Market Weston 75–6
Marlborough 14, 174–5, 236–7, 255, 258–9
Marlow 186
Marmion, Philip 142–3, 195, 254
Marmion, Ralf 185 n.178
Marmion, William 156 n.151, 247 n.21
marriage 6, 25–7, 34–6, 38–43, 45–6, 50–2, 58, 66–9, 75–6, 81–4, 102 n.100, 104–5, 104 n.114, 107–8, 121–2, 128–31, 133–5, 140–1, 140 n.69, 154, 169–71, 175–6, 186–7, 212, 246, 251–3, 258–9, 264–7, 269–70
Marsh, Adam 200–4
Marshal, Gilbert 25–6, 47–8
Marshal, Maud 71–2
Marshal, Reginald 76
Marshal, Richard 17–19, 39–40, 219
Marshal, Stephen 172
Marshal, Thomas le 184–5
Marshal, William (elder) 15–16, 18, 39–40, 51–2, 60–1, 71–2, 117, 149, 175–6, 188–9, 191
Marshal, William (younger) 16, 18–19, 61, 151–2
Marsh, John de 168–71
Marston Montgomery 104 n.110
Marsworth 63–4
Martinwas, William de 100
Martival, Anketin de 95–6, 100, 109–11, 120, 124–5, 140–1, 144–5
Masschaele, James 53–4, 53 n.74, 239–40, 240 n.54
Massingham 149
Matham 99–100
Mauduit, William 56–7
Maulay, Peter de 17–19, 36
McFarlane, K. B. 12, 71–2, 154–5, 253
Medmenham 60 n.105
Meldreth 62–3
Melrose chronicler 8, 48, 203 n.47
Mendham 76 n.43, 101 n.94
Menill, Thomas 139–41
Meopham, Adam de 178
mercenaries 16, 117–18, 158–61, 220
merchants 194–5, 210, 212–16, 265–6, 270–1
Merk, Robert de 149, 153
Merke, Henry de la 188–9
Merlawe, Roger de 147–8
Merton 210–11
Merton Priory 158
Merton, Walter de 48–9, 174, 210–11, 247–8

Meuland, Roger 207–8
Meysy, Robert de 102–3, 109–11, 111 n.58, 149, 170 n.65
Michael, Thomas fitz 124 n.224
Michaelmas 67–8, 103, 112–13, 119–20, 122–3, 138, 150–1, 158, 192, 258–9
Michaelmas parliament 216–17, 233–5, 256–7, 264–5
Middlesex 97 n.59, 123–4, 151, 209–10
Middleton 97
military
    action 160–1
    aid 250
    apparatus 252
    aptitude 17
    balance 194–5
    campaign 189–90, 221
    designs 252
    duties 90–1
    experience 133–4
    forces 124–5
    positions 249–50
    preparations 118
    prowess 20–1
    resources 230–1
    retinue 145–6, 208
    service 68–9, 117–18, 259, 269–70
    skill 37, 161, 250
    support 129–30, 133–4
    tenants 68–9, 79–80, 90–1, 146–7, 208
    tenure 78–9
    threat 189–90
ministers 15, 18–20, 22–4, 29–32, 40–1, 47–8, 50, 54, 67–8, 81–3, 85, 173 n.83, 178, 186–7
Minsterley 58
Missenden 61, 185 n.179, 187–8
Missenden Abbey 61, 186–7
Mitten, Philip de 142–3
Moeles, Nicholas de 171–2
Mohun, Joan de 78
Moigne, William le 125 n.226
Molins, John de 175–6
Molins, Nicholas de 175–6
Molis, Roger de 187–8
monasteries 70–1, 106–7, 141–2, 161, 186–7, 205, 221, 254
monastic boroughs 203–4, 212
monastic chronicles 218
Mondeville, John de 71
money 26–9, 33–4, 39–40, 43–6, 49, 51–2, 61–2, 64, 68–9, 78, 83, 135–6, 158–9, 168, 175, 177–8, 182, 185–6, 191, 194, 210, 215–16, 221, 231–3, 260–1, 265–9, *see also* exchequer, finances, income, revenues, taxation/ tallage, treasurers

INDEX 307

monks/canons/friars 40–1, 104–8, 134, 151,
    161–2, 162 n.26, 188–9, 222 n.166, 222–3,
    269 n.105
  Augustinian 212
  Franciscan 199–204
Monmouth, John de 168–9
Montalt, Adam de 249–50
Montchesney, Hubert de 109–11, 111 n.157
Montchesney, William de 149, 149 n.125,
    156 n.151
Montferrand, Imbert de 128–9, 133–4, 157–8
Montfichet, Richard de 137 n.54
Montfort, Amaury de 251
Montfort, Eleanor de 251
Montfort, Guy de 223
Montfort, Henry de 165
Montfortian
  activist 179–80
  agents 181–2
  barons 222–3
  bishops 188–9
  cause 141–2, 153, 208
  cavalry 227
  churchmen 207–8
  enigma 197
  enterprise 121, 242–3
  government 70, 189–90, 250
  heartlands 100, 124, 165–6, 237–8
  henchmen 117
  lieutenants 142, 161
  parliament 208–9, 247
  party 141–2, 145, 155–7, 189, 204–5, 208,
    216, 221–2
  period 13–14, 211–12
  position 193–4
  programme 221
  propaganda 219
  rebellion 117, 205–6, 210
  regime 74–5, 84 n.88, 120–1, 180, 196–7, 207–8
  riot 193–4
  statute 218–19
  supporters 134, 223–5, 245
  sympathies 120, 238–9
  victory 172
Montfortians 2, 115, 119–26, 138, 141–2, 144, 152,
    157, 160–1, 164–5, 173–4, 183–7, 189–92,
    215–19, 221, 223, 225, 247–50
Montfort, Peter de 97, 100, 109–11, 134–6,
    139–45, 155–6, 159–60, 207–8
Montfort, Simon de 2–3, 6–14, 36–7, 39–43, 45,
    49–51, 59–61, 71–2, 74–6, 78–80, 91–2, 100,
    103, 103 n.109, 107–8, 117, 119 n.201, 123–5,
    127–33, 137–41, 143–7, 157–62, 164–5, 170–1,
    173–8, 189–92, 193 n.227, 194, 196–230,
    237–8, 247–8, 250, 274

Montfort, Simon de (the younger) 117, 144–5,
    155–6, 159–60, 190, 193–4, 208, 212–16,
    215 n.122, 223, 225–7
Montgomery 56–7, 251
Montgomery, William de 103–4, 123–4
Montibus, Ebulo de 47–8, 128–30, 133–4, 157–8
More, Bartholomew de la 146
More, Robert de la 151 n.129, 175–6
Morevill, John de 120–1
More, William de la 49 n.57
Morris, Marc 71–6, 260–1
  King John: Treachery, Tyranny and the Road
    to Magna Carta 10
Mortimer, Edmund 251
Mortimer, Geoffrey 150–1, 185–6
Mortimer, Roger 96 n.58, 97–8, 119–20, 134–5,
    158, 162, 178–9, 190–3, 202–3, 227,
    245–6, 250–1
Mortimers 56, 58–9, 95–6, 253
mortmain 81–4, 205, 236–7, 258–9, 265–6, 269–70
Morton 60–1, 63–4, 104 n.110, 184
Morton, Gilbert de 185–6
Mot, William 178
Moulton 149
Moulton, Thomas de 74 n.37
Mount St Katherine 184–7
Moyne, William le 106, 120–1, 151
Mulcaster, Robert de 110 n.154, 125 n.227
Munchensey, Joan de 41–2, 51–2, 77
Munchensey, Warin de 51–2
Munteny, Arnold de 151 n.129
Munteny, Robert de 151 n.129, 249–50
Mursley 60–2, 183–4, 238–9
Musgrave, John de 171–2
Musson, John 174
Mustel, Hugh 101, 102 nn.100, 102
Mutton, Ralf de 105 n.118

Nacton 75 n.42
Nailsea 151–2
Napton, Adam de 95–6
Netley 52–3
Neuton, Richard de 123–4
Neville, Christine de 123
Neville, Hasculf de 123
Neville, John de 146–7, 146 n.106
Neville, Peter de 123
Neville, Ralph de 6
Neville, Robert de 123, 158–9
Neville, Stephen de 123, 146 n.106
Neville, Thomas de 123
Nevill, Gilbert de 264–5
Newbold, Geoffrey de 78
Newbury 140 n.69
Newcastle on Tyne 269

308 INDEX

Newenden 150
Newenton, Richard de 169 n.63
Newman, J. E. 70–1
Newmarket, Adam de 117, 156 n.151, 207–8,
    247 n.21
Newport Pagnell 61, 63–4, 185–6
Newton Longueville 60 n.105, 184, 186–7
Newton, Richard de 169 n.63
Neyrnuit, Geoffrey 181–2, 184
Neyrnuit, John 181–2
Neyrnuit, Walter 184, 187–8
Nicholas, Ralph fitz 24, 44–5, 47–8, 60 n.104
Nigel, Richard fitz 183–4
Nigel, Robert fitz 60 n.104, 181–6, 188, 238 n.47
nobility/nobles 13, 15, 25–6, 33–4, 37–65, 92–4,
    109, 115–16, 128–9, 161–2, 196, 198–202,
    202 n.38, 216–18, 230, 249–50, 252–3, 258–63,
    270–5, see also aristocracy/aristocrats
Noble, William le 184
Noers, Robert de 146
Norbury 104 n.115, 142–3
Norfolk 55, 66–76, 82–3, 101–3, 111–12, 111 n.158,
    114–15, 119–20, 123–4, 131–2, 149, 151–2,
    155–6, 160–1, 260–3, 261 n.66
Norman Conquest 4, 33 n.97, 60–1, 104 n.114,
    106, 221–2
Normandy 218
Normandy, duke Robert of 128 n.5
Normanvill, Ralph de 119–21
Norreys, John le 152
Northampton 20, 48–9, 72–3, 79 n.64, 88,
    114–15, 119–20, 141–2, 144–7, 150 n.128,
    155–7, 160–1, 164–5, 185–6, 188–90, 211–14,
    249–50, see also battles
Northamptonshire 44–5, 67, 69–70, 83, 95,
    111 n.158, 115, 117, 120, 139, 140 n.69, 142 n.76,
    144, 149–50, 154, 166 n.46, 170–1, 185, 191
Northill 70
Northumberland 29, 39–40, 42, 77 n.49,
    111 n.158, 120–1, 125–6, 269–70
Norton 169 n.63, 171
Norton, John de 168–71
Norwich 48–9, 73 n.30, 82–3, 119–20, 134, 158–9,
    207–8, 211–12, 214, see also bishops
Noseley 100
Notley 182–3
Notley Abbey 182–3, 186–7
Nottinghamshire 40 n.13, 44–5, 95–6, 103–4,
    112 n.162, 117, 123–4, 142, 144, 191, 208
Nutley 60 n.105
Nutting, Adam 185 n.176

Odiham 39–40
Odiham, John de 176

Offa, King 60–1
Okeburn, Henry of 185–6
Oketon, John de 125 n.226
Oldbury 97–8, 98 n.69, 102 n.100
Olney 184
Olney, William of 184
Ombersley, Maurice de 96 n.57
Ombersley, Richard de 95–6
Ordinance of the Magnates 91–2
Ordinance of the Sheriffs 87–9, 233
ordinances 189–90, 205–6, 210–11, 218–19,
    246, 267–8
Ortiary, William de 152
Orwell 75–6
Osney Abbey 60–1, 108, 178–9
Osney chronicler 225–7
Oswestry 56, 58–9
Otford 67
Otto, Cardinal 24–5, 33–4, 40 n.14
Ottobuono, Cardinal 246–7, 249–50
Oxenedes, John of 203 n.47
Oxford 20, 41–2, 60 n.105, 61, 78–9, 87, 155–6,
    158–61, 162 n.28, 164–5, 168, 184, 187–8,
    206–7, 211–14, 218–19, 231–3, see also
    Provisions of Oxford
Oxford, earl of 4 n.10, 121, 193, 225, 225 n.183,
    246 n.10
Oxford Parliament 2–3, 12–13, 85, 135–6, 233
Oxfordshire 46–8, 56, 69–70, 95–6, 105–6, 108,
    112 n.162, 123–4, 150, 164–5, 166 n.46,
    180–7, 192
Oxnead 119–20, 149

Page, Richard 169
Pakenham, William of 111–12
Palmer, Walter le 215 n.124
Palmer, William le 215 n.124
papacy/popes 135–6, 157, 203–7, 218, 220,
    231–3, 249–50
papal
    absolution 158–9
    bulls 48–9, 132–3, 158, 159 n.8
    chaplain 49
    clerk 205
    court 36, 48, 128–9
    Curia 199
    debts 27–8
    ideology 31–2
    legate 15–16, 33–4, 40 n.14, 189–90, 194–5,
        207–8, 246–7, 249–50
    livings 70–1
    offer 26–7
    policy 16
    provisions 205, 218

rhetoric 31–2
sanctions 12–13, 189–90
taxes 204–5
Paper Constitution 27–8
Papworth 62–3, 188 n.198
Paris, Matthew 25–6, 29, 31, 31 n.88, 32 n.95,
    33 n.96, 33–6, 42–3, 45–8, 47 n.48, 50–1,
    72–3, 77, 87 n.4, 91–2, 98, 106 n.125, 125–6,
    130, 132–3, 197, 203 n.47, 206–7, 218, 230–1
  Chronica Majora 29–31, 35
  Historia Anglorum 35
Parles, William de 142–3
Parliamentary Roll of Arms 270–1
Parliament Rolls 267–8
parsons 75–6, 146–7, 167–8, 173–5, 179–81, 184,
    186–8, 208, 269 n.105
party 13–14, 41–2, 115–16, 123, 127–57, 164–5, 173,
    181–3, 185–9, 185 n.178, 204–5, 207–8, 216,
    219, 221–2, 237–9, 242–3
Passelewe, Robert 48–9
Passelew, John 238 n.47
Passelew, Simon 210
Passel, Luke 60 n.104, 61–2
Passenham 180–1, 185
patent rolls 49 n.57, 97, 104–5, 111–12, 122,
    131, 145
patriciate 209–10, 214
patronage 12–13, 18–20, 23–8, 38–65, 41 n.22,
    70–1, 78, 82–3, 128–30, 136–7, 139–40, 150–1,
    157–8, 160–1, 190, 219–20, 223, 229, 252–5
Patshull 107
Pattingham 142
Pattishall, Simon de 95, 102–3, 111–12, 115,
    119–20, 124 n.225, 144–7, 149, 151–2, 185–6,
    225, 248
Paul of Tarsus 198–9
Paunton, Baldwin de 105–6
Paunton, James de 105–6, 107 n.137, 123–4
Pauntons 108
Paveleys 169
Paveley, William de 168–71
Paynel, Katherine 254
peace 12–13, 16, 18, 25–6, 50–1, 53–4, 70, 73–4,
    78, 100, 115–18, 120–5, 146, 153, 159–60,
    165–6, 168, 188–9, 191–2, 194, 207, 215–16,
    218–19, 223–5, 246–7, 254–5
  form of peace 158–9, 207–8, 222–3
Peace of Canterbury 189–90, 221
Peace of Worcester 189–90, 223
Peasenhall 73 n.31
Peatling Magna 217, 242–3
Pecche, Aimery 174
Pecche, Batholomew 135 n.42
Pecche, Hugh 185–6

Pecches 171–2
Pedami, John 176
Pembroke 41–2, 66, 77
Pembroke, countess of 64
Pembroke, earl of 16, 18–19, 47–8, 59–60
Pembrokeshire 190
Penifader, Robert 145–6
Penkridge 107
Penne, Hugh de la 129–30, 180–1, 185
Penne, John de la 185 n.175
Peopleton 146–7, 149
Percy, Henry de 137 n.54
Percy, Walter de 249–50
Perigord 78
Peter, Reginald fitz 171–2, 175, 179–80, 251
Peterborough Abbey 144
Petition of the Barons 41, 83–5, 88, 92–4, 205,
    218–19, 231–4, 236–7, 258–9
petitions 84, 154, 209–10, 212–14, 233, 257,
    262–4, 267–70
Pevensey 40–1, 108 n.143
Peverel, Hugh 60 n.104
Peyforer, Fulk 96 n.55, 103, 111 n.158, 120–1,
    124–5, 125 n.228
Peyvre, John 147–8, 180–1, 184
Peyvre, Paulinus 46–7, 47 n.48, 58–9, 60 n.104, 64
Piddington 182–3
Pimhill 56–7, 59
Pincote 62–3
Pinkeni, Henry de 60 n.104
pipe rolls 67–8, 111–12
Pirot, Ralph 117
Pitstone 184, 187–8
Pitstone Lee 184
pleas 53–5, 58–9, 61–4, 74 n.39, 77, 86, 166 n.43,
    183, 257, 260–1
Plessetis, William de 145
Plessis, Hugh de 188
Plessis, John du 111 n.158, 120–1, 125 n.229
Plessy, John de 56–7
Plucknet, Hugh 173–4
Plumstead 101
Pocklington, Remy de 109–11
Poer, William le 102 n.100
Poitevin interlude 15–16
Poitevins 43–5, 51–2, 77, 129–30, 154, 157–8,
    218–19
Poitevin scutage 72–3
Poitou 15–17, 26–8, 36, 38–9, 42, 46–7, 72–3
Polden, Anne 46–7, 183–4
Polesworth Abbey 107 n.137
Popping, William 184
Porter, Peter le 100, 120–1, 139–40
Portsmouth 215–16

310 INDEX

Poughley 169–70
Poulton, Thomas de 151 n.129
Powicke, F. M. 12–13, 17 n.7, 44 n.31, 90 n.20, 207
 King Henry III and the Lord Edward 3, 116
Powis 58
Powys 2–3, 56 n.90
Preston 56–7, 119–20, 152
Prestwich, Michael 135 n.39, 136–8, 250 n.31,
 252–5, 265–6
Prestwold 104 n.110
priories 61, 73–4, 158, 215–16, 215 n.116, *see also*
 abbeys
priors 32 n.95, 57, 60–1, 67–8, 75 n.40, 107–8,
 107 n.137, 117–18, 169–70, 173, 184, 186–8,
 194–5, 208, 215–16, 222–3, 225 n.184,
 see also abbots
privatization 13, 38–65, 272–3
Protestantism 10–12
Provence, Sanchia of 25–6, 38–9
Provisions of Oxford 48–9, 64–5, 85–6, 88–90,
 101, 131, 157–8, 189, 194–5, 202–3, 210, 230
Provisions of the Barons (*Providencia Baronum*)
 91–2, 234
Provisions of Westminster 14, 85, 222–3, 229–43
public authority 14–15, 29–31, 94, 163,
 229–43, 258
Pugeia, Humbert de 60 n.104, 61
Pugeys, Imbert 47–8, 128–9, 131, 133–4
Puleston, Thomas 210
Purslow 57, 97–8

Quarines, Thomas de 151
Quedgley 163
Quincy, Margaret de 200–1
Quincy, Roger de 101 n.91, 139–41

Raby 123
Radclive 61
Radnor 142–3, 203 n.45
Raleigh 103 n.109
Raleigh, William de 22–3
Ralph, Ralph fitz 4, 214
Ramsey Abbey 106, 178–9
ransom 68–9, 130 n.16, 150 n.128, 164–5, 172, 174,
 178, 189, 223–5, 237–8, 270
Ranulf III, earl of Chester 80–1, 139–40
Raunds 144 n.88
Ravel, Robert 185 n.177
Reading Abbey 60 n.105, 174, 178–9
Ree, Ralf de 58
reformers 1, 73–4, 87–8, 90–5, 101, 109–16,
 118–20, 135–40, 255
reform movement 4–5, 8, 103–4, *see also*
 baronial reform

Reginald the Carpenter 177
religious houses 34, 59–60, 70–1, 81–4, 106–7,
 236–7, 258–9, 269–70, *see also* abbeys,
 priories, monasteries
Reuter, Tim 25 n.52, 202–3
revenues 16, 21–4, 27–9, 39–40, 43–5, 54–6,
 67–9, 88–9, 263–4, *see also* exchequer,
 finances, income, money, taxation/tallage,
 treasurers
Reydon 149
Ribbesford, Henry de 96 n.58
Ribbesford, Simon de 95–6
Richard I, King 21–2, 55–7, 60–1
Richard, Hugh fitz 51–2
Richardson, H. G. 233 n.25
Richmond 40–1, 133
Ridgeway, Huw 8, 32 n.93, 41, 43–4, 77–8, 85,
 96 n.55, 102–3, 108 n.142, 109–11,
 111 nn.158–159, 116 n.186, 118–19, 124–5,
 127, 129 n.13, 135–6, 220
 'A Study in Faction' 135–6
Rigaud, Eudes 200–1
Ringeslowe 103 n.107
Ripple 103 n.107
Risborough 184
Risby 75–6
Rishanger, William 202 n.37
Rivallis, Peter de 6–7, 15–17, 59
rivers
 Severn 158–9, 190
 Thames 173–4, 210
 Trent 269–70
 Waveney 75–6
Rivers family 106
Rivers, John 119–20, 122
Rivers, Walter de 112 n.162
Rivers, William de 175
Riviere, Walter de 124 n.224
robbery 122–3, 167–9, 173–80, 182–8, 238–9
Robert, Robert fitz 103 n.107
Robert the Smith 184, 238–9
Robert the Tailor 171–2
Robert, Thomas fitz 95
Rochelle, Richard de la 249–50
Roches, Peter des 15–17, 20–1, 24–5, 48–9, 219
Rochester 41 n.18, 48–9, 60–1, 207–8, *see also*
 bishops
Rochford, Guy de 44–5
Rodmarton 102 n.100
Roffa, Richard de 103–4
Rokele, Richard de la 150, 261 n.66
Rooshall 104–5
Ros, Robert de 72–3, 104–5, 156 n.151
Ros, William de 18–19, 36

Roshale, John de 97
Roshale, Thomas de 95, 97
Roshale, Vivian de 97–8
Rossall 97
Rostand, Master 49
Rothwell 67, 69–70, 144
Rouen 184–7, 200–1, *see also* archbishops
Ruddock, Robert 178
Rudham, Walter de 185 n.176
Rushall, Henry de 75–6
Rushbrook 106
Rus, Peter le 152
Russel, John 187–8
Russell, Ralph 215–16
Russel, Simon 185 n.176
Rutland 56, 95–6, 105–6, 107 n.137, 108–11, 120–1, 123–4, 149
Ryston, William of 88

Salden 183–4
Salines, Stephen de 129–30
Salines, William de 128–9
Salisbury 83, 180–1
Salisbury, earl of 6, 19–20, 49
Saluzzo, marquess of 42
Salwarpe 109–11
Sampson Foliot 105–6, 123–4
Sancta Ermina, William de 44–5
Sancto Leodegario, Geoffrey de 151 n.129
Sanders, I. J. 6–7, 91–2
Sandwich 145–6
Sandwich family 106
Sandwich, Henry de 103
Sandwich, John de 103, 119–20
Sandwich, Ralph de 103 n.107
Sanzavar, Ralf de 123–4
Sapcote 117, 139–41, 144–5, 155–6, 247 n.21
Saukervill, Jordan de 185 n.176
Sauvage, James le 109–11
Savage, William le 171–2
Savoy, Amadeus of 252–3
Savoyard faction 134–5, 157–8, 160–1
Savoyards 26–7, 40–4, 47–8, 127–31, 133–6, 138, 157–8, 180–1, 218–20
Savoy, Beatrice of 130 n.16, 133
Savoy, Bernard of 128–9
Savoy, Boniface of 40–1, 43–4, 130–1, 204–8
Savoy, Peter of 12–13, 40–1, 49–51, 71–4, 103–4, 127–31, 133–6, 140–1, 157–9, 210–11, 216
Savoy, Thomas of 40–1, 130 n.16
Savoy, William of 24–5, 28–9
Sawtry 62–3
Saxton 121
Say, Geoffrey de 225

Sayles, G. O. 233 n.25
Say, William de 137 n.54, 148 n.119, 150
Scalariis, John de 125 n.228
Scarborough 123–4
Scoland, Geoffrey de 103
Scotland 34, 45, 72–3, 109–11, 139–40, 218, 253
Scredington 101
Scudamore, Geoffrey de 120–1, 124–5
Scudamore, Peter de 171 n.75
Seagrave, Gilbert de 139–41
Seagrave, Nicholas de 139–40, 155–6, 185–6, 193 n.227, 246, 247 n.21
Seagrave, Stephen de 139–40, 144–5
Searle, Eleanor 107–8
Sedgelaw 61–4
Sedgewick 159–60
Seething 75 n.42
seizure/replevin/confiscation 27–8, 36, 44–5, 59–61, 73–4, 98–9, 104–5, 115–16, 119–25, 134, 147–52, 149 n.125, 158–63, 165–9, 171 n.70, 172, 174, 180, 187–8, 190, 192, 195, 208, 211, 215–16, 223, 245–7, 254–5, 267
Semer 76 n.43
Senghenydd 70
Seyton, Richard de 185–6
Seyton, Roger de 146 n.106
Shapwick 140–1, 140 n.69
Shelsay Walsh 146–7
Shenley 183–4
Sherborne 152
Sherington 184–5
Sherstone 164–5
Shotford 76 n.43
Shotford, Thomas de 75–6
Shottesbrooke 146–7, 174, 179–80
Shottesbrooke, Henry de 179–80
Shottesbrooke, Robert de 161
Shottesworth 208
Shoulden 149
Shrewsbury 142–3, 215–16, 264
Shrewsbury Abbey 57, 97–100, 98 n.76
Shropshire 29, 56 n.90, 56, 58–9, 80–1, 95–8, 100, 108–11, 119 n.201, 123–4, 142–3, 147 n.113, 170–1, 191, 210, 269–70
Shutford 150
Sicilian
    adventure 204–5
    ambitions 229
    business 35–6, 47–8, 206–7, 231–3
    enterprise 193 n.227, 206
Sicily 12–13, 26–8, 48
Simon, Simon fitz 150
Siward, Richard 70, 80–1
Slaughter 18–19

312 INDEX

Snowdonia 251
Somerset 69–70, 77 n.53, 95–6, 101 n.96, 102–3,
    120–1, 123–4, 149, 152, 170–1, 173, 191, 193 n.228
Somery, Alan de 188, 237–8
Somery, Joan de 41
Somery, Roger de 63–4, 79–80, 137 n.54, 141–2,
    195, 246
Southampton 168–9, 215–16
Southoe 62–3, 66–7, 69–71
Southwark 130
Spelho 149
Spencer, Andrew, M. 6 n.23, 54, 252, 254–5, 260–3
Spigurnel, Nicholas le 191
Stacey, Robert 21–2, 48 n.50, 265
Stafford 142–3
Stafford, Robert III de 103–4
Staffords 107
Staffordshire 58, 97–8, 103–7, 123–4, 142–3,
    195, 248
St Alban 106–7
St Albans 20, 60–1, 104–5, 115–16, 218
St Albans Abbey 60–1, 106–7, 186–7
St Albans chronicler/chronicles 20–1, 33–4,
    72–3, 106–7
St Amand, Aimery de 47 n.48, 151
Stamford 134–5
Standon, Robert de 142–3
St Andrews, Saher of 139–40
St Andrew, Thomas de 146, 153
Stanford 167–8
Stanho, Hervey de 111–12, 124–5
Stanton Harcourt 180–1
Stapleford Tawney 108, 121–3
Stapleton, Philip de 170 n.65
Statute of Acton Burnell 265–6
Statute of Gloucester 257
Statute of Marlborough 14, 236–7, 255
Statute of Merchants 265–6
Statute of Mortmain 258–9, 265–6
Statute of *Quia Emptores* 259–60, 264–5, 267
Statute of Rhuddlan 251
Statute of Westminster 239–40, 242 n.68, 255–7
St Augustine Abbey 103, 103 n.107, 106
Staunton, William de 120
St Edmund 203–4
St Edward 119–20, 128–9
Steventon 173
Stewart, Susan 241
St Frideswide 60–1
St Helens 174–5
St Helens, Beatrice de 169–70
St Helens, John de 151, 169–70, 177–8, 185 n.176
St Hilary 66–7
Stilton 62–3

St John hospital 60 n.105, 61
St John, Roger de 103 n.107, 156 n.151, 247 n.21
St Laud, Gilbert de 123–4
Stobinton, William de 147–8
Stockwell, Nicholas de 212–14
Stodfold 61
Stoke 61, 108, 184
Stoke Dry 123
Stokes, Theodore de 150
Stokes, William de 185–6
Stowe 60–1
Strapel, Ralph 169
Stratfield Mortimer 178–9
Stratton 63–4
Stratton, Adam de 266–7, 269–70
Strode, John de la 123–4, 169
Strood 103 n.109
St Thomas hospital 130
Stubbs, William 7, 258
Sturmer 149
Stutevilles 95–6
Stuteville, William de 59
St Valery 60–2
St Valery, John de 111–12
Sudbury, William de 95
Suffolk 67–70, 73–6, 87 n.5, 101–3, 111–12,
    111 n.158, 117, 119–20, 123–4, 131–2, 151–2
Sulhamstead 176
Surrey 29, 40–1, 52–3, 67, 69–70, 77, 83, 89, 95–7,
    108–11, 111 n.158, 112 n.162, 117–21, 117 n.193,
    123–4, 131–2, 159–60, 166 n.43, 167–8, 191,
    211 n.87, 234, 241, 247
Surrey, earl of 41–2, 135–6
Sussex 40–1, 69–70, 77, 89, 107–11, 111 n.158,
    112 n.162, 117, 123–4, 131–2, 138 n.59, 191, 223,
    247, 262–3
Sutherland, Donald 53–5, 59 n.101
Suthese, Thomas de 150–1
Sutton 99 n.77, 108 n.143, 184
Sutton, Robert de 122–3, 208
Swanscombe 51–2

Tadlow 62–3
Taillard, Roger 146–7
Talbot, Gilbert 109–11, 111 n.156
Tannington 75 n.41
Tany, Gilbert de 122 n.214
Tany, Peter de 122 n.214
Tany, Richard de 112 n.162, 119–23, 124 n.225,
    191, 246
Tany, Richard de (the younger) 122–4
Tarrington 102 n.100
Tattenhoe 61
Tattingstone 75 n.42

INDEX 313

Tatton 152
Tatton, Andrew de 152
taxation/tallage 5–6, 9–10, 15–17, 24, 26–9, 38–9,
    44–5, 62, 67–9, 96 n.55, 173, 204–10, 212–14,
    217 n.134, 218, 221–3, 229–30, 239–40,
    263–7, *see also* exchequer, finances, income,
    money, revenues, treasurers
Templars 60 n.105, 222–3
Temple 158–9, 210, 269–70
Terry, Henry 171–2
Tewkesbury 67–70
Tewkesbury Abbey 70, 96 n.57
Tewkesbury annalist 206–7
texts
    Book of Fees 101, 105 n.120
    Flores Historiarum 114 n.171, 115–16
    Fouke le Fitz Waryn 79–80
    Laudes Regiae 32–3
    Leges Edwardi Confessoris 230–1
    Liber de Antiquis Legibus 114–15
    Life of William Marshal 79–80
    Song of Lewes 188–9, 200–1, 221–2
Thame Abbey 186–7
Thanet 103 n.107
Thedmar, Arnold fitz 208–11, 223, 233
Thetford 73–4, 75 n.40
Theydon Mount 122–3
Thickbroom 76 n.43
Thirkelby, Roger 111–12
Thistleton 149
Thomas, Hugh 78–9
Thomas, Thomas fitz 158–9, 208–10
Thornborough 61, 186–7
Thornbury 67–8
Thornton 61, 140–1
Thornton, Gilbert de 262–3
Thorpe Arnold 139–40
Thorrington 51–2
Thweng, Robert de 220
Tickford 60 n.105
Tingewick 184–7
Tiptoft, Robert 249–50
Tixall 105 n.118
Toddington 46–7
Tonbridge 66–70, 151 n.131
Tonney, Nicholas 176
Towy Valley 134–5
Tracy, William de 115–17, 151 n.129, 162–3, 191
Tralbe, Ralph 171–2
Tralbe, Richard 171–2
Trayly, John de 60 n.104, 145–6
treasurers 27–8, 48, 64–5, 85, 102–3, 111–12, 131,
    see also exchequer, finances, income,
    money, revenues, taxation/tallage

treaties 18, 136–7
    Treaty of Aberconway 251
    Treaty of Kingston 117–18
    Treaty of Paris 26–7, 132 n.30, 197
Tregoz, John 168–72
Tregoz, Robert 170–1
Treharne, R. F. 2–4, 6–8, 11–14, 87, 89–94, 97 n.61,
    108–9, 111–17, 111 n.157, 127, 136–7, 207
    The Baronial Plan of Reform 1, 10–11, 85
Trenchemele, William 169
Trevelyan, G. M. 7
Trussell, William 140–2
Tuckscary 152
Tuddenham, Hugh de 76
Tulhuse, William de 185 n.177
Turberville, Robert de 249–50
Turin 130 n.16
Turpin, John 102 n.100
Tutbury 80–1, 103–4
Tyrel, Richard 97–100
Tyrel, Roger 99–100, 269–70
Tyringham 64, 185 n.179
Tyringham, John de 64

Uffington, Adam de 179–80
Uffington, David de 179–80
Uffington, Robert de 179–80
Umfraville, Gilbert de 39–40, 269–70
Upavon 17–19
Upnor, Thomas 175–6
Upper Winchendon 60–1
Usk 66–7

Vache, Richard de la 175–7, 181–4, 185 n.176
Valence, Aymer de 49, 51–3, 130, 135–6, 186–7
Valence, William de 25–7, 40–1, 44–5, 51–2,
    59–61, 63–4, 83, 133–6, 140–1, 151, 167–8
Valente, Claire 125 n.231, 199
Valognes, Robert de 101
Vauchez, André 199
Vautort, John 97 n.59, 123–4
Vaux, John de 134–8
Vaux, Petronilla de 101
Vaux, Robert de 75–6
Vaux, Roger de 158–9
Vavasour, John le 119–20
Vavasour, Mauger le 119–20
vavasours 88–93, 111–12, 117, 141–2, 231–3
Verdon, John de 188, 237–8
Verdon, Robert de 143–4
Verdon, Theobald de 64
Verdun, Henry de 142–3
Vere, Hugh de 60 n.104, 61–4
Vere, Robert de 225 n.183, 247 n.21

314 INDEX

Verney, Ralf de 182
Vernon, John de 195
Vernon, Richard de 103–4, 120–1, 180
Vescy, John de 156 n.151, 247 n.21
Vescy, William de 42
Villa, Baldwin de 133–4
Vincent, Nicholas 8–9, 33, 219–20
Vipont, Robert de 61, 252–3
Viponts 109–11
Vylayn, Hugh 215–16

Wake, Baldwin 144, 185–6, 193–4
Walcote, Henry 169
Walderne 108 n.143
Walerand, Robert 47–8, 133–7, 158–9, 192, 245–6
Wales 26–7, 39–42, 47–8, 58–9, 66–7, 71–2, 77,
    80–1, 109–11, 128–9, 134–6, 146–7, 158–9,
    160 n.12, 163–4, 218, 235, 247–8, 250–5,
    260–1, 264–5, see also Welsh Wars
Waleys (Welshman), John le 146–7, 187–8
Waleys (Welshman), Philip le 174–5
Waleys (Welshman), Ralph le 171
Wallingford 38–9, 60–1, 63–4, 80–1, 162, 166–7,
    173–5, 179–80, 185–6
Walsingham 67–8
Walton 62–3, 181–2, 186
Walton, John de 125 n.229
Walton, Robert de 48–9, 95, 158–9, 207–8
Wantage 167–71
Ware, John de la 149
Warenne, John de 40–2, 50–1, 101, 134–8, 146,
    154, 158–61, 190, 215–16, 223, 249–50, 253,
    260, 262–3
Warin, Fulk fitz 161, 170–1
Warin, William fitz 249–50
Warmington, William de 167–8
Warminster, William 167–8
War, Philip la 152
Warwick, earl of 59–60, 139–44, 187–8, 251, 261
Warwickshire 40 n.13, 45–6, 79–80, 95–6,
    108–11, 115, 117, 119–20, 123–4, 139–45,
    150 n.128, 183–4, 193 n.229, 237–8, 248
Warwick, William de 176
Wasteneys 105–6
Wasteneys, John de 105 n.118
Wasteneys, Payn de 103–4, 105 n.118
Wasteneys, Walter de 105 n.118
Waterville, Reginald de 144
Watford, Eustace de 83, 95, 111 n.158, 119–20,
    124–5, 191
Waugh, Scott L. 49–50, 82–3, 154–5, 253–4
Wauton, John de 95–6, 112 n.162, 117–21, 123–5
Wauton, Roger de 119–20
Waverley Abbey 223–5

Waver, Robert de 95–6
Waver, William de 95, 119–20
Weber, Max 198–9, 199 n.22, 201–2
Weedon, John de 95, 120–1
Weiler, Björn 25 n.52, 25–7, 35–6
Wellesbourne 143–4
Welsh Wars 146–7, 250 n.31, 253, 255–6
Wendover 183, 186
Wendover, Roger of 20–1, 218, 231 n.8
Wenlock 57
Weobley 98–100
Westbury 61
Westcliff 151
West Corscombe 152
West Dene 108 n.143
Westgate 103 n.107
Westminster 21–2, 25–6, 35–6, 39, 42, 50–3, 87,
    106–7, 109–11, 119–20, 192, 206–7, 210–11,
    266–7, see also Provisions of Westminster,
    Statute of Westminster
Westminster Abbey 26–8, 32–3, 60 n.105, 81–2,
    96 n.57, 102 n.100, 209–11, 264–5
Westminster Hall 7, 235
Westmorland 109–11, 120–1, 191
Weston 183–4
Weston, Hugh de 97–8, 142–3
West Peckham 103
West Wycombe 186–7
Wexford 41–2, 77
Weybridge 73 n.30
Weyland, Thomas 260–3, 266–7
Wherstead 75 n.42
Whig interpretation 1–14, 19–20
Whitchurch 139–40, 143–4, 184
Whitfield, Robert de 171–2
Whytepens, Laurence 145–6
Wickham 150
Wigmore 56–9, 98, 162, 190, 203 n.45
Wigmore Abbey 57
Wild, Benjamin 31–2
Williams, Daniel 139–40, 199, 202–3
Williams, Gwyn Alf 209–11
William the Cook 76
William the Conqueror 128 n.5
Willingale Doe 150
Wilton, William de 136–7
Wiltshire 17–19, 40 n.13, 56, 69–70, 77, 77 n.49,
    102–3, 105–6, 111, 111 n.158, 120–1, 164–5,
    170–2, 177 n.105
Wimple 104–5
Winchester 32 n.95, 34–6, 46–7, 49, 51–2,
    60 n.105, 119–20, 130, 168–9, 186–7, 192,
    212–16, 245–6, see also bishops
Winchester, countess of 200–1

Winchester, earl of 72 n.19, 101 n.91, 139–40, 144
Windle, Alan of 111–12
Windsor 36, 41–2, 115–16, 128–9, 146–7, 166, 173–86, 210–11
Wingrave 180–3
Winslow 60–1
Winterbourne 168–9
Wittenham 151
Woburn 60 n.105, 184, 187–8
Wolverton 183–4
Woodham, Gilbert de 180–1
Woodstock 35–6, 88
Woolstone 61, 147–8, 184
Woolvey 62–3, 71
Worcester 50–1, 100 n.85, 114–16, 189–90, 200–1, 206–8, 223–5, 251, *see also* bishops, Peace of Worcester
Worcestershire 67–70, 95–6, 100 n.85, 108–11, 146–7, 149, 248, 261
Wormeton 99–100
Wormingford 149
Worminghall, Geoffrey de 146 n.106

writs 21–3, 49–55, 59–61, 60 n.105, 63–4, 81–2, 87–8, 94–5, 99 n.81, 131–2, 186–7, 235, 264–6, 270
Wychbold 108
Wycombe 186
Wykes, Thomas 193, 212–14
Wykewan, William de 180–1
Wylmersley 144 n.87
Wyre Forest 96 n.58
Wyverstone 75–6

xenophobia 13–14, 218–23, 274, *see also* aliens, anti-alienism, foreigners

Yardley Hastings 144 n.87
Yattendon, Nicholas de 165–6, 171–3
York 35–6, 48, 180–1, 206–9, 212–14, 223, *see also* archbishops
Yorkshire 40–1, 70–3, 74 n.39, 76, 109–11, 117, 156 n.151, 191, 205, 214, 220, 258–9

Zouche, Alan la 136–7, 154, 190
Zouche, William la 123–4, 136–8